COLLECTOR'S ENCYCLOPEDIA OF

VOGUE DOLLS

IDENTIFICATION AND VALUES

Judith Izen • Carol Stover

COLLECTOR BOOKS

A Division of Schroeder Publishing Co., Inc.

The current values in this book should be used only as a guide. They are not intended to set prices, which vary from one section of the country to another. Auction prices as well as dealer prices vary greatly and are affected by condition as well as demand. Neither the authors nor the publisher assumes responsibility for any losses that might be incurred as a result of consulting this guide.

On the cover

Clockwise from top left: Jill, courtesy Peggy Millhouse.
Ginny, courtesy Peggy Millhouse.
Painted Eye Ginny, courtesy Peggy Millhouse and Carol Stover.
Ginnette, courtesy Carol Stover.

Cover design by Beth Summers
Cover photos by Peggy Millhouse
Book design by Holly C. Long

Collector Books
P.O. Box 3009
Paducah, KY 42002-3009
www.collectorbooks.com

Values Updated, 2000

Contents

Acknowledgments

Ginny dolls were our childhood dolls and we loved playing with them. Even as children we appreciated the quality of the dolls and their clothing. We are fortunate to have talked with the many people who were responsible for making these lovely dolls during the course of our research.

We would like to thank the relatives of Jennie Adler Graves, the founder of Vogue Dolls, who agreed to be interviewed, lent archival material, and their memories for this book. We would especially like to thank Virginia Graves Carlson, the long-time dress designer and ultimately vice president of Vogue, for all of her help.

We would also like to thank June and Edwin (Ted) Nelson, Joe Kingston, and Carol Ann Lee for their help. We would also like to thank these former employees of Vogue — members of the Vogue extended family who felt working there was like working for a family business, and business associates for talking with us and sharing their memories: Mary A. Bate, Loretta Beattle, Paul Brogan, Carol Conlon Coakley, Joan Cornett, Julia Della Gatta, Ruth Doyon, John Flanagan, Arthur Grobe, Joel Lesser, Evelyn F. Meehan, Grace Meehan, Julie Navarro, George Olsen, Florence Phillips and her daughter, Helen Carlson, Eleanor Skinner, Ruth Sheppard, Henry Weisser.

We also would like to thank the many collectors who were willing to share their knowledge and lovely Vogue dolls with us and helped to make this book possible: Johana Gast Anderton, Kathy Bailey, Sherry Baloun, Kathy Barry-Hippensteel, Ann Bergin, Shirley Bertrand, Carol Black, Robi Blute, Mary Bono, Vicki Broadhurst, Diane Buck, Millie Caliri, Laura and Ronald Colpus, Marlene Dantzer, Mary Davis, Carolyn DeMatteo, M. Ceil Eastman, Grace Evans, Audrey Fletcher, Maureen Fukushima, Jane Gaumond, Margaret Groninger, Susan Haynes, Susie Heilman, Barbara and Nick Hill, Sue Johnson, Sandy Johnson-Barts, Vicki Johnson, Pam and Polly Judd, Laura Kussmaul, Chree Kysar, Ida Labaki, Ruth and Fred Leif, Heather Lennon, Maureen Lizdas, Nancie Mann, Anita Maxwell, Ellen McDonald, Marge Meisinger, Ursula Mertz, Peggy Millhouse, Mary Miskowiec, Shirley Niziolek, S. Ogilvie, Judy Ormsbee, Veronica Phillips, Shirley Rice, Tina Ritari, Barbara Rosplock-Van Orman, Marge Ruppel, Marian Schmuhl, Dot Smith, Marcie Smith, Kathy Schneider, Nadine Steele, Susan Steelman, Ann Tardie, Trudy Taylor, Mary Lu Trowbridge, Iris Troy, Betty Wallace, Wenham Museum, Eleanor Thompson, director; Lorna Lieberman, Diane Hamblin, and Diane Buck, doll curators; GiGi Williams, Valerie Zakszewski, Joyce Zambuto, Pam Zampiello.

We would also like to thank the new owners of the Vogue Doll Company, Inc. especially Linda Smith, for their cooperation.

Finally we would like to thank our families for their support and understanding. Judy would like to thank her wonderful husband Myles H. Kleper; her great children Shulamit Elisheva, Seth Edward, and Naomi Ruth for their help and understanding; her mom and dad, Melvin and Shirley Izen; her mother-in-law Rozz Kleper; and her entire loving family.

Carol would like to thank her wonderful husband, Frank, who has been so supportive as well as her great children Jason and Adam for their help. She also thanks her loving parents, Lowell and Louise Gibbs, and her entire family for their encouragement. She also wishes to thank her grandmother, Ora Adams, who along with her mom sewed little dresses for her, providing the spark that began her interest in Ginny and her fashions.

We would be most grateful for any corrections, pictures, or additional information about Vogue dolls, especially those not pictured in this book. You may write to Judy Izen at P.O. Box 623, Lexington, MA 02420 or Carol Stover at 81 E. Van Buren, Chicago, IL 60605.

About the Authors

Judith Izen, a doll historian and toy industry researcher, has degrees from Boston University and Harvard School of Public Health. She specializes in Baby Boom era dolls. Ms. Izen is the author of *Collector's Guide to Ideal Dolls* published by Collector Books. Her articles have appeared in many publications including *Doll Reader, Doll News, Doll World, Contemporary Dolls, New England Antiques Journal,* and *Antiques & Collecting* magazines. Ms. Izen is also a lecturer on and guest curator of collectible dolls.

Carol Stover researches and lectures about early 1950s hard plastic dolls, specializing in Vogue dolls. She is a professional marketing consultant and has a degree from the Cornell University School of Hotel Administration. Her articles have appeared in numerous publications including *Antiques & Collecting, Dolls,* and *Doll Reader* magazines. Mrs. Stover is an avid doll collector and her dolls have been featured in numerous articles.

Introduction

Vogue Dolls Incorporated made many lovely dolls. Vogue's most popular creation was Ginny — an 8" doll with an extensive wardrobe. In addition, Vogue Dolls created an entire family for Ginny including baby sister Ginnette; baby brother Jimmy; big sister Jill; big brother Jeff; and Jill's friend, Jan. There were also many cousins added to the Vogue line in the 1960s including Wee Imp, Li'l Imp, and Brikette. Other successful dolls included the Baby Dear family including Baby Dear, Baby Dear-One, and Too Dear.

Before Ginny came along, Vogue had sold other dolls such as Velva, a latex rubber doll they developed; Toddles, a composition Ginny precursor; even stuffed animals. Vogue Dolls had started in business by dressing bisque, composition, rubber, and even celluloid dolls manufactured by other companies.

Vogue was, in essence, the brain child of one woman, Jennie H. Adler Graves, who began simply by sewing clothes for dolls in her home in Somerville, Massachusetts. Under her guidance and inspiration Vogue Dolls Inc. grew to become the biggest doll company in the United States by 1957.

Under different owners, Vogue has continued making dolls up to the present time. This book will cover all dolls made by the Vogue Doll Company, including Ginny and her family, her predecessors, and the dolls that were produced concurrently with Ginny.

Vogue Doll "Herstory"

Vogue Dolls Incorporated was founded by Mrs. Jennie H. Graves of Somerville, Massachusetts. Her story is one of courage, determination, talent and vision. Ironically, Mrs. Graves might never have started the company except for the unknowing help of a "friend." The story is that the "friend," knowing of Mrs. Graves's talent in sewing dresses for her daughters, asked her to dress dolls for a charity bazaar. When the "friend" kept coming back for more dolls, Mrs. Graves became curious. It wasn't long until she discovered that the "friend," instead of giving the dolls to charity, was selling them! Mrs. Graves figured if the "friend" could sell the dolls, so could she. She began selling dressed imported German dolls to Jordan Marsh, a Boston department store, in 1922 out of her home on 77 Liberty Ave. in Somerville. Thus, Vogue's forerunner, The Vogue Doll Shoppe, was founded.

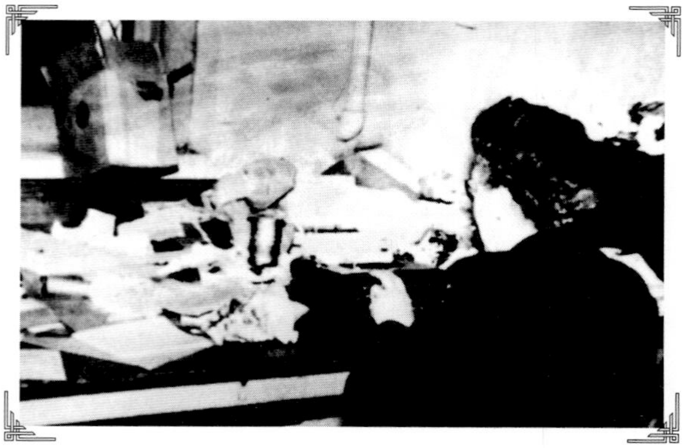

Mrs. Graves (1951) at work. Vogue had just moved into their Ship Avenue factory. Courtesy Mrs. Virginia Carlson.

Starting in 1925, Mrs. Graves worked out of her house on 152 Willow Ave. Her first floor was her sewing room, the basement was the shipping room, and a toy cart was for interoffice transportation. Her business grew rapidly. Mrs. Graves employed Mrs. Ethel Clarke, a neighbor, as her main sewer who would sew the sample dresses as well as the socks and shirt material. Mrs. Clarke's daughter, Pauline, would help her mother with the work and would take the finished items down to Mrs. Graves's house on her roller skates. Pauline and her friend, Mrs. Eleanor Buckley Skinner, were allowed to come in and take items from a box of sample clothes, seconds, and ends of ribbons and lace that Mrs. Graves kept in the corner of the cellar where she worked on her dolls.

Price list of the Vogue Doll Shoppe (1933– 34). Courtesy Mrs. Virginia Carlson.

As her business grew, Mrs. Graves began to rely on home sewers to make the dolls' outfits. According to Ruth Doyan who worked at Vogue for 30 years as forelady of the home sewers, Miss Helen Sanborn from Somerville was one of the very first employees. Miss Sanborn would make up the original samples, seeing how much time they took to be made, and then figure out how much to pay the home sewers based on a per piece basis. She would also cut the patterns. There were only a few workers in the early days, mostly women from the neighborhood who would come in part-time to dress the dolls, finishing 50 or 60 per hour. Mrs. Graves would work right alongside them. Sales peaked at around $15,000 a year.

Vogue Doll Shoppe (1936) located in Mrs. Graves's home, showing small bisque and large bisque and composition dolls; also showing rubber babies, Sunshines, and Valerie. Courtesy Wenham Museum, Wenham, Mass.

In 1939 Mrs. Graves moved to Wildwood Road in Medford where she established the operations of the Vogue Doll Shoppe.

By 1941 Vogue had moved to 108 Medford Street in Magoun Square, Somerville, in a house just for dolls. Women worked in a storefront and overhead apartment in a two-family house. By 1942 sales increased to $55,000. Her daughter, Virginia Graves, joined the firm as a designer in 1942. A large dependence on home-sewers developed during the World War II years since the government did not allow Vogue to have factory workers.

Mrs. Graves herself designed the clothes for Vogue dolls herself for over 20 years. She loved to wear hats, and was seldom seen without one, so her dolls almost always had hats in their wardrobes. Many hats were designed by milliner Humpert Green of Brooklyn, New York, who was glad to have the business during times when ladies' hats were on the decline.

In 1945 Mrs. Graves incorporated her company as Vogue Dolls, Inc., and moved to their first factory on 4 Mystic Ave. in Medford. The following year sales reached $224,000.

In 1946 sales declined and Mrs. Graves decided to come up with a line of eight-inch plastic dolls that them, saying they were too small for U.S. tastes. Finally Mrs. Graves found the Commonwealth Plastics Company in Leominster, Mass., to produce the hard plastic Ginnys. They also manufactured Ginny's shoes and little accessories such as pocketbooks, headbands, and belts. Vogue never did any on-premises doll manufacturing. All their molding was done by outside firms.

By 1949 Vogue had moved into a 15,000 square foot factory on Ship Avenue in Medford, which employed 50 people plus 100 to 200 home-sewers. Mrs. Graves was involved with every aspect of her company from inspecting Ginnys at the factory to marketing. Sales jumped to $239,000 a year.

In order to gain acceptance of her dolls as a gift suitable for any occasion not just a holiday gift, Mrs. Graves launched a series of promotions in the spring of 1952 designed to build off-season sales. These promotions were cooperative ventures with Vogue paying 50 percent of the cost of running half-page newspaper ads and supplying material and advice in return for the retailer's purchase of a sizable order and his agreement to engage in specific store promotions. The promotion was centered on the then novel ideal of having the sale of a basic doll separate from the outfit. Having purchased the doll, the customer could then purchase as many outfits and accessories as they wished from a selection of over fifty outfits. The retailer agreed to have a selling counter on the main floor as well as in the toy department and to devote one ground floor window exclusively to the display of the dolls.

Virginia Graves (1953) on television with Virginia Graham; notice Coronation Ginny. Courtesy Wenham Museum, Wenham, Mass.

Other gimmicks such as doll birthday parties and coloring contests were timed to coincide with the promotion so that the attendance of children with the parents would be assured. Vogue got manufacturers of Talon® zippers and soft drinks to share in the expense of the promotion since they had put zippers in some of Ginny's clothes and gave out soft drinks at the birthday parties. The hope was that large impulse sales would be made by the large customer flow attracted by the advertising.

Vogue produced signs which read "Hi! I'm Ginny...A Vogue doll and the fashion leader in miniature doll society. I have fifty outfits for you to select from. I'm unbreakable plastic, and you may wet-set-and-comb my hair. I am just $1.98 in panties and slippers. Outfits $1.00 to $2.98." Retailers such as Stewart's of Baltimore; Elder & Johnson Dayton, Ohio; Auerbach's in Salt Lake City; F & R Lazarus, Columbus, Ohio; White House, San Francisco; Gimbels in New York; Blacok's in Indianapolis; Mandel Brothers in New York; and Joseph & Loeb Birmingham, Alabama all reported sell-outs or near sell-outs of Ginny when they did the special promotion. This was during the off-peak toy selling season. Some of the stores had to close down their booths due to lack of stock. A toy buyer at Lansburgh's of Washington D.C., Al Lowen drove all night to Boston to pick up additional merchandise to continue the promotion in his store since he couldn't wait for the usual ordering and shipping channels. Stewart's of Baltimore sold out in four hours and had to borrow stock from another branch. One retailer's doll sales increased over 790 percent for the month of April between 1951 and 1952 due to the promotion.

Virginia Graves (circa 1954) on WSB-TV television show *Woody Willow*. Courtesy Wenham Museum, Wenham, Mass.

This novel idea of promoting dolls in April and May required lots of cajoling from Mrs. Graves. Buyers hesitated since it was considered untried and risky to commit money to such a novel idea of selling dolls in the off-season. However, the buyers and Vogue were both surprised with the tremendous response to their promotions. Orders poured in as dealers sought to join the bandwagon. July shipments even exceeded the previous year's peak month. A happy consequence of the promotions was that large consumer preference for the product was built (over other dolls) so gross sales which amounted to only $433,000 in 1951 rose to over $2,113,904 by 1953. Vogue was successful in reducing the importance of holiday sales to total production of only 48 percent of total year's sales. Production was stabilized and layoffs only affected 30 percent of the employees in 1953 for a maximum of nine weeks.

Mrs. Jennie H. Graves, age 64. Courtesy Ruth Doyon.

To deal with the torrent of

orders, Mrs. Graves had an industrial engineering firm of Anderson-Nichols adjust production and hired a general manager. She also hired talented designer Joan Cornette, beginning in 1956, to assist with wardrobe design. She leased another factory in Malden on 184 Commercial Street which was headed by her daughter Virginia Graves who was by then vice president of Vogue.

In order to finance Vogue's tremendous growth Mrs. Graves had to secure a bank loan in 1953 to get through the growth crisis safely. This allowed 80 percent of the Vogue stock to remain in the Graves's family hands.

Vogue also had to weather another type of storm in 1955. Hurricane Diane caused the Mystic River to flood the Vogue factory on Ship Ave., Medford, in 1955, and the board of health made Mrs. Graves throw out the thousands of Ginnys that were stored in the basement.

Mrs. Graves with Mr. and Mrs. Pat O'Brien and their daughter Brigid, age 10, during the 1955 Hollywood trip. Courtesy Wenham Museum, Wenham, Mass.

Mrs. Graves with Ronald Reagan, Nancy Reagan, and their daughter Patty, age 3, on a business trip to Hollywood (1955). Courtesy Wenham Museum, Wenham, Mass.

By 1955 Mrs. Graves had more than 300 home sewers working for her in addition to the factory workers who cut out the clothing from the fabric and did assembly and packing. Mrs. Graves was a wonderful employer. Factory employees remember her sending them roses on their birthdays, treating them to holiday parties at a country club, or hosting them at her summer home in Westwood. Even more than that, Mrs. Graves was a special person. Paul Brogan, a Vogue employee in the 1950s, remembers her giving him an inspirational talk when his infant was sick with tuberculosis. "You could talk to her, she was like a regular person," he recalls. Mrs. Graves was so beloved by her employees that they rejected union attempts to organize at Vogue because she treated them so well.

The Ginny doll was getting so popular she spawned many competitors, chief of which was Ginger made by the Cosmopolitan Doll Company of New York founded by Kathryn Kay in 1955. Ms. Kay who had been a sales representative for Vogue even used the same plastics manufacturer as Vogue — Commonwealth Plastics. Vogue felt Ginger was a knock-off and reduced their business with Commonwealth Plastics.

Mrs. Graves's uncle, Alfred Fuller, founder of the Fuller Brush Company, provided his expertise and advice to Vogue over the years.

Mrs. Graves with Wendell Corey and Ginny during the 1955 Hollywood trip. Courtesy Wenham Museum, Wenham, Mass.

Mrs. Graves with Bonita Granville and daughter Linda, age 5, inspecting new Ginny outfits during a visit to Bonita's home in Beverly Hills (1955). Courtesy Wenham Museum, Wenham, Mass.

Mrs. Graves and Mrs. Barbara Daly Anderson of *Parents' Magazine* inspecting straight leg Ginny dolls at the Vogue factory (c. 1956). Courtesy Wenham Museum, Wenham, Mass.

Mrs. Graves and Virginia Carlson at factory showing new designs (Dec. 1957). Courtesy Wenham Museum, Wenham, Mass.

Mrs. Graves inspecting a carton of Ginny dolls at the Vogue factory (c. 1957). Courtesy Wenham Museum, Wenham, Mass.

Mrs. Graves watching workers comb dolls' hair at the Vogue factory (c. 1956). Courtesy Wenham Museum, Wenham, Mass.

Factory sewers at Vogue factory (c. 1957). Courtesy Wenham Museum, Wenham, Mass.

The period of Ginny's highest production was 1957. Vogue had grown to employ well over 300 home sewers and several hundred employees at their Medford plant and was selling thousands of dolls and costumes a year. Vogue became the largest doll manufacturer in the United States in 1957, selling over five million dollars worth of merchandise, an extraordinary accomplishment for entrepreneur Mrs. Jennie Graves who started the company sewing doll clothes on her kitchen table. Mrs. Graves had accomplished this growth entirely on her own talent and courage since her husband died in 1939.

In 1957 Mrs. Graves spoke to 3,500 industrialists at the 61st annual Congress of American Industry sponsored by the National Association of Manufacturers in the Waldorf-Astoria in New York City early in December. In her talk, "The Impact of Taxation on Small Business," Mrs. Graves outlined her tax experience at the start of her business career. She was the only woman featured as a speaker on the program.

Mrs. Graves always realized the value of promotion. Each year as the new line of dolls and their wardrobes came out, she threw lavish fashion shows in Hollywood or at New York's Stork Club. Hordes of celebrities and their daughters showed up and were gifted with Ginnys and their accessories. Celebrities such as Ronald Reagan, Jack Palance, Jayne Mansfield, Jean Crane, Esther Williams, and Maureen O'Sullivan crowded these festivities with their children.

Vogue also organized fashion shows in department stores with girls modeling the child-size versions of the Ginny doll clothes. Peggy Schoenfelder-Schwarz remembers having a black velvet dress with a pink flower at the waist (child size 6) — an exact replica of a Ginny dress from 1957. Her aunt was a buyer for Edwards Department Store of Rochester, New York.

Mrs. Graves also organized a Ginny fan club complete with newsletter and contests for Ginny owners who comprised about 25 percent of the entire population of girls aged three to ten in the United States.

Always concerned about their Ginny dolls and the girls who played with them, Vogue officially started its doll hospital. They had been unofficially repairing Ginnys for quite some time. A child would send her broken Ginny doll to Vogue, Vogue would repair her, usually putting on a new wig and replacing broken parts, and return the little patient to her owner with a sticker on the box showing a Ginny Nurse saying "Hi, I'm the Vogue Dolls' Nurse! Now that your doll is all better...she's coming home to you. She had good care and lots of fun, but she missed you. Please take good care of her so she won't have to go away again!" (see page 14).

The history of Vogue dolls could have been different if the negotiations between Vogue and Mattel had come to fruition. Ruth and Elliot Handler of Mattel wanted to buy Vogue and started discussions with Mrs. Graves in 1958 – 59 (before Barbie hit it big). Fortunately or unfortunately for the doll world (no one will ever know), the two companies couldn't come to terms and the deal was not completed.

Jennie H. Graves and Mrs. Virginia Carlson, dress designer, discussing new 1958 line at their Malden plant (Dec. 1957). Courtesy Wenham Museum, Wenham, Mass.

Brownies touring Malden plant (Dec. 1957). Courtesy Wenham Museum, Wenham, Mass.

Mrs. Graves and Eleanor Roosevelt (c. 1957) when she donated $50,000 worth of dolls to Save the Children Federation through Mrs. Roosevelt to Miss Faith Baldwin, author (left). Courtesy Virginia Carlson.

In 1958 Vogue decided to expand their miniature doll line (Ginny) to larger dolls and bought the Arranbee Doll Company of New York. In 1959 Vogue's gross sales were over $6 million.

With Vogue's acquisition of Arranbee dolls, many new dolls were added over the next several years including Li'l Imp, Littlest Angel, Baby Dear, Brikette, and Ginny Baby. Vogue used Prima Vinyl Company in New York who did the molding on the vinyl Littlest Angel dolls and some of the vinyl Ginnys. Vogue also used Arrow Plastics in New Jersey for some of their vinyl dolls.

Mrs. Graves's company was given an honor when she was chosen to exhibit her dolls at the 1959 American National Exhibition in Moscow's Sokolniki Park. At that point nine million little girls throughout the nation owned Ginny dolls so Vogue was judged most representative of the toy industry for the fair. Ginny dolls got into the political realm since Vice President Richard M. Nixon, Premier Nikita Khrushchev, and future Premier Leonid Breshnev showed up for the exhibit.

In 1960, Mrs. Jennie Graves retired from the company, turning to her daughter, Mrs. Virginia Graves Carlson, and son-in-law, Mr. Edwin (Ted) Nelson, to lead the company. Many of Vogue's growth strategies continued right up until Mrs. Carlson's retirement in 1966.

In 1961 Vogue advertised in *Playthings Magazine,* magazine of the toy trade, that "We will not be on TV! NO PRICE LEADERS! JUST FULL MARK-UP!" which means that all of their dolls would be profitable to the toy retailers. Vogue was following Mrs. Graves's policy of not advertising on television even after her retirement. This was mainly due to lack of capital to finance a television campaign.

In 1965 Vogue introduced their 1965 line early to help prestigious department stores and independent toy retailers freshen up their carry-over doll inventory with all new merchandise to stimulate the traffic created by after-holiday clearance sales. Vogue's entire early line sold for $1.00– 5.00 to stay within price groups most successful in the non-Yule selling season. Featured in the line were the original 8" hard plastic Ginny with vinyl head and a complete group of garments to fit various occasions. In 1966, Mrs. Carlson retired, leaving the management of Vogue entirely to her brother-in-law, Edwin W. Nelson, Jr., the president of Vogue dolls. He ran the company for several years before selling the Vogue name to Tonka Corporation in 1972. He remained with Tonka Corporation for three years while Tonka continued to produce the Ginny dolls in Hong Kong.

In 1977 Lesney Products Corporation of Moonachie, New Jersey, purchased the rights to the Ginny doll and Vogue name from Tonka. Lesney was already well known primarily for their Matchbox cars and other toys. The rights to the other Vogue doll names such as Baby Dear, Brikette, and other dolls were bought by Playmates, a company with offices in California and manufacturing in China. Playmates changed the name of its company with rights to the Vogue dolls (other than Ginny) to Tiara Dolls and Mr. Joel Lesser, formerly Vogue's executive vice president, became president of the U.S. company Playmates World Wide. In 1982 Lesney went into receivership and both factory and warehouse were emptied out.

In 1984 Meritus® Industries of Florham Park, New Jersey, bought Vogue and for three years produced Ginny dolls, including a porcelain Ginny in 1984 – 86.

In the fall of 1986, R. Dakin & Company of San Francisco, California, bought the rights to the Ginny and Vogue names and doll molds from Meritus and produced Ginnys until 1995. The company was sold to The Vogue Doll Company Inc., founded in 1995 and headed by Linda and Jim Smith, Wendy and Keith Lawton, Nancy Cordary, David Smith, and Susanne de Groot. The future looks bright for Ginny, the lovable toddler doll.

Fashion Shows in 1957 starring Ginny

Vogue sponsored fashion shows with matching Ginny and Jill fashions. Courtesy Wenham Museum, Wenham, Mass.

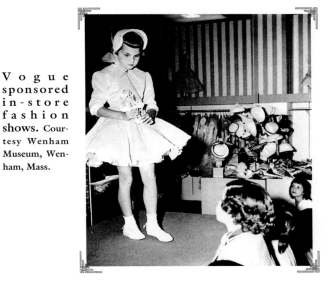

Vogue sponsored in-store fashion shows. Courtesy Wenham Museum, Wenham, Mass.

Girls and their Ginny-look-alike dresses at Vogue-sponsored fashion show.

Wouldn't you like to be that girl getting a Ginny from Mrs. Graves at a Vogue-sponsored fashion show? Courtesy Wenham Museum, Wenham, Mass.

Hollywood Party at the Beverly Hills Hotel

Mrs. Graves and some of the 114 children and their celebrity parents who attended the Hollywood Ginny Club Party. All girls attending received a Ginny doll.

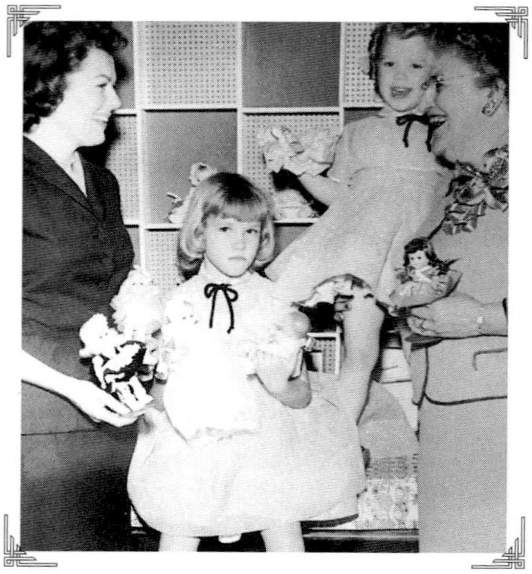

Barbara Hale and daughters and Mrs. Graves. Courtesy Wenham Museum, Wenham, Mass.

Mrs. Graves hosted a Vogue party in Hollywood at the Beverly Hills Hotel on Feb. 10, 1957, for children of movie stars, including Dana Andrews, Joan Bennett, MacDonald Carey, Robert Cummings, Dennis Day, Joan Fontaine, Mona Freeman, Margaret Hayes, Bob Hope, Ruth Hussey, Elyse Knox and Tom Harmon, Barbara Lawrence, Art Linkletter, Jayne Mansfield, Angelea Green Martin, James Mason, Robert Mitchum, Ken Murray, Maureen O'Sullivan, Pat O'Brien, Jack Palance, Ronald Reagan, Nancy and Tina Sinatra, Barry Sullivan, Phyllis Thaxter, Esther Williams, and Bonita Granville Wrather. Chucko the TV Clown entertained. All girls received a Ginny doll. What a wonderful treat for all!

Esther Williams and daughter and Mrs. Graves. Courtesy Wenham Museum, Wenham, Mass.

Girls waiting for their Ginny at the party. Courtesy Wenham Museum, Wenham, Mass.

Hollywood Party at the Beverly Hills Hotel

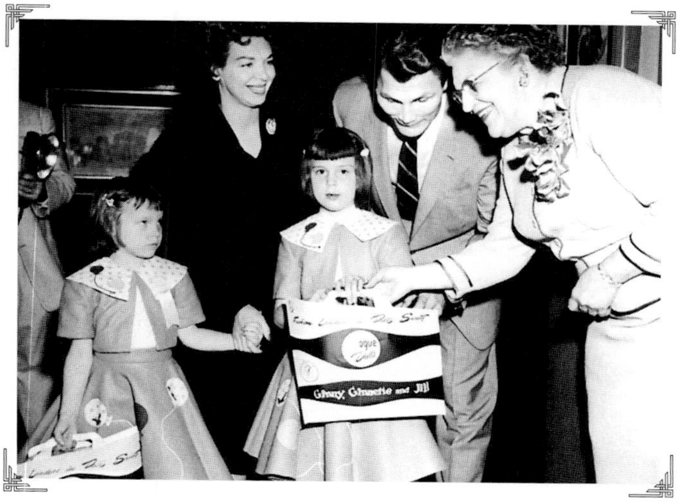

Mr. and Mrs. Jack Palance and daughters with Mrs. Graves. Courtesy Wenham Museum, Wenham, Mass.

Mrs. Graves with Mr. and Mrs. James Mason and their daughter, Portland and friend, Laurie Burke. Courtesy Wenham Museum, Wenham, Mass.

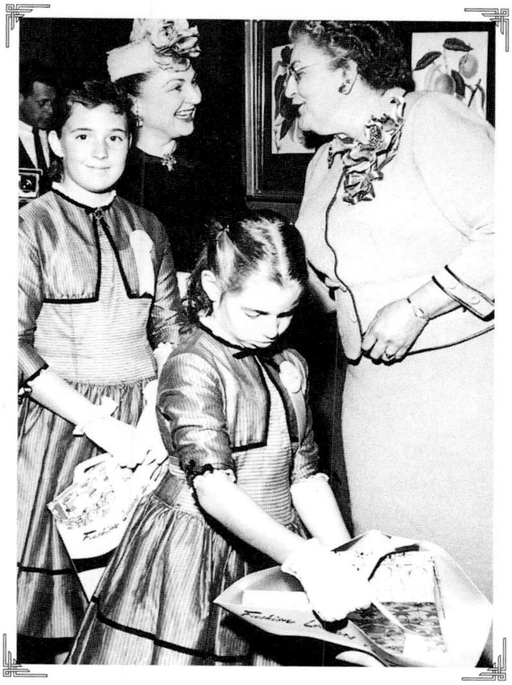

Mrs. Graves with Mrs. Art Linkletter and daughters, Diane and Sharon. Courtesy Wenham Museum, Wenham, Mass.

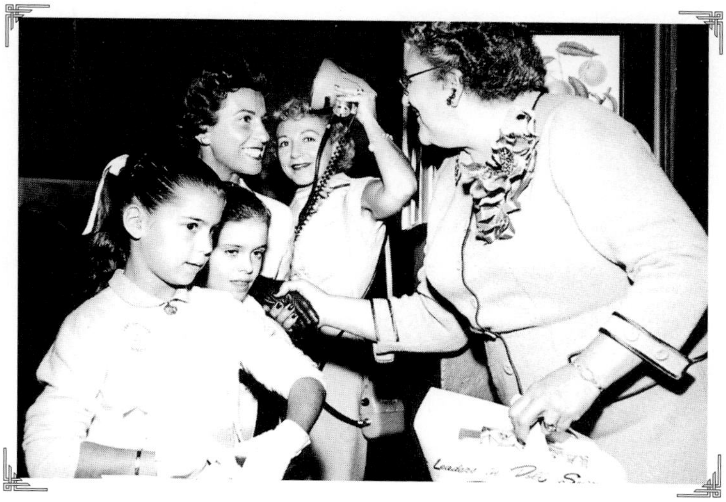

Mrs. Graves with Nancy Sinatra and daughter, Tina, and friend Shelley Wanger. Courtesy Arthur Grobe.

Maureen O'Sullivan and daughters Mia (in back), Prudy, Steffi, and Tisa Farrow at party. Courtesy Arthur Grobe.

Ginny Doll Hospital sticker (1957) was put on dolls after they returned from the doll hospital. Courtesy Ruth Doyon.

Store display of Ginny, Ginnette, and Jill (1957). Wesley Swadley photograph. Courtesy Arthur Grobe.

Ginny dolls in Macy's window (1957). Wesley Swadley photograph. Courtesy Arthur Grobe.

Display of Ginny, Ginnette, and Jill (1957) at toy show for retail trade. Notice shipping boxes under table. King's Photo Service. Courtesy Arthur Grobe.

Mrs. Iva Erlach and Mr. George Olsen (sales representatives for Vogue) and Mrs. Graves, Feb. 10, 1957.

Jeff, Jill, Jimmy, and Ginnette display at Jordan Marsh, Peabody, Mass. (1958). Courtesy Wenham Museum, Wenham, Mass.

Mrs. Graves looking at Ginny's Party Package (1957). Courtesy Wenham Museum, Wenham, Mass

Mrs. Graves and her trademark hats (circa 1958). Courtesy Wenham Museum, Wenham, Mass.

Ginny dolls on a TV game show with Bill Cullen (1958). Courtesy Wenham Museum, Wenham, Mass.

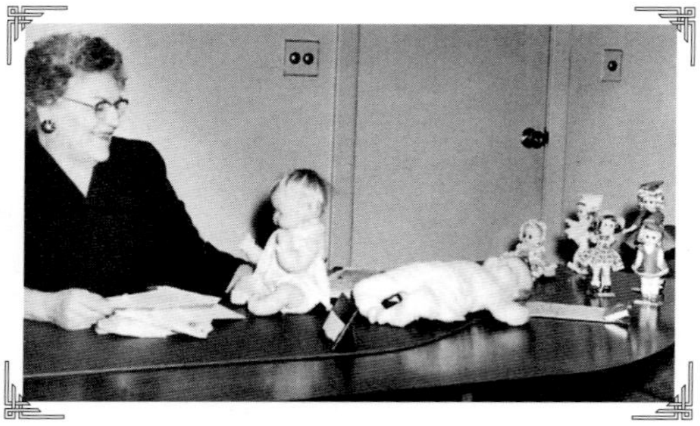

Mrs. Graves and Baby Dear, Ginny, Jill, Ginnette, and Brikette (1960). Courtesy Wenham Museum, Wenham, Mass.

Mrs. Graves getting the dolls ready for the American National Exhibition in Moscow's Sokolniki Park, summer 1959, as Walter Brown, shipping clerk, looks on. Courtesy Wenham Museum, Wenham, Mass.

Vogue delivery truck (c. 1952). Vogue's delivery truck was decorated with the new graphic design introduced in 1952 – 53. The truck made deliveries to department stores and possibly assisted with deliveries to and from home sewers. Wouldn't we love to have the Vogue truck make a delivery to our house! Courtesy Wenham Museum, Wenham, Mass.

The 1960 Vogue line. Vogue publicity photo.

Brikettes in the window of F.A.O. Schwarz (1960). Courtesy Arthur Grobe.

The Vogue line (1962) showing the extended Vogue family including Ginny, Ginnette, new Jill, Ginny Baby, Miss Ginny, Littlest Angel, Baby Dear, Baby Dear-One, and Bobby Dear-One. *Playthings Magazine* ad.

Arthur Grobe (left) and George Olsen (right), sales representatives, shown with Mr. and Mrs. Edwin Nelson, Jr. of Vogue Dolls (1961). Dolls in the Vogue line that year included Ginny, Ginnette, Ginny Baby, Baby Dear, Littlest Angel, and Brikette. *Toys and Novelties Magazine.* Courtesy Arthur Grobe.

Vogue Clothing Production

Jennie H. Graves and her daughter, Virginia Carlson, built Vogue into "The Fashion Leaders In Doll Society."

Mrs. Graves's well-made doll clothes were beautiful as well as action oriented (e.g., cowgirls, roller skaters, etc.). Also, she believed that coordinated accessories were very important, and always completed an outfit with a matching hat, bow, or purse. Even the shoes with snaps or bows had to match and were ordered in coordinating colors. In short, Vogue's outfits always had a certain unique look, which was comprised of an appealing use of color, fabric texture and pattern, and trim.

Virginia Carlson, who joined the company in 1942 and oversaw dress design, recalls the process she used in creating Ginny outfits. First came the ideas for outfits, which often materialized from actually watching children at play in the community or from fashion magazines. As Mrs. Carlson would get an idea, she would actually drape the fabric on the doll itself to style the outfit. She then sat down at the sewing machine to create a sample outfit. Next she would carefully assess the sample. Not only would it have to be attractive, but it would have to be easily made in quantity. Occasionally Vogue would create a design which would take longer than average to sew, such as the Mistress Mary outfit in 1950. If the outfit was needed to complete a theme, Vogue would include it anyway. Profit was not always the overriding concern.

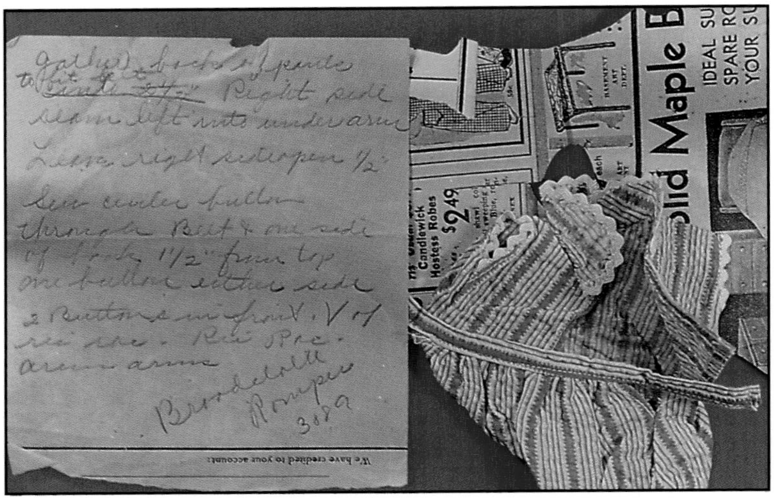

Instructions, sample outfit, pattern pieces for Broadcloth Romper #3089 (1940s). This close-up shows Mrs. Graves's hand written sewing instructions for a romper. Note the very early pattern was cut out of newspaper. Courtesy Virginia Graves Carlson.

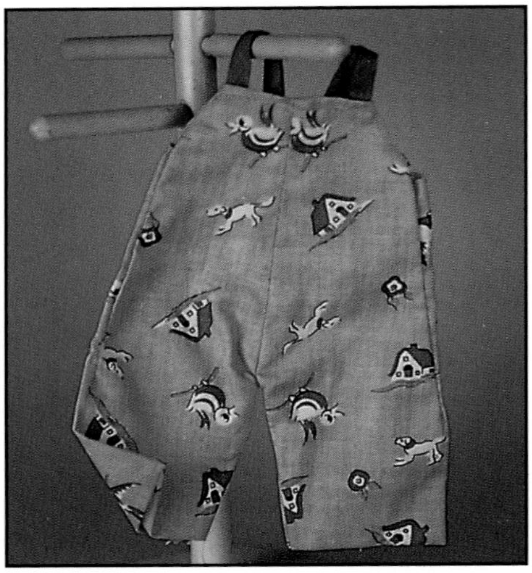

Overall (1940s). Early cotton printed overall from Vogue's separate outfits sold in a cardboard chest with a drawer. The simple pattern design was easy for home sewers to complete and to sew on a hook and eye as a closure. The 1949 Playmate's broadcloth pedal pusher outfit #8-9 & 10-C used a similar pattern. Courtesy Marge Meisinger.

Once the idea for the outfit was agreed upon, a final pattern was created from the sample and the fabric was then cut. In the early days (1930s and '40s) patterns were made from brown or colored paper, and the fabric was cut on a table by the sewer. As the business grew, an exact pattern was drawn for cutting in the factory by professional fabric cutters. In creating a pattern, they considered the talents of their growing workforce of home sewers as well as the capabilities of their equipment.

Originally, Mrs. Graves would sew the outfits with the assistance of her daughter, Virginia, and neighbors would be called in to help. As the business expanded in the 1930s and 1940s, Mrs. Graves had to devise a plan to increase production, yet maintain the quality that she required. She increasingly turned to the talented pool of sewers who were her friends and neighbors, and thus began the cottage industry of home sewers.

While a variety of sewing equipment was allowed, professional or factory-type machinery was not allowed to insure Vogue's quality standards. For example, one will not find factory stitched oversewing on early Vogue interior waist seams in the 1950s. The placement of each little hook and eye as well as careful edging, seaming, and detailing, created the truly finished outfit look. This exact attention to detail was vitally important to Mrs. Graves. Mrs. Ruth Doyon, the supervisor of all sewers at Vogue from 1950 through its sale to Tonka in 1972, recalls many discussions with Mrs. Graves and Mrs. Carlson about the design options and means to allow their sewers to achieve a finished look inside and out. These details in the early 1950s included such features as finished interior side seams or loops to keep little belts in place, hand-fed drawstring neck treatment of Crib Crowd Baby outfits, and separately stitched petticoats. It was just such details that made the early Vogue outfits so appealing.

Mrs. Carlson recalls that as a teenager she was already assisting her mother with the business. She would personally drive deliveries around to the sewers. Deliveries

Sunshine Baby Outfit (1940s). Home sewers assisted Vogue with fine detail work, such as on this lovely cotton outfit for a composition Sunshine Baby. Mrs. Graves's fine design included inset embroidery and lace trim.

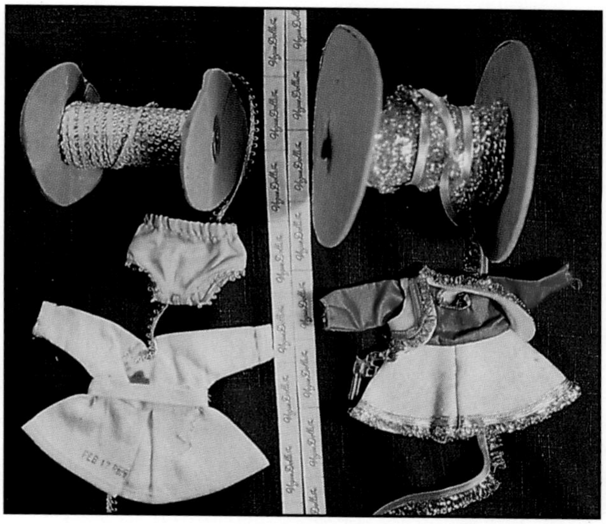

Vogue trims and labels (1950s). Vogue supplied trims and labels to home sewers for their use in completing outfits. Upper left: Picot trim, used for edging on dresses and accessories, such as panties shown. Lower left: Felt appliqué to glue on, such as on the red cross on 1955 Ginny Gym Kids #31 Nurse outfit. Upper and lower right: Fringe such as the gold fringe used on 1956 Playtime #6056 Cowgirl outfit. Center: These labels were used from 1957 to the mid '60s. Original spools of trim and outfits. Courtesy Helen Carlson and Florence Phillips.

included carefully detailed instructions for an outfit, a sample of the outfit itself, a bolt of cloth, and sufficient trim and hooks, eyes, and thread for their use. When the outfits were completed, young Virginia would then collect them, which appeared to her as "beautiful little puffs of clothing," and take them home.

Ruth Doyon reviewed all sewing applicants and gave them a test garment to sew in order to assess their talent. Once accepted, a Vogue truck would deliver supplies and pick up finished products for sewers within 15 miles of the plant. Those outside of that area received materials by mail. Some home sewers have described goods being mailed in egg crates, while others refer to students' laundry baskets. Packages were meticulously packed with enough supplies for four dozen outfits. All hooks and eyes, labels, trimmings, etc. were wrapped separately and included. At first pre-Ginny or Ginny garment pattern pieces were supplied. Later Ginnette, Jill, Ginny Baby, or other separate outfits were supplied as they were added to the line. Mrs. Doyon remembers personally assembling these materials for shipment and allowing some overage for the sewer's use.

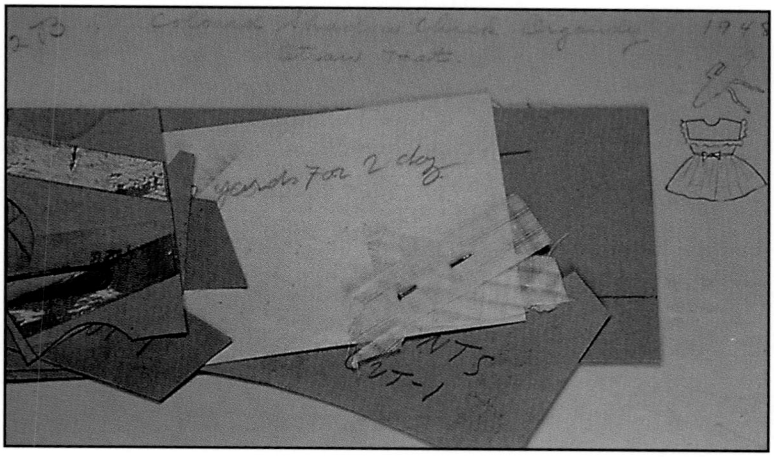

Home sewer's materials and instructions (1948). Sewers received envelopes containing sewing instructions and simple pattern pieces, as shown here. Fabric bolts were supplied in the '40s, but in the '50s cut fabric was supplied with a sample outfit. Courtesy Wenham Doll Museum, Wenham, Mass.

Fabrics – Trimming and Talents

As early as 1932 we find that Vogue fashions were comprised of fabrics as basic as broadcloth or muslin and as delicate as flocked organdy. Most of these same fabrics continued to be used into the 1950s and '60s. In the early 1950s fabrics such as wool jersey and corduroy were included in Vogue designs.

Mrs. Graves and Mrs. Carlson made annual buying trips to New York as well as abroad to view fabrics and fashion trends. Mrs. Graves was proud that Vogue chose "the finest materials, trimmings, ..." and had perfect workmanship in their outfits. All material was pretested to make sure it was washable and could withstand wear. All of these fine fabrics were cut to pattern specifications, at first by hand by the sewers. Later as the business grew in the '50s, special cutting dies were created and the talents of Mr. Tom Morrisette and others at the plant cut fabric using a linoleum cutter. Everything from pattern pieces to little felt bunnies and shiny gold cowboy cuffs were pre-cut for the sewers. Home sewers were not at liberty to make substitutions or change the fabrics or fittings supplied to them for any

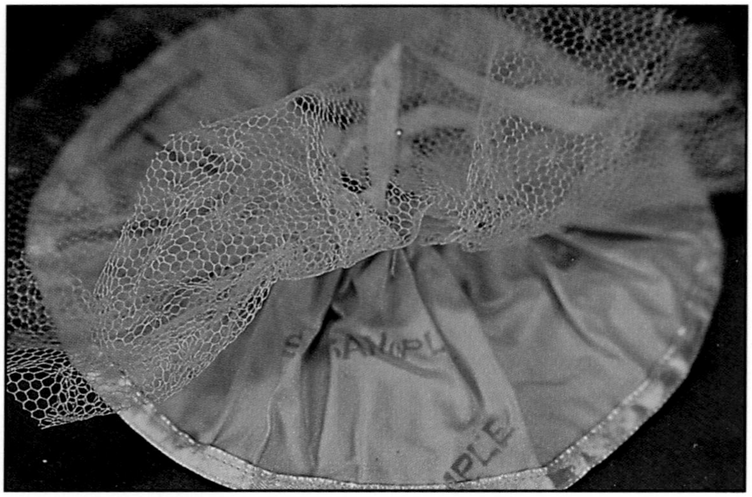

Sample dress (1956). Vogue provided its home sewers with a sample outfit, such as this 1956 aqua Formals outfit #6061, along with instructions and a sufficient quantity of material, trims, etc. to complete the order. Some sample outfits were stamped "SAMPLE," and others were stamped with Vogue's name and address. All samples were returned with completed outfits and any leftover trim. Courtesy Sue Johnson.

reason. For example, the dress attributed to Margie, #28 of the Kindergarten series, is sometimes found with a different braid than was shown in the catalog. This change would have had to have been made and supplied by Vogue, according to Mrs. Doyon.

The Sewing Process

Some sewers recall working on multiple outfits simultaneously, while others recall one outfit being supplied to them at a time. Each shipment of supplies also included a completed outfit which was stamped "sample" for the seamstress to use as a guide. Meticulously written directions for completing each outfit were supplied as well. Most sewers followed the directions exactly, however some devised their own versions. This was acceptable to Vogue as long as the end product was the same as the sample supplied. Occasionally a sewer would have a few supplies left at the end of a project. Materials left over at the end of a project were returned to Vogue with completed outfits. However, some home sewers cherish a few leftover pieces to this day as a fond reminder of their work with Vogue.

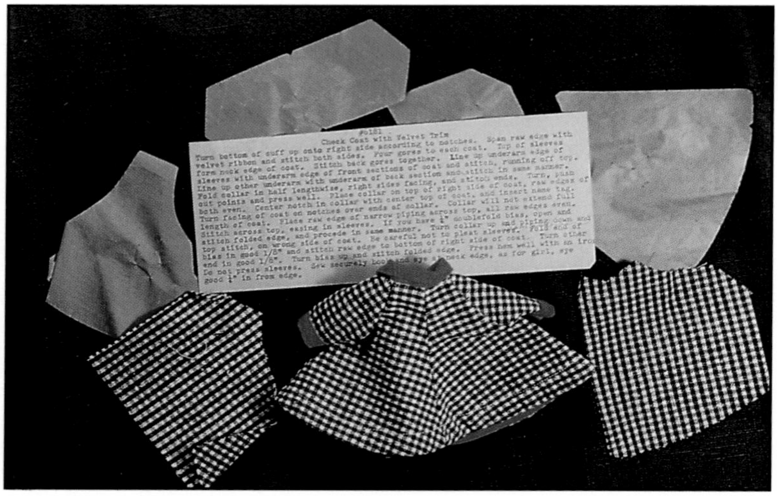

Sample coat (1956), #6181:C, with instructions and pattern. Courtesy Helen Carlson and Florence Phillips.

Some sewers preferred the assembly line process, whereby each sewing step was completed at one time for materials supplied. Other sewers were more at ease completing one frock entirely before beginning the next. Many times a combination of methods was employed. Some sewers recall completing all garments except for attaching hooks and eyes, and then gathering with the other sewers for socializing while completing the task. Loretta Beattle recalls getting together with neighborhood sewers for coffee while stitching hooks and eyes, and found that the time passed quickly that way.

The inclusion of Talon™ zippers into outfits in the 1953 line offered a challenge to home sewers. While they had used the product in their own outfits, the tiny size of Ginny's zippers required great dexterity and ingenuity for the women sewers. These zippers are still in working order today and are prized by collectors.

When the fashion or pattern necessitated talents beyond the capabilities of the sewer, specialists were enlisted. For example, bridal fashions were often done by Mrs. Polly Gagnon from Manchester, New Hampshire, who excelled in handling such work. Likewise, the smocking seen in the 1952 Debutante series was hand done by a talented smocker, such as Miss Helen Sanborn from Somerville. These delicately fashioned pieces were then supplied to the home sewer to utilize in completing the outfit. The hand smocked feature was then prominently promoted to dealers on price lists and in literature.

While home sewers were not permitted to make changes to materials, patterns, etc., occasionally it was necessary for the plant to do so mid-year. This was particularly true as the business grew, and systems called for placing all fabric orders only one time per year if possible. To accomplish this, firm estimates of fabric quantity were made annually. If a fabric ran out due to unanticipated demand, then pattern changes utilizing less fabric

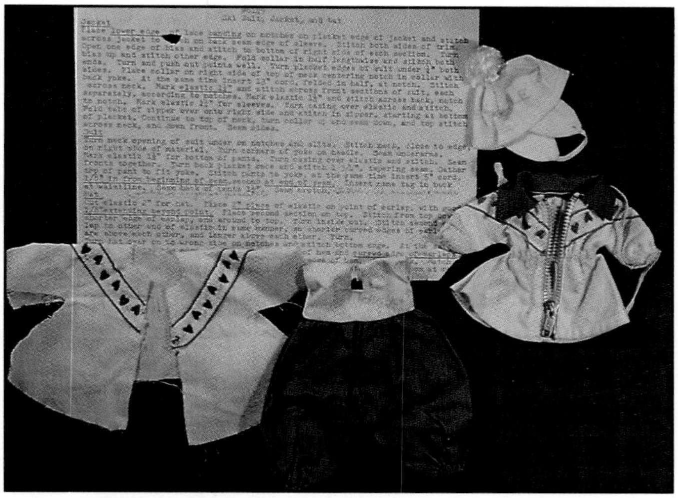

Home sewer instructions and sample (1956). #6149 Ski outfit marked "SAMPLE" was delivered to home sewers along with fabric to sew. Early sewers in the '40s cut the fabric from patterns, but '50s sewers received cut fabric like the piece at lower left. Courtesy Helen Carlson and Florence Phillips.

Home sewer's sample outfit (1958). Ginny's Country Fair Gown #1180 is stamped with Vogue's address on the skirt and sleeves, indicating that it is a sample outfit for sewers to use as a guide and to return with the completed outfit. Courtesy Sue Johnson.

were considered in order to supply dealers' requests. Thus, the home sewer could be called on to use two different methods to make the same outfit in the same year. This could be a possible explanation for the existence of two different designs for the 1954 roller skating outfit #347, one utilizing less velvet surface fabric than the other by substituting knit panties.

Running short of fabric was not a serious problem at Vogue. Likewise, neither were fabric overages, but overages did occur despite the best annual estimates. One solution to this situation was to create budget dress designs utilizing the leftover fabric for cost-conscious little customers and parents. Home sewers were given these projects to complete. Another solution was to utilize the fabric in the next season's design. For example, the brown check cotton fabric in the 1954 separate coat #181 was utilized again as a top in the 1955 Merry Moppets dress #233.

Occasionally an elaborate outfit requiring fine details took more time than usual to complete. This was particularly true in the early years through 1956 when each costume fit into a series of six (such as Kindergarten School series or Twin series). The Bridal costume #464 in the 1954 My First Corsage style series, while costly for sewers to produce, was carried anyway if omitting it would have been detrimental to its series. In these cases, a conscious decision was made by Mrs. Carlson prior to production to set standards allowing the sewers valuable time needed to complete the outfit. This was consistent with Mrs. Carlson's high standards in fashion and for quality workmanship.

Hats and Home Sewers

Mrs. Graves's love of hats in completing outfits became well known and hats and/or bows were an integral part of each costume design. In the 1940s when costly hats were not consistent with war-time fashion trends, many costumes called for hats of matching dress fabric instead. Home sewers were often called upon to complete these fabric hats along with outfits. They were also involved in stitching headband-type pieces. Some sewers recall vividly making little Tyrolean hats or Indian headdresses. Hats for early military costumes and straw

Majorette outfits (1956 vs. 1957). The two majorette outfits shown illustrate the snap closures used on outfits beginning in 1957, (left) vs. hooks and eyes (at arrow) sewn by hand onto the 1956 majorette outfit (right). Note: the "star" pattern on the outside metal portion of the snap is distinctive to Vogue.

Bowtie maker (1950s). Vogue sewers used this apparatus to tie bows for Vogue outfits by looping ribbon over the pegs. Courtesy Ruth Doyon.

hats were subcontracted to outside suppliers. Mr. Humpert Green of New York is reported to have made Vogue hats, after having made hats for ladies for years.

Sewers Produce Fashion Profits

Vogue derived its highest profit margin from Ginny's little garments rather than from the doll itself. When the Dress Me doll was introduced in 1952, the market for even more separate costumes was created, and the home sewers were called upon to increase production. Likewise, when Ginnette was introduced in 1955 and yet more separate costumes were needed, it was the sewers who enabled this to happen. Studies indicate that in the mid 1950s each little customer bought five outfits for each undressed Ginny doll alone, not including the wardrobe needs of other members of Vogue family added to their household. Obviously, the additional production required to fill store shelves with these outfits yielded valuable additional revenues for Vogue. Thus, the home sewer's value to the company was insured in the 1950s and well into the 1960s. Vogue was able to draw from this vast pool of talent to meet production demands. It is reported that Vogue utilized the efforts of home sewers until the final days of sale to Tonka in 1972.

Sewing Standards and Inspections

A study completed by a student of the Harvard Graduate School of Business Administration in 1956 reveals that home sewers' work fell into four standard categories. Once the company became familiar with their work and their speed, they assigned the sewers into four categories: fast, medium, slow, and last resort. The timing was reported by the sewers on the honor system.

Time standards for these categories were established by Vogue for the sewers according to time judged sufficient to complete a garment. This standard was the average of the time required by the medium and slow workers to complete a garment. One can imagine that sewers whose capabilities were above average had no problem completing tasks according to standard times. Those in low categories, however, undoubtedly had to devise work efficiencies in order to be retained by Vogue. In any case, no worker was ever allowed to work more than 40 hours a week at home. These standards were a very sensitive subject at the time due to pressure by organized labor who questioned the use of home sewers at all. The majority of home sewers, on the other hand, enjoyed earning a livelihood from their homes. They enjoyed the flexibility and ability to involve their families in their schedules.

Once sewers completed their work, there were systems in place to collect their finished outfits and to complete the production process. The first step was a rigid inspection process. Mrs. Doyon oversaw the inspection process and recalls Vogue's high quality standards. For example, edging stitching had to be within ⅛" of the finished edge, and the stitch gauge could not exceed the standard number of stitches per inch. As previously mentioned, the honor system was used to determine the number of garments per hour completed by the sewer. If the standard was exceeded, sewers were paid at the piece work rate for the overage. The amount paid in 1956 for the standard number of pieces was $1.00 minimum wage per hour. Supervisors for home sewers had their own pay scale as well as a bonus system as an incentive to production.

Box used to deliver home sewing material (1950s). Courtesy Ruth Doyon.

Garments which did not meet the rigid requirements were returned to the sewer to be redone. On occasion, however, these garments were purchased as-is and they were sold to employees at discount rates. Obviously, sewers producing this substandard work were not retained in the future.

It should be pointed out that Vogue did maintain some sewers in the factory primarily for preparation work for home sewers, for repetitive processes, or for use in emergencies. Factory sewers were called upon to produce additional accessories and panties. Different time standards applied to these factory sewers. Mrs. Graves was very proud of Vogue's labor relations policies and was considered an authority on this and other issues such as small business taxation, and other issues relating to cottage industries.

Routing, Tracking, and Budgeting

Despite the many advantages outlined, there was one major disadvantage to the home sewers system. This was that a substantial amount of goods remained in the home sewers' homes during the sewing process. This resulted in large inventories of work in process for Vogue which lengthened the time between cutting the fabric and turning it into saleable goods. In order to minimize this gap, another system was necessitated for the routing and accounting of supplies allocated to sewers, and for the return of their completed work. By the mid 1950s, a manual IBM system existed which tracked goods in and out of inventory. Returned goods were immediately deducted from work in process and reassigned to finished goods inventory. Not only did Vogue establish this and other sophisticated controls, but they also constantly improved upon them to insure prompt payment for the sewers and accurate inventories for the company.

Machine cut fabric pieces (1960s). These felt and denim pieces date from the 1960s; however Vogue began to machine cut fabric in the 1950s. Before then home sewers hand cut fabric.

Another of Vogue's systems necessitated by the home sewers was tracking their contribution to the budgeted cost of each garment. For this task, Vogue designed a routing system which sent the hours reported by the sewers to the appropriate personnel. This routing insured that sewers' time reports reached accounting and were analyzed. If a garment was determined to be too expensive to produce, ways to produce the piece more economically without sacrificing design were considered. For example, Mrs. Doyon recalls that just such an analysis led to a change from a three-piece yoke pattern which required two shoulder seams and three hooks, to a one-piece yoke which eliminated shoulder seams and needed only one hook. The one-piece yoke saved sewers time and saved Vogue labor cost. Since Vogue's storage facilities in the mid 1950s allowed only sufficient space for a 24- to 48-hour period, turnaround was especially important. All of these systems increased efficiency, helped organize the home sewing effort, and got outfits and dressed dolls into the market place faster.

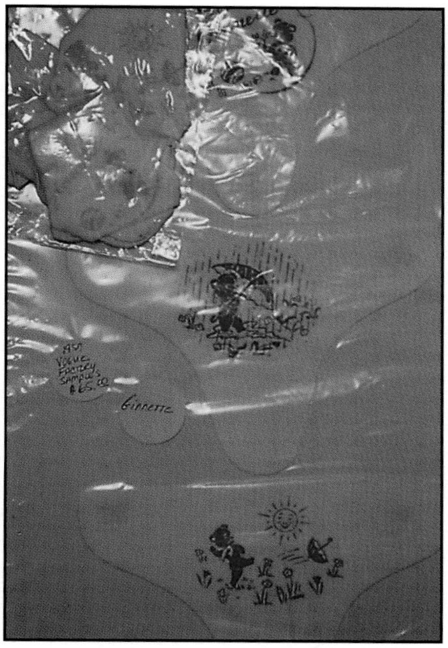

Diapers (mid 1950s). Factory sewers usually sewed machine over-stitched borders on Ginnette's flannel diapers.
Courtesy Robin Randall.

One final problem remained to be solved which both the home sewers and Vogue shared: seasonality. In Vogue's early days, the holiday season was the busiest, and the rest of the year experienced peaks and valleys for orders. Summer was the slowest season. Mrs. Graves's introduction of the undressed Dress Me Ginny in 1952 drastically increased demand for separate costumes. This kept the home sewers busier than ever before, and, indeed, additional sewers were added to meet production demands. However, it was a clever promotion with department stores nationwide which really helped to increase slow season demands. In late 1951 and early 1952, Vogue encouraged department stores to devote window space to Ginny and her many outfits by promising cooperative advertising dollars and other marketing assistance. Stores such as Macy's in New York and Loveman's in Birmingham reported a sell-out of merchandise on the first day of the promotion! Thus, Vogue's entry into off-season promotions in the winter and at other slow times was in full swing, increasing profitable business for Vogue and for their home sewers as well.

Conclusion

Vogue's home sewing network began as a solution to a business problem for Vogue — labor shortage — and became a valuable addition to the community in general, affording many women the opportunity to earn a livelihood from their homes. Undoubtedly, the home sewer system created additional logistical and production challenges for the company. However, in the final analysis, the home sewers greatly enhanced Vogue's production of their fine doll fashions and contributed to the growth of the company.

Vogue Tags and Labels

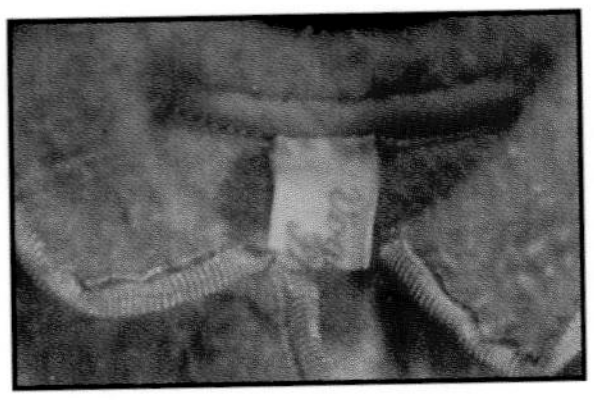

1930s: "Vogue" or "Vogue Doll Shoppe," yellow/gold on white cloth tag.

1930s – 1947 or 1948: "Vogue" in black script on round gold paper label glued on front of clothing.

1944 – 46: "VOGUE DOLLS INC./MEDFORD MASS." in blue lettering on white cotton tag (not shown).

Mid to late 1940s – 1950: "Vogue Dolls, INC.; MEDFORD MASS." in white on a blue background on cotton tag. Called "Ink spot" label by collectors.

1950 – 1951: "Vogue Dolls" printed horizontally in blue on white rayon tag; wavy line design upper left, lower right.

1952: "Vogue" printed in blue on thin white rayon tag.

1953: "ORIGINAL/Vogue/DOLLS INC." in blue writing (Vogue in script) on white rayon tag.

1954 – 1956: "VOGUE DOLLS Inc.*/MEDFORD, MASS, U.S.A.;* REG. U.S. PAT. OFF." in black print on white rayon tag.

1957 – 1965: "Vogue Dolls, Inc." in blue script on white cotton tag.

1978 – 82: "MADE IN HONG KONG" black print on white rayon (Ginny Outfits).

1966 – 71: "Vogue Dolls, Inc./MADE IN U.S.A." in blue script (Vogue) and print on white cotton tag.

1972 – 77: "MADE IN/HONG KONG" in green print with a green border on white paper on Hong Kong Produced Ginnys.

1978 – 1982: "MADE IN HONG KONG," red print with a red border on white paper (Far Away Lands outfits).

1981 – 82: "MADE IN CHINA," black print on white ribbon (on Sasson Ginny outfits). (not shown)

1984–86: "Vogue dolls, inc. /1984," black print on white rayon.

1987 – 1995: "VOGUE DOLLS, INC." with date of outfit with black print on white tag. (same as 1984 – 86 tag)

Ginny® ©1995
THE VOGUE DOLL
COMPANY, INC.

1995 – current: "GINNY ® ©1995/THE VOGUE DOLL/COMPANY INC." in black print on white cloth tag

*Note: During early years of production, especially early 1940s and 1950 – 52, labels were occasionally left off outfits; also, label and tag dates frequently overlap.

Early Dolls Dressed by Vogue

Bisque Dolls

1922 – mid 1930s

Jennie H. Graves began designing and sewing doll clothing in 1922 on a treadle sewing machine in a corner of her bedroom in Somerville, Massachusetts. The dolls she dressed were the large German bisque head dolls such as the Kammer & Reinhardt (K star R) dolls. She also dressed smaller dolls such as the 8" and 10½" Armand Marseille Just Me character doll, the 8" Peggy Jean, who was a little sister to Just Me, and Bokaye Babies from Germany.

Kammer & Reinhardt

K star R (early 1920s)

Description: Large (approximately. 36") Kammer & Reinhardt (K star R) large German bisque head dolls
Marks: Variations of the K star R mark

Mrs. Graves's forte was fashion design and she outfitted the dolls in dresses and hats that reflected the latest fashions. At first she dressed huge 36" Kammer & Reinhardts with great big heads. The clothes were all crepe de chine with smocking.

The first dolls were so large they might have been display dolls, taking a children's size four or five clothing. They became too cumbersome to deal with and Mrs. Graves turned to dressing smaller dolls such as the Armand Marseille Just Me doll. Eventually the Vogue Doll Shoppe, as she called her business, sold dolls to Jordan Marsh department store in Boston and many other stores. These outfits have a Vogue tag.

Large K star R imported German bisque doll dressed by Mrs. Graves (1920 – 30s). Courtesy Wenham Museum, Wenham, Mass.

Large imported German bisque K star R dolls dressed by Mrs. Graves (1920 – 30s). Notice fitted case. Courtesy Wenham Museum, Wenham, Mass.

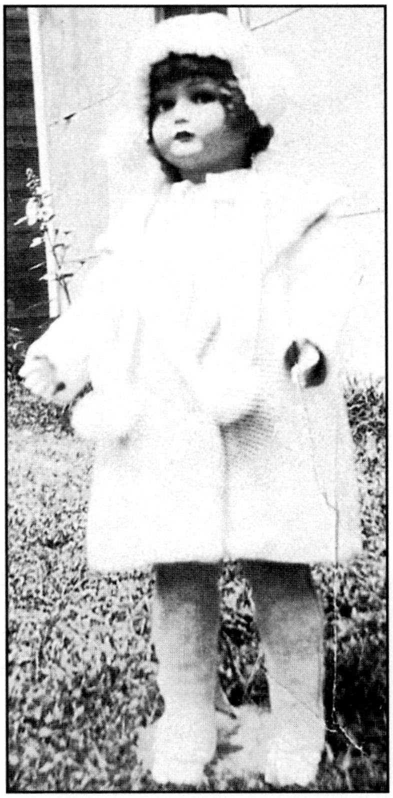

Large imported German bisque K star R doll dressed by Mrs. Graves (1920 – 30s). Courtesy Wenham Museum, Wenham, Mass.

Prices:
Too few examples seen

Just Me

(1920s – 1930s)

Armand Marseille 8" and 10½" Just Me, 8" Peggy Jean, 11" Suzanne, unknown size Nancy Lee (1930s)

Description: 8" and 10½" Just Me had a fired or painted bisque head, and a five-piece jointed composition body, sleep eyes, open crown, and glued-on curly wig.

Marks:

Fired Bisque	Head:	Just ME//Registered//Germany//A//310//5//0//M	
	Back:	None	
Painted Bisque	Head:	Just ME//Registered//Germany//310/7*/0,	*7 or 10 or 11 seen
	Back:	None	

Clothing White cotton tag sewn with gold lettering with "Vogue" in script was sewn folded in the outfit.

The Armand Marseille Doll Company of Germany produced the 8" and 10½" Just Me doll that had a bisque head and a five-piece composition body, sleep eyes, open crown, and glued-on curly wig. Mrs. Graves imported the doll, dressed it, and sold it under the Vogue label. She designed and individually sewed the lovely dresses, many with smocking or embroidered flowers, and matching hats. The white cotton tag sewn with gold lettering with "Vogue" in script was sewn folded in the outfit in the 1930s.

Just Me had two types of bisque heads: a fired bisque head or a painted bisque head. The fired bisque were the earliest dolls Mrs. Graves used. These dolls have pale skin color. The 10½" fired bisque head Just Me doll was marked "Just ME// Registered// Germany// A//310//5//0//M." The painted bisque, which means the facial painting was not fired into the bisque, were the later dolls and usually found after 1930. The painted bisque have shinier, brighter facial color. The painted bisque head marks were Just ME// Registered// Germany// 310/7/0. The last version of Just Me was all composition that Vogue dressed from the mid to late 1930s.

The 1933 – 34 Vogue catalog offered Just Me in nine different outfits: a wool jersey coat and beret with figured muslin dress; a zephyr print ensemble with a plaited skirt and beret; a wool jersey sweater with plaited skirt and beret; a four-piece ensemble of crepe piqué and organdy with embroidery, trimmed in ribbon; a colored dimity dress and bonnet with embroidery, trimmed in ribbon; checked organdy dress and bonnet with white organdy ruffling trim; a colored organdy dress and hat with hemstitched white organdy bows and trimming; a wool bathing suit ensemble with a terrycloth cape, watering pot, and towel; and a striped broadcloth dress and beret with felt trimmed buttons. Vogue also offered Just Me in a wicker basket with a matching wardrobe in 1933 – 34.

DRESSED JUST ME DOLL—(IMPORTED)
10½" with Curly Wigs and Closing Eyes

278B	Wool Jersey Coat and Beret, Figured Muslin Dress	$16.50
279B	Zephyr Print Ensemble, Plaited Skirt with Beret	16.50
280B	Wool Jersey Sweater with Plaited Skirt and Beret	16.50
281B	Four-piece Ensemble, Crepe Pique and Organdy, Embroidery and Ribbon Trimmed	16.50
282B	Colored Dimity Dress and Bonnet, Embroidery and Lace Trimmed	16.50
283B	Checked Organdy Dress and Bonnet, White Organdy Ruffling Trimmed	16.50
284B	Colored Organdy Dress and Hat, Hemstitched White Organdy Bows and Trimming	16.50
285B	Ensemble Wool Bathing Suit with Terry Cloth Cape and Watering Pot and Towel	16.50
286B	Striped Broadcloth Dress and Beret, Felt Button Trimmed	16.50

DRESSED SUZANNE DOLL—(IMPORTED)
11" with Curly Wigs and Closing Eyes
Big Sister to Just Me

514B	Colored Gingham Plaited Dress with White Organdy Hat, Hemstitched Organdy Trimmings (Lamb on Arm)	19.50
516B	Boy's Suit, Colored Gingham Pants, White Blouse, Hat to Match (Tennis Racket on Arm) (Twin to 517B)	19.50
517B	Colored Gingham Plaited Skirt, White Blouse, Hat to Match (Tennis Racket on Arm) (Twin to 516B)	19.50
520B	Chinchilla Coat and Hat, Novelty Voile Dress, Ribbon and Button Trimmed	19.50
521B	Crepe Pique Ensemble, Smocked Dotted Swiss Dress, Hat to Match	19.50
522B	Red or Blue Dotted Dimity Dress and Hat, Felt Flower Trimming, Week-end Bag on Arm with Soap, Towel, Tooth Brush and Mirror	19.50
523B	Colored Organdy Plaited Dress and Hat with Dainty Embrodiered Rose Buds and Ribbon Trimmed, Hat Box on Arm with Nightie, Towel, Mirror	19.50
524B	Colored Handkerchief Lawn Dress and Hat, Featherstitched and Embroidered Rose Buds, Pocket Book on Arm	19.50
525B	Wool Jersey Zipper Ski Suit, White Jersey Scarf and Beret with Wool Pom-poms, Romper under Suit	19.50
526B	Sun or Garden Pajamas, no back, Leather Bag with Garden Tools	16.50
527B	Riding Habit	19.50

DRESSED PEGGY JEAN DOLL—(IMPORTED)
Little Sister to Just Me, 8" with Curly Wigs
and Closing Eyes

		Per Doz.
650B	Colored Dimity Dress and Hat, Embroidered Flowers and Lace Trimmed	$12.00
651B	Striped Broadcloth Dress and Beret, Felt Button Trimmed	12.00
652B	Colored Organdy Dress and Hat, Insertion Down Front and Around Bottom, Lace Around Crown of Hat	12.00
655B	Colored Batiste Dress and Bonnet, Pointed Collar Featherstitched and Embroidered Flowers	12.00
656B	Smocked and Embroidered White Batiste Dress, Colored Dimity Bonnet and Band Around Bottom	12.00
657B	Smocked and Embroidered Colored Organdy Dress with Round Yoke, Bonnet to Match	12.00
658B	Wool Jersey Jumper Dress with Beret, Dotted Dimity Blouse and Bloomer. Can be used for Separate Romper	12.00
659B	Ensemble Bathing Suit with Sailor Pants and Hat	10.80

10½" Just Me, 8" Peggy Jean, and 11" Suzanne doll listed in the 1933 – 34 Vogue Doll Shoppe price list. Courtesy Mrs. Virginia Carlson.

DRESSED DOLLS AND FITTED BASKETS

Just Me (Jointed--Composition)
10½", Curly Hair, Closing Eyes (All outfits come with Hats)

283	Novelty Hemstitched Org. Ruffle with Featherstitching and Roses	21.66 Do
284	Col. Dimity, Smocked Front, Org. Trim, Lace	21.66
285	Col. Org., Ribbon Sash, Emb. Roses, Ruffles	21.66
286	Smocked Batiste, Wh. Org. Yoke, Emb. Roses	21.66
287	Col. Batiste, Wh. Org. Collar, Sash and Lace	21.66
288	Col. and Wh. Dotty Stripe - Bolero Jacket, Felt Flowers	21.66
289	Red Riding Hood, Silk Cape, Smocked Dotted Dimity Dress	24.76

Peggy Jean 8"
Little Sister to Just Me

640	White Dimity, Tyrolean Bias on Bottom, Smocked	15.47
642	Col. Batiste, Lace and Roses	15.47
643	Col. Batiste, Smocked Front, Roses	15.47
644	Col. Organdy, White Inserts in Skirts, Emb. Roses	15.47
645	Col. Dimity, Wh. Org. Yoke Emb. Lace	15.47
646	Col. Org. Old Fashioned Pantalette Dress	18.57

The Just Me and her family's shoes were leatherette and tied with little pom-pons attached to the front. They came in plain cardboard boxes lined with paper doilies and marked "Made in Germany" at the end of the box.

Just Me also came in a wicker basket ensemble or metal trunk with six outfits and little accessories such as hats and towels (see page 33). There was also a bisque head Just Me in a large Easter egg dressed in a pink cotton batiste outfit trimmed with pink taffeta ribbon. The beautiful egg is imported from Germany and came with a tiny chick and bunny with pink crepe paper lining inside.

Prices:

Just Me

Early fired bisque doll, composition body	$1,000.00+
Painted bisque, later bisque doll. Composition body	$950.00+
Easter Egg Just Me	$1700.00+

Peggy Jean , Suzanne and Nancy Lee — too few examples to price

Prices shown are for mint, complete, all original dolls. Dolls which have been played with, have messy hair or are faded will have substantially reduced prices. Likewise, MIB dolls, with original boxes, tags, and booklets will have increased prices.

These pricing standards apply to this and all other chapters.

Just Me (1924) 10½" bisque head with composition body in white dress with pink smocking and embroidered pink flowers. Swivel socket head, composition body with jointed arms and legs, curly mohair wig, glass eyes. Vogue Sample dressed by Jennie Graves. Marks: "JUST ME/ REGISTERED/GERMANY/A310/50/M." Courtesy Wenham Museum, Wenham, Mass.

Just Me (1930s) 8" bisque head, composition body wearing blue dress with pleats and embroidered pink flower on neckline and hat. Painted bisque, a later doll. Marks: "JUST ME/Registered/ Germany/A310/7/0 /M" (on head). "JUST ME" on bottom of shoe. No Vogue tag on dress. Courtesy Pam Zampiello.

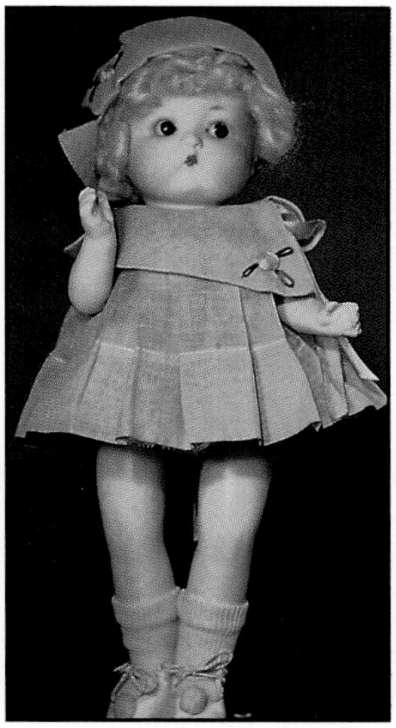

Just Me (1931) 9" bisque head, composition body, floral dress, curly hair. Missing shoes and socks. Marks: JUST ME/ REGISTERED/ GERMANY/ A310/7/0/M. Bought from Jennie Graves herself, Nov. 1931. Courtesy Wenham Museum, Wenham, Mass.

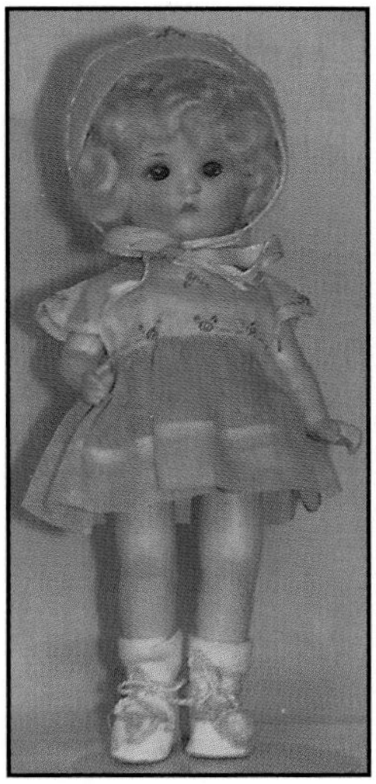

Just Me (1933) 8" bisque head, jointed composition body, sleep eyes, glued-on curly light blonde mohair wig. Yellow organdy dress with blue flower embroidery decoration and matching tie bonnet. Tie shoes with pom-pons. Marks: JUST ME/REGISTERED/GERMANY/A 310/11/O.M (on head), none on body. Courtesy Maureen Fukushima.

Just Me (late 1930s) 7" painted bisque head and jointed composition body. Sleep eyes, mohair wig, wearing green and orange striped dress. Marks: "JUST ME/REGISTERED/ GERMANY/A 310/11/O.M" (on head), none on body. Courtesy Maureen Fukushima.

Just Me (1933) 7¾" bisque head, jointed composition body, sleep eyes, glued-on curly brunette mohair wig. Wearing white smocked dress with blue hem and hat. Marks: "JUST ME/REGISTERED/GERMANY/A 310/11/O.M" (on head), none on body. Shown with silk lined wicker trunk fitted with Vogue's handmade bedtime and play outfits. Courtesy Maureen Fukushima.

Just Me (probably 1924) 8" bisque head, composition body. Wearing blue dress with smocking front and blue bonnet with lace in front. Marks: "JUST ME/ REGISTERED/GERMANY/A310/11/OM." Dressed by Jennie Graves. Date of 1938 is on doll in museum, it is questionable whether bisque was used so late. Courtesy Wenham Museum, Wenham, Mass.

Just Me (1930s) 8" painted bisque, later bisque doll used. Composition body, sleep eyes. Wearing blue dress with white netting on front, hem, and neckline. Marks: "Just Me/Registered Germany/A. 310/11/O.M." Dress not tagged. Courtesy Ann Tardie.

Just Me (1920s – 1930s) 9" bisque head, composition body, brown glass eyes, brown wig. Wearing white organdy dress with flannelette jacket and organdy hat. Doll dressed especially for Mrs. Skinner by Mrs. Clark for Christmas. Marks: "REGISTERED/GERMANY/A 310/7/0/1" (on head). Clothes untagged. Bottom of shoe stamped "Made In ?—erland." Courtesy Mrs. Eleanor Skinner.

Just Me (mid to late 1930s), 8" painted bisque head, jointed composition body, sleep eyes, glued-on curly mohair wig. Wearing red dotted white dimity skirt with white cottom bodice trimmed with red embroidery. Marks: "Just Me/Reg/Germany/A310/11/0" on head, none on body. Courtesy Barbara Rosplock-Van Orman.

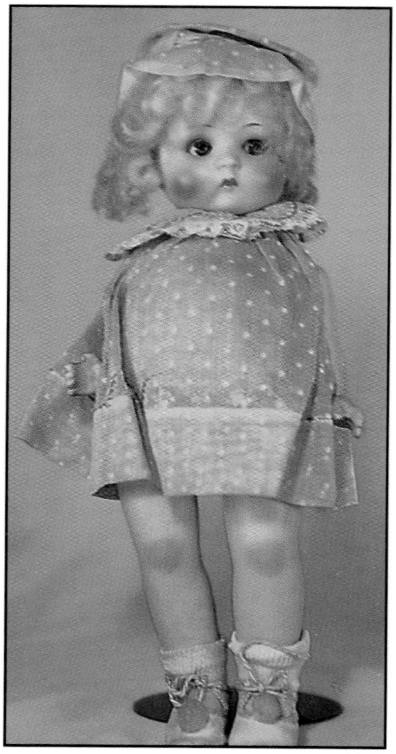

Just Me (c. 1930s) 9½" bisque head and jointed composition body, sleep eyes, mohair wig, wearing a white dress and hat with polka dots and blue and pink embroidery and lace collar. Marks: "JUST ME/ REGISTERED/ GERMANY/A 310/7/OM" (on head), none on body. Courtesy Veronica Phillips.

Just Me (1930s) 9" bisque head and jointed composition body, sleep eyes, mohair wig, wearing a white dimity dress with red, yellow, and blue smocking and felt appliqué bands at hem, red cape. Marks: "JUST ME/ REGISTERED/ GERMANY/A 310/11/O.M" (on head), none on body. Courtesy Maureen Fukushima.

Just Me (1930s), 9½" bisque head, jointed composition body, sleep eyes, mohair wig, blue dress and hat with white printed flowers, blue and pink embroidery, near lace collar, replaced shoes and socks. Marks: "JUST ME/Reg/Germany/A 310/11/OM" (on head), none on body. Courtesy Veronica Phillips.

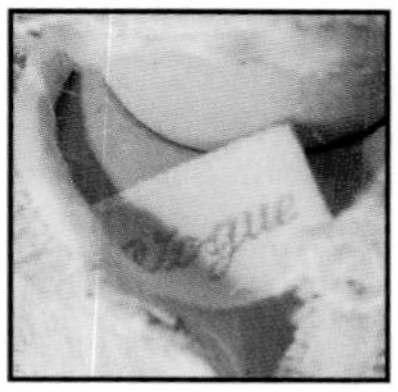

Just Me (1930s) detail of Vogue gold thread label on 9½" bisque head and jointed composition body. Courtesy Veronica Phillips.

Easter egg with Just Me is imported from Germany and came with a tiny chick and bunny with pink crepe paper lining inside. Courtesy Polly Judd.

Peggy Jean
(Just Me)

Description: 8" with a bisque head and five-piece jointed composition body, sleep eyes, open crown, and glued-on curly wig, 1933 – 34 (see page 26).

Marks:

Head: Just ME/Registered Germany/A. 310/11/O.M.
Back: None

Just Me had a younger sister called Peggy Jean who was 8" tall. Peggy Jean was marked "Just ME/Registered Germany/A. 310/11/O.M." The doll had a five-piece jointed composition body with a bisque head, sleep eyes, open crown, and glued-on curly wig.

In the 1933 – 34 catalog Peggy Jean is offered in seven different outfits including a colored dimity dress and hat with embroidered flowers and trimmed in lace; a striped broadcloth dress and beret trimmed in felt buttons; a colored organdy dress and hat with front insertion and lace around crown of hat; a colored batiste dress and bonnet with pointed featherstitched collar and embroidered flowers; a smocked and embroidered white batiste dress with colored dimity bonnet with band around bottom; a smocked and embroidered colored organdy dress with round yoke and bonnet to match; a wool jersey jumper with beret and dotted dimity blouse and bloomer; and an ensemble bathing suit with sailor pants and hat. Peggy Jean also came in a metal trunk with six changes in 1933 – 34. Wardrobe determines whether an 8" doll is Peggy Jean or Just Me.

Peggy Jean (1933 – 34) 8" bisque head and five-piece jointed composition body, sleep eyes, open crown, and glued-on curly wig. Marks, head: "Just ME/Registered Germany/A. 310/11/O." Mint in box, notice little doily around edges. Courtesy Veronica Phillips

Suzanne
(Just Me)

Description: The 11" big sister to Just Me. In the 1933 – 34 Vogue catalog she is offered in 11 different outfits (see page 26).

Marks: Unknown

Suzanne was the 11" big sister to Just Me. In the 1933 – 34 Vogue catalog she is offered in 11 different outfits. These outfits were unique and Suzanne was the most expensive doll Vogue, sold at $1.62 each.

Suzanne came in a colored gingham pleated dress with white organdy hat, hemstitched organdy trimmings with a lamb on her arm; a boy's suit of colored gingham pants, white blouse, hat to match and tennis racket on her arm (a twin to the next outfit); a colored gingham pleated skirt, white blouse, hat to match and tennis racket on her arm; a chinchilla coat and hat with a novelty voile dress trimmed with ribbon and button; a crepe piqué ensemble, with a smocked dotted Swiss dress and hat; a red or blue dotted dimity dress and hat with felt flower trim carrying a weekend bag on her arm containing soap, towel, toothbrush, and mirror; a colored handkerchief lawn dress and hat, with embroidered rosebuds and a pocketbook on her arm; a wool jersey ski suit with a zipper, white jersey scarf and beret with wool pompons and romper undersuit; sun or garden pajamas with no back with a leather bag with garden tools; and a riding habit. Suzanne also came in a metal trunk with seven changes.

Nancy Lee

(Just Me)

Description: Unknown size. Nancy Lee doll was an older sister to Suzanne. In 1933 – 34 she came in a 18" metal trunk with six changes of clothes. The trunk was red and all the fittings are red and white.

Baby BoKaye

(and Bonnie Babe Dolls)

Description: 5" bisque BoKaye Babies from Germany had painted eyes and painted shoes with straps and socks. They had chipmunk cheeks. They are listed in 1933 – 34 catalog.

Marks: Unmarked, may have sticker on torso

Mrs. Graves also dressed 5" bisque BoKaye Babies she imported from Germany. They had painted eyes and painted shoes with straps and socks. They had chipmunk cheeks. There were two boys' outfits and four girls' outfits in the 1933 – 34 catalog.

The two boys' outfits were cotton suit with plaiting and buttons with a shovel and pail; and #25B, a wool jersey suit and beret, shovel and pail. For the girls there was a colored handkerchief lawn plaited dress with round collar and lace trimmed bonnet to match; a colored dimity smocked dress and hat with pointed collar; a white nainsook smocked dress with colored nainsook bonnet; and a colored dimity dress with three rows of feather stitching down the front with rosebuds, bows on shoulder, and hat to match.

The BoKaye doll also came in a trunk and a hat box. The trunk was 5¾" and came with three changes. She also came in two hat boxes: a small patent leather hat box with eight changes, and a black paper-covered oval hat box with a strap with four changes: a nightie, two dress sets, and a bathing suit.

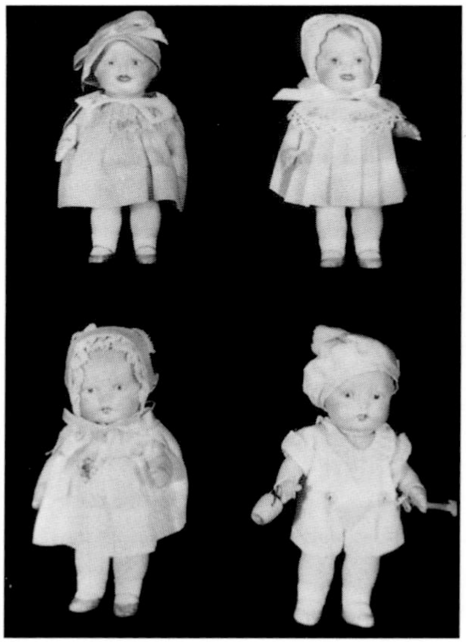

BoKaye Babies (1933 – 34) 5" all bisque, manufactured by BoKaye, Germany. There were six in total, two not shown. Courtesy Mrs. Virginia Carlson.

DRESSED 5' BISC BABY BOKAYE AND BONNIE BABE DOLLS (IMPORTED)

		Per Doz.
20B	Boy's Cotton Suit, Plaiting and Buttons, Shovel and Pail	10.80
21B	Colored Handkerchief Lawn Plaited Dress, Round Collar, Featherstitched and Embroidered, Lace Trimmed Bonnet to Match	$10.80
22B	Colored Dimity Smocked Dress and Hat, Pointed Collar	10.80
23B	White Nainsook Smocked Dress, Lace Trimmed, Colored Nainsook Bonnet	10.80
24B	Colored Dimity Dress, Three Rows of Featherstitching Down the Front with Rose Buds, Bows on Shoulder, Hat to Match	10.80
25B	Boy's Wool Jersey Suit and Beret, Shovel and Pail	10.80

Baby BoKaye in the 1933 – 34 Vogue Doll Shoppe price list. Courtesy Mrs. Virginia Carlson.

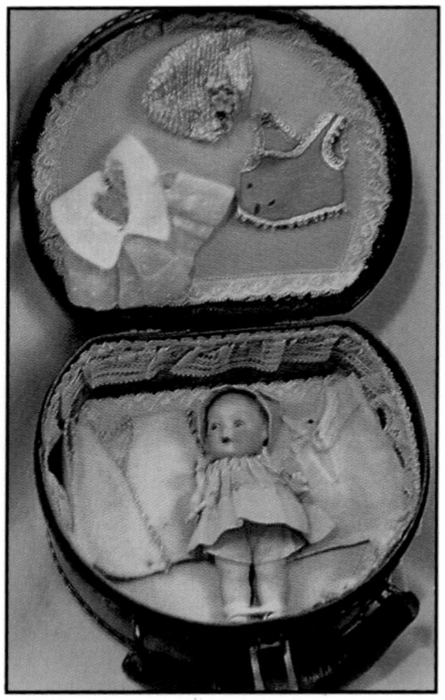

Baby BoKaye (1933 – 34) 5", all bisque, manufactured by BoKaye, Germany wearing the colored dimity dress with three rows of featherstitching down the front with rosebuds, bows on shoulder and hat to match. In the black paper-covered oval hat box with a strap with four changes: a nightie, two dress sets, and a bathing suit. Courtesy Veronica Phillips.

Baby BoKaye (1933 – 34) 5", all bisque, close-up of doll. Notice the painted shoes and open mouth with two painted teeth. Courtesy Veronica Phillips.

Baby BoKaye (1933 – 34) close-up of the black paper-covered oval hat box with a strap in which the doll came. Courtesy Veronica Phillips.

Prices

BoKaye Baby	$1,000.00+

Other Bisque Dolls

(Less than 7" tall)

The Vogue Doll Shoppe catalog offered a 4½" "bisc" baby doll wearing a short smocked dress and bonnet with a pacifier in 1933 – 34. Also in 1933 – 34 Vogue sold a 5" Kammer & Reinhardt (K star R) Company of Germany doll listed as Toddles who was offered in three outfits: a white smocked batiste dress; a colored dimity dress and bonnet to match; and a wool jersey dresses with pleated skirt, felt button trim with beret.

Prices
Too few examples seen.

Sweet Pea

(Less than 7" tall)

Description: Sweet Pea was a 3" bisque doll dressed by Mrs. Graves.

Marks:
Head: "Japan"
Back: "JAPAN" painted vertically

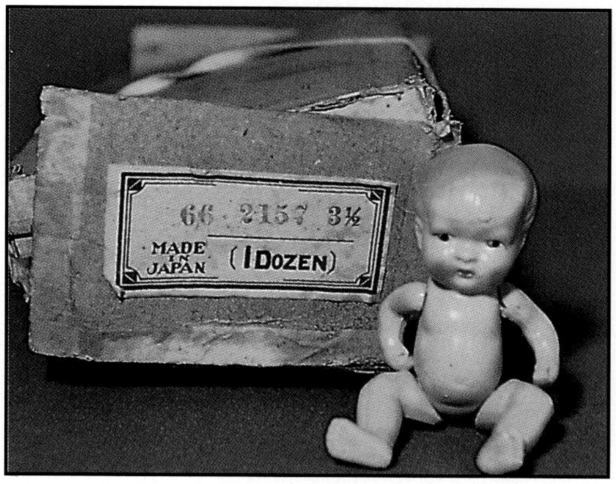

She was dressed in fluffy organdy dresses with lace with matching organdy hats. Mrs. Graves would buy the dolls in boxes and dress them.

The 1933 – 34 Vogue Doll Shoppe catalog lists 3" bisque jointed dolls with long hair wearing organdy dresses and felt berets. They came packed 12 to a box.

Prices
Too few examples seen.

Sweet Pea (1920s – 1930s) 3" bisque doll used by Mrs. Graves. Marked: "Japan" (on head); "JAPAN" painted vertically (on back), shown with her box. Courtesy Eleanor Skinner.

Valerie

(Less than 7" tall)

These were thin dolls with painted eyes, and socks and shoes. The dolls offered in 1942 had dresses and straw hats, painted eyes, and mohair wigs. It is likely they are composition dolls although this conjecture is undocumented.

Valerie (1942) 8"– 9". Courtesy Mrs. Virginia Carlson.

Prices
Too few examples seen.

Celluloid Dolls

1933 – 1934

Celluloid – Pyroxylin Head

(K star R dolls)

Description: 15", 21", 26", 31" pyroxylin head, composition body, rolling eyes, baby type dolls.

Marks: Head: Unknown
Back: Unknown
Clothing : Unknown

The 1933 – 34 Vogue Doll Shoppe catalog offered a K star R doll 15" baby doll with a Pyroxylin head dressed in six different outfits. Pyroxylin is a trade name used for celluloid.

These imported dolls were dressed by Vogue in an imported dotted Swiss dress and bonnet with rosebuds and trimmed in lace. Another doll listed in the brochure was a 21" doll with Pyroxylin head wearing a dotted Swiss or embroidered batiste dress with round yoke with a featherstitched hat with flowers to match. She also came with a fitted weekend case containing crepe-de-chine pajama and negligee.

There was also a 21" doll wearing wool chinchilla coat with hat and mittens; a 26" doll wearing a serge coat and beret and gingham dress underneath; a 26" doll wearing a blue velvet coat with cape and a white fur trimmed hat to match with a smocked crepe-de-chine dress underneath; and a 31" doll wearing a chinchilla coat, poke bonnet, and zipper leggings with white fur and ribbon and a dotted Swiss smocked dress underneath.

Also offered was an all Pyroxylin jointed doll with a Dutch haircut and five changes, including a romper and nightie in 1933 – 34.

	DOLLS LESS THAN 7" TALL—(IMPORTED)	Per Doz.
901B	4½" Bisc Baby Doll, Short Smocked Dress and Bonnet, Pacifier (one to a box)	$7.50
902B	3" Bisc Jointed Dolls, Long Hair, Doll House Size, Organdy Dresses and Felt Berets (12 to a box)	4.00
304B	Toddles (5" K&R) White Smocked Batiste Dress, Colored Dimity Dress and Bonnet to Match	12.00
305B	Toddles (5" K&R) Wool Jersey Dresses, Plaited Skirts, Felt Button Trim with Beret	12.00
	GORGEOUSLY DRESSED K&R DOLLS WITH PYROXYLIN HEADS AND ROLLING EYES—(IMPORTED)	**Each**
480B	15" all Pyroxylin Babe, Imported Dotted Swiss Dress and Bonnet, Finest of Featherstitching and Dainty Rose Buds, Lace Trimmed	$8.00
478B	21" Imported Dotted Swiss or Embroidered Batiste Dress, Round Yoke, Featherstitched Hat to Match with Flowers. A fitted Week-end Case hangs on her arm with a Crepe-de-Chine Pajama and Negligee, French Binding, Lace and Embroidery	12.50
476B	21" Wool Chinchilla Coat and Hat and Mittens, Coat and Hat Embroidered in Wool, Nainsook and Colored Dimity Dress, Smocked and Embroidered	12.50
474B	26" Serge Coat and Beret, Brass Buttons and Emblems, Gingham Dress, Featherstitched, Embroidered Roses	15.00
472B	26" Blue Velvet Coat with Cape, White Fur Trimmed Hat to Match, Smocked Crepe-de-Chine Dress	19.50
470B	31" Chinchilla Coat, Poke Bonnet and Zipper Leggings, Trimmed with White Fur and Ribbon, Imported Dotted Swiss Smocked Dress	33.00
	FITTED TRUNKS, HAT BOXES AND SUIT CASES	**Per Doz.**
212B	12" Metal Trunk with Travel Stickers, Just Me Doll, Six Changes, Three Dress Sets, Romper, Coat, Hat, Nightie with Brush and Comb	$54.00
214B	11" Metal Trunk with Travel Stickers, Baby Dear Doll, Six Changes, Three Dress Sets, Romper, Nightie and Cape, with Lamb, Brush and Comb	42.00
220B	14" Metal Trunk with Travel Stickers, Suzanne Doll, Seven Changes, Chinchilla Coat and Hat, Wool Jersey Ski Suit, Four Dress Sets, Nightie, Brush and Comb	66.00
221B	9" Metal Wardrobe Trunk with Peggy Jean Doll, Six Changes, Coat and Hat, Three Dress Sets, Nightie and Kimono	36.00
222B	18" Metal Trunk with Travel Stickers, Nancy Lee Doll (older sister to Suzanne) Six Changes, Cape and Beret, Ski Suit, Nightie with Feet, Cotton Pajamas, Two Dress Sets, Brush, Comb, Mirror. This is a real Christmas trunk. The trunk itself is red and all the fittings are red and white	90.00
225B	5¾" Wardrobe Trunk with 5" Bokaye Doll, Three Changes, Two Dress Sets, Bonnet and Nightie	16.50
226B	Small Patent Leather Hat Box with 5" Bokaye Doll, Eight Changes, Nightie, Kimono, Ensemble Coat and Hat with Dress, Bathing Suit, Boy's Suit, Two Dress Sets, Silk Pads, Lace and Ribbon	36.00
227B	Black Paper Covered Oval Hat Box with Strap, 5" Bokaye Doll with Four Changes, Nightie, Two Dress Sets, Bathing Suit	21.00
327B	Baby June on Pillow with Novelty Paper Covered Suit Case, done up in Cellophane and packed in individual cartons ready to ship. The Case contains Nightie with Feet, Dress, Slip, Bonnet, Powder, Soap, Towel and Patch Work Puff	21.00
327BB	The same as 327B but Doll with Closing Eyes	24.00
328B	Travel Kit (paper covered suit case) with all Pyroxylin Jointed Doll, Dutch Cut, Five Changes, Three Dress Sets, Romper, and Nightie	27.00
	BASSINETTES	**Each**
330B	Finest Grade Reed Bassinette, basket measures 27" by 15" and sets into a stand with crook which measures 45" from the ground. Beautifully decorated with Net, Lace, Rose Buds, and Ribbon. Fitted with Mattress, Sheets, Blanket and Crepe-de-Chine Puff. Ribbon run through the beading in the basket and gorgeous bow in front	$18.00
331B	Reed Basket with two handles, the Modern Way to Carry a Baby. Lace and Ribbon trimmed. Fitted with Mattress, Sheets, Blanket and Silk Puff. Accessories, Powder, Soap, Towel, Hot Water Bottle, Nursing Bottle. (24" by 15")	10.00
332B	Reed Bassinette with hoops over top, covered with Net, Lace and Ribbon. Fitted with Mattress, Sheets, Blanket, Silk Puff (22" by 15"—without stand)	10.00

Vogue Doll Shoppe catalog 1933 – 34 listing Pyroxylin head K star R doll offered in six different outfits. Courtesy Mrs. Virginia Carlson.

Prices
Too few examples seen.

Rubber Dolls

1922 – 1937

Description: 6½" all rubber child doll or 7" all rubber baby dolls
Marks: Jr. Rubber Doll
Head: None
Back: "MF'D BY/THE SUN RUBBER CO/BARBERTON O"
Other Rubber Dolls
Head: Unknown
Back: Unknown
Clothing: Round gold Vogue sticker

Price
Mint $300.00 – 500.00

Mrs. Graves dressed rubber dolls manufactured by the Sun Rubber Company of Barberton, Ohio, from about 1922 – 1937. The Junior Rubber dolls were 6½" tall and made of soft rubber.

The Vogue Doll Shoppe also sold outfits only for rubber dolls in 1933 – 34. They produced 12 "short clothes baby outfits to fit the rubber dolls or dolls of similar size" as quoted in their brochure. These included Dr. Denton nightie with feet, an eiderdown coat and bonnet, and white organdy dress and bonnet.

These rubber dolls have deteriorated over time and it is very rare to find one in good condition with a Vogue gold sticker.

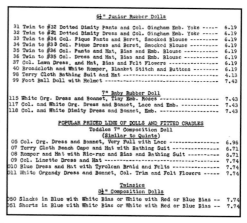

6½" Junior Rubber Dolls

31	Twin to #32 Dotted Dimity Pants and Col. Gingham Emb. Yoke -----	6.19
32	Twin to #31 Dotted Dimity Dress and Col. Gingham Emb. Yoke -----	6.19
33	Twin to #34 Col. Pique Pants and Beret, Smocked Blouse ---------	6.19
34	Twin to #33 Col. Pique Dress and Beret, Smocked Blouse ---------	6.19
35	Twin to #36 Col. Pants and Hat, Bias and Emb. Blouse -----------	6.19
36	Twin to #35 Col. Dress and Hat, Bias and Emb. Blouse -----------	6.19
37	Col. Lawn Dress, and Hat, Bias and Felt Flowers ----------------	6.19
40	Broadcloth and White Romper, Blanket Stitch and Buttons --------	6.19
98	Terry Cloth Bathing Suit and Hat -------------------------------	4.13
99	Foot Ball Doll with Helmet -------------------------------------	7.43

7" Baby Rubber Doll

115	White Org. Dress and Bonnet, Tiny Emb. Roses ------------------	7.43
117	Col. and White Org. Dress and Bonnet, Lace and Emb. -----------	7.43
118	Col. and White Dimity Dress and Bonnet, Emb. ------------------	7.43

POPULAR PRICED LINE OF DOLLS AND FITTED CRADLES
Toddles 7" Composition Doll
(Similar to Quints)

05	Col. Org. Dress and Bonnet, Very Full with Lace ---------------	6.96
07	Terry Cloth Beach Cape and Hat with Bathing Suit --------------	6.71
08	Romper and Hat with Ric-rac and Bias and Bathing Suit ---------	6.71
09	Col. Linetto Dress and Hat ------------------------------------	7.74
010	Blue Dress and Hat with Tyrolean Braid and Felts --------------	7.74
011	White Organdy Dress and Bonnet, Col. Trim and Felt Flowers -----	7.74

Twinsies
8½" Composition Dolls

050	Slacks in Blue with White Bias or White with Red or Blue Bias --	7.74
051	Shorts in Blue with White Bias or White with Red or Blue Bias --	7.74

Vogue Doll Shoppe price list showing 6½" Junior Rubber and 7" Baby Rubber dolls (1922 – 37). Courtesy Mrs. Virginia Carlson.

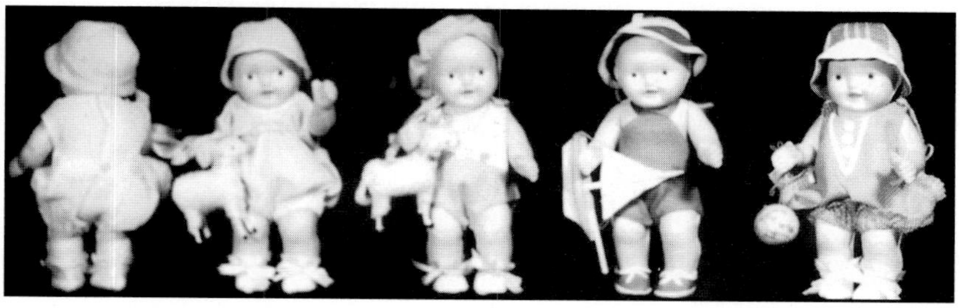

Junior Rubber dolls (1922 – 37). Shown are #30 front and back with lamb, #40 with lamb, #20 with sailboat, and #50 with ball. Courtesy Mrs. Virginia Carlson.

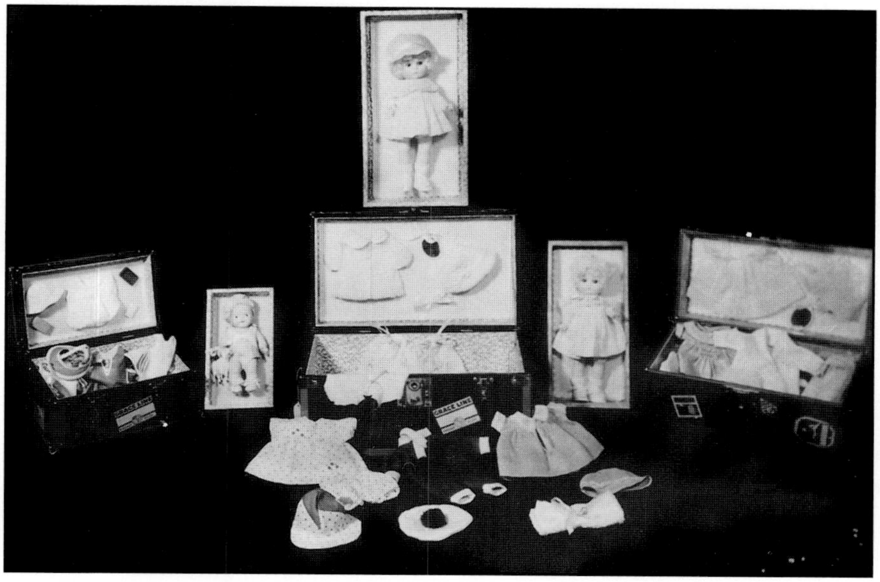

Vogue photo of Junior Rubber doll (on left) with layette. Also shown are two Just Me dolls (1922 – 37). Courtesy Mrs. Virginia Carlson.

Junior Rubber doll (1922 – 37) #23 (or 27). Rust cotton frock with matching hat, embroidery trimmed yoke, small plastic animal was in original box with doll as shown. Vogue round gold tag. Box is pale pink with darker pink line drawings of nude babies, ducks, balls, pails, and dogs. Balls and blocks in blue and red. End panel ½" x 1¼", handwritten "Jr. Rubber/27 (or 23) Rust."

Composition Dolls

1930s – 1948

Composition Just Me
(1937)

Mrs. Graves had been dressing the bisque head Armand Marseille "Just Me" dolls in the 1920s and 1930s. The all composition version of "Just Me" became available in 1937 and Mrs. Graves also dressed and sold this doll.

Prices
Too few examples seen.

Large Composition Dolls
(Produced by Arranbee, Ideal, and Madame Alexander companies)

Mrs. Graves bought, costumed, and sold large composition dolls manufactured by other doll companies such as Arranbee, Ideal, and Madame Alexander under the Vogue label. Most of these larger size composition dolls (13" and up) are unmarked or are just marked with letters and numbers such as "R & B" (for the Arranbee Doll Company).

Vogue would dress the dolls and offer them in series such as Make-Up dolls, Young Folks, or Junior Miss. Each year Vogue would advertise various size dressed composition dolls for sale in *Playthings Magazine*, the magazine of the toy trade. In 1942 Vogue offered composition dolls up to a 24" size. In 1943 a complete line of 7" to 20" composition dolls was advertised. In 1946 they advertised fully jointed all composition dolls with silky mohair wigs in 13", 17", 20", and 21" sizes.

Priscilla/Pickaninny*

Description: Priscilla – 9½", 1926
Pickaninny – 9", 1920s – 1930s

In 1926 Mrs. Graves sold a 9½" unmarked composition doll she called Priscilla. Priscilla came in a wooden cradle with a patchwork quilt and mattress and wore a gray flannel cape. Filene's Department Store in Boston had a display of Priscilla for the Sesquicentennial in 1926.

Mrs. Eleanor Skinner, former Vogue employee, also remembers dressing a 9" all composition black pickaninny* doll as a baby. The doll is unmarked.

*term used by Vogue in 1920s – 1930s.

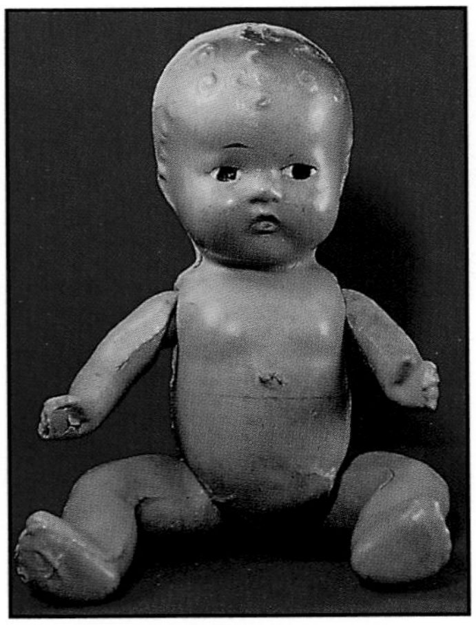

Priscilla (1926) 9½" unmarked composition doll. Priscilla came in a wooden cradle with a patchwork quilt and wore a gray flannel cape. Courtesy Eleanor Skinner.

9" black pickaninny* (1920 – 30s). Courtesy Mrs. Eleanor Skinner.

Prices
$250.00

Baby June, Chuckles, and Cuddles
(1933-1934)

The Vogue Doll Shoppe also offered Baby June, Chuckles and Cuddles composition dolls dressed in Vogue outfits in the 1933 – 34 catalog. Chuckles was a composition head doll with a cloth body. Cuddles was manufactured by the Ideal Toy Company from 1928 to 1940. Cuddles came in various sizes and was a composition doll who also came with rubber arms and legs.

Baby June came with either painted or sleep eyes. A pillow with a novelty paper-covered suitcase containing a footed nightie, dress, slip bonnet, powder, soap, towel, and puff came with the doll.

Prices
Too few examples seen.

BABY JUNE, CHUCKLES AND CUDDLES

324B	Baby June in Crepe Romper, Ricrac Braid and Button Trimmed, Boat in Doll's Hand	12.00
325B	Plain Colored Percale Romper, Bias Tape and Crocheted Button Trimmed, Lamb in Doll's Hand	12.00
462B	Cuddles, Soft Bodied Babe, Composition Head, Closing Eyes, Voice, White Organdy Dress, Colored Organdy Side Yoke, Lace Trimmed	21.00
464B	Chuckles, Soft Bodied Babe with Pyroxylin Head and Hands, Voice, White Organdy Dress and Bonnet, Lace and Ribbon Trimmed	21.00

Vogue Doll Shoppe price list (1933 – 1934) showing Baby June, Chuckles, and Cuddles. Courtesy Virginia Carlson.

Dora Lee
(mid 1930s – 1940s)

Description: 11" all composition jointed doll. Closed mouth with wistful expression, sleep eyes.
Marks:
Head: Unmarked
Back: Unmarked
Clothing: Gold Vogue tag with Vogue in black writing. Dora Lee printed on bottom of shoe
Box: Blue foil with light stars, peach end label with Vogue in script

Dora Lee was a lovely, thin 11" composition doll with a mohair wig and a rather sad, wistful expression. She is quite hard to find and is a fine example of Vogue's sewing talent.

Prices:

11" MIB	$800.00 – 1,000.00

MIB dolls have original boxes, tags, and booklets.

Dora Lee (1939) 11" composition in pink dress with red flowers. Notice reddish light brown eyes. Unmarked. Courtesy Anita Maxwell.

Dora Lee (c.1939) 11" composition in nurse's outfit, with Vogue gold circle sticker on front. Notice reddish light brown eyes. Doll is unmarked, with molded ear-length hair under wig. "Dora Lee" stamped on bottom of shoe. Courtesy Kathy Schneider.

Dora Lee (1939) 11" composition Bathing Beauty showing original blue Vogue box. Courtesy Jennifer Dettay.

Dora Lee (1939) 11" composition, showing underpants are tied to slip which is attached to dress. Courtesy Anita Maxwell.

Dora Lee (1939) 11" composition Bathing Beauty in red polka dot outfit. Doll is unmarked. Courtesy Jennifer Dettay.

Make-Up Dolls

13" Mary Jane, 16" Betty Jane, 19½" Jennie
(1940s)

Description: 13", 16", 19½", 20" all composition jointed dolls. Closed or open mouth with teeth. Sleep eyes and lashes.

Marks:

Head:	Unmarked
Back:	"13" (on 13" doll)
Back:	"USA/16" (on 16" doll)
Clothing tag:	"VOGUE DOLLS, INC./ Medford, Mass." or no tag
Outfit closures:	Hooks or ties
Box:	Plain cardboard box with blue Vogue label, "Vogue Dolls: FASHION LEADERS IN DOLL SOCIETY"

The Make-Up dolls came with a little bag of cosmetics tied around their wrists which held a mirror, a powder puff, and a cardboard container of powder. The Make-Up dolls all came with hats and adorable outfits with the Vogue tag. Their names were Mary Jane (13"), Betty Jane (16"), Jennie (19½"), and Mary Ann (20").

Mary Jane. Mary Jane was a 13" composition doll that came in at least two versions, open mouth and closed mouth. The open mouth doll had four teeth, a curly mohair braided wig, and painted dark lower lashes. Her body is marked "13." There was also a same size closed-mouth version. Apparently the size was the most important attribute in determining the doll's name.

Betty Jane. Betty Jane was a 16" fully jointed composition doll with blue sleep eyes, mohair wig and open mouth with teeth. She is marked on her back "USA/16" and was probably manufactured in 1943.

Jennie. The unmarked 19½" Jennie was composition with either closed or open mouth with four teeth and sleep eyes. She had dark eye shadow above her eyes. She was manufactured in early to mid 1940s and appears on the 1943 price list, (see photo bottom page 38) but not in the 1947 – 49 price list.

Mary Jane – 13"

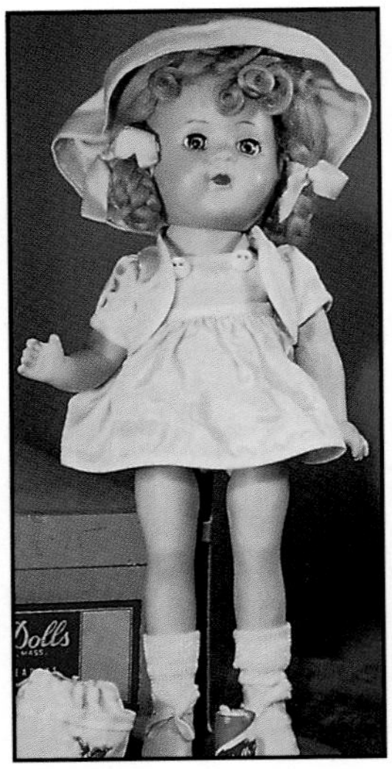

13" all composition, closed mouth, sleep eyes, mohair wig, pink dress, shoes, hat, ribbons. Came with pink bag with powder, powder puff, and mirror. Head marked faintly "A L or R." Tag on clothes: "Vogue Dolls Inc./Medford, Mass."

13" all composition, open mouth with teeth, sleep eyes, mohair wig, in blue cotton dress, showing variation in mouth and color of outfit. Marks: "X" or "Y" in a circle (on head); "13" (on back) Clothes are tagged "Vogue Dolls Inc./Medford, Mass." in blue ink on white cotton tag. Courtesy Mary Lu Trowbridge.

13" all composition, open mouth with teeth, sleep eyes, mohair wig, wearing white organdy dress hat. Notice different make-up bag. Doll unmarked, looks like something has been rubbed out on back. Clothing tagged "Vogue Dolls, Inc. /MEDFORD, MASS." in blue ink on white cotton tag outside of dress. Courtesy Mary Lu Trowbridge.

Prices
Make-Up Dolls

13" MIB	$250.00 – 345.00
16" MIB	$300.00 – 375.00
19½" MIB	$400.00 – 475.00
20" MIB	$500.00+

MIB dolls, with original boxes, tags, and booklets will be more.

13" all composition, closed mouth, sleep eyes, mohair wig, wearing green dress with white lace-up front, matching hat and bag carrying make-up. Notice variation of make-up bag. Courtesy Mary Lu Trowbridge.

13" all composition, sleep eyes, mohair wig, blue dress with white lace down front, yellow, blue, pink flowers with matching bonnet, blue leatherette shoes, and socks. Doll is unmarked. Vogue Dolls, "INC./MEDFORD, MASS." ink spot tag on outside of dress. Courtesy Wenham Museum, Wenham, Mass.

13" composition doll in dress with pink ribbon with Vogue tag. Doll is unmarked. Courtesy Judy Armitstead.

13" all composition, closed mouth, sleep eyes, mohair wig, white long gown with flower print and yellow ribbons, matching bag. Notice gold Vogue round label. Courtesy Veronica Phillips.

Red velvet shorts outfit for 13" with matching make-up bag, probably a skating outfit. Notice white sewn-on mittens. Notice Vogue white tag with blue printing on outfit. Courtesy Veronica Phillips.

13" composition in plaid. Courtesy Susan Haynes.

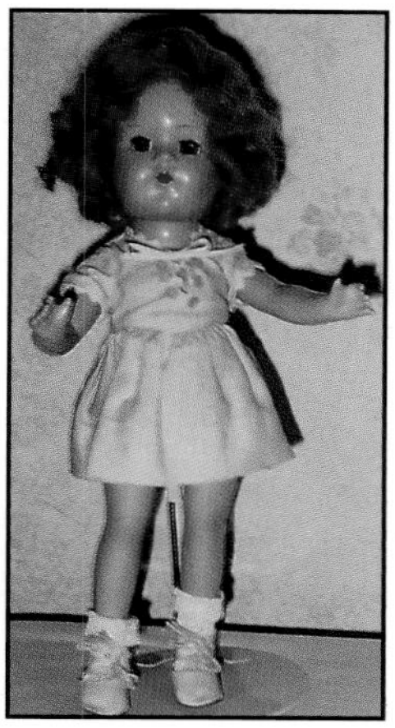

13" composition in yellow dress with yellow felt flowers and tie in front. Marks: "Ideal" rubbed out (on head). Courtesy Jan Nickel.

Betty Jane (or Jean) – 14"

Betty Jane (1943) 14" composition, sleep eyes, closed mouth with braids. Blue dress with pinafore sleeves and inset flowered apron front. Dressed by Vogue for the Toy Fair in 1942 – 43. Doll is unmarked.

Jennie – 19"

Jennie (1943 – 44) 19" composition in white fake lamb coat and muff with red felt trim and mittens. Underneath wearing white wool dress with red felt panel in front, trimmed with pale blue rickrack, red knit underpants, white ankle socks, red leatherette tie shoes. Doll is unmarked. Courtesy Ursula R. Mertz.

Jennie (c. 1943) 19" composition wearing gray felt coat and matching hat. Doll is unmarked. Courtesy Ursula R. Mertz.

Jennie (1943 – 44) 19" composition doll, fully jointed, sleep eyes, open mouth with four teeth, mohair wig. Dressed in pink printed organdy dress with blue velvet lacing in front and lace trim, #770 in Vogue publicity photo. Doll is unmarked. Courtesy Shirley Niziolek.

Jennie (1940s) 19½" Southern Belle with rose print and carrying bag. Doll is unmarked. Clothes are tagged "Vogue Dolls Inc./Medford, Mass." in blue ink on white cotton tag. Courtesy Mary Lu Trowbridge.

WAAC-ette and WAV-ette

(1943 – 1944)

Description: 13" all composition jointed dolls. Closed or open mouth with teeth. Blue or brown sleep eyes with lashes.

Marks: Unmarked

Clothing: Round gold Vogue tag on front

Outfit closures: Hooks or ties

Mrs. Graves designed a set of World War II military characters in 1943 – 44 called Lieutenant WAV-ette and Lieutenant WAAC-ette. It seems that at least two different unmarked composition dolls, perhaps by different manufacturers, were used for these armed forces dolls. One WAAC-ette doll appears to be made by the Ideal Toy Company. Another WAAC-ette doll has a faint A R blotted out on her back, possibly for Arranbee Doll Company. Both are stamped WAAC-ETTE (on bottom of shoe).

Vogue obtained official permission from the armed services to produce the replicas of the uniforms of the women's branches of the armed services. A news clipping in the Vogue archive at the Wenham Museum in Wenham, Massachusetts, tells how both the director of the WAVES, Miss Mildred MacAfee, and the director of the WAACS, Mrs. Ovleta Hobby, came to Boston for a preview of the dolls at the Parker House Hotel. Both Miss MacAfee and Mrs. Hobby are quoted as saying that the dolls were important for the war effort.

Vogue publicity flyer (1943 – 44) showing WAAC-ette and WAV-ette (top photo) along with Linda (bottom left) #468, #790, and #30 from left to right; and 19" Jennie dolls (bottom right) #700s. Vogue photo courtesy Mrs. Virginia Carlson.

Lieutenant WAV-ette and Lieutenant WAAC-ette (1943 – 44) 13" composition open mouth with teeth. WAV-ette has blue eyes, WAAC-ette has brown eyes. Dolls are unmarked. Courtesy Ursula R. Mertz.

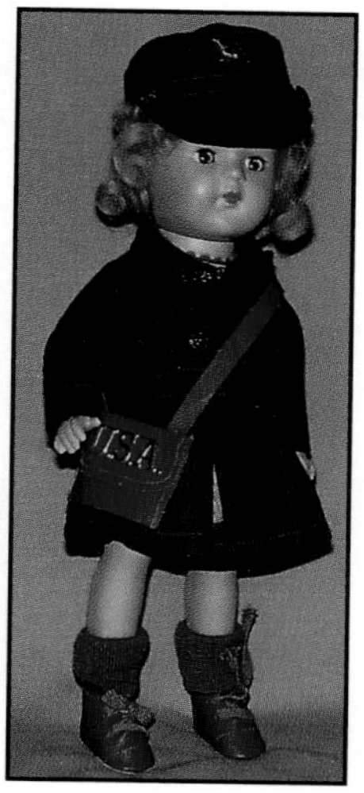

Lieutenant WAAC-ette (1943 – 44) 13" composition closed-mouth version of Lieutenant WAAC-ette. Doll is unmarked. Courtesy Anita Maxwell.

Lieutenant WAAC-ette (1943 – 44) 13" composition. Showing the brown and white striped dress that was under the coat. Doll is unmarked. Courtesy Anita Maxwell.

Lieutenant WAV-ette (1943 – 44) 13" composition doll. Navy cotton coat with brass buttons and WAVE insignia on cap, brown cotton stockings, and tie shoes. Round gold Vogue tag on coat. Courtesy Maureen Fukushima.

Prices:

WAV–ette and WAAC-ette	$350.00 – 400.00

Prices shown for mint, complete, all original dolls.

Cynthia
(1940s)

Description: 13" and 18" all composition jointed dolls. Closed or open mouth with teeth. Blue or brown sleep eyes with lashes. Wig in various styles and colors including tosca and blonde.

Marks: Unmarked
Clothing tag: Unknown
Box: Blue foil with light stars, peach end label with Vogue in script

Cynthia was a 13" and 18" composition doll that came in various outfits such as plaid jumper and beret, and long gowns with pantalettes. Her hair was tosca or blonde in various styles.

Prices
Cynthia

13"	$350.00
18"	$450.00

Prices shown are for mint, complete, all original dolls.

Cynthia (1940s) Vogue publicity photo. Courtesy Mrs. Virginia Carlson.

Cynthia (1940s) 13" composition with tosca hair and brown eyes wearing yellow satin gown, pantaloons, petticoat, and gold shoes. Doll is unmarked. Box features doll's name. Courtesy Joan Nickel.

Cynthia (1940s) 13" in plaid jumper and beret (left) and 13" in long gown with rickrack and pantalettes (right), and 18" in pink dress with flower on front (middle). Courtesy Marge Meisinger.

Young Folks

(1947 – 1948)

Description: 13" jointed composition dolls, sleep eyes, mohair wig, pantalettes. Original price $4.00 – $4.50.

Marks: Unknown

Also typical of Vogue's production was the 1947 and 1948 Young Folks series of 13" jointed composition dolls with sleep eyes, mohair wigs and pantalettes. The 1947 dolls were named Jean, Judy or Joan, depending on the outfit they wore.

As described in a 1947 Vogue price list, Jean was dressed in a "Col. Org. (colored organdy) dress, felt jacket, and hat with plume and flowers." Judy came in "a flowing dotted Swiss dress and hat and had braids," and Joan wore "a white challis dress and hat with rickrack and net mitts." Their cost was $4.00 – $4.50 each wholesale. An ad from the 1947 Montgomery Ward's catalog shows Jean as she is described, but she was called Pantalette Doll in the catalog.

The 1948 Young Folks were Joyce, Linda, Joan, Ellen, Mitzi, and Ginger. Joan, the only name used from 1947, was wearing a different dress this year a "flowered lawn dress and hat, eyelet peplum and collar." In 1948 Vogue sold a fitted weekend case for the 13" dolls consisting of a sunsuit, hat, party dress, nightie, towel, face cloth, soap, powder, and two barrettes.

Pantalette Doll, could also be Jean from Young Folks (1947), 13" composition head and body, glassine sleep eyes, real lashes, mohair wig. Organdy skirt over lace trimmed pantalettes and petticoat. Felt jacket, poke bonnet. Originally cost $6.69. Advertised as Pantalette Doll in Montgomery Ward catalog. Courtesy Marge Meisinger.

Jean from Young Folks, also called Pantalette Doll (1947). This 13" composition doll with "glassine sleeping eyes" was shown in the 1947 Ward catalog and wears an organdy skirt over lace trimmed pantalettes and petticoat with a felt jacket and bonnet.

Jean from Young Folks, showing Vogue ink spot tag.

Telephone MYStic 7030

Vogue Dolls, INC.

JENNIE H. GRAVES
Style Consultant

New York Office and Showrooms
1107 BROADWAY
ROOM 400
Tel. Chelsea 2-3993

Factory and Main Office
4 MYSTIC AVENUE
MEDFORD 55, MASS.

PRICE LIST

Effective March 1, 1947

STYLE NO.	DOLLS' NAME	DESCRIPTION	DOZ.	EACH	STANDARD PACKAGING (APPROX. WGT.)
		8" Fully jointed Composition Doll — Mohair Wig			
TODDLERS					
8-1A	Dobby	Wh. Dress, Col. Batiste Pinafore & Bonnet	$ 24.00	$ 2.00	
8-2A	Penny	Col. & White Org. Dress & Bonnet, Flowers	24.00	2.00	12
8-3A	Trudy	Col. Org. Dress & Bonnet, Hand Smocked Panel	24.00	2.00	Weigh
8-4A	Pinky	Hand Smocked Col. Batiste dress & Bonnet	24.00	2.00	7 lbs.
8-5A	Cookie	Col. Org. Dress & Bonnet, Lace Trimmed	24.00	2.00	
8-6A	Bobsy	Wh. Organdy Dress & Bonnet, Silk Loop & Flow. Trim	24.00	2.00	
PLAYMATES (Twins, sold only in pairs)					
8-7A	Bunky	Col. Jersey Suit & Hat (Pastel Shades)	24.00	2.00	
8-8A	Binky	Col. Jersey Dress & Hat (Pastel Shades)	24.00	2.00	12
8-9A	Jerry	Jersey Overalls & Hat, Stripe Sweater, Garden Tool	24.00	2.00	Weigh
8-10A	Julie	Jersey Overalls & Hat, Stripe Sweater, Garden Tool	24.00	2.00	7 lbs.
8-11A	Alpine	Felt Suit, Alpine Hat	24.00	2.00	
8-12A	Alpine	Felt Dress & Hat	24.00	2.00	
SPECIALTY GROUP					
8-15A	Bride	White Ninon, Lace, Net Veil, Bouquet	27.00	2.25	6
8-16A	R.R.Hood	Red Hooded Cape, Wh. Dress, Felt Basket	27.00	2.25	Weigh
8-18A	Colonial	Col. Batiste Dress, Pantalets, Flowered Head Band	27.00	2.25	5 lbs.
		13" Jointed Comp. Doll — Closing Eyes — Mohair Wig — Pantalets			
YOUNG FOLKS					
13-5A	Jean	Col. Org. Dress, Felt Jacket & Hat, Plume, Flowers	54.00	4.50	6
13-6A	Judy	Flow. Dotted Swiss Dress & Hat, Lace & Beading—(Braids)	48.00	4.00	Weigh
13-7A	Joan	Wh. Challie Dress & Hat, Col. Ric-Rac, Net Mitts	48.00	4.00	10 lbs.
		17" Jointed Comp. Doll — Closing Eyes — Mohair Wig — Pantalets			
JUNIOR MISS					
17-5A	Patty	Col. Gingham Dress, Wh. Dotted Pinafore, (Braids)	84.00	7.00	4
17-6A	Peggy	Col. Flow. Batiste Dress & Hat, Rib. Bows & Beading	84.00	7.00	Weigh
17-7A	Polly	Stripe Gingham Peplum Jacket, Skirt & Hat	84.00	7.00	11 lbs.
		21" Jointed Comp. Doll — Closing Eyes — Mohair Wig			
YOUNG MODERNS					
21-6A	Gail	Col. Ck. Tissue Gingham Dress & Sun Bonnet, (Braids)	99.00	8.25	
21-7A	Audrey	Fig. Ninon Party Dress, Lace Trim — Bows on Hair	99.00	8.25	4
21-8A	Sue	Col. Polka Dot Dress & Bonnet, Wh. Org. Blouse	99.00	8.25	Weigh
21-9A	Sandy	Col. Check Gingham Dress & Hat, Hand Smocked Blouse	99.00	8.25	12 lbs.
21-10A	Miss Vogue	Col. Felt Coat & Hat, Silk Braid, Button, Plume Trim Col. Org. & White Serge Dress, Lace & Ribbons	120.00	10.00	
		Fitted Week-End Acetate Case for 8" Vogue Dolls			
		Sunsuit — Skirt — Cape — Hat — Beach Bag Towel — Face Cloth — Soap — Powder Nightie — Bathrobe — Slippers with Pom Poms	27.00	2.25	4 Weigh 3 lbs.

1947 Vogue price list showing Young Folks, Junior Miss, and Young Moderns. Courtesy Wenham Museum, Wenham, Mass.

PRICE LIST

Effective March 1, 1948

Style No.			Doz.	Each
SPECIALTY GROUP				
8-14B	Bridesmaid	Col. Org. dress & hat, ribbon bow & lace trim	27.00	2.25
8-15B	Bride	White Ninon dress—lace trimmed—net veil—bouquet	27.00	2.25
8-16B	Sunsuit	Fig. Percale sunsuit—white eyelet trim—braids pinned up—pail	18.00	1.50
CHARACTER GROUP				
8-17B	R. R. Hood	Red hooded lined cape—white striped dimity dress—basket	27.00	2.25
8-18B	Alice	Alice in Wonderland blue dress—white org. apron lace trimmed—ribbon in hair	22.50	1.87½
8-19B	Willie	Wee Willie Winkie, flannelette fig. pajamas, stocking cap, candle in holder—pom poms	18.00	1.50
WEE LASSIE GROUP				
8-20B	Ging. Girl	Plaid Gingham dress—ruffle trimmed red Velvet jacket and bonnet	30.00	2.50
8-21B	Coat	Velvet coat & bonnet—feather—fur trimmed—fig. lawn dress	30.00	2.50
8-22B	Spring	Wh. Org. dress & hat—hand embroidered with wool	30.00	2.50
8-30		**Fitted Week-end Acetate Case for 8" Vogue Dolls** Sunsuit—Skirt—Cape—Hat—Beach Bag—Towel—Face Cloth—Soap—Powder—Nightie—Bathrobe—Slippers with Pom Poms—Party Dress and Bonnet — Plastic Comb and Mirror	27.00	2.25
		13" Jointed Comp. Dolls—Closing Eyes—Mohair Wigs		
YOUNG FOLKS				
13-1B	Joyce	Col. dotted Swiss dress & bonnet—lace flower & ribbon trim	48.00	4.00
13-2B	Linda	Col. Shadow checked Org. dress & bonnet—lace & novelty braid trim	48.00	4.00
13-3B	Joan	Flow. Lawn dress & hat, eyelet peplum and collar	48.00	4.00
13-4B	Ellen	Plain & striped gingham dress & hat—ric-rac trim	48.00	4.00
13-5B	Mitzi	Col. suiting dress & hat—circular skirt—eyelet ruffle & lace trim ribbon bows	48.00	4.00
13-6B	Ginger	Plaid dress & beret—circular skirt—eyelet ruffle trim—braids	48.00	4.00
13-20		**Fitted Week End Acetate Case for 13" Vogue Dolls** (Packed 4 to a box only) Sunsuit—Hat—Party Dress—Nightie—Towel—Face Cloth—Soap—Powder—Two Barrettes	33.00	2.75
		17" Jointed Comp. Dolls—Closing Eyes—Mohair Wigs		
JUNIOR MISS				
17-1B	Peggy	Four piece sun dress—striped broadcloth—ric-rac & bias trim	60.00	5.00
17-2B	Polly	Col. broadcloth skirt & batiste blouse—ruffled eyelet trim ribbon bows	72.00	6.00
17-3B	Lassie	Plaid Gingham dress—white & plaid ruffles—lace trim—braids	72.00	6.00
17-4B	Patty	Wh. Org. blouse—button & lace trim—Velvet skirt	72.00	6.00
17-5B	Dixie	Long. Flow. Chintz dress & hat—ruffles—eyelet trim—ribbon bows	90.00	7.50
17-6B	Judith	Velvet coat & lined hood—Jersey dress—novelty trim	90.00	7.50

Approximate Weight per Dozen

8 inch dolls — 6 lbs.
17 inch dolls — 27 lbs.
13 inch dolls — 21 lbs.
18 inch Velva Baby Dolls — 40 lbs*

Fashion Leaders in Doll Society

*Includes individual corrugated mailing boxes and outside carton.

1948 Vogue price list showing Young Folks and Junior Miss. Courtesy Wenham Museum, Wenham, Mass.

Prices
Young Folks $250.00 – 300.00

Junior Miss
(1947-1948)

Description: 17" jointed composition dolls, sleep eyes, mohair wig, pantalettes.
Original price $7.00
Marks: Unknown

Jr. Miss were 17" composition dolls sold in 1947 – 48. The 1947 series consisted of Peggy, Polly, Lassie, Patty, Dixie, and Judith. Each doll was the same basic doll with mohair wig and sleep eyes but was dressed in a different outfit with a different hair color or style. The 1948 Jr. Miss dolls were Peggy, Polly, Lassie, Patty, Dixie, and Judith. The Polly and Patty dolls although named the same as the 1947 dolls were wearing different outfits this year.

Prices
Junior Miss $300.00 – 350.00

Young Moderns
(1947)

Description: 21" jointed composition dolls, sleep eyes, mohair wig.
Original price $8.25.
Marks: Unknown

Dolls were called Gail, Audrey, Sue, Sandy, and Miss Vogue in 1947. See price list shown above.

Prices
Young Moderns $350.00 – 400.00

Sportswomen Series

(1940s)

Description: 14" composition doll, unmarked.

Another adorable series of composition dolls dressed by Vogue is the sportswoman series including the 14" Skater, Golfer, Tennis Player, and Skier. These unmarked dolls are of excellent quality and the attention to detail and the quality of the clothes and accessories are amazing.

The Skater has auburn hair that blends perfectly with the tan corduroy two-piece outfit with matching cap with lace-up skates. The Golfer wears a stylish golfing outfit topped by a turban, carries her golf bag and clubs, and even has fringed golf shoes. She indeed captures the fashions of the day and has the round Vogue paper tag on her pants. The Tennis Player sports a blue and white striped tennis dress with matching hat and a tennis racket in her tennis bag. The Skier's velvet parka hood features real feathers and she has wooden skis and poles. These fantastic outfits really capture the essence of young adulthood of the 1940s.

Tennis Player and Golfer 14" composition. Doll is unmarked. Notice gold round Vogue tag on clothes. Courtesy Wenham Museum, Wenham, Mass.

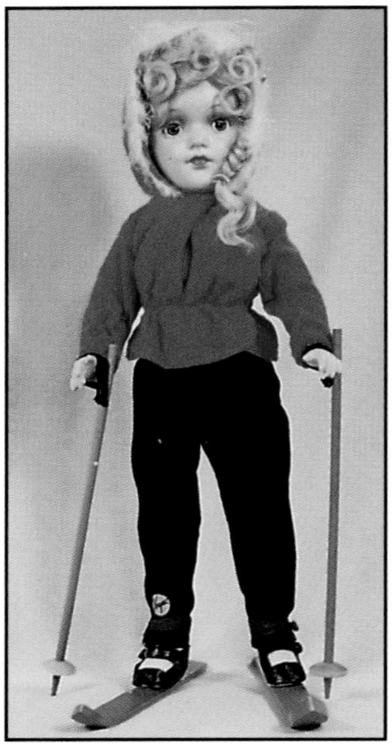

Skier 14" composition. Doll is unmarked. Gold round Vogue tag on pants. Courtesy Wenham Museum, Wenham, Mass.

Skater 14" composition. Doll is unmarked. Courtesy Wenham Museum, Wenham, Mass.

Prices
$400.00

Composition Dolls

Unknown as to date or series

Composition (1948 – 50) 13" with mohair wig. Doll is unmarked. Dress has ink spot label. Courtesy Millie Caliri.

Composition doll (1940s) in a blue pinafore and beret. Doll is unmarked. Dress marked "Vogue." Courtesy Wenham Museum, Wenham, Mass.

Little Bo-Peep (1944 – 46) 12½" composition, brown eyes, brown mohair wig. Doll is unmarked. Clothes are tagged "Vogue" in blue print on twill tag. Courtesy Pam Zampiello.

Composition (1948 – 50) 13" with blonde mohair wig and brown sleep eyes, closed mouth, wearing yellow coat and hat with white fur trim. Doll is unmarked and from collection of former Vogue employee. Courtesy Veronica Phillips.

Composition (1948 – 50) 13" with dark blonde mohair wig and painted eyes, closed mouth, wearing blue dress with attached panties and white, green, and yellow felt flower trim, and white tie shoes. Doll is unmarked and from the collection of former Vogue employee. Courtesy Veronica Phillips.

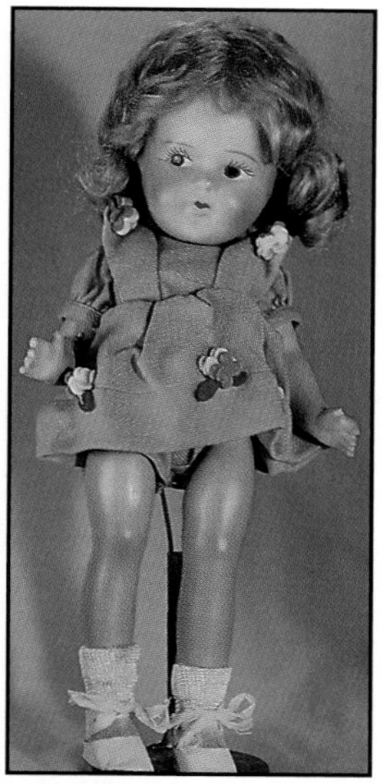

Composition (1948 – 50) 13" with blonde mohair wig with braids and blue sleep eyes, closed mouth, wearing pink dress with pink, blue, and green flower trim, and pink tie shoes. Doll is unmarked and from collection of former Vogue employee. Courtesy Veronica Phillips.

Composition (1948 – 50) 13" with blonde mohair wig with braids and brown sleep eyes, closed mouth, wearing red, green, and yellow print dress and red snap shoes. Doll is unmarked and from the collection of former Vogue employee. Courtesy Veronica Phillips

Mint Prices

13"	$350.00

Patsy Family Outfits

(1933 – 1934)

The 1933 – 34 Vogue Doll Shoppe catalog offered outfits for the composition Patsy doll family produced by the Effanbee Doll Company from 1928 on. Mrs. Graves sewed outfits for Patsy Lou (22"), Patsy Ann (19"), Patsy Joan (17"), Patsy (13"), and Patsykins (11"). There were at least 42 outfits for these dolls in 1933 – 34. Vogue also sold 16 outfits for the 9" Patsyette. Vogue sold just the outfits, not the dressed dolls.

Prices

Too few examples seen

Outfits for the Patsy Family

THESE PRICES INCLUDE UNDERWEAR WITH ALL DRESS SETS AND COME IN ASSORTED COLORS

ALL PRICES NET, F.O.B. FACTORY

Style No.	ROMPERS	Lou /22 Doz.	Ann /19 Doz.	Joan /17 Doz.	Patsy /13 Doz.	Kins /11 Doz.
120B	Print Romper, White Collar, Bias Tape	$6.00	$5.00	$5.00	$4.00	$4.00
	SEPARATE COATS, FOUR PIECE ENSEMBLE SUITS SLEEPING PAJAMAS AND BATHROBES					
122B	Figured Outing Flannel Bathrobe with Slippers	6.00	5.00	5.00	4.00	4.00
124B	Four-piece Ensemble, White Organdy and Crepe Pique, Embroidered Front of Dress, Collar, Hat	12.00	10.80	10.80	9.00	7.50
125B	Coat and Hat with Bag (Assorted Wool Tweeds) Trimmed with Felt Flowers	12.00	10.80	10.80	9.00	7.50
126B	Blue Wool Serge Coat and Beret, Brass Buttons and Emblems	16.50	15.00	15.00	10.80	9.00
127B	Colored Crepe Pique Coat and Hat, Ribbon and Pearl Buttons	9.00	7.50	7.50	6.00	5.00
128B	Red Cotton Tweed Cape and Beret	7.50	6.00	6.00	5.00	4.00
129B	Pink or Blue Eiderdown Coat and Aviator Hat with Mittens	12.00	10.80	10.80	9.00	7.50
130B	Dr. Denton's Nightie with Feet	5.00	4.00	4.00	3.00	3.00
134B	Two-piece Gingham Sleeping Pajamas, Loops and Buttons	6.00	5.00	5.00	4.00	4.00
	BEACH TOGS					
135B	Print Beach Pajamas, Sun Hat, Bias Tape, Felt Flowers	7.50	6.00	6.00	5.00	4.00
136B	Three-piece Ensemble, Bathing Suit, Terry Cloth Cape and Hat with Pail and Towel	10.80	9.00	9.00	7.50	6.00
137B	Print Sun Suit with Hat and Beach Sandals	9.00	7.50	7.50	6.00	6.00
	DRESS SETS					
139B	Colored Dotted Swiss Dress and Hat, Lace Embroidery and Ribbon	10.80	9.00	9.00	7.50	7.50
140B	Checked Organdy Dress and Hat, White Organdy Collar, Organdy Ruffling and Buttons	12.00	10.80	10.80	9.00	7.50
143B	Figured Dimity Smocked Dress and Hat	10.80	9.00	9.00	7.50	6.00
144B	Zephyr Print Suspender Dress and Hat with Detachable Cape, Novelty Edging Trim, Crocheted Buttons	12.00	10.80	10.80	9.00	9.00
145B	Smocked Colored Broadcloth Dress and Hat	9.00	7.50	7.50	6.00	5.00
147B	Colored Organdy Dress and Hat Trimmed with White Organdy Edging, Bows and Crocheted Buttons	12.00	9.00	9.00	7.50	6.00
148B	Gingham Dot, and White Organdy Dress and Hat, Embroidery	9.00	7.50	7.50	6.00	5.00
149B	Figured Cross Bar Muslin Dress and Hat, Bias Tape Trim	10.80	9.00	9.00	7.50	7.50
150B	Smocked Wendy Batiste Dress and Hat, Ruffle around Collar and down Front, Pocket	10.80	9.00	9.00	7.50	6.00
151B	Plaid Gingham Dress and Hat, Six Pointed Collar, Pocket Book	9.00	7.50	7.50	6.00	5.00

Style No.		Lou /22 Doz.	Ann /19 Doz.	Joan /17 Doz.	Patsy /13 Doz.	Kins /11 Doz.
152B	Figured Gingham Dress and Hat, White Broadcloth Trim and Crocheted Buttons	10.80	9.00	9.00	7.50	6.00
153B	Figured Gingham Dress and Hat, Collar Laced up in Front with Ribbon	9.00	7.50	7.50	6.00	6.00
154B	Red or Blue Dotted Dimity Dress and Hat, Felt Flower Trim	9.00	7.50	7.50	6.00	5.00
155B	Smocked Crepe-De-Chine Dress, Side Yoke, Lace Trimmed	13.50	12.00	12.00	10.80	9.00
156B	Stripe Broadcloth Dress and Hat, Round Yoke, Felt Trim	9.00	7.50	7.50	6.00	6.00
157B	Gingham Jumper Dress with Hat, Checked Batiste Blouse and Tie	9.00	7.50	7.50	6.00	6.00
158B	Zephyr Gingham Dress and Hat, Featherstitched with Embroidered Roses	9.00	7.50	7.50	6.00	6.00
159B	Checked Gingham Dress and Hat, Cross Bar Muslin Blouse, Novelty Braid Trim	9.00	7.50	7.50	6.00	6.00
160B	Cotton Tweed Suspender Dress and Beret, Pongee Blouse	9.00	7.50	7.50	6.00	5.00
161B	Jersey Sweater, Skirt, and Beret, Felt Button Trim	10.80	9.00	9.00	7.50	6.00
162B	Wool Jersey Jumper Dress and Beret, Felt Flowers and Wool Pom-poms	15.00	13.50	13.50	12.00	10.80
	BOY'S AND NOVELTY SUITS					
163B	Scout Suit	$9.00	$7.50	$7.50	$6.00	$6.00
164B	Gym Suit, Wool Bloomers, White Broadcloth Top, Red Tie	9.00	7.50	7.50	6.00	6.00
165B	Boy's Sailor Suit with Long Pants and Beret	9.00	7.50	7.50	6.00	5.00
166B	Riding Habit	15.00	13.50	13.50	12.00	10.80
167B	Graduate Nurse's Uniform	10.80	9.00	9.00	7.50	7.50
168B	Maid's Uniform	9.00	7.50	7.50	6.00	6.00
169B	All Wool Jersey Ski Suit and Beret, Zipper Front, Wool Pom-poms on Hat and Ends of Scarf	15.00	12.00	12.00	10.80	9.00
170B	Alice-in-Wonderland Dress, with Apron and Ribbon	9.00	7.50	7.50	6.00	5.00
175B	Boy's Blouse and Pants		9.00	9.00	7.50	

OUTFITS FOR PATSYETTE

Style		Per Doz.
761B	Wool Jersey Bathing Suit, with Terry Cloth Cape and Hat	$5.00
763B	Sun or Beach Pajamas of Printed Percale	5.00
765B	Colored Handkerchief Lawn Dress and Hat, Featherstitched and Embroidered Roses	6.00
770B	Four-piece Ensemble, Crepe Pique Coat and Hat, with Smocked Dotted Swiss Dress	7.50
771B	Four-piece Zephyr Print Ensemble, Plaited Skirt	6.00
772B	Colored Organdy Plaited Dress and Hat, Embroidered Roses	6.00
773B	Red or Blue Dotted Dimity Dress and Hat, Felt Button Trim	6.00
775B	Colored Dimity Dress and Bonnet, Embroidered Roses	6.00
776B	Smocked and Embroidered White Bastiste Dress with Colored, Dimity Band Around Bottom and Bonnet to Match	6.00
777B	Smocked Colored Organdy Dress and Hat, Round Yoke with Featherstitching	6.00
778B	Colored Batiste Dress and Hat, Embroidered Pointed Collar	6.00
779B	Smocked Crepe-de-Chine Dress	6.00
780B	Wool Jersey Sweater and Beret with Plaited Skirt	6.00
781B	Wool Jersey Coat and Beret, Brass Buttons	5.00
782B	Wool Jersey Jumper Dress and Beret, Dotted Dimity Blouse and Bloomers (can be used for Separate Romper)	6.00
783B	Dr. Denton's Nightie with Feet	2.50

1933 – 34 Vogue Doll Shoppe price lists showing outfits for Patsy and her family and Patsyette. Courtesy Mrs. Virginia Carlson.

Cloth Dolls

1942

Description: 7" to 24" all-cloth dolls, painted side glancing eyes, hair in curly ringlets, and large cloth feet.

Marks:

Head:	Unknown
Back:	Unknown
Clothing:	Unknown

Vogue advertised three large cloth dolls in a 1940s era publicity photo. The dolls had painted side glancing eyes, hair in curly ringlets, and large cloth feet. One was dressed in a short sleeve print dress with white pinafore and matching print bonnet, white socks with ribbon ties around ankle; one with a polka-dot short sleeve dress and cap; and one with a jacket with rickrack down the front and matching bonnet.

In March 1942 Vogue advertised Composition and Soft Dolls 7" to 24" high in *Playthings Magazine*.

Large cloth dolls from the 1940s are shown in a Vogue publicity photo; also shown are composition Sunshine Babies. Courtesy Mrs. Virginia Carlson.

Prices
Too few examples seen

Hard Plastic Dolls

1949 – 1950

Description: 14" all hard plastic, mohair wig, sleep eyes.

Marks:

Head:	"14"
Body:	"MADE IN USA"
Clothing:	Late 1940s ink spot labels
	1950 – 1951 "Vogue Dolls" in script

Prices
Mint $250.00 – 300.00

Vogue also dressed large hard plastic dolls manufactured by other companies, such as the Arranbee Doll Company and the Ideal Toy Company, and sold them under the Vogue label.

Vogue sold their hard plastic dolls in series, as they did their large composition dolls. The first year Vogue sold large hard plastic dolls was 1949. The 1949 hard plastic dolls were sold in a series called Young '49ers; they were Peggy, Polly, Patty, Penny, Bridesmaid, and Bride.

There were three dolls in the set: a mother and two daughters with matching outfits. A brochure from 1949 promotes these dolls as a family, the 14" doll as the mother, 8" toddler as the daughter, and the 8" Crib Crowd baby as the baby (see page 67). It is unclear whether there were large hard plastic dolls sold in 1950, but by 1951 they were no longer on the price list. These dolls show Mrs. Graves's attention to quality and detail in costumes and are evidence of her motto that Vogue Dolls Incorporated be the "Fashion Leaders in Doll Society."

PRICE LIST

Effective April 1, 1949

Style No.			Doz.
8" FULLY JOINTED PLASTIC BABY WITH RINGLETS (FOUNDATION WIGS) RUBBER PANTS AND TINY HAIR BOWS			
CRIB CROWD			PER DOZ.
830	Nancy	Col. dotted swiss dress—lace & bow trim	24.00
832	Tootsie	Col. dimity dress with collar—bow trim	24.00
834	Sally	Col. ninon—lace trim	24.00
836	Ruthie	Col. flocked organdy—eyelet & medallion trim	24.00
14" ALL PLASTIC DOLL — CLOSING EYES — MOHAIR WIGS			
YOUNG '49ers			PER DOZ.
*14-20C	(Mother)	Col. broadcloth dress—headband (mate to Daughter 8-20C)	$54.00
*14-21C	(Mother)	Plaid dress—white organdy apron (mate to Daughter 8-21C)	54.00
14-22C	Peggy	Col. organdy pinafore dress—bow and flowers in hair	54.00
14-23C	Polly	Col. chambray dress—black bow trim—headband	54.00
14-24C	Patty	Flocked organdy dress—lacn & flower trim—bows in hair	54.00
14-25C	Penny	Taffeta & ninon dress—gold & silver trim—flowers in hair	54.00
14-30C	Bridesmaid	Old-fashioned gown of taffeta & ninon—picture hat & rosebud trim	84.00
14-31C	Bride	Satin gown—white veil—lace & flowers	72.00

*Mother & Daughter 14-20C & 8-20C
*Mother & Daughter 14-21C & 8-21C

1949 Vogue price list for 14" hard plastic dolls with closing eyes, mohair wigs. Courtesy Mrs. Virginia Carlson.

Mother 14" in #14-21C plaid dress with white apron. Mohair wig in braids (should be on top of head). Marks: "14" (on head); "MADE IN USA" (on body). Tag on dress is 1950 – 51 label "Vogue doll" (in script) on a diagonal. Courtesy Millie Caliri.

Patty (1949) 14" hard plastic in #14-24C flocked organdy dress.* Marked: "14" (on head). Courtesy Dyan Murphy. * blue color variation.

1949 Vogue hard plastic from publicity photo. Polly #14-23C pink dress, black ribbon, Mother #14-20C blue dress, and Mother #14-21C plaid dress with braids atop head. Courtesy Wenham Museum, Wenham, Mass.

14" Mother (right) and 8" child (above) #14-20C and #8-20C, dressed alike in Vogue publicity photo (1949). Courtesy Wenham Museum, Wenham, Mass.

Hard plastics from 1949 brochure. Patty #14-24C flocked organdy yellow dress, Penny #14-25C blue dress with gold ribbon, and Peggy #14-22C pink dress. Courtesy Wenham Museum, Wenham, Mass.

Peggy (1949) 14" hard plastic in #14-22C pink organdy pinafore dress and teddy, pink cotton slip attached to skirt. Pink leatherette snap shoes. With Vogue hang tag. Sleep eyes. Marks: "14" (on head); "MADE IN USA" (on body). Sewn in tag on dress "Vogue Dolls." Courtesy Shirley Niziolek.

Bride and Bridesmaid (1948 – 49) 14" hard plastic (#14-31C and #14-30C, respectively) from Vogue publicity photos. Courtesy Wenham Museum, Wenham, Mass.

Dolls and Toys Developed by Vogue

Velva

1948 – 1951

Description: 15", 18", and 22" composition head and latex foam stuffing in a Neoprene® latex body. Hard plastic head and drink and wet features added later. Velva was molded to the dimensions of a nine-month-old baby.

Marks:
- Head: "VOGUE DOLL"
- Body: None
- Clothing: "Vogue Dolls, INC.; MEDFORD MASS." in white on a blue background on cotton tag (ink spot tag)

Mrs. Graves wanted to sell a baby doll that children could really hug, wash, and play with. Not content with the quality and playability of other doll manufacturers' baby dolls, she developed her own baby doll with a composition head and latex rubber body stuffed with latex foam. She named the doll "Velva" and introduced her at the 1948 New York Toy Fair.

Velva came in 15", 18" and 22" sizes and was adopted by Mrs. Graves to fit the proportions of a nine-month-old baby. Velva was sculpted by Bernard Lipfert. Vogue applied for a patent on the sanitary latex foam stuffing in a Neoprene® latex body. Velva is marked "VOGUE DOLL" on her head.

In 1949 Velva was advertised in *Playthings Magazine* as "Velva Wetting Baby with all plastic fittings, foamed rubber filling, with fittings made and tested by the Fuller Brush Company." Interestingly, the Fuller Brush Company was owned by Mrs. Graves's uncle, Alfred Fuller. Testing of the doll got rather drastic as she was advertised as so sturdy as to not pull apart under 65 pounds of pressure! Velva's Neoprene® skin was supposed to withstand oxidation and tearing and having fingers and feet chewed off!

Velva was sold dressed in five different outfits: a panty and bib; a ruffled eyelet romper; an organdy dress; a flowing ninon dress and bonnet; and a jersey nightie. Three separate outfits could be bought such as "a colored lawn nightie, white astrachan bunting, or knitted jersey nightie" as specified in the 1948 price list. A layette which included rompers, a sleeper, plastic pants, shoes, and a washcloth in an acetate case could also be bought separately. Velva cost $5.50 to $7.50, depending on her outfit. She was the first doll that Vogue sold with separate outfits; the company did not begin selling separate outfits for Ginny until the early 1950s.

Velva was the first doll that Mrs. Graves had designed, developed, and manufactured to her specifications. We have the privilege to review Velva's birth process since Mrs. Graves donated Velva, her molds, and reference material to the Vogue archives at the Wenham Museum in Wenham, Massachusetts.

Mrs. Graves used the production of the rubber-filled dolls as an opportunity to employ a small number of blind workers, who would stuff the dolls with the granular material that came out of a long hose from a vat that chewed up the rubber. Former employees report that the seeing-eye dogs would rest under the tables and get covered with rubber while their masters or mistresses worked.

Vogue Velva Baby
The only all-latex-body doll on the market . . . so human to the touch it feels like real flesh. Designed by Vogue craftsmen for extreme play value, Vogue Velva Baby combines heavier working parts, lasting adhesives, air-molded foam latex stuffing and tested neoprene skin to produce a durable companion for the child who really plays with her toys. There is nothing to rust or break down from contact with moisture. The play-tested Vogue Velva Baby can be sold to your customers with pride!
Length, 18".
Sold with diaper, bib, sunsuit, shoes and stockings.
A Vogue Dolls, INC. ORIGINAL
4 Mystic Avenue
Medford 5, Mass.

Velva ad touting all latex Neoprene® skin (July 1947). Courtesy Mrs. Virginia Carlson.

Velva was cuddly and well-made. Vogue improved upon Velva and gave her a hard plastic head and ability to wet in 1950. There aren't many examples of Velva around today for collectors because the "magic skin" latex has deteriorated.

Vogue determined as other doll companies did, that although the latex rubber was an advancement over composition, holes would develop and the stuffing would come out or it would dry up and crack. Because of the lack of long-term endurance of this material, Vogue phased the latex rubber out after 1951 and the production of Velva came to an end.

Prices

Composition Head	$250.00
Hard Plastic Head	$300.00

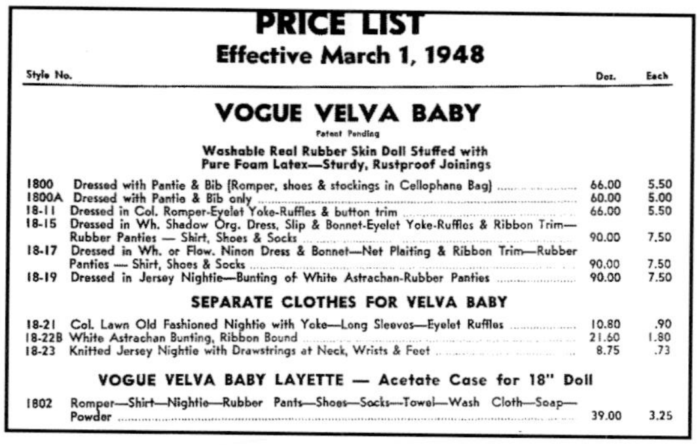

PRICE LIST
Effective March 1, 1948

VOGUE VELVA BABY
Patent Pending
Washable Real Rubber Skin Doll Stuffed with Pure Foam Latex—Sturdy, Rustproof Joinings

Style No.		Doz.	Each
1800	Dressed with Pantie & Bib (Romper, shoes & stockings in Cellophane Bag)	66.00	5.50
1800A	Dressed with Pantie & Bib only	60.00	5.00
18-11	Dressed in Col. Romper-Eyelet Yoke-Ruffles & button trim	66.00	5.50
18-15	Dressed in Wh. Shadow Org. Dress, Slip & Bonnet-Eyelet Yoke-Ruffles & Ribbon Trim—Rubber Panties — Shirt, Shoes & Socks	90.00	7.50
18-17	Dressed in Wh. or Flow. Ninon Dress & Bonnet—Net Plaiting & Ribbon Trim—Rubber Panties — Shirt, Shoes & Socks	90.00	7.50
18-19	Dressed in Jersey Nightie—Bunting of White Astrachan-Rubber Panties	90.00	7.50
	SEPARATE CLOTHES FOR VELVA BABY		
18-21	Col. Lawn Old Fashioned Nightie with Yoke—Long Sleeves—Eyelet Ruffles	10.80	.90
18-22B	White Astrachan Bunting, Ribbon Bound	21.60	1.80
18-23	Knitted Jersey Nightie with Drawstrings at Neck, Wrists & Feet	8.75	.73
	VOGUE VELVA BABY LAYETTE — Acetate Case for 18" Doll		
1802	Romper—Shirt—Nightie—Rubber Pants—Shoes—Socks—Towel—Wash Cloth—Soap—Powder	39.00	3.25

Vogue price list for Velva (1948). Courtesy Wenham Museum, Wenham, Mass.

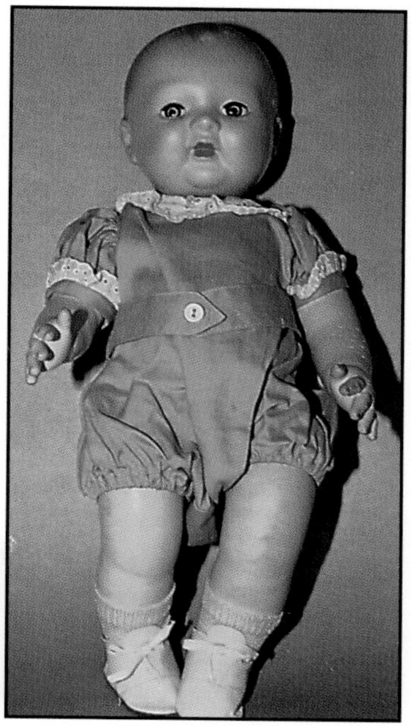

Velva (1948). 16½" hard plastic head and magic skin stuffed latex body and limbs. Wearing blue romper. Marks: "Vogue Doll" (on head). Courtesy Wenham Museum, Wenham, Mass.

EVERY CHILD WILL WANT TO HAVE THIS NEW 15" VOGUE VELVA

WETTING BABY....
WITH PLASTIC HEAD

Don't fail to have this wonderful new addition to Vogue Doll Society ready for immediate sales. She's slated for big things! She'll be asked for all over the country!

Check and see WHY ...

- Drinking-wetting feature
- Sanitary foam latex stuffing. (Originated by Vogue Dolls, Inc.)
- Natural Rubber Skin (withstands oxidation).
- Plastic arm and Leg joinings eliminate water seepage, rusting, or arms and legs from pulling off.

PRICE LIST

		Doz.	Each
15-12	Dressed in White shadow Org. dress and Bonnet with Emb. Org. bib, slip, shirt, diaper, shoes and socks and nursing bottle	64.80	5.40
15-22	Separate white Astrachan Bunting with attached hood, bound with colored satin ribbon and bows	14.40	1.20
15-23	Separate White knitted jersey nightie with drawstrings at neck, wrists and feet	6.80	.57
	15" VOGUE VELVA BABY LAYETTE with Acetate Case (packed four to a box only)		
1502	Jersey knit nightie — colored romper — rubber pants — towel — facecloth — soap — powder	24.00	2.00

Approximate weight per dozen — 27 lbs. including individual corrugated mailing boxes and outside cartons.

NEWSPAPER MATS FURNISHED UPON REQUEST

Velva Wetting Baby (1950 – 51). 15" plastic head, rubber body stuffed with foam rubber. With layette. Clothes have ink spot tag "Vogue Dolls, INC.; MEDFORD MASS," in white on a blue background on cotton tag. Vogue publicity photo courtesy Wenham Museum, Wenham, Mass.

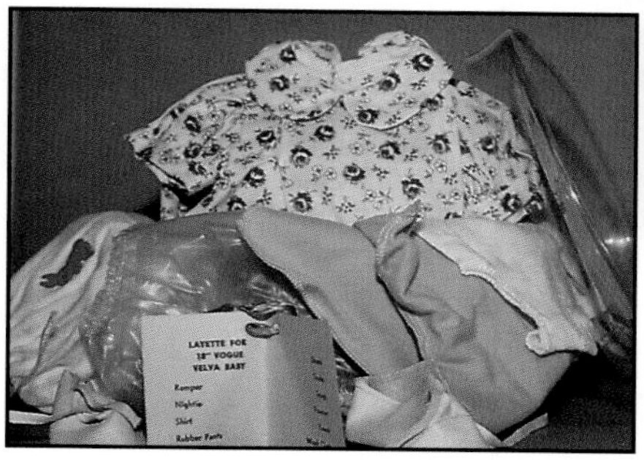

Velva layette. Courtesy Wenham Museum, Wenham, Mass.

15" Velva with hard plastic head (1950). Courtesy Wenham Museum, Wenham, Mass.

VELVA MOLDS

Photos courtesy Wenham Museum, Wenham, Mass.

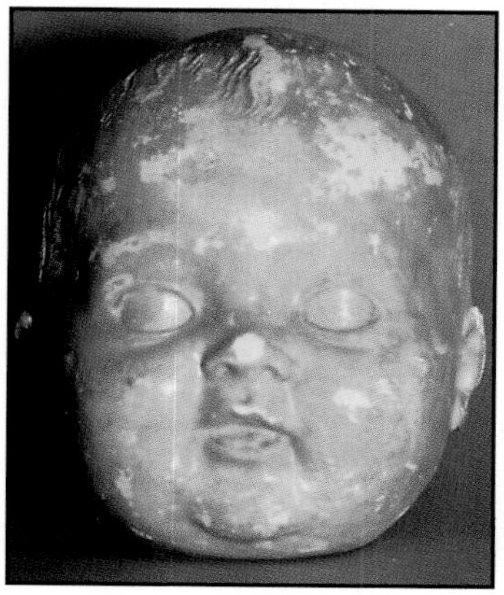

Velva head mold.

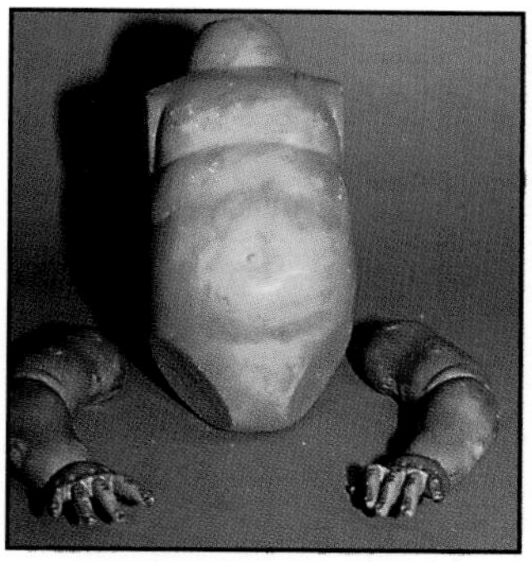

Velva body and arm mold.

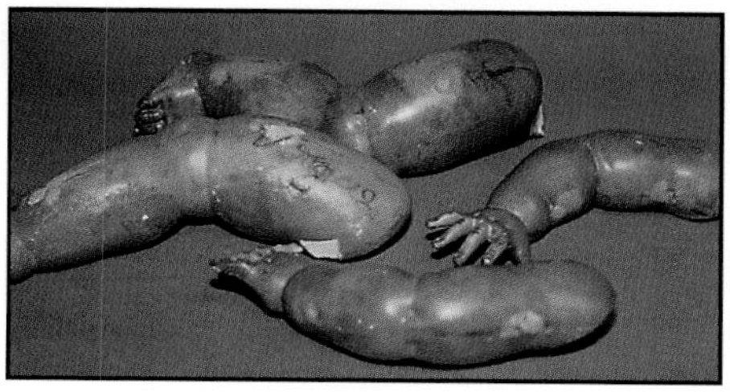

Velva limb mold.

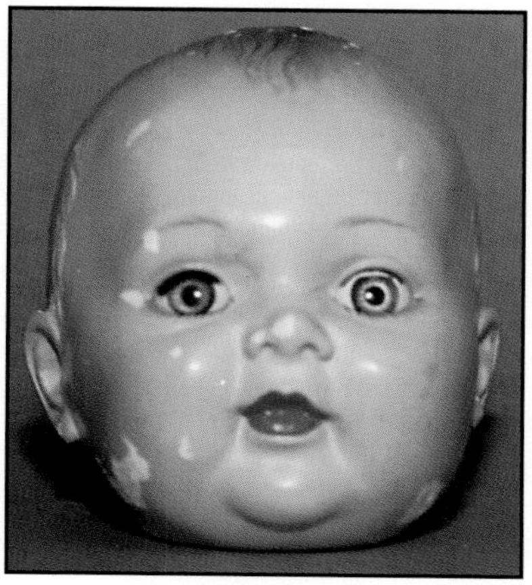

Velva composition face prototype, notice one blue eye and one green eye.

Stuffed Animals

1949 – 1952

Description: 14" and 12" Wooley Baa-Baa, astrachan lamb stuffed with pure foamed rubber (1949).
1950 Pee Wee, 9" astrachan lamb, was added.
1951 Honey Bunny, Scottie, Wooley Baa-Baa (in both 9" and 12" versions) and Snoozie Kitty were added.
1952 Teddy Bear added to line.

Marks: None on animal, had Vogue silver paper tags tied to them or a Vogue pink paper booklet with blue print tied to their necks.

In 1949 Vogue introduced stuffed animals into their line. Their first stuffed animal was a lamb called Wooley Baa-Baa. He was 14" and came in black or white astrachan stuffed with pure foamed rubber wearing a ribbon and bell. A 12" size was called Wooley Baa-Baa, Jr. Both sizes were washable and individually boxed. Vogue had bought out a factory in 1949 – 50 to get materials for the stuffed animals. Wooley Baa-Baa came in assorted colors in 1950 and Pee Wee, a 9" version, was added. The lambs had plastic hearts that said, "I Love You," tied around their necks on a ribbon. Wooley Baa-Baa was a success and more stuffed animals were added to the line.

In 1951 the stuffed animals were Honey Bunny, Scottie, Wooley Baa-Baa (in both 9" and 12" versions), and Snoozie Kitty (spelled Snoozy Kitty in 1952). Most animals were available in black or white and Wooley Baa-Baa also came in red. In 1952 Pee Wee Lamb was returned to the line and an 8" Teddy Bear was added.

Vogue produced the lambs on site at the factory in Medford on the receiving platform. They had a huge hose that put sponge material into the animals. The lambs and stuffed animals were very appealing, but unfortunately there was a problem in their production. The material used for the stuffing was very flammable. John Flanagan, a Vogue driver who delivered material to the home sewers, smelled fumes from the foam when he returned to the plant one day. He immediately showed Virginia Graves and they stopped production of the stuffed animals. The Vogue stuffed animals became a short and almost unknown chapter in Vogue's illustrious production.

Vogue Animal Kingdom

1949

Wooley Baa-Baa, 14" astrachan lamb with pure foamed rubber, black or white, ribbon and bell.
Wooley Baa-Baa, Jr.,12" astrachan lamb with pure foamed rubber, black or white, ribbon and bell.

1950

Wooley Baa-Baa, Jr., 12" astrachan lamb with pure foamed rubber, assorted colors, ribbon, heart, and bell.
Pee Wee, 9" astrachan lamb stuffed with foamed rubber, assorted colors.

1951

Astrachan animals stuffed with foamed rubber (washable)
Honey Bunny, 8" long, white. Cost $1.40.
Scottie, 9" long, black. Cost $1.40.
Wooley Baa-Baa, 9" tall, assorted colors. Cost $1.40.
Wooley Baa-Baa, 12" tall, white, black, red. Cost $2.40.
Snoozie Kitty, 12" long, white. Cost $2.00.

1952

Honey Bunny, 8" long, white and pastels. Cost $1.40.
Scottie, 9" tall, black and white. Cost $1.40.
Wooley Baa-Baa, 12" tall, white, black, pastels. Cost $2.40.
Snoozy Kitty, 12" long, white. Cost $2.00.
Pee Wee Lamb, 9" tall, pastels, black, white. Cost $1.40.
Teddy Bear, 8" sitting down, pastels, black, white. Cost $2.00.

Prices
$120.00 – 250.00

Pee Wee (1950) 9" pink astrachan lamb. He came in assorted colors. Has an "I LOVE YOU" pink heart tied around neck on a ribbon. Marks on large silver tag: "STUFFED WITH PURE FOAM RUBBER/WASHING INSTRUCTIONS/WASH CAREFULLY IN LUKE-WARM WATER AND WHITE SOAP FLAKES." On other side: "VOGUE/DOLLS/INC." (in script). On small silver tag: "A VOGUE DOLL." Courtesy Betty Wallace.

Pee-Wee (1950 – 52). 9" black lamb, notice ribbon and place where bell should be. Courtesy Sue Johnson and Betty Wallace.

Wooley Baa-Baa, black and white (1949). Courtesy Wenham Museum, Wenham, Mass.

Toddles

1937 – 1948

Description: Toddles were 7½" to 8" composition dolls with molded hair and/or mohair wigs, with chubby little legs and bodies, and painted side-glancing eyes. The mold was sculpted by Bernard Lipfert.

Marks: Vogue used dolls with at least six different markings for Toddles. It is unclear whether there is an exact chronology to the markings.; it is known that the Arranbee (R & B) dolls were first. However, Vogue seemed to have used unmarked doll parts interchangeably with Vogue marked parts. It is known that in 1943 there are dolls with at least three different markings for the same Military Group series. The dolls in the Military Group series are marked:

1) Vogue (on head), Doll Company (on body)
2) None (on head), Doll Company (on body)
3) Vogue (on head), none (on body).

Starting in 1937 Mrs. Graves bought small composition dolls from the Arranbee Doll Company to dress and sell under her own Vogue label. She called these dolls Toddles. She later commissioned noted doll sculptor Bernard Lipfert of New York to develop a small 8" doll with more realistic features, reminiscent of the 8" Armand Marseille Just Me and the 8" Arranbee dolls she had been dressing. Toddles has molded hair and most dolls have a wig applied over the molded hair. The dolls have painted eyes with eyelashes, closed mouth, and are jointed at the neck, shoulders, and hips. The fingers are molded together and are slightly curled. The face and bodies are chubby.

Even though Mrs. Graves met with initial disapproval from her suppliers and store buyers, her intuition was right that a little girl would want a small doll she could play with. Toddles was the name chosen for the 8" composition doll with painted eyes and a blonde, brown or black mohair wig. Toddles was produced from 1937 – 48.

Toddles is made of composition, a material made of cowhide, liquid glue, wood flour (not sawdust), resin, and cornstarch. Many collectors call Toddles the "#1 Ginny" although Vogue did not give the name Ginny to their 8" hard plastic doll until 1953.

Toddles came in series such as Nursery Rhyme, Fairy Tales, Bridal Party, and Far Away Places. Named groups include American Workers' group, Patriotic group, Nursery Rhyme group, Fairy Tale, Foreign Costume, Historical, Brother and Sisters. Each doll in a group had a different catalog number and a separate name, e.g., Jerry (#8 – B) and Julie (#8 – 10B) are from the 1947 Playmates group.

Separate clothes were available only in small flowered boxes containing a party dress and bonnet, nightie, shoes, soap, and towel. The emphasis was on selling a completely dressed doll.

A well-known group of dolls was the Military group from 1942 – 44. An ad from the March 1942 *Playthings Magazine* says there were two series: a "Civilian Defense" which included an Air Raid Warden, a male doll wearing a denim suit with an armband marked "C.D." (Civil Defense), a nurse, a fireman, and a policeman. The second series was the Service series in 1942 which had an aviator (Air Corps), draftee (Army), and a sailor (Navy). The 1943 – 44 Service series also included a Navy captain.

Also in 1942 there was a related series called United We Stand which included Uncle Sam, Miss America, and the "allies," Russian, English and Chinese boy and girl dolls. Uncle Sam and Miss America wore red, white, and blue patriotic outfits and came with little American flags. The other couples wore outfits appropriate to their countries.

Vogue also produced a Character and Nursery

Rhymes Series in 1942. Mrs. Graves's daughter, Virginia Graves Carlson, joined Vogue in 1945 as the chief dress designer.

In 1947 the named group of dolls were Toddlers, six girl dolls in dresses with mohair wigs; Playmates, three set of twins; and Specialty group, three dolls, Bride, Red Riding Hood, and Colonial. In 1948 the named group of dolls were Toddlers (Debby, Penny, Trudy, Pinky, Cookie and Bobsy); Playmates, twins (Bunky and Binky, Jerry and Julie, and Alpine boy and girl); Specialty group (Bridesmaid, Bride, Sunsuit); Character group (Red Riding Hood, Alice, and Willie Winkie); and Wee Lassie group (Gingham Girl, Coat, and Spring).

Fitted Nautical Hamper (1937 – 39). 8", twin compo dolls in sailor suits packed in basket with capes, red and blue berets, brass buttons, knit swimsuits, embroidered white organdy frocks, and bonnets. From Vogue Doll Shoppe, West Somerville, Mass. Courtesy Wenham Museum, Wenham, Mass.

Storybook Lamps

Vogue produced Storybook Lamps which were Toddles dolls clipped onto lamps in 1943 – 44. The lamps were 14" with a wooden base. The shades were ruffled and the dolls could be unclipped from the base. The dolls were Red Riding Hood, Little Bo Peep or Toddles. They sold for $5.50.

Toddles dolls are collectible in their own right due to their cute expressions, bodies, and well-made outfits. They are also interesting because they are precursors of Ginny. One can see many Toddles fashions carried over into the hard plastic Ginny, including the Fairytale series, the couples series, and various styles of dresses.

Prices

Toddles marked by Arranbee or Vogue	$250.00 – 300.00
MIB	$350.00+
Special Costumes	
Air Raid Warden	$400.00 – 550.00+ in box
Military Group	$325.00+
Chinese Girl	$375.00
Robin Hood	$375.00
Uncle Sam	$400.00

Prices shown are for mint, complete, all original dolls.

Toddles
(1937 – early 1940s)

Description: 8" composition, large eyes and features, both arms very slightly bent, mohair wig over molded hair,manufactured by the Arranbee (R & B) Doll Company, New York.

Marks: On doll R & B/DOLL CO. (on back).
Outfit: Vogue gold circle sticker label on front of outfit
String closure on blouse, hook and eye, panties attached to dress
Shoes: Tie shoes, center snap shoes, name stamped on bottom of shoe

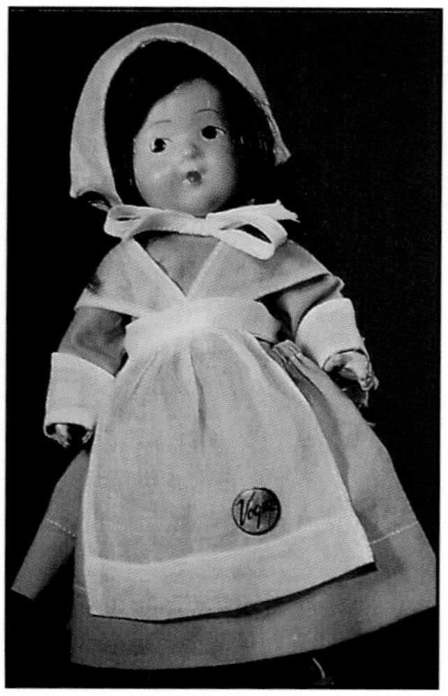

Priscilla, 8" compo molded curl on forehead. Marks: "R and B/DOLL CO" (on back). No marks on head. Priscilla stamped on bottom of shoe. Vogue round gold tag (on dress). Courtesy Pam Zampiello.

Toddles, 8" compo, molded hair. Marks: "R & B" (on back). No tag on dress. Panties attached to dress. Courtesy M. Smith.

NOTE: Dolls are arranged chronologically. When dolls' years are unknown, they are arranged under their marks.

Peasant, 8" composition. String closure on blouse, skirt and apron are separate pieces. Hook and eye closure on apron, elastic on skirt. Marks: "R & B Doll Co" (on body). Gold Vogue sticker on front. Clothes untagged. "Peasant" stamped on bottom of shoe. Courtesy M. Smith.

Vogue publicity shot (1942) showing R&B marked doll group Far Away Lands series. From left to right: Dutch girl and boy, American girl in plaid, Alpine girl and boy. Courtesy Mrs. Virginia Carlson.

Little Red Riding Hood, 8" no marks on head, R & B (faintly on back). Gold Vogue sticker on dress, untagged dress. "Red Riding Hood" stamped on bottom of left shoe. Courtesy Mary Lu Trowbridge.

Toddles, 8" gypsy? Doll unmarked, may have faint R & B. Clothes untagged. String closure on back of blouse. Blouse attached to white panties, apron separate from skirt, ties in back. Earring sewn to scarf. Courtesy M. Smith.

Toddles

(1942 – 1943)

Description: 8" composition, manufactured by Vogue, bent right arm, finer facial features and limbs, mohair wig over molded hair

Marks:

On doll:	None on head, DOLL CO. (on body)
Outfit:	Gold round sticker on front of outfit, clothing untagged
Shoes:	Side snap shoes, name stamped on bottom of shoe.

How a Vogue Doll is Made: composition material and molds of how Toddles was made. Notice face mold in top row. Disregard plastic body (in middle of top row) that was added later. Courtesy Wenham Museum, Wenham, Mass.

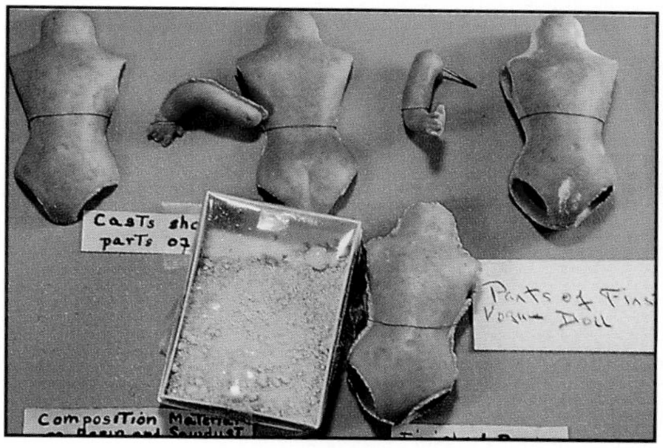

How a Vogue Doll is Made: body and arm mold in top row and raw composition material of sawdust and resin in bottom row. Courtesy Wenham Museum, Wenham, Mass.

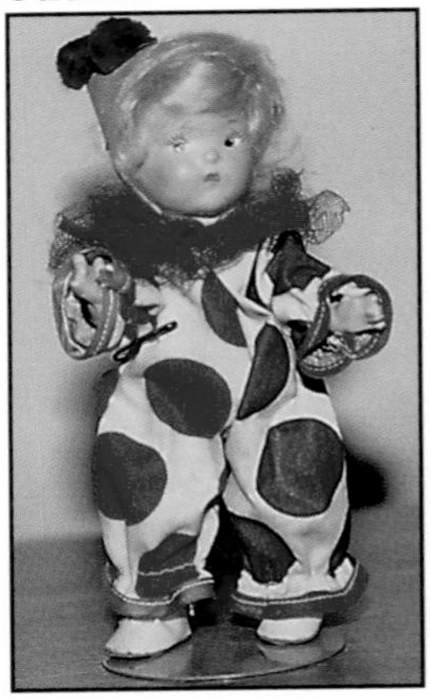

Clown (1942) 8", in red and navy blue polka dot outfit. Came in blue box with Vogue label. Marks: VOGUE (on head); DOLL CO (on back). No tag on clothes. Courtesy Judy Ormsbee.

Air Raid Warden (1942 – 43) from Military Group, 8", in blue denim outfit with white stitching and matching cap. Marks: VOGUE (on head); DOLL CO (on body). "Air Raid Warden" stamped on bottom of right shoe. Original price 89¢. Courtesy Sandy Johnson Barts.

Mr. America (1942 – 44) Marks: VOGUE (on head); DOLL CO (on back). Clothes untagged. No marks on shoe. Courtesy Mary Lu Trowbridge.

Jill (1943), Character and Nursery Rhyme series, 8", girl in blue and white checked dress with yellow top and blue and white checked hat, metal pail. Marks: None on head; DOLL Co. (on back). Dress untagged but gold Vogue circle sticker on front. Courtesy M. Smith.

Jack (1943), Character and Nursery Rhyme series. Missing pail. Marks: None on head; DOLL Co. (on back). Dress untagged but gold Vogue circle sticker on front. Courtesy Wenham Museum, Wenham, Mass.

Indian (1943), Character and Nursery Rhyme series 8" composition. Marks: VOGUE (on head); DOLL CO. (on body). Clothes untagged. "Indian" stamped on bottom of shoe. Courtesy Kathy Schneider.

Bo Beep, Character and Nursery Rhyme series. Bo Peep on left (1943) wearing yellow flowered skirt gown with side panniers. Bo Peep (1944 – 45) on right wearing blue organdy gown with satin panniers and pantaloons. Courtesy Maureen Fukushima.

Toddles (1943), #046, 8", composition, wearing smocked dotted red organdy dress and bonnet. Clothes untagged, panties attached to the dress, hook and eye closing, leatherette shoes. Marks: VOGUE (on head); DOLL CO. (on body). Courtesy Wenham Museum, Wenham, Mass.

Boy and girl (1943), #047 and #048, 8", composition, in rose jersey shorts or skirt and shirt. Missing jersey caps. Marks: VOGUE (on head), DOLL CO (on body). Clothes untagged. Courtesy M. Smith.

Toddles (1943), #152, 8", girl twin in blue dimity dress with white rickrack and embroidered flower in front, and matching hat. Shown on box. Courtesy Betty Bourgault.

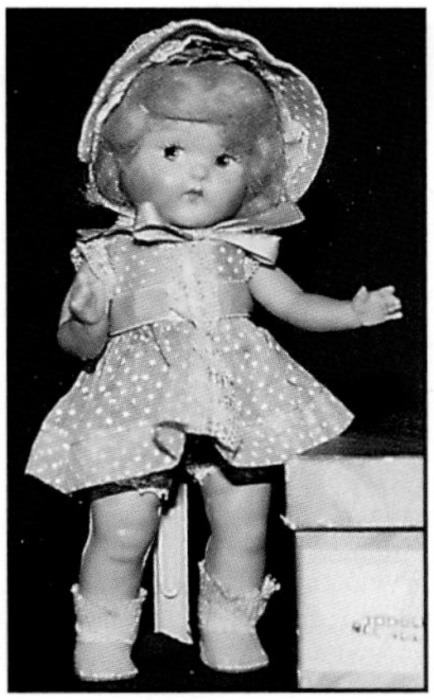

Toddles (1943), #049, 8", girl in blue dotted organdy dress and bonnet with box showing number. Marks: VOGUE (on head), DOLL CO. (on body). Clothes untagged. Courtesy Kathy Schneider.

Toddles in pink shorts (1943), #153, in pink dimity, had matching twin sister #152. Marks: none (on head); DOLL CO (on body). Clothes untagged. Vogue gold sticker. "Toddles" stamped on bottom of left shoe. Courtesy Mary Lu Trowbridge.

Toddles (1943), 8", bent right arm and molded hair: #150 and #151 girl and boy twins in matching striped gingham outfits with hats; #152 and #153 girl and boy twins in pastel dimity outfits with white rickrack trim and embroidered flower in front and matching hats; #164 pastel organdy dress with square edging and bonnet; and #166 with wig in striped gingham sunsuit and bonnet, and beach pail. Vogue publicity photo courtesy Mrs. Virginia Carlson.

Fairy Godmother (1943), Cinderella Group, wearing pink gown with pink satin panniers and pink cone hat. Marks: none (on head); DOLL CO (on body). Clothes untagged. Shoe marked: "Fairy Godmother" on right sole. Courtesy Mary Lu Trowbridge.

Prince Charming (1943), Cinderella Group, 8", composition in blue cotton tights with attached white organdy shirt with lace jabot. Pink satin with matching hat. Marks: VOGUE (faintly on head under wig); DOLL CO (on back). Clothes untagged. Courtesy Mary Lu Trowbridge.

TODDLES
(1940 – 1943)

Description: 7½" composition manufactured by Vogue, right arm bent at almost a right angle, left arm only slightly bent, wig over slightly molded hair, medium-sized painted eyes, delicate eyelashes with light brown line above eyes, closed mouth, second and third fingers molded together and slightly curled.

Marks:

On doll: VOGUE (on head); DOLL CO (on middle of back)
Or None (on head)

Outfits: String closure on top neck, dress attached to panties or slip, hook and eye closure, some panties not sewn onto dress
No tag; or white tag with blue lettering:
"Vogue Doll Inc./MEDFORD, MASS" or ink spot tag
Vogue Nurse and War era (1943) had gold sticker

Shoes: Side snap shoes, center snap shoes, center tie shoes, name stamped on bottom of shoe

AMERICA ON THE MARCH TO VICTORY GROUP

Nurse (1943), America on the March to Victory group, 7½", composition, missing hot water bottle. Courtesy Kathy Schneider.

Vogue publicity shot showing America on the March to Victory group (1943), left to right, Soldier, War Nurse, Miss America, Sailor, and American Indian. Marks: VOGUE (on head), DOLL CO. (on body). Courtesy Mrs. Virginia Carlson.

Miss America (1943), America on the March to Victory group, 7½", composition, with tosca hair complete with flag and flower on hat. Shown with her box. None (head); DOLL CO. (on body). Courtesy Barbara Rosplock-Van Orman

Sailor (1943), America on the March to Victory group, 7½", composition. Marks: VOGUE (on head), DOLL CO. (on body). Clothes untagged. "Sailor" stamped on bottom of shoe. Hat not original. Courtesy M. Smith

Draftee (1943), America on the March to Victory group, green felt clothing. No marks on head, unknown on body. Clothes untagged. "Draftee" stamped on bottom of left shoe. Missing gun. Courtesy Mary Lu Trowbridge.

Indian (1943), America on the March to Victory group, 7½", girl with long black braids. Brown dress with detailed embroidery, embroidered headband and decoration on dress. Long brown pantaloons matching top. Missing some red feathers on headband. Marks: VOGUE (on head); DOLL CO (on back). No tag on clothes. Courtesy Marcey Smith.

Military Group

Military group (1943), Navy Captain, Sailor, Uncle Sam, and Soldier. Some of the military dolls (nurse, soldier, and sailor) also appeared in the America on the March to Victory group. Courtesy Wenham Museum, Wenham, Mass.

Aviator (1943), Military group, 7½", in brown felt, notice plane. Courtesy Wenham Museum, Wenham, Mass.

Uncle Sam, Military group (1943 or 44), 7½", composition. Marks: VOGUE (on head); DOLL CO (on back). Clothes untagged. "Uncle Sam" stamped on bottom of left shoe. Courtesy Mary Lu Trowbridge.

Air Force (1943), Military group, 7½", in brown jacket and khaki pants. Marks: VOGUE (on head); DOLL CO (on body). Courtesy Marge Meisinger.

Policeman (1943) 7½", composition. Marks: none (on head); DOLL CO (on body). Notice little billy club. Outfit untagged but gold Vogue circle sticker on front. Courtesy Marge Meisinger.

Toddles (1943), 7½", composition, in cotton print playsuit with smocked inset yoke and matching cap. An example of Mrs. Graves's action-oriented outfits. Marks: None (on head); Doll Co. on back. Courtesy Barbara Rosplock-Van Orman.

Mexican (1943), 7½", composition. Marks: None (on head); DOLL CO (on body). Clothes untagged. Black side snap shoes. Courtesy M. Smith.

Toddles (1940 – 1943). Girl in navy blue hat, white with blue print dress. Marks: VOGUE (on head), DOLL CO. (on body). Dress untagged. Courtesy M. Smith.

Hansel and Gretel (1943), Fairy Tale set, 7½", composition, red and blue felt with yellow hats. Replaced red leatherette shoes. Marks: VOGUE (on head); DOLL CO (on body). Courtesy Kathy Schneider.

Farmer (1943), in case with extra clothes. Notice pink dress, red and white checked outfit, and garden tool. In blue suitcase. Courtesy Veronica Phillips.

Farmerette (1940 – 1943), 7½", composition. Marks: VOGUE (on head), DOLL CO. (on body). Clothes untagged. "Farmerette" stamped on bottom of shoe. Original garden tools. Courtesy M. Smith.

Cowboy (1943 – 1944), #3361, from Americana Character and Nursery Rhyme series. 7½", composition, molded hair. Plaid cotton shirt, brown leatherette chaps, cowboy hat, and yellow scarf. Round gold Vogue sticker. Toy gun sewn to chaps. Clothes untagged. End label on box says "Suttons Importers Vogue Dolls, Medford, Mass." Courtesy Barbara Hill.

Toddles girl (1940 – 1943), 7½", composition. White dress with navy and red edging and white cap with same edging. Marks: VOGUE (on head), DOLL CO. (on body). Clothes untagged. Dress and slip attached to panties. Replaced shoes. Courtesy M. Smith.

Bridesmaid (1940 – 1943), 7½", composition. Long gown with rose and blue print flowers, pink bow in front, flowers on front. Marks: VOGUE (on head), DOLL CO (on body). Clothes untagged. Bottom of shoe stamped "Bridesmaid." Courtesy M. Smith.

Miss America (1943), in case with extra clothes. Notice brown bucket, playsuit, and red and white checked outfit. In blue suitcase. Courtesy Veronica Phillips.

1944

Vogue publicity shot showing Far Away Lands Miss Scotland and the rest Americana (left to right), Victory Gardener Girl and Boy, and Cowgirl and Cowboy. Marks: VOGUE (on head), DOLL CO. (on body). Courtesy Mrs. Virginia Carlson.

Scotch (1944 – 46), 8", composition. Marks: VOGUE (on head), DOLL CO. (on body). Clothes tagged with white tag with Vogue in blue writing. "Scotch" stamped on bottom of shoe. Skirt separate from white body suit. Courtesy M. Smith.

Cowboy, Americana group, 8", composition. Notice green belt. Marks: VOGUE (on head); DOLL CO (on back). No tag on clothes. Courtesy Judy Ormsbee.

Oriental Girl, Far Away Lands group, black mohair wig, pink print kimono, worn over pink one-piece string tie closure jumpsuit. Black felt hat, yellow organdy obi, ivory leather tie shoes. Courtesy Barbara Hill.

Fire Chief (1944 – 46), 8", composition. Black jacket with red fire hat, black and white check pants, black leatherette shoes with leatherette inset to make it look like boot. "Fireman" stamped on bottom of shoe. Courtesy Ruth Lief.

Cowgirl, Americana group, 8", composition. Marks: VOGUE (on head), DOLL CO. (on body). Clothes untagged. String closure on dress, vest is separate, replaced hat. Courtesy M. Smith.

Cowboy (1944), Americana group, 8", composition, blonde wig. Showing variation in neckerchief. Notice lasso. "Cowboy" stamped on bottom of left shoe. Courtesy Mary Lu Trowbridge.

Toddles
(1940 – 1943)

Description: 7¼" composition, manufactured by Vogue, slim body jointed at neck, shoulders and hips, right arm bent at almost a right angle, left arm only slightly bent, deeply molded hair with curls around face, medium-sized painted eyes, delicate eyelashes with light brown line above eye.

Marks: On doll: VOGUE (on head), none (on body)
Outfit: Ink spot tag
Shoes: Center snap

Toddles
(1945 – 1949)

Description: 8"composition, manufactured by Vogue, chubby body and face, round painted eyes, thick eyelashes with lash nearest outer eye painted longer, fingers molded together and slightly curled, both arms almost straight.
A sub-set of Toddles was advertised as Toddlers.

Marks: On doll: VOGUE (on head) VOGUE (upper back)
Outfit: Twill ink spot tag
String closure on top, hook and eye closure
Shoes: Snap shoes

Exact Date Unknown

Toddles (early to mid – 1940s), 8", composition. Blue dress with white inset with pink and green and white embroidery, blue cap. Marks: VOGUE (on head), DOLL CO. (on body). Clothes untagged. Panties separate from dress. Courtesy M. Smith.

Russian Girl (early to mid – 1940s), 8", composition. Marks: VOGUE (faintly on head under wig); DOLL CO (on back). Clothes untagged. Courtesy Sue Johnson.

Farmerette (1943), 8", composition. Marks: VOGUE (on head); DOLL CO (on body). Round Gold Vogue tag on clothes. Original garden tools. Courtesy Wenham Museum, Wenham, Mass.

Toddles Girl (1940 – 1943), 8", composition. Short pink dress with house, dog, flower print, white apron. Dress attached to panties. Marks: VOGUE (on head), DOLL CO (on body). Clothes untagged. Replaced shoes. Courtesy M. Smith.

Gypsy Lady (1944), wears cotton outfit with red print skirt and white blouse with yellow bodice; apron is trimmed with ribbon and yellow cotton scarf is tied over mohair wig. Marks: VOGUE (on head); unknown (on back). Courtesy Barbara Rosplock-Van Orman.

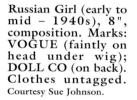

Toddles (mid – late 1940s), 7½", girl in red plaid. Mohair wig. Marks: Vogue (on head); none (on body). Blue ink spot label. Courtesy Millie Caliri.

Chinese Boy (1944), wears red cotton pants and top edged with yellow bias tape and stenciled with gold symbol; mohair wig is tied in a single pigtail in the back. Note original black and gold foil Vogue tag on pants leg. Marks: none (on head), VOGUE (on back). "Chinese Boy" marked on sole of shoe. Courtesy Barbara Rosplock -Van Orman.

Toddles (mid – late 1940s), girl, light blue side-glancing eyes, bent right arm, wearing blue and white lightly striped dress with two pink flowers and black stems. Marks: Vogue (on head) very faint. Dress untagged. Hook and eye closure, panties attached to dress. Courtesy M. Smith

Tyrolean (mid – late 1940s), boy in gray felt with green trim and yellow felt flowers, missing cap. Marks: VOGUE (on head), VOGUE (on back). Clothes have ink spot tag. Courtesy M. Smith.

Toddles (1945 – 47), composition doll with straight arms. White organdy dress trimmed with navy woven laced trim and matching bonnet. Attached pants. Marks: VOGUE (on head); VOGUE (on body).

Tyrolean (mid – late 1940s), orange felt skirt and hat with white blouse. Marks: none (on head); VOGUE (on back). Medford ink spot tag. Courtesy Anita Maxwell.

Toddles (1946+), composition doll with straight arms. Mohair wig. Blue organdy dress with lace trim, yellow ribbon tie at waist, and matching bonnet. Attached pants. Shown with box. Marks: VOGUE (on head); VOGUE (on body).

Southern Belle (1944 – 46), 8", composition in long blue gown with flower print. Straight arm. Long ankle-length pantaloons are sewn to dress. Came with a nosegay of flowers. Marks: VOGUE (on head), VOGUE (on body). Clothes tagged: Vogue Doll Inc./Medford Mass., white tag with blue letters. Pink slippers. Courtesy M. Smith.

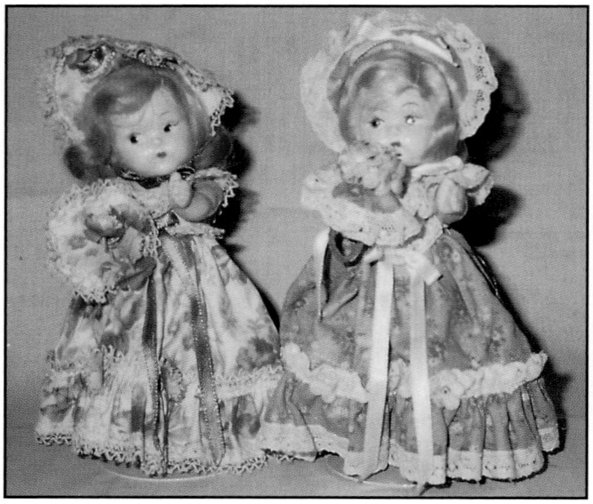

Southern Belles (1944 – 46), 8", composition wearing printed linen gowns with lace trim and matching bonnets and nosegay holders. The large print on the left is unusual since small-scaled prints were more typical. Marks: VOGUE (on head); VOGUE (on body). Courtesy Maureen Fukushima.

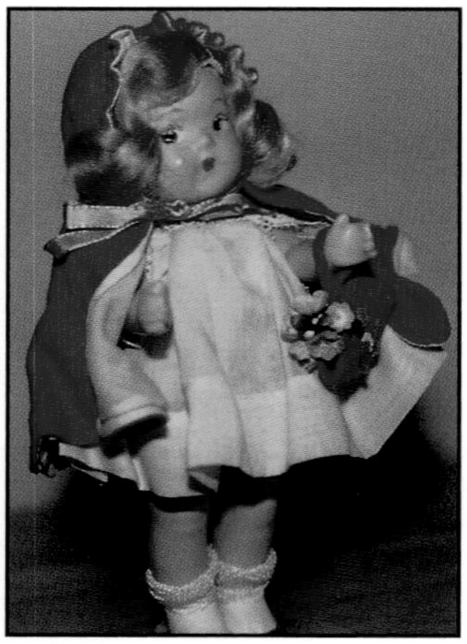

Red Riding Hood (1946 or 47), red hooded cape, white dress, felt basket. Marks: None (on head); VOGUE (on back). Ink spot tag. Courtesy Judy Ormsbee.

Miss Muffet (1946), blue long dress with red and white flowers and matching cap. Shown with blue Vogue box. Marks: None (on head); VOGUE (on back). No tag on dress. Courtesy Mary Lu Trowbridge.

Preacher (1940s) from Wedding Party. Black felt outfit and hat. Holds a little Bible. Marks: VOGUE (on head), DOLL CO. (on body). Round gold Vogue label. Courtesy Wenham Museum, Wenham, Mass.

Fairy Godmother (mid – late 1940s) from the Fairy Tale set. Pink with black polka dot. Marks: none (head); VOGUE (on body). Ink spot tag on outside of clothes. Courtesy Wenham Museum, Wenham, Mass.

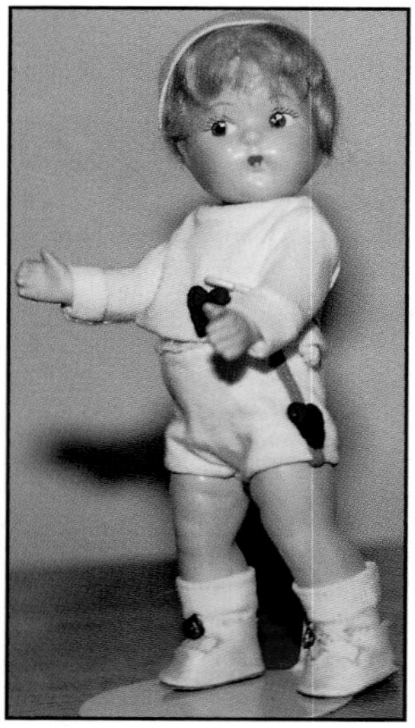

Boy in white with green felt hearts (mid – late 1940s), doll with red felt hearts was a Valentine Special doll. Marks: None (on head); VOGUE (on back). Ink spot tag on outfit. Courtesy Judy Ormsbee.

Fairy Godmother (before 1947) from the Fairy Tale set. Pink with black polka dot with pink overlay and pink hat. Marks: none (head); VOGUE (on body). Ink spot tag on outside of clothes. Courtesy Wenham Museum, Wenham, Mass.

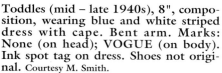

Toddles (mid – late 1940s), 8", composition, wearing blue and white striped dress with cape. Bent arm. Marks: None (on head); VOGUE (on body). Ink spot tag on dress. Shoes not original. Courtesy M. Smith.

1947

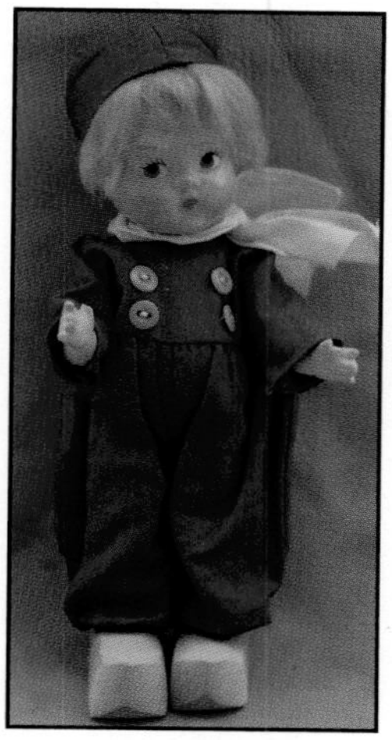

Dutch boy (1947), 8", composition. Marks: VOGUE (on head), DOLL CO. (on body). Clothes untagged. String closure on neck. Courtesy M. Smith.

Little Red Riding Hood (1947) from the Fairy Tale set. 8" composition. Marks: VOGUE (on head); DOLL CO (on body). Courtesy Wenham Museum, Wenham, Mass.

Hansel and Gretel from the Fairy Tale Set (1947) 8" composition. Red felt with yellow rickrack, red leatherette shoes. Clothes are tied on top, hook and eye on felt. Marks: VOGUE (on head); DOLL CO (on body). No tag. "Hansel," "Gretel" stamped on bottoms of shoes. Courtesy Wenham Museum, Wenham, Mass.

Wee Willie Winkie (1947), 8", composition Marks: VO last 3 letters unclear (on head); DOLL CO (on back), clothes untagged, "Wee Willie Winkie" stamped on bottom of shoe. Replaced candle and candleholder. Courtesy Mary Lu Trowbridge.

Ice Skater (1947), 8", all composition in aqua ice skating outfit with white feather trim. Courtesy Mary Lu Trowbridge.

Debby (1947), #8 – 1A, in pink dress showing ink spot tag sewn on outside of dress. Courtesy Barbara Rosplock-Van Orman.

Debby (1947), #8 – 1A, in pink dress with flowers with ink spot tag sewn on outside of dress. Shown with plain cardboard box with Vogue sticker. Marks: None (on head); VOGUE (on body). Courtesy Barbara Rosplock-Van Orman.

Alice In Wonderland (1947), #8 – 18B, from Character group. Composition with mohair wig. Wearing blue cotton dress with white trim and white organdy pinafore apron with lace trim, ribbon in hair. Marks: None (on head); VOGUE (on body). Courtesy Barbara Rosplock-Van Orman.

Colonial girl (1947), #8-18A, Specialty group, wears a pink batiste dress, pantalettes, and flowered cap. Mint in box. Marks: Vogue (on neck). Courtesy Barbara Rosplock-Van Orman.

1947 or 1948

Pinky (1947 or 48) #8-4A or B from Toddlers series, 8", composition, blue dress with smocking. Marked: none (on head) Vogue (on back). Ink spot tag. Courtesy Pam Zampiello.

Jerry (1947 – 48) #8-A or B from Playmates series 8", composition. Showing variation of shirt's jersey material. Original garden tool. Marks: VOGUE (on head), VOGUE (on body). Round gold Vogue tag on clothes and ink spot tag on clothes. Courtesy Carol Stover.

Bunky and Binky (1947 – 48), Bunky 1947: #8-7A or B; Binky: 1947 #8-8A or B from Playmates series. Twins in yellow jersey outfits. Marks: VOGUE (on head), VOGUE (on back). Clothes have ink blot tag. Courtesy M. Smith.

Jerry and Julie (1948), Jerry #8-9B, and Julie #8-10B, from Playmates series, 8", composition. Twins in green jersey overalls, red, green, yellow, and blue jersey caps and shirts. Each came with a garden tool. Can date Julie because 1948 price list says "stocking cap" whereas 1947 list just says "hat." Marks: VOGUE (on head), VOGUE (on body). Ink spot tag on clothes. Hook and eye closure. Courtesy M. Smith.

Alpine (1947 – 48), #8-11B and #8-12B from Playmates series. Light blue felt with gold hats and aprons. Marks: VOGUE (on head), VOGUE (on body). Courtesy M. Smith.

Little Red Riding Hood (1947 – 48), # 8-16A, 1947; #8-17B, 1948, 8", composition. Marks: VOGUE (on head), DOLL CO. (on body). Clothes tagged white tag with blue writing: VOGUE DOLL INC./MEDFORD, MASS. String closure on dress, separate panties. Courtesy M. Smith.

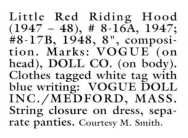

1948

Sunsuit (1948), #8-16B from Specialty group. 8", composition in blue flowered percale sunsuit with white eyelet trim, braids pinned up. Missing pail. Marks: None (on head); "VOGUE" (on back). Ink spot tag on clothes. Courtesy M. Smith.

8" Fully Jointed Composition Dolls —Mohair Wigs

TODDLERS				
8-1B	Debby	Striped Chambray Dress & Bonnet, Checked Dimity, pinafore apron, ruffled trim	22.50	1.87½
8-2B	Penny	Col. shadow Org. dress & eyelet ruffles, straw hat with flowers, ribbon trim	22.50	1.87½
8-3B	Trudy	White Org. dress with col. fig. lawn, col. bonnet—lace trim	22.50	1.87½
8-4B	Pinky	Hand smocked col. dimity dress and bonnet—lace trim	22.50	1.87½
8-5B	Cookie	Col. Org. dress & Bonnet, white eyelet inserts & pockets, loop trim	22.50	1.87½
8-6B	Bobsy	Col. Batiste dress & bonnet, col. embroidered trim	22.50	1.87½
PLAYMATES		(twins sold only in pairs)		
8-7B	Bunky	Col. striped jersey suit & hat (pastel shades)	22.50	1.87½
8-8B	Binky	Col. striped jersey dress & hat (pastel shades)	22.50	1.87½
8-9B	Jerry	Jersey overalls & hat, striped sweater, garden tool	22.50	1.87½
8-10B	Julie	Jersey overalls & stocking cap, striped sweater, garden tool	22.50	1.87½
8-11B	Alpine	Felt suit, novelty trim, alpine hat with feather	22.50	1.87½
8-12B	Alpine	Felt dress & hat—novelty trim	22.50	1.87½

Approximate Weight per Dozen

8 inch dolls — 6 lbs.
17 inch dolls — 27 lbs.
13 inch dolls — 21 lbs.
18 inch Velva Baby Dolls — 40 lbs*

Fashion Leaders in Doll Society

*Includes individual corrugated mailing boxes and outside carton.

Vogue price list (1948) showing Toddles in groups: Toddlers and Playmates. Courtesy Marge Meisinger.

VOGUE VELVA BABY LAYETTE — Acetate Case for 18" Doll

1802 Romper—Shirt—Nightie—Rubber Pants—Shoes—Socks—Towel—Wash Cloth—Soap—Powder 39.0

8" Fully Jointed Composition Dolls —Mohair Wigs

TODDLERS			
8-1B	Debby	Striped Chambray Dress & Bonnet, Checked Dimity, pinafore apron, ruffled trim	22.50
8-2B	Penny	Col. shadow Org. dress & eyelet ruffles, straw hat with flowers, ribbon trim	22.50
8-3B	Trudy	White Org. dress with col. fig. lawn, col. bonnet—lace trim	22.50
8-4B	Pinky	Hand smocked col. dimity dress and bonnet—lace trim	22.50
8-5B	Cookie	Col. Org. dress & Bonnet, white eyelet inserts & pockets, loop trim	22.50
8-6B	Bobsy	Col. Batiste dress & bonnet, col. embroidered trim	22.50
PLAYMATES		(twins sold only in pairs)	
8-7B	Bunky	Col. striped jersey suit & hat (pastel shades)	22.50
8-8B	Binky	Col. striped jersey dress & hat (pastel shades)	22.50
8-9B	Jerry	Jersey overalls & hat, striped sweater, garden tool	22.50
8-10B	Julie	Jersey overalls & stocking cap, striped sweater, garden tool	22.50
8-11B	Alpine	Felt suit, novelty trim, alpine hat with feather	22.50
8-12B	Alpine	Felt dress & hat—novelty trim	22.50

Approximate Weight per Dozen

8 inch dolls — 6 lbs.
17 inch dolls — 27 lbs.
13 inch dolls —
18 inch Velva Baby Dolls —

Fashion Leaders in Doll Society

*Includes individual corrugated mailing boxes and outside carton.

Vogue price list (1948) showing Toddles in groups: Specialty, Character, and Wee Lassie. Courtesy Marge Meisinger.

Debby (1948), #8-1B blue, pink and yellow striped chambray dress and bonnet, pinafore apron with ruffled trim. Shown with box. Courtesy Mary Miskowiec.

Bobsy (1948), # 8-6B from Toddlers group in white pinafore with embroidered lace around hem, waist, and sleeves, with bonnet. Marks: VOGUE (on head); DOLL CO (on back). Ink spot tag on outfit. Box says "Toddlers" #8-6B blue/blonde, BO..?" Courtesy Ann Tardie.

Sunsuit (1948), #8-16B from Specialty Group. 8", composition in red flowered percale sunsuit with white eyelet trim, braids were pinned up. Missing pail. Marks: None (on head); VOGUE (on back). Ink spot tag on clothes. Courtesy Judy Ormsbee.

ACCESSORIES

Wardrobe items in box with pull-out drawer (early 1940s). Contains hand-sewn Vogue clothing and accessories. Inventory on the lid. A rake and shovel were included in a later version. Courtesy Marge Meisinger.

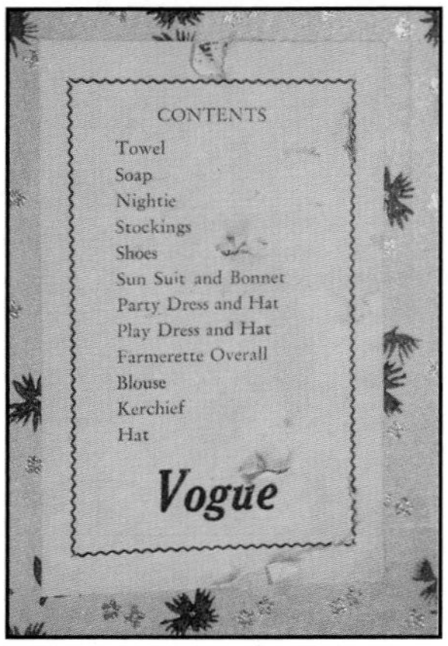

Wardrobe items in box with pull-out drawer (early 1940s) showing variation of purple foil covering.

STORYBOOK LAMPS

Storybook Lamps, Toddles dolls clipped on lamps, 1940s. The lamps were 14" with wooden base. Courtesy Mrs. Virginia Carlson.

Sunshine Babies

late 1930s – mid 1940s

Description:	8" composition baby dolls with molded hair; had the same head and body as Toddles but with curved baby legs.
Marks:	Head: Vogue
	Back: Doll Co.

Vogue sold 8" composition baby dolls that had the same head and body as Toddles but with curved baby legs during approximately the same time that the Toddles were produced (late 1930s – mid 1940s). These Sunshine Babies had molded painted hair. They had side-glancing painted blue eyes. Sunshine Baby's right arm is bent at the elbow and the legs are curved at the knee with toes pointing slightly inward. Sunshines were marked Vogue on back of head and Doll Co. on their back (the same as some of the Toddles).

Sunshines came in dresses of organdy and fine quality cotton with attached or separate slips, and one-piece chemises. They wore little rayon socks tied with ribbons. Most outfits came with a matching bonnet. Dresses had string ties in back and some had the blue and white Vogue Dolls label while others had the small round gold Vogue paper tag on the front of the dress.

The six outfits available in 1937 were typical of Sunshine Baby's clothing. They were a colored organdy dress and bonnet with embroidered organdy bands down the front; a colored batiste dress with poke bonnet with lace and ribbon; a colored organdy dress and bonnet with white yoke insert and embroidered roses; a white organdy dress and bonnet with narrow lace and felt flowers; a white dotted organdy dress and bonnet; and a colored dimity smocked dress and poke bonnet. The wholesale cost of each doll was 65¢. The Sunshine Babies are delightful dolls. They are hard for collectors to find in excellent condition and are therefore valuable.

Sunshine Baby (late 1930s – mid 1940s), 8", composition, bent leg, molded hair, outfit has no label. Whiteish dress. Marks: Vogue (on head). Courtesy Millie Caliri.

Prices	
Sunshine Baby	
Mint	$400.00
MIB	$500.00+

Sunshine Baby (1943 – 47), 8", composition, wearing blue dimity printed dress with lace and inset embroidery flowers on organdy trim. Matching bonnet. Side snap shoes, most had booties tied with a ribbon. Courtesy Shirley Niziolek.

Sunshine Baby (late 1930s – mid 1940s), 8", composition, red polka dot dress and bonnet. Showing suitcase which was fitted with layette. Courtesy Wenham Museum, Wenham, Mass.

Sunshine Baby (late 1930s – mid 1940s), 8", composition, red polka dot dress and bonnet. Courtesy Wenham Museum, Wenham, Mass.

Sunshine Babies (1943) middle row: #513 colored organdy dress and bonnet with embroidered roses; #515 sheer organdy dress and bonnet. Front row: #526 frosted white organdy dress with puffy sleeves, lace trim and embroidered roses and bonnet; #512 pale dimity dress with puffed sleeves and smocked yoke, matching bonnet with ribbon bow; #514 white organdy dress trimmed with lace, ribbon and felt flowers at the hem; #511 pastel printed organdy dress with rosebuds, matching bonnet. All babies have molded hair. Vogue publicity photo.

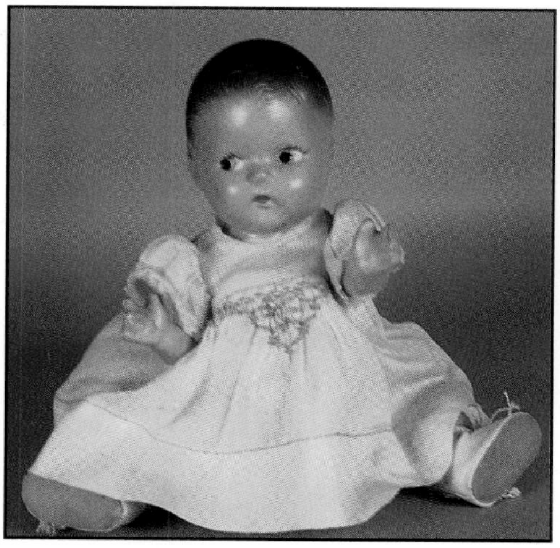

Sunshine Baby (1943 – 47), 8", composition, molded hair, wearing blue dimity outfit with embroidered smocking trim, tiny pink flower, and puffed sleeves. Courtesy Shirley Niziolek.

Sunshine Baby (1943 – 47), 8", composition, molded hair, wearing pink dress with pink embroidery and blue flower. Courtesy S. Ogilvie.

Sunshine Baby (1943 – 47), 8", composition, molded hair, wearing blue dress with white panels with pink and green embroidered flower. This is R&B's doll head used by Vogue. Notice the distinctive eyes and single center curl. Courtesy Veronica Phillips.

Crib Crowd

1948 – 1952

Description: 8" hard plastic baby dolls with the same head and body as painted eye hard plastic doll but with curved baby legs.
The first Crib Crowd babies (1948 – 50) had painted eyes and mohair wigs. Later Crib Crowd babies (1950 – 51) had sleep eyes with lambskin (caracul) wigs.

Marks: Head: VOGUE
Back: VOGUE DOLL

Vogue marketed the adorable hard plastic Crib Crowd baby in 1948 – 52. Crib Crowd babies had the same body as the 8" painted eye hard plastic doll, except they had curved baby legs. Vogue used the curly mohair wig on the doll to achieve the baby look on their painted eye doll produced from 1948 – 50.

Vogue introduced the sleep eye Crib Crowd dolls with curly lambskin (caracul) wigs in 1950. Thus, both painted eye and sleep eye Crib Crowd babies were produced in 1950. In 1951 only the sleep eye version was produced. In 1950 and 1951, many dolls had delicate bisque-like plastic colors and transitional face colors, as Vogue experimented with colors and various materials for the 8" doll.

It should be noted that Vogue did not consistently assign the term "Crib Crowd" to the promotion of the baby version of the Painted Eye Hard Plastic doll from the start. In some early 1949 advertisements the doll was referred to simply as a baby doll or "mighty mite," but in another 1949 advertisement and a price list, the term "Crib Crowd" was used. However, in 1950 price lists it was only assigned a category called "Curved Baby Legs" and it was in some 1950 advertising copy that the doll was described as: "The Crib Crowd With Special Ringlet Wigs." Apparently, Vogue finally adopted the term "Crib Crowd," because all subsequent material referred to the dolls' name as Crib Crowd dolls.

In addition to being advertised separately in 1949, the Crib Crowds were advertised as part of a family along with a 14" mother doll, an 8" doll in its matching daughter dress, and the Crib Crowd as the baby. However, this approach was abandoned in 1950, and the Crib Crowd dolls were sold separately.

Wardrobe

The first Crib Crowd Dolls wore distinctive gowns with gathered necks and/or high waists and matching bonnets or ribbons. The painted eye hard plastic Crib Crowd doll also came with rubber pants and knit booties tied at the ankles. Sometimes the Crib Crowd dolls were also shown in snap shoes, especially in 1950.

In 1949 there were four different outfits each with a different name. They were Nancy in a colored dotted Swiss dress with lace and bow trim; Tootsie in dimity with a collar and bow trim; Sally in colored ninon and lace trim; and Ruthie in pastel flocked organdy, eyelet, and medallion trim. Their wholesale price was $2.00 each.

In 1950 and 1951 the sleep eye Crib Crowd doll came dressed as an Easter Bunny for a special Easter promotion. This Easter Bunny is a very desirable doll to collectors.

There were six different outfits in 1950, three dresses and three play outfits: Tootsie (#8 – 1L) dimity romper with eyelet ruffles; Nancy (#8 – 2L); Sally (#8 – 3L) dimity dress in either plain or pattern print with shawl collar trimmed with lace); Ruthie (#8 – 4L) drawstring printed organdy gown with eyelet ruffled trim); Barbie (#8 – 5L); and Betsy (#8 – 6L) ninon dress (hooded satin cape was added as a seasonal promotion). All had hair bows.

The three outfits in 1951 were Dora (#45) a romper with eyelet trim, carrying a tiny toy with a bow in her hair; and Judy (#46), a pale pastel organdy dress and matching bonnet with lace trim and satin bows; and Peg (#47), a dotted Swiss apron dress with matching bonnet. Crib Crowd does not appear on the 1952 price list but a painted eye Judy was available in a round case with extra clothing (#823).

Today Crib Crowd Babies are in great demand by collectors because of their cuteness and rarity.

Prices

Crib Crowd, mint	$475.00 – 500.00+
Easter Bunny	$1,500.00+

Crib Crowd Baby – Painted Eye (1949), light blue dimity dress with lace trim and blue satin bow at yoke and in hair. Mohair poodle wig. Nylon sock booties and rubber pants.

Crib Crowd Baby – Painted Eye (1949), Nancy #830, curly blonde mohair wig with bow matches blue dotted organdy dress with lace trim. Knit booties tied with blue ribbon. Courtesy S. Ogilvie.

Crib Crowd Baby – Painted Eye (1950), (from left) (#1-L) Tootsie in blue dotted romper; (#4-L) Ruthie in dress with blue ribbon trim; (#3-L) Sally in yellow dress; (#5-L) Barbie in blue dress with white polka dot trim. Vogue stuffed animal (top row). Courtesy Virginia Carlson.

Crib Crowd Baby – Painted Eye (1949), advertised as part of a family along with 14" mother doll, an 8" doll in its matching daughter dress, and the Crib Crowd as the baby.

Crib Crowd Baby – Painted Eye (1949), Ruthie #836, wears the pale yellow version of the flocked organdy gown gathered at the neck and trimmed with lace and medallions; wears rubber pants and booties. Courtesy Barbara Rosplock-Van Orman.

Tootsie (1950) #8-1L, Crib Crowd doll wears the pink version of a dimity romper with ruffled eyelet trim. Note the curly mohair wig used in the first "transitional" sleep eye Crib Crowds. Courtesy Barbara Rosplock-Van Orman.

Crib Crowd Baby – Painted Eye (1950), platinum blonde curly hair with pink bow stapled to the head. Pale pink dimity dress with lace trimmed yoke. Courtesy Maureen Fukushima.

Crib Crowd Baby – Transitional Painted Lash (1950), yellow dimity with printed dimity hem and yoke with ruffle trim. Yellow ribbons trim the blonde curly hair and the shoulder. Courtesy S. Ogilvie.

Crib Crowd Baby – Painted Lash (1950), special Easter Bunny released to promote sales at Easter time. Outfit came in pastel colors of pink, yellow, and green. Suit and felt-lined ears are made of poodle cloth. Some earlier transitional Easter Dolls had wigs to match the outfit. Courtesy Shirley's Dollhouse.

Crib Crowd Baby – Painted Lash (1950 – 51), white dimity dress with ruffle cap sleeves, smocking, and lace edging with matching bonnet. Yellow blonde poodle wig. Similar to 1947 Toddles "Pinky" outfit. Courtesy Barbara Rosplock-Van Orman.

Crib Crowd Baby – Transitional Painted Lash (1950 – 51), white printed organdy dress with blue ribbon trim. A blue bow is stapled to the doll's curly poodle wig. The pale facial coloring with early hand-painted lashes combine to create a true baby look.

Crib Crowd Baby – Painted Lash (1950), Easter Bunny costumes; notice pastel pink, blue, green, and yellow. Courtesy Kathy Bailey.

Crib Crowd Baby (1950), Fluffy box. Courtesy Tina Ritari.

Crib Crowd Baby (1950), Fluffy, a special Easter Bunny doll issued by Vogue for a seasonal promotion. This doll is mint with no fading and all original. Courtesy Tina Ritari.

Crib Crowd Baby – Painted Lash (1950 – 51), Judy #46 in pale blue organdy dress and matching bonnet with lace trim. Bonnet and shoulders are tied with blue satin bows. Notice wrist tag and pink box with "ink spot" label. Also came in pink. Courtesy Ann Tardie.

Crib Crowd Baby – Painted Lash (1950 – 51), Judy #46 in pale pink organdy dress and matching bonnet with lace trim. Bonnet and shoulders are tied with pink satin bows. Notice wrist tag. Also came in blue. Courtesy Shirley's Dollhouse.

Crib Crowd Baby –Painted Lash (1950), brunette in pink satin dress trimmed with organdy and flowers and a matching bonnet. Courtesy Kathy Bailey.

Crib Crowd Baby – Painted Lash (1951), Judy #46 in yellow organdy dress. Notice yellow bow on head. Missing bonnet. Courtesy S. Ogilvie.

Crib Crowd Baby – Painted Lash (1950), printed cotton dress with eyelet cap sleeves and ruffle trim with ribbon laced braid and matching cotton print bonnet. Fabric is a nice example of Vogue's tiny scale prints. Courtesy Maureen Fukushima.

Crib Crowd Baby – Painted Lash (1951), red head in pale green dotted Swiss romper with eyelet trim and hair ribbon. Plastic toy was original to doll. Shown in pink Vogue box. Courtesy S. Ogilvie.

Crib Crowd Baby – Painted Lash (1950 – 52), in round case #823 containing doll and extra clothes and baby accessories. This case is shown in early brochures through 1952 with a painted eye doll. Courtesy S. Ogilvie.

Crib Crowd Baby – Painted Eye (1952), Judy in round case #823 containing doll and extra clothes and baby accessories. Courtesy Wenham Museum, Wenham, Mass.

Vogue Outfit Identification

1948 – 1956

Collectors enjoy knowing that the costume on their doll is an authentic Vogue outfit, and that it is correct for the year the doll was produced. However, Vogue's costume styles and construction changed over the years. Also, outfits for 8" dolls, such as Muffie, Ginger, and Pam manufactured by other doll companies, can be confused with Ginny clothes. Let's examine the different characteristics of Vogue's outfits, and how they changed her wardrobe over the years, so we can learn to identify original Vogue outfits.

Fabrics

Outfits from the 1948 – 56 period have a special look, due in great part to the fine quality of fabric Vogue utilized. Collectors can usually obtain a clue from the fabric, such as the small prints and the types of taffeta, as to whether their untagged outfit could be an early period costume.

Vogue often used the same types of fabrics found in children's clothes, except that patterns were on a very small scale. School girl, play, and sport outfits used diminutive print and polished cotton, pastel and brightly colored felt, waffle piqué, and cotton knits. However, many other companies producing doll clothes at this time also used these fabrics. More distinctive debutante, and ballgown outfits from 1948 – 1956 are fashioned from fine, expensive fabrics, including fine dimity, satin, organdy, taffeta, and velvet, as well as elaborately embroidered cotton. All of these fabrics were often effectively used with dotted or plain nylon, or thin voile-like ninon as overskirts or bodice materials.

Vogue frequently used specialty fabrics or treatments to give an outfit a unique or customized look. Beginning in the mid 1940s rabbit fur was occasionally used to trim skating and other outfits. In 1952 fur was also used for a coat and matching hat and muff. Beginning in 1950 the popular "poodle cloth" (a looped fabric) of the day was utilized in the widely sought-after Easter Bunny costume, as well as for cowboy chaps and later for coats and trim for Ginny.

Plastic material was not often used by Vogue. However, as early as 1952 a plastic fisherman raincoat was produced, and thereafter plastic was used for belts, with real functioning brass buckles. Leatherette was used throughout the 1940s and 1950s; in 1952 silver and gold foil surface leatherette was introduced for belts. In 1955 a special cotton jersey with "Ginny" woven in it was utilized in the Whiz Kids group and was used in 1956 and thereafter as well. Whether the fabric was a simple cotton or taffeta or a specialty fabric, it was always fine quality. This quality was selected not only for beauty, but in order to withstand a lot of play action by little hands.

Trims

Vogue trims are also easily recognized by collectors familiar with the look of early Ginny outfits. For example, an outfit with a tiny looped picot trim edging neck or arm openings has a good chance of being an early Ginny outfit. Likewise, delicate lace, tulle trims, rickrack, and braids frequently edged openings or were stitched as borders around hems. These trims were also commonly sewn on the bodice suspender style from front waistband, over the shoulder, to back waist. Wide trims were often sewn or inset into the skirt or bodice for extra interest.

Colors of trims were delicate pastels, bold primary or hot colors. Gold or silver metallic, or satin threaded trims were common, particularly for braid, rickrack and picot edging.

Ribbons and bows were favorite accent treatments used by Mrs. Graves and her daughter, Virginia. Satin, velvet, or other fabric bows were often sewn into trim or seams — never stapled or pinned. Ribbons were almost always satin with woven edges, never cut edge flat rayon.

Pattern Construction

Some outfits were simple, and others were quite elaborate, but all had to be easily sewn by Vogue's sewers in their homes. In order to accomplish this, basic patterns were developed by Vogue with most outfits using variations on basic neck, sleeve, and skirt designs. These designs help us identify some Vogue outfits from 1948 to 1956 primarily the 8" dolls.

Underpants

•Dresses or gowns were sold with separate matching underpants or bloomers. Most outfits prior to 1948 had underpants attached to the skirt, but these were for the composition Toddles doll, the forerunner of the Ginny doll.

•In 1953 the Dress Me Ginny doll was sold in white, blue or pink taffeta underpants with picot trim which were not designed to match any specific outfit. If your outfit has these pants, the original matching pants are undoubtedly missing.

•Most underpants are full, short bloomers type, and helped to keep full skirts full. However, some were cut straight, matching the outfit fabric. Key to identifying Ginny underpants are the waist elastics, which are not exposed, but drawn through a channel or pocket casing, like a drapery rod through the top of a curtain.

Bodices and Sleeves:

•The bodice and the sleeves, long or short sleeve, are cut from one piece and then stitched under the arm, rarely using a shoulder or arm hole seam.

•Beginning in 1948, the sundress style outfits were frequently shown for both the 8" and Crib Crowd baby dolls (8" doll with curved baby legs). This charming, high waist style uses a high waistband under the arms into which fabric over-shoulder bands are sewn.

•Cap sleeves were often fashioned from lace or wide trim, and sewn onto short bodice sleeves or sundress straps.

•Some of the outfits with long sleeves of delicate nylon, organdy or other sheer fabric did have set-in sleeves, and/or were elasticized at the wrist for a "balloon" sleeve effect. This was particularly true with 1956 ballgowns.

Neck Openings

•Square or round necks have turned, stitched, and finished edges; raw edges are never exposed and inexpensive bindings are never stitched over neck openings.

•Neck openings are either trimmed (as described above), plain, or with attached collars. Attached collars were usually part of patterns to keep them simple. However, when they were used, they were usually large round yokes or Bertha collars or small shirt collars.

Opening Fasteners

•1948 – 1956 Vogue used a hook and eye to close the backs of dresses.

•Even if a ribbon tie or sash was tied around the waist, a hook and eye was also sewn underneath the tie to close the garment.

•Snaps were not used to close garments until 1957.

•In 1953 Vogue introduced the Talon zipper series, closing outfits with small zippers. A few of the outfits used these zippers thereafter.

Skirts and Hems

•All of the outfits produced by Vogue's home sewers were inspected and had to meet pattern standards. Most hems were 1-1½". All hems had to be turned under at the raw edge and stitched evenly. Therefore, no raw edges were exposed on the underside of skirt hems.

•Felt skirts were not hemmed.

•Nylon, lace, or fabric with embroidered edges was often used and were not hemmed.

•Inside waist seams were straight stitched on home sewing machines and were not finished with zigzag or overcast sewing. (This zigzag type of factory sewing was not begun until 1957, and was used only on a very few Ginny dresses.)

•Inside skirt seams are limited to a single, center back seam which is turned and finished.

Painted Eye Hard Plastic 8" Doll

1948 – 1950

Description: 8" hard plastic, painted side-glancing eyes, strung and jointed at head, arms and straight legs, mohair wigs. The mold was sculpted by Bernard Lipfert.

Marks: Head: VOGUE
Back: VOGUE DOLL

Dress labels: Two Types

1. Mid – late 1940s, white cotton twill tag with "Vogue Dolls Inc., Medford, Mass." in blue or in white on a blue ink spot shaped background (collectors today refer to this tag as the "ink spot" label); usually sewn into a back seam.
2. In 1950, may have a white rayon label with blue lettering, Vogue Dolls, with wavy lines at upper left and lower right of logo. Note: During this period it was not uncommon for tags to be left off the dress. It is wise to become familiar with Vogue outfits and dress construction to verify authentic outfits.

Dress closures: Hooks and eyes.

Tags: Small, round silver tags with navy printing "A Vogue Doll" hang from the wrist.

Boxes: Ginny came in pastel colored pink and blue boxes with Vogue ink spot end labels which were bought from Packard Paper Box Company in Somerville, Mass.

Innovation and Growth

Hard plastic: Vogue's 8" composition dolls (now popularly called Toddles) were popular in the late 1940s. However, it became apparent to Mrs. Graves and her daughter that hard plastic, perfected during World War II, was an advancement that could be used for doll-making. Hard plastic had none of the problems of crazing due to humidity fluctuation which were such a problem for composition dolls. Therefore, in 1948 Vogue replaced Toddles with an 8" hard plastic doll in time for the 1949 holiday selling season.

The technical term for the plastic material used was "cellulose acetate" which was injected into a doll mold under high pressure. The mold was then opened, and the halves of the doll were glued together. The plastic used for these early dolls varied from very pale, bisque-like shades to pink tones, all very appealing.

Painted eye hard plastic dolls by Vogue have a sweet look, and are difficult to find today in mint condition with boxes and tags. However, they are among the most prized, and well worth the search.

Mohair wig: The painted eye hard plastic doll's wigs were made of mohair which was machine stitched at the part and then glued over the plastic molded hair. The most common colors were blonde, light brown or auburn. Hair styles included short flips with either a side part or bang. Some braided styles existed, and a few had braids drawn up and stapled on top of the head and secured with a bow. A short, curly mohair was used to achieve the darling ringlet look.

Unfortunately, one of the only drawbacks of the doll was the fragile quality of the mohair wig. The original set was always lovely. However, since Vogue intended for their dolls to be played with, the little owners would invariably comb out the hair, and it would frequently become matted and almost impossible to restore to its original look. It is a real treat to find a doll with a mint mohair set today.

Move to larger building: In 1949 Vogue announced in *Playthings Magazine* that it had moved to larger quarters at 33 Ship Avenue, in Medford, Massachusetts, where 15,000 square feet of modern workroom and other conveniences would make economical production and fast service easier to render to their customers. Obviously business was thriving, and it was further reported that the new line featured hard plastic bodies with the added features of the unusual and stylish clothes which had made the Vogue Doll line outstanding for many years. "Nothing has been spared of skill, time and imagination to give the doll trade something new to sell but with the real old fashioned quality which is part and parcel of the Vogue Dolls reputation." These accolades from *Playthings* turned out to be the beginning of great things to come for Vogue.

Wardrobe, Special Styles, and Accessories

Wardrobe: Mrs. Graves's daughter, Virginia, had joined the company in 1942, and she was well established as Vogue's chief designer at the time hard plastic painted eye dolls were introduced. Together with her mother, she created incredibly detailed outfits that were beautifully trimmed with matching accessories for the painted eye doll. They were still skillfully hand sewn by Mrs. Graves and her daughter, sometime staying up all night to complete an order. However, they increasingly depended on a growing team of local home sewers to help with jobs. These neighbors and friends sewed according to meticulously typed instructions which were delivered to them along with fabric and trim. This was an exciting time for the family and for Vogue as it continually achieved recognition from the doll buying public and orders began to increase.

In 1948 – 50 price lists, Vogue described their many types of outfits which included "dainty afternoon fashions," school dresses, nursery rhyme outfits, sleep wear, bride and groom, and boy and girl playmates.

Popular outfits from the Toddles period were carried over. For example, the Red Riding Hood outfit can be found on both the composition doll as well in the Character group for hard plastic dolls. Boxed outfits were also sold and are a rare find today.

Vogue used center snap shoes primarily; however, tie shoes were also used for a period of time.

Special styles: Vogue offered painted eye hard plastic dolls in special outfits at Christmas, Valentine's Day, and Easter. For example, in 1950 they featured Valentine dolls, #1 Vogue Sweetheart, and #2 Queen of Hearts; Easter dolls, #21 Springtime, and #24 Easter Parade. Special dolls were also created in connection with department or toy store promotions. Two of Vogue's 8" dolls in 1949 were offered in daughter outfits, #8-20C and #8-21C (in the Toddlers gingham school dress category on the price list). These mother and daughter dolls were featured in an advertisement, along with baby doll (later called Crib Crowd dolls), inviting dealers to visit Vogue's show room during the Toy Fair. This 14" mother doll was discontinued in 1950, as was the daughter approach to marketing the 8" doll. A unique series was the One-Half Century group which features seven painted eye dolls, one for each decade from 1900 – 1950, plus the year 2000, (usually a sleep-eyed doll) whose futuristic outfit is very prized today. All sleep-eye sets have also been found.

Accessories: Over the years 1948 – 50 Vogue also offered assorted fitted cases of clothes. Some were contained simply in round acetate cases with a Vogue tag tied on. For example, in 1949, the price list included: #8-30C fitted weekend case for 8" doll, complete with sunsuit, skirt, cape, hat, beach bag, towel, face cloth, powder, nightie, bathrobe, slippers with pom-pons, party dress and bonnet, soap, plastic comb and mirror. Also, #8-50-C acetate case with doll and clothes: 8" doll dressed in taffeta robe with silk cord, slippers with pom pons, bow in hair. Also, socks, shoes, panties, dress, straw hat, play suit, nightie, mirror. In 1950, the list of outfits which was put into each doll's box also referred to as "fitted chest of clothes (with doll)."

In a letter to dealers in 1950, Vogue offered other accessories such as a Hat Box #820 and a Chest #875.

Marketing

Advertisements: In 1948 – 49 Vogue did not market the new hard plastic toddler doll under one particular name. Instead, they simply referred to the doll as a "playmate" in promotional material. The doll was advertised as one of The Vogue Family of Dolls, which even included a 14" mother doll for the little 8" doll. In 1948 – 1950 merchants' price lists and fliers simply called the doll an "all plastic doll." It was the doll's wardrobe that was given strong billing in advertising. Vogue stressed individually designed, custom made clothes and beautifully designed dolls.

Price lists: In featuring the wardrobe to dealers and customers, Vogue continued to assign categories on price lists. For example, in 1948 and 1949, categories such as Playmates and Toddlers were used. They also assigned sub-categories, such as Dainty Afternoon Dresses to keep track of the outfits on the doll. Within each sub-category, Vogue also designated a character name (e.g., Cowboy) or a first name (e.g., Debbie), as well as a sales code/number for ordering purposes. In 1950, the category names were changed somewhat. However, since Vogue did not give the line of entire dolls one name at this time, (as they later would with Ginny). Most customers simply referred to the doll by the individual doll name that was printed on the box's label.

Apparently, during the entire painted eye hard plastic period of 1948 – 1950, these broad categories, sub-categories, names, and codes became confusing for Vogue and its customers, and the system was simplified in 1951.

Brochure: Vogue did not produce a brochure for the painted eye doll with photographs of all outfits. Instead price lists were produced for dealers, and they briefly described each outfit. However, flyers with pictures of some outfits were produced to promote birthday present sales, as well as seasonal sales of dolls, such as summer sales. Also, flyers were produced with pictures of special holiday outfits (primarily in connection with Christmas, Easter, and Valentine's Day). These flyers were mailed to dealers, and today they provide a valuable record of outfit design. In addition, Vogue would produce a special outfit at the request of a department or toy store, and participate in the promotion.

Boxes, logo: The boxes used for the dolls over this period were solid pink with lids, and the labels used the ink spot Vogue logo as it had since the mid 1940s. Also, the company tag line, "Fashion Leaders In Doll Society," was widely used in all promotional material.

Prices

Painted Eye Ginny

Year Produced	Outfit	Mint Price
1948 – 50	Painted Eye Ginny	$300.00+
	Holidays	$400.00+
	Bride and Groom	$350.00+
	Cinderella group	$400.00+
	Crib Crowd	$450.00+
	One-Half Century group each	$1,000.00+

1948 – 1950

Painted Eye Hard plastic dolls came out in 1948 in time for the 1949 holiday selling period. They first appear on the 1949 price list.

PRICE LIST
Effective April 1, 1949

Style No.			Doz.
8" ASSORTED — FULLY JOINTED — ALL PLASTIC DOLLS — MOHAIR WIGS			
PLAYMATES			DOZ. PAIRS
8-7C & 8-8C	Binky & Bunky	Jersey Boy & Girl—pastel colors	$42.00
8-9C & 8-10C	Sonny & Susie	Chambray pedal pushers—plastic wheelbarrow	42.00
8-11C & 8-12C	Steffi & Sven	Alpine Boy & Girl—felt outfits—asst. col.	42.00
			PER DOZ.
	Red Riding Hood	Satin Cape, white dress, straw basket	$27.00
8-18C	Jean	Taffeta coat & straw hat—fig. ninon dress—pastel colors	27.00
8-19C	Jo-An	Velvet coat & hat—fur trimmed—rosebud ninon dress	27.00
	Cinderella	Spangle dress, Cinderella hat with veil	27.00
	Godmother	Spangle dress, taffeta paniers, Godmother hat	27.00
	Prince	Satin coat & hat with plume—pillow with slipper	24.00
	Bride	White satin dress, lace trimmed, veil & prayer book	27.00
	Bridesmaid	Rosebud taffeta & ninon, picture hat, rosebud trim	27.00
	Groom	Full dress-suit—tall hat—boutonniere	24.00
8-16C	Laury	Taffeta dress & Bonnet—French val lace trim—pastel colors	24.00
	Bo-Peep	Flowered dotted swiss & taffeta dress with hat & crook	24.00
TODDLERS (dainty afternoon dresses)			
8-1C	Debby	Broadcloth & ninon pinafore dress & bonnet	21.60
8-2C	Judy	Flocked organdy dress—straw hat—pastel colors	21.60
8-3C	Trudy	Shadow organdy dress & bonnet—lace & bow trim—pastel colors	21.60
8-4C	Pinky	Hand-smocked white organdy dress & bonnet	21.60
8-5C	Cooky	Colored organdy dress & bonnet—eyelet pockets & trim	21.60
8-6C	Bobsy	Flocked dot. organdy dress & bonnet—lace & ribbon trim	21.60
TODDLERS (party dresses)			
8-14C	Joyce	Flowered taffeta rosebud—headband with flowers	21.60
8-15C	Christy	Sparkle ninon—gold and silver trim. headband with roses	21.60
TODDLERS (gingham school dresses)			
*8-20C	(Daughter)	Col. broadcloth dress & headband (mate to Mother 14-20C)	21.60
*8-21C	(Daughter)	Plaid dress with organdy apron—braids (mate to Mother 14-21C)	21.60
8-22C	Pam	Col. chambray dress & bonnet—plaid pockets & trim	21.60
	Clown	Two-tone taffeta suit & hat with pom-poms—asst. colors	21.60
8-25C	Julie	Col. broadcloth playsuit & bonnet—rhumba ruffles (watering pot)	21.60
	Alice in Wonderland	Blue dress—white organdy apron—ribbon on hair	21.60
	Cowboy	"With all the fixins"	21.60
	Cowgirl	"With all the fixins"	21.60
	Wee Willie Winkie	Flannette pajamas—stocking cap—candle & holder	18.00
8-24C	Mitzi	Sunsuit—asst. percale print—eyelet ruffling—braids with bow—pail	18.00

Fashion Leaders in Doll Society

ALL DOLLS INDIVIDUALLY BOXED

(Approximate shipping weights without outside cartons.)

Twelve 8" dolls weigh 6 lbs. Twelve 14" dolls weigh 14 lbs.
Twelve 15" Velva Babies weigh 26 lbs.

Price list (1949). Courtesy Mrs. Virginia Carlson.

Painted Eye Hard Plastic Doll (1948 – 50), pink dimity dress with embroidered trim and pleated net trim at yoke and skirt sides and matching tie on hat. The side part mohair wig is in its original flip style popular with later Ginnys. Courtesy Shirley Niziolek.

Painted Eye Hard Plastic Doll (1948 – 50), flowered cotton dress with attached pants and a matching bonnet. Notice pale facial coloring. Courtesy Peggy Millhouse.

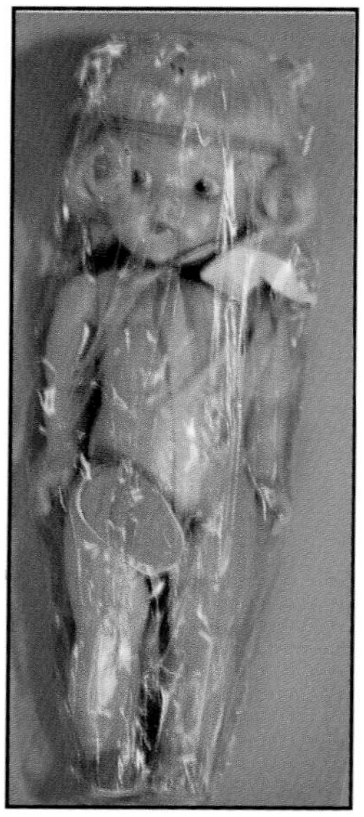

Painted Eye Hard Plastic Doll (1948 – 50), undressed doll packaged in cellophane in white leatherette tie shoes. Note original elastic still holds the bangs in place. Usually the dolls were dressed at the factory, so significance of original cellophane is unclear.

Painted Eye Hard Plastic doll (1948 – 1950), pale blue dimity dress with rickrack trim and matching hat. Notice the unusually dark mohair wig. Courtesy Shirley Niziolek.

Painted Eye doll, (1948 – 50), white organdy dress with rickrack trim and flowers at the waist and on the matching hat. Courtesy Kathy Schneider.

Toy Fair Display (1949), painted eye dolls. Front row: Brother and sister sets. Courtesy Mrs. Virginia Carlson.

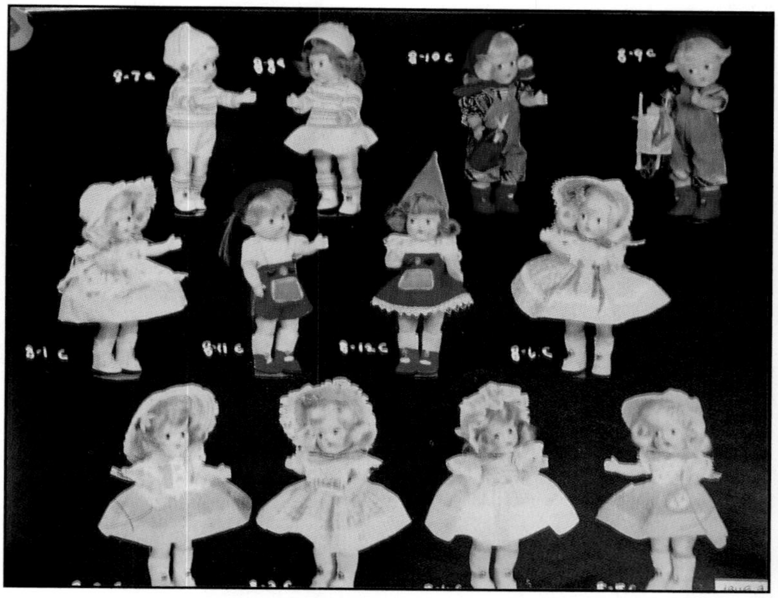

Painted eye hard plastic doll outfits (1949). (From top left to right): Playmates: #8-7C and #8-8C Binky and Bunky in pastel jersey outfits; #8-10 C and #8-9C Susie and Sonny in denim overalls; (center): #8-1C Debby in broadcloth and ninon pinafore; #8-11C and #8-12C Steffi and Sven in Alpine outfits; #8-6C Bobsy in flocked organdy dress and bonnet; (bottom) Toddlers: #8-2C Judy in flocked organdy dress and straw hat; #8-3C Trudy in shadow organdy dress and bonnet; #8-4C Pinky in hand smocked dress and bonnet; #8-5C Cooky in organdy dress and bonnet, with eyelet trim. Note that the 1949 outfits were modeled by composition Toddles dolls probably since the hard plastic dolls were not available at time photo was taken. Vogue photo courtesy Wenham Museum, Wenham, Mass.

Binky and Bunky (1949), #8-7c and #8-8C from Playmates series in white jersey outfits with matching socks and center snap shoes. This outfit is usually seen in pastel colors and is rare in white. Courtesy Barbara Rosplock-Van Orman.

Painted eye hard plastic doll outfits (1949). (Top left to right): Bridesmaid, Groom, Bride; Toddlers series (middle row): #8-24C Mitzi in playsuit with pail, #8-18C Jean in pink coat, #8-15C Christy in sparkle ninon, #8-14C Joyce in flowered taffeta dress, #8-25C Julie in playsuit with watering can. (Bottom): Bo Peep, Cowgirl and Cowboy, and unidentified party dress from Toddlers series. Note that the 1949 outfits were modeled by composition Toddles dolls since the hard plastic dolls were probably not available at time photo was taken. Vogue photo courtesy Wenham Museum, Wenham, Mass.

Jean (1949) #8-18C from Playmates series wearing a pink taffeta coat and broad brim straw hat, dress with felt flower trim. Notice silver Vogue wrist tag and plain blue box with Vogue ink spot label on end. Courtesy Ann Tardie.

Cinderella and Prince (1949), Cinderella in silver dotted ninon gown and hat with silver braid trim. Prince is in pink satin outfit and hat with organdy blouse and carries pillow and slipper. Courtesy Barbara Rosplock-Van Orman.

Bride (1949), wearing a white satin gown with white picot trim, ribbon sash with a spangle tiara trimmed with gold picot over a net veil. Note the dark lip color. Courtesy Kathy Schneider.

Bridal Series (1949), back, left to right: Bridesmaids; front, left to right: Groom, Bride, Ringbearer. Courtesy Mrs. Virginia Carlson.

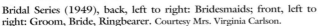

Bridesmaid (1949), wearing pink rosebud taffeta and ninon dress with blue rosebud trim and a picture hat. Note the beautiful wave on the mohair wig. Courtesy Kathy Bailey.

Clown and Laury (1949), clown in a pink and blue taffeta suit (also came in other colors) and Laury #8-16C in taffeta dress and bonnet. Vogue photo courtesy Wenham Museum, Wenham, Mass.

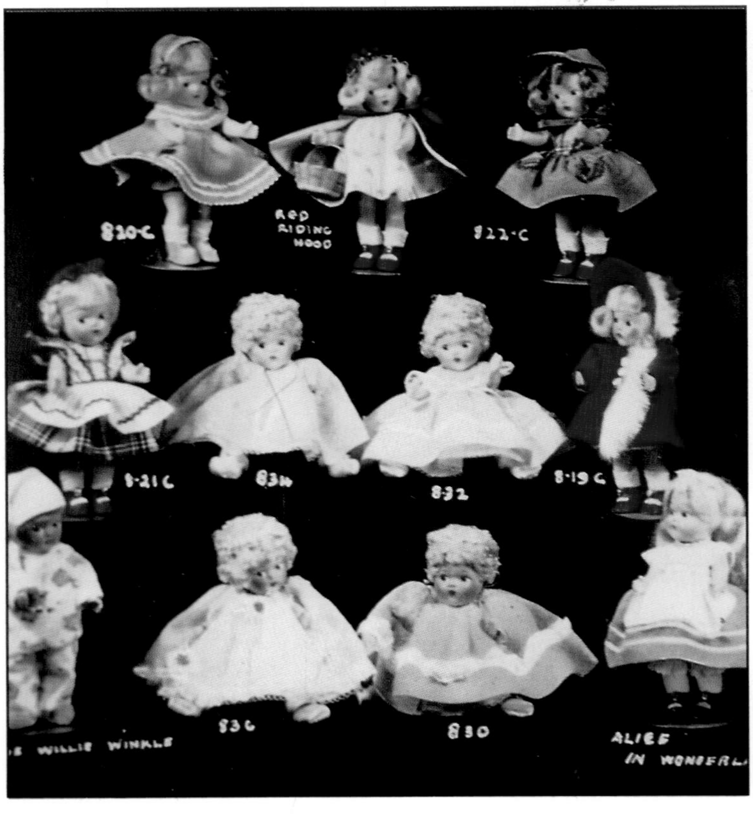

Painted eye hard plastic doll outfits (1949). Toddlers series (Top, left to right: Daughter #8-20C in blue cotton dress with rickrack and headband, #8-22C Pam in blue chambray dress with plaid pockets. Center: Daughter #8-21C, plaid dress with apron. (Top center) Red Riding Hood and (center right) Jo-An #8-19C in red velvet coat. Bottom row: Wee Willie Winkie and Alice in Wonderland. Also shows Crib Crowd. Note that the 1949 outfits were modeled by composition Toddles dolls since the hard plastic dolls probably were not available at time photo was taken. Vogue photo courtesy Wenham Museum, Wenham, Mass.

Vogue ad (1949), showing mother and daughter dolls (14" and 8"). 8" in outfit #8-20C. Also showing other 1949 dolls in the line. *Playthings Magazine.*

Daughter (1949), #8-21C wearing plaid dress with organdy apron, braids are fastened to the top of her head. This doll was daughter to a matching 14" hard plastic mother doll #14-21C advertised by Vogue. Courtesy Maureen Fukushima.

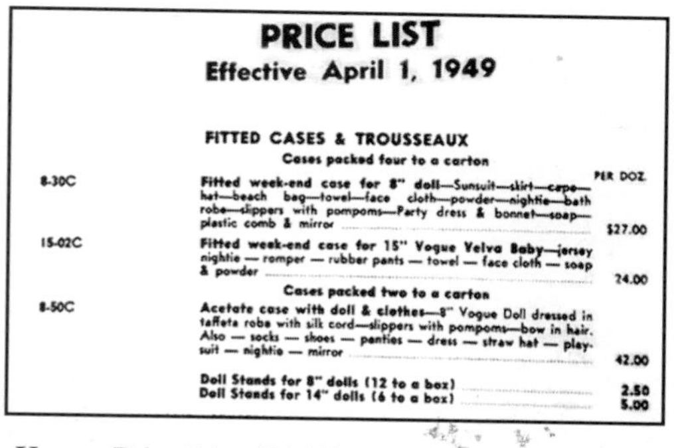

PRICE LIST
Effective April 1, 1949

FITTED CASES & TROUSSEAUX

Cases packed four to a carton

		PER DOZ.
8-30C	Fitted week-end case for 8" doll—Sunsuit—skirt—cape—hat—beach bag—towel—face cloth—powder—nightie—bath robe—slippers with pompoms—Party dress & bonnet—soap—plastic comb & mirror	$27.00
15-02C	Fitted week-end case for 15" Vogue Velva Baby—jersey nightie — romper — rubber pants — towel — face cloth — soap & powder	24.00
	Cases packed two to a carton	
8-50C	Acetate case with doll & clothes—8" Vogue Doll dressed in taffeta robe with silk cord—slippers with pompoms—bow in hair. Also — socks — shoes — panties — dress — straw hat — play-suit — nightie — mirror	42.00
	Doll Stands for 8" dolls (12 to a box)	2.50
	Doll Stands for 14" dolls (6 to a box)	5.00

Vogue Price List (1949), showing 8" dolls with fitted cases. Courtesy Virginia Graves Carlson.

Cowboy and Cowgirl (1949), no number, in red satin shirts, felt vests with braid trim, felt hat, yellow neck ribbons, poodle cloth chaps. Originally shown with center snap shoes in Vogue photo. Courtesy Barbara Rosplock-Van Orman

Susie (1950) #8-4E from Brother and Sister group (also called Gardener Girl in a 1950 summer promotional flyer), wears a red checked shorts set with matching sunbonnet and a plastic watering pot. Courtesy Chree Kysar.

Group E – Brother and Sister series (1950) #8-1E Binky and #8-2E Bunky; Cowboy and Cowgirl, #8-4E Susie and #8-3E Sonny; #8-5E Sven and #8-6E Steffie. Notice continuation of themes from previous year with minor variations in clothing. Courtesy Virginia Graves Carlson.

Group K Afternoon Dresses (1950) (from left) #8-1K Pam, #8-2K Peggy, #8-3K Polly, #K-4 Edie, #K-5 Beth, #K-6 Penny. This slide was given to Vogue representatives to show dealers the new lines. Courtesy Mr. and Mrs. Edwin Nelson.

Bobsy (1950) #8-6D from Afternoon group in flowered ninon dress with pink ribbon trim and pink hair ribbon. Courtesy Peggy Millhouse.

Group K Evening Dresses (1950), (back, left to right): #8-11K Gail, #8-12K Betty, #8-10K Libby. (Front, left to right) Gingham: #8-8K Sandy, #8-9K Bonnie, #8-7K Jo-An. Courtesy Virginia Graves Carlson.

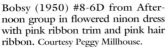

Prince Charming (1950), notice Vogue label identifies him simply as "Pink." Courtesy Shirley's Dollhouse.

Fairy Godmother (1950) from the Cinderella group. Wearing a red taffeta dress and hooded cape, white spangle apron and bodice. Notice unusual platinum mohair wig. Also note this outfit was shown on a hard plastic doll in Vogue brochure in 1950 (shown in 1950 sleep eye chapter). Courtesy Sandy Barts-Johnson.

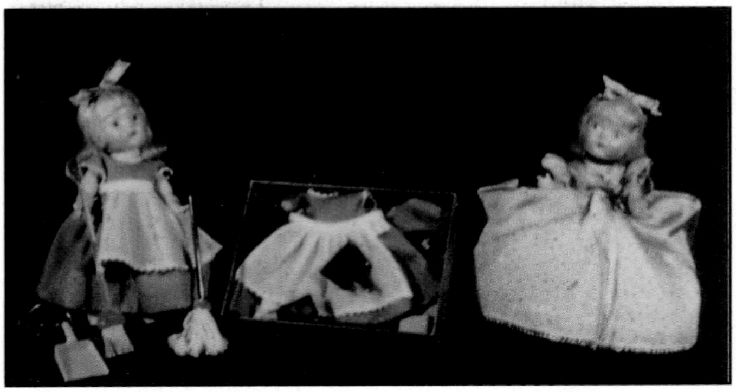

Cinderella in gown and "Cinder" (1950). "Cinder" Cinderella outfit complete with broom, dustpan and mop. Courtesy Mr. and Mrs. Edwin Nelson.

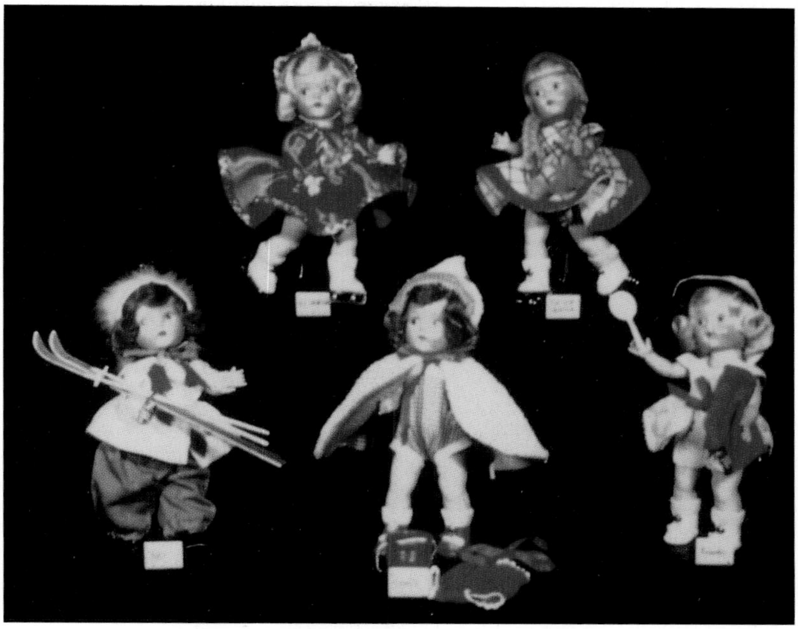

Sports Fashion group (1950), back, left to right: Ice Skater, Roller Skater; front, left to right: Ski, Beach, Tennis. Courtesy Virginia Carlson.

Dutch Boy and Girl (1950) from Character group. Courtesy Virginia Carlson.

Mary Lamb (1950) from Character group wearing a yellow organdy dress with cotton checked apron and bloomers with matching bonnet, white tie shoes. Courtesy Judy Ormsbee.

Group R (1950), (front, left to right) #8-1R Cindy in felt coat, #8-3R Ginny in red velvet coat, #8-2R Ellen Cotton Coat. (Back left to right) #8-4R Glennie Plaid Cape, #8-5R Jean in Raincape. Courtesy Virginia Carlson.

Julie (1950), #8-6R from Group R, straight legs in red and white checked gingham playsuit trimmed with eyelet ruffles. A curly mohair poodle-cut wig and bow are glued to the head. Courtesy Maureen Fukushima.

Vogue flyer sent to dealers (1950) to promote Valentine's sales. Outfit #1 is the Janie #8-10D. Vogue adapted the Betty Outfit #8-12K for outfit #2 with a heart-shaped headpiece. Dolls came with plastic hearts that said "I Love You" tied to wrists. Outfits came on both painted eye and sleep eye dolls. Courtesy Virginia Graves Carlson.

Valentine Special Outfit #2 (1950) red taffeta with white organdy apron and matching tie on hat in the shape of a heart. Notice "Love You" charm tied to wrist. Courtesy Peggy Millhouse.

Vogue flyer sent to dealers (1950) to promote Easter sales. They adapted existing outfits from the K and D series to pastel colors and added a little chick to the doll's outfit for the promotion. Courtesy Virginia Graves Carlson.

Vogue flyer sent to dealers (1950) to promote summer sales. Vogue featured outfits from their regular line. These outfits were also sold on their sleep eye dolls offered in 1950. Courtesy Virginia Graves Carlson.

Miss 1900, Miss 1910, Miss 1920 (1950) from One-Half Century group. Courtesy Wenham Museum, Wenham, Mass.

Miss 1930, Miss 1940, Miss 1950 (1950) from One-Half Century group. Courtesy Wenham Museum, Wenham, Mass.

Miss 2000 (1950), One-Half Century group. Usually a sleep-eye doll. Courtesy Wenham Museum, Wenham, Mass.

Painted eye hard plastic (1950), wearing a yellow cotton dress with flower print and rickrack, matching bonnet. Missing plastic purse. Also came in blue. Courtesy Sue Johnson.

Judy (1949), #8-2C, printed organdy dress with eyelet trim at waist, sleeves and bodice. A pale pink straw hat tied with pink satin ribbon. Strawberry blonde side part flip mohair wig.

Ginny Dolls

Strung Sleep Eye Ginny

1950 – 1953

Description: 8" hard plastic strung dolls, painted lashes and eyebrows, varied coloring. The color of early lashes may be various shades of brown and irregular since they were literally handpainted. 1950 – 1952 are called early transitional dolls with light coloring.

- 1950 Vogue produced both painted eye dolls with mohair wigs as well as sleep eye dolls with painted lashes, pale coloring, and either mohair or Dynel synthetic wigs.
- 1951 and 1952 produced sleep eye dolls with transitional coloring (e.g., painted lashes and light lip and face coloring), Nutex or Dynel wigs.
- Late 1952 and 1953 sleep eye dolls with darker lip and cheek coloring and Dynel wigs, the lashes are reddish brown and uniform in painting because lashes were applied using stencils at the factory. "Greenish" lashes are lashes whose pigment has changed with time.

Marks: Head: VOGUE
Back: VOGUE DOLL

Dress labels: Blue print on white rayon as follows:

- 1951: Vogue Dolls
- 1952: Vogue
- 1951 and 1952: some outfits were not tagged.
- 1953: Original Vogue Dolls, Inc., all of the outfits were tagged.

Dress closures: Hooks and eyes.

Tags: Little round, silver wrist tags with the Vogue logo in navy on most dolls from 1950 – 1953.

- Special square, hanging tags were also used in 1951 on the Ginny #80 with the Wavette Hair. The white tag had a pink border and was printed in black, "Hi! I'm Ginny!" and had a drawing of the doll in her famous flip hair style. This tag continued to be used in 1952 and 1953 on dolls with curlers, (e.g., 1952 Ginny series and others) as part of the promotional campaign of the Ginny name.
- White paper tags circling the wrist of the doll, with Vogue Dolls Inc. in pink print were used on some dolls as early as 1952. In 1955 the doll's series number was added to the tag, and it was used until the early 1960s.

Boxes: In 1950 – 1952 the doll came in pastel colored pink or blue boxes with Vogue end labels (the same box as the late 1940s painted eye hard plastic dolls). Boxes were bought from the Packard Paper Box Company in Somerville, Mass. Vogue introduced the fuchsia, black, and white colored boxes with paper doll design in late 1952 and 1953.

Innovation and Growth

Sleep eyes: Vogue was very pleased with their hard plastic toddler doll with painted eyes, and sales were good as the company approached 1950. However, Mrs. Graves and her daughter, Virginia, continually sought ways to improve their little doll. In 1950 they introduced a major innovation to their doll design, sleep eyes. They knew that the sleep eyes were very popular in their larger composition dolls in the 1940s. They were delighted that new, lightweight plastic eyes now made this feature practical for the smaller dolls, too. However, they were very careful not to change the adorable look of the toddler doll when they added the new eyes.

There is some discussion as to whether Vogue actually commissioned a new doll mold, or simply adapted their mold from the old painted eye dolls which had been created for Vogue by the renowned sculptor, Bernard Lipfert. We know that Mr. Lipfert was involved in the new sleep eye doll mold in some way, since subsequent 1950s promotions proclaimed that the doll was created by a world famous sculptor. In any case, the new hard plastic toddler doll with sleep eyes was every bit as cute a toddler doll as the one with painted eyes had been. It is unlikely that either Mrs. Graves or her daughter realized, at that time, that they had just moved one step closer to the creation of one of the most popular dolls of all time!

In order to assure the doll's success, Vogue concentrated all of their efforts on promoting the new sleep eye doll, virtually abandoning the production of the 14" and other dolls. Interestingly, the new eyes seemed to be the only feature added, since their 1950 brochure still promoted the old mohair wigs which had been used on the painted eye doll in 1948 and 1949. This undoubtedly explains why we find early sleep eye dolls with old mohair wigs today. Also, Vogue was careful not to totally abandon the painted eye doll in 1950. Perhaps this was due to the doll's popularity, or was an effort to use up painted eye doll stock. Whatever the reason, early promotional fliers offered doll prices to dealers for Easter and for Valentine dolls with either painted eyes or moving eyes.

Transitional Plastics and Colors: The years 1950 – 1952 were "transitional" years for Vogue. The plastic used for the face and body was either pale bisque, orange tone, or flesh color. The cheek color was either pale or bright pink. The eyes came in two or three combinations of blues and browns, some with black or brown rings around the iris. Some dolls even had violet eyes.

Wigs: Wigs were another area of change in the transitional years 1950 – 1952. In 1950 various synthetic wigs were tried, and while they were attractive, some were stiff and mannequin-like. In 1951 Vogue finally made significant improvements over the hard-to-manage mohair and synthetic wigs. They promoted Nutex wigs, introducing the innovation of a washable wig that could actually be more easily combed and styled. The dolls' hairstyles were quite varied in 1951. For example, an upswept hairdo was created for the Canasta Hostess and ponytails for Nan #32 in the Kindergarten Kiddies series. The most common were the somewhat short and fluffy versions of the flip and braids styles. However, most importantly, in 1951, Vogue featured one special doll, Ginny #80, as a Wavette Hair doll. In 1952 Vogue created an entire sales campaign to feature the new Dynel wigs, and the doll's "comb, curl, and set," and hair capabilities.

In 1951 and 1952, some 8" dolls had curly lambskin (caracul) wigs. These dolls have what Vogue called the pixie haircut. The hairstyle was named after Mrs. Graves's granddaughter, Marcia Nelson, daughter of her daughter June Nelson. This cute Ginny with the short curly hairstyle is very sought after today by collectors.

By 1953 brochures and ads had popularized Ginny's traditional, very set, ear length flip, and brochures advertised three hairstyles: Ginny bangs, pigtails, or side parts. In addition, a variety of blonde shades was tried in addition to brunette, and auburn. In regard to braided styles, one of the only ways to distinguish a 1953 braided wig from a 1952 braided wig is that the braid is thicker, as is the ribbon used to tie the braid.

Colored Ginny: In 1953 an undressed Ginny labeled "Colored" on the box was introduced made of brown tone hard plastic with a dark brunette or black wig and brown eyes. This doll had limited production for some geographical areas. A Hawaiian doll with brown skin tone was also issued but was not marked "Colored" on the box. There were possibly other dolls with brown skin tone issued in other outfits but they were not marked "Colored" on the box. Today, these dolls are sought after by collectors.

All of these innovations resulted in continued growth for Vogue. They moved to even larger quarters in Medford, Massachusetts. By 1951 Vogue had moved into a factory with twice as much space and employed 50 people. At this point, Mrs. Graves was still involved with every aspect of her company, including inspecting dolls at the factory.

Wardrobe, Special Styles, and Accessories

Wardrobe and special styles: Vogue continued to produce wonderfully detailed and trimmed series of outfits from 1950 – 53 in addition to some very exciting special series of costumes.

Also, in 1950 and 1951, very creative seasonal dolls were sold. Up to this time most (65 percent) of Vogue's dolls were sold in the pre-holiday selling period. This meant that the factory was practically idle in the winter and had to lay off employees. So Vogue decided to diversify and try to increase off-season demand for dolls. Vogue sold several specials dressed in holiday outfits such as for Christmas, Valentine, and even St. Patrick's Day. In addition, Indian and Pilgrim dolls were made in order to exploit the huge New England tourism market.

Vogue's mainstay, however, seemed to be the moderately priced dolls in darling little dresses. A category simply called Colored Dresses in 1950 became the Kindergarten Kiddies in 1951, the Kindergarten series in 1952, and both Kindergarten Afternoon, and Kindergarten School series in 1953. Many other popular themes, such as nursery rhymes, and brother/sister outfits were similarly developed over these years. The hallmark of each outfit was a special basic Vogue look of quality, beautiful trimming, hook and eye closure, and some kind of head piece, either a matching hat or bow, with each and every outfit. Mrs. Graves loved hats and her daughter shared this enthusiasm for lovely dress designs.

The action oriented outfits in the sports series were also very popular, and helped to set Vogue's line apart from others. Little girls, often not encouraged to be active in the 1950s, enjoyed the action play and fantasy with their dolls.

Very special dolls continued to be released, as well. In 1952, for one year only, five dolls named Square Dance series was released. In 1953, a doll called The Coronation Queen was released. Designed by Mrs. Graves and her daughter well in advance of the actual event, the exquisite beaded, satin brocade gown was remarkably like the one actually worn by Queen Elizabeth II in her coronation that year. The doll with her crown and scepter came in a unique gold box with a goldtone cardboard base and a plastic display top. This doll was heavily advertised to dealers in full page ads in *Playthings* and other dealer publications, and really put the spotlight on Vogue. Anyone who had not heard of Ginny by that time more than likely did during this campaign.

The popularity of Vogue's 1953 Coronation Queen was not unnoticed by Alexander and they introduced their own version in 1954. It should be noted, however, that while Alexander was a heavy competitor to Vogue, Ginny costumes were primarily little girl outfits from the 1950s era. Alexander tended to specialize in costumes of famous characters in literature and history.

Finally, one of the most unique style promotions in the doll world was Vogue's 1953 collection of six Ginny outfits featuring Talon Zippers. This series exemplified Mrs. Graves's and her daughter's understanding that the little Ginny owners wanted to play, but also wanted to be "just like Mommy and Daddy."

Vogue was also in the forefront of using special fabrics in their fashions. Very special nylons were sought out for their beauty as well as ease of washing, which was always an important feature for Vogue. The party outfit of the 1953 Talon Zipper collection (#74) is one of the prettiest examples of nylon fabric found. Likewise, a very special ribbon-like fabric was used in the Gretel Twin series outfit #34 in 1953, as well as in the famous Ballet Gadabout series #45 (e.g., Rainbow Ballerina). Mrs. Graves and her daughter, Virginia Carlson, Vogue's chief designer, relied increasingly on the group of community sewers they had enlisted to hand stitch doll clothes in their homes. Due to Vogue's many innovations in the early 1950s, demand grew steadily and the need for sewers grew rapidly. Vogue eventually utilized over 300 women by the mid 1950s throughout New England, forming a substantial cottage industry in the region.

Accessories: Beginning in 1950, Vogue introduced a line of separately boxed clothing, including shoes, and socks, for their 8" dolls. Shoes were smooth bottom center snap or fuzzy bottomed. The packaging of virtually all of their outfits separately truly made them unique.

Furniture: Vogue sold a wooden E-Z Do Wardrobe in 1953 to hold the doll's clothes. A letter to dealers also offered a Hat Box #820, and Chest #875. Merchandising was outstanding, and outfitted cases of clothes, etc. were readily available as gift items from Vogue.

Marketing

Vogue continued to market their 8" doll from 1950 – 1953 as a child's playmate with outfits that are "easily changeable, just like a real child's." Children were encouraged to "make your doll's wardrobe as smart as your own." Vogue also recognized the child's interest in older play, and the Talon Zipper outfits, gowns, sports outfits, etc., gave the them a chance to play grown-up, as did the many promotions offering the child the fun of washing and setting their doll's hair "just the way Mother gets hers done." Vogue carefully tailored the doll's image to the child's role in society at the time, and they perfectly positioned the doll to the public through a series of very clever promotions through which the name Ginny gained worldwide recognition.

Promotions:

1950: Actually, the name Ginny was first used by Vogue in 1950, on one of the dolls (#8-3R in a red velvet coat with white fur trim) in Series R.

1951: In 1951, Vogue named the Wavette Hair doll #80 Ginny, in the first widely distributed promotion to dealers. The promotion's flyer had Ginny saying, "Our hair is so Beautiful (naturally curly NUTEX) you just can't resist Fixing it on our real plastic curlers...." The doll was sold with a plastic case with curlers and a plastic cosmetic cape. This promotion was a huge success and the orders for Ginny (still just one doll among many series of dolls) poured in!

1952: Vogue leaped on the promotional opportunities begun so successfully the previous year. They began to feature the doll's fantastic hair, in addition to its already acclaimed wardrobe. Vogue featured Dynel wigs on their 1952 dolls, apparently in an effort to make styling the wig even easier for the little owner. This time they created an entire Ginny series of four dolls (#80, #81, #85, #86) each with the curlers and plastic cape. However, Vogue still did not promote a single name for the entire 8" doll line.

After the success of the various promotions using the name Ginny in 1951 and 1952, the name Ginny really stuck with dealers. Whatever the reason, by the end of 1952 everyone, dealers and customers alike, was calling all of the dolls Ginny regardless of the names, numbers or series assigned by Vogue. Everybody thought it was a good idea to have one name for all of the dolls. Dealers, suppliers, and customers began to suggest their favorite names. At that point, Mrs. Graves wisely, and sentimentally, chose the nickname of her own daughter, Ginny, already so popular through Vogue's promotions.

1952 – 53: Vogue followed up on their successful 1951 Wavette Hair Ginny promotions. In 1952, they heavily promoted the name Ginny for the entire line of 8" dolls, and sales took the doll world by storm. (However, they still assigned dolls individual names, as well.) The wash and set wig feature was clearly established at this point, so advertisements returned to the unique feature upon which the company was founded: Vogue's fashions.

In the spring of 1952, to increase sales, Vogue featured the undressed doll boxed in its underpants. Over 50 outfits were available separately. The campaign was centered on the then novel idea of having the sale of the basic doll separate from the outfit. The label on the doll box read "Undressed Doll," and sold for $1.98.

Dealers rapidly sold out dolls and the outfits packaged separately for the "dress me" doll. Each little Ginny owner bought an average of four to five outfits per year for her doll. Mrs. Graves and her daughter traveled widely during the promotion, as the company sponsored coloring contests, doll birthday parties, fashion shows, and increased their line of Ginny accessories.

Growth: Based on the spring success, July orders were 1⅓ times the value of shipments during the previous year's peak month. Such name recognition was achieved for the doll that gross sales rose to over $2,113,904 by 1953 from $433,000 in 1951. Christmas sales were reduced to only 45 percent of production, employment was stabilized for employees, and layoffs affected only 30 percent of the employees in 1953 for a maximum of nine weeks.

Vogue and Ginny were becoming household names. In order to finance Vogue's tremendous growth, Mrs. Graves secured a bank loan. Eighty percent of the Vogue stock remained in the Graves family's hands. Her uncle, Alfred Fuller of the Fuller Brush Company, took a personal interest in the company and provided advice. Mrs. Graves's sound business and marketing decisions allowed Vogue to lead the mid-priced doll market and paved the way for further growth and fame.

Note: Today, the dolls from 1950 – 1953, when Vogue still named individual dolls, are very collectible. Also, since the 1953 line featured the darker cheek and lip coloring, the transitional pale coloring of 1950 – 52 has become very popular. Since Vogue also reduced the number of hairstyles as well as the eye colors in 1953, the earlier dolls seem to have a unique look.

New logo and box: Vogue realized they would need a new look for their tags and boxes to help promote the new Ginny name. In 1952 Vogue's New York advertising agency created a fuchsia box with a black and white paper doll design, and this box was introduced in 1952. The new design was heavily promoted in 1953 as a Carry All box for the Talon Zipper series, with a handle as part of the lid. The "Fashion Leaders In Doll Society" slogan, adopted long ago by the company, was prominently displayed on all promotional material, and Vogue dropped the Vogue ink spot design logo entirely.

Brochures: In 1950 and 1951, no Vogue brochure featuring the dolls was produced, but lists with categories of dolls were placed in doll boxes. Some sales promotional fliers (i.e., holiday, summer, birthday, etc.) were produced for dealers which showed photographs of dolls in regular or special outfits. Also, promotional photos of entire series were taken. These are valuable to us in identifying outfits. In 1952 Vogue created the first extensive brochure with photographs organized by series, but it was not generally released for some reason. In 1953, Vogue created a brochure capitalizing on the name, Ginny. A photograph of Ginny was on the cover saying, "Hi, I'm Ginny...the Fashion Leader in Doll Society," with actual photographs and names of each series doll. One was put into each doll box to promote sales of additional dolls, boxed outfits and accessories.

It should be noted that the hairstyle shown in the photographs for a particular outfit were actually available for all of the various dolls, and in other colors. This still gave the little customer lots of choices.

The years from 1950 – 1953 were fantastic growth years for the company. Ginny was born and would continue to gain popularity into the mid 1950s just by being an adorable, active toddler.

Prices

Strung Sleep Eye Ginny Dolls

Year Produced	Outfit	Mint Price *	Year Produced	Outfit	Mint Price *
1950 – 53	Ginny, all original	$375.00 – 450.00	1952	Kindergarten/Tiny Miss	$300.00 – 400.00+
1950	MIB	$2,000.00	1952	Poodlecut	$600.00
1950	Queen of Hearts	$500.00+	1952	Square Dance	$425.00+
1950	Holidays	$400.00+	1952	Ginny series	$375.00+
1950	Character group	$350.00+	1952	Frolicking Fables	$250.00 – 400.00+
1950 – 51	Cinderella group	$350.00+	1952 – 53	Debutante	$425.00+
1950 – 51	Bridal group	$350.00+	1953	Gadabout	$350.00+
1950 – 51	Sport group	$350.00+	1953	Zipper series	$350.00 – 375.00
1950 – 53	School & play outfits	$110.00	1953	Kindergarten School/Tiny Miss	$350.00+
1950 – 53	Party & fancy outfits	$135.00	1953	Bridal	$375.00 – 400.00
1951	Kindergarten/Tiny Miss	$325.00+	1953 – 54	Coronation Queen (Mint)	$900.00
1951	#80 Wavette Ginny	$400.00+		MIB	$1,300.00+
1951	Brother/Sister	$900.00+ a pair	1953	Black Ginny	$2,000.00+

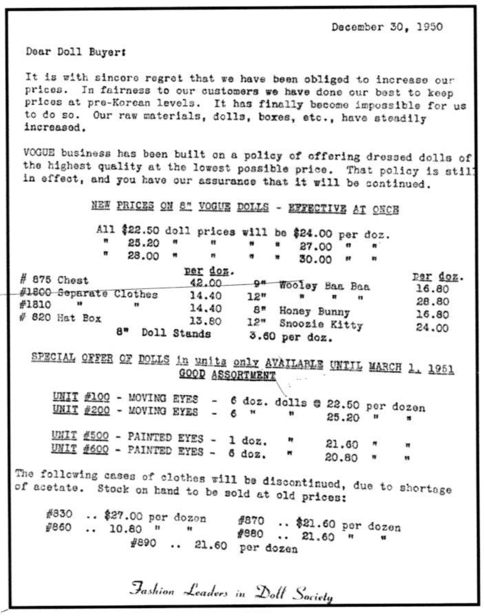

December 30, 1950

Dear Doll Buyer:

It is with sincere regret that we have been obliged to increase our prices. In fairness to our customers we have done our best to keep prices at pre-Korean levels. It has finally become impossible for us to do so. Our raw materials, dolls, boxes, etc., have steadily increased.

VOGUE business has been built on a policy of offering dressed dolls of the highest quality at the lowest possible price. That policy is still in effect, and you have our assurance that it will be continued.

NEW PRICES ON 8" VOGUE DOLLS - EFFECTIVE AT ONCE

All $22.50 doll prices will be $24.00 per doz.
" 25.20 " " " " 27.00 " "
" 28.00 " " " " 30.00 " "

	per doz.		per doz.
# 875 Chest	42.00	9" Wooley Baa Baa	16.80
#1800 Separate Clothes	14.40	12" " " "	28.80
#1810 " "	14.40	8" Honey Bunny	16.80
# 820 Hat Box	13.80	12" Snoozie Kitty	24.00

8" Doll Stands 3.60 per doz.

SPECIAL OFFER OF DOLLS in units only AVAILABLE UNTIL MARCH 1, 1951
GOOD ASSORTMENT

UNIT #100 - MOVING EYES - 6 doz. dolls @ 22.50 per dozen
UNIT #200 - MOVING EYES - 6 " " 25.20 " "

UNIT #500 - PAINTED EYES - 1 doz. " 21.60 " "
UNIT #600 - PAINTED EYES - 6 doz. " 20.80 " "

The following cases of clothes will be discontinued, due to shortage of acetate. Stock on hand to be sold at old prices:

#830 .. $27.00 per dozen #870 .. $21.60 per dozen
#860 .. 10.80 " " #880 .. 21.60 " "
#890 .. 21.60 per dozen

Fashion Leaders in Doll Society

1950 Vogue Flyer to dealers showing both painted eye and moving eye dolls offered in 1950. Notice acetate dresses were being phased out due to shortages. Courtesy Virginia Graves Carlson.

Strung transitional painted lash doll (1950 – 52), some of the synthetic eyes used by Vogue have turned shades of red. Courtesy Peggy Millhouse.

Strung transitional painted lash doll (1950), some of the transitional eye colors appear to be two-tone such as this brown and blue eyed doll. Courtesy Peggy Millhouse.

Strung transitional painted lash doll, some transitional eye colors appear to be a solid color such as this black eye. May have been an experimental color or blending of unstable colors. Courtesy Peggy Millhouse.

Strung transitional painted lash doll (1950) in white organdy skirt and plaid cotton bodice and trim on the skirt with straw hat. Outfit not listed in any Vogue brochure. Notice plaid band around hat, also has red ribbon in back sewn into the plaid band. Plaid is similar to #7K Jo-An. Courtesy Sandy Johnson Barts.

Ginny (1950), #8-3R from Group R wearing red velvet coat with white fur collar and matching beret style hat with white feather trim. This is Vogue's first recorded use of the name Ginny. It wasn't until 1952 that a series of dolls was named Ginny.

Judy (1950), #8-2D from Afternoon series wearing a red organdy dress with lace edging and heart trim and a red bow on her head. The dress came in several colors. Courtesy Maureen Fukushima.

Sonny (1950), #8-3E from Brother and Sister series has sleep eye, painted lash, tosca dutch cut mohair wig, white leather vest with red rickrack, red leatherette shoes, green plaid flannel shirt sewn to curly poodle cut white chaps, white leather cuffs sewn to the shirt. Came in a pink (almost peach color) box. Courtesy Barbara Hill.

Sven #8-5E (left), and Steffie #8-6E (1950) from the Brother and Sister group, with pale transitional coloring. Both wear felt outfits with cotton organdy blouses and embroidered braid trim; Steffie's skirt has a lace trimmed hem. This outfit was also shown in 1951 as Sten #37 and Stina #38. Note that this may have been a special holiday version of the outfit, since the 1950 and 1951 Vogue salesmen's photos show the outfits with blue felt skirts and hats, and gold vests. Courtesy Veronica Phillips.

Mary Lamb (1950) from the Character group wears a yellow outfit and matching hat. Note the original plastic lamb which was shown with the doll in promotional material. Courtesy Sandy Johnson Barts.

Alice in Wonderland (1950) from the Character group wears a dress with white organdy top and apron edged with lace and a blue cotton skirt with white bands. White pantalettes and socks are worn underneath. The doll's long hair is tied with a ribbon. Courtesy Veronica Phillips.

Cinderella group (1950). Notice Cinderella has a hair ribbon instead of the 1949 cone hat. Vogue brochure which came in dolls' boxes. Courtesy Marge Meisinger.

Prince (1950 – 52) from Cinderella group, felt outfit and hat with gold braid trim with brass buttons on shoulders. Some had capes.

Strung transitional painted lash doll (1950), pale pink dress with flowers at hem and matching bow. This dress was included in the 1953 Rich Uncle fitted red suitcase #828. Courtesy Peggy Millhouse.

Holly Boy (1950 – 52), a special doll produced by Vogue as a Christmas present for their employees. Note felt appliqué on shirt and felt boots and belt. Courtesy Ruth Doyon, former supervisor of Vogue's home sewers.

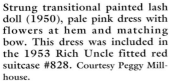

Holly Boy and Girl (1950 – 52), special holiday outfits of red and white felt. Note the bells on the boy's felt slippers. Courtesy Vicki Johnson.

Strung (1950) Vogue flyer, showing Vogue Sweetheart Valentine #1 and Queen of Hearts Valentine #2. Also Springtime Easter #21 and Easter Parade #24. Dolls came in both painted eye and sleep eye. The Easter Parade #24 was used again in 1951 as Beryl – Tiny Miss #43. Courtesy Virginia Graves Carlson.

Strung transitional painted lash doll (1950). Vogue Sweetheart Valentine #1 in a taffeta dress with printed hearts. Courtesy Darlene Foote.

Miss 1900 (1950), from One Half-Century group wearing pink gown with cape of dotted dimity trimmed in lace, poke bonnet with felt brim. See entire collection of One Half-Century group on page 80. They came with both painted and sleep-eye versions. Courtesy Maureen Fukushima.

1951

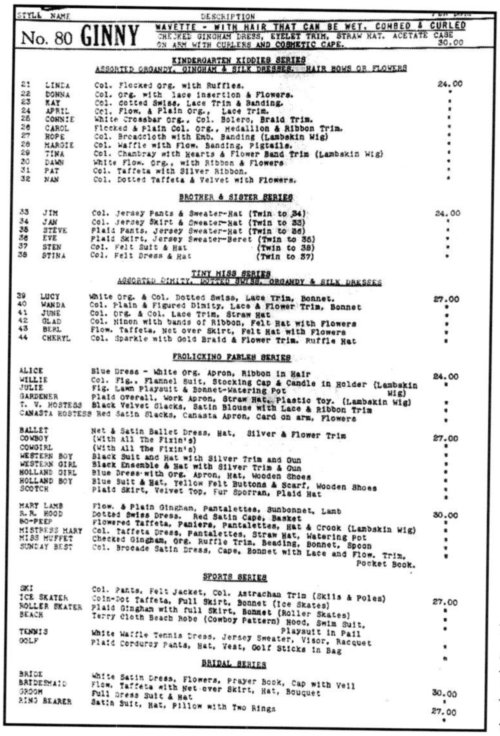

STYLE	NAME	DESCRIPTION	[illegible]
No. 80	GINNY	WAVETTE - WITH HAIR THAT CAN BE WET, COMBED & CURLED CHECKED GINGHAM DRESS, EYELET TRIM, STRAW HAT. ACETATE CASE ON ARM WITH CURLERS AND COSMETIC CAPE.	30.00
		KINDERGARTEN KIDDIES SERIES ASSORTED ORGANDY, GINGHAM & SILK DRESSES. HAIR BOWS OR FLOWERS	
21	LINDA	Col. Flocked Org. with Ruffles.	24.00
22	DONNA	Col. Org. with lace insertion & Flowers.	.
23	KAY	Col. dotted Swiss, Lace Trim & Banding.	.
24	APRIL	Col. Flow. & Plain Org., Lace Trim.	.
25	CONNIE	White Crossbar Org., Col. Bolero, Braid Trim.	.
26	CAROL	Flocked & Plain Col. Org., Medallion & Ribbon Trim.	.
27	HOPE	Col. Broadcloth with Emb. Banding (Lambskin Wig)	.
28	MARGIE	Col. Waffle with Flow. Banding, Pigtails.	.
29	TINA	Col. Chambray with Hearts & Flower Band Trim (Lambskin Wig)	.
30	DAWN	White Flow. Org., with Ribbon & Flowers	.
31	PAT	Col. Taffeta with Silver Ribbon.	.
32	NAN	Col. Dotted Taffeta & Velvet with Flowers.	.
		BROTHER & SISTER SERIES	
33	JIM	Col. Jersey Pants & Sweater-Hat (Twin to 34)	24.00
34	JAN	Col. Jersey Skirt & Sweater-Hat (Twin to 33)	.
35	STEVE	Plaid Pants, Jersey Sweater-Hat (Twin to 36)	.
36	EVE	Plaid Skirt, Jersey Sweater-Beret (Twin to 35)	.
37	STEN	Col. Felt Suit & Hat (Twin to 38)	.
38	STINA	Col. Felt Dress & Hat (Twin to 37)	.
		TINY MISS SERIES ASSORTED DIMITY, DOTTED SWISS, ORGANDY & SILK DRESSES	
39	LUCY	White Org. & Col. Dotted Swiss, Lace Trim, Bonnet.	27.00
40	WANDA	Col. Plain & Figured Dimity, Lace & Flower Trim, Bonnet	.
41	JUNE	Col. Org. & Col. Lace Trim, Straw Hat	.
42	GLAD	Col. Ninon with bands of Ribbon, Felt Hat with Flowers	.
43	BERL	Flow. Taffeta, Net over Skirt, Felt Hat with Flowers	.
44	CHERYL	Col. Sparkle with Gold Braid & Flower Trim. Ruffle Hat	.
		FROLICKING FABLES SERIES	
	ALICE	Blue Dress - White Org. Apron, Ribbon in Hair	24.00
	WILLIE	Col. Fig., Flannel Suit, Stocking Cap & Candle in Holder (Lambskin Wig)	.
	JULIE	Fig. Lawn Playsuit & Bonnet-Watering Pot	
	GARDENER	Plaid Overall, Work Apron, Straw Hat, Plastic Toy. (Lambskin Wig)	.
	T. V. HOSTESS	Black Velvet Slacks, Satin Blouse with Lace & Ribbon Trim	.
	CANASTA HOSTESS	Red Satin Slacks, Canasta Apron, Card on arm, Flowers	.
	BALLET	Net & Satin Ballet Dress, Hat, Silver & Flower Trim	
	COWBOY	(With All The Fixin's)	27.00
	COWGIRL	(With All The Fixin's)	.
	WESTERN BOY	Black Suit and Hat with Silver Trim and Gun	.
	WESTERN GIRL	Black Ensemble & Hat with Silver Trim & Gun	.
	HOLLAND GIRL	Blue Dress with Org. Apron, Hat, Wooden Shoes	.
	HOLLAND BOY	Blue Suit & Hat, Yellow Felt Buttons & Scarf, Wooden Shoes	.
	SCOTCH	Plaid Skirt, Velvet Top, Fur Sporran, Plaid Hat	.
	MARY LAMB	Flow. & Plain Gingham, Pantalettes, Sunbonnet, Lamb	
	R. R. HOOD	Dotted Swiss Dress. Red Satin Cape, Basket	30.00
	BO-PEEP	Flowered Taffeta, Paniers, Pantalettes, Hat & Crook (Lambskin Wig)	.
	MISTRESS MARY	Col. Taffeta Dress, Pantalettes, Straw Hat, Watering Pot	.
	MISS MUFFET	Checked Gingham, Org. Ruffle Trim. Beading, Bonnet, Spoon	.
	SUNDAY BEST	Col. Brocade Satin Dress, Cape, Bonnet with Lace and Flow. Trim, Pocket Book.	.
		SPORTS SERIES	
	SKI	Col. Pants, Felt Jacket, Col. Astrachan Trim (Skiis & Poles)	
	ICE SKATER	Coin-Dot Taffeta, Full Skirt, Bonnet (Ice Skates)	27.00
	ROLLER SKATER	Plaid Gingham with full Skirt, Bonnet (Roller Skates)	.
	BEACH	Terry Cloth Beach Robe (Cowboy Pattern) Hood, Swim Suit, Playsuit in Pail	.
	TENNIS	White Waffle Tennis Dress, Jersey Sweater, Visor, Racquet	.
	GOLF	Plaid Corduroy Pants, Hat, Vest, Golf Sticks in Bag	.
		BRIDAL SERIES	
	BRIDE	White Satin Dress, Flowers, Prayer Book, Cap with Veil	
	BRIDESMAID	Flow. Taffeta with Net over Skirt, Hat, Bouquet	
	GROOM	Full Dress Suit & Hat	30.00
	RING BEARER	Satin Suit, Hat, Pillow with Two Rings	27.00

Vogue price list (1951) sent to dealers, describes Ginny #80 Wavette with hair that can be wet, combed, and curled. Courtesy Virginia Graves Carlson.

Ginny the Wavette Hair Doll (1951) #80 had Nutex hair. Red and white gingham dress with eyelet trim and straw hat. Cape and curlers are in little acetate case. Courtesy Robi Blute.

1951 Vogue press photo promoting the first 8" doll actually named Ginny. The promotion was such a success that in 1952 Vogue had a Ginny Series of four dolls each with plastic curlers and cape. Courtesy Virginia Graves Carlson.

Not Shown
#21 Linda
#22 Donna
#24 April
#25 Connie

Kay (1951) #23, Kindergarten Kiddies series. Red dotted Swiss dress with lace trim.

Kindergarten Kiddies series (1951), (from left): #30 Dawn, #27 Hope, #28 Margie, unclear, #31 Pat, #29 Tina, #32 Nan. Courtesy Virginia Carlson.

Carol (1951) #26, Kindergarten Kiddies, wearing dress of yellow organdy with lace trim. Shown in box with original cardboard insert and Vogue brochure. Courtesy Tina Ritari.

Nan (1951) #32, Kindergarten Kiddies series, wearing blue version of dotted taffeta dress with a velvet top. The special ponytails wig style is tied with flowers and ribbons to match the skirt. Courtesy Chree Kysar.

Margie (1951) #28, Kindergarten Kiddies, wearing blue waffle weave dress with gathered cap sleeves, white woven band trim with blue flower design, and matching bloomers.

Tina (1951) #29, Kindergarten Kiddies wearing red chambray dress with woven hearts and flowers trim and white rickrack at sleeves and neck. Poodle cut wig has a stapled red bow. Courtesy Barbara Rosplock-Van Orman.

Brother & Sister Series

Brother and Sister series (1951), (back from left): #33 Jim and #34 Jan; #36 Steve and #35 Eve; (front) #37 Sten and #38 Stina. Courtesy Virginia Carlson.

Tiny Miss Series

Tiny Miss series (1951) (from left): #42 Glad, #39 Lucy, #40 Wanda, #43 Berl, #41 June, #44 Cheryl. Courtesy Mr. and Mrs. Edwin Nelson.

Glad (1951) #42, Tiny Miss series, wearing a pink dress with blue satin ribbons and pink felt bonnet trimmed with flowers. Notice exceptional cheek color on this mint doll in original pink box. Courtesy Robi Blute.

Frolicking Fables Series

Frolicking Fables (1951), (from left): Dutch girl and boy, Ballet, Western girl and boy, Scotch. Courtesy Virginia Carlson.

Berl (1951) #43, Tiny Miss series, wearing a flowered taffeta dress with net overskirt and cap sleeves. The pink felt hat ties at the neck with a satin ribbon and is trimmed with gathered net and flowers. This doll was also shown on the 1950 – 51 Easter promotional flyer wearing this "I Love You" wrist charm. Courtesy Maureen Fukushima.

Frolicking Fables (1951), (from left): Gardener, Alice in Wonderland, Wee Willie Winkie, TV Hostess, Julie, Canasta Hostess. Courtesy Virginia Carlson.

Ballet (1951), Frolicking Fables series, wearing tulle costume with silver band and flower trim, matching headpiece, silver ballet slippers. Courtesy Kathy Bailey.

Frolicking Fables (1951), (from left): Mistress Mary, Mary Lamb, Red Riding Hood, Miss Muffet, Bo Peep, Sunday Best. Courtesy Virginia Carlson.

Red Riding Hood (1951), Frolicking Fables series, wearing dotted red organdy dress with lace trim and red satin cape lined with white. Original basket and red center snap shoes. Courtesy Barbara Rosplock-Van Orman.

Canasta Hostess (1951), Frolicking Fables series, wearing red satin slacks and white satin canasta print apron and top trimmed in gold rickrack. A playing card is tied on her wrist and flowers trim her unusual upswept hairdo. A rare doll. Courtesy Maureen Fukushima.

Sunday Best (1951), Frolicking Fables series, wearing brocade satin dress with lace trim and matching bloomers, cape, and hat. She also carries a plastic purse. Pale blue box with ink spot label predates 1953 fuchsia paper doll design box. Courtesy Maureen Fukushima.

Sports Series

Miss Muffet (1951), Frolicking Fables series wears a yellow checked outfit with beaded eyelet trim and matching cap. Courtesy Sandy Johnson-Barts.

Sports series (1951), (from left): Beach, Ski, Ice Skater, Tennis, Roller Skater, Golf. Courtesy Virginia Carlson.

Golfer (1951), Sports series, wearing plaid corduroy pants and matching cap, red blouse, blue vest. A miniature golf bag with tiny golf clubs hang over doll's shoulder. Courtesy Maureen Fukushima.

Not Shown

Frolicking Fables: Cowboy and Cowgirl.

Bridal Series: Bride, Bridesmaid, Groom, Ringbearer.

Cinderella Series: Cinderella, Fairy Godmother, Prince

Sweetheart #1 (1951), Valentine special wearing a white satin skating costume with red heart print and faced with red bias tape at hem, matching tie bonnet, center snap skates. Saran wig was used during the transitional years.

Other Outfits

Strung transitional painted lash doll (1951), checked red and white cotton dress with hearts and flowers band and eyelet trim with matching panties. Braided hairstyle is pulled up and stapled with a bow. Courtesy Kathy Bailey.

Strung transitional painted lash doll (1951) in yellow piqué dress with white ninon apron tied in the back with large bow and matching bonnet. Dress is identical to a blue cotton Toddles dress with a 1945 – 50 tag.

Strung transitional doll (1951), in yellow cotton pinafore dress with unusual blue silkscreened hem design.

Strung transitional painted lash doll (1950 – 1951), in blue cotton dress with white printed ninon pinafore, matching bonnet. The dress's tag is an identical style to a yellow piqué version issued with a 1951 tag. Courtesy Sandy Johnson-Barts.

Strung transitional painted lash doll (1950 – 1951), in yellow sunsuit with ties at the neck and a flowered print overskirt with elastic waist, cape, and hat. Comes with a drawstring purse.

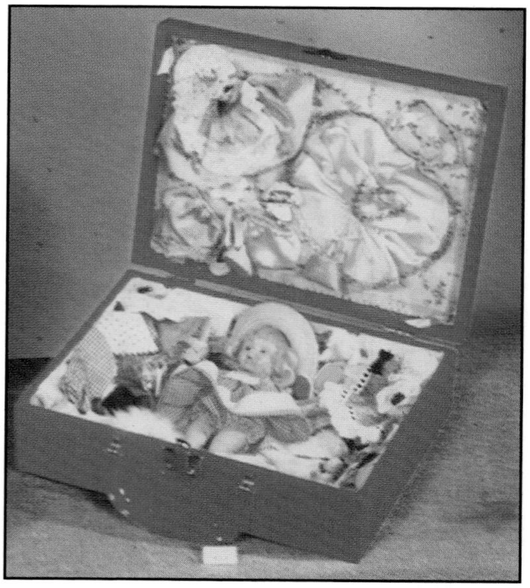

Ginny (1951), in case #828. Courtesy Virginia Carlson.

Ginny Series

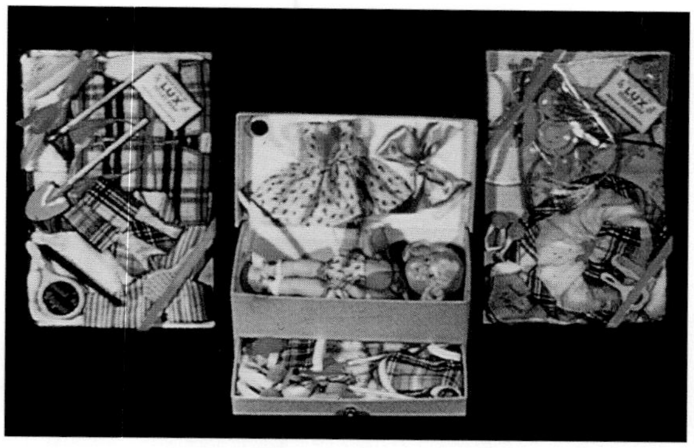

Box of clothing (1951) #880 set for boys, #875 painted eye doll in box with drawers, and #870 set for girls. Courtesy Virginia Carlson.

Later strung transitional painted lash dolls began to use darker lip colors and cheeks of sleep eye hard plastic dolls. Courtesy Peggy Millhouse.

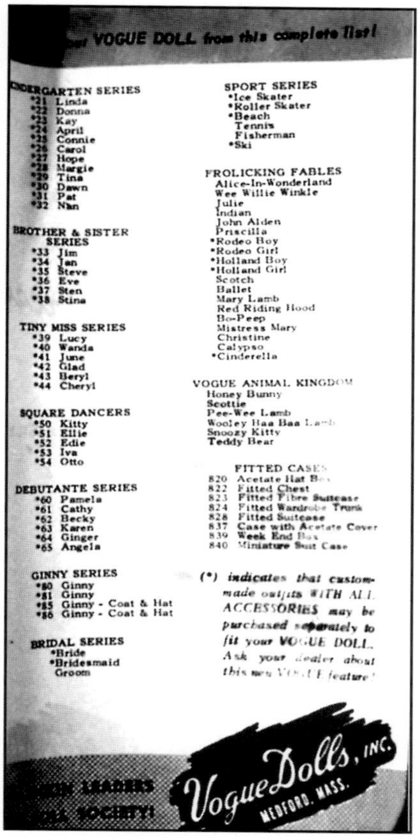

VOGUE DOLL from this complete list!

ERGARTEN SERIES
*21 Linda
*22 Donna
*23 Kay
*24 April
*25 Connie
*26 Carol
*27 Hope
*28 Margie
*29 Tina
*30 Dawn
*31 Pat
*32 Nan

BROTHER & SISTER SERIES
*33 Jim
*34 Jan
*35 Steve
*36 Eve
*37 Sten
*38 Stina

TINY MISS SERIES
*39 Lucy
*40 Wanda
*41 June
*42 Glad
*43 Beryl
*44 Cheryl

SQUARE DANCERS
*50 Kitty
*51 Ellie
*52 Edie
*53 Iva
*54 Otto

DEBUTANTE SERIES
*60 Pamela
*61 Cathy
*62 Becky
*63 Karen
*64 Ginger
*65 Angela

GINNY SERIES
*80 Ginny
*81 Ginny
*85 Ginny - Coat & Hat
*86 Ginny - Coat & Hat

BRIDAL SERIES
*Bride
*Bridesmaid
Groom

SPORT SERIES
*Ice Skater
*Roller Skater
*Beach
Tennis
Fisherman
*Ski

FROLICKING FABLES
Alice-In-Wonderland
Wee Willie Winkle
Julie
Indian
John Alden
Priscilla
*Rodeo Boy
*Rodeo Girl
*Holland Boy
*Holland Girl
Scotch
Ballet
Mary Lamb
Red Riding Hood
Bo-Peep
Mistress Mary
Christine
Calypso
*Cinderella

VOGUE ANIMAL KINGDOM
Honey Bunny
Scottie
Pee-Wee Lamb
Wooley Baa Baa Lamb
Snoozy Kitty
Teddy Bear

FITTED CASES
820 Acetate Hat Box
822 Fitted Chest
823 Fitted Fibre Suitcase
824 Fitted Wardrobe Trunk
828 Fitted Suitcase
837 Case with Acetate Cover
839 Week End Box
840 Miniature Suit Case

(*) indicates that custom-made outfits WITH ALL ACCESSORIES may be purchased separately to fit your VOGUE DOLL. Ask your dealer about this new VOGUE feature!

VogueDolls, INC.
MEDFORD, MASS.

1952 Vogue list of doll series which was included in each doll box.

Ginny series (1952), #80 red checked gingham dress with white eyelet trim and straw hat. This dress came in several colors and the outfit was used in a Ginny flyer promoting the doll's wash and set wig. Notice acetate case containing plastic curlers and cosmetic cape.

Ginny series (1952), #81 wearing a dress with a black velvet skirt and colored organdy top with lace sleeve and neck trim. Panties are black velvet with lace trim. Straw hat has black velvet band on brim edge. Black center snap shoes.

Ginny series (1952), #85 white fur coat and hat with pink taffeta dress; cosmetic cape and curlers, mint in box. This outfit also came with a blue dress. Courtesy GiGi's Dolls.

Ginny series (1952), (from left), #86 pink or blue poodle cloth coat and beret, silk dress; #81 black velvet skirt with organdy blouse; #80 pin check gingham dress (also came in red, yellow, blue, and green); #85 white furette coat and beret, silk dress. These slides were given to Vogue representatives to show to dealers. Courtesy Mr. and Mrs. Edwin Nelson.

Kindergarten Series

Linda (1952), #21, Kindergarten series, wearing printed pale blue organdy pinafore dress with gathered cap sleeves, trimmed with black ribbon- laced braid. Flowers in hair. Courtesy Peggy Millhouse.

Kay (1952), #23, Kindergarten series, wearing red organdy dress with white medallion shoulder trim and red hair ribbon. Notice silver wrist tag and ink spot label on the pink box. Courtesy Ann Tardie.

April (1952), #24, Kindergarten series, in poodle wig wearing shadow yellow organdy dress with ribbon tie at waist and Bertha collar. Also came in blue. Venetian lace trim on dress. Missing flowers and twin bows on poodle wig. Courtesy Shirley Niziolek.

Carol (1952), #26, Kindergarten series, in checked dimity dress with a large separate white piqué collar with lace trim and a blue patent leather belt. Notice horse tails hairstyle is from Nan #32, same series. Courtesy Judy Ormsbee.

Not Shown

Kindergarten Series:
- #22 Donna – colored dotted swiss dress, eyelet trim
- #27 Hope — striped cambray strap dress
- #31 Pat — colored ninon and sparkle, gold braid trim
- #32 Nan — flocked bows on a satin skirt, black velvet bodice

Connie (1952), #25, Kindergarten series, in poodle wig wearing pink glazed piqué dress with yellow and blue bias trim, and felt "buttons" glued on bodice front. The matching hair ribbon was sold with boxed outfit.

Margie (1951), #28, Kindergarten series (on left), and Margie (1952), #28, (on right) showing differences in blue waffle weave dress.

Brother & Sister Series

Tina (1952) #29, Kindergarten series, in dimity dress with multi-colored coin dots, a novelty red felt border, and a laced felt bodice with flower trim, showing variation of outfit color. Courtesy Peggy Millhouse.

Dawn (1952), #30, Kindergarten series, in green velvet dress with tiny felt bow trim on bodice and unique petal-shaped skirt over satin. Also available in pink. Notice silver wrist tag. Courtesy Barbara Rosplock-Van Orman.

Jan (1952), #34, Brother and Sister series, in pink jersey skirt and cap and pink and white top. The tag dates from 1953. The style was shown in the 1952 sales flyer with a different striped top. Outfit is not listed in 1953 price list. Goes with #33 Jim, wearing colored jersey, sweater and hat, but wears pants. Both available in various pastel colors.

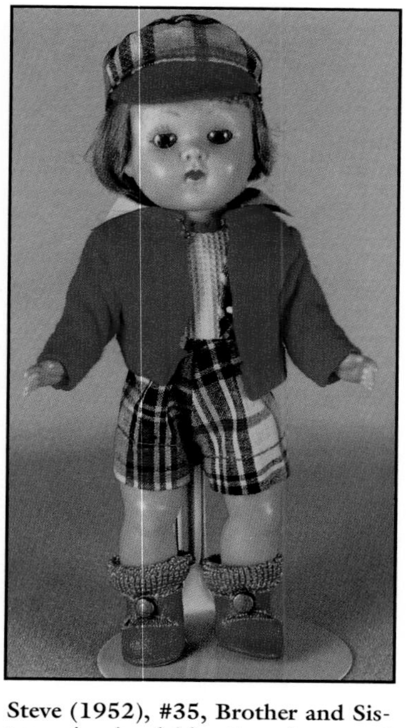

Steve (1952), #35, Brother and Sister series, in plaid cotton shorts and cap with felt brim, white piqué top edged with red rickrack. A red cotton knit shirt and white vinyl collar, center snap shoes. Goes with #36 Eve.

Eve (1952), #36, Brother and Sister series, in plaid cotton skirt and beret, white top, red knit sweater with white vinyl collar, center snap shoes. Goes with #35 Steve. Courtesy Barbara Rosplock-Van Orman.

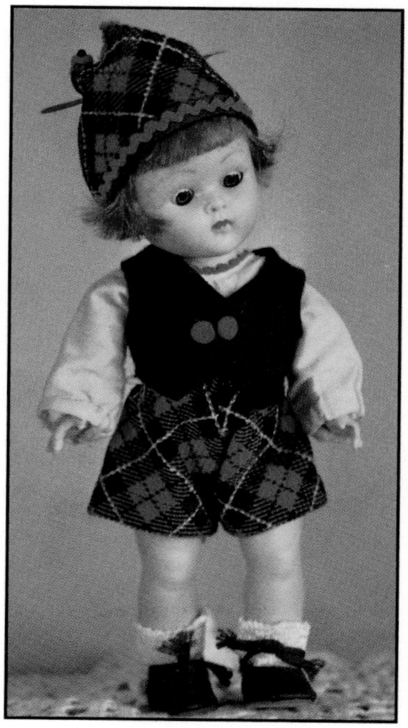

Sten (1952), #37, Brother and Sister series, in plaid corduroy shorts, hat, and navy felt vest. Goes with #38 Stina. Courtesy Peggy Millhouse.

Tiny Miss Series

Lucy (1952), #39, Tiny Miss series, in blue dotted dimity dress with attached white organdy apron edged with lace, and blue bow trim. Peach color straw hat with blue ribbon. Courtesy Sue Johnson.

Wanda (1952), #40, Tiny Miss series in plaid pinafore dress with navy band trim over white organdy hem and bodice band. Blue straw hat is trimmed with red cherries. Red center snap shoes. This dress also came with a red hem trim. The price lists describes this outfit as plaid silk taffeta with dotted Swiss banding. The 1950 K-7 dress is similar but without the blue braid hem trim.

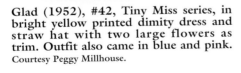

Glad (1952), #42, Tiny Miss series, in bright yellow printed dimity dress and straw hat with two large flowers as trim. Outfit also came in blue and pink. Courtesy Peggy Millhouse.

June (1952), #41, Tiny Miss series, in white organdy dress with green pin-striped trim on hem and bodice, white lace edging and blue bows. Poodle cut wig, although price list does not mention poodle cut for June. Also came in blue and red. Courtesy Ann Tardie.

Beryl (1952), #43, Tiny Miss series, in pale lavender/pink printed organdy dress edged with lace and a ribbon waist tie. Pleated net trims the pink straw hat and petticoat. Originally had two woven flowers on skirt's lace trim.

Cheryl (1952,) #44, Tiny Miss series, in white flowered satin dress, gathered lace trim, and a pink ribbon sash, matching bloomers. Pink straw hat has velvet flowers under brim. Wrist tag has her name and number on it. Courtesy Maureen Fukushima.

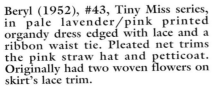

Square Dancers

Ellie (1952), #51, Square Dancers series, in red dotted cotton dress with long full skirt trimmed with rickrack and eyelet ruffle. Black patent belt. Also came with hearts and flowers band in place of rickrack. All square dancers had a "dance card" tied to their wrists. Courtesy Judy Ormsbee.

Edie (1952), #52, Square Dancers series, in green print suspender dress with rickrack trim. Note the excellent face color. This doll is shown with pigtails as described on Vogue's original dealer price list. (Toy violin not original.) Courtesy Kathy Schneider.

Iva (1952), #53, Square Dancers series, in blue cotton flower print dress with long, full skirt trimmed with black beading, with ruffled eyelet at hem and neckline. Also came in white print. Courtesy Peggy Millhouse.

Otto (1952), #54, Square Dancers series, in denim jeans, plaid shirt, kerchief, handkerchief, and a straw hat. Accessories not original to doll. Courtesy Maureen Dantzer.

Not Shown

Square Dancer #50 Kitty – white organdy long sleeved top with black flowered cotton skirt, pink bias trim.

Debutante #62 Becky – white organdy dress with embroidered blue flowers, straw hat with ribbons.

Debutante Series

Pamela (1952), #60, Debutante series, in white embroidered dress with lace trim. Dress and hat have sprays of heather flowers and a fluffy white feather decorates brim of hat. Courtesy Judy Ormsbee.

Cathy (1952), #61, Debutante series, in pastel embroidered dress with ruffled lace trim and a spray of flowers at the waist and on the pink straw hat. Courtesy Sue Johnson.

Karen (1952), #63, Debutante series, in dress with green velvet yoke and yellow organdy skirt decorated with roses and green velvet leaves, matching bonnet. Courtesy Kathy Bailey.

Ginger (1952), #64, Debutante series, in a white organdy dress with embroidered multi-colored coin dots, trimmed with red ribbon and berries on the straw hat. Also shown by Vogue with berry trim at waist. Courtesy Peggy Millhouse.

Angela (1952), #65, Debutante series, in a hand smocked blue organdy pinafore dress with a white felt bonnet with flowers and an ostrich plume trim. Also came in pink. Courtesy Robi Blute.

Sports Series

Sport series (1952), (from left), Fisherman, Beach, Ice Skater, Roller Skater, Tennis, Ski. Courtesy Mr. and Mrs. Edwin Nelson.

Fisherman (1952), Sport series, in a yellow plastic slicker and a black rain hat with denim pants. Original red plastic fishing pole. Courtesy Sandy Johnson-Barts.

Beach (1952), Sport series, in a green print three-piece midriff set of shorts, halter top, and skirt with a matching sunhat. The plastic sunglasses and imported straw fan are original. Notice the rare horsetail wig style. Courtesy Shirley's Dollhouse.

Roller Skater, (1952), Sport series, in a red quilted gingham outfit with yellow bias edging, felt flower sprays on skirt and headband. Courtesy Millie Caliri.

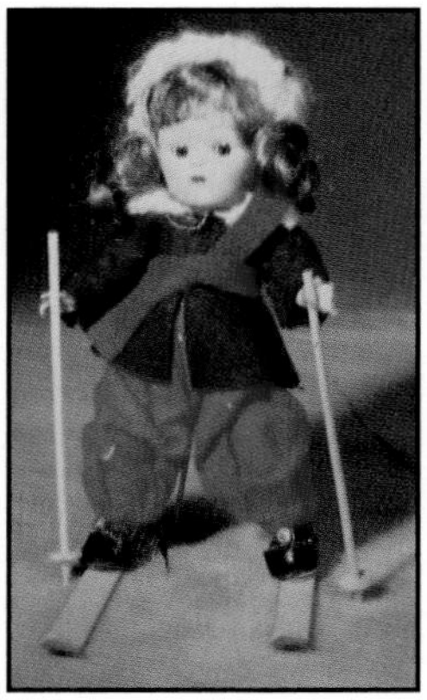

Ski (1952), Sports series, red pants, felt jacket, astrachan trim, skis and poles. Courtesy Marge Meisinger.

FROLICKING FABLES

Frolicking Fables series (1952), from left (back row): Julie, Wee Willie Winkie, Alice-In-Wonderland, Indian, Priscilla, John Alden. Front row: Rodeo Girl, Rodeo Boy, Scotch, Holland Boy, Holland Girl. Courtesy Mr. and Mrs. Edwin Nelson.

Wee Willie Winkie (1952), Frolicking Fables series, in printed cotton flannel pajamas and white knit cap. Lambskin wig. Pom pons trim the slippers, neck and knit cap. Brass candle holder and candle are original. Wrist tag simply says "Willie." Courtesy Shirley's Dollhouse.

Indian (1952), Frolicking Fables series, in a white felt outfit with bright thread trim, beads, and feather headband. Notice bright cheeks, reddish-brown eyes, and pale plastic as an example of transitional coloring. Courtesy Sue Johnson.

John Alden and Priscilla (1952), Frolicking Fables series, in gray traditional outfits with white collars, cuffs, and hats. Courtesy Kathy Bailey.

Rodeo Girl (1952), Frolicking Fables series, in a white outfit printed with gold, with gold braid and fringe trim at hem, gold belt at waist, black boots, plastic gun, magenta ribbon scarf, and green felt hat.

Scotch (1952), Frolicking Fables series, in a red and blue plaid skirt, scarf, and hat with a blue velvet top. Sleeves and neck are edged with gold rickrack, white fur sporran, black center snap shoes. Courtesy Maureen Fukushima.

Holland Boy (1952), Frolicking Fables series, in blue cotton suit with matching cap. Wooden shoes. Missing yellow felt scarf. Courtesy Shirley's Dollhouse.

Frolicking Fables series (1952), from left (back row): Bo Peep, Mistress Mary, Ballet, Mary Lamb. Front row: Red Riding Hood, Calypso, Christine. Courtesy Mr. and Mrs. Edwin Nelson.

Mary Lamb (1952), Frolicking Fables series, in a pale blue shadow striped dimity dress with a fuzzy lamb decoration on hem. Woven straw hair decoration. Courtesy Ann Tardie.

Promotional Dolls

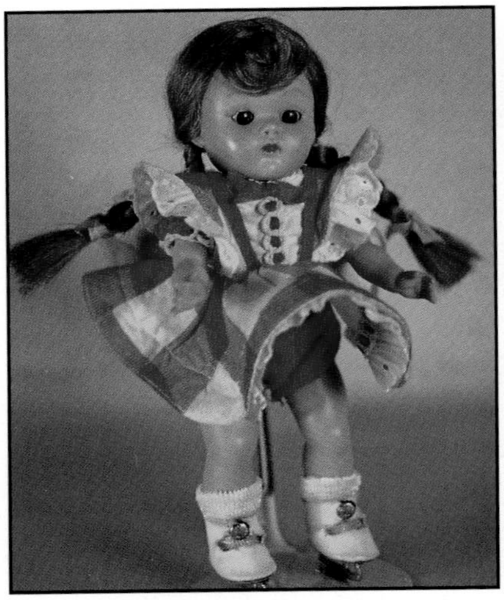

A special souvenir doll (1952) sold at the Ice Capades to promote skating star Barbara Ann Scott. A red and white checked outfit edged with ruffled eyelet on shoulder. A picture of the star wearing this outfit came with the doll. Outfit courtesy Marian Schmuhl.

Candee (1952), Valentine's promotion in red organdy with white eyelet embroidery. The dress is a red version of the special 1952 Pixie doll, the namesake of Mrs. Graves's granddaughter. Notice "I Love You" plastic heart tied on the wrist. Courtesy Barbara Rosplock-Van Orman.

Christine (1952), Frolicking Fables series, in a printed organdy dress with long skirt trimmed with silver threads and multi-colored ribbon, pleated net trim edging hem and magenta velveteen cap. Courtesy Barbara Rosplock-Van Orman.

Not Shown

Bridal series:
- Bride – white satin gown, flowers, prayer book, cap, veil and blue garter
- Bridesmaid – bouffant net skirt over taffeta, flower and gold braid trim, cap
- Groom – dress suit and hat

Frolicking Fables:
- Cinderella – long organdy dress with net plaiting, conical hat and veil, side panniers.

Separate Clothing

Separate coat (1952), #88C, blue waffle weave with white cuffs and bertha collar edged with lace, and matching bonnet. Also came in pink and yellow. There were four coats sold separately.

Painted lash doll (1952), printed organdy dress not found in a 1952 series. Has Vogue tag. This special separate dress probably utilized extra trim from 1952 Kindergarten series #28 which had the same trim.

Painted lash doll (1952), tagged separate dress with striped multicolored skirt and waist band and white cotton top, used fabric from Kindergarten series #27 Hope and was sold as a separate boxed outfit.

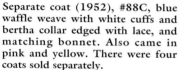

Tiny Miss #42, boxed outfit (1952). Courtesy Shirley Bertrand.

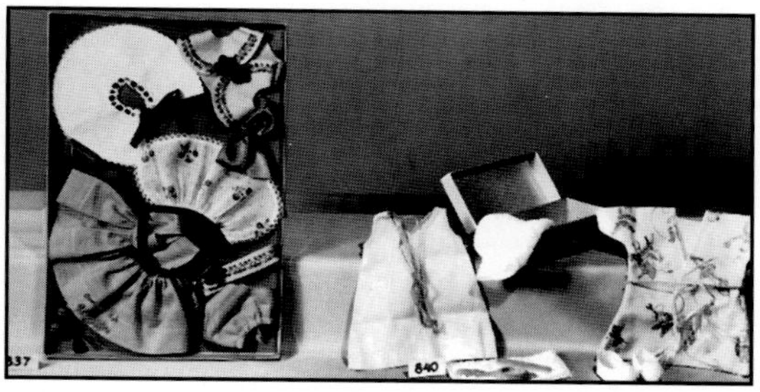

Vogue (1952) photo of boxed interchangeable clothes #837 with acetate lid and suitcase #840. Courtesy Wenham Museum, Wenham, Mass.

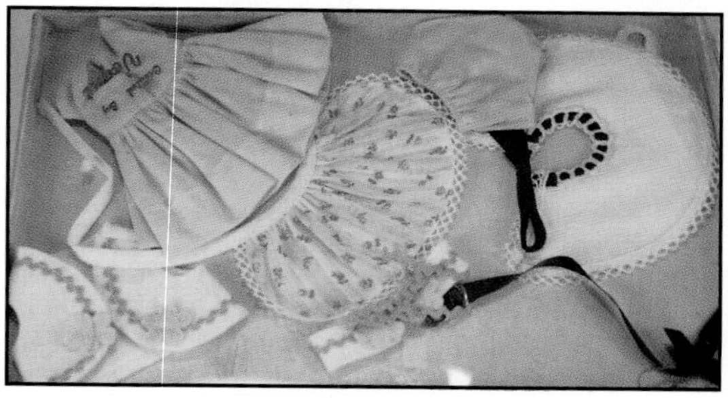

Tiny Miss #837, boxed outfit (1952) interchangeable clothing offered in various patterns with dress, apron, tie-on collar, felt vest and belt, belt, and panties. Courtesy Ann Tardie.

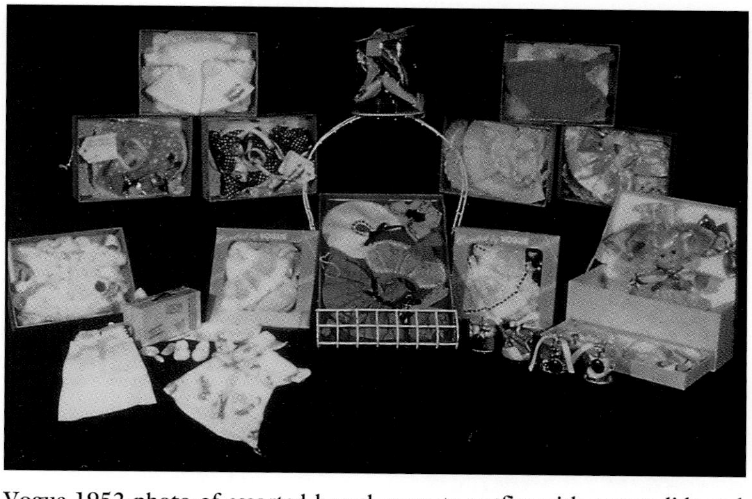

Vogue 1952 photo of assorted boxed separate outfits with acetate lids and #822 chest with Ginny and extra outfits, also shows additional separate shoes, hats, etc. Courtesy Mr. and Mrs. Edwin Nelson.

Fitted fiber case #822 (1952 – 54), made of cardboard with a pull-out drawer and tilt-up lid. Contained a doll in underpants, extra outfits, ribbons and shoes, white cosmetic cape and curlers, yellow dress. Courtesy Maureen Fukushima.

Rich Aunt fitted fiber case (1952), #824, came with doll and several outfits. Courtesy Wenham Museum, Wenham, Mass.

Rich Uncle (1952), #828, fitted with Ginny dressed in yellow and white checked outfit #80 from Ginny series, ski and ice skater outfits, organdy and cotton dresses, bonnets, coat, nightie, pocketbooks, extra shoes, slippers. Courtesy Ann Tardie.

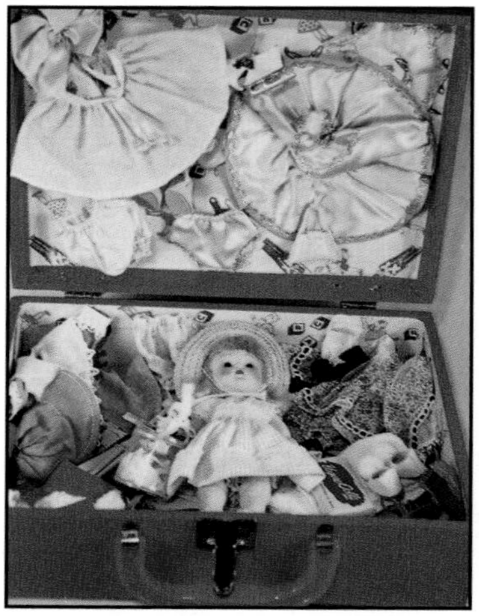

1953

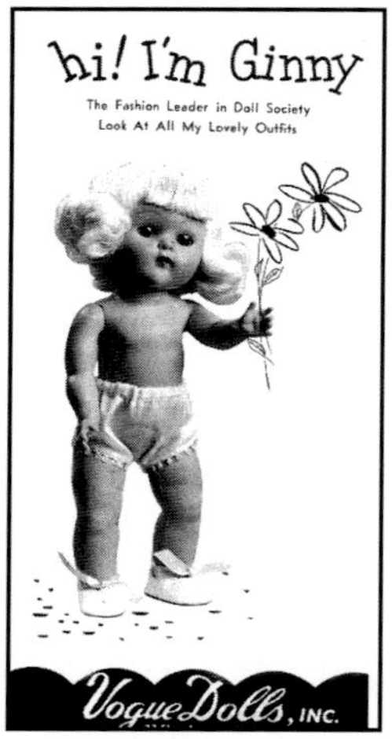

Ginny (1953) Hi! I'm Ginny cover of Vogue brochure.

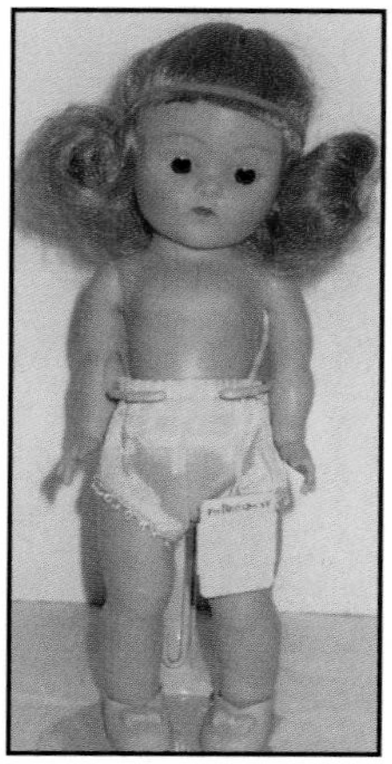

Basic undressed painted lash Ginny (1953) wearing panties and vinyl shoes. Interestingly, while the 1953 catalog cover showed the undressed doll in tie shoes, many all original dolls wore vinyl shoes with molded bows. Courtesy Gigi's Dolls.

By 1953 Vogue's doll manufacturer utilized stencils to hand paint the lashes and brows on the doll. This close-up shows a uniform effect was achieved with this method. Over time, paint pigments could turn greenish if exposed to strong light. Courtesy Peggy Millhouse.

Kindergarten Afternoon Series

Linda (1953), #21, Kindergarten Afternoon series, wearing dress of flowered chintz skirt and velvet ribbon waist tie. White bodice has a gathered eyelet trim with ribbon laced braid. Green hair bow was sold with the separate outfit.

Donna (1953), #22, and Kay #23, Kindergarten Afternoon series. Vogue brochure.

April (1953), #24, Kindergarten Afternoon series, wears a crisp white organdy dress with dotted organdy and lace trim and matching bows. Doll still has original band on bangs and wrist tag. Notice Vogue Paper Doll pink box. Courtesy Robi Blute.

Connie (1953), #25, Kindergarten Afternoon series, wears an organdy dress with printed hem and shawl collar trimmed with lace and satin bows. Courtesy Kathy Bailey.

Carol (1953), #26, Kindergarten Afternoon series, wears dotted cotton organdy dress with gathered cap sleeves. The skirt border is printed with an A-B-C design. The separate outfit was sold with a hair bow. It also came in orange, a harder to find color.

Kindergarten School Series

Hope (1953), #27, Kindergarten School series, in a white cotton dress with green checked top-facing on skirt, and suspender trim at shoulders, with black plastic belt and black ribbon neck trim. Courtesy Kathy Schneider.

Margie (1953), #28, Kindergarten School series, in a plaid cotton skirt and suspenders, the white top is edged with blue rick rack. The hem has white angle-pleated edging. Matching blue center snap shoes. Courtesy Barbara Rosplock-Van Orman.

Tina (1953), #29, Kindergarten School series. Vogue brochure.

Dawn (1953), #30, Kindergarten School series, in a pink cotton pinafore dress with decorative band depicting teddy bear and balls, etc. Pink hair ribbon. Purse and plastic shoes not original. Courtesy Marlene Dantzer.

Pat (1953), #31, Kindergarten School series. Vogue brochure.

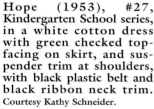

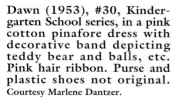

Nan (1953) #32, Kindergarten School series, in a frilly lavender cotton pinafore dress edged with eyelet and pink rickrack. Pink hair ribbon.

Twin Series

Hansel and Gretel (1953), #33 and #34, Twin series, wearing white organdy tops with ribbon ties at wrists and magenta velveteen cloth hats. Hansel wears velveteen shorts and Gretel's skirt is trimmed with multi-colored ribbons.

Dutch Boy (1953), #35, Twin series. Vogue brochure.

Dutch Girl (1953), #36, Twin series, wearing long blue dress with organdy apron and eyelet trim and shoulder ties. Dutch cap matches apron. Also wears wooden shoes. Matches Dutch Boy #35. Courtesy Barbara Rosplock-Van Orman.

Cowboy (1953), #37, Twin series. Vogue brochure.

Cowgirl (1953), #38, Twin series wearing felt skirt and vest with silk-screened western design, green boots, and chartreuse felt cowgirl hat complete the outfit. Vogue pink box with ink spot label. Courtesy Judy Ormsbee.

Tiny Miss Series

Lucy (1953), #39, Tiny Miss series, wearing green and white cotton fern print dress with white organdy apron edged with lace. Peach straw hat with green bow, green center snap shoes. Courtesy Peggy Millhouse.

Wanda (1953), #40, Tiny Miss series, wearing white cotton dress with yellow flower print and ribbon laced trim and gathered eyelet on sleeves. Yellow straw hat with matching black velvet trim.

June (1953), #41, Tiny Miss series, wearing white organdy dress with plaid bands on the gathered skirt, square neck bodice with red rickrack trim. Red straw hat has white and navy bands around the brim. Courtesy Peggy Millhouse.

Glad (1953), #42, Tiny Miss series, wearing red pinafore dress with white band trim, red and green berries trim waist and green straw hat. Hat also shown with rounded crown.

Beryl (1953), #43, Tiny Miss series, wearing dress with pink and black cotton checked skirt and pale pink organdy top trimmed with lace. Black velvet ribbon ties at wrists and in a bow at the neck. Peach straw hat has a black woven band.

Cheryl (1953), #44, Tiny Miss series, wearing blue taffeta dress with pleated taffeta band at the skirt hem, silver braid trim on cap sleeves and skirt band. Straw hat and bodice are decorated with a spray of flowers. Notice silver wrist tag. Courtesy Ann Tardie.

Gadabout Series

Ballet (1953), #45, wearing multi-colored ribbon and net tutu skirt over gathered net, with top and skirt trimmed with silver braid. Separate panties with net underskirt attached. Flowers trim the waist and headband. Outfit called "Rainbow Ballerina" by collectors and is hard to find in good condition due to fragile nature of net and ribbon. Outfit came with silver slippers. Courtesy Barbara Hill.

TV (1953), #46, wearing lounging outfit of black velvet pants and polished cotton coral top with black velvet collar and cuffs with gold picot trim. Gold belt and slippers, and eyeglasses complete the outfit.

Roller Skater (1953), #47, wearing purple velvet costume with gold flowers and braided fringe trim, matching headband. Outfit is hard to find in good condition since it was prone to cracking. Courtesy Barbara Rosplock-Van Orman.

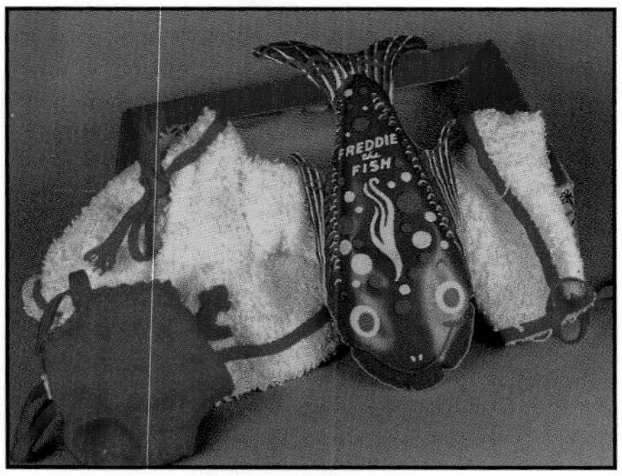

Beach (1953), #48, boxed separate outfit with red knit swimsuit, terry cloth robe and hood with inflated Freddie the Fish as shown in the 1953 Vogue brochure. The outfit was sold with a blue knit swimsuit and robe variation in 1954 for Fun Time dressed doll #48.

Ski (1953), #49, Gadabouts series. Vogue brochure.

Ice Skater (1953,) #50, wearing red velveteen costume with attached pants, fur and silver rickrack trim, matching headband and white skates. Courtesy Barbara Rosplock-Van Orman.

Fable and Bride Series

Red Riding Hood (1953), #52 and Bo Peep #53, Fable and Bride series. Vogue brochure.

Mistress Mary (1953), #54, Fable and Bride series, wears a blue taffeta dress with pleated net edging on hem and matching pantalettes. Flowers trim the hem and the straw hat. Missing plastic watering can. Outfit has also been shown with pleated net trim on the hat brim.

Alice (in Wonderland) (1953), #51, Fable and Bride series, wearing pale blue taffeta dress with white organdy apron trimmed with ruffled eyelet. Black velvet ribbon trims the skirt and adorns the hair. Hard to find in original blue, most fade to lavender. Courtesy Kathy Bailey.

Bride (1953), #55, Fable and Bride series, in satin long-waisted gown with gathered lace skirt, white waist. The original headpiece was a white satin peaked band trimmed with lace and tulle veil. Courtesy Barbara Rosplock-Van Orman.

Bridesmaid (1953), #56, Fable and Bride series, wears a pink taffeta gown with a ruffled collar and overskirt both of pink tulle; an open crown nylon and straw hat trimmed with flowers. Mint in box with original tag. Courtesy Barbara Rosplock-Van Orman.

Debutante Series

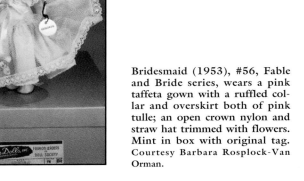

Pamela (1953), #60, Debutante series, in pink organdy skirted dress with woven ribbon and lace trim at hem, green velvet top, and flower trim on plastic purse, at waist, and on distinctive straw hat tied with green ribbon.

Cathy (1953), #61, Debutante series, in coin dotted organdy dress with beaded braid and ruffled lace trim and a black velvet waist tie. The straw hat and dress hem are trimmed with a flower bouquet. Courtesy Judy Ormsbee.

Becky (1953), #62, Debutante series, in white embroidered dress with a black velvet bodice. Pink purse and bodice are trimmed with roses and the black straw hat is tied with pink satin ribbon. Courtesy Robi Blute.

Karen (1953), #63, Debutante series, in pinafore dress with apron and straw hat with flowers. Vogue brochure.

Ginger (1953), #64, Debutante series, in red velvet dress with embroidered flower band and red cherries on the purse and matching hat which also has a white feather trim. In pink box with silver tag and brochure. Courtesy Robi Blute.

Angela (1953), #65, Debutante series, in full-skirted dress of blue cotton with a white organdy blouse, trimmed with pink and blue embroidered band, a black silk bow, and a bouquet of flowers. Courtesy Peggy Millhouse.

Talon Zipper Series

Talon Zipper series (1953). Four of the six outfits in series (from left): Afternoon #73; #71 P.M. blue flowered percale robe; #70 AM blue denim jeans; #74 Party white nylon dress with lace ruffles.

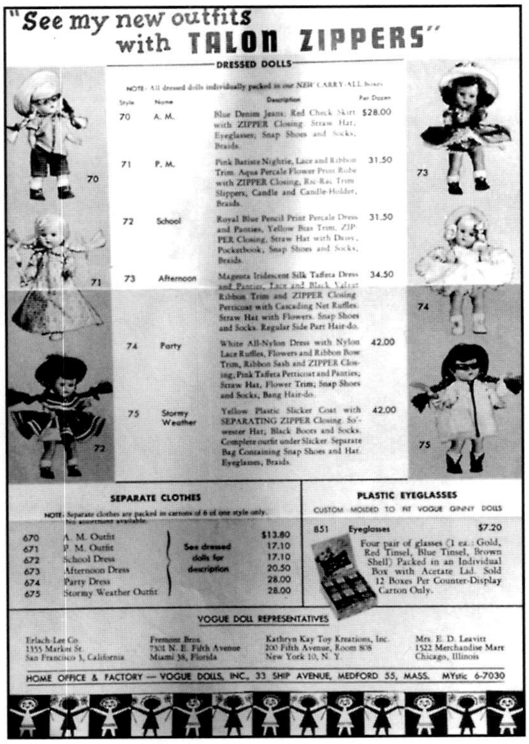

"See my new outfits with TALON ZIPPERS"

DRESSED DOLLS

NOTE: All dressed dolls individually packed in our NEW CARRY-ALL Boxes

Style	Name	Description	Per Dozen
70	A. M.	Blue Denim Jeans; Red Check Skirt with ZIPPER Closing; Straw Hat; Eyeglasses; Snap Shoes and Socks; Braids.	$28.00
71	P. M.	Pink Batiste Nightie, Lace and Ribbon Trim. Aqua Percale Flower Print Robe with ZIPPER Closing, Ric-Rac Trim Slippers, Candle and Candle-Holder, Braids.	31.50
72	School	Royal Blue Pencil Print Percale Dress and Panties, Yellow Bias Trim, ZIPPER Closing, Straw Hat with Daisy, Pocketbook, Snap Shoes and Socks, Braids.	31.50
73	Afternoon	Magenta Iridescent Silk Taffeta Dress and Panties, Lace and Black Velvet Ribbon Trim and ZIPPER Closing. Petticoat with Cascading Net Ruffles. Straw Hat with Flowers. Snap Shoes and Socks. Regular Side Part Hair-do.	34.50
74	Party	White All-Nylon Dress with Nylon Lace Ruffles, Flowers and Ribbon Bow Trim, Ribbon Sash and ZIPPER Closing; Pink Taffeta Petticoat and Panties; Straw Hat, Flower Trim; Snap Shoes and Socks, Bang Hair-do.	42.00
75	Stormy Weather	Yellow Plastic Slicker Coat with SEPARATING ZIPPER Closing. So'-wester Hat; Black Boots and Socks. Complete outfit under Slicker. Separate Bag Containing Snap Shoes and Hat. Eyeglasses, Braids.	42.00

SEPARATE CLOTHES

NOTE: Separate clothes are packed in cartons of 6 of one style only. No assortment available.

670	A. M. Outfit	See dressed dolls for description	$13.80
671	P. M. Outfit		17.10
672	School Dress		17.10
673	Afternoon Dress		20.50
674	Party Dress		28.00
675	Stormy Weather Outfit		28.00

PLASTIC EYEGLASSES

CUSTOM MOLDED TO FIT VOGUE GINNY DOLLS

851 Eyeglasses $7.20

Four pair of glasses (1 ea.: Gold, Red Tinsel, Blue Tinsel, Brown Shell) Packed in an Individual Box with Acetate Lid. Sold 12 Boxes Per Counter-Display Carton Only.

VOGUE DOLL REPRESENTATIVES

Erlach-Lee Co.
1355 Market St.
San Francisco 3, California

Fremont Bros.
7301 N. E. Fifth Avenue
Miami 38, Florida

Kathryn Kay Toy Kreations, Inc.
200 Fifth Avenue, Room 808
New York 10, N. Y.

Mrs. E. D. Leavitt
1522 Merchandise Mart
Chicago, Illinois

HOME OFFICE & FACTORY — VOGUE DOLLS, INC., 33 SHIP AVENUE, MEDFORD 55, MASS. MYstic 6-7030

Talon Zipper series (1953). Vogue flyer sent to merchants promoting complete series of six outfits. Notice eyeglasses on bottom right. Courtesy Virginia Graves Carlson.

Stormy Weather (1953), #75, Talon Zipper series, yellow plastic slicker with a separate pack containing snap shoes and hat. Courtesy Sandy Johnson-Barts.

Afternoon (1953), #73, Talon Zipper series, in magenta iridescent silk taffeta dress and panties, lace and black velvet ribbon trim, zipper closing. Petticoat with cascading ruffles. Straw hat with flowers. Courtesy Robi Blute.

Party (1953), #74, Talon Zipper series, shown on two dolls as described in sales flyer, "White all-nylon dress with nylon lace ruffles, flowers and ribbon bow trim ribbon sash and zipper closing, pink taffeta petticoat and panties, straw hat, flower trim."

Special Dolls

"Colored" (1953), undressed doll, a rare example of a mint in the box undressed black Ginny. Note Vogue's designation of "colored" doll. Courtesy Ann Tardie.

Coronation Queen (1953), special doll issued to commemorate the coronation of Queen Elizabeth II of England. Complete and all original including exceptional beading on the gown and the replica of St. Edward's Crown. Courtesy Shirley's Dollhouse.

Coronation Queen (1953), in brocade gown beaded with pearls and sequins across the front. Fur-trimmed purple cape is fastened with gold ties. Metal scepter with handmade medallion. This box (with its plastic cover not shown) was also used in 1954. Courtesy Maureen Fukushima.

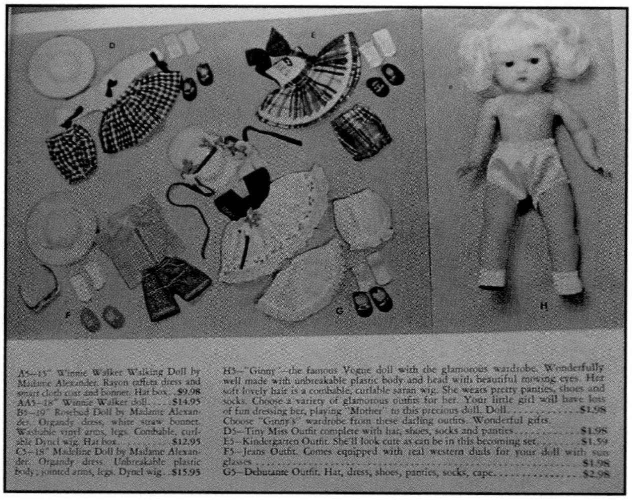

Advertisement for undressed Ginny wearing vinyl shoes, and separate outfits (1953). Herpolsheimer's (Grand Rapids, Michigan) Christmas catalog. Courtesy Marge Meisinger.

Furniture

E-Z-Do Cabinet (1953 and 1954) #850 (wooden doors and cardboard interior). Called E-Z-Do Wardrobe in 1954. Shown with Jill clothes.

Straight Leg Walker Ginny

1954

Painted Lash

Description: 8" all hard plastic, sleep eye, painted lashes, walker with turning head mechanism, Dynel wig.

Marks: Head: VOGUE
Back: GINNY/VOGUE DOLLS/ INC./PAT. PEND./MADE IN U.S.A. Some dolls have the patent number on their back.

Dress labels: Clothing had white rayon labels with black print, "Vogue Dolls Inc./Medford, Mass., U.S.A./*Reg U.S. Pat. Off."; labels were sewn into the inside of the outfit, usually at the waist in the back.

Dress closures: Hooks and eyes.

Tags: Round, silver, hanging wrist tags were still used in 1954 on some dolls, however, white tags encircling the wrist reading, "Hi! I'm Ginny," were on some dolls as well.

Boxes: Hot pink, white, and black Vogue paper doll logo with black end labels with white writing "Hi! I'm Ginny ®."

Innovations And Growth

In 1954 Vogue was clearly established as one of the most successful doll companies in the country, competitive with much larger companies. In fact, Madame Alexander was clearly positioning their 8" doll against the Ginny Doll. However, Vogue's doll captured the mid-priced market, and she was the doll that was truly played with by little owners. Vogue could have remained content with this success, but, instead continually sought ways to grow and maintain their sales momentum.

Vogue realized that one way to keep customers interested in the doll, and to give them a reason to buy another doll, was to periodically introduce a new feature. This is what they had done with the sleep eyes in 1950, and then with the various improved, "comb, curl, and set," glued-on wigs in 1951 – 53. These features were too popular to change, nor did they want to change the washable, unbreakable, hard plastic construction of the doll. However, they decided that what they could do to enhance the product was to introduce a Ginny that could walk.

John Flanagan, a Vogue driver who delivered material to the home sewers, remembers being called into Mrs. Graves's office one day. Mrs. Graves was there with Alvin Fuller, Mrs. Graves's uncle, and Chet Lawson, of Lawson Machine and Tool Co. They took the walking Ginny out of the vault and asked him what he thought of the doll before they put the doll on the market. Apparently, they were pleased with his and others' responses, because in 1954 they produced a straight leg walking doll, utilizing a new patent, jointed at the hip, whose head turned from side to side as it walked.

The new doll looked just like the darling little toddler doll, so popular the previous year. It still had sleep eyes and painted eyelashes. However, the walking mechanism gave it a slightly stiff look, and it could not be posed as easily as the strung version. Fortunately, this did not hinder sales. In fact, in general, the walking Ginny was as popular as ever, and growth had not yet peaked. The company had a well-thought-out image for the doll, and their customers, both big and little, loved the doll.

In 1954 Mrs. Graves's daughter, Virginia, was married to Mr. Stanley Carlson and she continued her role as chief dress designer at Vogue, producing a lovely collection of outfits for Ginny.

Wardrobe, Special Styles, And Accessories

Wardrobe: The walking mechanism in the 1954 doll necessitated a change in the doll's foot wear. The center snap shoes had already proven to be fragile, and they certainly would not provide enough traction for the doll's walking. Therefore, Vogue switched to vinyl shoes in 1954. Unfortunately, the new shoes were not available to be photographed for the 1954 brochure, so the company cleverly drew the shoes on the doll for the cover photograph. However, on the inside of the brochure, the dolls had center snap shoes with the new outfits. This can be confusing to the collector. To add to the confusion, some of the 1954 dolls were actually issued with the center snap shoes, using up existing stock. For the record, vinyl shoes were the ones intended to go with 1954 outfits. The 1954 vinyl shoes marked "Ginny" had a smooth, flat bottom which was different from the 1955 shoes which had a heel.

In 1954, Vogue produced over 50 different outfits for Ginny. They also advertised, "....sun, rain and snow outfits, play clothes, school dresses, dainty nylon lace party dress...I'm the best dressed doll in the world!" They advertised that "trimming, flowers, and hats are imported from fashion centers in Europe." The fine outfit design and detail by Mrs. Graves's daughter, Virginia, combined with sewing talents of the ever-growing pool of home sewers, to produce a wonderful assortment of Ginny costumes in 1954. One of Ginny's most unique fashions from 1954 – 1955 was a Davy Crockett outfit featuring a fur hat with a special button.

Separate boxed outfits, vinyl shoes, hats, etc., were sold for all of the 1954 styles. These sales were very important to the company since they had a higher margin of profit than the dolls themselves.

Special styles: Notably, the Candy Dandy series of six dolls, #51 – 56, was introduced, with a variety of lace and ribbon trimmed dresses and coordinating straw hats.

Also, six My First Corsage Styles, #60 – 65, included beautiful printed organdy Bride and Bridesmaid gowns, as well as a delightful collection of four dresses with frilly petticoats trimmed with bright ribbon, peaking out from under full skirts. Each one carried a plastic corsage case with flowers. The new Whiz Kids group included three of the Talon Zipper styles: A.M. (#70); Stormy Weather (#75); and Party, (#74); plus three new creative styles with zippers, #71 – 73. However, the popular Debutante series of 1951 and 1952 disappeared, as did the Fable characters (e.g., Red Riding Hood, etc.) for the first time since the composition Toddles doll. Today, these discontinued series are very much in demand by collectors.

Accessories: The line of Ginny accessories was numerous in 1954. A plastic case with curlers and a cosmetic cape could be purchased for the new Dynel wigs. An unfitted train case #823; fitted wardrobe trunk #826; and weekender suitcase #829, the Trip Mates #830 were issued in a plaid vinyl that was to become a popular Ginny accessory material. One of the most popular new items was Ginny's little puppy #831, a stuffed toy by Steiff, destined to be one of the most popular collectibles, next to Ginny.

Furniture: The E-Z-Do Wardrobe #850 was continued in brown wood and Vogue introduced pink Ginny furniture with a youth bed, table, and chairs. A pink clothes-tree with a Ginny cut-out face design on top was sold, and it is almost impossible to find intact today.

Marketing

In 1954, the new brochure featuring the doll's outfits read, "Hi! I'm Ginny – Now I walk!" A flyer was also placed in each box with clear instructions about how to make Ginny walk "just like any little girl walks....Besides walking I sit, stand, and sleep." Thus, Ginny was still presented as a little companion, just like themselves.

Another flyer included in merchandise that year was from Ginny who announced, "You can have me with either brown or blue eyes and my hair comes in lovely shades of blonde, brunette or auburn. You can buy me with either bangs or pigtails....." They continued to emphasize the beautiful hair, and switched to life-like Dynel wigs in 1954. However, the unusual hairstyles of the early fifties, for the most part, were gone, as was the variety of colors of the eyes from the transitional years. However, the plastic was of a very good quality and a healthy looking color, though perhaps somewhat shinier. The cheek color was bright. It should be noted that, while Vogue advertised two eye colors, blue is much easier to find than brown today, probably reflecting production demands.

We notice in the 1954 brochure that, for the first time, Vogue did not assign first names or character names to the dolls. This was entirely consistent with the campaign to call all of the dolls Ginny, rather than individual names. Also, this undoubtedly simplified record keeping for Vogue.

Vogue continued the new logo in 1954 with the paper doll pattern on bright fuchsia boxes. However, they returned to lids, rather than Carry All boxes. The "Hi! I'm Ginny!" theme was continued on all box labels and literature, as well as the Fashion Leaders in Doll Society. Dressed doll boxes were wider than undressed doll boxes.

In 1954 Ginny was still the leader in the mid-priced doll market, and Vogue was growing and prospering.

Prices
Straight Leg Walker

Year Produced	Outfit	Mint Price
1954	Ginny, All original	$350.00+
	Tiny Miss/Kinder Crowd	$275.00
	Fun Time/Rain or Shine	$275.00 – 300.00
	My First Corsage	$350.00 – 400.00
	Candy Dandy	$300.00 – 350.00
	Whiz Kids	$275.00 – 300.00
	Black Ginny	$1,800.00+
	Coronation Queen	$750.00+
	MIB Coronation Queen	$1,300.00
Accessories:	Ginny's Pup	$225.00+
Special:	Davy Crockett	$500.00
Outfits (Mint in Box)		
	School, sports and play outfits	$100.00
	Party and fancy outfits	$115.00

Undressed Ginny (1954), #5, with auburn braids shown in special lift-out box. The pink paper with walking instructions was included in the box by Vogue since this was the first year the walking Ginny was offered. Courtesy Veronica Phillips.

My Kinder Crowd Dresses

My Kinder Crowd Dresses (1954), #22, blue and white nautical dress with red felt anchor trim. The 1954 Dynel wig had thicker braids than previous years. Courtesy Ann Tardie.

My Kinder Crowd Dresses (1954), #25, green organdy square neck dress with green velvet trim and linen flowers on the skirt. A green satin bow is stapled to the wig which is set in a flip style with bangs. White plastic shoes.

My Kinder Crowd Dresses (1954), #21 – 26. Vogue brochure.

For Rain or Shine

For Rain or Shine (1954), #27 – 32. Vogue brochure.

For Rain or Shine (1954), #29, striped overalls with denim shirt and trim. Courtesy Judy Ormsbee.

For Rain or Shine (1954), #31, nurse's uniform with hot water bottle and brochure. Mint in box. Courtesy Peggy Millhouse.

For Rain or Shine (1954), #32, dotted cotton organdy dress with red hem and woven trim, tie on vinyl polka dot rain cape. Red suede boots.

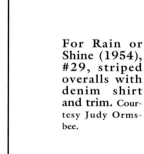

My Twin Sets

My Twin sets (1954), #33 – 238. Vogue brochure.

My Twin sets 1954), #38, Cowgirl, and #237 Cowboy, wearing green felt skirt or chaps, coral cotton top, chartreuse hat, yellow ribbon neckties, gold belts and tie-on cuffs, plastic toy gun, and green boots. This outfit was also issued in the 1953 Twin series.

My Tiny Miss Styles

My Tiny Miss styles (1954), (from left), #40, plaid cotton and white organdy top dress with felt vest; #41, pineapple cotton print dress; #43, bright pink pinafore with pink print dress; #42, green print dress with felt tie vest.

My Tiny Miss styles (1954), #39, cotton stripe dress with red patent belt and vinyl Scottie dog trim. Missing straw hat. Courtesy Shirley Niziolek.

My Tiny Miss styles (1954), #44. Vogue brochure.

For Fun Time

#45 Ballerina (1954), For Fun Time series, with white net tutu and net over taffeta bodice trimmed with silver braid edging. Silver tie slippers. Headband of silver leatherette petals and velvet flowers. Also came with a silver metallic snood head covering.

#46 Tennis (1954), For Fun Time series, with green tennis design knit jacket and cap, white tennis dress with green rickrack trim. Doll is newer than dress. Racket is replaced. Courtesy Shirley Niziolek.

#47 Roller skater (1954), For Fun Time series, in two-piece velveteen backed fabric with tied-on skirt; matching hat and costume are trimmed with gold braid and gold fringe is on the skirt and bodice. Suede cloth roller skates.

#347 Roller skater outfit (1954), For Fun Time series, in one-piece version with knit panties. This is an example of how Vogue would occasionally vary a pattern.

#48 Beach outfit (1954), For Fun Time series, blue knit swimsuit with sailboat design, white terry cloth jacket and hat lined with coral cotton. Missing a Freddie the Fish inflated toy (shown under accessories).

#49 For Fun Time (1954). Vogue brochure.

#50 Ice Skater (1954), For Fun Time series, outfit of green velveteen backed fabric with silver rickrack edging and silver braid and fur trim on skirt hem. Fur headband with silver braid ties on. Doll is a newer doll. Courtesy Shirley Niziolek.

The Candy Dandy Series

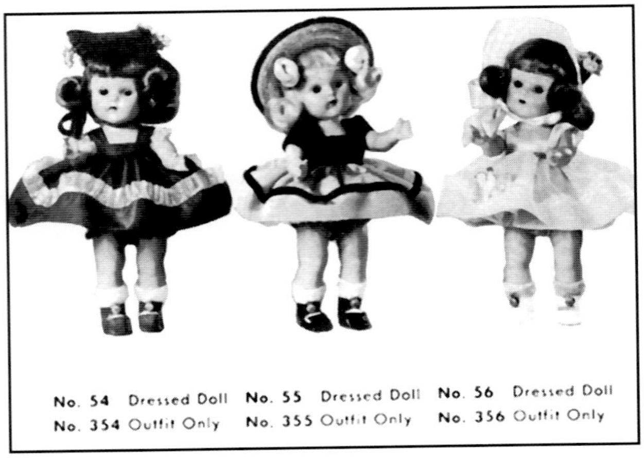

The Candy Dandy series (1954), #51 – 56. Vogue brochure.

The Candy Dandy series (1954), #52, printed organdy dress trimmed with yellow and green band and ruffles at neckline and hem. Missing yellow straw hat. Courtesy Shirley Niziolek.

The Candy Dandy series (1954), #53, hot pink polished cotton dress with lace trim at hem and on shoulder. Black velvet ribbon ties at the waist and around the straw hat crown.

My First Corsage Styles

My First Corsage styles (1954), #61, green and pink flowered cotton skirt with matching peach taffeta top and straw hat. All outfits in this series had satin ribbon trimmed petticoats and an acetate corsage case. Courtesy Judy Ormsbee.

My First Corsage styles (1954), #60, (on left), red organdy party dress with lace trim and coordinating net slip with red and white ribbon trim. Red straw hat with white woven border and embroidered butterfly trim. Carries a plastic case with flower corsage. (On right) #63 gold velveteen square neck party dress with black iridescent silk taffeta skirt, net slip with gold and green ribbon trim, black straw hat with flower trim, and a plastic corsage box with flower inside.

My First Corsage styles (1954), #62. Vogue brochure.

My First Corsage styles (1954), (on left), #65, bridesmaid gown of pink printed organdy with lace and ribbon trim and a straw hat with flowers and pleated net trim. Bride #64 (in center) in white long sleeved gown, sweetpea trim, and lace cap.

The Whiz Kids Group

The Whiz Kids group (1954), #70, denim short pants, red check shirt with zipper, straw hat. Glasses not shown. This outfit was also sold as 1953's Talon Zipper outfit #70 A.M., and 1955's Merry Moppets #34. Courtesy Barbara Rosplock-Van Orman.

The Whiz Kids group (1954), #71, #72. Vogue brochure.

The Whiz Kids group (1954), #73, lounging outfit of yellow velvet slacks trimmed in gold picot with polished cotton top with fur trim and zippered front. Gold slippers and belt, and glasses. Headband not shown.

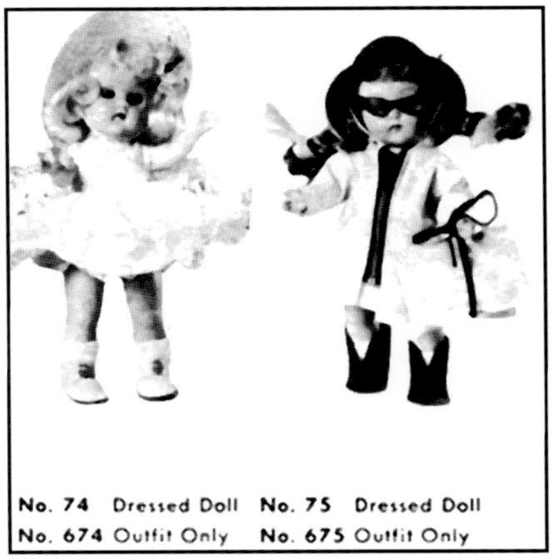

The Whiz Kids group (1954), #74, #75. Vogue brochure.

Special

Hawaiian Ginny (1954), #80, outfit comes with a grass skirt, two-piece cotton shorts and halter top, flower hair trim and necklace. Courtesy Tina Ritari.

Coronation Queen (1954), in same brocade gown as 1953 except that beading on front was eliminated. Fur trimmed purple velvet cape, metal crown and scepter. This box (with its plastic cover not shown) was also used in 1954. Courtesy Barbara Rosplock-Van Orman.

Hawaiian Ginny (1954), #80, box showing label. Note there is no designation as a colored doll as on the box of the undressed black Ginny. Courtesy Tina Ritari.

Separates

Another Ginny Fashion separate (1954 – 56), aqua dress with black ribbon and flower at waist has 1954 – 56 rayon tag. In original package. Cost 89¢.

Separates (1954), #181, brown and white checked cotton coat with brown straw hat, sold separately.

No. 282
FELT COAT
For colder days you will love my rose or blue colored felt coat with matching fur trimmed hat.
No. 383
VELVET COAT
For very special occasions I like to wear my fur trimmed red or green velvet princess coat, hat and muff of white fur.
No. 484
FUR COAT
I'll be nice and warm in my white bunny coat, hat and muff.

Coats (1954). Vogue brochure.

Accessories

Trip Mates (1954), #830. Cover of Ginny's travel accessories. Courtesy Mary Davis.

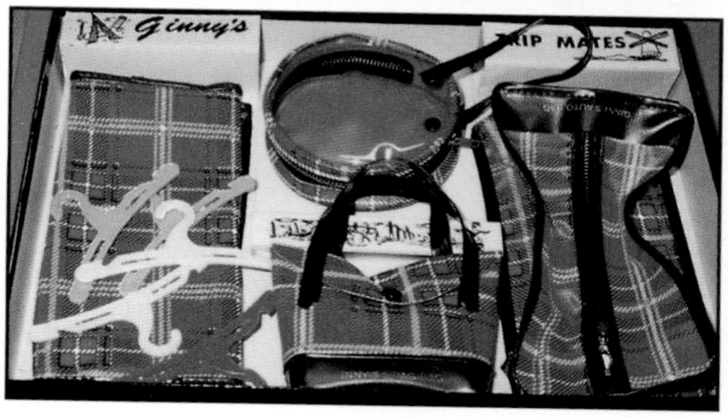

Trip Mates (1954), #830, Ginny's garment bag with hangers, car bag for traveling, a swag bag, and a hat bag in a plaid vinyl. Courtesy Mary Davis.

Ginny's Shoe Bag and Shoes (1954) (center), #842, holds two pair of shoes. Could be attached to E-Z-Do Wardrobe door with thumb tacks. Freddie the Fish inflated toy, For Fun Time #48 beach outfit (on left); package of roller skates (1955), #848 (on right).

Ginny's Pup (1954 – 55), #831, Steiff pup with ear tag, plaid plastic coat, black leash, bow, and bell. Courtesy Shirley's Dollhouse.

Ginny's Glasses (1954 – 55) #851; (1956) #6851; (1957) #7851, sold in set of four different colors. Courtesy Veronica Phillips.

Straight Leg Walker Ginny

Molded Lash
(1955 – 1956)

Description: 8", hard plastic, sleep eyes with plastic molded lashes, straight leg walker, head turns, wigs of Dynel and Saran.
Marks: Head: VOGUE
Body: GINNY/VOGUE DOLLS/INC./PAT NO. 2687594/MADE IN U.S.A.
Dress closures: Hooks and eyes.
Dress labels: Black print on white rayon ribbon, same as 1954;
VOGUE DOLL, INC.*/MEDFORD, MASS. U.S.A./*Reg.U.S. Pat Off
Tags: Same as 1954, round white paper tag circling the wrist, with pink print:
"Hi! I'm Ginny" with outfit number.
Boxes: Fuchsia, white and black Vogue paper doll design with pink end labels with white writing "Hi! I'm Ginny ®." Clothing came in Vogue hot pink window boxes with paper doll logo on side.

Innovations And Growth

In 1955 – 1956 Vogue added yet another improvement to their doll, molded eyelashes. The painted eyelashes from 1953 and 1954 faded with play and washing, so Vogue decided that the plastic molded lashes would add to the durability of the doll. The plastic used in the doll had good color, but some of the cheek coloring was not as bright as previous years. Some felt that the plastic lashes took away from the, sweet, wide-eyed, look of the painted lashes, but sales continued to grow, and Vogue was pleased with its improved doll.

In 1955 – 56, Vogue expanded their line of accessories and introduced a new doll, Ginnette, in 1955 as Ginny's baby sister. Vogue was really growing at this time.

Also in December of 1956, Mrs. Graves gained national prominence when she was asked to speak to 3,500 industrialists at the Annual Congress of American Industry, about the taxation of small businesses. She was the first woman ever to address the group. Clearly, she was a pioneer not only in the doll world, but also a woman of action in the business world!

Wardrobe, Special Styles, And Accessories

Wardrobe: In 1955 and 1956, while the plastic eyelashes were the newest feature, Vogue still continued to emphasize fashion as its main asset. On the cover of the 1955 brochure Ginny asks, "Hi!... I'm Ginny, what shall I wear today? See all my beautiful clothes." The Fashion Leaders in Doll Society theme had worked as a motto since the 1940s, and Vogue wisely stayed with their strength. Also, in 1956 Joan Cornette joined Vogue as a dress designer and contributed greatly, adding many new looks to the line. Her role was to expand as her excellent design talent was recognized by Vogue.

Once again Vogue revised the way categories of outfits were named. The term "Series" and "Group" were not part of the title itself. Instead, titles were kept very simple. For example, My Kinder Crowd Dresses in 1954 was simply called Kindercrowd in 1955 and 1956, offering, once again, charming cotton or organdy dresses with matching hair bows. However, other outfits were being phased out, such as the innovative zipper outfits. By 1955, only two of the original 1953 Talon Zipper outfits were shown. The dungaree outfit with red checked zipper shirt, formerly A.M. #70 in 1953, became Merry Moppets #34 in 1955. The Stormy Weather #75, a yellow zippered rain slicker, was sold as a separate, #182, in 1955. The Talon Zipper outfits were dropped altogether in 1956. Again, this demonstrates how Vogue continued to simplify and streamline in response to competitive pressures.

Vogue also began to cut costs in ways that were not obvious to Ginny fans. Outfits would be designed with one less pleat or buttons were eliminated. Through this economizing Vogue could continue to produce mid-priced dolls. In fact, to further cater to the cost conscious market, a budget line of dresses, #188, was added. Unfortunately, some regular dressed doll outfits also began to have an unadorned look. However, this was not true of most outfits, and the dress line was actually expanded.

Special styles: In this process of updating outfits, Vogue did add some very desirable and popular categories. One notable new title was Bon-Bons #80 – 85, produced in 1955 only, which featured six frilly nylon party dresses, and plastic parasols in coordinating colors. Added in 1956 were the very popular Formals #6060 – 6065, featuring lovely taffeta and net 3/4 length gowns, and imaginative velvet head pieces, hard to find today. Also added in 1956 was Debs # 6070 – 6075, a collection of beautiful full-length gowns with coordinating hats. Both of these collections offer lovely design and detail.

Furniture and Accessories: To spur profits, Vogue counted on sales from an increased line of accessories. A gym set #925 was added in 1955, encouraging several dolls to be purchased to play together. Also new was a hardwood wardrobe finished in pink and white enamel and monogrammed with Ginny's name and picture #922; matching chair #920; and bed #910 with personalized bedding #912. The ultimate accessory in 1956 was Ginny's own dollhouse complete with a doghouse for her pup. The dollhouse was made of cardboard printed with white shingles, red trim, and blue roof. Even green shrubbery grew around the sides.

Fabulous fitted wardrobe cases were also available, such as #865, with Ginny in an ice skating costume, along with five outfits and pajamas and an unfitted case #864, "...big enough to hold me and lots of my clothes." The years 1955 – 56 were truly growth ones for Vogue's accessories.

Marketing

Vogue seemed to have made all of the right marketing decisions for her doll in an increasingly competitive field. By 1955 every little Ginny owner bought five outfits each year for her little doll. Ginny's wonderful clothes and adorable toddler features were still very appealing to children. Letters sent to Vogue confirmed that children enjoyed their little doll, a playmate who could wear pretty clothes one minute, skate and ski the next, and then suddenly become a cowgirl. Society at the time strongly advocated children having good manners and dressing properly, and Ginny could share that behavior, and yet be as playful and active as any child could imagine.

However, in 1955 – 56 Vogue began to be affected by other companies who had increased production of separate outfits, attracting the very market which Vogue had created. In response, Vogue advised on their 1955 brochure: "Look for this label.... you'll be sure you are buying outfits that are made to fit me perfectly." Nonetheless, lost sales were beginning to be felt, and this began to have some impact on the design of Vogue outfits in general. Admirably, Vogue never resorted to lowering their high marketing standards, and never sold to discount stores.

To maintain their growth, Vogue created a number of marketing innovations in 1956. These innovations were:

1. The beginning of the Ginny Doll Club. Members were encouraged to write to Ginny, and received a "Hi! I'm Ginny!" button for joining as well as a newsletter.
2. Production, in cooperation with *Parents' Magazine*, of an educational advertising short film, "The Dolls In Your Life," hosted by Faye Emerson. It was shown around the country and to groups touring Vogue's factory. Unfortunately, it was not used as a commercial on television. The decision not to advertise on television would later prove to be detrimental to Vogue.
3. A multitude of store promotions, coloring contests, and fashion shows were sponsored around the country.
4. Mrs. Graves continued to visit with celebrities and have their photos sent to newspapers in order to garner publicity for her dolls.

Vogue continued to use the bright pink box and lid with paper doll design. The labels with logo was the same as 1954: "Hi! I'm Ginny; Fashion Leaders in Doll Society," printed on the label.

By the end of 1956, Ginny sales were strong, but Vogue was implementing cost cutting measures, as well as marketing initiatives, to stay ahead of the competitors and to maintain their strong mid-priced lead in the doll market. The name Ginny was still magic in the doll world.

Prices

Straight Leg Walker Ginny Dolls (1955 – 56)

Year Produced	Type/Outfit	Mint Price
1955 – 1956	Ginny/All original	$225.00 – 350.00+
1955	Bon-Bons	$400.00+
1955	Davy Crockett	$500.00
1956	Formals/Debs	$350.00 – 400.00
	12 Star Plan	$250.00 each
Boxed Outfits (Mint-In-Box)		
1955 – 56	School/Play/Sports	$70.00
	Formals/Debs	$95.00
Accessories		
	Furniture	$45.00 – 75.00
	Trousseau Tree	$175.00
	Gym Set	$500.00+
	House	$1,200.00
	Trousseau Chest	$1,500.00
1955	Heart Shaped Chair, #920	$75.00
	Wardrobe, #922	$60.00 – 70.00
	Dream Cozy, #912	$75.00
	Skates, #847	$30.00
	Trunk, #860	$600.00+
1956	Bed, #6910	$60.00 – 65.00
	Rocking Chair, #6914	$75.00
	Wardrobe, #6922	$75.00
	Christmas Stocking, #6834	$400.00+
	Ginny and Mother pearls	$75.00

Cover of 1955 Vogue brochure.

Kinder Crowd (1955) (left to right) #21 – 26. Dressed dolls are numbered #21+; outfits only #121+. Vogue brochure.

Kinder Crowd (1955), #21, in a black and white cotton dress with white rolled collar, accented with a green vinyl belt and shoes. A white ribbon was sold with outfit.

Kinder Crowd (1955), #24, wearing red organdy full skirt dress with white organdy hem trimmed with white lace at bodice, waist, and sleeves. Red vinyl shoes and a red bow were shown in the brochure on a molded lash walker.

Kinder Crowd (1955), #26, wearing lavender organdy dress with lace bow at the bodice. Pink bow is original to the outfit and was included with boxed outfits sold separately. Courtesy Shirley's Dollhouse.

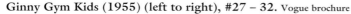

Ginny Gym Kids (1955) (left to right), #27 – 32. Vogue brochure

Ginny Gym Kids (1955), #28, wearing navy shorts outfit with red and white striped trim, white blouse, white vinyl belt and red felt hat with a white pompon. Note the red vinyl pup on the shorts. Courtesy Kathy Schneider.

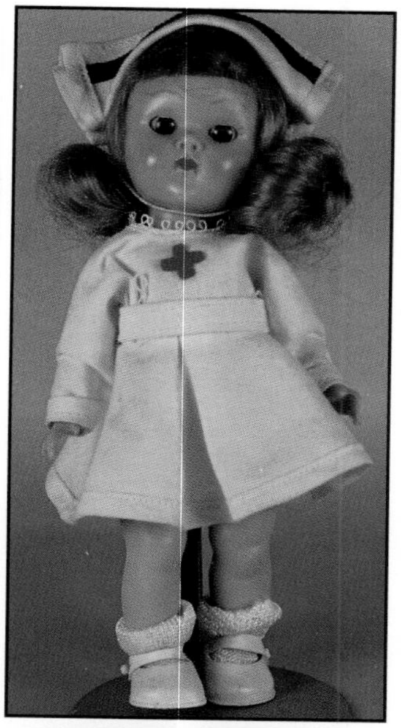

Ginny Gym Kids (1955), #31, nurse's outfit with a red felt cross and white picot neck trim. Matching cap has a black braid trim. Missing long cotton stockings. Should be on molded lash walker. Courtesy Shirley Niziolek.

Ginny Gym Kids (1955), #32, chartreuse romper outfit trimmed with red rickrack and matching felt hat. Shown in 1955 brochure on molded lash walker. Courtesy Shirley Niziolek.

Merry Moppets (1955) (left to right), #33 – 38. Vogue brochure.

Merry Moppets (1955), #33, chartreuse cotton chintz dress with suspender design, black vinyl belt, and brown and white checked cotton blouse.

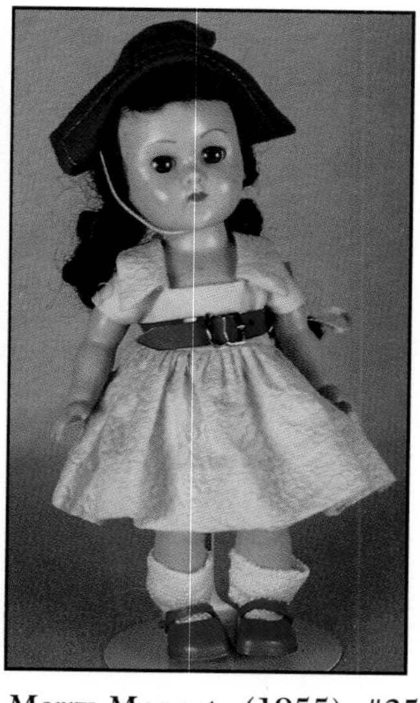

Merry Moppets (1955), #35, cotton dress with yellow skirt and collar and white square neck bodice. Green vinyl belt and shoes match the green felt hat with white stitching.

Merry Moppets (1955), #36, school girl outfit with a red, white, and black checked skirt and red jersey top. Black felt vest matches the red and black felt beret. Notice the doll's brown eyes which are hard to find.

Merry Moppets (1955), #38, Cowgirl outfit of purple felt hat and skirt, green cotton top and bright pink felt vest. Gold braid fringe trims the outfit. The gold cuffs tie on. Courtesy Barbara Rosplock-Van Orman.

Tiny Miss

Tiny Miss (1955), #39, (on left), in a flowered cotton dress with a purple border and trim and a light purple straw hat. Tiny Miss #44, (on right) white organdy apron over a cotton print dress, straw hat with green velvet and flower trim.

Tiny Miss (1955), #40, in red checked cotton dress with white organdy and black velvet bows, matching hat. Courtesy Shirley Niziolek.

Tiny Miss (1955), #41, in a blue and black checked top with matching panties and blue cotton skirt. Black picot trims the neck and sleeves. Black straw hat.

Tiny Miss (1955), #42 – 43. Vogue brochure.

Fun Time

Fun Time (1955), #45, Ballerina in a multi-colored organdy costume with gold braid trim and a flower headband. Courtesy Chree Kysar.

Fun Time (1955), #46, Dutch Girl, in short lavender taffeta dress with white cotton organdy apron trimmed with silver braid and pleated net. Matching Dutch cap and wooden shoes. Also found in blue taffeta which may have faded to lavender. Courtesy Shirley Niziolek.

Fun Time (1955), #47, Roller Skater, in gray cotton costume and hat with red lining. Notice Vogue paper doll motif box and wrist tag. Courtesy Ann Tardie.

Fun Time (1955), #48, Beach outfit with red candy stripe swimsuit and matching terry cloth robe and hat. Came with personalized wooden pail. Also shown is 1955 trunk #860 with Ginny lining. The Colored* Ginny (*Vogue's designation) is a 1954 painted lash walker. Courtesy Shirley's Dollhouse.

Fun Time (1955), Ski #49, in lime green felt two-piece suit with zipper front. Woven flower braid trims the front and red knit stocking style hat. Wooden skis and poles.

Fun Time (1955),#50. Vogue brochure.

And Away We Go

And Away We Go (1955), #51, in red vinyl jacket and hat with white linen dress with pleated skirt. White socks, red necklace, and red vinyl shoes complete the outfit.

And Away We Go (1955), #52 – 53. Vogue brochure.

And Away We Go (1955), #54, in flocked blue net dress trimmed with lace and a rose. Straw hat, plastic beads, a case of plastic curlers and a cosmetic cape are part of the outfit. Notice wrist tag and original box. Courtesy Ann Tardie.

And Away We Go (1955), #55, in a black velvet top with pink organdy skirt with black lace trim. Matching bonnet has a pink taffeta lining and pink feather trim and ties with a pink ribbon. Black vinyl shoes are worn with pink socks.

And Away We Go (1955), #56, dress of turquoise velvet top and yellow organdy skirt with gold picot trim, and a gold braid tie at the waist. A matching tie-on hat and gold slippers complete the outfit. Should be on molded lash walker.

Bridal Trousseau (1955), #60 – 62. Vogue brochure.

Bridal Trousseau (1955), #63, outfit with purple velvet top and long skirt with gold, purple and white stripes. Matching pantaloons with pleated net trim and gold slippers. Purple straw basket and hat trimmed with flowers.

Bridal Trousseau (1955), #64, bride's gown of white lace over taffeta trimmed with white picot and sweetpea flowers at the waist. Lace crown and white veil. Courtesy Nancie Mann.

Bridal Trousseau Ginny (1955), #65, wears the less common deep rose version of the outfit. Should be on molded lash walker. Courtesy Barbara Rosplock-Van Orman.

Bon-Bons

Bon-Bons (1955), #80, dress of blue nylon with flocked dots and ribbon trim on the shoulder straps and tie waist. Nylon net petticoat and straw hat with ribbon trim and blue satin slippers. Not shown is coordinated plastic parasol. All Bon-Bons had nylon dresses, parasols, and satin tie slippers.

Bon-Bons (1955), #81, dress of flowered nylon with velvet inset on bodice and sleeves, both trimmed with lace. Purple straw hat with feather trim. Personalized pink plastic parasol. Should be on molded lash walker.

Bon-Bons (1955), #82, pink flocked nylon dress with picot trim and flower trim at waist and on pink straw hat. Coordinating pink umbrella. Necklace is Ginny's but not original to outfit. Courtesy Peggy Millhouse.

Bon-Bons (1955), boxed Ginny outfit #582, pink flocked nylon dress with petticoat, panties, slippers, straw hat and plastic Bon-Bon umbrella. It is very rare to find a boxed Bon-Bon outfit today. Courtesy Chree Kysar.

Bon-Bons (1955), #83, (dressed doll), yellow nylon dress with flocked white heart pattern trimmed with white lace at yoke and black velvet tie at waist. Yellow straw hat. Notice Vogue paper doll design box. Courtesy Barbara Rosplock – Van Orman.

Bon-Bons (1955), #84, mint in box with wrist tag. Blue printed nylon dress with matching blue straw hat and rosebud trim. All Bon-Bon outfits came with coordinating plastic umbrellas. Courtesy Chree Kysar.

Bon-Bons (1955), #85, a gray cotton version of the nylon outfit shown in the sales flyer. Perhaps this is a budget version of the outfit as it is unlikely that the nylon fabric featured in the series was changed by Vogue. Doll is earlier.

Coats

Coats #180 – 184. Vogue brochure.

Separates

Separate outfit (1955), yellow printed organdy dress with Medford black print tag matching Ginnette 1955 #002 from that year. Ginny dress number unknown since not listed in catalog.

Separate outfit (1955), #186, flowered cotton robe with zipper front, pleated net trim at hem, sleeves and neck.

Special Dolls

Davy Crockett (1955), #990, sold on both painted lash and molded lash walker dolls. Wearing a fringed suede cloth outfit and fur cap, metal toy Kentucky rifle, a button and a jacket emblem. Doll was created to boost summer sales. Should be on molded lash walker.

Accessories

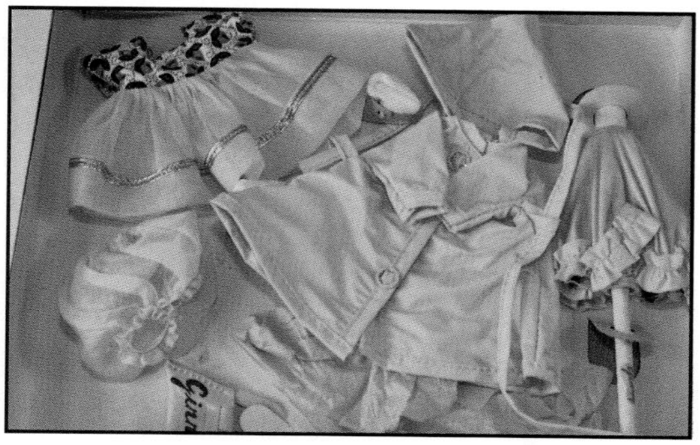

Bridal Trousseau boxed set (1955), #460, dress with pink organdy skirt and cotton top, pink plastic rain coat and umbrella; pink vinyl purse, shoes and socks. The top of the box had a cellophane window. Courtesy Chree Kysar.

Ice Skates (1955), #847, white skates in their package.

Fitted Wardrobe Trunk #862, (1955), pink and white metal trunk with Ginny's monogram and picture. Contains dressed doll plus four additional outfits. Also sold in 1956 as #6862. Courtesy Chree Kysar.

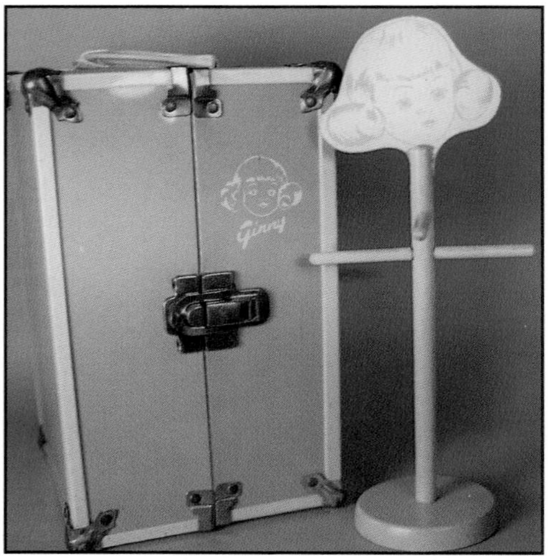

Unfitted travel case (1955), #864, in pink and white metal shown with #915 Trousseau Tree, wooden with removable Ginny top.

Fitted Bridal Chest (1955), #866, shows Ginny as bride doll #64 from the Bridal Trousseau series; separate blue checked suit #461; yellow knit outfit #130 from the Gym Kids group; parasol #833, and rain cape. Courtesy Veronica Phillips.

Fitted Bridal Chest (1955), #866, (1956), #6866, made of pink painted hardwood, had Ginny's picture and name in white. Note that the white lattice design was also offered on Ginny's furniture that year. 1956, #6866 chest did not have heart design on front. Courtesy Veronica Phillips.

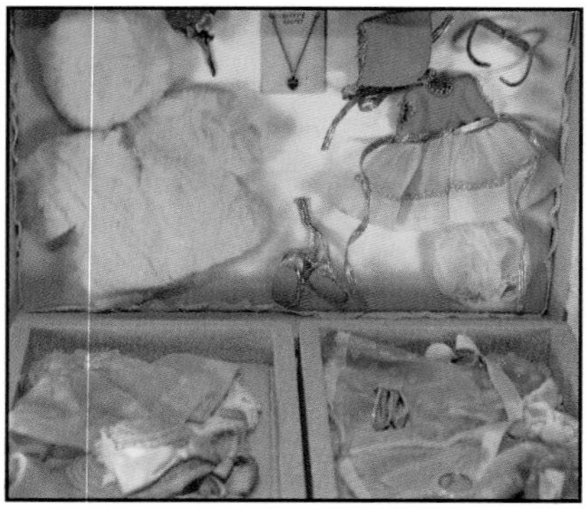

Fitted Bridal Chest (1955), #866, with lid open showing Ginny's trousseau outfits on the fold-away trays and on the lid. Courtesy Veronica Phillips.

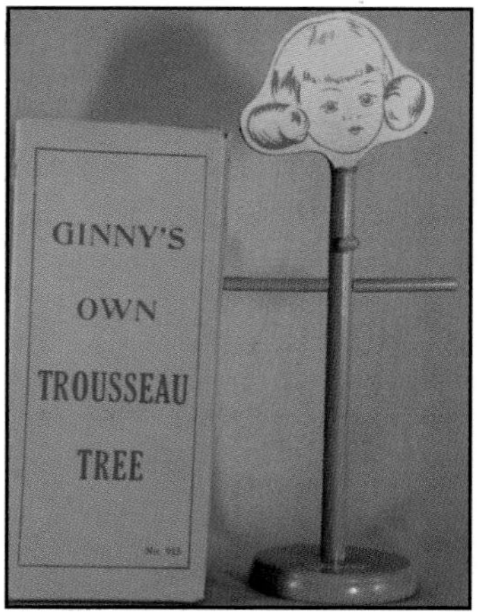

Ginny's Own Trousseau Tree (1955), #915, in its original box. Courtesy Veronica Phillips.

Furniture

Boudoir chair (1955), #920, lattice design wood in pink and white. Courtesy Judy Armitstead.

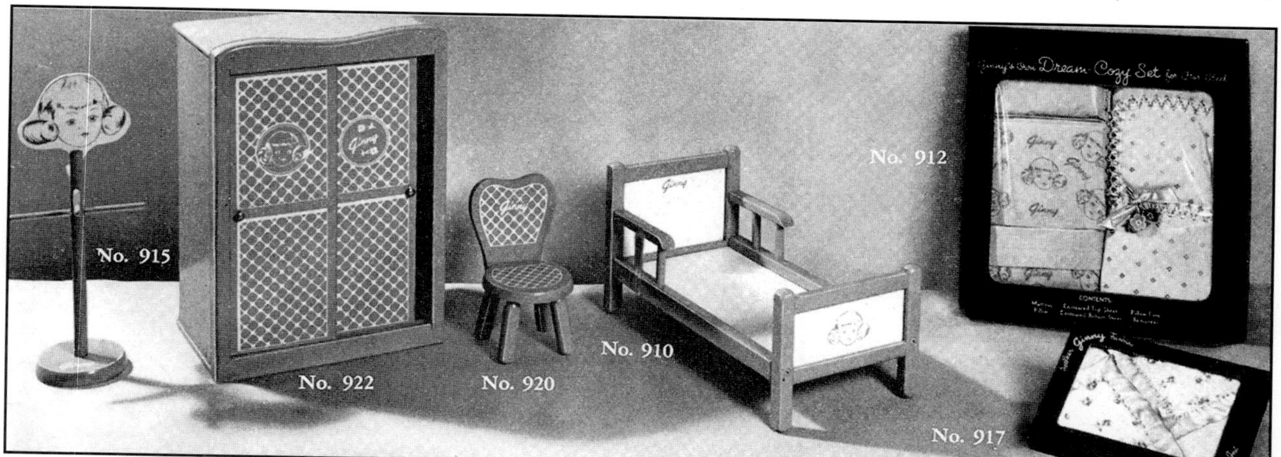

Furniture (1955), #910 – 922. Vogue brochure.

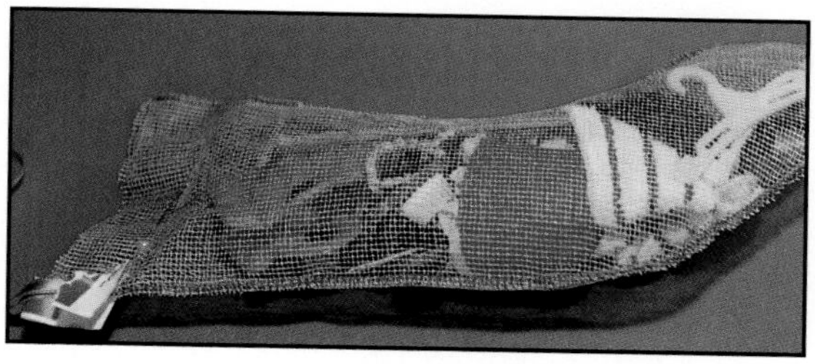

Christmas Stocking (mid 1950s), #1580, containing Ginny goodies such as vinyl shoes, beads, head bands, etc. $300.00. Courtesy Sue Johnson.

Ginny's Gym Set 1955, #925; 1956, #6925; 1957, #79251; and 1958, #1890, with swing, slide, and glider. Courtesy Barbara Rosplock-Van Orman.

1956 — Kinder Crowd

Kinder Crowd (1956) (left to right) #6021, #6022 (matches Ginnette outfit), #6023, #6024, #6025, and #6026. Dressed dolls numbered #60+; outfits only, #61+. Vogue brochure.

Kinder Crowd (1956), #6022, wearing a dotted pink organdy dress with pink and white braid trim on skirt and shoulders. Matching pink plastic headband. Courtesy Barbara Rosplock-Van Orman.

Kinder Crowd (1956), #6025, wearing a yellow cotton dress with lace trim and a black velvet waistband decorated with a rose. Yellow Ginny headband and black vinyl shoes. Note original Vogue paper doll motif box, wrist tag, and elastic around bangs. Courtesy Robi Blute.

Gym Kids

Gym Kids (1956), (from left), #6027, wearing dungaree shorts with cuffs matching cotton print shirt; #6029, aqua overalls with kitty appliqué, cotton knit jersey; #6028, tan shorts, plaid top one-piece outfit with green vinyl belt. All had matching plastic caps. #6029 was also sold in 1957 on a bent knee walker.

Gym Kids (1956), #6031, riding outfit with brown felt jodhpurs, a horseshoe print top, and a black riding cap. Courtesy Shirley Niziolek.

Gym Kids (1956), #6032, advertised as "Camp Outfit." Collectors call it Brownie.

Gym Kids (1956) (left to right), #6027, #6028, #6029 (matches Ginnette outfit), #6030, #6031. Dressed dolls numbered #60+; outfits only, #61+. Vogue brochure.

Merry Moppets

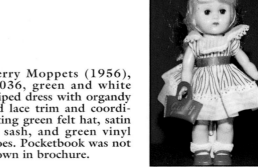

Merry Moppets (1956) (from left to right), #6033, #6034, #6035 and #6036, #6037 nurse, and #6038. Vogue brochure.

Merry Moppets (1956), #6033, red and blue plaid dress and yoke trim with white organdy top, red ribbon wrist ties, and lace trim, red felt hat. Courtesy Candice Zake.

Merry Moppets (1956), #6035, school dress with white organdy top with lace trim and a navy skirt with ABC block print. Straw hat.

Merry Moppets (1956), #6038, gray organdy dress with pink and white lace trim on the hem and broad collar. Pink satin ribbon at the waist and pink straw hat with flowers.

Merry Moppets (1956), #6036, green and white striped dress with organdy and lace trim and coordinating green felt hat, satin tie sash, and green vinyl shoes. Pocketbook was not shown in brochure.

Tiny Miss

Tiny Miss (1956) (left to right) #6039, #6040, #6041, #6042, #6043 (matches Ginnette outfit), and #6044. Vogue brochure.

Tiny Miss (1956), #6039, pink cotton print dress with organdy apron and pink straw hat. Courtesy Kathy Schneider.

Tiny Miss (1956), #6040, navy and green plaid cotton dress trimmed in white rickrack, matching blue vinyl shoes, and navy blue felt hat with green pompons. Should be on molded lash walker. Courtesy Shirley Niziolek.

Fun Time

Fun Time (1956) #6045, #6046, #6047, #6048 (matches Ginnette outfit), #6049 (matches Ginnette outfit) and #6050 skater. Vogue brochure.

Fun Time (1956), #6047, Roller Skater with printed cotton outfit with gold braid trim, matching hat with gold pompons, suede cloth roller skates. Courtesy Barbara Rosplock-Van Orman.

Fun Time (1956), #6049, Skier in pink cotton jacket with zipper and woven braid trim, gray pants, hat, and wooden skis. Replaced shoes. Elasticized waist detail is unique. Not original are "mittens" which are Ginnette's booties from her matching snowsuit outfit.

Fun Time (1956), #6045, Ballerina(on right), pink taffeta top and net skirt, flower headband. Also shown for comparison is (left), 1955 For Fun Time #45, and (middle), 1954 For Fun Time #45. Note 1956 ballet outfit should be on a molded lash walker. Courtesy Kathy Bailey.

Fun Time (1956), #6050, Ice Skater in red velvet one-piece outfit and hat with plaid pleated skirt.

Play Time

Play Time (1956) #6051, #6052, #6053, #6054, #6055, and #6056. Vogue brochure.

Play Time (1956), #6052, red plaid skirt with matching felt jacket trimmed in white braid. Replaced felt hat. Shown on earlier doll. Courtesy Shirley Niziolek.

Play Time (1956), #6054, blue felt suspender style skirt and matching hat with pink and green felt flower trim, white organdy blouse, vinyl shoes. Shown on an earlier doll. Courtesy Shirley Niziolek.

Play Time (1956), #6056, Cowgirl outfit with blue cotton top, white felt skirt and vest trimmed in gold braid and fringe, gold belt, hat, and suede cloth boots. She had a plastic toy gun hanging from her skirt. Courtesy Barbara Hill.

Formals

Formals (1956), #6061, pale green dress with pink tulle overskirt and satin ribbon trim, coordinated velvet

Formals (1956), #6060, plaid taffeta skirt with black velvet bodice and trim, lace edging; matching black velvet headpiece. Courtesy Chree Kysar.

Formals (1956), #6062, coral taffeta skirt topped with matching tulle overskirt and matching shawl, black velvet bodice and hat.

Formals (1956), #6063, yellow crayon dotted organdy dress trimmed in yellow ribbon. Unique yellow velvet headpiece and yellow satin slippers. Circular wrist tag shows outfit number. Courtesy Nancie Mann.

Formals (1956), #6065, pale pink cotton and tulle gown with flower trim; pink velvet headpiece trimmed with flowers, usually found in blue. Courtesy Chree Kysar.

Not Shown

#6064 Bride
#6065 Nun

Debs

Debs (1956), #6071, blue cotton gown with nylon apron and lace trim; white straw hat with rosebud trim. Courtesy Chree Kysar.

Debs (1956), #6072, yellow calico print gown with nylon apron, with eyelet and beaded trim; black straw hat with flowers. Matches Ginnette outfit. Courtesy Chree Kysar.

Debs (1956), #6073, flowered nylon gown with black velvet bodice; pink straw hat with flowers. Matches Ginnette outfit. Courtesy Chree Kysar.

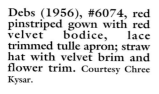

Debs (1956), #6074, red pinstriped gown with red velvet bodice, lace trimmed tulle apron; straw hat with velvet brim and flower trim. Courtesy Chree Kysar.

Debs (1956), #6075, flowered nylon gown with puffed sleeves, ruffled tulle hem, lavender velvet bodice; stiffened lace trimmed hat. Courtesy Chree Kysar.

Special Outfits

Valentine's outfit (1956), Vogue promotional piece to dealers advertising outfits for Ginny and Ginnette. Note special "I Love You" plastic hearts around their wrists. Outfits were not in the regular line. Courtesy Wenham Museum, Wenham, Mass.

Separates and Furniture

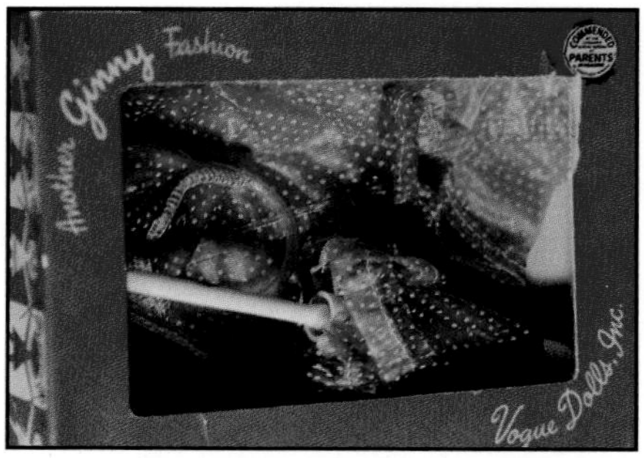

Separate outfit (1956), #6182, plastic raincoat, hood, bag, and umbrella in box. Courtesy Sue Johnson.

Dream Cozy Set (1956), #6912, contains a pink and white matching bed linen set including mattress, pillow, contoured top and bottom sheets, a pillow case, and bedspread with Ginny's name. Courtesy Veronica Phillips.

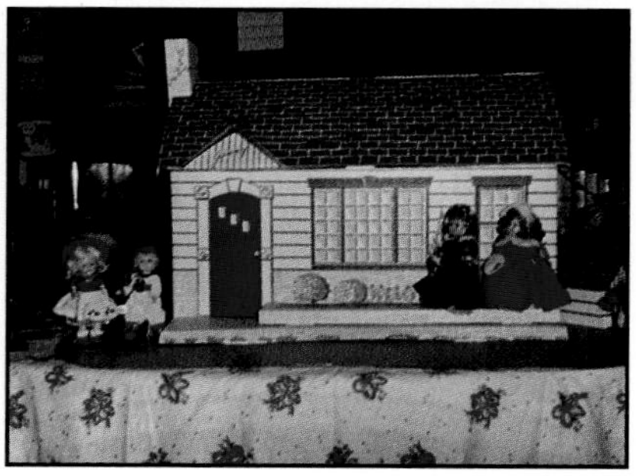

Ginny's Dollhouse and Doghouse (1956), #6926, made of corrugated cardboard, four color printed, required assembly. Courtesy Veronica Phillips.

Hi-Fi Fashions Gowns (1956) #6222 – 6224. Also showing Furniture available, #6910 Bed, #6912 Dream Cozy Set, #6922 Wardrobe, #6914 Rocking Chair. Vogue brochure.

Separate coats (1956), #6180 – 6186. Note coat #6181 check (2nd from left) has a different check and raincoat #6182 is slightly different and comes with umbrella. This photo is different than the Vogue brochure photo and may have been taken prior to final changes in 1956 line. Vogue Publicity Photo.

Accessories

Birthday tablecloth (1956), for Ginny, packaged by Party Papers by Parkay, contains a 60" x 102" paper cloth with Ginny dolls, Ginnette, and Ginny's Pup design. Courtesy Veronica Phillips.

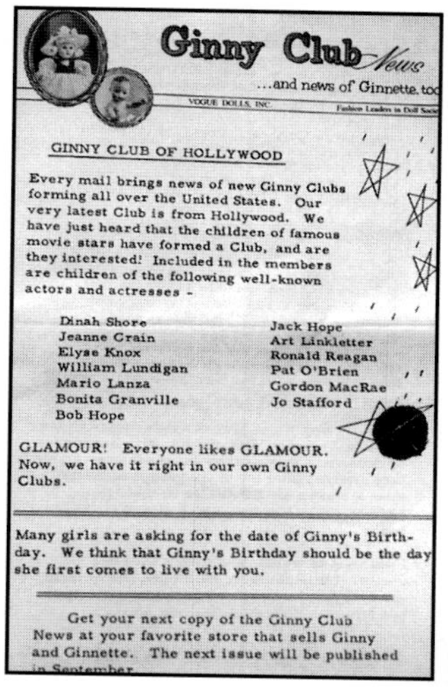
Ginny Club News
...and news of Ginnette, to[o]
VOGUE DOLLS, INC.

GINNY CLUB OF HOLLYWOOD

Every mail brings news of new Ginny Clubs forming all over the United States. Our very latest Club is from Hollywood. We have just heard that the children of famous movie stars have formed a Club, and are they interested! Included in the members are children of the following well-known actors and actresses -

Dinah Shore	Jack Hope
Jeanne Crain	Art Linkletter
Elyse Knox	Ronald Reagan
William Lundigan	Pat O'Brien
Mario Lanza	Gordon MacRae
Bonita Granville	Jo Stafford
Bob Hope	

GLAMOUR! Everyone likes GLAMOUR. Now, we have it right in our own Ginny Clubs.

Many girls are asking for the date of Ginny's Birthday. We think that Ginny's Birthday should be the day she first comes to live with you.

Get your next copy of the Ginny Club News at your favorite store that sells Ginny and Ginnette. The next issue will be published in September.

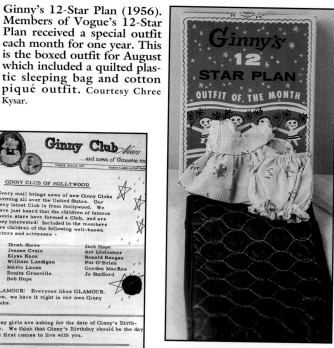

Ginny Club News (1956), sent quarterly to over 6,000 members of the Ginny Doll Club throughout the country until 1960. Courtesy Shirley Niziolek.

Ginny's 12-Star Plan (1956). Members of Vogue's 12-Star Plan received a special outfit each month for one year. This is the boxed outfit for August which included a quilted plastic sleeping bag and cotton piqué outfit. Courtesy Chree Kysar.

Paper plate, napkin, and cup (1956) manufactured by Parkay, a division of Gibson Greeting Cards. Courtesy Veronica Phillips.

Matching Pearl Set (1956, #6834; 1957, #7834; 1960, #1611). For Ginny and her mother: matching pearls, beads, and bracelets. Courtesy Chree Kysar.

Bent Knee Walker Ginny

1957 – 1962

Description:	8", hard plastic, sleep eyes, molded lashes, bent knee walker, walking doll with turning head and bending knees; blonde, brunette, or auburn saran wig. Blue or brown eyes. In 1961 all Ginnys came with green eyes and freckles with blonde, brunette, or auburn wigs.
Marks:	Head: VOGUE Back: GINNY/VOGUE DOLLS/INC./PAT.NO.2687594/MADE IN U.S.A.
Dress labels:	White cotton tape with blue print: Vogue Dolls, Inc.
Dress closures:	A gripping snap fastener, with a circular star-like imprint on exposed metal top; snap was machine applied to outfit.
Tags:	White, circular, tag around wrist with "Hi! I'm Ginny!" and outfit number.
Boxes:	1957 – 60 Ginny dolls came in boxes with a fuchsia, white and black Vogue paper doll design with pink or black end labels with white writing "Hi! I'm Ginny®." Clothing came in Vogue fuchsia window boxes with paper doll design on the side. The 1959 Far Away Lands series came in hinged lid, one-piece fuchsia boxes. 1961 – 62 Ginny dolls came in aqua blue one-piece box with pink writing, with a large white paper doll logo on front.

Growth, Innovations

Growth: In 1957 Vogue added bending knees to the Ginny doll walker and had one of the greatest years ever of Ginny sales. However, to truly appreciate the changes introduced in the Ginny line beginning in 1957, one must first understand the four primary factors that influenced and/or created the need for change:

1. Even though 1957 was one of greatest years of Ginny production, competitive forces in the doll and toy industry increasingly cut into Vogue's corporate profits. Other companies continued to produce separate doll clothing and 8" play dolls, a market pioneered by Vogue. Many of these new competitors placed more emphasis on profitability than on the doll's quality. In order to survive in this new business climate, as early as 1955 Vogue was forced to economize to maintain competitive prices. Thus, we begin to find fewer pleats, trims, etc., on some outfits in the Vogue line. This, of course, was in direct conflict with Vogue's tradition of quality and detail.

2. The growth and development of the Ginny doll line in 1957 was a reflection of the increased growth and development of Vogue overall. Essentially, since 1950, Vogue had devoted all of its energies to developing and improving the 8" Ginny doll. Ginny had Vogue's full attention until 1955 when a new member of the family, baby Ginnette, was introduced. To be competitive in the mid 1950s doll market, Vogue introduced three teenage dolls and another baby doll. Ginny's older teenage sister Jill was added in 1957. This necessitated marketing Ginny in a way that was compatible with Jill's new teen concept. For example, Jill and Ginny had to have matching outfits, and other sister marketing themes. Then, in 1958, two other teen friends, Jan and Jeff, were added as well as baby brother Jimmy.

   In the 1960s more dolls were added including Brikette, Littlest Angel, Ginny Baby, Dream Baby, and Li'l Dear as well as a host of other dolls. Unfortunately, the new dolls took time and energy away from Ginny, the very doll that had given the company such prominence in the first place.

3. Vogue management changes: In 1960, Mrs. Jennie Graves retired from the company, turning to her daughter, Mrs. Virginia Graves Carlson, and son-in-law Edwin (Ted) Nelson to lead the company. Many of the growth strategies resulted from the new leadership, and it continued right up until Mrs. Carlson's retirement in 1966.

In light of the above events and factors, we review in more detail the changes Vogue made in 1957 to Ginny which lasted until 1962 when the doll itself was changed again.

Bent Knee Walking Mechanism: In 1957 Vogue added an innovation to their walking Ginny doll. A newly patented mechanism enabled the doll's knee to bend. This allowed the doll to be posed in the kneeling position, and added play value to the doll. However, many felt that it took away from the cute look of the doll.

In 1957 Vogue began to use a decal to apply Ginny's brow and used plastic molded lashes instead of painted ones. Courtesy Peggy Millhouse.

Plastics, Coloring, Wigs: Beginning in 1957, Vogue changed the type of plastic used to produce the doll. By 1959, the doll had a less natural skin tone, despite the application of good cheek color. Some felt that the overall effect of the doll's new coloring, combined with the molded plastic lash, lacked the fresh, appealing wide-eyed look of the original Ginny.

Vogue continued to use Dynel wigs, but increased the use of Saran wigs, using them almost exclusively by 1959. Saran wigs were appealing from the standpoint of washing and combing, but less manageable than the Dynel wigs. Some had a wiry look, and were very difficult to curl. Undoubtedly, some of these changes were made in an attempt to economize, and to maintain a mid-market price lead. However, the changes also had the unfortunate effect of eliminating some of the appeal of the doll's look, which Vogue had always strived to maintain.

Wardrobe, Special Styles, and Accessories

Wardrobe and Special Styles: Ginny's wardrobe continued to be the focus of Vogue's Ginny promotions. One major change in Ginny's wardrobe was the closures, as Vogue switched to gripper type snaps. Home sewers had previously sewn hooks and eyes by hand to outfits. Obviously, it is very easy to date Vogue outfits with snaps as 1957 or later. A new factory was added in Laconia, New Hampshire, and Ginny's bed linen began to be sewn by factory workers, along with selected doll clothing for Jill, Jan, etc. Factory workers did not sew Ginny clothing until the mid 1960s to early 1970s.

Also, Vogue made another change which helps to date and categorize Ginny's wardrobe. Beginning in 1957, Vogue assigned a number to each outfit produced, and virtually eliminated naming series of outfits. The noteworthy features of the collection for the bent knee walker Ginny follow, year by year:

1957: Mrs. Carlson created many lovely school girl outfits, utilizing plastic headbands instead of bows or coordinating straw hats. Also, Joan Cornette, a talented designer who joined the company in 1956, designed many lovely outfits, including creative felt outfits and a number of gowns. In fact, 10 of Vogue's loveliest gowns were produced in 1957, including a much sought after red velvet gown #7175, with matching white fur headpiece, collar, and muff. Mrs. Carlson increasingly relied on Joan Cornette to be the Ginny and smaller dolls designer while Mrs. Carlson designed the clothing for the new larger dolls included in the soon to be acquired Arranbee line (e.g., Littlest Angel).

Action oriented outfits were continued in 1957, including, a salmon colored roller skating outfit #7147, a bright yellow felt ice skating skirt with black knit top #7150, and a swimming outfit #7148 complete with glasses, fins, and life jacket.

A number of Ginny's outfits matched Jill and/or Ginnette. For example, a strapless net gown over blue taffeta with ribbon trim and hair bow, #7162, matched the same gown for Jill, as did wedding gown #7164. Ginny's white felt ski jacket and hat with red cotton pants #7149 matched Ginnette's ski outfit.

1958: Included in the 36 outfits featured in the 1958 brochure, were school girl, dress up, and sports outfits. The outfits were very cute, but the designs were less elaborate, a direct result of cost-cutting measures. Also, only two formals were offered, #1381 and #1390, in addition to a County Fair gown #1380, a bridal gown #1364 (same as 1957), and bridesmaid gown #1165.

A new concept was introduced in 1958: Patterns from Vogue Patterns (not to be confused with Vogue Dolls) for mothers to make for little girls. There were eight patterns that matched Ginny's special outfits. The Vogue brochure touts, "Now you can have that dress-alike look." The patterns were only available in pattern departments of stores.

1959: Vogue featured 24 new Ginny outfits in its 1959 brochure, including school girl and sport outfits. However, it did not include evening gowns, with the exception of a net over white taffeta bridal gown #1460. The promotion with Vogue Patterns continued in 1959, featuring patterns for little girls' for dress-alike outfits to match Ginny.

Ginny's Costumes from Far Away Lands series was introduced with seven outfits: Scandinavia, Hawaii, Holland, Israel, the Orient, Alaska, and the British Isles. Outfits could be purchased separately, and a colorful display was available for stores and dealers. These outfits were very detailed and an educational brochure was enclosed with each one which explained what the outfits were and a little bit about the country. For example, Ginny in her British Islander costume speaks in the first person and explains what a sporran, jabot, and doublet are. "Hoot mon! (as my Highlander friends would say) I nearly forgot to tell you about my white spats! Aren't they smart?" says Ginny in the brochure. Ginny in her Alaskan costume says, "Doesn't my costume look cozy and warm?....You guessed it, I've been to Alaska — our new 49th state." Vogue was always trying to educate as well as entertain little girls.

1960: Vogue created 24 outfits for Ginny in the 1960 catalog. Interestingly, while Ginny now had the bending knee feature for more active play, Ginny's outfits were getting less active and by 1960 none of the outfits were sports outfits. (This was true in 1961 and 1962 as well). In 1960, a special doll called Wee Imp was sold for one year only. The doll had a carrot red wig, green eyes, and freckles. It could be purchased in a special green Ginny box in one of four special Wee Imp outfits. These Wee Imp outfits were coordinated with outfits for Li'l Imp, Vogue's special carrot top version of the Littlest Angel doll (see Wee Imp section).

1961: Ginny dolls were issued with green eyes and freckles, with regular colored and styled Ginny wigs, perhaps using up the left-over Wee Imp stock. Thirteen outfits were created for the doll. No sports outfits were included but notable was a bridal outfit #18445, and a lovely green velvet dress with pantalettes #18446. As before, the basic undressed doll was sold as well as separate outfits.

1962: Only 16 outfits were issued for Ginny. Three of the outfits matched outfits for a new 16" doll issued, Miss Ginny: a red and white candy striped outfit #18345, an aqua jersey outfit #18342, and a yellow cotton dress with green velvet sash #18335.

Accessories: Accessories continued to be a valuable source of revenue for Vogue. The following are the most notable of those sold:

1957: Ginny Party Pack #7859 included the doll, two outfits, Ginny Club Kit and accessories; Fitted Wardrobe Case #7860, pink wood case with the doll and two outfits; Fitted Wardrobe Trunk # 7862 and Fitted Travel Trunk #7865, both pink metal cases with a Ginny doll and three outfits; Fitted Trousseau Chest #7866, an elaborate case with side hinged top shelf included Ginny in bride outfit with fur coat and five outfits. Also, a clever Knit Kit #7869, contained instructions and yarn for three cardigan sweaters.

Furniture: included a wooden table and chairs #7921, rocking chair #7914, wardrobe #7922, and chest of drawers #7920 with Ginny's name on it.

1958: Most of the above accessories and furniture items were continued but a new type of personalized bed #1850, and a vanity table with matching bench #1860 were introduced. Also available was Ginny's Week-Ender #1750 with a doll in party dress plus four ensembles packaged similarly to the 1957 Party Pack.

1959: The complete line of accessories and furniture was continued. Also, a little charm bracelet #3690 with Ginny, Ginnette, and Jill charms was offered. Ginny's Gym set, first available in 1955, was offered as well.

1960: A number of Ginny's furniture and accessory items were discontinued, but the Weekender and Party Packages were continued, as well as most other accessories.

1961 – 62: Vogue dropped all accessories except for doll stands and replacement wigs.

Marketing

Brochures: Ginny and the new Jill doll, along with Ginnette, were heavily marketed in 1957. An extensive 16-page brochure with a four-color cover photograph of the dolls, and black and white photographs inside were included in doll boxes. It was anticipated that cross merchandising would occur with each purchase. In 1958, an even larger brochure was produced with a page devoted to the other dolls. "Hi! We're the Vogue Doll Family...We're Ginny, Ginnette, Jill, Jan, Jimmy and Jeff." Catalogs were now also produced separately for Ginny, Jeff, Jill, etc. In 1959 a brochure was produced for Ginny's outfits. However, they were only shown in line drawings (except for photos of the new Far Away Lands outfits), and no advertising for the other dolls was included; these had their own brochures.

Advertising: In 1957, Vogue had a lot at stake in the success of Ginny with her new walking bent knees. To insure maximum dealer awareness of the new product, they launched a major advertising campaign in *Playthings Magazine* prior to the winter Toy Fair. "Pop up" cut outs were attached between double page spreads, one each for Ginny, Ginnette, and Jill. Copy for Ginny's pages reads, "This year, more than ever, Ginny's wardrobe is the most exquisite line ever created." A page promoting all three dolls dressed in the same sundress read, "...We at Vogue Dolls are proud to have three such beautiful dolls represent us. Ginny, the original Fashion Leader in Doll Society, and the most popular doll in the country, Ginnette, Ginny's baby sister, who is acclaimed as the most life-like baby doll ever created and now Jill, Ginny's teen-age sister. This is the Vogue Doll family....the family of High Fashion...the Key to High Profit!" Clearly, Vogue covered all marketing bases in this ad.

Vogue also made some magnificent public relations moves in 1957, including Mrs. Graves's presentation of $50,000 worth of dolls and their accessories to the Save the Children Federation, and to Greer Garson who accepted $25,000 worth of dolls for the Child Welfare League of America. Vogue also continued their promotional parties around the country, including high profile Hollywood parties.

However, one notable absence in Vogue's attempt to promote their doll line was television advertising. As Mattel heavily promoted Barbie, Vogue lost ground because Mrs. Graves was unwilling or unable to advertise on television. The company struggled to revive interest and to boost their profits by introducing a vinyl headed Ginny in 1963, but, sadly, the golden age of the 1950s Ginny was over.

#7021 (1957), red, green, and black striped dress with red hem. Marks on back: GINNY/VOGUE DOLLS/ INC./ PAT.NO.2687594/ MADE IN U.S.A.

#7022 – 7026 (1957). **Vogue brochure.**

Prices
Bent Knee Walker Ginny Dolls

Year Produced	Outfit	Mint Price *
1957 – 59	Ginny	175.00 – 225.00
	Formals	225.00+
1960	Ginny	$125.00 – 175.00
	#1160 Formal	$250.00
	#1152 Sugar N Spice	$270.00
	#1130 Cook	$350.00
1961	Ginny	$150.00
	#18246	$175.00
1962	Ginny	$150.00+
Outfits Mint In Box		
1957		$65.00
1958 – 1959		$55.00
1957 – 59	Gowns	$80.00
1960 – 61		$45.00
1960	Cook #1330, Popover #1331, Sugar N Spice, #1352, Gowns	$75.00+
1961	Red velvet frock #18446, Bride #18445	$75.00
Special accessories:		
	Tablecloth, MIB (1956 – 57)	$300.00
	Individual plate/cup/napkin (1956 – 57)	$35.00 each
	Trousseau Chest	$1,000.00+

#7027, #7029, #7031, #7033 – 7037, and #7039, #7040, #7042, #7043 and #7044 (1957). Vogue brochure.

#7028 (1957), red and blue plaid shorts with attached red jersey shown with original box and brochure included.

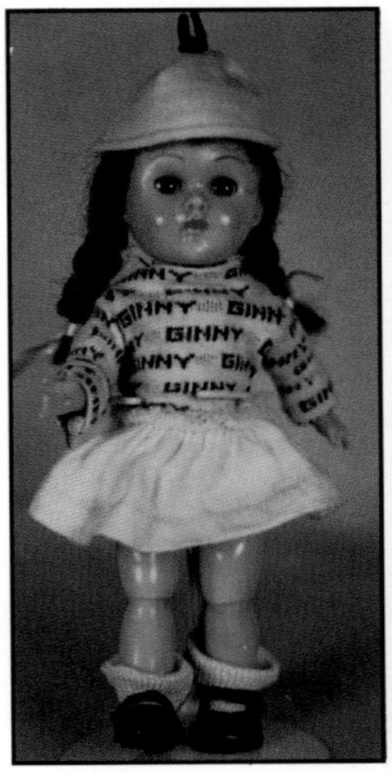

#7030 (1957), yellow knit outfit with Ginny pattern top jersey. Outfit was also available in 1954 and 1958 in various colors.

#7032 (1957), Camp outfit and brown felt cap. Also offered in 1956 Gym Kids #6032. Courtesy Shirley Niziolek.

#7038 (1957), black velvet dress with lace trim and organdy apron. Rose flowers trim the waist and white straw bonnet. Doll shown is earlier, should be a bent knee walker. Courtesy Shirley Niziolek.

#7041 (1957), blue polished cotton dress with black braid and white lace trim. Straw hat has a black ribbon trim. Courtesy Barbara Rosplock-Van Orman.

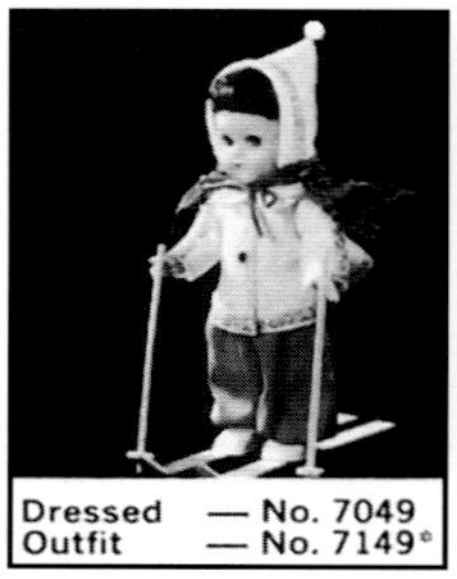

#7045, #7047, #7048, #7049, #7050, #7051, #7054 and #7056 (1957). Vogue brochure.

#7046 (1957), Majorette in white outfit with blue cotton lining and gold braid. Blue pants trimmed in gold rickrack, brass tipped baton, red felt hat with blue plume and boots. Snap closure. Same design as 1956 Fun Time #6046 with hook and eye closure.

#7052 (1957), yellow organdy dress with white lace trim and petticoat, yellow ribbon trim on bodice and on straw hat. Courtesy Barbara Rosplock-Van Orman.

#7053 (1957), pink felt jumper over a pink checked top and petticoat. Matching felt hat has a pompon. Shown on earlier doll, should be a bent knee walker.

#7055 (1957), white organdy dress with pink satin trim and cape; tie-on hat with net and rosebud trim. Courtesy Chree Kysar.

#7061 (1957), black velvet tie-on cape over a pale pink dress; matching black velvet headpiece with sequin trim. Courtesy Chree Kysar.

#7062 (1957), formal of blue taffeta under silver flecked net, trimmed with silver rickrack and blue satin ribbon, matching blue ribbon bow and flower stapled to the head. Matches Jill's gown #7409.

#7060, 7063 (1957). Vogue brochure.

#7064 (1957), bridal gown of white tulle skirt and bodice trimmed with lace over satin with a chapel length veil and white straw headpiece. She carries a bouquet of flowers. Matched Jill outfit.

#7065 (1957), blue flowered taffeta gown with blue straw hat decorated with flowers and satin ribbon. Courtesy Chree Kysar.

#7070 (1957), blue gown topped with embroidered nylon skirt and puffed sleeve top, lacy straw hat tied with peach satin ribbon.

#7071 (1957), gown with white organdy skirt over black and white striped cotton, pink velvet bodice; with wrist tag. Black hat with pink rosebud trim. This doll has an unusual low ponytail hairstyle. Courtesy Chree Kysar.

#7072 (1957), embroidered nylon over pink taffeta gown with pink satin trim; pink straw picture hat. Courtesy Chree Kysar.

#7073 (1957), gown of tulle lined gold taffeta with a brown velvet jacket and bows on the skirt and fur hat. Courtesy Maureen Fukushima.

#7074 (1957), blue taffeta gown with flounce skirt over white nylon; pearl tiara, with wrist tag. Courtesy Chree Kysar.

#7075 (1957), red velvet gown with white bunny fur cape, hat and muff. This is a very hard to find outfit today. Courtesy Chree Kysar.

Dressed No. 7091 $4.50 Outfit No. 7191 $2.50

Nighty and Slippers Outfit Only No. 7221 — $1.00

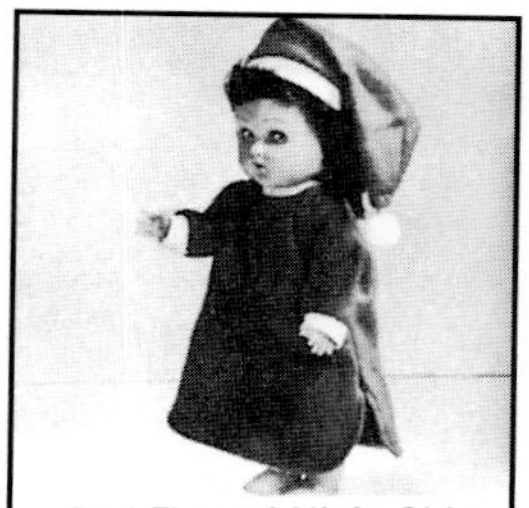

Red Flannel Night Shirt and Cap — Outfit Only No. 7222 — $1.00

3 Piece Pajama Set Outfit Only No. 7223 — $2.00

Housecoat Outfit Only No. 7224 — $1.00

(1957) #7091, #7221, #7122, #7223 and #7224. Vogue brochure.

No. 7180 Coat and Hat — $1.50

No. 7181 Coat and Hat — $1.50

No. 7182 — Coat Umbrella, Bag — $2.00

No. 7183 Coat and Hat — $2.50

No. 7184 Coat, Hat, Muff — $3.00

No. 7185 Coat and Hat — $2.0

°Matching Ginnette Coat

#7180 – 7185 (1957), coats, from Vogue brochure, available as outfits only.

#7092 (1957), nun outfit available only on dressed doll. Courtesy Marlene Dantzer.

#7186 (1957). Vogue brochure. Available as outfit only.

No. 7186 — Borgana Coat, Hat, Muff — $2.50

#7187 (1957), aqua felt car coat with toggle closings and hat. Available as outfit only.

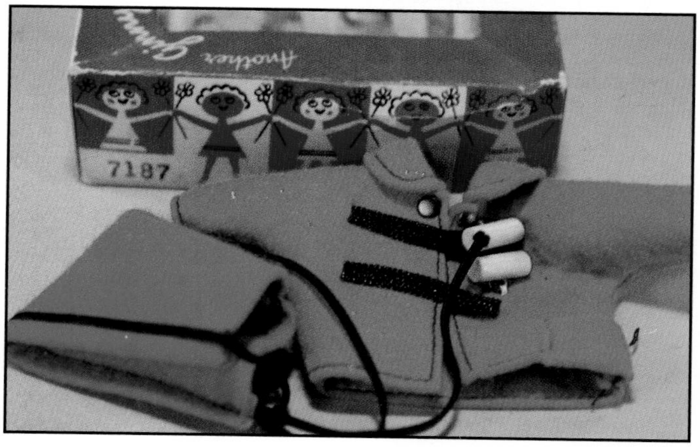

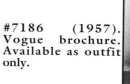

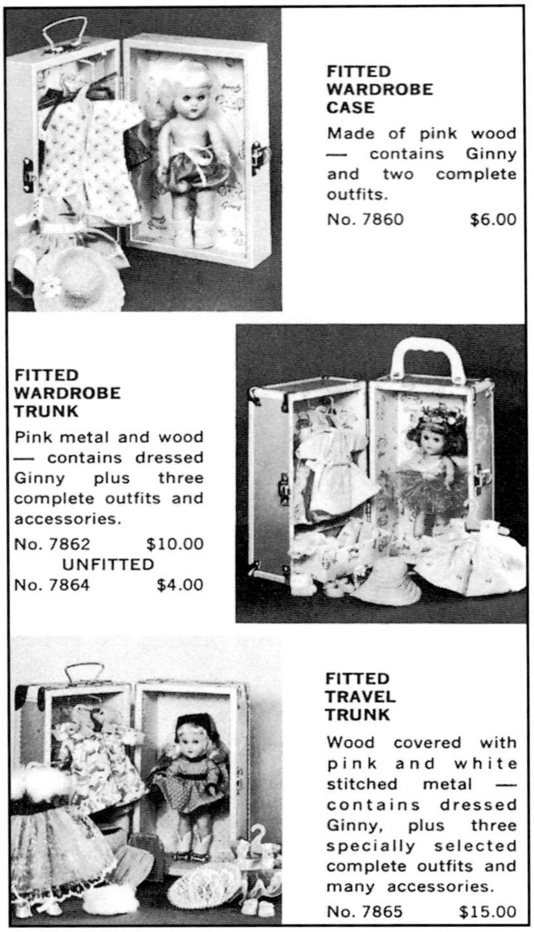

FITTED WARDROBE CASE
Made of pink wood — contains Ginny and two complete outfits.
No. 7860 $6.00
FITTED WARDROBE TRUNK
Pink metal and wood — contains dressed Ginny plus three complete outfits and accessories.
No. 7862 $10.00
UNFITTED
No. 7864 $4.00
FITTED TRAVEL TRUNK
Wood covered with pink and white stitched metal — contains dressed Ginny, plus three specially selected complete outfits and many accessories.
No. 7865 $15.00

#7860 – 7865 (1957). Vogue brochure.

FITTED TROUSSEAU CHEST
Pink and white hardwood — includes Ginny in Bride Outfit, five additional outfits, fur coat, raincoat, umbrella, many accessories.
No. 7866 $29.95
WARDROBE
No. 7922
$3.00
CHEST OF DRAWER
No. 7920
$3.00
GINNY'S YOUTH BED
No. 7910
$2.00
GINNY'S DREAM COZY BED SET
No. 7912
$2.00

#7866 – 7912 (1957). Vogue brochure.

Accessories

#7837 (1957), Apron set with matching aprons for Ginny and her mother. Courtesy Chree Kysar.

#7849, Rain bonnet and boots, made of transparent plastic and sold for 60¢. Courtesy Veronica Phillips.

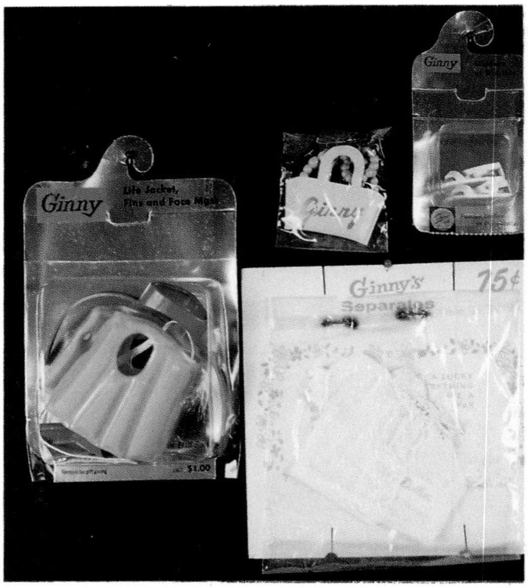

Accessories (1957 – 60), including #7226 separate blouses; #7836 beads, bracelet, and bag; #7842 slippers or sandals; and #7850 life jacket and fins.

Gadabout Case (1957), #7863, yellow canvas with a magic fold window to carry Ginny. Has a separate accessory compartment.

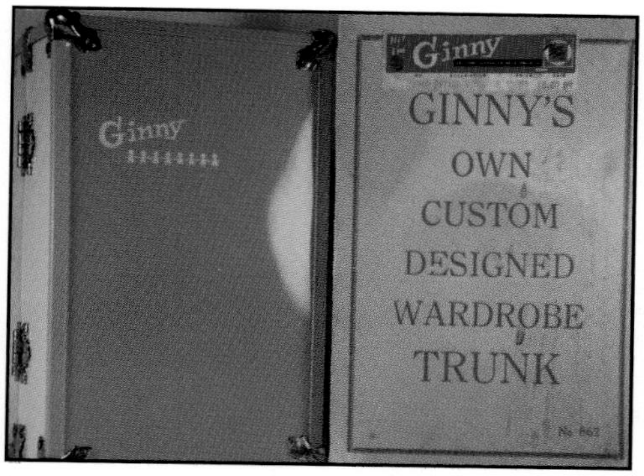

Fitted Wardrobe Trunk #7862 (1957), pink metal and wood trunk contained Ginny, three outfits, and eight accessories. Note: Vogue reused 1955 cardboard box and put 1957 label on it. Courtesy Veronica Phillips.

Party Package #7859 (1957), Ginny and two extra outfits including a navy felt cowboy outfit only found in this package including a birthday invitation and Ginny Club Kit. Courtesy Chree Kysar.

Trousseau Chest (1957), #7866, cover contains Ginny in a bridal gown with five additional outfits. Courtesy Laura Kussmaul.

Trousseau Chest (1957), #7866, contains Ginny in a bridal gown with five additional outfits, including some from 1956. Among the outfits displayed is blue fur coat #7184 plus many accessories. Courtesy Laura Kussmaul.

Trousseau Chest (1957), #7866, close-up showing variations in color of jersey. This is lower level of case. Courtesy Ann Tardie.

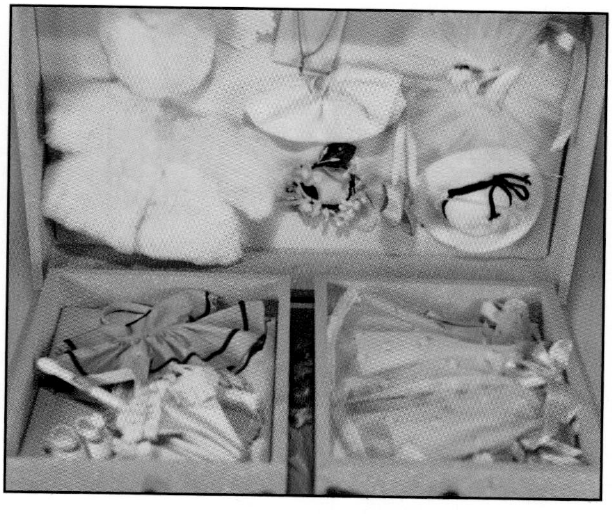

Trousseau Chest (1957), #7866, showing variations in fur coat and straw hat. This is upper level of case. Among the outfits displayed are turquoise dress #7141. Courtesy Ann Tardie.

Knit Kit (1957), #7869, contained yarn and instructions for a sweater and cap each for Ginny, Jill, and Ginnette or three sweaters for one. This novelty was prepared as part of the overall campaign to promote the new 10" Jill doll in 1957. Courtesy Chree Kysar.

Furniture

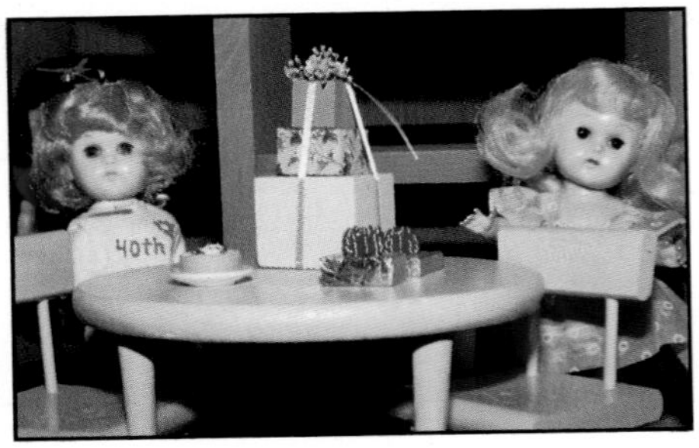

Ginny's round table (1957, #7921, and 1958 – 1959, #1861). Courtesy Vogue Review Luncheon, Worcester, Mass.

Ginny's rectangular table. Unusual shape not shown in Vogue catalog. Courtesy Sue Johnson.

Items of Interest

Promotional piece (1957) with a Ginny Birthday Party photo offer promoting the Ginny Doll Family. Courtesy Sue Johnson.

Two page pop-up advertisement (1957) in *Playthings Magazine* announcing the arrival of the bent knee Ginny. Ginny is wearing outfit #7025 brown and white cotton. Courtesy *Playthings Magazine*.

1958

Paper tote given out to attendees of the Ginny parties sponsored by Vogue. Courtesy Judy Armitstead.

These and photos on the next page are from 1958 Vogue brochure.

Cover (1958). Vogue brochure.

Outfit 1300 $1.00†
Here's Ginny, cute as a button i her cotton jersey leotard and tin satin ballet slippers. Her leotar in pink, black or red.

Outfit 1301 $1.00‡
Now off to dreamland and Ginny wears her shortie pajamas. They're colorful cotton, lace trimmed, with full-blown jacket.

Outfit 1302 $1.00
Pretty flowery housecoat with full, full skirt. Sparkling white cotton splashed with roses and edged with delicate white lace.

Outfit 1303 $1.00
Let's play! And Ginny can wear her princess dress of crispy, colorful cotton. The skirt is full and flary and edged in scalloped rick rack.

Outfit 1304 $1.00
This is Ginny's little shirtmaker dress . . . crisp and new as Spring in sparkling, colorful cotton with convertible collar and full skirt.

Outfit 1305 $1.00
What fun when Ginny wears her new yoke dress! The skirt falls to gentle fullness from the shoulders, and the colors are so bright and gay.

Dressed 1110 $3.50 Outfit 1310 $1.50†
How Ginny loves a sundress! This one is crispy white polished cotton banded with black on the skirt and tied with a bow on the shoulders.

Dressed 1111 $3.50 Outfit 1311 $1.50‡
It's party time . . . and what could be prettier than a frilly little dress of bright red dotted Swiss tied with satin and trimmed with lace!

Dressed 1112 $3.50 Outfit 1312 $1.50†
What a sweet little cotton this is! Every line so new and smart. The blouse is aqua . . . the skirt white with aqua flower print.

Dressed 1113 $3.50 Outfit 1313 $1.50†
Pretty as a picture, this red and white polka dot dress has a flaring skirt, black belt and black ribbon beading on sleeves and neckline.

Dressed 1114 $3.50 Outfit 1314 $1.50†
For warm summer days Ginny wears a dress of primrose yellow cotton. The skirt is full, the neck-line and sleeves edged with lace.

Dressed 1115 $3.50 Outfit 1315 $1.50†
Red and white candy striped cotton, gay as a summer day with swirling skirt, lace edged sleeves and spar-kling white belt to circle the waist.

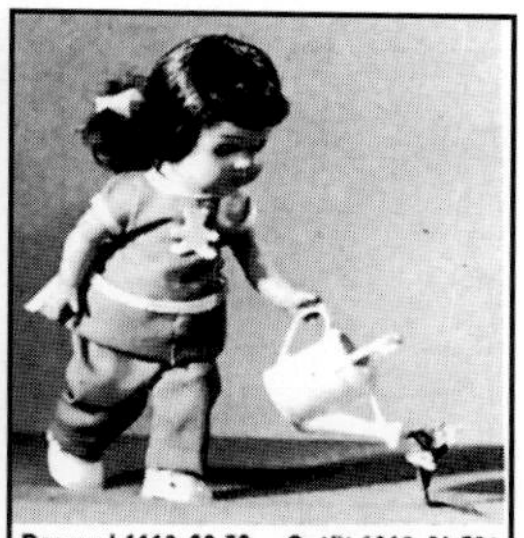

Dressed 1116 $3.50 Outfit 1316 $1.50*
A-gardening we will go! And Ginny can wear her pretty rose play-apron and matching pants. She even has her own watering can!

Dressed 1117 $3.50 Outfit 1317 $1.50†
All ready for "Coke"** and Ginny wears a white cotton shirt and blue denim jeans. Her glasses are white plastic.

Dressed 1118 $3.50 Outfit 1318 $1.50†
Ginny has fun-times when she dresses in her Ivy League striped Bermudas, black belt, red jersey shirt and matching socks.

Dressed 1119 $3.50 Outfit 1319 $1.50
When the air is nippy Ginny feels cuddly-warm in her aqua knit "Ginny" sweater and skirt of white polished cotton.

Dressed 1120 $3.50 Outfit 1320 $1.50†
Beige twill jodhpurs for riding or relaxing. With them a colorful print blouse, bright collar pin, brown belt and brown boots.

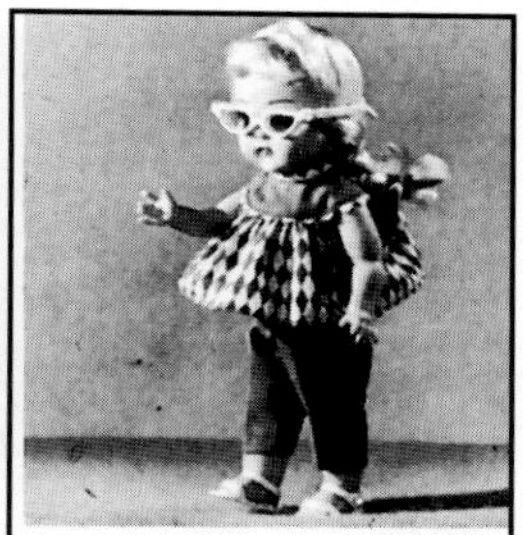

Dressed 1121 $3.50 Outfit 1321 $1.50†
This is one of Ginny's favorites! Bright red Capri pants and match-ing harlequin pattern overblouse. Her glasses are white plastic.

Outfit 1325 $1.50‡
This is Ginny's red felt cape, full and beautiful with flower trim on the collar. For her hair, a colorful flower felt band.

Outfit 1326 $1.50
For dress-up Ginny wears this aqua coat with gold and black flower print. Her hat, black velveteen faced with matching print.

Dressed 1130 $4.00 Outfit 1330 $2.00†
The gayest little dress we know, this bright red cotton sailor with white trim, white satin tie. Her hat, white felt banded with red.

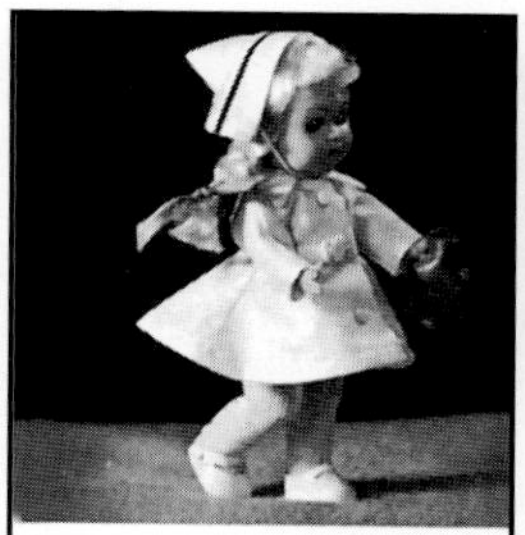

Dressed 1131 $4.00 Outfit 1331 $2.00
Here Ginny wears a crisp white nurse's uniform and just-like-real nurse's cap. In her hand she carries a hot water bottle.

Dressed 1132 $4.00 Outfit 1332 $2.00‡
Luscious lavender dress with lace edged collar. On her head a cotton eyelet mop cap. In her hand, a white purse and white gloves.

Dressed 1133 $4.00 Outfit 1333 $2.00
For birthday parties a pretty, pretty yellow flocked taffeta, lace trimmed and tied with satin. Match-ing bonnet trimmed with lace.

Dressed 1134 $4.00 Outfit 1334 $2.0
This is Ginny's green and whit gingham, trimmed ever-so-daintil with white eyelet embroidery. He big hat is natural straw.

Dressed 1135 $4.00 Outfit 1335 $2.00‡
How lovely Ginny looks in gleam-ing black velveteen and sheer pink organdy. Her bonnet is rose trimmed, tied beneath the chin.

Dressed 1136 $4.00 Outfit 1336 $2.00‡
Party pinafore in rose cotton with sheer flowered apron that is lace edged and tied with rose satin. Her white straw sprouts a perky flower.

Dressed 1137 $4.00 Outfit 1337 $2.00
Ginny in white cotton organdy trimmed with black rick rack and sashed with black velveteen. Straw hat has red flower.

Dressed 1138 $4.00 Outfit 1338 $2.00† Pretty little sleeveless cotton in pale pink with a bouquet of flowers at the waist. Matching pink jersey shrug and hat of pink straw.

Dressed 1139 $4.00 Outfit 1339 $2.00† Ginny in trim, slim slacks of tartan plaid. The white bulky knit sweater bright with brass buttons. On her head a white straw bowler.

Dressed 1140 $4.00 Outfit 1340 $2.00 How Ginny loves her swirling blue corduroy skirt, sheer white top and black felt bolero jacket. Her cap is

Outfit 1345 $2.00 This is Ginny's navy felt Regulation Coat . . . brass buttoned and trimmed with red eagle emblem. Her hat is navy, her purse is white.

Dressed 1150 $4.50 Outfit 1350 $2.5 Ballet is fun! Here Ginny wears a frilly white tulle costume with silver lamé bodice. Her ballet slippers and flower wreath are pink.

Dressed 1152 $4.50 Outfit 1352 $2.5 Ginny struts in her drum majorette costume of white cotton with sparkly gold braid trim. Gold panties, visor hat, baton.

Dressed 1153 $4.50 Outfit 1353 $2.50 Here we see Ginny ready for underwater exploring in a white suit, orange life jacket, face mask and fins. Towel and pail are for fun!

Dressed 1155 $4.50 Outfit 1355 $2.50† Ginny's beautiful coral skating dress gleams with silver threads. Her matching hat sports a real feather. Skates included.

Outfit 1358 $2.50‡ Ginny, dressed for party-ing in a brilliant red velveteen coat with detachable hood that is lined with black velvet. Her purse is white.

Outfit 1359 $2.50 Ginny's toasty warm coat is made of cloud-light beige dynel and lined with crispy taffeta. Close fitting headband to match.

Dressed 1160 $5.00 Outfit 1360 $3.00 Beautiful navy linen coat over a cotton dress of red and blue print. Coat is lined with matching print. Flower-pot hat in white straw.

Dressed 1161 $5.00 Outfit 1361 $3.00 Ginny says "I like lollypops and ice-cream cones" on this skirt of pale pink felt. With it, a matching felt jacket and pink hat.

Dressed 1163 $5.00 Outfit 1363 $3.0 Pretty little princess dress of bright red velveteen with lace from shoulders to hemline. Her hat layer upon layer of white tulle.

Dressed 1164 $5.00 Outfit 1364 $3.00† Ginny's beautiful bridal gown of gleaming white satin and tulle. She wears a chapel length veil and carries a bouquet of flowers.

Dressed 1165 $5.00 Outfit 1365 $3.00 Ginny as a bridesmaid in beautiful blue tulle with whispery underskirt of blue taffeta. She wears a circlet of flowers, carries a bouquet.

(1958), #1141, red felt top and hat and red and white checked skirt outfit had a matching Dress-Alike Vogue Pattern #2741 for girls to match their dolls.

(1958), #1151, pink felt roller skating costume with Ginny silk screened in black on the skirt; matching pink felt hat. Courtesy Chree Kysar.

(1958), #1154, two-piece blue polished cotton ski outfit with faux fur trim on hat and mittens. Matches Jill's and Ginnette's outfits. Courtesy Shirley Niziolek.

Outfit 1367 $3.00
Ginny's snow white, real bunny fur is beautiful and cozy warm. Her perky little hat in matching bunny fur.

Dressed 1169 $5.00
Ginny dressed in her nun's habit of black. Gold-like cross hangs from the waist.

Dressed 1181 $6.00 Outfit 1381 $4.00
Isn't Ginny beautiful in her full length party pinafore? Fantasy green with lace edged organdy apron. Her hat a natural straw.

From 1958 Vogue brochure.

(1958), #1156, cowgirl outfit, white felt skirt with attached panties, pink satin shirt, silver trim, belt and boots, missing silver cuffs. Toy gun hangs from skirt. White felt cowgirl hat. Courtesy Barbara Hill.

(1958), #1162 dress of nylon skirt with embroidered pattern and scalloped edges, black velvet top, and net sleeves. Black straw hat ties with pink ribbon. Courtesy Barbara Rosplock-Van Orman.

(1958), #1180, Country Fair gown with flowered cotton skirt, black basque bodice, and white dimity blouse; matching mauve straw purse and hat with flower trim. Courtesy Chree Kysar.

(1958), #1190, gown of white organdy skirt and red velvet jacket with snap front. Tie-on bonnet and matching purse. Pleated net trims the hat, sleeves, and hem. Variations of trim pattern have been seen.

Separates

(1958), Separates #1550, nylon blouse and #1552, green felt skirt, each sold separately for 75¢.

Accessories

(1958), Christmas stocking, #1580, smaller of two versions, contains Ginny accessories of pink plastic suitcase, hot water bottle, rain boots, pink fur hat, flippers, headband, glasses, green vinyl shoes, note paper, and a white jockey cap. Courtesy Veronica Phillips.

Furniture

(1958 – 1959), Ginny's Pink Vanity Table #1860, with matching bench has lift-up mirror and plastic comb. Shown with 1956 Green Kinder Crowd dress #6123 and 1954 Candy Dandy #52.

1959

(1959), #1001 – 1426, Ginny line from Vogue dealer catalog; numbers are outfit numbers. #1401, 1401, 1402, 1403, and 1426 were available as outfits only, not on dressed dolls. Dressed dolls are #1210+. Courtesy Marge Meisinger.

(1959), #1430 – 1269, Ginny line from Vogue dealer catalog. #1445 and #1446 were available as outfits only, #1269 was available as dressed doll only. Courtesy Marge Meisinger.

(1959), #1253 – 1259 Ginny's Costumes from Far-Away Lands from Vogue dealer catalog. Numbers are outfit numbers. Dressed dolls are #12+. Courtesy Marge Meisinger.

(1959), undressed Ginny #1005, bent knee walker with molded lashes and auburn braids. The doll wears panties, socks, and vinyl shoes. Courtesy Veronica Phillips.

(1959), #1255 Israeli, Ginny's Costumes from Far-Away Lands, striped dress with metallic banding on the bodice, sleeves, and skirt. White veil and golden chain with the Star of David. Courtesy Kathy Schneider.

(1959), #1434 pink cotton checked with white apron. Courtesy Beulah Franklin.

(1959), #1256 British Islander Ginny's Costumes from Far-Away Lands. Plaid kilt, sporran, white lace jabot, black wool felt doublet, plaid scarf on shoulder, black felt tam o'-shanter, white spats.

Ginny's Costumes from Far-Away Lands

Hoot Mon! I'm Ginny in my British Islander Costume

Did you ever dance the Highland Fling? Did you ever hear t skirl of bagpipes? Ah, what a stirring sound.

But first, shall I tell you about my costume? (Mine was given me by a little friend who lives in Aberdeen, Scotland, the beauti sea city lying between the mouths of the rivers Dee and Don). called a kilt in Scotland and the Highlanders wear them, be t lads or lassies.

Most kilts are made in very special plaids. You see, long the Scots had a habit of banding together in close family gro called clans. And so, every clan had a special plaid (or tartan its own.

Do you see what I have around my waist? It's called a "spor The jabot at my throat is white lace — the doublet is black felt. The scarf (or shawl) at my shoulder is made of the same as my kilt. The jaunty cap? A "tam-o'-shanter", of course!

Hoot, mon! (as my Highlander friends would say) I nearly to tell you about my white spats! Aren't they smart?

And now that I have told you all about my kilt, would y me to teach you the Highland Fling? Good! I just knew we have lots of fun playing together.

P. S. Don't forget to see the other authentic, native costu gathered for you from all over the world. You'll love ea every one.

AN CAMERON

CLAN MacLEOD

CLAN FORBES

VOGUE DOLLS

(1959) #1256 British Islander, educational sheet included in box.

(1959), #1258 Alaskan parka with white fur, separate brown furry hood with snap banded in white, one-piece furry pants with blue sleeveless top, white mukluks.

1960

Vogue Dolls
Hi, I'm Ginny
BASIC DOLL $2.00
I'm 8" tall and can sleep, sit, stand, kneel and walk. I'm available in two hair styles — bangs or braids — in blonde, brunette or auburn. Dressed in panties, shoes and socks.
OUTFIT 1301 $1.00
Ginny takes a stroll in this afternoon dress with gayly checked yoke and flary white skirt. Lace edges the neckline and sleeves.
OUTFIT 1302 $1.00
It's time for school and Ginny wears a colorful cotton dress. The skirt is full and the yoke trimmed prettily at the waist.
OUTFIT 1303 $1.00
Ginny has sweet dreams when she wears these 2-piece pajamas of brightly assorted fabrics.
DRESSED 1110 $3.50
OUTFIT 1310 $1.50
How sweet Ginny looks in her dainty pink checked dress with lace trimmed organdy pie-plate collar and flower motif. Pink plastic headband.
DRESSED 1111 $3.50
OUTFIT 1311 $1.50
There's fun-time ahead for Ginny when she wears her colorful felt jodphurs and long-sleeved white jersey.
DRESSED 1112 $3.50
OUTFIT 1312 $1.50
Ginny looks like a drop of golden sun in white organdy and yellow polished cotton. Frosty lace trims skirt and on the yoke — a flower motif. Pearly yellow headband.
DRESSED 1113 $3.50
OUTFIT 1313 $1.50
Ginny can climb trees in her faded blue denim jeans with red and white checked shirt. Her hat is a natural straw roller.
DRESSED 1114 $3.50
OUTFIT 1314 $1.50
How Ginny loves to dress up in this crisp aqua dress of polished cotton. The striped crop top is prettily edged with white lace.
OUTFIT 1325 $1.50
Ginny doesn't mind the rain at all when she wears her hooded plastic raincoat. She carries a matching tote bag and umbrella that really works!
OUTFIT 1326 $1.50
For Sunday or visiting Ginny loves to wear her scarlet red velveteen coat and hat. She carries a white purse.
OUTFIT 1327 $1.50
When it's freezy cold Ginny is cozy and warm in her snow white bunny fur coat with matching beret and muff.
DRESSED 1130 $4.00
OUTFIT 1330 $2.00
Ginny has a cookout and wears a perky white apron with rooster motif over a sleeveless red and white checked dress. And see her matching white chef's hat!
DRESSED 1131 $4.00
OUTFIT 1331 $2.00
Ginny looks like a French schoolgirl in her blue felt popover trimmed with white braid and red sailboat worn over white jersey leotights. Her matching felt sassy beret sports a pom-pom.

DRESSED 1132 $4.00
OUTFIT 1332 $2.00
Darling little party dress with lace edged black velveteen yoke and swirling skirt of white taffeta with flower motif. Gauzy bows trim her pink straw hat and she carries her own pink pocketbook.
DRESSED 1133 $4.00
OUTFIT 1333 $2.00
Bright and gay is Ginny in this lace-edged afternoon dress of cherry-red cotton. Her flower trimmed hat ties on top with a perky satin bow.
DRESSED 1134 $4.00
OUTFIT 1334 $2.00
Ginny dons a yellow felt hat and carries a yellow handbag when she wears this print dress. Skirt and yoke are smartly trimmed with cotton lace.
DRESSED 1135 $4.00
OUTFIT 1335 $2.00
Ginny enters the Land of Nod wearing this colorful candy-striped pajama set with full blown top. And doesn't her nite cap look cute? Pink pom-pom slippers.
DRESSED 1150 $4.50
OUTFIT 1350 $2.50
Here's Ginny sweet in her quaint little white pinafore worn over a turquoise dotted dress. See her matching white bloomers and long cotton stockings?
DRESSED 1151 $4.50
OUTFIT 1351 $2.50
Ginny totes a gun when she wears her gold-fringed red and white cowgirl outfit. Belt and holster, white felt hat and boots complete the Western costume.
DRESSED 1152 $4.50
OUTFIT 1352 $2.50
Sugar and spice . . . frosty ruffles and rosebuds trim this dainty white organdy frock. Worn with the laciest pantalettes and pink satin slippers. Her hat is white straw with matching trim and pink satin ribbon ties.
DRESSED 1160 $5.00
OUTFIT 1360 $3.00
Ginny steals the scene in a blue nylon gown daintily frosted with white lace. She carries an old-fashioned nosegay and wears a circlet of blue flowers in her hair.
DRESSED 1161 $5.00
OUTFIT 1361 $3.00
Here comes the bride in lace-trimmed satin and tulle. Her chapel-length veil is held in place by a pearl crown. Her bouquet — white, of course!
DRESSED only 1169 $5.00
Ginny wears a Nun's habit of black broadcloth. A golden cross hangs from the waist.

Bent Knee Walker Ginny (1960), dressed dolls #1132 – 1169.

Bent Knee Walker Ginny (1960) outfits #1301 – 1331, dressed dolls #1110 – 1131.

1961

18430 OUTFIT $1.00
Ginny is comfy warm for bed time in her full-length cuddly pink flannelette nightie.
18431 OUTFIT $1.00
For anytime, a favorite with Ginny is a white pleaty skirt with colorful yoke.
18432 OUTFIT $1.00
Ginny loves fun time in durable play slacks and her own "Ginny" jersey sweater.
18438 OUTFIT $1.50
A "must" for every wardrobe is Ginny's comfy camel coat with brass buttons and cuddle-scarf.
18240 DRESSED $4.00
18440 OUTFIT $2.00
Ginny adores her red check French school smock, with blue legotards and red rollerbrim.
18241 DRESSED $4.0
18441 OUTFIT $2.0
It's party time and Ginny steals the scene in he frosty blue nylon, pett coat and straw hat.

Bent Knee Walker Ginny (1961) outfits #18430 – 18441, dressed dolls #18240 – 18241.

18236 DRESSED $3.50
18436 OUTFIT $1.50
18237 DRESSED $3.50
18437 OUTFIT $1.50
For afternoon tea, isn't Ginny sweet in her cheery rosy check with organdy and lace
18245 DRESSED $4.50
18445 OUTFIT $2.50
Happy Ginny in her bridal gown of tulle and taffeta with chapel length
18246 DRESSED $4.50
18446 OUTFIT $2.50
It's dress-up time in Ginny's velvety red frock and bonnet with lacy pantalettes.

Bent Knee Walker Ginny (1961) outfits #18435 – 18446, dressed dolls #18235 – 18250.

1962

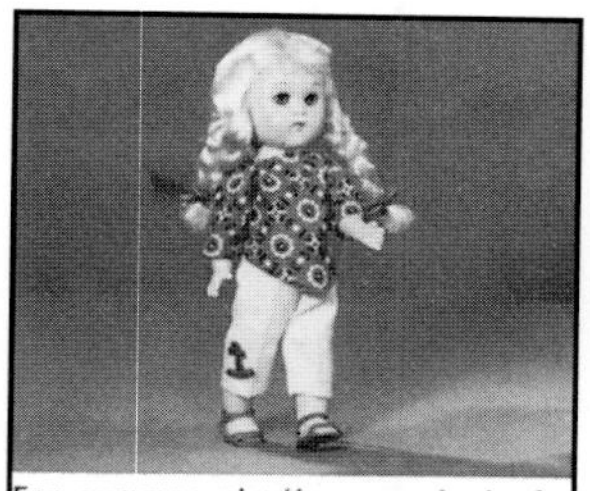

For summer playtime or picnic fu
white cotton deck pants with re
print overblouse are just the thing
Doll 18131 $3.00 Outfit 18331 $1.0

For school or play, a simple basi
cotton with lace-trimmed collar i
a fundamental must.
Doll 18132 $3.00 Outfit 18332 $1.0

or school, Ginny adores her sunny
ellow cotton with soft green velve
ash and yellow rosebuds.
oll 18135 $3.50 Outfit 18335 $1.5

or the girls' club meeting, a brigh
se velvety jumper dress with whit
ylon blouse will be the envy of all
oll 18137 $3.50 Outfit 18337 $1.5

Around the house on cooler day
calls for Ginny's aqua cord slack
with matching angel top.
Doll 18138 $3.50 Outfit 18338 $1.5

or a country fair or special wear
inny wears her provincial lace
rimmed red print ensemble.
oll 18140 $4.00 Outfit 18340 $2.0

arty best for adorable Ginny is a
uffly white organdy dress with
olorful flowered banding and lace.
oll 18141 $4.00 Outfit 18341 $2.00

ere comes the bride in her full
ylon gown with chapel length lace
eil, cap and traditional bouquet.
oll 18150 $5.00 Outfit 18350 $3.00

For collectors, Ginny is dressed i
a traditional nun's habit.
Doll only 18151 $5.00

(1962), #18146 pink organdy dress with felt top and hat.

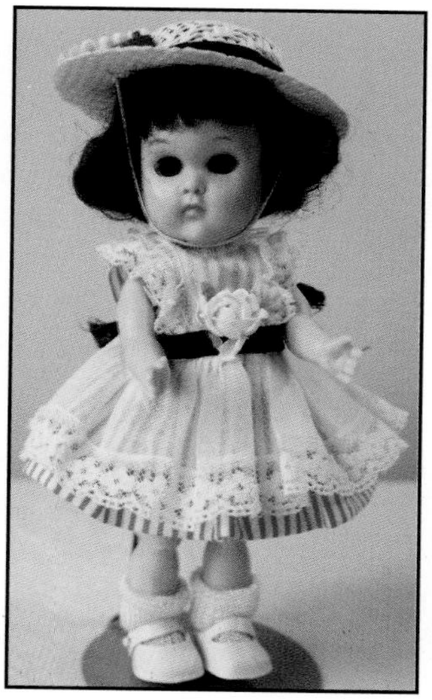

(1962), #18145 red and white candy striped pinafore dress with black velvet waist tie; white straw skimmer hat. Courtesy Chree Kysar.

For slumber-time at home or visit
ing, Ginny is a love in her dainty
print two-piece pajammas.
Outfit only 18330 $1.00

o wardrobe is complete without a
retty pink lace trimmed felt coat
with matching cuddle cap.
utfit only 18339 $1.50

From 1962 Vogue brochure. Dressed dolls numbered #18131+; outfits only #18330+.

(1962), #18136 blue dotted cotton dress with eyelet apron. Notice new blue Vogue box.

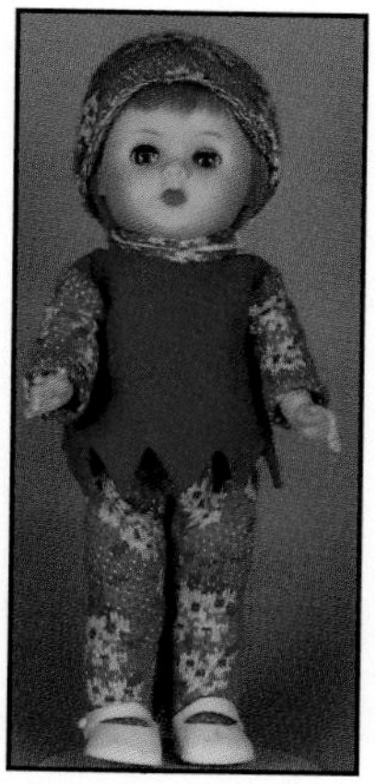

(1962), #18142 pixie outfit of flowered aqua jersey knit slacks and kerchief. Shown on later doll. The unusual elfin hairdo and felt top were created to match the 16" Miss Ginny #86181. Courtesy Barbara Rosplock-Van Orman.

fashion
leaders
in doll
society
1962
A quality family of dolls
and their outfits
cherished by little mothers everywhere,
created by Vogue Dolls, Incorporated

Cover 1962. Vogue brochure.

Ginny's Book

Ginny's First Secret

1958

Ginny even had her own book. The Phillips Publishing Company of Newton, Massachusetts, published a book on May 8, 1958 titled *Ginny's First Secret*, an endearing book about Ginny as a little girl having lots of adventures. The book, written by Lee Kingman, portrays wonderful values such as being open and positive. The book's lovely pictures of Ginny wearing clothes from the 1957 line are by Hazel Hoecker, a West Coast artist.

The publisher commissioned Lee Kingman to write under the terms of work for hire, which means the author received a flat fee. The Phillips Publishing Company was a small toy company run by two men whose daughters played with Ginny. They had previous success with a game called Spill and Spell and the Ginny book was their first attempt at publishing.

The publishers gave Lee Kingman the Ginny doll with the 1957 line of outfits and asked her to create a story using all the outfits. Ms. Kingman chose the phrase "look for the best" as the theme of the book. The secret is that Ginny is told to look for the best and that's what she'll find.

There was no editor on Phillips' first publishing project. Although Ms. Kingman did not meet her illustrator Hazel Hoecker or Mrs. Graves from the Vogue Company, the book manages to capture the essence of Ginny and is a charming story about a little girl's adventures.

The story is aimed at girls younger than age eleven. Ms. Kingman used adventures that she would like to experience as a child and made them happen for Ginny. She decided to represent all of the United States in the book. Ginny had a western costume; that is why a ghost town appears in the book. She even had Ginny go on a riverboat, another adventure which Ms. Kingman had never done.

The book begins with Ginny riding a horse at her aunt's Arizona ranch. Ginny finds out that she has to move with her family to a new home and is, understandably, not very happy. Lying in bed in her blue print nightgown with pom-pon slippers snuggling her dog, Sparkie, she wonders why she has to move. The next morning finds Ginny dressed in her red and white checked blouse and blue jeans outfit with straw hat setting out on an adventure with old Mr. Prospect over the desert and into the canyon to town. That night Ginny camps out under the stars and is told a secret by Mr. Prospect. When they arrive in the ghost town, Ginny, dressed in her yellow cotton dress with white and yellow flowers, talks to the hotel manager who tells her another secret. She then sends a message to her sister Jill who is home taking care of twin baby sister and brother Ginnette and Jimmy. Boarding a bus wearing her brown and white striped dress, Ginny meets a Navajo Indian girl holding a lamb who tells her another secret.

Staying overnight in a hotel in Gallup, New Mexico, Ginny wears her pink with white polka dot dress. The next day finds Ginny standing on a dock in her white dress with pink flowers and black bow tie and white hat. Her next stop on her adventures was New Orleans to visit her Aunt Nora. The next adventure was on a riverboat up the Mississippi River to St. Louis, with Ginny wearing a white with blue polka dot pants outfit and kerchief. Captain Dan tells her another secret on the riverboat. After staying one day with Aunt Lillian in St. Louis, Ginny, wearing her green dress with white lace trim and pink bow, and her mom go on a plane .

They are met at the airport at home by Jill wearing her yellow dress with white puffy sleeves and yellow ribbon print, pushing Jimmy and Ginnette in their strollers wearing their red and white checked shirt and romper outfits. Ginny wears her navy coat with white cuffs and collar and pink hat. Seeing her new home in Clearview Cove, Ginny says it is "the nicest place in the entire world." Her new house is replete with a lake and an apple tree with a swing in the yard. The next day sitting at her desk writing letters Ginny, wearing her white jumper with flowers and red top tells her secret to Jill who is wearing her orange and white striped dress with black trim, while Jimmy and Ginnette play outside in the sandbox. Ginny's secret was "Open your heart – Open your mind –

Look for the best, and that's what you'll find!"

Written in the first person by Ginny's mother, the book was very different from other books Ms. Kingman had written. Looking back on her experience writing the book, Ms. Kingman says it was a fun thing to do and that she can feel professional about it today even though it was so far from her usual writing style that it wasn't comfortable for her. She wishes she had further contact with the book and the publishers. Ms. Kingman went on to write 27 more books, including one illustrated by her own daughter.

Ginny's First Secret originally cost $2.75 and is now a collectible book worth around $125 with dust jacket. The dust jacket is white with pictures of Ginny and several of the people she meets in the book. The linen finish liner cover has a lovely orange print of Ginny's fashion accessories such as skis, necklaces, skates, gloves, hat boxes, sunglasses, mittens, golf bag, watch, and cowboy hat. The book was listed in the 1958 and 1959 Ginny brochure along with the furniture and accessories. It was also listed on the 1960 dealer price list. We thank Ms. Kingman for her precious story which captures the excitement and enthusiasm of a young girl whom we all love — Ginny.

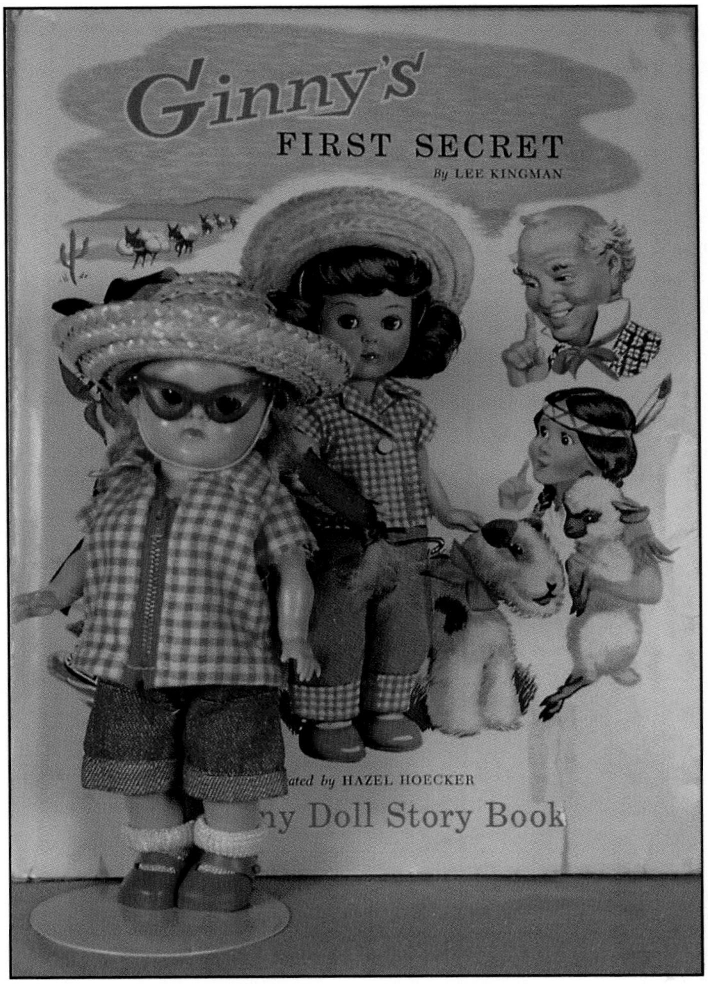

Cover of *Ginny's First Secret* by Lee Kingman, illustrated by Hazel Hoecker, published by Phillips Publishing, Newton, Mass., 1958. Current value is $125.00+ with dust jacket. The strung Ginny is wearing 1953 Talon Zipper Outfit "A.M." #70. The book cover illustrates 1957's similar outfit #7140.

Vinyl Head Walking Ginny

1963 – 1965

Description: 8", soft vinyl head, hard plastic body, bent knee walker but no head-turning mechanism, sleep eyes, molded lashes. The straight rooted hair was advertised as a pixie style.
Marks: Head: GINNY
Back: GINNY/VOGUE DOLLS, INC./PAT. NO.2687594/Made in U.S.A.
Dress Labels: Vogue Dolls, Inc., blue script on white twill tag
Dress closures: Gripper-style snaps with fluted metal design exposed on outside.
Tags: White paper hang tag tied to wrist with a string.
Printed on side one: "Hi! I'm Ginny/Created by Vogue Dolls Incorporated/Malden Mass."
Printed on side two: "Ginny Doll Family."
Boxes: Navy blue, pink and white one-piece boxes marked A Vogue Dolls Original.
Also one-piece whitish boxes, with teardrop-shaped acetate on lid; pink and navy blue Vogue logo is below window display.

Innovations And Growth

Vinyl Head and Rooted Hair: In 1963 Vogue put a soft vinyl head with rooted hair on Ginny's hard plastic, bent knee body. The doll itself was cute, but did not have the same quality and appeal as the all hard plastic dolls. The vinyl head Ginny's rooted pixie hairstyle was cut very short, quite a departure from earlier attractively set styles. While this vinyl headed version did have a certain charm, the doll just didn't look like the famous Ginny any more. Today, the doll's value to collectors is in having an example to complete their Ginny collection.

Management in Transition

Mrs. Graves retired from actively running Vogue in 1960. She remained chairman of the board of Vogue Dolls, Inc. while her daughter, Virginia Graves Carlson and son-in-law, Edwin Nelson ran the company. However, Mrs. Carlson concentrated on costume design and Mr. Nelson as president, concentrated on management.

Vogue actively promoted and developed other types of dolls, such as baby dolls and teen dolls. The baby dolls such as Ginnette and Ginny Baby, were both issued in new versions; Li'l Dear was introduced in 1963 and Bunny Hug was introduced in 1964. Vogue was focusing less and less on Ginny, and this was obvious with the new doll design and minimal fashions in 1963. Ginny had come a long way from the active little toddler with the beautiful wardrobe. Also, she was becoming a bit too tame for America's children who were increasingly being influenced by the exciting new television shows. In addition, Vogue was still attempting to capture a portion of the high-heeled teen doll market from competitor, Barbie dolls, and issued new versions of Jill and Jan in 1961 and 1962, respectively. Vogue was concentrating on the teen and larger doll market as a priority over Ginny.

Wardrobe, Special Styles, and Accessories

Fifteen simple new outfits were created for the vinyl head Ginny doll. Vogue's cost cutting efforts in order to stay competitive with the other doll makers were primarily responsible for the modest outfit designs. One exception in 1963 was a party outfit, #18545, with a white organdy skirt and black velvet bodice with matching hat. In fact, Vogue chose to use this outfit design for a matching outfit for their 16" Miss Ginny produced that year. Ginny also had two other outfits that matched Miss Ginny: #18542 white eyelet dress and bonnet, and #18540 white fleece jacket and pink pants. However, for the most part, Vogue could no longer count on Ginny's wardrobe to attract sales. Also, since only a few outfits were action styles, e.g., slacks, and none were sports styles, the market that enjoyed Ginny as an active little playmate was declining.

In such a lackluster sales environment, Vogue issued no accessories for Ginny in 1963 – 1964.

Marketing

Vogue marketed the new vinyl headed Ginny doll to consumers in 1963 and 1964 as "..a tiny toddler molded in the image of all sweet little girls." They marketed Ginny to the dealers as "the original miniature doll that continues to set standards again and features a hard plastic unbreakable body with walking features and bending knee with soft vinyl head and sleeping eyes and rooted hair. In her brand new pixie and side ponytails hairstyles she'll continue to command a strong following and profitable sales." Vogue created a sizable cardboard counter top display to help merchants attract business on the sales floor. However, all of these marketing efforts were not to provide the sales results that Vogue wished, and the doll was redesigned once again in 1965.

Prices	
Vinyl Head/Hard Plastic Body Ginny	
1963 – 1965	$150.00+

1963

Vinyl Head Bent Knee Ginny (1963) line shown in Vogue brochure. Courtesy Marge Meisinger.

Vinyl Head Bent Knee Ginny (1963), #1821, (-3 on box) undressed doll with soft vinyl head with rooted hair, hard plastic bent knee walker body. Did not have head-turning mechanism. Marks: GINNY (on head); GINNY/VOGUE DOLLS/INC/ PAT. NO. 267594/ MADE IN USA. Courtesy Ann Tardie.

Vinyl Head Bent Knee Ginny (1963), soft vinyl head and hard plastic bent knee walker body. Short blonde pixie hair cut. Red plaid dress, red bow is stapled into the head.

Vinyl Head Bent Knee Ginny (1963 – 65), aqua and blue checked dress with eyelet trim and black bow at the neck. Courtesy Cathy Schneider.

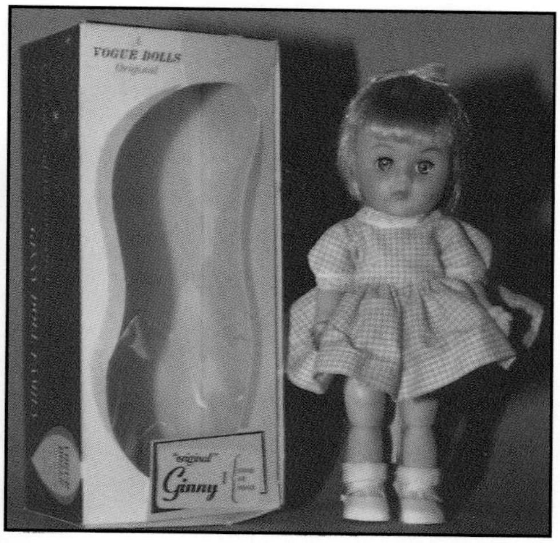

Vinyl Head Bent Knee Ginny (1963 – 65), pink checked dress with lace trim; mint in original box with acetate window lid. Courtesy Kathy Schneider.

Nun (1963) #18551, outfit for Vogue's vinyl head bent knee walker is the same as the previous year's all hard plastic Nun. Courtesy Barbara Rosplock-Van Orman.

1964

Vinyl Head Bent Knee Ginny (1964) line shown in Vogue brochure. Courtesy Marge Meisinger.

Vinyl Head Bent Knee Walker (1964) #1822, in panties as she came in her box. Courtesy Kathy Barry-Hippensteel.

Vinyl Head Bent Knee Walker (1964) #18630 in cotton gown. Courtesy Kathy Barry-Hippensteel.

1965

Vinyl Head Bent Knee Ginny (1965) #18143, red Valentine outfit with white fleece hooded top; #18141, black velvet pants outfit. Courtesy Marge Meisinger.

Ginny's Last USA Production Years

1965 – 1972

Description: 8", all vinyl doll, jointed arms and straight legs, non-walker, rooted hair, sleep eyes, molded lashes.

Marks: Head: GINNY
Back: GINNY/VOGUE DOLLS, INC.

Dress labels: Vogue Dolls, Inc. Made in U.S.A. in blue print on white cotton tag

Dress closures: Gripper snap with outside fluted metal design.

Tags: White paper tag print hung from doll's wrist with a string. Printed in black on side one: "Hi! I'm Ginny"; side two: name of doll or character.

Boxes: Navy blue, pink, and white one-piece boxes marked "A Vogue Dolls Original." Also, clear plastic with navy and hot pink cardboard label inside.

1965 – 69 White box with a doll in an oval design. Some of these boxes had irregular shaped, acetate window openings on the lid.

1972 Hot pink cardboard box with white writing "An Original Vogue Doll is Made to be Loved."

Innovation and Growth

Vinyl body: In 1965 Vogue introduced the Ginny Fairytale Land and Far-Away Land series dolls with a new all vinyl, straight leg body and a new head mold. Interestingly, Vogue still issued the 1965 little girl fashions on a Ginny with the previous year's vinyl head and a hard plastic body with bending knees. However, in 1966 all dolls (including the Fairytale Land and Far-Away Land series, as well as little girl Ginny) were all vinyl dolls with straight legs and rooted hair. The new soft vinyl Ginny head had a blushing glow color, and was molded with a sweet expression that was closer to the toddler look of the 1950s Ginny. The doll was very appealing and quite popular.

Made in USA Vinyl Ginny (1965), (from top left), Fairytale Land: Red Riding Hood, Mistress Mary, Mary Lamb, Jack and Jill, Cinderella, Little Bo Beep. (Bottom from left) Far-Away Land: France, Indian, Ireland, Tyrolean, Scotland, Dutch, Oriental (Spain and Italy not shown). Courtesy Wenham Museum, Wenham Mass.

These dolls continued to be produced in the United States by Vogue until 1969, when they discontinued production in this country. They then began to manufacture the all vinyl Ginny in Hong Kong as a further cost cutting measure. Company records from that time quote Mr. Nelson, president of Vogue, describing the process of manufacturing the new dolls. "The body and legs are blow molded vinyl and the arms and head are rotational molded. This differs only from the American made 1965 doll in that the earlier one was entirely rotational molded. The company has found that the blow molding process eliminates possibility of one leg being longer than the other...the new process provides us with better quality." However, while Vogue used this improved process on the USA vinyl Ginny mold, some of the Hong Kong vinyl used was a poorer quality. Consequently, while some of the dolls produced still had a good, pinkish color, many of the dolls were pale, and over time, some even produced a greenish cast. Vogue's attempt to take advantage of the reduced labor cost in Hong Kong resulted in some poorer quality dolls. This undoubtedly confused the consumer and began to have a negative impact on sales.

Management/competition: In 1966, Mrs. Carlson retired, leaving the management of Vogue entirely to her brother-in-law, Edwin W. Nelson, Jr., president of Vogue dolls. By the early 1970s competitive forces in the business were keen and the influence of television advertising was great. Vogue had chosen not to advertise on television for financial and other reasons. Competitors who did advertise on TV were gaining sales. The Barbie doll had captured the teen doll market, and Alexander-kins had assumed leadership in the 8" doll market. In addition to this, labor costs continued to grow. These factors among many others finally influenced Vogue to become a subsidiary of Tonka, officially selling the company and the Vogue name to Tonka Corporation in 1972. Tonka's name appears along with Vogue's on catalogs beginning in 1973.

Wardrobe, Special Styles, And Accessories

Wardrobe and special styles: In general, the styles from this era were simply made, yet quite appealing:

1965: In 1965 Vogue revived the Fairytale Land series with eight adorable outfits and Far-Away Lands dolls with nine new outfits that are charming and well-detailed.

1966: The Fairytale Land and Far-Away Lands series were released again in 1966 along with a collection of 10 little girl casual and party outfits.

1967: Far-Away Lands series were released.

1968: The Far-Away Lands dolls were released, along with a number of unique outfits: Stewardess #518, Pilgrim #519, Cowboy #520, Ballerina #522, and Bride #523. These outfits are much sought after today. Many Far-Away Lands outfits are also in demand, especially the American Indian in #501 in a white leather beaded dress. Of the eight 1968 little girl outfits, #1822 with the unusual Swedish braided hairstyle is one of the most unique.

1969 – 70: In 1969 Ginny had 12 Far-Away Lands dolls, and 10 little girl outfits, which were sold separately as well.

1971 – 72: In 1971 Vogue continued to produce Far-Away Lands dolls, switching production to Hong Kong, and officially selling to Tonka in 1972. Tonka's name appears on promotional material in 1973.

Marketing

Vogue attempted to draw on the past reputation of Ginny in their consumer marketing efforts with phrases such as: "Famous Ginny, the first miniature with her fully-jointed all skin-soft body, rooted hair and sleeping eyes..." In Ginny catalog pages to dealers Vogue featured, "Hours and hours of fun – and multiple sales – with the original miniature dolls and their undressable and washable wardrobes."

The pink paper doll design box had been dropped in 1961 in favor of a blue box with an adapted string of paper dolls and a solid lid flap. In 1965, a white box with doll in an oval design was instituted with an irregular oval-shaped acetate opening in the lid or lid flap to display the doll. This box was retained from 1965 through 1969. In addition, a clear plastic case was also issued for some dolls. Clothing boxes adopted a wood grain frame or TV screen design in the 1960s.

1965 had started out to be promising for Vogue, with the popular new vinyl doll mold generating greater interest than the vinyl head/plastic body version of the doll tried in 1963 and 1964. However, despite Vogue's attempt to produce an attractive mid-priced doll with exciting outfits, sales were not great enough in the competitive market. Ginny had lost her drawing power, little customers continued to be drawn to high-heeled teenage and other dolls. Vogue was ready to move to another stage and Ted Nelson, the last remaining member of Mrs. Graves's family in Vogue management, turned ownership over to Tonka in December, 1972. Tonka's name appeared on Vogue literature beginning in 1973.

Prices
All Vinyl Ginny
(1965 – 72)

Ginny (USA)	$100.00+
Far-Away Lands	$75.00
Fairytale Lands	$80.00
American Indian	
1965, 1966,	
1968 (felt dress)	$100.00+
1969 – 71 (leather dress)	$125.00

1965

Fairytale Land (1965 – 1966), Mary Had a Little Lamb #102, red checked skirt with eyelet overskirt and pantalets. Straw hat. The head mold was closer to the doll of the 1950s than the vinyl head hard plastic doll had been.

Fairytale Land (1965), all vinyl dolls made in USA. (Left to right) #102 Mary, #103 and #104 Jack (front) and Jill, #100 Red Riding Hood. Courtesy Marge Meisinger.

Fairytale Land (1965), Little Bo Peep #105, wears a pink polished cotton dress with lace trim and flowered side panniers. Courtesy Sandy Johnson Barts.

Far-Away Lands (1965 – 66), Little Dutch Girl #205 wearing an eyelet overskirt and lace cap, blue dress with ribbon of Dutch children near hem. Notice the 1960s Vogue wrist tag.

Far-Away Lands (1965) #200, France in red and white long cotton skirt and lace trim. Replaced hat. This outfit is reminiscent of the 1957 long gown #7071.

Far-Away Lands (1965), #206, Oriental outfit with a lovely upswept hairstyle decorated with flowers. Original paper parasol and plastic fan.

Far-Away Land (1965), American Indian #201 and Tyrolean Miss #203. Courtesy Marge Meisinger.

1966 – 1972

All Vinyl Ginny (1966 – 72), #181, in yellow romper and plastic pail. Note wrist tag and navy blue and purple Vogue box. Courtesy Ann Tardie.

All Vinyl Ginny (1966 – 69), red suede cloth apron over dotted cotton dress not shown in brochure but tagged, similar to 1968 #1826.

Fairytale Land (1966), (from left), Wee Willie Winkie, Hansel and Gretel. Courtesy Marge Meisinger.

Nun (1966) in special plastic case used by Vogue for a short time.

1968

All Vinyl Ginny (1968), #1822, yellow cotton dress with lace trim, one of eight little girl outfits produced in addition to the numerous Far-Away Lands costumes in 1968. Note unusual braided upswept hairdo.

Far-Away Lands (1968), #518, Turkish style costume with knife pleated nylon hat, brass hoop earrings, felt vest, and special black shoes with turned-up toes.

Far-Away Lands (1968), #509 and #510, Tyrolean girl and boy wear felt shorts or skirt with braid suspenders and cotton blouses.

1969

Far-Away Lands line, (from top left): #501 The American Indian; #502 Ireland; #503 Mexico; #504 Scotland; (from center left): #505 Dutch; #506 Russia; #507 Spain; #508 Italy; (from bottom left): #509 Tyrolean; #511 Scandinavia; #513 Germany; #517 India. Vogue catalog courtesy Marge Meisinger.

Far-Away Lands (1969), #501, the American Indian in white leather dress with beading, moccasins, headband and a papoose on the back. Courtesy Joe Kingston.

Far-Away Lands Ginny (1969), #509, Tyrolean; #504 Scotland. Courtesy Marge Meisinger.

Made in USA All Vinyl Ginny (1969) line, (from top left): #522 Bride; #523 Nun; (from center left) #1850; #1851; #1852; #1853; (from bottom left): #1854; #1855; #1856; #1857. Vogue catalog courtesy Marge Meisinger.

Ginny Bride #522, all vinyl doll, all original with satin gown, lace trim, and veil with flower attached to head.

Made in USA Vinyl Ginny (1969), #1852, pleated dress. Courtesy Marge Meisinger.

1972

Made in USA All Vinyl Ginny (1972), Gift Pack #1001, contains a dressed doll and two extra outfits. Note pink Vogue box. Courtesy Ann Tardie.

Vogue: A Subsidiary of Tonka

1972 – 1977

Description:	8", all vinyl, jointed at neck, arms and legs, non-walker, sleep eyes, molded lashes, some with painted lashes under the eye, rooted hair.
Marks:	Head: GINNY Back: VOGUE DOLLS © 1972/MADE IN HONG KONG/3
Dress labels:	MADE IN HONG KONG with green print and border on white paper
Dress closures:	Two types of snaps: 1. Round snap with smooth painted exterior on outside of outfit. 2. Unexposed metal snap sewn in dress opening.
Tags:	No wrist tags or other display tags on the doll itself.
Boxes:	1972, hot pink cardboard box with white writing, "An Original Vogue Doll is Made to be Loved."

Innovations and Growth

Doll mold/wigs: In 1972 Vogue was bought by Tonka Corporation. Tonka's official date of incorporation for Vogue was Dec. 18, 1972. However, Tonka's name first appeared on a Vogue catalog in 1973. Ted Nelson, president of Vogue since 1966, remained with Tonka Corporation for about three years while Tonka continued to produce the Ginny dolls in Hong Kong. By the mid 1970s there was no longer a member of Mrs. Graves's family managing the company.

Some of the Hong Kong Ginny dolls found today, mint in Tonka's box, have excellent coloring, with lashes painted under the eye, in addition to the molded lash. This is the case with #1820 Scotland and #1837 Dutch Girl dolls. However, other dolls found in Tonka's box, such as the #1899 Mexico doll, have poor coloring and no lashes painted under the eye. Also, some dolls have full, attractive hair and yet other Tonka dolls had hair rooted more sparsely than previous Vogue dolls.

Obviously, these variations can be attributed to Tonka's use of Vogue's remaining stock, to their use of vinyl with inconsistent quality in new doll production, and to their economizing on hair and rooting treatment. Unfortunately, the consumer could not have helped but notice this product inconsistency. Consequently, in 1975, Tonka attempted to rectify the problem of the inferior dolls, and they advertised in their 1975 catalog: "...new skin tones and hairstyles. Vogue knows that the more lifelike a doll looks, the more loveable she is to a little girl. Softer-looking, more colorful and more alive faces will be seen on our dolls this year." It was true that the doll color was a vast improvement. Nevertheless, they had already lost market share which proved difficult to recapture.

Tonka management: As Tonka endeavored to produce and market an appealing Ginny for a profitable cost, they were able to make some economies that Vogue was not able to make. For one thing their distribution and delivery channels were larger and very well developed. Also, they had an established, nationwide direct sales force to reach dealers regularly in an efficient way. Vogue had always rated high on dealer and customer service, and Tonka upheld this tradition. Tonka also put considerable time and energy into selling the entire Vogue line of dolls in this way.

Wardrobe, styles, and accessories: Tonka issued Ginny from Far-Away Lands in outfits from 16 countries. At first, some outfits were virtually the same as Vogue's outfits, (e.g., Spain #1859) while others were changed entirely, and some new outfits were added. In 1975 Africa #1802 was introduced in a cotton print wrap dress with a green top that is popular with collectors today. Also in 1975, Tonka produced a new version of the Ginny North American Indian #1840 in a brown suede cloth outfit and moccasins. In general, the outfits were inexpensively made, but most were appealing, nonetheless.

Marketing

Tonka paid a lot of attention to attracting and communicating with dealers. Recognizing that Vogue still carried great name recognition with dealers, they produced sales flyers with both the Vogue Dolls logo along with their own Tonka logo beginning in 1973. Also, they created new, attention grabbing, fuchsia colored packaging and promoted it to the dealer in sophisticated sales terms such as "maximum shelf impact," "purchase-motivating sales copy and graphics, and structural design for physical package strength and visibility." They also created a type of display that allowed the dealer to choose the specific Vogue dolls they wanted to be displayed.

While actively selling the toddler Ginny, no attempt was made to embellish the Ginny line beyond the Far-

Away Lands series, and a limited number of little girl outfits and gift packs. Unfortunately, dolls in international costumes did not spark the child's imagination to the extent that the active Ginny toddler once did. Perhaps Tonka recognized that the marketing climate was not right for the toddler doll, as the hot dolls on the market continued to be the high-heeled teen dolls, and not little girl dolls.

The Vogue doll line was not entirely consistent with Tonka's toy product line in general, and was not the most important contributor to their sales volume. Finally, in 1977 Tonka decided to sell the Vogue line, leaving the task of reviving Ginny to an eager Lesney Corporation.

Prices
Tonka

Year Produced	Type/Outfit	Mint Price
1973 – 77	Ginny (Hong Kong)	$75.00
	Far-Away Lands	$45.00+
	Africa	$95.00

Tonka Ginny from Far-Away Lands (1973 – 75), (from left), #1865 Switzerland, #1876 Poland, #1887 Tyrolean. These costumes are simply but attractively made. Unfortunately the vinyl on some of the Tonka dolls discolored or faded over time as these dolls show.

Tonka Ginny from Far-Away Lands (1975), #1802, Africa new this year.

Tonka Ginny from Far-Away Lands (1973), #1837 Dutch Girl 8", all vinyl. Made in Hong Kong with sleep eyes. Note Tonka's bright pink box.

Ginny Gift Pack (1973), #1000 contains a vinyl Ginny wearing a blue velvet jumper and white blouse, white stockings, and vinyl shoes, plus two other outfits. This was essentially the same as Vogue Gift Pack #1001, sold in 1972. Courtesy Veronica Phillips.

Tonka Ginny from Far-Away Lands (1974 – 75), #1899 Mexico, wears a hat similar to Vogue's 1968 doll. The 1973 Mexico was shown with basically the same costume but with a cloth head scarf instead of a hat.

Tonka Ginny from Far-Away Lands (1975), 8", all vinyl, made in Hong Kong with sleep eyes. (From top left) #1802 Africa, new this year; #1814 Russia; #1815 Ireland; #1819 Italy; #1820 Scotland; #1826 Canada. (From bottom left): #1837 Little Dutch Girl; #1840 North American Indian; #1841 Scandinavia; #1848 France; and #1859 Spain. Vogue catalog courtesy Marge Meisinger.

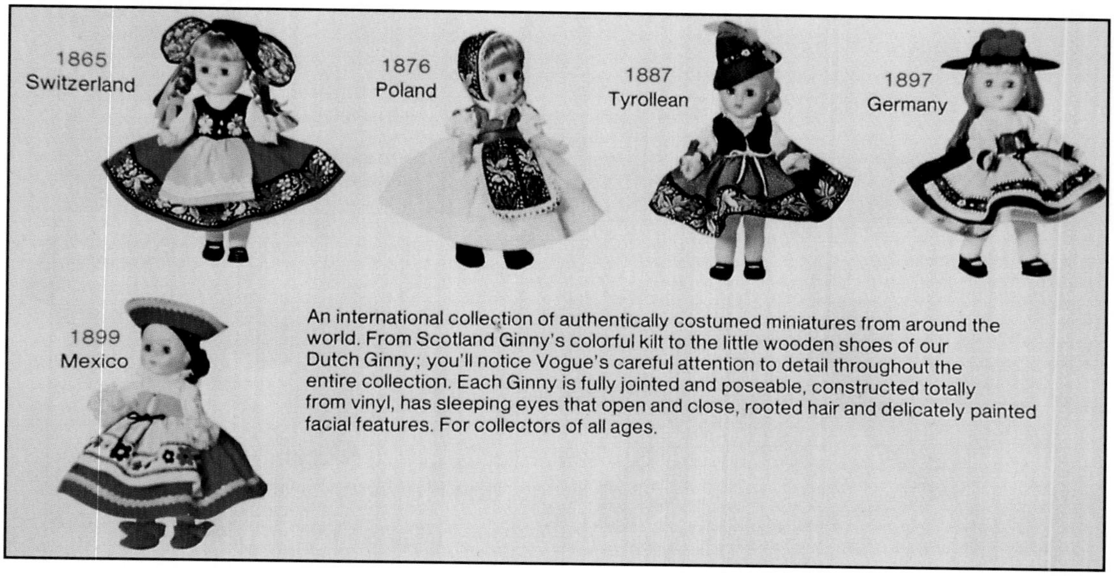

1865
Switzerland
1876
Poland
1887
Tyrollean
1897
Germany
1899
Mexico
An international collection of authentically costumed miniatures from around the world. From Scotland Ginny's colorful kilt to the little wooden shoes of our Dutch Ginny; you'll notice Vogue's careful attention to detail throughout the entire collection. Each Ginny is fully jointed and poseable, constructed totally from vinyl, has sleeping eyes that open and close, rooted hair and delicately painted facial features. For collectors of all ages.

Tonka Ginny from Far-Away Lands (1975), 8", all vinyl, made in Hong Kong with sleep eyes. (From top left) #1865 Switzerland; #1876 Poland; #1887 Tyrolean; #1897 Germany; (bottom) #1899 Mexico. Vogue catalog courtesy Marge Meisinger.

Tonka's France #1848 (left) was reissued as Lesney's (1977) #301848 in red skirt, white blouse, and hat. (Right) New Spain #301852 (1975) had new red dotted costume introduced in 1975. Prior Spanish costume had lace skirt.

Tonka Ginny from Far-Away Lands (1975), #1840, North American Indian, was introduced in brown suede cloth costume with braid trim and moccasins. Missing headband and matching arm braid.

Lesney Re-creates Ginny

1977 – 1982

In 1977 Lesney Products Corporation, well known for their Matchbox cars, purchased the rights to the Ginny name from Tonka. At the 1978 Toy Fair, Lesney surprised the doll world by announcing a brand new version of Ginny. This was their first of numerous changes for Ginny, including variations that were unique:

A. 1977 – 1982: Ginny from Far-Away Lands. Lesney initially promoted the Tonka series with sleep eyes until 1980. In 1980 they issued the series on their painted eye slim body Ginny.

B. 1978 – 1982: The World of Ginny. The big story from Lesney was their introduction of a revolutionary new Ginny design with the look of a much thinner 5- to 8-year-old girl.

C. 1981 – 82: Sasson Ginny. Lesney added the designer appeal of a Sasson Ginny. The doll had sleep eyes in 1981 and painted eyes in 1982.

D. 1982 – 83: International Brides. Using the same doll as the painted eye Sasson Ginny, Lesney created a series of brides elaborately attired in bridal outfits from around the world.

Lesney Friends from Far-Away Lands (1977). 8" all vinyl (from top left) #301865 Switzerland, #301803 Poland, #301815 Ireland, #301826 Scotland; (from bottom left) #301848 France, #301821 Greece. Vogue catalog courtesy Marge Meisinger.

Ginny From Far-Away Lands

(1977 – 1982)

Description: The Ginny from Far-Away Lands doll underwent three style changes, using different combinations of heads and bodies from other Ginny dolls produced under Lesney's direction:

1977 – 1979

(sleep eyes, chubby body)

Description: 8", all vinyl; sleep eyes; jointed head, arms, legs; chubby body (same as Tonka) non-walker; rooted hair. Same doll as Tonka overall.

Marks: Head: GINNY
Back: VOGUE DOLLS 1972/MADE IN HONG KONG/3*
(or same with 1977 date; *note some early dolls did not have "3")

Wardrobe: From 1977 – 1979 Lesney issued a series which it called Ginny from Far-Away Lands consisting of 12 international costumes. While this was essentially the same chubby Tonka doll, Lesney dropped some styles (Africa, Russia, Canada, North American Indian, Tyrolean, and Mexico) from the Tonka collection. However, some styles were released exactly as Tonka had designed them. These were: Ireland, Scotland, Dutch, Scandinavia, France, and Switzerland. In addition, Lesney redesigned the Spanish outfit from lace to a red dotted cotton gown with a ruffled hem. Also, Lesney added a doll from Greece, and a Little Pioneer Girl #301870 doll.

Box: Upright box, navy with white picture frame display front.

Lesney Friends from Far-Away Lands (1980), 8", all vinyl #301807 Jamaican Girl.

Lesney Friends from Far-Away Lands (1977), 8", all vinyl (from top left), #301805 Germany; #301841 Scandinavia; #301890 Italy; #301852 New Spain; (from bottom left) , #301870 Little Pioneer Girl; #301837 Little Dutch Girl. Little Pioneer Girl was new this year. Vogue catalog courtesy Marge Meisinger.

1980 – 1981

(painted eye, chubby body)

Description: A new 8", vinyl doll with painted eye head with rooted hair on the chubby body.

Marks:
Head: VOGUE DOLLS/ © GINNY TM/1977
Back*: VOGUE DOLLS © 1977/MADE IN HONG (or same with 1972 date)
(Note:* The chubby body for the painted eye Far-Away Lands doll was the same as for the sleep eye doll, but the 1977 date distinguishes it; however, as old stock was used up, some painted eye doll bodies have a 1972 date.)

Box: Same as 1977 – 79 (navy and white display box).

Wardrobe: Outfits were changed again in 1980 when Lesney changed to the painted eye dolls for the series. For example, Lesney added Jamaican Girl doll (#301807); an Austrian Girl (#301846) and Boy (#301839); and an English Girl (#301834). A number of dolls were dropped from the sleep eye Far-Away Lands doll series, including Poland and Spain.

Lesney's unique contributions to the Ginny from Far-Away Lands series were the Jamaican Girl (in her bright yellow cotton dress with orange and green rickrack), the Pioneer Girl (in gold print dress and green calico print poke bonnet), and the Austrian boy and girl (in their coordinated red, white, and blue outfits). All are popular with collectors.

Lesney designed a variety of boxes to promote various Ginny's looks over time, (from left) Far-Away Lands painted eye doll in navy and white box (1980 – 81); newly designed slim Ginny (1978 – 82) in dark and light pink stripe box; Sasson Ginny painted eye version in gray and pink box.

Ginny by Lesney (1978 – 1979), styles from Group A #301930 and Group B #301911. Note Lesney called black Ginny "Ginnette." Vogue catalog courtesy Marge Meisinger.

1982

(painted eye, slim body)

Description: 8", painted eye vinyl head with rooted hair; slim body (same as new slim Lesney Ginny doll); jointed at head and arms and flush joint at legs (same as International Bride).

Marks: Head: GINNY ®/VOGUE DOLLS/1977
Back: HONG KONG

Dress labels: White paper label with red type and border: O/MADE IN HONG KONG; usually sewn into inside seam of skirt petticoat; some do not have labels. (Also used up old Vogue stock labels with green ink.)

Dress closures: Primarily metal snaps sewn into back seam opening.

Tags: None on the doll itself.

Boxes: White upright box with red print, blue trim and fanciful balloon drawing on the front.

Wardrobe: In 1982 the Ginny from Far-Away Lands doll was changed to the painted eye, slim style dolls (like the new Lesney Ginny), and the collection came in 12 international styles. The Dutch style was similar to the original Lesney style, and the Spanish doll had a red dotted gown, reminiscent of the original Lesney look. However, the other dolls were new designs altogether or were for countries not previously represented, such as the Japanese and Polish dolls.

Marketing Far-Away Lands

Lesney continued to market Tonka's Far-Away Lands sleep eye, chubby body doll from 1977 – 79. The company added its own painted eye version beginning in 1980. In order to take advantage of any awareness of the original Ginny doll, they described the various forms of the chubby Far-Away Lands doll as the original 8" Ginny Collector Doll, and stressed Ginny from Far-Away Lands on the box. (Interestingly, the dealers catalog called the same doll "Friends from Far-Away Lands" with no promotion of the Ginny name at all.) Lesney redesigned Tonka's bright magenta box to a dignified blue and white box with cellophane display area, and changed the Tonka promotional line for Vogue from: "Vogue Dolls Are Made To Be Loved," to "Vogue Dolls... made with love." Lesney also designed an attractive four-color catalog page for dealer's information. These Far-Away Lands dolls, while inexpensively made, are very attractive and popular with collectors today.

Interestingly, Lesney's initial Far-Away Lands Ginny with a chubby body bore no resemblance to their new slim body Ginny. In 1982, perhaps to be consistent with the slim style of their regular Ginny doll, they changed the chubby Far-Away Lands doll to the slim, painted eye version too. They also redesigned the box with red print on a basic white box with blue trim, with a look very similar to the International Brides.

Ginny From the World Of Ginny

(1978 – 1982)

Description: 8", all vinyl; fully jointed neck, arms, legs (hip joint is square); poseable with bendable knees;
Dynel rooted hair in long straight or pulled beck styles in blonde, dark and light brown; molded lash, sleep eyes with three short painted lines in the outside corners and two under the eye.

This doll was designed by Marcy Burtula, and was more slender than Vogue's original Ginny toddler concept, and was designed to look like a 5- to 8-year-old child. They created an identical black doll #301930 named Ginnette, with dark hair, in a short, curled, style. (The 1978 Ginny brochure points out: Note: Black doll is called Ginnette™).

Marks: Ginny:
Head: GINNY ®/VOGUE DOLLS/1977
Back: 1978 VOGUE DOLLS/MOONACHIE NJ/MADE IN HONG KONG

Marks: Ginnette (black doll):
Head: GINNY ®/VOGUE DOLL CO/1977
Back: same as Ginny above

1978 – 82 World of Ginny also sold in a navy window display box with white lettering.

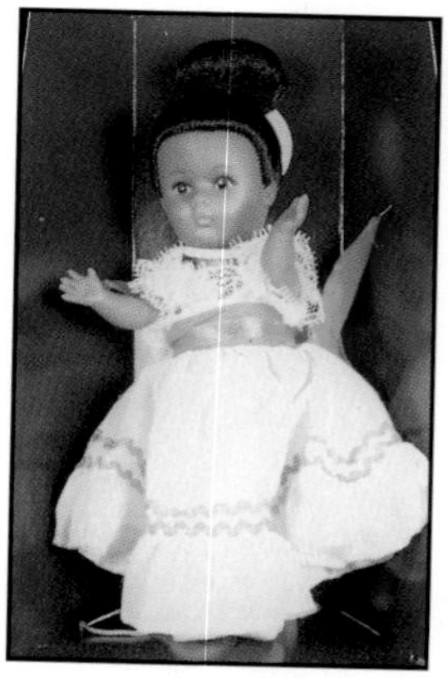

Lesney Friends from Far-Away Lands (1980), 8", all vinyl #301807 Jamaican Girl.

Lesney Friends from Far-Away Lands (1977), 8", all vinyl (from top left), #301805 Germany; #301841 Scandinavia; #301890 Italy; #301852 New Spain; (from bottom left) , #301870 Little Pioneer Girl; #301837 Little Dutch Girl. Little Pioneer Girl was new this year. Vogue catalog courtesy Marge Meisinger.

1980 – 1981

(painted eye, chubby body)

Description: A new 8", vinyl doll with painted eye head with rooted hair on the chubby body.

Marks:
Head: VOGUE DOLLS/ © GINNY TM/1977
Back*: VOGUE DOLLS © 1977/MADE IN HONG (or same with 1972 date)
(Note:* The chubby body for the painted eye Far-Away Lands doll was the same as for the sleep eye doll, but the 1977 date distinguishes it; however, as old stock was used up, some painted eye doll bodies have a 1972 date.)

Box: Same as 1977 – 79 (navy and white display box).

Wardrobe:
Outfits were changed again in 1980 when Lesney changed to the painted eye dolls for the series. For example, Lesney added Jamaican Girl doll (#301807); an Austrian Girl (#301846) and Boy (#301839); and an English Girl (#301834). A number of dolls were dropped from the sleep eye Far-Away Lands doll series, including Poland and Spain.

Lesney's unique contributions to the Ginny from Far-Away Lands series were the Jamaican Girl (in her bright yellow cotton dress with orange and green rickrack), the Pioneer Girl (in gold print dress and green calico print poke bonnet), and the Austrian boy and girl (in their coordinated red, white, and blue outfits). All are popular with collectors.

Lesney designed a variety of boxes to promote various Ginny's looks over time, (from left) Far-Away Lands painted eye doll in navy and white box (1980 – 81); newly designed slim Ginny (1978 – 82) in dark and light pink stripe box; Sasson Ginny painted eye version in gray and pink box.

Ginny by Lesney (1978 – 1979), styles from Group A #301930 and Group B #301911. Note Lesney called black Ginny "Ginnette." Vogue catalog courtesy Marge Meisinger.

1982

(painted eye, slim body)

Description: 8", painted eye vinyl head with rooted hair; slim body (same as new slim Lesney Ginny doll); jointed at head and arms and flush joint at legs (same as International Bride).

Marks: Head: GINNY ®/VOGUE DOLLS/1977
Back: HONG KONG

Dress labels: White paper label with red type and border: O/MADE IN HONG KONG; usually sewn into inside seam of skirt petticoat; some do not have labels. (Also used up old Vogue stock labels with green ink.)

Dress closures: Primarily metal snaps sewn into back seam opening.

Tags: None on the doll itself.

Boxes: White upright box with red print, blue trim and fanciful balloon drawing on the front.

Wardrobe: In 1982 the Ginny from Far-Away Lands doll was changed to the painted eye, slim style dolls (like the new Lesney Ginny), and the collection came in 12 international styles. The Dutch style was similar to the original Lesney style, and the Spanish doll had a red dotted gown, reminiscent of the original Lesney look. However, the other dolls were new designs altogether or were for countries not previously represented, such as the Japanese and Polish dolls.

Marketing Far-Away Lands

Lesney continued to market Tonka's Far-Away Lands sleep eye, chubby body doll from 1977 – 79. The company added its own painted eye version beginning in 1980. In order to take advantage of any awareness of the original Ginny doll, they described the various forms of the chubby Far-Away Lands doll as the original 8" Ginny Collector Doll, and stressed Ginny from Far-Away Lands on the box. (Interestingly, the dealers catalog called the same doll "Friends from Far-Away Lands" with no promotion of the Ginny name at all.) Lesney redesigned Tonka's bright magenta box to a dignified blue and white box with cellophane display area, and changed the Tonka promotional line for Vogue from: "Vogue Dolls Are Made To Be Loved," to "Vogue Dolls... made with love." Lesney also designed an attractive four-color catalog page for dealer's information. These Far-Away Lands dolls, while inexpensively made, are very attractive and popular with collectors today.

Interestingly, Lesney's initial Far-Away Lands Ginny with a chubby body bore no resemblance to their new slim body Ginny. In 1982, perhaps to be consistent with the slim style of their regular Ginny doll, they changed the chubby Far-Away Lands doll to the slim, painted eye version too. They also redesigned the box with red print on a basic white box with blue trim, with a look very similar to the International Brides.

Ginny From the World Of Ginny

(1978 – 1982)

Description: 8", all vinyl; fully jointed neck, arms, legs (hip joint is square); poseable with bendable knees;
Dynel rooted hair in long straight or pulled beck styles in blonde, dark and light brown; molded lash, sleep eyes with three short painted lines in the outside corners and two under the eye.

This doll was designed by Marcy Burtula, and was more slender than Vogue's original Ginny toddler concept, and was designed to look like a 5- to 8-year-old child. They created an identical black doll #301930 named Ginnette, with dark hair, in a short, curled, style. (The 1978 Ginny brochure points out: Note: Black doll is called Ginnette™).

Marks: Ginny:
Head: GINNY ®/VOGUE DOLLS/1977
Back: 1978 VOGUE DOLLS/MOONACHIE NJ/MADE IN HONG KONG

Marks: Ginnette (black doll):
Head: GINNY ®/VOGUE DOLL CO/1977
Back: same as Ginny above

1978 – 82 World of Ginny also sold in a navy window display box with white lettering.

Dress labels: White cloth with black print label: MADE IN HONG KONG
Dress closures: ⅜" diameter exposed white metal snap.
Tags: None on the doll itself.
Boxes: 1978 – 82 World of Ginny sold in a pink, green and/or blue pin-striped design on the front of upright window display box; Ginny written in white script on acetate display panel.

Wardrobe, Special Styles and Accessories

Wardrobe and Special Styles: The new Ginny wardrobe in 1978 had 18 new styles and was well designed. Interestingly, Lesney borrowed some elements of design from original '50s and '60s Ginny outfits, including an eyelet dress and apron, plaid skirt and beret, lace trim, and even a popover and tam outfit. However, the overall look was very modern, and the white tights and plastic hats gave a look that was updated, now, today, per the sales brochure. These outfits were also packaged and sold separately.

In 1979, there was a problem with the manufacturer in Hong Kong and very few Ginnys appeared, and only six new outfits appeared.

Collectors wanting at least one Lesney Ginny to complete their Ginny collection tend to seek out outfit #301944, a lace trimmed, pink party dress with a white straw hat, which was widely featured in Lesney advertisements, and resembled '50s Ginny dresses (except for inset sleeves). Also, #301930 Ginnette (black Lesney Ginny) in overalls is popular. The Special Gift Pack containing Ginny and two extra outfits in a cellophane covered display package is also popular for Lesney Ginny fans.

Accessories: In 1978 Lesney introduced a number of imaginative plastic accessories for the new Ginny, including # 302084 bed; #203088 wardrobe; #302096 vanity; #302083 student desk; #203097 moped (not shown again until the 1980 catalog). In 1979, two new accessories were introduced, a cute, vinyl house-design Ginny Carry Case in pink and blue, holding the doll and outfits, and the Ginny Sweet Shop with tables and chairs to sit and sip a soda, and even a poster to hang in the owner's room. The desk and the moped are hard to find today, and are much sought after by collectors. In 1980 Lesney marketed a High Bar (doll not included) which had a crank handle to turn while Ginny did the most difficult of gymnastic feats with the greatest of ease.

Marketing Ginny

Doll design: Lesney truly surprised Ginny lovers with the creation of a new doll which did not look at all like the original doll. This doll had a thin face and body with the look of a 5- to 8-year-old little girl. Lesney's new concept for Ginny was clearly stated in a four-color brochure found in each box: "The Wonderful World of Ginny has been updated for the now look and comes dressed in the fashions you dream of having today." Indeed, each Ginny outfit was very stylish, and Ginny dresses had grown-up white stockings instead of anklets, which were reserved for sports or slacks outfits. Lesney wisely promoted features that had been popular with the original Ginny in the 1950s. For example, printed on the box was: "Poseable doll with bendable knees, moving eyes and combable hair," and also, "...lots of pretty new clothes and accessories." While these were not the jointed knees of the 1957 Ginny, they encouraged action-oriented play, and Lesney recognized that promoting a Ginny that was active in addition to well dressed was very important.

Advertising

Lesney used its vast network of distribution and retail channels to market the doll. In addition to their dealer and merchant contacts, Lesney tied in with a number of mail order catalog houses, and these mail order dolls were shipped in plain boxes, and separate outfits in plain brown packages. Many special outfits were exclusive to these mail order outlets, such as Montgomery Ward's catalog, and are very interesting dolls to collect today.

Advertising was vigorous in consumer magazines, such as *Doll Reader*, *Woman's Day* and *Good Housekeeping*, and in trade magazines such as *Playthings*. However, Lesney had a basic problem with the new promotional concept. While Lesney had changed the look of the doll itself to a slim doll, they still expected advertising to take full advantage of the popularity of the 1950s and 1960s Ginny, which had a cute little toddler body. The little girls who loved the original doll were now mothers themselves, and Lesney attempted to convert their loyal following into sales for the new doll. The brochure said: "The World of Ginny ... The precious doll that mother played with as a child is now back for you to play with and treasure just as Mommy did." The box said, "Chances are you will love me as much as your Mom did." Apparently, this was an optimistic stretch for the new Ginny owners, and, more importantly, for their mothers. As adorable as the new doll was, and as well thought out as the marketing approach was, the doll was not accepted as a replacement for the old Ginny and sales reflected this.

Interestingly, Lesney initially saw no contradiction to advertising and promoting two Ginnys simultaneously: one from the Far-Away Lands series which was essentially the chubby Tonka Ginny in international costumes, and another one with a slim new design in the same little girl outfits. Finally, in 1982, Lesney changed the Far-Away Lands doll to the slim design, too. All of these changes probably confused the customer and inhibited sales.

It is also interesting that Lesney saw no contradiction in marketing their black doll as Ginnette, a name long used for their 8" baby doll.

The new Ginny did not sell as well as they hoped. Some current doll collectors register their lack of appreciation for the Lesney Ginny by dubbing it "the skinny Ginny" while others go out of their way to acquire the doll. Since it is a doll with a lot of style and charm, it will one day undoubtedly develop its deserved following.

World of Ginny by Lesney (1978 – 1979), styles from Group B #301944, an assortment of six outfits offered in 1978 and 1979 for the new slim body Ginny. Vogue catalog courtesy Marge Meisinger.

World of Ginny by Lesney (1978 – 1979), styles from Group C #301977, an assortment of six styles. Vogue catalog courtesy Marge Meisinger.

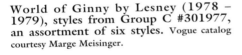

World of Ginny by Lesney (1978), separate outfits were sold on cards and included shoes, sneakers, tights, and panties. Vogue catalog courtesy Marge Meisinger.

Ginny Goes Sasson

(1981 – 1982)

Description: 8", all vinyl, fully jointed legs, head, arms; poseable doll with bendable knees, rooted Dynel hair in long styles with pulled back side braided style around the crown, blonde and brunette color. The Sasson Ginny was introduced in the 1981 brochure with sleep eyes, which was later changed to painted eyes in 1981 – 82. Two observations about the doll design should be noted:

1. The Sasson body is the same as the new, slim Lesney Ginny doll body, with either the sleep eye or the painted eye head.
2. The painted eye design on Sasson dolls had two versions. Some painted eyes have four lashes above the eyes, and a white dot to indicate a twinkle or sparkle. Other painted eyes utilize a painted eye with brown shading above the eye and an "x" design to indicate a twinkle. (This second version of eye paint also had a deeper shade of vinyl. It was apparently the same head used on the International Bride series, but with the pulled back braids of the Sasson style.)

Marks: Sasson Ginny (painted eye and sleep eye):
Head: GINNY ®/VOGUE DOLLS/ 1977
Back: 1978 VOGUE DOLLS INC/MOONACHIE N.J./MADE IN HONG KONG

Dress labels: Early sleep eye Sasson: White ribbon with black print, MADE IN HONG KONG. Later painted eye Sasson: White label ribbon printed in black, MADE IN CHINA sewn inside outfit.

Dress closures: Mostly pull-on styles with ties or belts, etc.

Tags: None on the doll itself.

Boxes: Gray and white window box with a drawing of a Ginny seated on the pink outline of a hand on a special side flap: Ginny script in blue at the top of the box; braiding diagrams on the back of the box. Large gift boxes had a pin stripe design on the cardboard box with an acetate top.

Wardrobe, Special Styles, and Accessories

Lesney turned to the popular design house, Sasson, (of Sasson Jeans, Inc.) by 1981 to give life to the Ginny doll line. An entire collection of Sasson fashions was created, the most popular of which featured detailed Sasson jeans, a designer T-shirt, designer belt and buckle. This was the outfit featured in most advertisements, promotions, and in the 1981 Lesney catalog. Extra Sasson outfits could be purchased on specially designed blister cards. Special Gift Pack Sets were sold which contained the dressed doll and two extra outfits. All the Sasson Ginny outfits required active footwear, such as running shoes or disco roller skates. Even the skirt outfits had fashionable go-go boots, and the stylish cowboy outfit had a plastic cowboy hat and boots. Obviously, all of the regular Ginny accessories could be used by the new Sasson Ginny.

Ginny by Lesney (1980), Special Gift Pack #302092, Ginny dressed to play sports with two extra outfits. Courtesy Shirley Niziolek.

Marketing

The new sleep eye Sasson Ginny was given prominence in the 1981 Lesney catalog, and was shown side by side with the slim Ginny introduced in 1980. Numerous newspaper features appeared around the country on the new Sasson Ginny outfits. The doll was marketed with the promotion line: Ginny goes Sasson. A very creative box was designed for the new doll, promoting her features: Sasson outfits, and braids. In fact, the box featured a diagram of three different braiding styles for Sasson Ginny's hair. Owners were encouraged to brush, comb, and braid her hair to compliment her many new and exciting fashions.

It is interesting that, while this Sasson Ginny used the same body as its new 1978 slim Ginny, they got an entirely different look for the Sasson doll with braids, particularly when Vogue changed the Sasson doll to painted eyes. Perhaps they were trying to create a cuter Ginny while injecting the excitement of the Sasson outfits. In any case, sales were disappointing, even after they changed to Sasson Ginny with painted eyes.

Sasson Ginny by Lesney (1981). Sleep eyes were introduced on the all vinyl Sasson Ginny in 1981. In 1982 Sasson Ginny was changed to painted eyes. Courtesy Trudy Taylor.

INTERNATIONAL BRIDES
(1982)

Description: 8", soft vinyl, painted eyes with a little white x-shaped sparkle mark, rooted Dynel hair in long, pulled back or upswept styles, fully jointed with a flush hip joint, arms, and head. While the doll and its outfits are inexpensively made, the bright, cleverly designed international bride costumes distinguish the doll.

Note:

1. Head: The head on this doll is basically the same head as the Sasson painted eye head, with varied eye painting styles.
2. Eyes: Some dolls have painted lashes above the eyes, and some do not, but all use a little white "x" mark to indicate a sparkle in the eye.
3. Vinyl: The vinyl on some international dolls is a deep shade of tan with glowing cheek color, according to the nationality depicted. Unfortunately, the vinyl on some dolls has changed color over time.
4. It should be pointed out that, while the body mold appears to be the one used for the slim body Ginny, it is not. It has a flush hip joint instead of the squared off joint of the other slim Ginny dolls. Also, the body of the International Bride itself is distinguished by the different mark: HONG KONG, as detailed below.

Marks: Neck: GINNY ®/VOGUE DOLLS/ 1977
Back: HONG KONG (lower back)

Dress labels: Black print on white ribbon: MADE IN CHINA

Dress closures: Metal snaps, both exposed and unexposed, and circular snaps.

Tags: None on the doll itself.

Box: White box with a three-sided altar display front; drawings of Ginny bride on the front; Ginny/Bride in red print and International in blue print.

International Brides by Lesney (1981), Brazilian #30-16-04, 8", painted eye vinyl doll in yellow and white costume. The window altar box with colorful graphics was used for all International Brides.

International Brides by Lesney (1981). Chinese is one of the most colorful costumes in the series. The stand was included in the box.

Wardrobe

While the series was rather inexpensively made, the authentic bridal costumes from 12 countries were quite attractive. The American Bride in a white nylon gown with lace trim and net veil trimmed with flowers is one of the most popular in the series. Also, the Chinese Ginny #30-16-13, with her colorful metallic head piece and lovely brocade and silk gown is very attractive. Some consider the International Brides Lesney's most outstanding series.

Marketing

The International Bride series was Lesney's last attempt to rejuvenate Vogue Ginny dolls. A unique altar box was created with a three-sided, cellophane display case. The box enthusiastically encouraged collectors to buy the entire series, using an actual photograph with all 12 dolls: Mexican, Turkish, Brazilian, French, Chinese, English, Irish, Egyptian, Polish, German, American, and Israeli. Unfortunately, the line never got off the ground, since Lesney went into receivership in 1982. No catalog documentation has been found for 1983.

Ginny International Brides (1982), introducing 12 brides and three window display boxes that look like an altar. *Toys, Hobbies and Crafts Magazine* ad. Courtesy Marge Meisinger.

Code:
V – Vinyl
SL – Straight Leg
Bend – Bendable
Root – Rooted hair
Slp – Sleep eye
Mld – Molded lash

Prices

Lesney

Year Produced	Type/Outfit	Body	Eye	Mint Price
1977 – 1979	Far-Away Lands	V, SL	Slp, Mld	$25.00+
1978 – 1982	Ginny	V, Bend	Slp, Mld	$25.00+
1980 – 1981	Far-Away Lands	V, SL	Painted	$20.00+
1982	Far-Away Lands	V, Bend	Painted	$20.00+
1981	Sasson Ginny	V, Bend	Slp, Mld	$30.00+
1981 – 1982	Sasson Ginny	V, Bend	Ptd, Mld	$25.00+

Meritus® Rejuvenates Ginny

1984 – 1986

Vinyl Ginny
(1984 – 1986)

Description: 8", all soft vinyl doll with a new mold resembling Vogue's 1963 – 71 Ginny, fully jointed, non walker, sleep eyes, molded lashes, rooted hair in long and short styles, and braids.
Marks: Head: GINNY ®
Back: VOGUE DOLLS/(a star logo)/M.I.I 1984/Hong Kong
Dress labels: Black print on white satin labels: Vogue dolls, INC./ C 1984 (or 1985)
Dress closures: Metal snaps.
Tags: 1985/6 line: Gold foil two-sided heart shaped wrist tag, black print: a real Vogue Doll; reverse side: Ginny 1986.
Boxes: Navy blue with pink hearts in lattice design "Vogue dolls made with love"

Porcelain Ginny
(1984 – 1986)

Description: 1. Chinese Porcelain: 1984 – 1986
8" all porcelain mold with a slightly older, sophisticated looking face mold; jointed (In 1984 jointed at head, arms, legs, knees, ankles; in 1985 only jointed head, arms and legs); wigs (long styles on Ginny in Four Seasons costumes #75011 and side braided with buns hairstyle on porcelain ballerina #75003).
Marks: GINNY/® VOGUE DOLLS/INC/(a star logo)MII 1984/MADE IN TAIWAN
Description: 2. Heritage Collection: 1984
8" all porcelain, jointed at head, neck and legs; wig in long hairstyles.
It is a different mold than Chinese porcelain Ginny. It has a wide-eye look.
Beautiful lace trimmed gowns and dresses #78002 Party Time, #78003 Christmas Spirit, #78001 Southern Belle, #78004 Holiday Deluxe Doll with basket and extra outfits. A limited numbered edition.
Marks: Head: GW/SCD/5184

Innovations and Growth

In 1983, Walter Reiling, president of Meritus Industries, acquired the rights to the Ginny and Vogue names. From his many years of experience in the toy business, he recognized that Lesney's Ginny needed major revision. He felt that the time was right to restore Vogue's original cute little toddler-playmate concept for the doll and that this was the key to regaining the doll's popularity. He also recognized the importance to Ginny's market of well-made, adorable dress designs. Indeed, the doll market had come full circle from the high-heeled doll craze. The social climate fueling the great popularity of the teen doll since the mid 1950s was gradually changing. Consequently, tradition was once again becoming a viable approach to selling Ginny. Incredibly, this had been the approach Lesney had tried, but it had not worked. Now Meritus was in the right place and time with the right doll.

Meritus's new Ginny dolls were very successful at the 1984 Toy Fair and continued to be acclaimed in 1985 and 1986 by collectors and children alike. Meritus had brought back Ginny as the wide eyed, charming little play companion.

Wardrobe, Special Styles, and Accessories

In 1984 Meritus offered the basic doll in personalized Ginny panties, socks and shoes, #70016, as well as the dressed doll in outstanding outfits. The 1984 collection included Holiday Girl with a long flowing dress; Going Shopping, a tailored little two-piece outfit; and a lovely white Communion dress. In the tradition of Ginny, each outfit had a hat, headpiece or hair ribbon. In 1985 Meritus offered an extensive line, including the Ginny Collection #70001 consisting of 12 outfits, all reminiscent of outfits in the '50s and '60s. In addition they designed a Calendar Series #71501, with a special gown or long skirted outfit for each month of the year. Also, six Party Ensembles #72001, and six Play Ensembles included Bride and Groom #71005, Hansel and Gretel #71006, and Jack and Jill #71004. The outfits for these dolls were all beautifully detailed and resembled earlier Vogue outfits.

However, the most notable Ginny costume was the Coronation Queen #71007, with a royal pearl and gold crown, scepter, and long velvet robe trimmed in fur. The doll was a wonderful design in the tradition of Vogue's 1953 and 1954 Coronation Queen Ginny.

Accessories were released as well: a little plastic Shetland Pony # 7450 with a long, silky mane and tail; plastic Vanity #74403; Wardrobe # 74405; and Bed #74404.

Marketing

The Meritus marketing program was as clever and well executed as their wonderful doll collection. The doll box was changed to an eye catching royal blue with a white lattice border and pink heart design. Also, in addition to trade advertising, they produced an extensive four-color catalog, as well as a mini-catalog with an especially large distribution in 1985. Meritus president, Walter Reiling, took a personal role in the catalog's message. In an introductory note to dealers, reminiscent of Mrs. Graves's personalized dealer communications, he states, "....I thank you for your kind support and invite you to continue the Ginny experience with us. Warmest Regards, Wally." Meritus also instituted the Ginny Doll Club. Members received the *Ginny News* quarterly, a membership certificate, and a Doll Club Catalog with a charm with Ginny on it. Meritus also issued attractive calendars with wonderful photographs of both new and original Ginnys, reinforcing the link to the original doll. Watercolor paper dolls were also designed with reproductions of 1950 authentic collectors outfits and some new Ginny outfits to cut out.

These and other clever marketing programs contributed to the great acceptance of the new Ginny. Ginny was a success, but for personal reasons Walter Reiling decided to sell the rights to Ginny to Dakin, Inc. in 1986.

1984 – Vinyl

Ginny by Meritus (1984), 8", all vinyl, Ginny similar to original mold. Collection included: (counterclockwise from top): Sweetness, Holiday Girl, Communion, All Winds, Going Shopping, and Sweet Rosebud. All names were trademarked. Catalog courtesy Marge Meisinger.

Ginny by Meritus (1984), 8", all vinyl, Ginny similar to original 1950s mold. (Clockwise from top): Little One, Spring Time, Skating, Back to School, Antique Lace and Winter Chill. Notice Little One is reminiscent of Vogue's 1950s outfits updated with tights. Catalog courtesy Marge Meisinger.

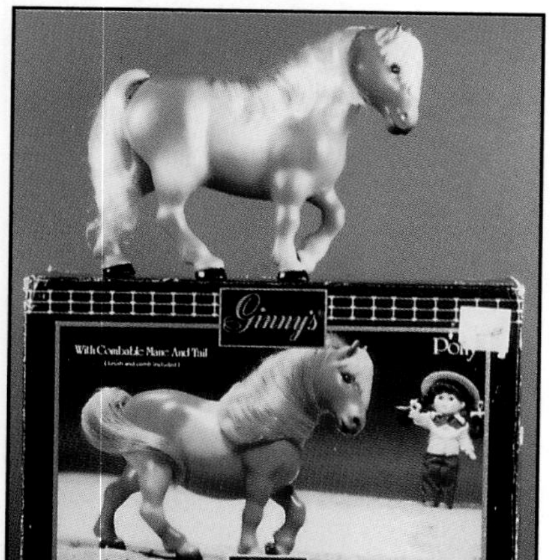

Ginny's Pony (1984), #7001, combable mane and tail, comb and brush included. Courtesy Barbara Hill.

Prices
Meritus

Year Produced	Type/Outfit	Body	Head	Mint Price
1984 – 86	Ginny/All orig.	V, SL	V, Root	$30.00 – 55.00
1984	Ginny/Porc./Heritage	P	P, Wig	$100.00+
1984 – 86	Ginny/Chinese Porc.	P	P, Wig	$55.00+
1984 – 86	Coronation Queen	V, SL	V, Root	$95.00+

Code:
V – Vinyl
P — Porcelain
SL – Straight Leg
Root – Rooted hair

1984 – Porcelain

Ginny by Meritus (1984), 8", porcelain from the Chinese Porcelain collection #75001, three dolls were offered: Satin Belle, Ballerina, and Midnight Pearl. All names were trademarked. Catalog courtesy Marge Meisinger.

Ginny by Meritus (1984), 8", porcelain from the Heritage Collection of Porcelain limited edition dolls. The outfits were produced in 1984 only. The dolls were marked: GW/SCK/5184 (on their heads). Catalog courtesy Marge Meisinger.

Ginny by Meritus (1983 – 85), 8", porcelain horse with brass Ginny name plate on the wooden base.

1985 – Porcelain

PorcelainGinny by Meritus (1985), 8", porcelain clown in plastic protective case. Special souvenir doll from the 1985 Modern Doll Convention. Courtesy Barbara Rosplock-Van Orman.

1985 – Vinyl

Ginny by Meritus (1985), 8", all vinyl Ginny Goes Country, a Shirley's Dollhouse Exclusive. Originally ordered from Meritus in 1985, the blue Meritus box is dated 1984 and the Meritus wrist tag is dated 1985. However, the doll was packaged and delivered in 1986 by Dakin.

1986 – Vinyl

Ginny by Meritus (1986), six of the 12 styles in the Ovation Collection. Note the return of the Ginny flip and braids hairstyles. Meritus President Wally Reiling added a personal greeting in the catalog. Catalog courtesy Marge Meisinger.

Ginny by Meritus (1986), Bride and Groom #71005, from Famous Pairs collection. Vinyl Ginny Bride has rooted hair. Courtesy Shirley Niziolek.

Ginny by Meritus (1986), styles from the Famous Pairs collection. Vinyl Ginny Bride has rooted hair. Catalog courtesy Marge Meisinger.

Ginny by Meritus (1986), styles from the Encore collection include #71007, a re-creation of the famous Ginny 1953 Coronation Queen. Also shown is the porcelain Ballerina #75003. Catalog courtesy Marge Meisinger.

Ginny Moves To R. Dakin Company

1986 – 1995

Description: 8", both all hard plastic and all soft vinyl, jointed at head, arms and legs; sleep eyes with molded lashes with and without painted lashes under the eye; rooted hair in long styles, braids, and poodle styles.

Marks: Soft Vinyl:
Back: VOGUE ® DOLLS/©1984 R.DAKIN INC./MADE IN CHINA
Hard Vinyl:
Back: VOGUE/®/DOLLS/©1986 R. DAKIN and CO./MADE IN CHINA

Dress labels: Vogue Dolls Inc./1987 or ©1988/Vogue R Dolls/A Division of Dakin or © 1989/Vogue ® Dolls/A Division of Dakin or, 1991, etc. in black print on white satin tag.

Dress closures: Metal snaps

Tags: Gold foil two-sided wrist tag black print: Vogue Dolls made with love; reverse side name and year of outfit.

Boxes: 1986 – Bright blue box, the same as Meritus.
1987 – Light pink with blue writing, "Vogue dolls made with love."
1988 – Pink and white striped with blue flowers.
1993 – Pink box with a new Doorway design.

Ginny by Dakin (1986), a limited edition 8", hard plastic, The Enchanted Doll #78 – 1410, produced for the Enchanted Doll House of Manchester, Vermont. Courtesy Iva Mae Jones.

Innovations and Growth

Ginny by Dakin (1987), 8", hard plastic Ginny dolls from Going Places collection. 1987 was the first catalog year that did not include any Meritus designs. Vogue catalog courtesy Marge Meisinger.

Management/Designs: In the fall of 1986 Dakin, a San Francisco manufacturer of plush animals, bought the rights to the Ginny and Vogue names and doll molds from Meritus Industries. At that time, however, Meritus had already produced most of the 1987 line to present to dealers at the Toy Fair. In the interest of time, Dakin showed the Meritus designs at the 1987 Toy Fair. Consequently, the first year that the entire line consisted completely of Dakin's own designs was not until the 1988 season. Dakin embellished the Ginny line with new features to attract both new buyers and collectors as well. For example, they announced, "We have added brown-eyed dolls, new hairstyles, new accessories, and more clothing assortments, all at the request of last year's enthusiastic customers." Dakin was committed to Meritus Industries's restoration of the Ginny line. Their designs were charming and, while not hand sewn, were still in the Vogue tradition of quality workmanship. However, their plan was to keep their mid-price advantage, averaging $10.00 less than the competition's retail price. Initially, Dakin issued both hard plastic Ginnys as well as vinyl Ginnys. In 1993 management limited doll production to hard plastic dolls. Most store special dolls were produced in hard plastic.

Plush additions: Dakin incorporated designs from their plush lines of animals to go with some Ginny outfits. For example, in the 1988 catalog a special black and white stuffed dog accompanied the Ginny's First Secret outfit #71 – 2080. This dog was Dakin's version of Ginny's Pup Sparky by Steiff, which Vogue introduced in the mid 1950s. (Ginny's pup was called "Sparkie" in the 1958 book "Ginny's First Secret.") By 1992 Dakin incorporated at least eight stuffed animals into all eight Ginny collections. These fuzzy additions definitely added play value to the line.

Vinyl/Hair: Dakin improved the hair rooting to allow fuller coverage and better hair play.

Wardrobe And Special Styles

1987: In 1987 Dakin's first catalog presented over 50 outfits which were mostly Meritus Industry designs. The collections featured were Going Places, 16 outfits including the signature outfit Let's Go Places #71 – 1020, which was used on the brochure cover showing Ginny in a white hat, and red traveling suit; Ginny Fantasy Collection of eight outfits featuring dress-up outfit Mommy's Attic #71 – 0513; Ginny Portraits and Famous Pairs Collections, featuring four pairs of sweet romantic duos; Holiday Collection with six outfits, Thanksgiving, Halloween, Christmas, Valentine's Day, Easter, and Fourth of July, which have become quite collectible; and a Lollipops collection of four sweet outfits, Lemon, Ice Mint, Berry, and Lime. In the Vogue tradition, the Dress Me doll #71 – 0021 was issued, as well as a monthly calendar collection of outfits.

1988: The 1988 catalog consisted of seven collections designed entirely by Dakin: Classics, Special Days, Going Places, Storybook, Fantasy, Party Time, and the Dress Me doll was continued. All of the dolls included a comb, brush, and doll stand. Some of these outfits were continued from 1987, such as Easter , Halloween, Thanksgiving, At The Round Up (cowgirl). Other outfits were changed slightly, such as Let's Go Places. Some of the new outfits were ingenious, such as the Court Jester #71 – 2280, with an elaborate headpiece decorated with bells, upturned toe jester boots, which was featured on Dakin's 1988 catalog cover. All of these 1987 and 1988 dolls have become quite popular since they are Dakin's first two years' collections.

1991: In 1991 Dakin celebrated Ginny's 40th birthday. A special outfit, 40th Birthday Party Special # 71 – 4080, was included with the Classics Collections. This was the best selling doll in 1991. Also, included in the Classics Collection were a Debutante outfit # 71 – 3690; and fur coat outfit, Strolling Down 5th Avenue #71 – 2000, both reminiscent of 1950s Vogue creations.

1992: In 1992, Victorian Romance #71497, designed by Jessica McClintock, was the centerpiece of the entire Ginny line, a beautiful white, romantic fashion in its unique clear plastic show box.

1993: 1993 marked a transition year for Dakin. Dakin president, Bob Solomon, announced that the company was improving the designs and quality of both their contemporary designs and their nostalgic little girl fashions, reminiscent of the original Vogue. Fabrics and Ginny shoes were particularly targeted for an upgrade. Also, an innovative new series was created, The Painter Series, six dolls each with their own famous painting from the impressionist era. The highlight of 1993 was Dakin's collection of three hand-painted porcelain dolls, all based on the original 1950s Kindergarten Series designs, and limited to 2,500 dolls.

Most importantly Dakin announced that it was phasing out the soft vinyl body, stating that collectors preferred the hard vinyl body and that their line would have a higher perceived value.

1994: In 1994, Dakin reissued the Painter Series.

Also, a second collection of three porcelain dolls was issued, re-creating Tiny Miss 1953, Fun Time 1956, and June 1951. These Ginnys were also a limited edition of 2,500 dolls, each with a numbered certificate of ownership. Dakin's most consistently best-selling collection over the years was the Ginny Calendar Collection, with each doll's dress matching the birthstone for the month. Boxed necklace sets were also available with birthstones for both the little girl and her Ginny calendar doll.

1995: In June 1995 Dakin sold the rights to the doll to the newly created Vogue Doll Company, Inc.

Marketing

Merchandising: Dakin executed the marketing of Ginny with creativity and energy. They retained Lesney's theme, "Ginny...Vogue Dolls made with love" and promoted it on all products and literature. They portrayed Ginny as a little girl who spoke directly to her little friends in letters, on boxes, and in newsletters, in much the same way the original Vogue Dolls, Inc. had done. Dakin employed their great merchandising skills to elevate Ginny's standing in the doll world. Initially in 1987, Dakin boxes continued the bright blue from Meritus Industries. However, in 1988 the color scheme was changed to pink in two styles. Soft vinyl dolls came with in window display boxes, and hard vinyl dolls came in closed collector boxes. In 1993, Dakin redesigned their pink box to incorporate an inviting doorway design. Substantial eye-catching wire racks and floor stand displays were available for purchase to help dealers promote all Dakin products.

Vogue Doll Club: The Vogue Doll Club (previously Ginny Doll Club) was continued, and each member received a certificate, a poster, and a Ginny gift to wear on the charm bracelet. Also, the *Vogue Doll Review*, a quarterly publication, was sent to members. The publication promoted Ginny pen pals, as well as a trading corner, and upcoming promotional events and contests.

Collectors: In the *Vogue Doll Reviews* issued in the spring of 1993, Dakin listed dolls being retired. In this clever attempt to cultivate the collectors' market, they further stated, "Remember, today's styles are tomorrow's collectibles." They also involved both collectors and customers in previewing doll designs at gatherings and conventions etc., soliciting their evaluation as well as suggestions for new dolls.

Dealers: Dakin also recognized the importance of being a partner to dealers in promoting Ginny. For example, when issuing their 1992 Victorian Romance doll designed by Jessica McClintock, they offered Show Party Kits, which included plans for a fashion show to introduce customers to the 1992 line, Design-A-Ginny Costume Contest forms, balloons, a poster, a media kit, news release, etc. Also, Dakin would assist dealers who were able to sponsor a customized Ginny design in substantial quantities. One such memorable event took place in June 1992 in Falmouth, Massachusetts, with Virginia Graves Carlson, daughter of the founder of Ginny, and Vogue's chief designer and Ginny namesake, presiding at a signing party at the Cranberry Patch doll store. Some of these store specials are very collectible.

Dakin admirably promoted Ginny, but finally decided to sell the rights to the doll in 1995 to the newly formed Vogue Doll Company, Inc.

Ginny by Dakin (1987), 8", hard plastic Ginny dolls from the Ginny Portraits and Famous Pairs collection include Pocahontas, Betsy Ross, Marie Antoinette, and Empress Josephine. Vogue catalog courtesy Marge Meisinger.

Ginny by Dakin (1987), 8", hard plastic Ginny dolls from Holiday collection: Thanksgiving, Halloween, and Christmas. Dakin was using bright blue boxes at this time. Vogue catalog courtesy Marge Meisinger.

Ginny by Dakin (1987), 8", soft vinyl Mr. and Mrs. Claus, a Shirley's Dollhouse Exclusive. Packaged to their specifications in 1987 by Dakin, wrist tag is dated 1987 and doll came in a blue 1986 box.

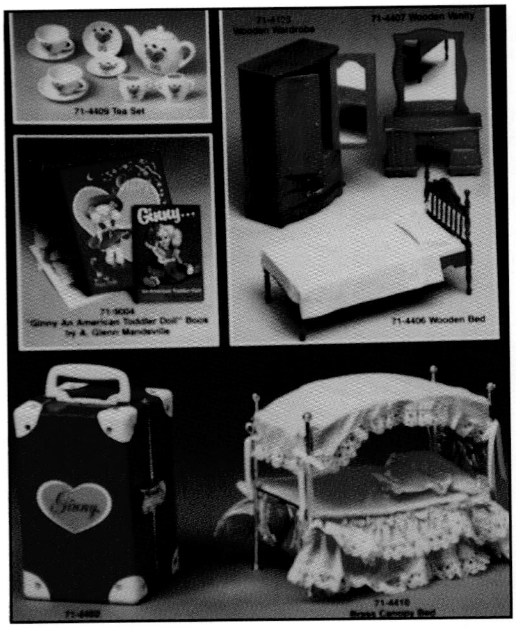

Ginny by Dakin (1987), accessories. The same items were shown by Meritus in 1986 and paper dolls were shown in 1985. Vogue catalog courtesy Marge Meisinger.

Ginny by Dakin (1987), 8", hard vinyl Swimsuit Ginny a Shirley's Dollhouse Exclusive. A black Ginny with a 1987 gold heart wrist tag. Note special life preserver and Ginny's pail.

Prices

Year Produced	Type/Outfit, Body	Mint Price
	DAKIN	
1986 – 1995	Ginny/All orig.	$40.00 – 50.00
1987 – 1988	#71 – 1020 Let's Go Places	$35.00+
	Holiday Collections	$60.00+
	#71 – 2280 Court Jester	$60.00+
1991	#714080 40th Birthday Party	$55.00+
1992	#71497 Victorian Romance	$45.00+
1993	Painter Series	$50.00
1993 – 1994	Porcelain Series	$90.00
	STORE SPECIAL DOLLS	
Shirley's Dollhouse, Wheeling, Ill.:		
1986	Ginny Goes Country	$95.00
1986	Ginny Goes to the Country Fair	$95.00
1987	Swimsuit Ginny, black doll	Retail
1987	Santa and Mrs. Claus	$90.00+
1988	Sunday's Best Boy and Girl	$60.00
1988	Ginny Babysits	$50.00
Gi Gi's Dolls, Chicago, Ill.:		
1987	Gi Gi's Favorite Ginny	$95.00
1988	Sherry's Teddy Bear Ginny	$95.00
Enchanted Doll House, Manchester, Vt.:		
1988	Limited Edition	$160.00
Meyer's, New Brunswick, N.J.:		
1986	Fairy Godmother	$210.00
1987	Cinderella and Prince Charming	$210.00

Year Produced	Type/Outfit, Body	Mint Price
1988	Clown	$95.00
1989	American Cowgirl	$95.00
Toy Village, Lansing, Mich.:		
1989	Ashley Rose	$130.00
Little Friends of Anchorage:		
1990	Alaska Ginny #78 – 6200	$85.00
	DOLL CONVENTIONS	
Modern Doll Convention:		
1986	Rose Queen	$200.00+
1987	Ginny at the Seashore	$75.00+
1988	Ginny's Claim	$80.00+
1989	Ginny in Nashville	$110.00+
1990	Ginny in Orlando	$95.00+
1991	Ginny in Las Vegas	$95.00+
1992	Poodle Skirt Ginny, Delaware	$75.00
1993	World of Elegance, Clearwater	$60.00+
1994	Fiesta, San Antonio	$65.00
Vogue Doll Review Luncheon:		
1989	*First Ginny Doll Revue Luncheon*	$100.00
1990	*Honoring Jenny Graves*	$110.00+
1991	*Ginny's 40th Birthday*	$95.00+
1993	*Special Christmas*	$75.00
1994	*Apple of My Eye*	$75.00
1995	*Secret Garden*	$75.00

Retail means still available in retail stores

1988

Ginny by Dakin (1988), 8", soft vinyl black Ginny from Dress Me collection #71 – 0070, with brown eyes introduced in 1988.

Ginny by Dakin (1988), 8", hard vinyl Princess Valentine from the Fantasy Collection, blue eyes. She was the Design-a-Ginny Costume winner.

Ginny by Dakin (1988), 8", hard vinyl Sunday's Best, a Shirley's Dollhouse exclusive black doll in yellow dress came in a solid widow display pink box with a 1988 gold heart wrist tag. Sold as a set with Sunday's Best Boy.

Ginny by Dakin (1988), 8", hard vinyl Queen of the Ball from the Fantasy Collection #71 – 2270. Has blue eyes, bouquet, dated satin ribbon, and pearl-like tiara. One of six dolls in the Fantasy collection.

Ginny by Dakin (1988), accessories. Note pink, blue, and white design on trunk. Doll was not included in trunk. Note new packaged accessories. Vogue catalog courtesy Marge Meisinger.

1990

Ginny by Dakin (1990), showing dolls costumed in modern interpretations of classic designs from the 1950s. Doll on top right is winner of the Design-a-Ginny costume contest. Vogue catalog courtesy Marge Meisinger.

Ginny by Dakin (1990 – 92), Special Days collection '50s, Bunny, hard plastic doll with blue eyes. Also issued in 1991 #71 – 3190, and 1992 as #71 – 319.

Ginny by Dakin (1990), accessories. Bed and furniture were introduced in 1990. Vogue catalog courtesy Marge Meisinger.

1991

Ginny by Dakin (1991), Vogue Doll Club Membership Special Doll, #71 – 3570, designed by Virginia Graves Carlson.

Ginny by Dakin (1991), Classics collection, (from left): hard vinyl Debutante #71 – 3690; hard plastic 40th Birthday Party Special #71 – 4080; soft vinyl Strolling Down 5th Avenue #71 – 2000, similar to 1950s costumes. Vogue catalog courtesy Marge Meisinger.

Ginny by Dakin (1991) Classics collection, hard plastic 40th Birthday Party Special #71 – 4080; designed by Judy Hernandez, on Vogue display unit. Courtesy Marge Meisinger.

Ginny by Dakin (1991 – 92), Ginny Calendar collection, styles matched boxed birthstone necklaces — one for Ginny and one for owner. This was a popular series and styles were periodically changed. Vogue catalog courtesy Marge Meisinger.

Ginny by Dakin (1991), Ginny and Friends collection, Sweet Dreams #71 – 3850, black Ginny with a teddy bear.

Porcelain Ginny (1991), wears a pink printed organdy gown with lace trim and straw hat reflecting the 1954 Bridesmaid. This doll was produced in a limited edition of 1,000. Courtesy Veronica Phillips.

Ginny by Dakin (1991), Mommy and Dolly fashion ensemble, #71 – 9010.

Ginny by Dakin (1991 – 94), Ginny Fantasy collection, Our Little Mermaid #71 – 3060, was the Design-a-Ginny Costume winner. Ginny One Million Years B.C. was offered in 1992. Note 1994 new box design. Vogue catalog courtesy Marge Meisinger.

1992

Ginny by Dakin (1992), International collection, two of the six costumes for hard vinyl dolls: #71 – 3750 Sari, and #71 – 4150 Chinese Ginny. Other costumes were Cherry Blossom, Dutch Girl, Africa Contempo Princess of the Nile, Ginny Al Mercado, Little Navajo. Vogue catalog courtesy Marge Meisinger.

Ginny by Dakin (1992), Victorian Romance #71 – 497, designed by Jessica McClintock, limited to 1992 production. Dakin designed numerous promotions for dealers promoting the 1992 line.

1993

Ginny by Dakin (1993), Painter's series: #71556 Renoir; #71570 Cassatt; and #71568 Monet; each hard vinyl Ginny came dressed appropriately to artist's picture which was included. Vogue catalog courtesy Marge Meisinger.

Ginny by Dakin (1993), Painter's series: #71549 Gauguin; #71569 Seurat; and #71567 Degas, each hard vinyl Ginny came dressed appropriately to artist's picture. Vogue catalog courtesy Marge Meisinger.

Ginny by Dakin (1993), Ginny Porcelain Kindergarten series (1993 – 94), 8", limited edition dolls patterned after the 1953 Kindergarten series. Each came with a numbered certificate of ownership. Vogue catalog courtesy Marge Meisinger.

1994

Ginny by Dakin (1994), Walking Spot Clothing package #70124. This outfit was offered on a dressed doll #71429 in 1993.

1995

Sparky by Dakin (1995). #70107 Sparky in his doghouse.

Ginny by Dakin (1995) Ginny's Secret Garden souvenir doll from 7th Annual Vogue Doll Review. Design by Susan and Kimberly Heilman, a limited edition of 350.

The Vogue Doll Company, Inc. Buys Ginny

1995 – current

Description: 8" hard plastic (Dakin's mold), jointed head, arms, legs, sleep eyes, molded lashes.
Marks: Head: None
Body: Ginny ®/© 1988/VOGUE DOLL COMPANY/MADE IN CHINA
Dress labels: Ginny ®/© 1995 THE VOGUE DOLL COMPANY/INC. in black on a white plastic label
Dress closures: Small plastic snap inside back openings.
Tags: Gold heart (on side one): "Hi! I'm Ginny," (side two) a triangle with an "!" in middle "WARNING:/CHOKING HAZARD – Small parts./Not for children under 3 years/The Vogue Doll/Company"

Innovations and Growth

Management: In July 1995 The Vogue Doll Company Inc. acquired the assets of Ginny from Dakin, Inc. From the new company's headquarters in Oakdale, California, a press release was issued in August 1995 stating, "The company has assembled TEAM GINNY, made up of some of the most respected names in the Doll and Toy Industry to take Ginny into the 21st Century. Team members are Linda and Jim Smith, Wendy and Keith Lawton, Nancy Cordary, David Smith, and Susanne de Groot." This distinguished team has many combined years in the modern doll industry, since Linda and Jim Smith and Wendy and Keith Lawton own the Lawton Doll Company, and the Smith's own Tide-Rider, distributor of fine doll lines. The company also stated, "Ginny's new director of design, Wendy Lawton, believes in the importance of historical context in planning Ginny's future." Indeed, the group has set about to capture the spirit and concept of the popular '50s doll.

Design/Wig: The new company utilized Dakin's hard plastic mold, but they modified key design features to more closely reflect the traditional Ginny look. For example, the painted features and coloring were given a more lifelike, natural look. However, one of the major changes came in the area of costuming. The 1995 – 1996 collections were very closely patterned after the original designs of Ginny's founder, Jennie Graves and her daughter, and Vogue's chief designer, Virginia Graves Carlson. Vogue also restyled the rooted hair, adding to the doll's play value and retaining one of the doll's most popular features from the '50s.

Wardrobe, Special Styles, and Accessories

Wardrobe/Special Styles: The 1995 Debut Collection of six outfits demonstrated that the new Vogue Doll Company, Inc. truly understood it was Ginny's fabulous wardrobe that originally drew little customers and their parents to Ginny. The new company's director of design, Wendy Lawton, re-created Ginny's adorable high waist dress patterns with full skirts and deep 1" hems, reminiscent of the Vogue's early outfits. Also, organdy and taffeta were generously used to further enhance the original look. The 1995 Debut collection outfits were named, Day at the Beach, Happy Birthday, Walk in the Park, Musical Recital, First Ballet, and Sunday Best.

In 1996, the Debut collection was repeated, and four new collections were added: On Stage, Town and Country, Ginny Cooks, and School Days. In addition, a collection of four Dress Me dolls was offered, three separate hair colors and one African-American doll; two newly offered collections of separate Clothing Packs were offered: 1. School Days Clothing Packs — Included Rain, Rain Go Away, which was reminiscent of the '50s; Sou'wester, yellow rain slicker; Soccer Uniform, and Cheerleader designs finding more modern inspiration in their cleverly designed styles with soccer ball and pom-pons included, respectively. 2. Dress Me Clothing Packs, six styles including traditional dresses, sleep, and overall outfits as well as a contemporary warm-up and a long-leg play outfit.

In 1997 Vogue added innovative outfits, such as "Farmer's Market" #7HP19, and "Bakes Bread" #7HP28, to their line. These pieces and the entire line are destined to be true collectibles.

Shoes were created for most outfits in the '50s center snap style with a newly monogrammed "G" on the snap, and were shown with nylons, white tights, or little white anklets.

Accessories: The 1996 catalog included three new accessories: Ginny Screen #6AC06, white with personalized pink Ginny Signature; Ginny's Trunk #6AC04 by General Fibre, a pink metal trunk with white trim; and Ginny Dress Form #6AC05.

Marketing

The new Vogue Doll Company, Inc. launched an aggressive promotional campaign including press releases to all media, and was featured in a cover story in the November 1995 issue of *Dolls: The Collectors Magazine*. The Ginny Doll Club was reinstituted to attract Ginny lovers, and members received a Redemption certificate to order the Charter Members-only Ginny, America's Sweetheart #6GC01, in a red organdy dress and hair ribbon, carrying a dozen roses. For the 75th anniversary of the Vogue Doll Company, Vogue issued the 1997 "Diamond Jubilee Princess" to members of the Ginny Doll Club. The doll is dressed in a lovely ice blue tissue taffeta gown and matching headpiece. Members also received *The Ginny Journal* quarterly.

The new Ginny is a great success, based on the popularity of the initial designs and promotions.

Prices
All dolls currently available on the retail market.
1996 America's Sweetheart Club Doll is sold out. $100.00
First Ballet (discontinued) $75.00

Vogue Doll Company (1996), Debut collection, includes Happy Birthday #9506, Walk in the Park #9502, Day at the Beach #9503. Marks: Ginny ®/1988©/THE VOGUE DOLL COMPANY/MADE IN CHINA. Courtesy Vogue Doll Company, Inc.

Vogue Doll Company (1996), Debut collection, includes Hot Chocolate #6HP14, Caramel Apples #6HP13, and Gingerbread Cookies #6HP12. A special recipe card is included with each of these dolls. Notice classic leatherette snap shoes. Courtesy Vogue Doll Company, Inc.

Vogue Doll Company (1996), On Stage collection, (left), Concert Pianist #6HP15, black velvet dress with keyboard hem; and (right), Puttin' on the Ritz #6HP16, top hat and gold lamé tuxedo. Courtesy Vogue Doll Company, Inc.

Vogue Doll Company (1996), America's Sweetheart #6GC01, available to charter members of the Ginny Doll Club™ with a redemption certificate. Also received a cloisonné pin, membership certificate, and four issues of *The Ginny Journal.* Courtesy Vogue Doll Company, Inc.

Vogue Doll Company (1996), School Days Ginny #6HP07, in navy monogrammed sweater and School Days African American Ginny #6HP08. Showing Ginny coming back home to her original concept as a little girl. Courtesy Vogue Doll Company, Inc.

Farmer's Market from Town & Country Collection (1997) #7HP19, bright cotton outfit with straw hat. Courtesy Vogue Doll Company, Inc.

Ginny Bakes Bread from Cooks Collection (1997) #7HP28, blue and white checked dress carrying loaf of bread on a tray. Courtesy Vogue Doll Company, Inc.

Ginnette

1955 – 1969
1985 – 1986

Description:	8", all vinyl, jointed doll, open mouth. 1955 – 1956: Dolls had painted eyes and lashes. 1956 – 1969: Dolls had sleep eyes with molded lashes and eyebrows. Drink and wet doll until 1962, then again in 1964.
Marks:	1955 – 1963: Head: None Back: VOGUE DOLLS/INC. 1964 – 65: Head: Numbers such as "6" or "19" or "13" Back: VOGUE DOLLS INC. 1967: Head: VOGUE DOLLS Back: VOGUE DOLLS INC. 1968 – 69: Head: VOGUE DOLL INC. © 1967 Back: VOGUE DOLLS INC. 1985 – 86 Head: None Back: GINNETTE © 1984/VOGUE DOLLS INC./MADE IN HONG KONG
Outfit labels:	1955 – 1956: White rayon with black block letters: VOGUE DOLLS, Inc./MEDFORD, MASS, U.S.A./*REG. U.S. PAT. OFF. 1957 – 1966: White twill with blue script: Vogue Dolls, Inc. 1967: Vogue Dolls, Inc./ MADE IN U.S.A.. 1985 – 1986: Vogue Dolls, Inc. c. 1985.
Outfit closures:	1955 – 1956: Hooks and eyes or ties 1957 – 60: "Dot starlet" snaps
Boxes:	Pastel blue, white, and pink using Ginny paper doll logo. Later ones were navy, pink, and white.

Innovations and Growth

Ginny was enjoying tremendous popularity with little girls everywhere. To capitalize on Ginny's success, Mrs. Jennie Graves, president of Vogue, decided to manufacture a baby sister for Ginny in 1955. Mrs. Graves named the new baby Ginnette and designed many costumes, including several matching outfits with Ginny. Ginnette was a 8" soft vinyl doll with jointed arms and legs, painted blue eyes, and molded brown hair. She had an open mouth and could drink and wet. Ginnette was marked VOGUE DOLLS INC. on her back. Vogue proclaimed Ginnette "the most life-like baby doll ever created." She came out in 1955 with seven outfits, in time for the 1956 holiday selling period. All basic Ginnettes came with a 4-ounce glass baby bottle with a rubber nipple and a paper label on it with "I'm Ginnette" on it until 1961. Ginnette was a success with little girls everywhere.

Vogue gave Ginnette sleep eyes with molded lashes in 1956. Ginnette had sleep eyes with tears in 1957 only. Ginnette with tears had a mechanism in her stomach with three tubes inside, two to her eyes and one to her mouth. When squeezed, water would come out of her eyes. Three different Ginnettes were available in 1957: the painted eye, the sleep eye, and the sleep eye that cried real tears. The crying and sleep eye Ginnettes had the same marks as the painted eye Ginnette. All Ginnettes came with a hole in their mouths and lower back so they could drink and wet.

Another version of Ginnette had a squeaker, a round metal circle with hole in the middle of their backs. These dolls also drank and wet. They are also marked VOGUE DOLLS on their lower backs. They came out about 1957.

Vogue designed approximately 20 different outfits for Ginnette each year between 1956 – 1960. Ginnette's basic wardrobe for each of these years included flannel pajamas, a topper diaper set, day dresses, party dresses, a pants outfit, and a pram suit usually made of fleece.

In 1956 Ginnette had 12 outfits, seven of which matched Ginny. In addition to outfits, Ginnette had all kinds of accessories, including a diaper set, a swim set and a baby bath. Ginnette's shoes were plastic and were marked GINNETTE on the heel.

In 1957 Ginnette had 21 outfits. Eight outfits matched Ginny's. One outfit matched both Ginny and Jill. The snap used starting in 1957 had a hole in the middle with lines coming out from it. It is called the "dot starlet" snap and can be used to identify untagged clothes. Ginnette's clothing box carried the "Commended by *Parents' Magazine*" logo. Barbara Daly

Anderson, editor of *Parents' Magazine*, visited the Vogue factory in 1956.

In 1958 Ginnette was advertised as drinking, wetting, and cooing. Ginnette had 22 outfits; of these one matched Ginny, one matched brother Jimmy, and one matched both Ginny and Jill. In 1959 Ginnette appears again in her painted eye version as well as a sleep eye version. She had 19 outfits; one matched Ginny, one matched Ginny and Jill, and two matched Ginny Baby, an 18" doll introduced this year by Vogue. After 1959 Ginnette was only available as a sleep eye doll. In 1960 Ginnette had 19 outfits.

The mid to late 1950s were Ginnette's heyday. She was a very popular doll and hundreds of thousands of dolls were sold. She was so popular she spawned several imitators, including a similar doll called Baby Vicky by Elite Doll Company, and an unmarked doll sold by the Commonwealth Plastics Corporation of Leominster, Massachusetts, who were the manufacturers of Ginnette for Vogue.

Furniture for the Vogue dolls was manufactured by Strombecker, the maker of Ginny furniture. Ginnette's furniture was white with a pink, blue, and yellow elephant, bear, and turtle logo. Ginnette was well cared for in a bathinette, crib, chest of drawers, a shoo-fly rocker, and a feeding table. In 1957 her crib had an inset panel; in 1958 it had a smooth head and foot board. The tender also was slightly changed in 1958 from a cloth seat to a vinyl seat and her name from script to block letters.

In 1961 Ginnette had only eight outfits, and seemed to be losing her popularity. Ginnette came with a vinyl bottle marked PERMA-NURSER with a pink removable top.

Rooted Hair Ginnette

In 1962, Ginnette, even though she came with a vinyl bottle, was not advertised as drinking and wetting in the Vogue brochure. The 1962 Vogue brochure only shows a molded hair Ginnette for $2.00 but the Vogue order blank contains a Ginnette with rooted Saran bob hairstyle (#28030) for $3.00. Ginnette had eight outfits that year also.

The 1963 Vogue order blank has several versions of Ginnette: sculptured hair, blonde rooted Saran bob, blonde rooted pixie cut, and platinum rooted chignon. The 1963 Vogue brochure shows eight outfits for Ginnette advertised as a drinking and wetting doll. They advertise the outfits as also fitting Li'l Dear.

The 1964 Vogue brochure shows eight outfits for Ginnette and a new version of Ginnette with rooted hair. This version had more hair which was fuller and pouffier. Ginnette was available in several different versions this year: a sculptured hair model, blonde rooted Saran bob, blonde rooted pixie, and a platinum rooted pixie.

Negro Ginnette

In 1964 Vogue introduced a Negro Ginnette who was a brown version of the old Ginnette. Negro Ginnette came in two versions: a sculptured hair doll with painted black hair and a rooted pixie hairstyle with black rooted hair and brown eyes. Both version used the same vinyl doll. Negro Ginnette did not squeak. Marks include a number on her head; 19, 13, or 6 has been seen with a "Vogue Dolls Inc." on her back.

The 1965 line of Ginnettes also included a Negro Ginnette. The basic Ginnette doll came in sculptured hair, blonde rooted Saran bob, a blonde rooted pixie, and a brunette rooted pixie. She was not a drink and wet doll. The Negro Ginnette came in sculptured hair or rooted pixie hairstyle. There were eight outfits in the line that year. The outfits included: #28330, a pink flannelette sleeper; #28331, morning dress in assorted colors; #28332, aqua checked creeper set; #28335, a white dot batiste with blue trim; #28336, a lacy red velvety stroller set; #28337, a crisp yellow dress with collar; #28340, a fluffy pink dress and bonnet; and #28341, a rose corduroy pram suit.

There was no Ginnette in 1966.

Note: Negro is the term Vogue used in 1964.

Remodeled Ginnette

Smaller eyes, distinctive curl in the middle of her forehead, remodeled Ginnette: When Ginnette returned in 1967, she was made from a different mold with smaller eyes and a distinctive large, molded curl in the middle of her forehead. Even the rooted hair dolls had this molded curl. The older Ginnettes had a curl in the middle of her forehead but it consisted of more strands. This remodeled Ginnette doll is marked VOGUE DOLLS (on head); VOGUE DOLLS INC. (on body).

Elongated head Ginnette: Vogue changed Ginnette again in 1968 and her head was cast from another new mold. This new Ginnette's head had a different look. Its head seems to be elongated, its painted molded hair was more reddish in tone, its lips were pink instead of red, its neck was elongated, and it had no eyebrows. There was no molded curl in front and it was not a drink and wet doll. This new Ginnette was marked: VOGUE DOLL INC. © 1967 (on head); VOGUE DOLLS INC. (on back). This elongated version of Ginnette was on the market for only two years.

Remodeled Ginnette had only four outfits made of synthetic fabrics numbered from #7820 to #7823 in 1968: a pink bathrobe, a yellow dress with flower on waistband, pink and white checked short top and panties, and a pink fleece hooded coat with pink ruffles, hem, and hood. The clothing was tagged: Vogue Dolls, Inc. MADE IN U.S.A.

The 1969 catalog has four of the remodeled head Ginnettes. The outfits were #2850, pink jersey sleeper with pom-poms; #2851, a blue dress; #2852, pink and white checked footed pants outfit and bonnet; and #2853, yellow pram outfit with hooded white fleece jacket. All the dolls came with bottles. This was the last year Ginnette, the baby doll, was produced until 1985.

Ginnette did not appear in the 1970 – 1977 Vogue catalogs.

Lesney Ginnette

The Ginnette name only was used again in 1978 by Lesney but this time it was used for the Afro-American Ginny who was the same size and had the same features of the Lesney Ginny girl doll, not for a baby doll. See the Lesney section for more information on the Lesney Ginnette.

Meritus Ginnette

In 1985 under Meritus, Ginnette the baby doll came back. Ginnette was from a different mold than before. She was 9" tall with a soft vinyl head and limbs with sleep eyes. This version of Ginnette (No. 80005) had rooted blonde, brunette or auburn hair which could be combed. Ginnette came in three different outfits: a blue dress with bonnet; a pink dress and bonnet; and an orange and yellow checked dress and bonnet. She resembles the 1963 – 64 version of Ginnette. She is marked: GINNETTE © 1984/VOGUE DOLLS INC./MADE IN HONG KONG (on her back).

In 1986 there were four vinyl Meritus Ginnettes: #80008, came in a lavender print dress; #80009, came in a pink dress; #80010, came in a blue dress and bib with heart motif; and #8011, came in a red plaid dress with a black ribbon in front. All came with bonnets and white sock booties. The outfits were marked: Vogue Dolls, Inc. c. 1985.

Porcelain Ginnette

Meritus also produced an all-porcelain version of Ginnette in 1985 and 1986. This all-porcelain Ginnette #85001 had yellow molded hair and eyes that seemed to bug out and wore a long christening gown and lace bonnet. She was #85001 in the catalog.

No Ginnettes have been produced since 1987. The later Ginnettes did not have the popularity and look of the earlier Ginnettes. Collectors seem to prefer the earlier Ginnettes, especially the Ginnettes that have matching outfits to Ginny and Jill. Ginnette is a very playable doll and the collector can have fun posing her in her furniture and dressing her in her myriad of outfits.

Prices

Ginnette mint condition, painted eye	$150.00
Ginnette mint condition, sleep eye	$60.00
Painted eye Ginnette MIB	$100.00 – 150.00
Sleep Eye Ginnette MIB	$75.00 – 150.00
Cries Real Tears Ginnette MIB	$125.00
Meritus Ginnette MIB	$40.00+
Porcelain Ginnette MIB	$60.00+
Outfits (MIB):	
plain early (1955 – 59)	$45.00 – 75.00
fancy early (1955 – 59)	$45.00 – 100.00
plain later (1960s)	$45.00 – 100.00
fancy later (1960s)	$45.00 – 100.00
Furniture:	
Chest of drawers MIB	$100.00
Other furniture MIB	$30.00 – 100.00
Baby beads MIB	$15.00 – 25.00

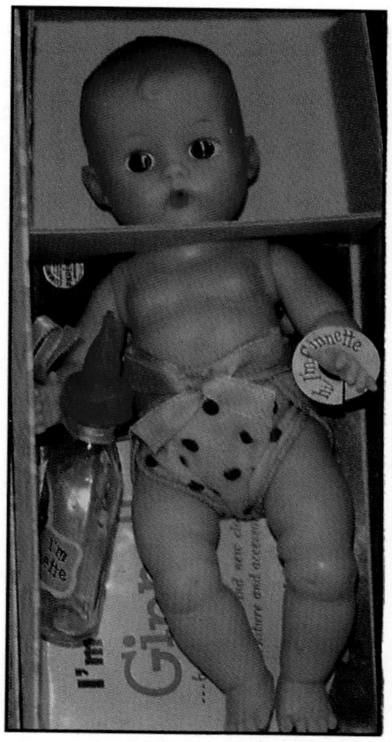

(1955) #170, Ginnette Basic Doll, 8", all vinyl, and has jointed neck, arms, and legs. She is marked VOGUE DOLLS INC. (on body only). Mint in box dressed in flannelette dotted diaper with ribbon tie came with bottle and painted eyes; she coos, drinks, and wets. Courtesy S. Ogilvie.

(1955) #002, yellow party dress with matching panties and diaper. Matches Ginny outfit. Courtesy Susan Steelman.

1955

Dressed dolls and outfits sold separately, had same number, #001+

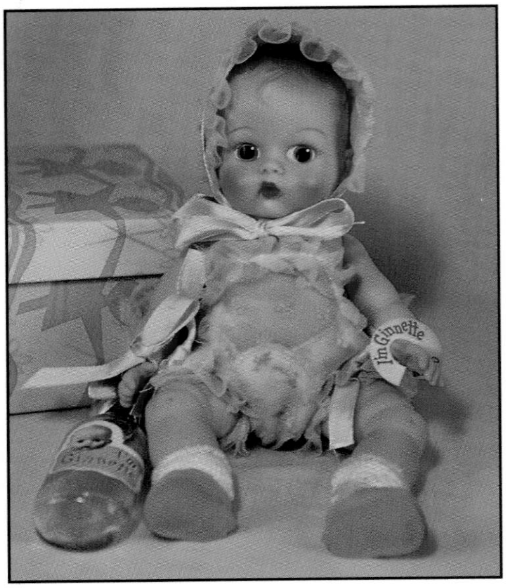

(1955) #003, ruffled nylon playsuit and bonnet, with diaper, came with bottle. Courtesy Ann Tardie.

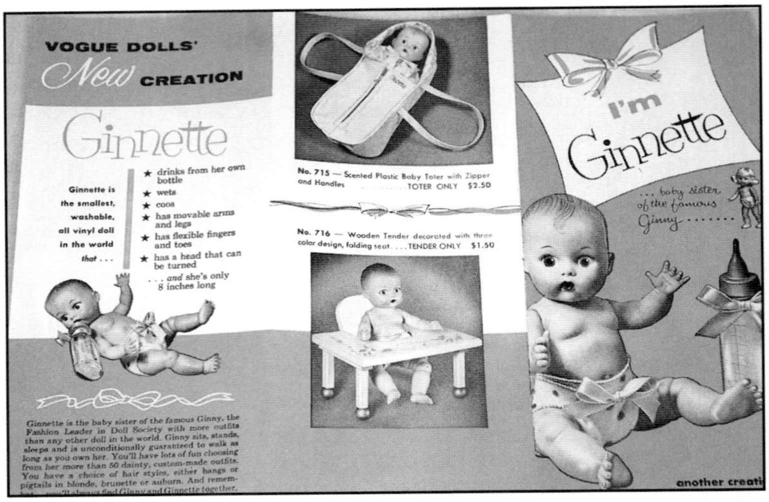

Ginnette brochure (1955), Vogue Dolls new creation: Ginnette – she drinks, wets, coos, has movable arms and legs, and a head that can be turned. Courtesy Ann Tardie.

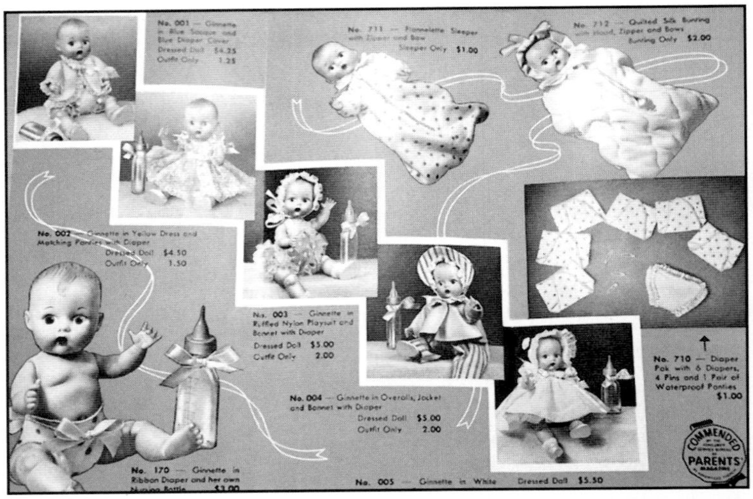

Ginnette brochure (1955), outfits: #001, blue sacque tie blouse with white lace and diaper cover; #710, Diaper Pak, six flannelette diapers, four pins, and one pair vinyl panties; #712, quilted silk bunting with hood, zipper, and bows.

(1955) #004, pink striped overalls, jacket and striped bonnet, with diaper, came with bottle.

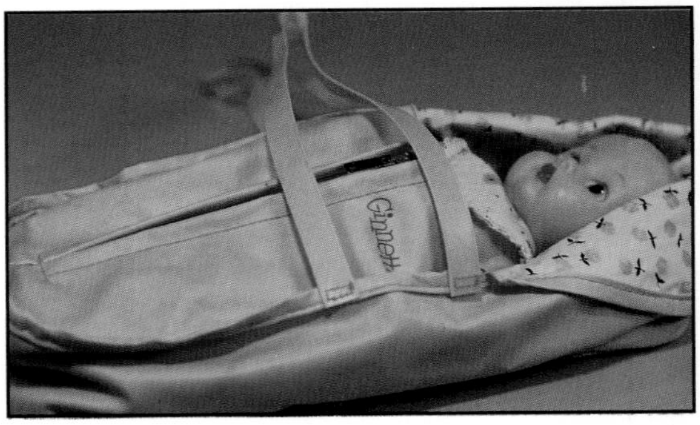

(1955) #715; 1956, #6750; 1957, #7770; 1958 — 1960, #2591; plastic Baby Toter, scented pink plastic with zipper and handles.

(1955) #005, white nylon party dress with tie and pink rose in front, petticoat, missing pink ribbon, diaper, and bonnet. Courtesy Judy Armitstead.

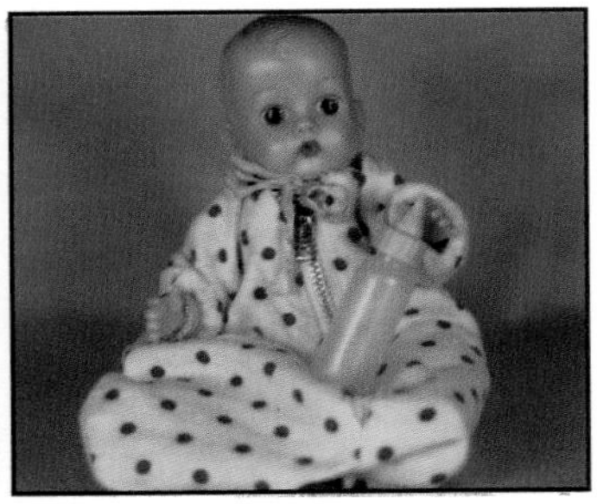

(1955) #711, flannelette sleeper, polka dot flannelette sleeper with zipper and bow.

(1955) #716, and (1956) 0#6775, Baby Tender, white wood decorated with animals, with folding top, printed cloth seat and blue balls on bottom of legs. Courtesy S. Ogilvie.

1956

Dressed dolls are numbered #65+; outfits only, #67+.

(1956) #6670, undressed Ginnette box.

(1956) Ginnette brochure, touting her new moving eyes. Vogue brochure.

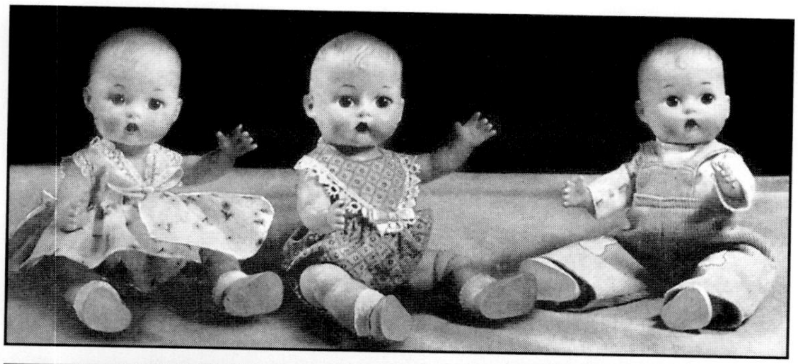

(1956) Ginnette brochure showing outfits, (top row), #6501, #6502, #6503, and (bottom row) #6504, #6505, and #6506. Vogue brochure.

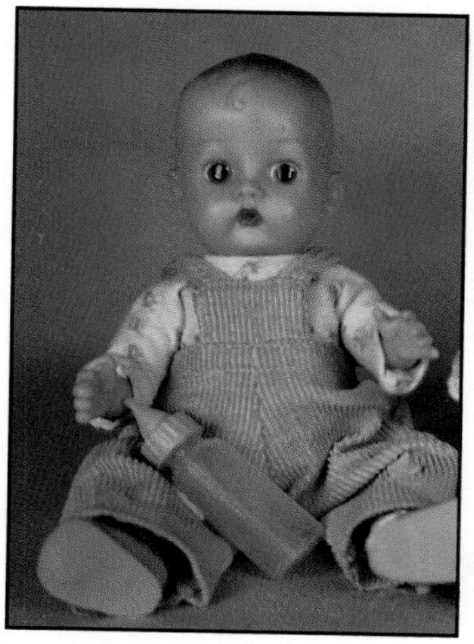

(1956) #6503, green corduroy overalls with felt bunny motif on knees and print jersey shirt. Matches Ginny outfit #6129.

(1956), #6506, sheer play dress, with printed material lace around yoke and skirt, bonnet with the rayon, black printed tag, hook closing.

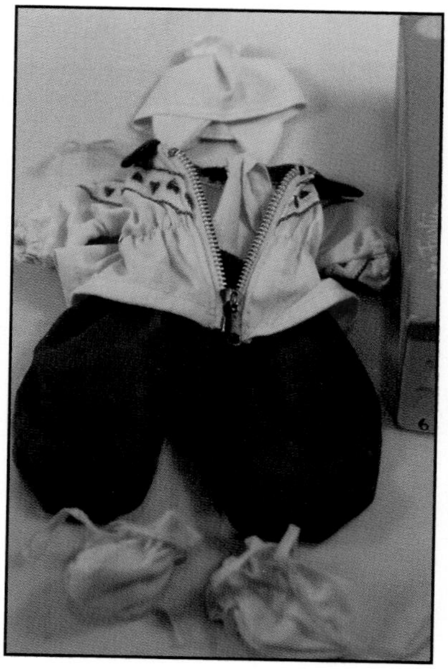

(1956) #6708, snowsuit, pink with gray snowsuit with zipper jacket, gray pants, booties, and cap. Courtesy Judy Armitstead.

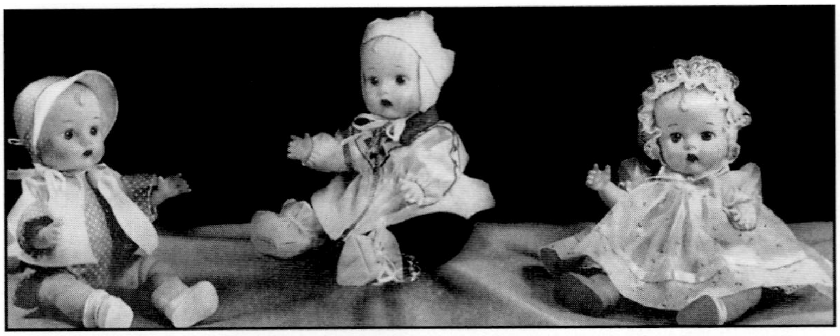

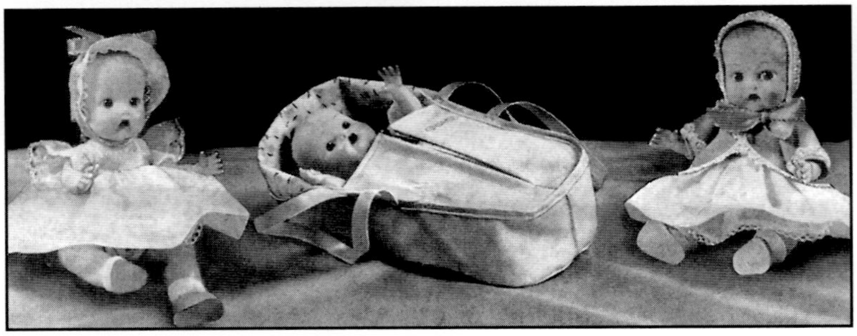

(1956) Ginnette brochure showing outfits (top row) #6507, #6508, #6509, and (bottom row) #6510, toter #6750, and #6511. Vogue brochure.

(1956) #6509, print sheer dress with ruffled bonnet. Courtesy S. Ogilvie.

(1956), #6512, Christening gown, long organdy gown with matching ruffled bonnet.

(1956) #6700, Valentine special outfit in red flowered white nylon dress and bonnet. A special Vogue promotion for Valentine's Day. Courtesy S. Ogilvie.

(1956) Ginnette brochure showing #6740, cotton waffle coat and bonnet; #6733 travel quilt; and #6741 felt coat and bonnet. Vogue brochure.

(1956) #6741, felt coat and bonnet with pom-pons. Shown in both pink and blue.

Accessories

(1956), #6731, bathrobe. Vogue brochure.

(1956) #6731, pink footed sleeper came with flannel bathrobe (shown at left).

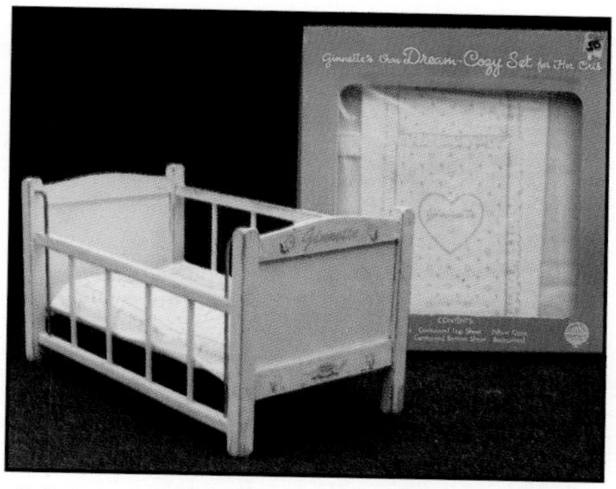

(1956), #6776, drop side white enameled crib with inset panel of turtle and flowers motif, shown with mint in box #6778 Dream Cozy Crib Set – mattress pad, pillow, bedspread. Courtesy Nadine Steele.

(1956), #6777; (1957), #7790; (1958 – 1959), #2850; Baby Bath, enameled white wood with plastic bath area.

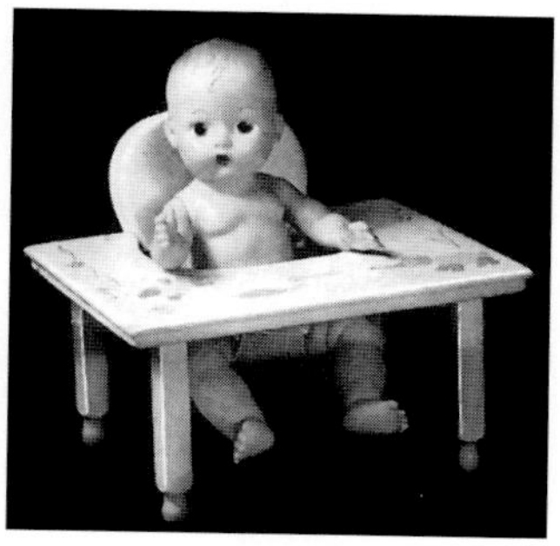

(1956), (left) #6775, wood tender; and #6780, bath set (right). Vogue brochure.

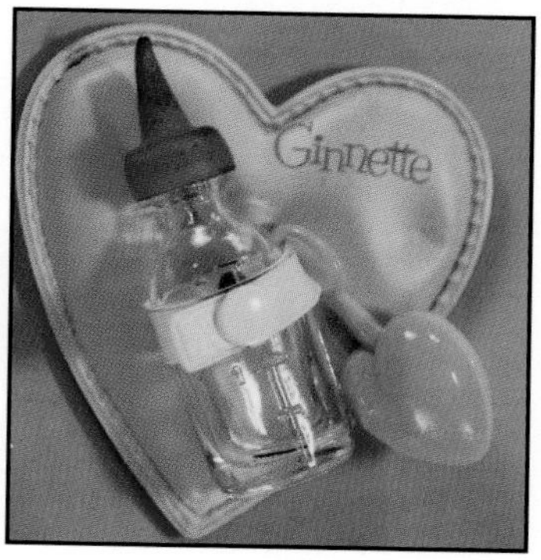

(1956), #6751; (1957), #7772; (1958), #2530; (1959 – 1960), #2510, glass bottle in plastic heart-shaped bottle holder with Ginnette in gold print, heart-shaped rattle.

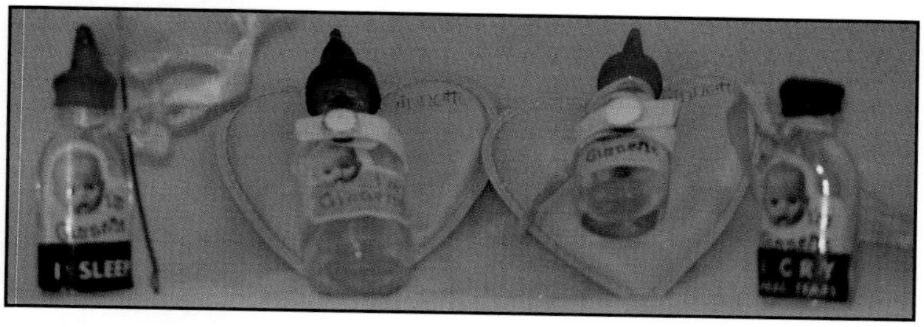

(1956), #6751; (1957), #7772; (1958), #2530; (1959 and 1960), #2510; glass bottle in plastic heart-shaped bottle holder showing variations in bottle and holder. Holder was generally blue but others can be found with pink on one side and blue on the other. Notice bottle on right saying Ginnette cries which is from later year. Courtesy S. Ogilvie.

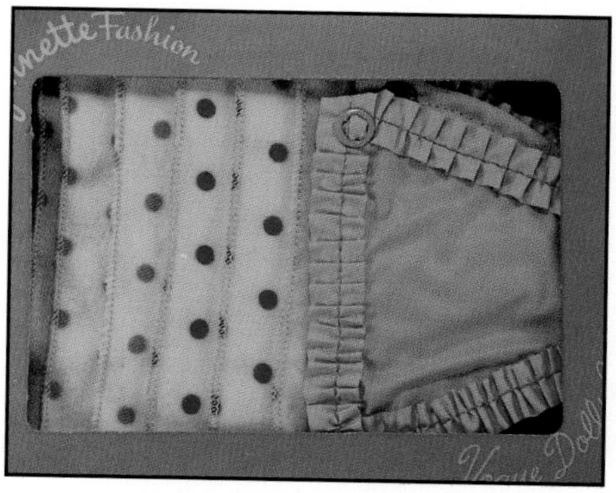

(1956) #6730 Diaper Pak – six felt printed diapers with flowers, four pins, plastic ruffled diaper cover.

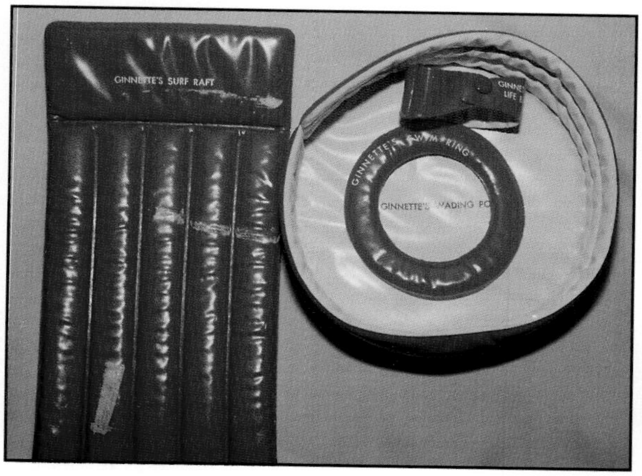

(1956), #6752; (1957), #7774; (1958), #2590; swim set had swimming pool, float, life belt, and swim ring. Courtesy Judy Armitstead.

Rattles, two types, one blue and round, the other heart-shaped and pink on one side, blue on the other. Courtesy S. Ogilvie.

(1956) #6752, Swim Set in its packaging, notice water safety rules. Courtesy Veronica Phillip.

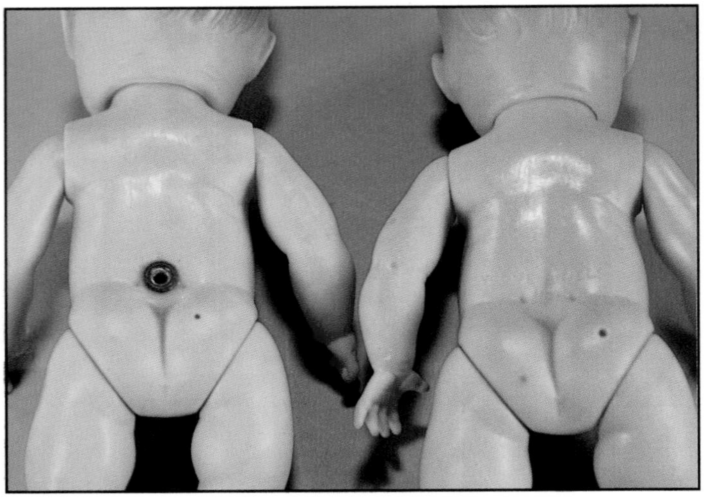

Comparison of Ginnette bodies. Doll on right is painted eye. Doll on left with "squeaker" is a sleep eye doll. Both are marked VOGUE DOLL.

1957

Dressed dolls were numbered #76+; outfits only, #77+.

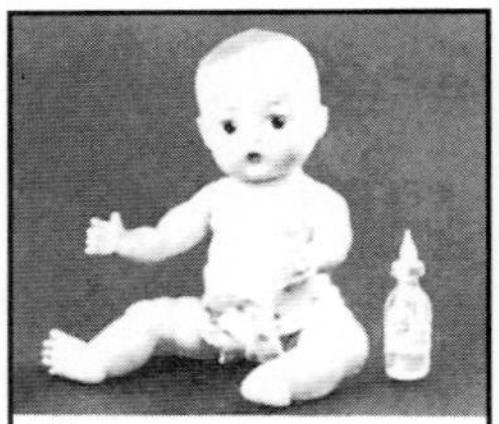

Ginnette in diaper with bottle — Non-moving eyes.
No. 7675 — $2.00

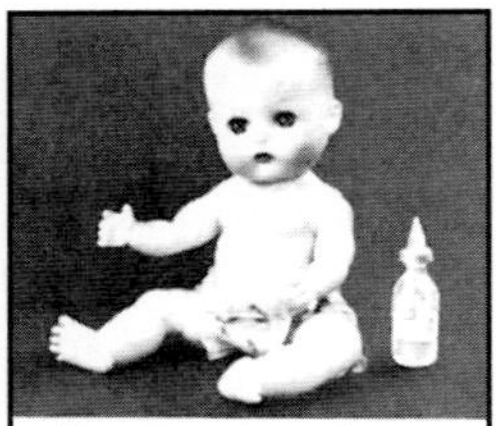

Ginnette in diaper with bottle — Moving eyes.
No. 7670 — $3.00

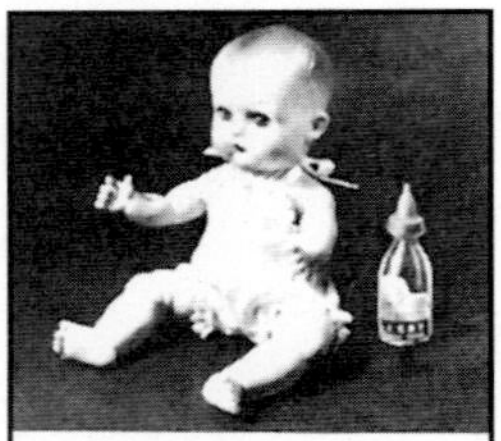

Ginnette in outfit with bottle — Moving eyes that cry real tears.
No. 7678 — $4.00

Ginnette (1957), three different dolls available that year, all came with bottle.

Ginnette (1957), in ad in *Playthings Magazine*.

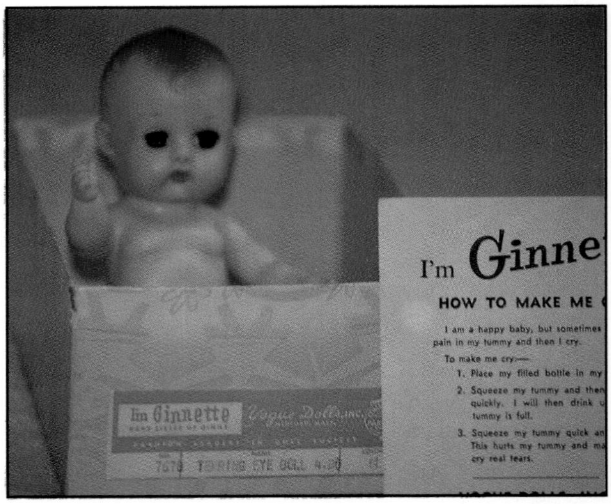

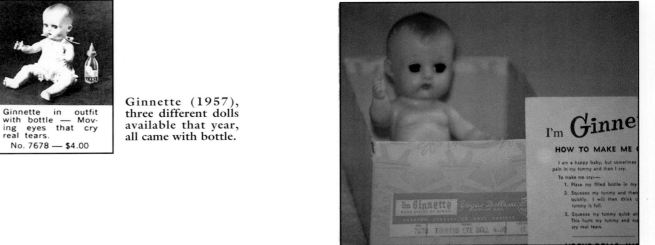

(1957) #7678, Tearing Eye Ginnette, Ginnette that cries real tears. Courtesy S. Ogilvie.

(1957) #7601, pink frilly sacque and panties, white socks with pink ties.

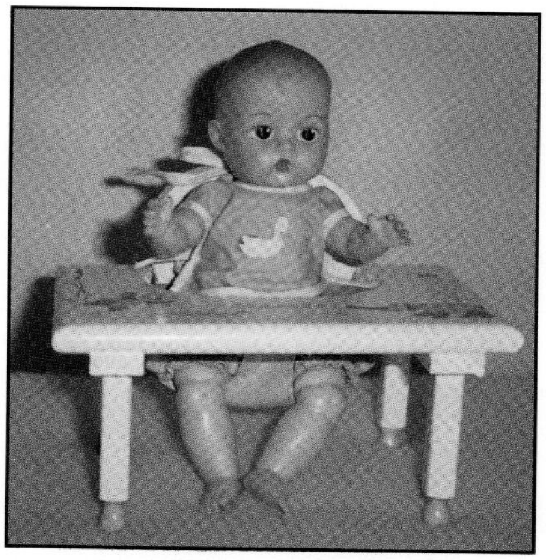

(1957) #7607, blue apron with felt bunny motif. Shown in Baby Tender. Courtesy Susan Steelman.

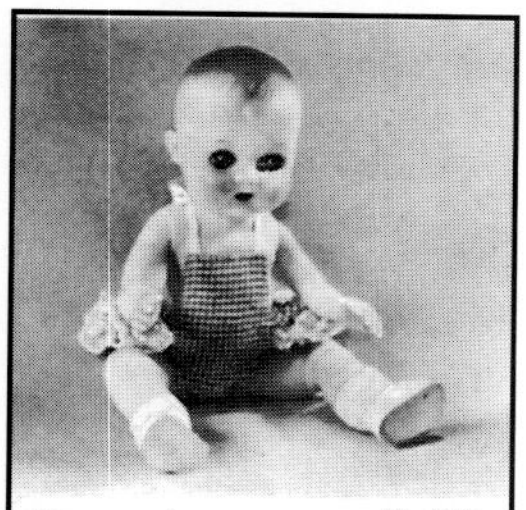

Dressed No. 7613 $4.50 Outfit No. 7713 $1.50

Dressed No. 7614 $4.50 Outfit No. 7714*† $1.50

Dressed No. 7615 $4.50 Outfit No. 7715* $1.50

(1957) #7616, yellow print sundress, matches Ginny.

(1957) #7619, blue dress and bonnet with pink flower in front, matches Ginny #7633.

Dressed No. 7620 $5.00 Outfit No. 7720 $2.00

Dressed No. 7621 $5.00 Outfit No. 7721 $2.00

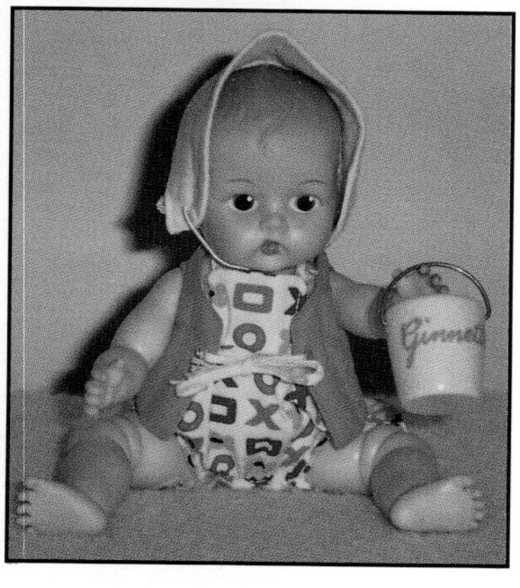

(1957) #7625, swimsuit, life jacket, bonnet, pail, matches Ginny #7048. Shown in catalog with shoes. Courtesy Susan Steelman.

Dressed No. 7627 $5.50 Outfit No. 7727* $2.50

(1957) #7626, snowsuit, white felt jacket and bonnet, snow pants, matches Ginny #7149. Courtesy Nadine Steele.

(1957) #7631, Party Dress with pink cape and bonnet, matches Ginny #7155. Courtesy S. Ogilvie.

(1957) #7632, white ruffled party dress and bonnet with pink underskirt and pink ribbon. Courtesy Veronica Phillips.

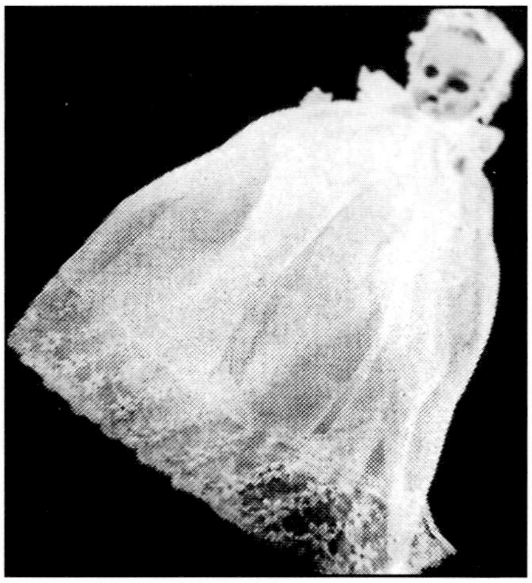

(1957) #7637, christening gown

(1957) #7650, sold as outfit only

(1957) #7751, felt coat and bonnet, matches Ginny. Came as outfit only. Courtesy Veronica Phillips.

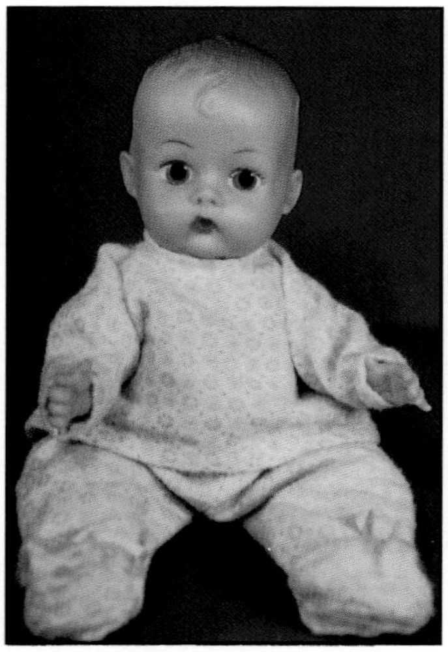

(1957) #7760, print footed p.j.s. Courtesy Sue Johnson.

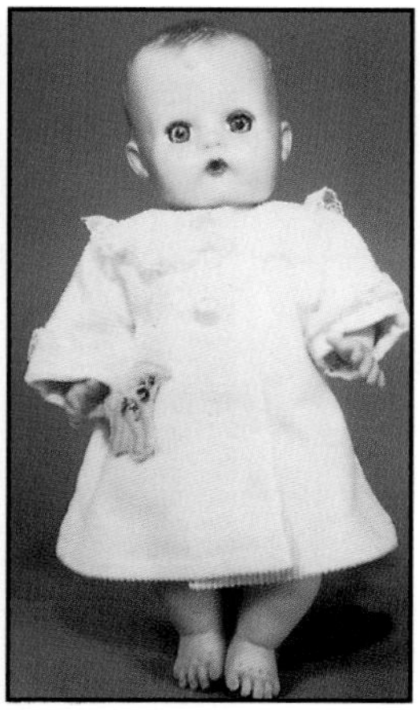

(1957) #7761; and (1958) #2317, white corduroy bathrobe.

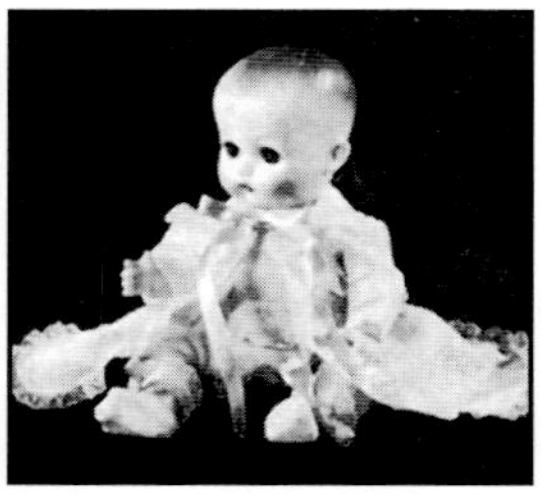

(1957) #7762, also available in 1968 #2318.

(1957) #7763 and 1958, #2363, white Dynel bunting with pink lining, matching bonnet.

(1957) #7764, Diaper Pak, three printed diapers saying "Baby Ginnette" with scenes of bears in pink and blue, pink vinyl diaper cover.

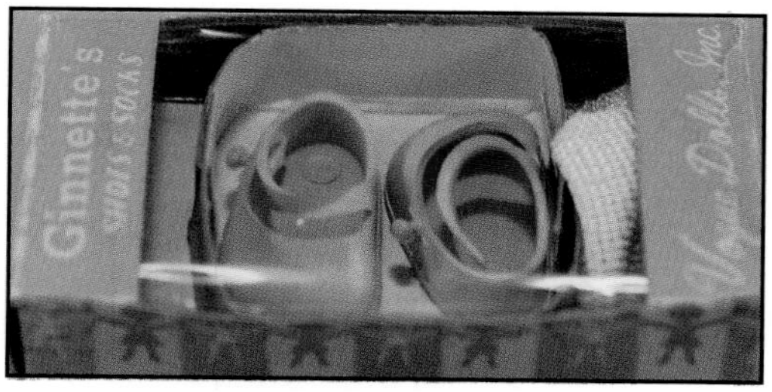

(1957) #7776; (1958 – 1960) #2500, shoes and socks in assorted colors. Most common were white, light blue, and pink. Rarer colors included red and black. Marked "Ginnette" on bottom of heel.

PLAY DAY PACKAGE
— Ginnette cries real tears in outfit with bottle plus 3 complete outfits.
No. 7779 $10.00
LAYETTE PACKAGE
— contains non-moving eyes Ginnette and layette items.
No. 7778 $5.00

(1957) #7779 Play Day package; and #7778 Layette package with painted eye Ginnette. Vogue brochure.

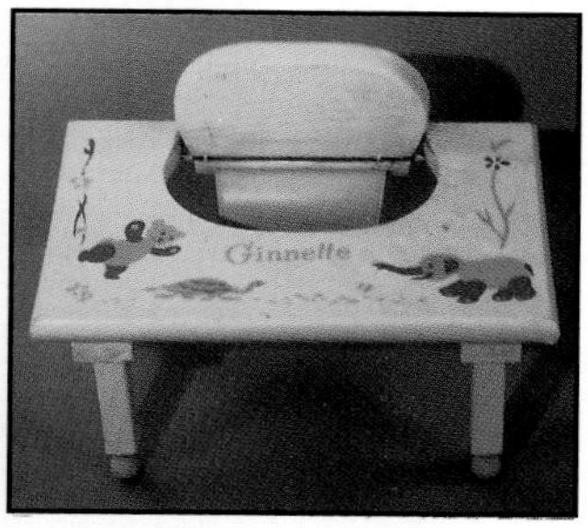

(1957) #7785, (1958) #2830, Baby Tender, white painted wood with animal motifs, top folds down to make a flat surface, plastic seat, pink balls at end of legs. Notice solid color pink vinyl seat, later version of 1956 cotton print seat.

(1957) #7787; (1958 – 1959) #2860, drop side white crib with animal motif, smooth headboard and foot board with Ginnette's name on it.

(1957) #7795, (1958 – 1959) #2851, Shoo-Fly Rocker, white painted wood with pastel color animal and flower motif.

1958

Dressed dolls were #21+; outfits only were #23+.

Ginnette (1958) Outfits . Vogue brochure.

Outfit 2300 $1.00
Saucy little plissé rompers i
peppermint pink with dainty lac
trim and shiny satin ribbon tha
circles the waist.

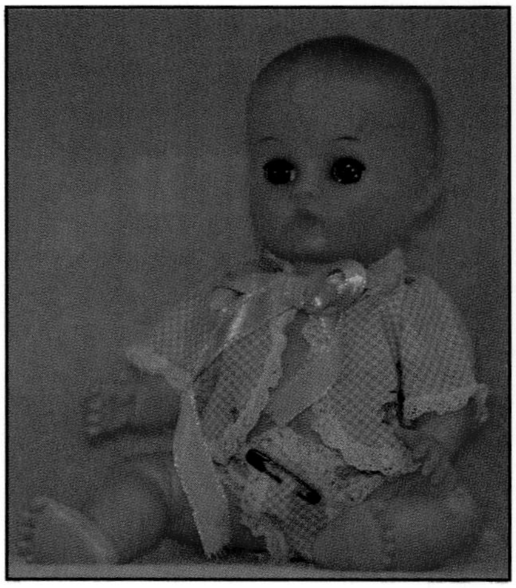
(1958) #2301, blue pin checked cotton sacque and diaper cover. Courtesy S. Ogilvie.

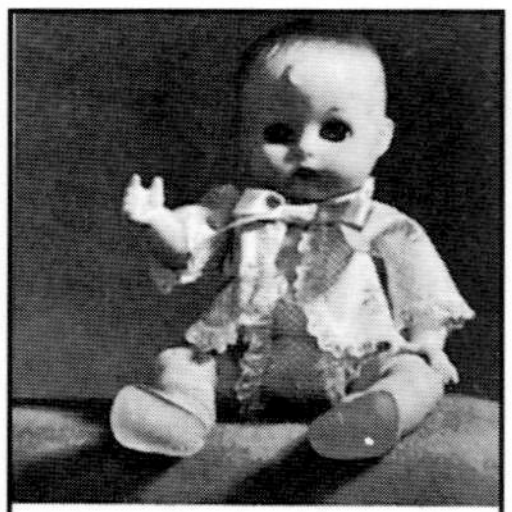
utfit 2301 $1.00
innette's sacque and diaper
over in blue pin checked cotton.
rimmed with white lace and tied
ith blue satin.

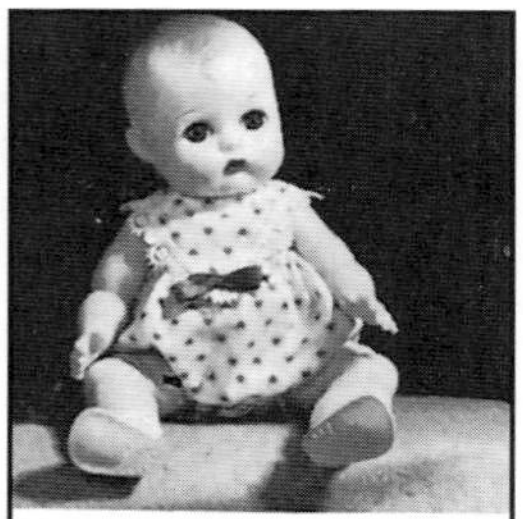
Outfit 2302 $1.00
How sweet Ginnette looks in he
pretty little sun suit! Red and white
cotton print trimmed with lace and
a saucy red bow.

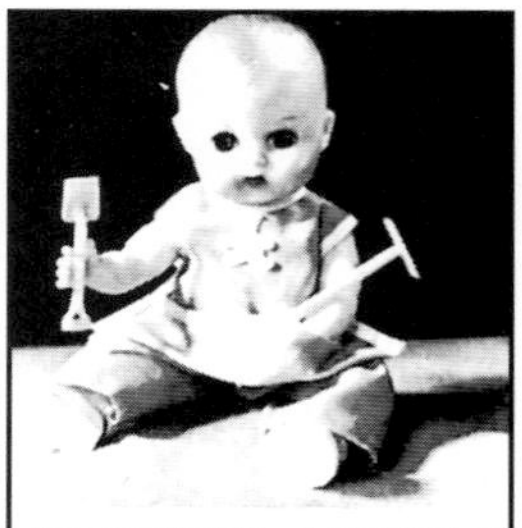
Dressed 2110 $4.50 Outfit 2310 $1.50
Let's go gardening! Ginnette ca
wear her coral play-apron and
matching pants. She even has he
own plastic garden tools.

Dressed 2111 $4.50 Outfit 2311 $1.50
Perky little sun dress and matching
bonnet in baby blue pique. White
rick rack trim and little kitty motif
at the hem.

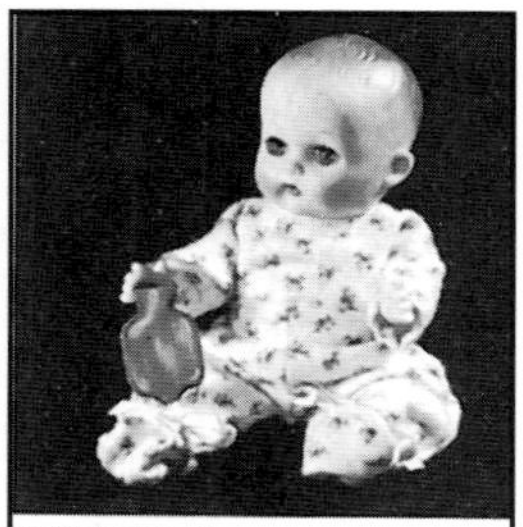
Outfit 2316 $1.50
Time for bed and Ginnette wears
cuddly warm flannelette sleepers
with feet. Available in pretty pastel
shades.

Dressed 2130 $5.00 Outfit 2330 $2.0
White pique topper set with re
duck and red rick rack trim. He
panties are red, her bonnet whit
pique with matching red trim.

(1958) #2303, batiste long nightgown with rosebud and lace trim. Courtesy Nadine Steele.

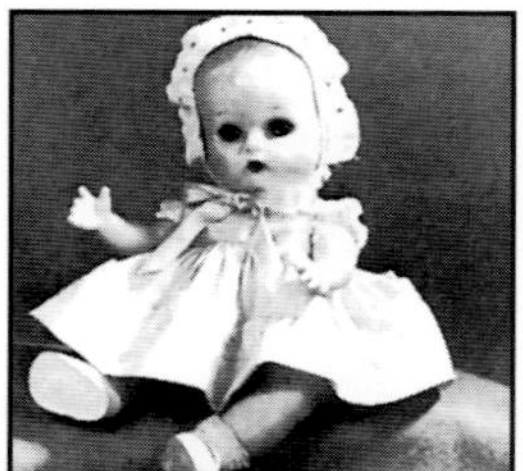
Dressed 2132 $5.00 Outfit 2332 $2.0
Pale pink polished cotton fo
warm, sunny days. Trimmed ever-
so daintily with embroidered eyelet ruffles and pink satin ribbon.

ressed 2133 $5.00 Outfit 2333 $2.00
innette wears a yellow gingham
uit, matching bonnet and yellow
erry lined jacket. Pail and glasses
or fun!

Outfit 2336 $2.00
How special Ginnette will look
when she wears her blue taffeta
dress-up coat. Matching bonnet is
trimmed with ruffly lace.

utfit 2337 $2.00
or a ride in her pram, Ginnette
ears this snowy white felt coat
nd bonnet that has pink buttons,
ink ribbons and rose bud trim.

Dressed 2150 $5.50 Outfit 2350 $2.5
Dressed for party-ing and Ginnette
wears pink organdy trimmed with
dainty lace and satin ribbon.
Petticoat and bonnet to match.

ressed 2151 $5.50 Outfit 2351 $2.50††
now-suit for freezy-cold days,
ashioned in aqua cotton with
utton-up jacket, separate pants,
arm fur trimmed hood and mitts.

Dressed 2180 $7.00 Outfit 2380 $4.0
Ginnette's Christening dress i
filmy white organdy with ribbo
and lace trim. Lace edged taffet
slip and matching bonnet.

(1958) #2112, pink cotton yoke dress with ruffle lace trim. Courtesy S. Ogilvie.

(1958) #2131, blue broadcloth overalls trimmed with lace, blue checked cotton blouse. Matches Jimmy outfit #4131.

(1958) #2160, white organdy dress and petticoat, pink lace trimmed quilted jacket and bonnet. Courtesy S. Ogilvie.

(1958) #2161, white nylon party dress with val lace, maize taffeta slip, and matching bonnet. Courtesy Veronica Phillips.

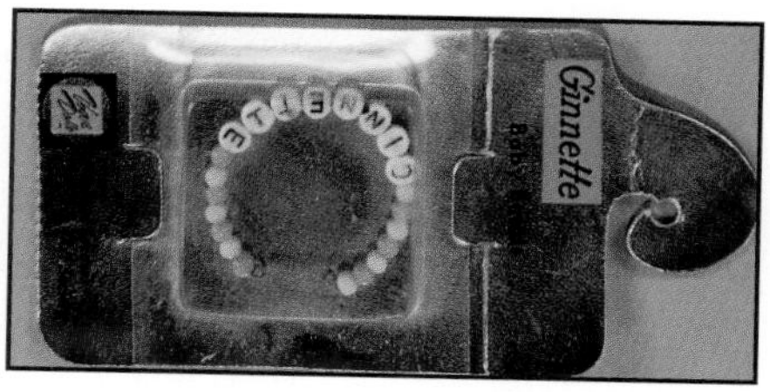
GINNETTE
Ginnette

(1958 – 1960) #2600, baby beads, a name bracelet, pink and blue beads with white beads which spell out Ginnette's name. Courtesy Sue Johnson.

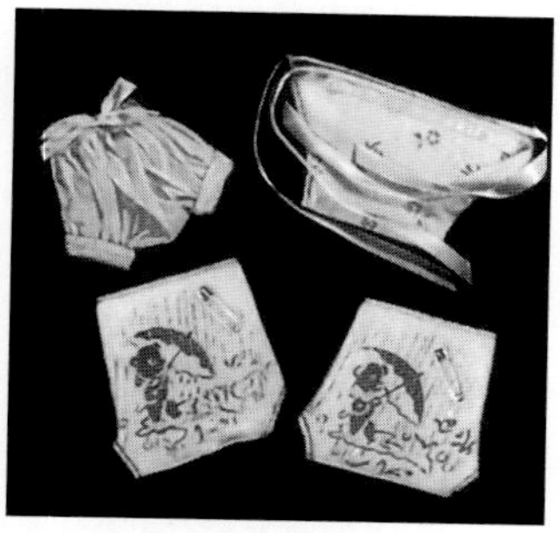

(1958) #2531 Ginnette's Diaper Pak contains three diapers, pins, and scented plastic panties. Vogue brochure.

2740 $6.00
Ginnette's Baby Pak contains Ginnette dressed in diapers, plus pretty nightie, sacque and diaper cover, bottle, bottle holder, Rubber pants, shoes and socks.
Ginnette's Baby Pak
Ginnette's play day
Ginnette

Ginnette (1958 –1959), #2740 Baby Pak, Ginnette in diapers plus sacque, diaper cover, bottle, bottle holder, rubber pants, shoes and socks; and Play Day #2750 1958 – 1959, Ginnette in diapers holding a bottle, baby bath and four-piece bath set including soap powder, hooded bath towel, and bath sponge, two-piece flannelette footed sleeper, play dress with matching shoes and socks. Vogue Brochure.

(1958) #2880, three drawer white dresser with animal motifs. Comes with dresser scarf and rattle.

1959

Dressed dolls were #22+; outfit only were #24+.

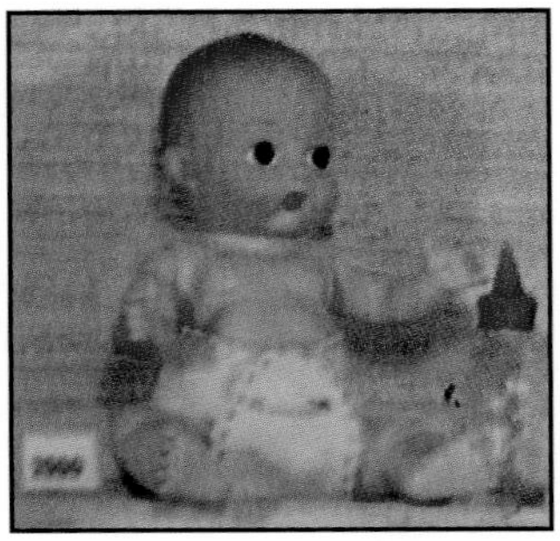

(1959) #2000, basic doll, 8" vinyl, painted eye baby doll dressed in diaper with bottle. 1959 Vogue catalog to retailers. Courtesy Marge Meisinger.

(1959) #2010, basic doll, 8", vinyl moving eye doll dressed in diaper with bottle. 1959 Vogue catalog to retailers. Courtesy Marge Meisinger.

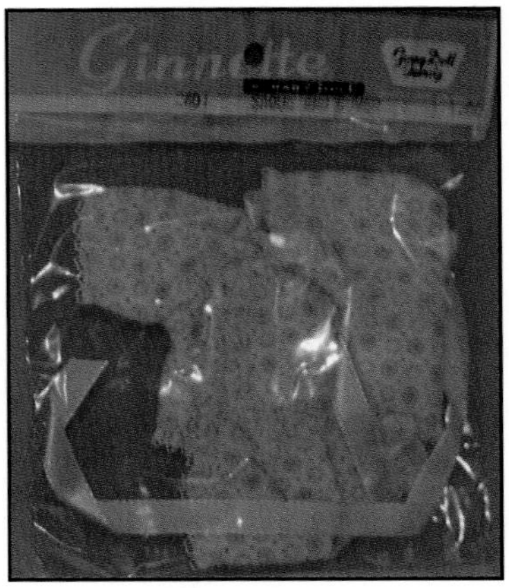

(1959) #2401, pink and white checked flannelette sacque and diaper cover with lace ruffle. Shown in hang package. Courtesy S. Ogilvie.

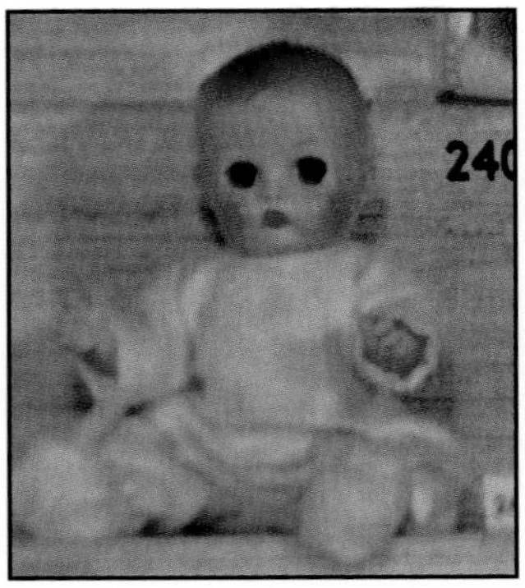

(1959) #2402, yellow flannelette one piece sleeper with feet (matches Ginny Baby). Came as outfit only. 1959 Vogue catalog to retailers. Courtesy Marge Meisinger.

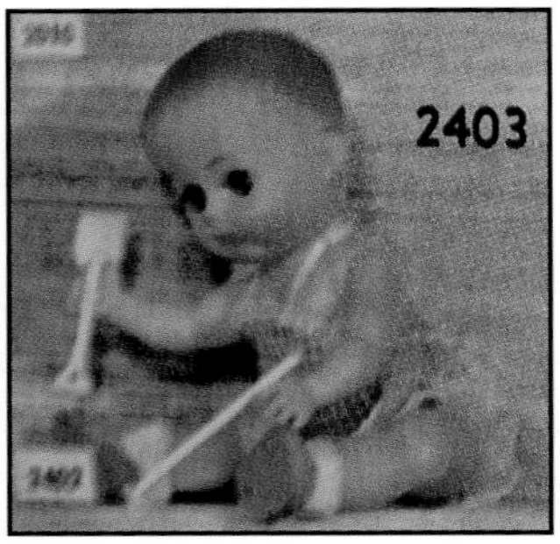

#2403, blue pin checked sunsuit with can-can ruffles, comes with rake and shovel. 1959 Vogue catalog to retailers. Courtesy Marge Meisinger.

(1959) #2210, white ribbed cotton romper with embroidered duck on front, red rickrack, and matching bonnet; #2211, pink organdy dress, pink satin shoulder ties, matching panties. 1959 Vogue catalog to retailers. Courtesy Marge Meisinger.

Not Shown

#2400, romper aqua rocking-horse print with white yoke with baby val lace trim. Came as outfit only.

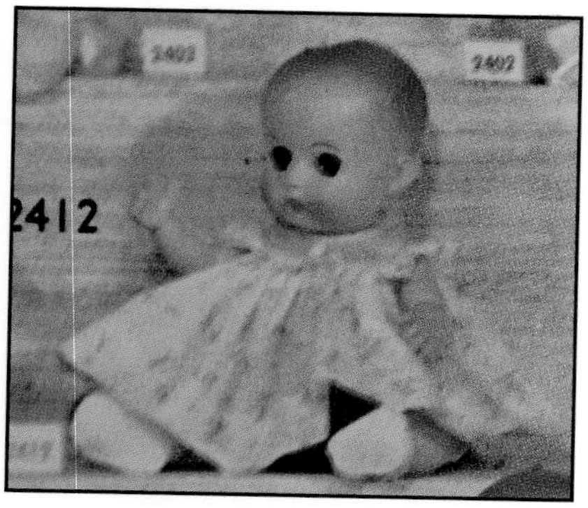

(1959) #2412 (#2212 dressed doll), white batiste dress with candy mint yoke with lace trim and matching panties. 1959 Vogue catalog to retailers. Courtesy Marge Meisinger.

(1959) #2213, sheer yellow organdy party dress with lace shoulder ruffles, beading lace and bow trim, matching panties (matches Ginny); (1959) #2214, pink plaid creeper with lace heart-shaped bib and bow in back, comes with beach pail with name on it. 1959 Vogue catalog to retailers. Courtesy Marge Meisinger.

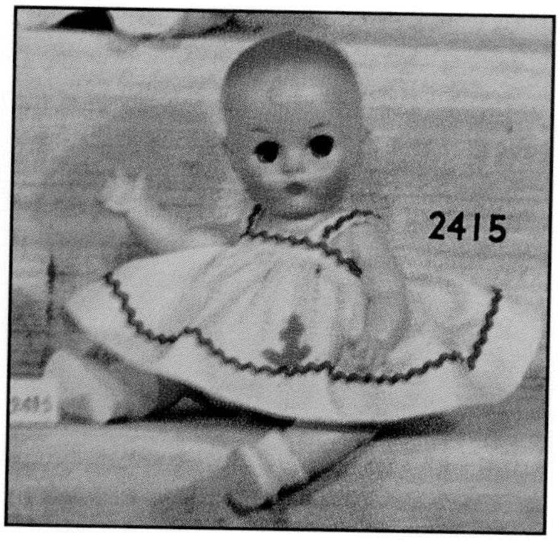

(1959) #2415 (#2215 dressed doll), white broadcloth sundress with blue rickrack trim, pink anchor motif, and matching panties. 1959 Vogue catalog to retailers. Courtesy Marge Meisinger.

Ginnette (1959) #2230, crawler set, pink striped pants, white blouse, pink wool felt jacket, came with sunglasses and watering can. Courtesy S. Ogilvie.

(1959) #2231, white organdy party dress with fluted sheer ruffle trim bonnet and petticoat to match, diapers. Courtesy Veronica Phillips.

(1959) #2232, dress with white top and pink skirt, matching bonnet and panties (Matches Ginny and Jill). Courtesy S. Ogilvie.

(1959) #2445, blue wool felt coat with white collar and pearly buttons, and bonnet trimmed with white. Came as outfit only. 1959 Vogue catalog to retailers. Courtesy Marge Meisinger.

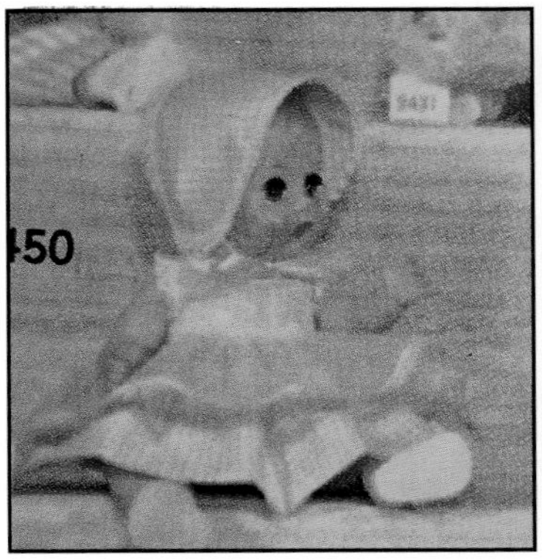

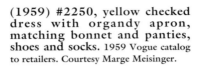

(1959) #2250, yellow checked dress with organdy apron, matching bonnet and panties, shoes and socks. 1959 Vogue catalog to retailers. Courtesy Marge Meisinger.

(1959) #2251, blue polka dot nylon dress with baby val lace ruffles, matching bonnet, separate petticoat, diapers, shoes and socks. Courtesy S. Ogilvie.

(1959) #2252, pink pram suit with zipper front and attached hood, trimmed in white rabbit fur (matches Ginny Baby). 1959 Vogue catalog to retailers. Courtesy Marge Meisinger.

(1959) #2260, pink flocked nylon dress with ruffled bonnet and matching nylon petticoat, diaper, shoes and socks. 1959 Vogue catalog to retailer. Courtesy Marge Meisinger.

(1959) #2261, white nylon christening dress over taffeta slip with lace ruffles, lace yoke and bonnet to match, diaper, booties. Courtesy Veronica Phillips.

Accessories

Not Shown

1959 – 1960, #2511, diaper set, three diapers and pins; #2852, Crib Bed Set, pillow, pillowcase, two contour sheets, and pink bedspread.

1960

Dressed dolls were #21+; outfits only were #23+.

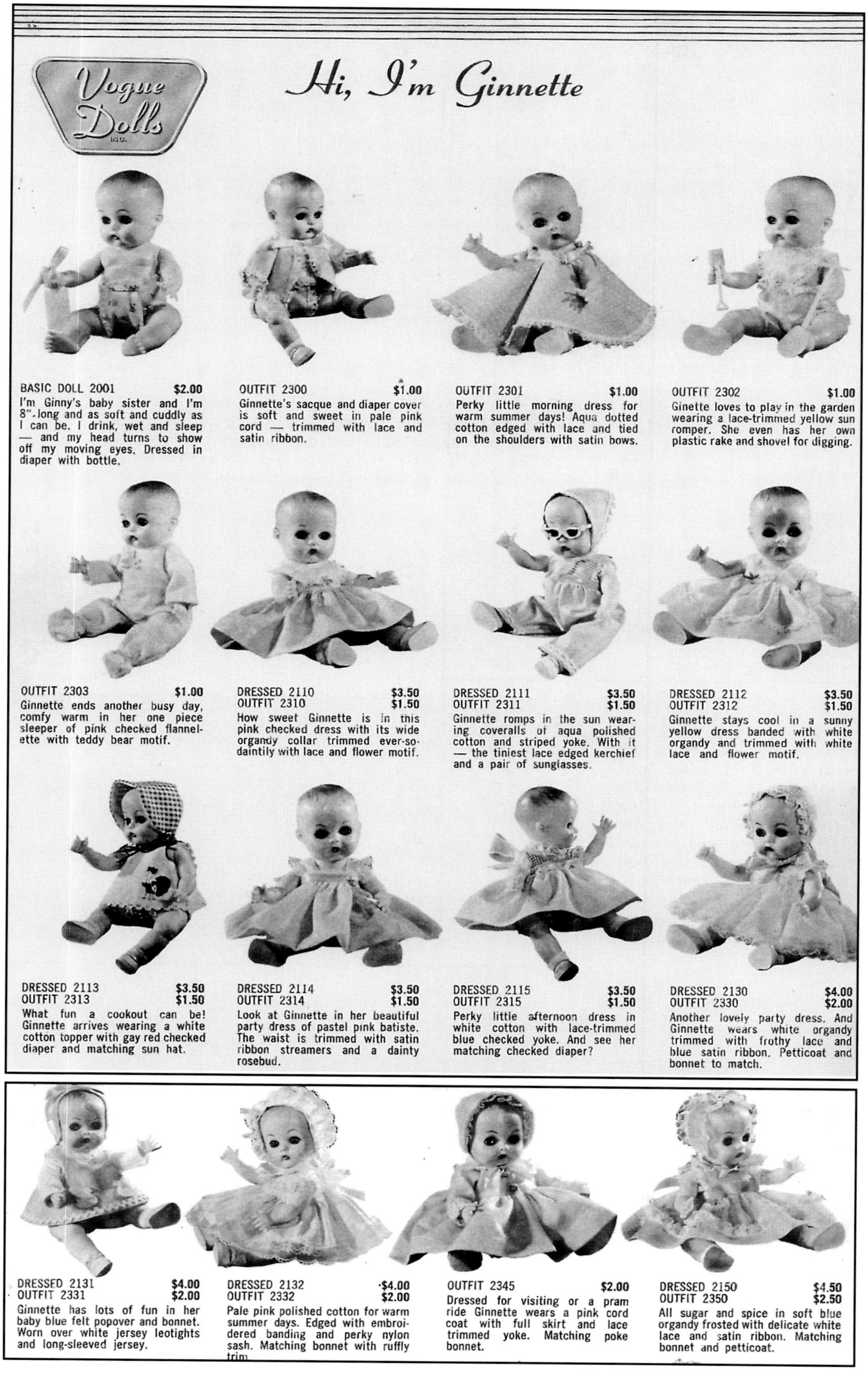

Vogue Dolls Inc.

Hi, I'm Ginnette

BASIC DOLL 2001 $2.00
I'm Ginny's baby sister and I'm 8"-long and as soft and cuddly as I can be. I drink, wet and sleep — and my head turns to show off my moving eyes. Dressed in diaper with bottle.

OUTFIT 2300 $1.00
Ginnette's sacque and diaper cover is soft and sweet in pale pink cord — trimmed with lace and satin ribbon.

OUTFIT 2301 $1.00
Perky little morning dress for warm summer days! Aqua dotted cotton edged with lace and tied on the shoulders with satin bows.

OUTFIT 2302 $1.00
Ginette loves to play in the garden wearing a lace-trimmed yellow sun romper. She even has her own plastic rake and shovel for digging.

OUTFIT 2303 $1.00
Ginnette ends another busy day, comfy warm in her one piece sleeper of pink checked flannelette with teddy bear motif.

DRESSED 2110 $3.50
OUTFIT 2310 $1.50
How sweet Ginnette is in this pink checked dress with its wide organdy collar trimmed ever-so-daintily with lace and flower motif.

DRESSED 2111 $3.50
OUTFIT 2311 $1.50
Ginnette romps in the sun wearing coveralls of aqua polished cotton and striped yoke. With it — the tiniest lace edged kerchief and a pair of sunglasses.

DRESSED 2112 $3.50
OUTFIT 2312 $1.50
Ginnette stays cool in a sunny yellow dress banded with white organdy and trimmed with white lace and flower motif.

DRESSED 2113 $3.50
OUTFIT 2313 $1.50
What fun a cookout can be! Ginnette arrives wearing a white cotton topper with gay red checked diaper and matching sun hat.

DRESSED 2114 $3.50
OUTFIT 2314 $1.50
Look at Ginnette in her beautiful party dress of pastel pink batiste. The waist is trimmed with satin ribbon streamers and a dainty rosebud.

DRESSED 2115 $3.50
OUTFIT 2315 $1.50
Perky little afternoon dress in white cotton with lace-trimmed blue checked yoke. And see her matching checked diaper?

DRESSED 2130 $4.00
OUTFIT 2330 $2.00
Another lovely party dress. And Ginnette wears white organdy trimmed with frothy lace and blue satin ribbon. Petticoat and bonnet to match.

DRESSED 2131 $4.00
OUTFIT 2331 $2.00
Ginnette has lots of fun in her baby blue felt popover and bonnet. Worn over white jersey leotights and long-sleeved jersey.

DRESSED 2132 $4.00
OUTFIT 2332 $2.00
Pale pink polished cotton for warm summer days. Edged with embroidered banding and perky nylon sash. Matching bonnet with ruffly trim.

OUTFIT 2345 $2.00
Dressed for visiting or a pram ride Ginnette wears a pink cord coat with full skirt and lace trimmed yoke. Matching poke bonnet.

DRESSED 2150 $4.50
OUTFIT 2350 $2.50
All sugar and spice in soft blue organdy frosted with delicate white lace and satin ribbon. Matching bonnet and petticoat.

(1960) Ginnette. Vogue catalog. Courtesy Jenny Henry.

DRESSED 2151 $4.50
OUTFIT 2351 $2.50
Pretty crispy little dress of white dotted nylon with ruffly lace and rosebud trim. How sweet her bonnet is with its pink satin bows. Matching petticoat.
DRESSED 2152 $4.50
OUTFIT 2352 $2.50
Ginnette doesn't mind the snow when she's dressed all comfy warm in her aqua polished sno-suit. White braid trims the jacket and matching hood.
DRESSED 2153 $4.50
OUTFIT 2353 $2.50
Ginnette loves to dress up! Here she is in a baby blue dotted dress with ruffly lace trimmed organdy apron with wide nylon sash. Matching bonnet.
DRESSED 2160 $5.00
OUTFIT 2360 $3.00
Ginnette's christening dress is sheer white nylon with embroidered banding and frothy lace trim. Dainty lace bonnet and yoke. White booties.

(1960) Ginnette. Vogue catalog. Courtesy Jenny Henry.

1961

Dressed dolls numbered #284+; outfits only, #283+.

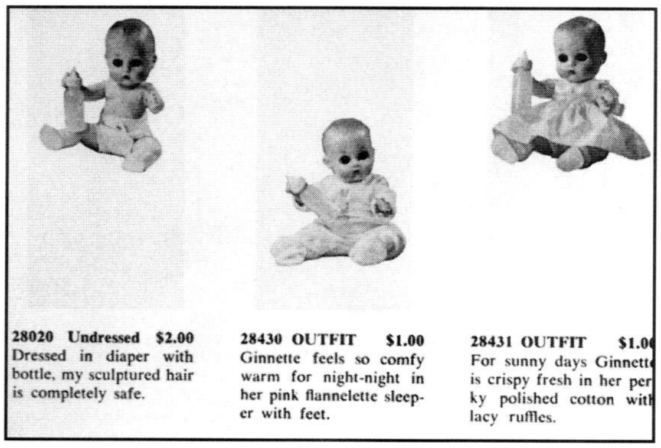
28020 Undressed $2.00
Dressed in diaper with bottle, my sculptured hair is completely safe.
28430 OUTFIT $1.00
Ginnette feels so comfy warm for night-night in her pink flannelette sleeper with feet.
28431 OUTFIT
For sunny days Ginnett is crispy fresh in her per ky polished cotton wit lacy ruffles.

Ginnette outfits (1961) from Vogue catalog: #28020, undressed Ginnette with sculptured hair; #28230, pink flannelette sleeper with cut-out felt bunny on front; #28231, polished cotton sundress with lacy ruffles. Vogue catalog. Courtesy Wenham Museum, Wenham, Mass.

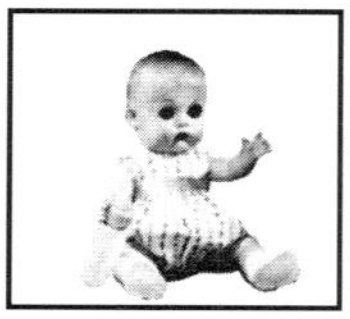

#28232, rosebud print romper with lace trim and bow.

#28235, pink polished cotton party dress with rosebud; #28236, white pleated cotton dress banded in blue with matching lace trimmed collar; #28237, lace trimmed choir girl top with rosy creepers; #28240, frilly blue nylon dress, petticoat, and matching bonnet; #28241, pink fleece jacket with bunny ears and pants. Vogue catalog. Courtesy Wenham Museum, Wenham, Mass.

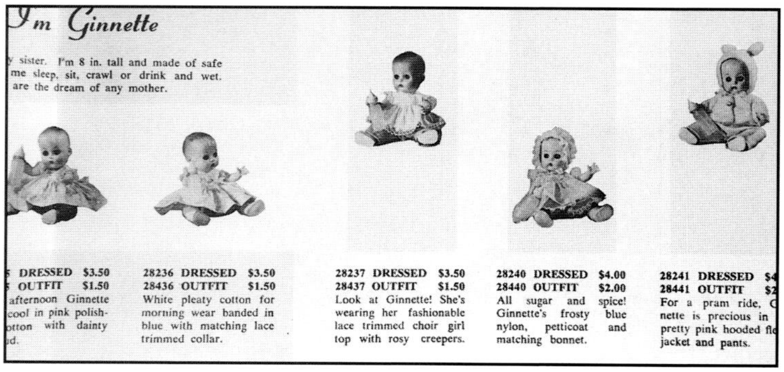
I'm Ginnette
sister. I'm 8 in. tall and made of safe
me sleep, sit, crawl or drink and wet.
are the dream of any mother.
DRESSED $3.50
OUTFIT $1.50
afternoon Ginnette cool in pink polish- otton with dainty
28236 DRESSED $3.50
28436 OUTFIT $1.50
White pleaty cotton for morning wear banded in blue with matching lace trimmed collar.
28237 DRESSED $3.50
28437 OUTFIT $1.50
Look at Ginnette! She's wearing her fashionable lace trimmed choir girl top with rosy creepers.
28240 DRESSED $4.00
28440 OUTFIT $2.00
All sugar and spice! Ginnette's frosty blue nylon, petticoat and matching bonnet.
28241 DRESSED
28441 OUTFIT
For a pram ride, nette is precious in pretty pink hooded jacket and pants.

1962

Dressed dolls numbered, #284+; outfits only, #283+.

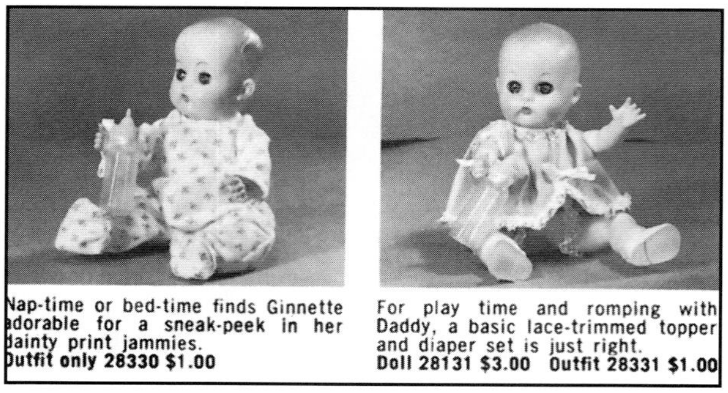
ap-time or bed-time finds Ginnette dorable for a sneak-peek in her ainty print jammies.
utfit only 28330 $1.00
For play time and romping with Daddy, a basic lace-trimmed topper and diaper set is just right.
Doll 28131 $3.00 Outfit 28331 $1.00

Ginnette (1962) outfit, #28330 print p.j.s and #28131, lace trimmed topper and diaper set.

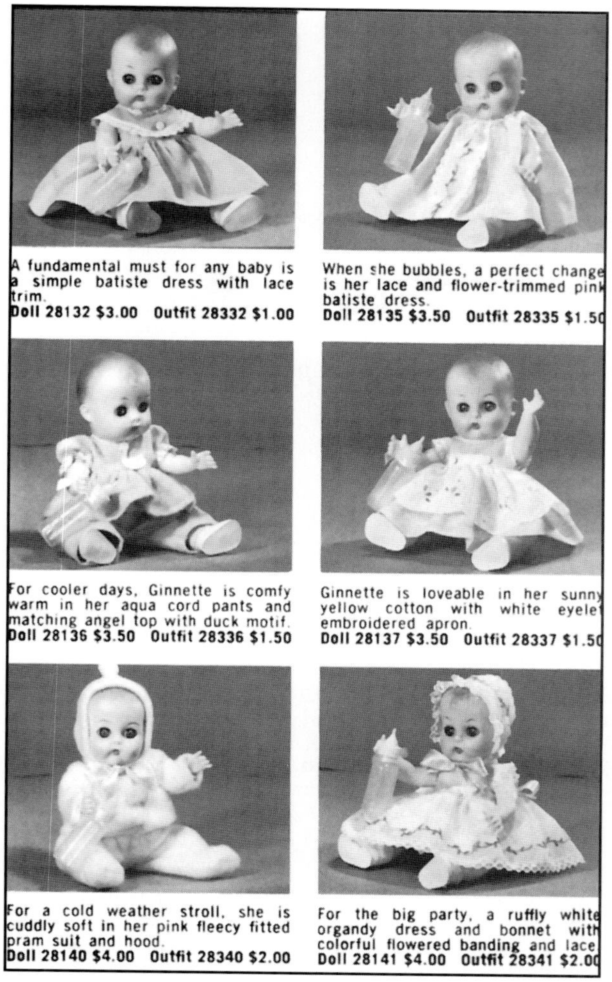

A fundamental must for any baby is a simple batiste dress with lace trim.
Doll 28132 $3.00 Outfit 28332 $1.00

When she bubbles, a perfect change is her lace and flower-trimmed pink batiste dress.
Doll 28135 $3.50 Outfit 28335 $1.50

For cooler days, Ginnette is comfy warm in her aqua cord pants and matching angel top with duck motif.
Doll 28136 $3.50 Outfit 28336 $1.50

Ginnette is loveable in her sunny yellow cotton with white eyelet embroidered apron.
Doll 28137 $3.50 Outfit 28337 $1.50

For a cold weather stroll, she is cuddly soft in her pink fleecy fitted pram suit and hood.
Doll 28140 $4.00 Outfit 28340 $2.00

For the big party, a ruffly white organdy dress and bonnet with colorful flowered banding and lace.
Doll 28141 $4.00 Outfit 28341 $2.00

Ginnette (1962) #28135, pink batiste dress with lace and flower trim. Courtesy S. Ogilvie.

Rooted hair Ginnette (1962) in 1961 #28237, variation of lace trimmed choir girl top with rosy creepers. 1962 price list is the first to list rooted hair Ginnette. Courtesy S. Ogilvie.

Ginnette (1962) outfits: #28132, batiste dress with lace trim; #28135, pink batiste dress with lace and flower trim; #28136, aqua corduroy pants and angel top with puffy short sleeves with duck motif; #28137, yellow cotton dress with white eyelet embroidered apron; #28140, pink fleece footed pram suit and hood; and #28141, white organdy dress and bonnet with flowered banding and lace.

Adorable Ginnette – 1963

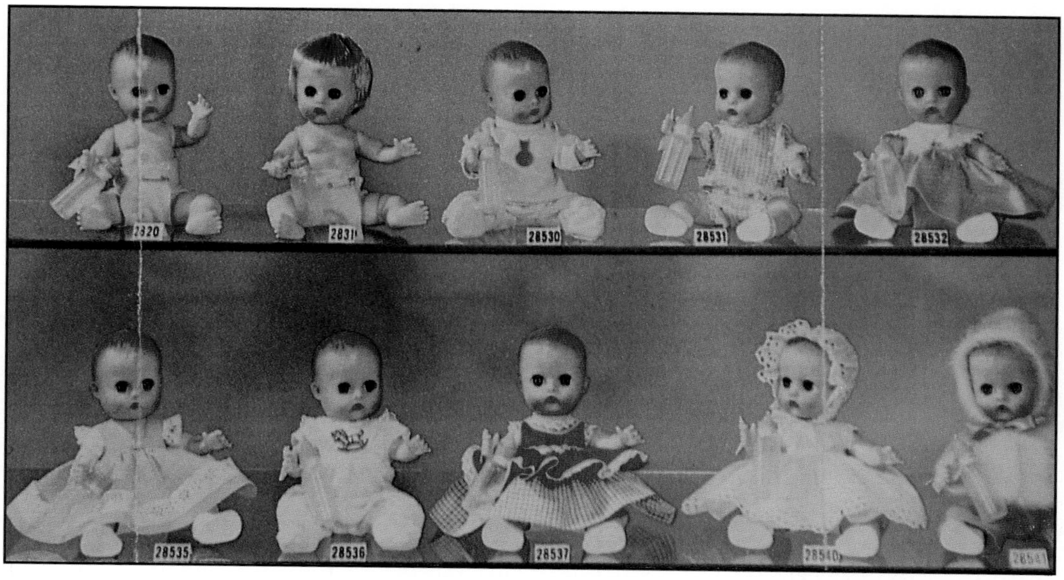

#2820 Basic Ginnette – molded hair, sleep eyes dressed in diaper, drinks and wets; #2831, Ginnette with rooted short blonde shag hair with bangs, sleep eyes, dressed in diaper, drinks and wets; #28530, footed blue flannelette p.j.s, felt cat cut-out on front; #28531, romper set, pink and white checked play set with white ruffle on front side and bottom; #28532, pink polka dot dress with white yoke; #28535, blue dress with white eyelet on sleeves and along edge of skirt; #28536, yellow footed romper with embroidered rocking horse over white jersey short sleeved blouse; #28537, dark pink and white checked dress with pink apron; #28540, white party dress with cotton lace with white ruffled bonnet with blue tie (matches Ginny and Sweetheart Jill); #28541, white fleece jacket with hood tied with pink ribbon with pink pants. All outfits and dolls came with bottle. Vogue brochure.

(1963) #28535, blue dress with white eyelet on sleeves and along edge of skirt. Courtesy S. Ogilvie.

(1963) #28537, dark pink and white checked dress with pink apron. Courtesy S. Ogilvie.

1964

Dressed dolls were #286+; outfits only were #288+.

(1964) #2820 Basic Ginnette, molded hair, sleep eyes, dressed in diaper with bottle; #2830, Ginnette with rooted hair, short dark blonde hair with bangs, sleep eyes, dressed in diaper; #28630, footed blue flannelette p.j.s with felt cat cut-out on front; #28631, red and white checked play set with red felt duck on front; #28632, blue polka dot dress with blue yoke and assorted budget dresses; #28635, yellow sundress with blue ribbon on front; #28636, blue overblouse with felt cat on front over white jersey blouse and bottoms; #28637, checked dress with sheer white apron; #28640, party dress with ruffled bonnet; #28641, yellow fleece jacket with hood with footed pants. All outfits came with bottle except #28641. Vogue brochure. Courtesy Marge Meisinger.

Negro Ginnettes (1964), #28930 – 41 brown vinyl versions of the old Ginnette. They wear the same outfits as Ginnette. Vogue brochure. Courtesy Marge Meisinger.

Ginnette (1964), in blue dress with pink appliqué flower and white lace trim, platinum pixie haircut. Outfit not shown in any price list, could be a store special. Courtesy Veronica Phillips.

Ginnette (1964), in pink topper with Baby heart motif, with platinum pixie haircut. Outfit not shown in any price list, could be a store special. Courtesy Veronica Phillips.

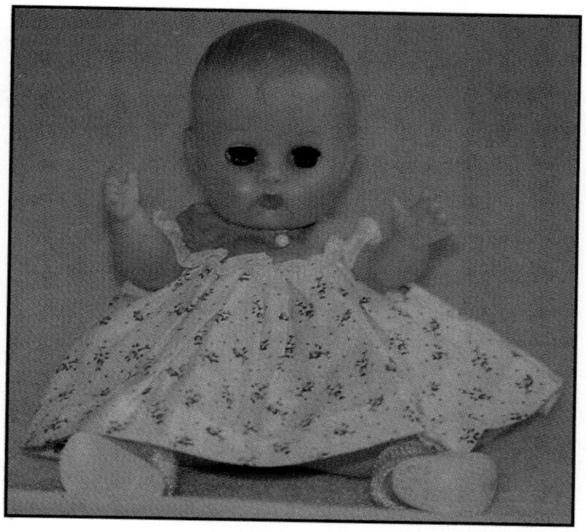

Ginnette (1964), #28632, blue polka dot dress with blue yoke. Courtesy S. Ogilvie.

Negro* Ginnette (1964), 8", all vinyl molded, painted black hair, wearing #28637, pink and white checked dress with white sheer apron. Marks: 19 (on head); VOGUE DOLLS INC (on lower back). Courtesy S. Ogilvie.

Negro* Ginnette (1964), 8", all vinyl rooted black hair, wearing #28637, pink and white checked dress with white sheer apron. Marks: 6 (on head); VOGUE DOLLS/INC (on lower back). Courtesy Wenham Museum, Wenham, Mass.

Negro* Ginnette (1964), 8", all vinyl rooted black hair, wearing pink and white topper outfit. Perhaps this was a unique outfit since outfit looks like it came off a display since it has glue on the back with traces of pink paper. Marks: None (on head); VOGUE DOLLS INC (on lower back). Courtesy S. Ogilvie.

NOT SHOWN:

1965 Ginnette and her eight outfits.
#28130, pink flannelette sleeper
#28131, morning dress in assorted colors
#28132, aqua checked creeper set
#28135, white dot batiste dress with blue trim
#28136, lacy red stroller set
#28137, yellow dress with collar
#28140, fluffy pink dress and bonnet
#28141, rose cord pram set

No Ginnette in 1966

* Vogue catalog term.

1967

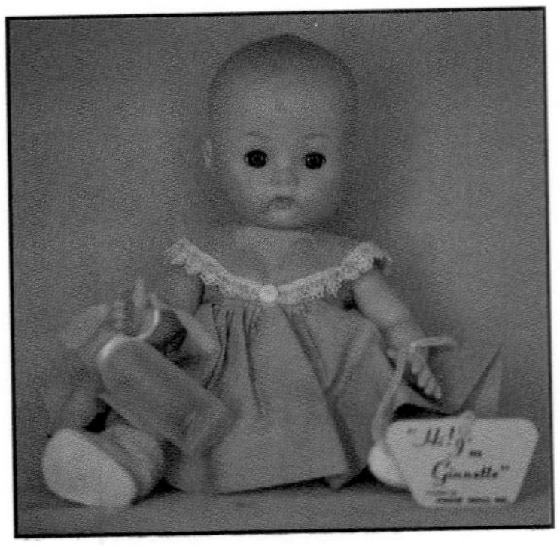

Ginnette (1967), with new smaller eyes and distinctive curl head mold with molded painted hair, blue dress. Marks: VOGUE DOLLS (on head); VOGUE DOLLS INC. (on back). Courtesy S. Ogilvie.

Ginnette (1967), with new smaller eyes and distinctive curl head mold with rooted hair, yellow romper. Marks: VOGUE DOLLS (on head); VOGUE DOLLS INC. (on back). Courtesy Veronica Phillips.

Ginnette (1967), with new smaller eyes and distinctive curl head mold with rooted hair, white fur jacket, pink velvet pants. Marks: VOGUE DOLLS (on head); VOGUE DOLLS INC. (on back). Courtesy Veronica Phillips.

1968

Ginnette (1968), with new remodeled elongated head mold. She came in four outfits: a pink bathrobe, yellow dress with flower on waistband, pink and white checked short top and panties, and a pink fleece hooded coat with pink ruffles on hem and hood. Courtesy Wenham Museum, Wenham, Mass.

Ginnette (1968), new remodeled elongated head mold with molded painted hair, yellow playsuit. Marks: VOGUE DOLLS INC/©1967 (on head); VOGUE DOLLS INC. (on back). Courtesy S. Ogilvie.

Ginnette (1968), new remodeled elongated head mold. with rooted auburn hair, pale pink lips, wearing yellow pants outfit. Courtesy S. Ogilvie.

1969

Remodeled Ginnette (1969), four outfits: #2850, pink jersey sleeper with pom-pons; #2851, a blue dress; #2852, pink and white checked footed pants outfit and bonnet; and #2853, yellow pram outfit with hooded white fleece jacket. All the dolls came with bottles. Vogue catalog. Courtesy Marge Meisinger.

1985 – 1986 Meritus Ginnette

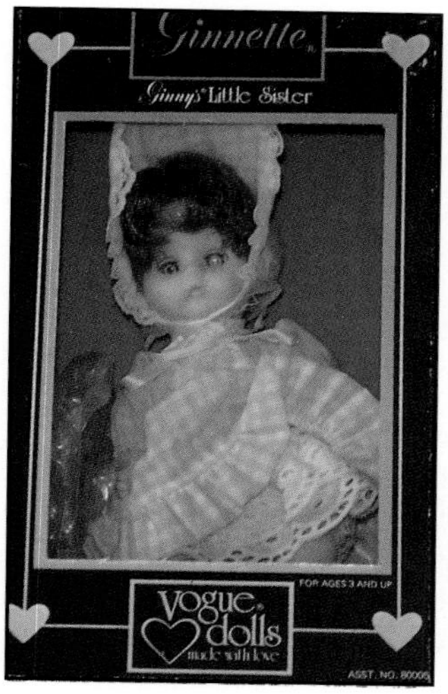

Ginnette (1985) #80005, Meritus Ginnette with sleep eyes and combable hair, in yellow and white checked dress and bonnet. Courtesy S. Ogilvie.

Ginnette (1985 – 86) #80005, Meritus Ginnette with sleep eyes and combable auburn hair, in white ruffled party dress with appliqué and bonnet. Courtesy S. Ogilvie.

Ginnette (1985 – 86) #80005, Meritus Ginnette with sleep eyes and combable blonde hair, in white dress with pink ribbons on front and bonnet. Courtesy S. Ogilvie.

Ginnette (1985) #80005, Meritus Ginnette with sleep eyes and combable blonde hair, in christening dress and bonnet. Courtesy S. Ogilvie.

Ginnette (1986) four vinyl Meritus Ginnettes with sleep eyes and combable hair. #80008, lavender print dress; #80009, pink dress; #80010, blue dress and bib with heart motif; #8011, red plaid dress with a black ribbon in front. Vogue catalog. Courtesy Marge Meisinger.

Porcelain Ginnette

Ginnette (1986), porcelain Ginnette with molded painted yellow hair. Vogue catalog. Courtesy Marge Meisinger.

Ginnette (1986), porcelain Ginnette in christening gown. Shown with box. Courtesy S. Ogilvie.

Jimmy

1958

Description:	8" all vinyl jointed doll. Open mouth. Painted eyes, some have no eyelashes.	
Marks:	Head:	None
	Back:	VOGUE DOLLS/INC.
Outfit labels:	White twill with blue script: Vogue Dolls, Inc.	
Outfit closures:	"Dot starlet" snaps	
Boxes:	Doll in medium blue, white, and pink using Ginny paper doll logo, clothing in navy blue box with red oval around Vogue logo.	

In 1958 Vogue introduced Jimmy as Ginny's baby brother. Jimmy was 8" all vinyl with painted eyes and moving arms and legs. He was a painted eye Ginnette dressed in boy's clothes; some Jimmys had no painted eyelashes.

Several mint in box Jimmys have been found with no eyelashes and he is pictured in Vogue's publicity material to the stores with no eyelashes. However, he appears in the 1958 brochure with eyelashes and Mrs. Carlson remarks that it was "such a hectic time for Vogue that they used whatever dolls they had." Jimmy is marked the same as Ginnette since he is the same doll.

Jimmy had six outfits. Some of his outfits matched Ginnette's clothes. Jimmy is portrayed as Ginnette's twin brother in the 1958 book, *Ginny's First Secret*. Jimmy did not come with a bottle and did not coo or wet. In the Vogue dealer's catalog he is offered at a lower price point ($2.00) so as to not compete with Ginnette who sold for $3.00. Jimmy was only manufactured for one year since he was not as successful as Ginnette.

Prices

Mint, painted eye, out of box	$60.00
Jimmy MIB	$125.00 – 150.00
Outfits MIB	$45.00 – 100.00
MIB clown	$60.00 – 150.00
MIB cowboy	$60.00 – 150.00

JIMMY

#1 Ginny's baby brother
JIMMY
An 8", all-vinyl baby boy. He has moving arms and legs and painted eyes. We are introducing him with outfits both for play and dress. Here is your opportunity to get extra sales without competing with the $3.00 Ginnette for this basic doll will retail at $2.00.

Jimmy (1958), Vogue dealer's catalog. Notice there aren't any eyelashes. Jimmy marked same as painted eye Ginnette. Courtesy Marge Meisinger.

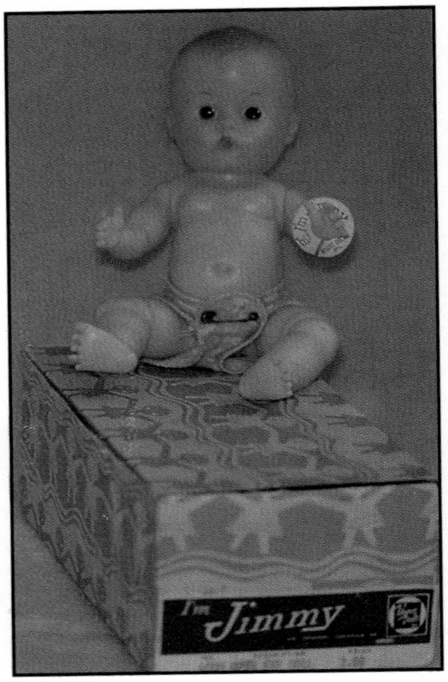

Jimmy (1958), #4000, undressed doll as he came with box. Notice box says "open eye doll." Courtesy S. Ogilvie.

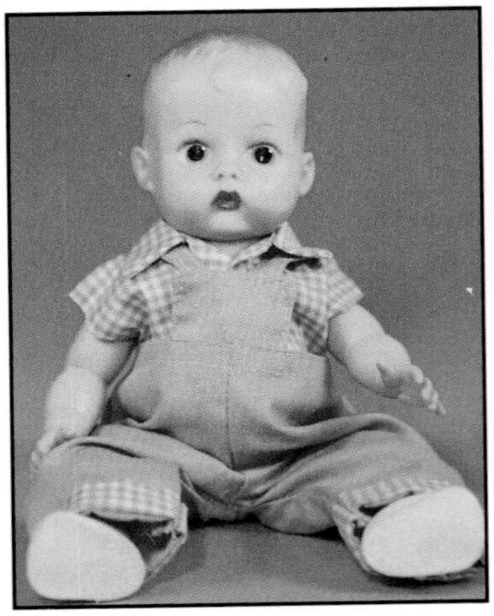

Jimmy (1958), #4131, blue cotton broadcloth overalls and checked shirt of blue and white matches Ginnette #2331 except hers had ruffles.

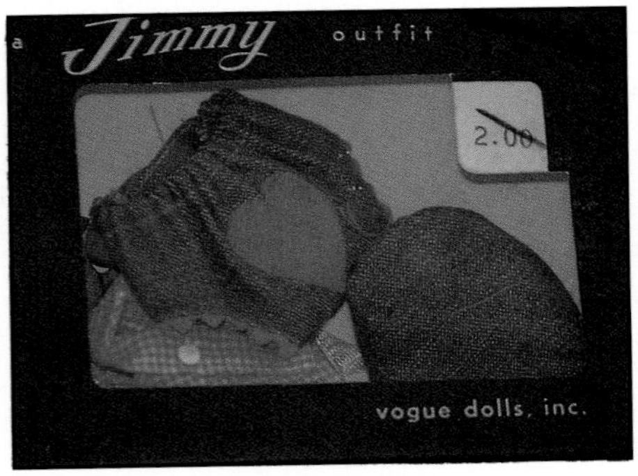

Jimmy (1958), #4130, denim shorts with red heart on rear, and red checked shirt, denim visor cap, mint in dark blue box. Courtesy S. Ogilvie.

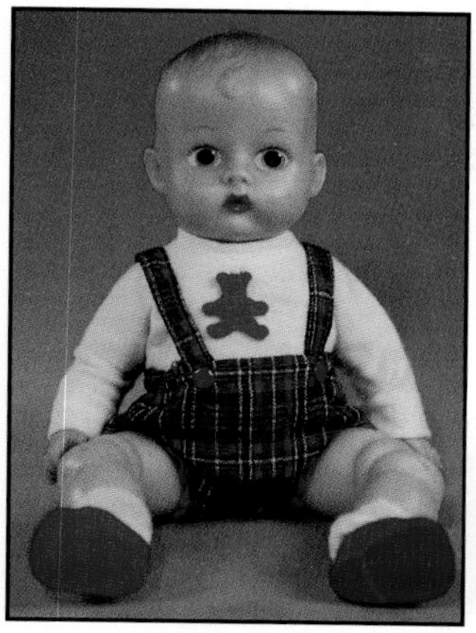

Jimmy (1958), #4132, red and blue plaid suspender shorts, white long sleeved jersey with bear motif.

Jimmy (1958), #4150, Ivy League, plaid shorts and white jersey shirt with red vest. Courtesy S. Ogilvie.

Jimmy (1958), #4151, clown outfit of taffeta with tulle ruff and matching peaked pompon hat. Did not come with rattle shown. Courtesy Sue Johnson.

Jimmy (1958), #4152, blue denim overalls with fringe, original outfit came with red jersey shirt, black felt cowboy hat, and gun. Not a squeaker. Notice wrist tag "Hi, I'm Jimmy." Marks: VOGUE DOLLS/INC (on lower back). Courtesy Wenham Museum, Wenham, Mass.

Jill

1957 – 1960, 1962 – 1963, 1965

1957 – 1960

Description: 10½", all hard plastic, bent knee walker dolls, sleep eyes. Blonde, brunette or auburn ponytail or angel cut wig. Metal loops in ears for pearl or metal teardrop earrings.

Marks:
Head: None
1957: Back: JILL/VOGUE DOLLS/ MADE IN U.S.A./©1957
1958 – 60 Back: JILL/VOGUE DOLLS INC./ MADE IN U.S.A./©1957

Outfit Labels: 1957 – 60: White twill with blue script: Vogue Dolls, Inc.

Outfit Closures: 1957 – 60: "Dot starlet" snaps marked dot starlet underneath. Other snaps used had raised squared edges, and button snap.

Boxes: Aqua with white paper doll logo and Jill in black writing; later one Ginny Doll Family blue box with large white paper doll logo in front and smaller ones on top and bottom.

In 1957 Mrs. Graves introduced a teenage doll called Jill as Ginny's big sister. Jill was a 10½" hard plastic walker with bent knees. She was produced in blonde, brunette, or auburn color hair in either Saran angel cut or ponytail hairstyle. The angel cut Saran wig had gold barrettes on either side. Jill had blue sleep eyes, some had brown eyes. She wore earrings and had little metal loops protruding from her ears so the earrings could be changed. Jill was very well-made and is eagerly sought today by collectors.

The early Jills were marked on back: JILL/VOGUE DOLLS/MADE IN U.S.A./C 1957. They did not have the "INC." after Vogue Dolls which the later doll had. These early Jills did not have the nice high color and rosy cheeks of the later models. Over the years their plasticizer has leached out and they have become shiny. In fact, they have a slightly yellow skin tone.

Jill came in a mint green box. The basic doll in 1957 wore a black leotard with a hankie tied at her waist. Mrs. Graves made a conscious decision not to sell the basic doll in her underwear because she did not want her little darlings standing around in their underwear in the stores, a business associate remembers.

Jill had outfits to match Ginny and Ginnette as well as her special teenage ones such as Record Hop, a felt skirt with soda pop and records printed on it. Jill rode on the crest of the wave of popularity of 10½" teen-age dolls such as Ideal's Little Miss Revlon and Madame Alexander's Cissette also introduced in 1957. Jill represented in Vogue's words "the elegance and grace of sophistication, charm, and exquisite styles." All Jill outfits are tagged "Vogue Dolls, Inc." on a white tag with blue script writing.

Jill's clothing was designed by Virginia Graves Carlson (for whom Ginny was named) and Joan Cornette who joined Vogue in 1956 and stayed until 1960. These talented designers planned over 100 outfits for Ginny and her family in 1957.

The adorable outfits were very fashionable and many came with matching hats or other little accessories. Jill had outfits for every occasion ranging from casual blue jeans to fancy prom gowns and a Dynel evening stole. Unusual outfits included a hostess outfit of velveteen slim-Jim pants with cummerbund, and a rodeo outfit complete with gun in holster. The outfits were usually available two ways: on the doll or outfit only, although some outfits were only available as separates. Accessories that could be bought separately included real nylon stockings, panty girdle and bra (in black or white), jewelry, and hat boxes. These items are very well-made and are a delight in their fashion and attention to detail.

Jill and her clothing came in a light blue box. In 1959 the box changed slightly to a darker blue, slimmer box. Outfits from 1959 and 1960 are harder to find than the earlier 1957 and 1958 ones; perhaps Jill was not as successful during these latter two years. Collectors prize these later outfits.

1960 was the last year the hard plastic Jill was made. There was no Jill in 1961. A redesigned all vinyl Jill was made from 1962 – 63. An all vinyl Jill called "History Land" was produced in 1965.

Wigs

Jill came in two basic hairstyles, an angel cut and a ponytail style. The angel cut has been called a Sandra Dee version of a short flip with bangs. The angel cut came with goldtone brass barrettes on either side of Jill's head. The angel cut length varied from short and curly, almost like a bubble cut, to a long flip. The ponytails came in two versions: a short curly ponytail tied high in the back, and a longer straighter ponytail tied nearer the neck. Some bangs on the ponytail version are long and come down to Jill's eyebrows and some bangs are shorter.

The colors of the wigs were blonde, brunette, and redhead. There were variations in the colors. The most common blonde was a yellow-gold, the most common color for Jill. There is also a honey blonde version which has a more golden color. The brunette wigs came in a very dark brown and a lighter brown of which there are at least two shades. There are also two redhead shades, one a dark orange tone which is the most frequent, and a rarer light strawberry auburn color.

Shoes

Jill's first shoes in 1957 were elastic high heels with a rhinestone in the front center. In 1958 Vogue added three styles of plastic shoes to Jill's wardrobe. These are identified by the "L" and the "R" on the inside of each shoe. The ankle strap sandals came in red, white, pink, black, and blue. Her closed toe high heels have a strap across the instep with an open back. Her casual wedge shoes came with all her sporty outfits. The wedge shoes came in three colors: black, white, and red. The shoes were made by Commonwealth Plastics in Leominster, Massachusetts. Jill's gold braid shoes for 1957's #7504 outfit were bought from same manufacturer in New York as the Nancy Ann storybook teen doll's shoes.

Patterns

There were Vogue patterns produced by the pattern-making company available for Jill in 1957.

Furniture

Furniture for the Vogue dolls was manufactured by Strombecker, a maker of doll furniture for many years. Paralleling Ginny's furniture which was all pink, Jill and Jan had mint green furniture including a bed, a desk, a wardrobe closet, and a vanity complete with a mirror and bench. The bed, vanity, and the wardrobe closet can be identified because "Jill and Jan" is painted on them. The desk had a little sign saying "Jill and Jan" on it.

Conclusion

Hard plastic Jill is the most widely collected Vogue doll after Ginny. Jill has an enthusiastic following of doll collectors who love her beautifully designed outfits. As Ginny's prices have soared, collectors have turned to Jill whose prices still remain reasonable for a 1950s doll.

Prices

Jill (1957 – 58)	
mint in basic dresses	$125.00 – 150.00
mint in gowns	$150.00 – 225.00
Jill (1959 – 60)	
mint in basic outfits	$150.00 – 175.00
mint in gowns	$175.00 – 250.00
mint in box	$200.00+
MIB outfits	$45.00 – 65.00
Rare outfits rodeo, cook out, sports outfits, 1960 rarer outfits	$75.00+
Accessories	$25.00 – 75.00
1957, 1958 and 1959 rhodium plated Jill head locket and chain	$50.00
Furniture	$45.00 – 75.00

1957

Dressed doll were numbered #74+; outfits only were numbered #75+.

Jill hard plastic bending knees walker. Her marks are VOGUE (on head); JILL/VOGUE DOLLS/ MADE IN U.S.A./ ©1957 (on back). Shown with original box. Jill came in a ponytail or a short bob hairdo in blonde, auburn, and brunette. Wore leotard with gaily colored hankies. Cost $3.00.

(1957) #7501, (#7401 dressed doll), pink polka dot sundress with white rickrack, #7502, (#7402 dressed doll), orange and white striped dress with black banding, and #7503 (#7403 dressed doll), white skirt with black velvet top short gown. First numbers shown are for outfit only. Pink polka dot dress had a matching Ginny outfit #7126. These photos were used to familiarize Vogue's sales force with the outfits in the Jill line. Courtesy Mr. and Mrs. Edwin Nelson.

(1957) #7401, pink polka dot sundress with white rickrack. Has matching Ginny and Ginnette outfit. Courtesy Mary Miskowiec.

(1957) #7402, orange and white striped dress.

(1957) #7403, formal black velvet top and white skirt with flower. Snaps are flat painted same color as material.

(1957) #7404, pink toreador pants, missing sash. Notice gold braid shoes.

(1957) #7405, navy polished cotton dress.

(1957) #7406, black felt record hop skirt with red jersey. Courtesy Mary Miskowiec.

(1957) #7407, gray pleated skirt and plaid top with red felt hat, missing red pocketbook. Has a matching Ginny outfit #7143. Courtesy Sue Johnson.

(1957) #7408, brown skirt, matching cape, and brown shiny blouse, hat. Showing fabric variation. Courtesy Vicki Broadhurst.

(1957) #7507 (#7407 dressed doll), #7508 (#7408 dressed doll), #7509 (#7409 dressed doll). These photos were used to familiarize Vogue's sales force with the outfits in the Jill line. Courtesy Mr. and Mrs. Edwin Nelson.

(1957) #7410, black toreador pants, white ruffled blouse. Courtesy Laura and Ronald Colpus.

(1957) #7510 (#7411 dressed doll), #7511 (#7411 dressed doll), and #7512 (#7412 dressed doll) notice ribbon bow hat on #7411, which is the more common hat found with this outfit. Vogue publicity shots. Courtesy Mr. and Mrs. Edwin Nelson.

(1957) #7412, short white organdy formal with blue ribbon sash and white hat. Has a matching Ginny #7042 and Ginnette #7627 outfit. Courtesy Ruth and Fred Leif.

(1957) #7513 (#7413 dressed doll), and #7514 (#7414 dressed doll).Has a matching Ginny outfit #7160. Vogue publicity shot. Courtesy Mr. and Mrs. Edwin Nelson.

(1957) #7415, Jill Bride.

(1957) #7515 (#7415 dressed doll). Jill Bride has a matching Ginny outfit #7064. Vogue publicity shots. Courtesy Mr. and Mrs. Edwin Nelson.

(1957) #7416, yellow taffeta with straw hat. Courtesy Ruth and Fred Leif.

(1957) #7516 (#7416 dressed doll), and #7517 (#7417 dressed doll). Vogue publicity shots. Courtesy Mr. and Mrs. Edwin Nelson

(1957) #7553, pink leather coat with hat. Only available as separate outfit, not on dressed doll. Courtesy Margie Hefler.

(1957) #7551, evening coat with hood with flower. Courtesy Mary Miskowiec.

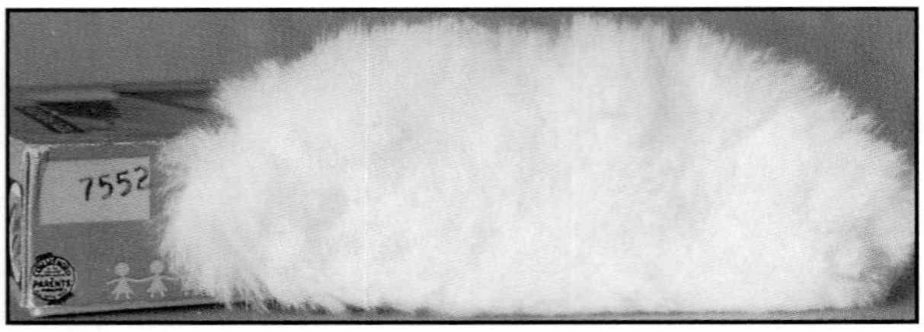

1957 – 1958, #7552, white stole. Courtesy Mary Miskowiec.

(1957) #7550, white vinyl raincoat and bag. Similar to Nancy Ann teen doll caot. Notice large snaps on raincoat. Has Vogue tag inside. Available as separate outfit only.

(1957) #7553, leather coat with hat in three colors: pink, red, and blue. Courtesy Vicki Broadhurst.

(1957) #7554, green velvet coat, collar and headband. Only available as separate outfit, not on dressed doll. Courtesy Laura and Ronald Colpus.

(1957) #7555, mink-like stole. Vogue brochure.

(1957) #7561, leotard. Courtesy Veronica Phillips.

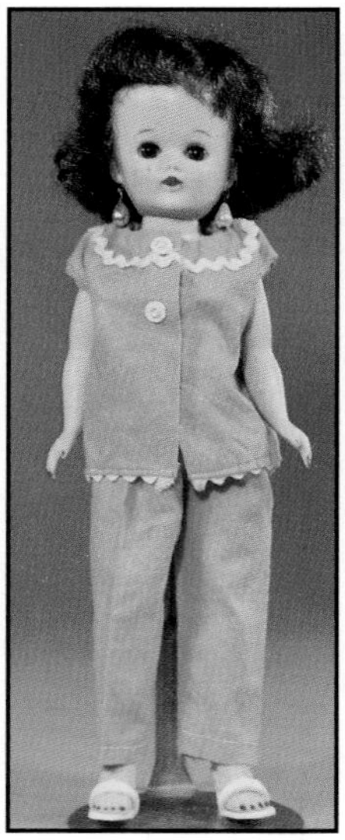

(1957) #7562, blue pajamas. Only available as separate outfit, not on dressed doll.

(1957) #7563, housecoat, blue print on white cotton. Only available as separate outfit, not on dressed doll.

Not Shown
1957 #7560 Pixie Panties.

(1957) #7564, honey undies. Courtesy Ruth and Fred Leif.

(1957) #7565, nightie and peignoir set, available only as separate outfit, not on dressed doll. Courtesy Ruth and Fred Leif.

(1957) #7571, shoes and stockings in cylinder package.

(1957) #7576, headbands and covers. Courtesy Ruth and Fred Leif.

(1957) #7577, 1958; and 1959, #3561, Jill hat box.

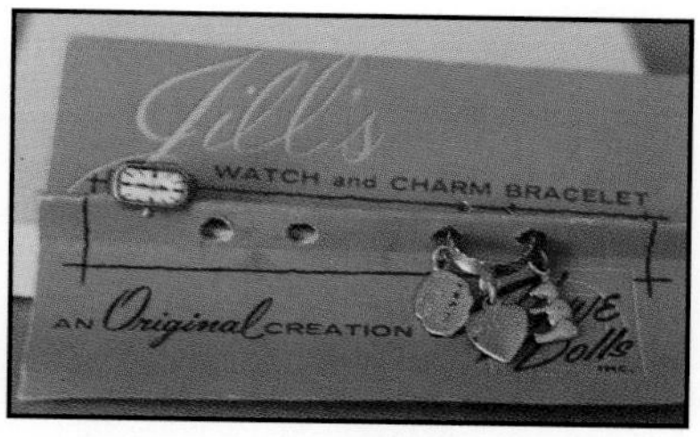

(1957) #7581; (1958) #3663; 1960, #3505, Jill charm bracelet and gold wristwatch. $75.00. Courtesy Mary Miskowiec.

(1957) #7580, pearl choker, bracelet, and earring set. $75.00. Courtesy Ruth and Fred Leif.

(1957) #7582; (1958 – 1959) #3661, rhodium plated Jill head locket and chain. Current value, $750.00. Courtesy Ruth and Fred Leif.

(1957) #7586; (1958 – 1959) #3651; (1960) #3602, pink pearl studded tiara and matching earrings. Also available in white. Courtesy Sue Johnson.

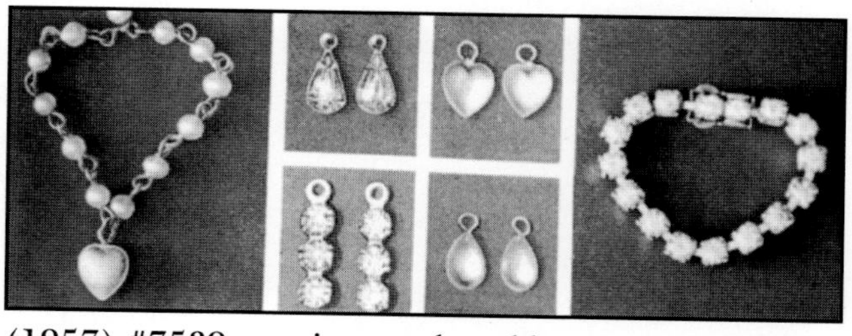

(1957) #7589, earrings and necklaces, showing pearl necklace also available. Vogue brochure.

1958

Dressed dolls were numbered #31+; outfits only were numbered #33+.

(1958) #3300, Jill in leotard, pink, black or red. Matches Ginny (1958) #1300. Courtesy Nadine Steele.

followed last year by Ginny's
big sister JILL
The marvelous 10½" action doll! In 1958, she will offer 46 gorgeous teen-age outfits with plenty of matching jewelry and accessories all to assure you traffic every day of the year.
and NOW...

Jill in 1958 Vogue dealer catalog. Courtesy Marge Meisinger.

(1958) #3302, lace-edged parchment nylon petticoat and cotton bra. Courtesy Ruth and Fred Leif.

(1958) #3304, red and white polka dot pajamas and 1958, #3305, robe in red and white kerchief design. Courtesy Ruth and Fred Leif.

(1958) #3311, pink nylon long nightgown. Courtesy Ruth and Fred Leif.

(1958) #3312, red Capri pants and harlequin overblouse. Has a matching Ginny outfit #1321. Courtesy Laura and Ronald Colpus.

(1958) #3313, pink cotton print dress with black ribbon straps. Courtesy Sue Johnson.

(1958) #3314, ballerina outfit, black nylon tulle over bodice of pink taffeta, flowers at waist. Courtesy Laura and Ronald Colpus.

(1958) #3315, blue jacquard taffeta skirt and blue velveteen bodice. Mint in box. Vogue brochure says it was supposed to be outfit only, not on a dressed doll. However, here it is with different shoes and with a necklace not shown in brochure. Courtesy Tina Ritari.

(1958) #3316, beige felt sheath skirt with brown cotton blouse. Courtesy Ruth and Fred Leif.

(1958) #3317, square dance outfit, goldtone print red skirt with eyelet embroidered blouse. Showing variation in red print. Courtesy Nadine Steele.

(1958) #3130, white cotton sundress with lace on square neckline. Has matching Ginny outfit #1310. Courtesy Ruth and Fred Leif.

(1958) #3131, pink fleece slim skirt with red jersey wrap-around blouse. Courtesy Ruth and Fred Leif.

(1958) #3132, aqua cotton dress with flower print skirt. Has matching Ginny outfit #1312. Courtesy Ruth and Fred Leif.

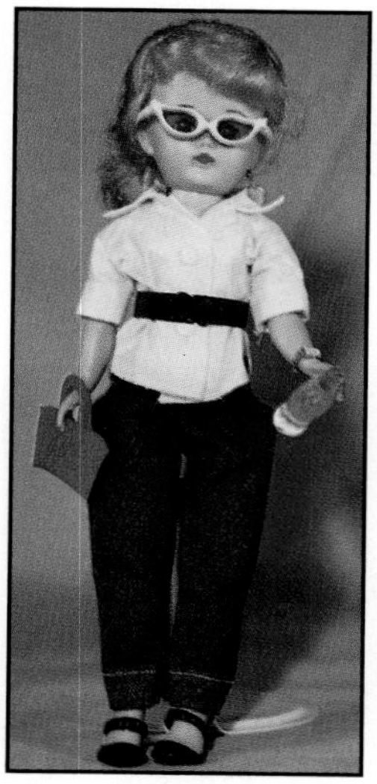

(1958) #3133, blue denim jeans, white shirt, belt, glasses and Coke™. Has matching Ginny #1317 outfit. Courtesy Laura and Ronald Colpus.

(1958) #3134, primrose yellow princess dress of yellow cotton. Has matching Ginny outfit #1314.

(1958) #3135, Ivy League striped shorts, red jersey shirt, knee socks. Has matching Ginny outfit #1318. Courtesy Ruth and Fred Leif.

(1958) 3136, red and white polka dot dress with black bow at neckline. Has matching Ginny outfit #1313. Courtesy Ruth and Fred Leif.

(1958) #3137, beige twill jodhpurs with print blouse, collar pin, and brown boots (boots shown not original). Has a matching Ginny outfit #1320. Courtesy Ruth and Fred Leif.

(1958) #3138, red and white striped dress with white belt and white at hem. Shown on brunette Jan. Has matching Ginny outfit #1315.

(1958) #3139, red, black, and white plaid pants and white sweater with brass buttons. Has a matching Ginny outfit #1339. Courtesy Ruth and Fred Leif.

(1958) #3140, pink print gown with butterfly hairclip. Courtesy Laura and Ronald Colpus.

(1958) #3345, print hooded raincoat under clear vinyl with handbag. Courtesy Ruth and Fred Leif.

(1958) #3160, cotton shirtmaker dress with white blouse, black pleated skirt, tie with gold thread, and black glasses.

(1958) #3161, pink cotton dress with pink jersey shrug. Has matching Ginny outfit, #1338. Courtesy Laura and Ronald Colpus.

(1958) #3162, white swimsuit with matching cape and red coolie hat, came with a terry towel. Courtesy Ruth and Fred Leif.

(1958) #3163, record hop, yellow felt skirt with black jersey. Notice charm bracelet.

(1958) #3164, coral jersey skating dress with feathered hat and skates. Has matching Ginny #1355 Skater outfit and a coordinating Jeff #6462 outfit. Courtesy Chree Kysar.

(1958) #3165, white lace over toast taffeta sleeveless short party dress. Courtesy Laura and Ronald Colpus.

(1958) #3166, red sailor dress with white felt hat. Shown on Jan. Has matching Ginny outfit #1330. Courtesy Laura and Ronald Colpus.

(1958) #3167, ski outfit, black felt pants, aqua jacket, black earmuffs, skis and poles. Has matching Ginny #1354 and Ginnette #2351 outfits. Courtesy Ruth and Fred Leif.

(1958) #3168, rose flowered print dress and pleated ribbon hat. Missing pink clutch purse. Courtesy Laura and Ronald Colpus.

(1958) #3169, plaid pleated skirt with red jersey top and white felt blazer with emblem. Courtesy Sue Johnson.

(1958) #3170, blue nylon strapless dress with lined jacket of silver lamé. Courtesy Laura and Ronald Colpus.

(1958) #3375, beige felt shawl collared coat with matching cloche. Came as outfit only. Courtesy Laura and Ronald Colpus.

(1958) #3180, long strapless apricot flowered print gown with green velvet trim with flower wreath. Also showing variation in the print. Courtesy Vicki Broadhurst.

(1958) #3181, blue fleece, two-piece suit with rhinestone button jacket, straw hat. Also came with black pocketbook and shoes. Courtesy Chree Kysar.

(1958) #3182, black velveteen skirt, pink lace top and straw hat. MIB doll $300.00. Courtesy Laura and Ronald Colpus.

(1958) #3385, red suedine coat, round fur collar, and flower trimmed beret of real rabbit fur. MIB doll, $250.00. Courtesy Barbara Rosplock-Van Orman

(1958) #3190, gown of eggshell brocade, cummerbund, petticoat, and aqua satin hat. Ranch mink muff. MIB doll $300.00. Courtesy Chree Kysar.

(1958) #3191, pink velveteen gown with fur cape and jeweled comb. Courtesy Laura and Ronald Colpus.

(1958) #3192, bridal gown, flowers not original. Has matching Ginny outfit #1364. Courtesy Laura and Ronald Colpus.

(1958) #3395, beige Dynel coat lined in taffeta with matching headband. Courtesy Laura and Ronald Colpus.

(1958) #3346, rabbit fur stole in white. Courtesy Ruth and Fred Leif.

(1958) #3303, cotton jersey panties. Courtesy Ruth and Fred Leif.

(1958) #3347; (1959) #3990; (1960) #3346; beige Dynel stole. Courtesy Chree Kysar.

(1958 – 1960) #3500 nylons. Came in assorted colors including pink and blue. Courtesy Sue Johnson.

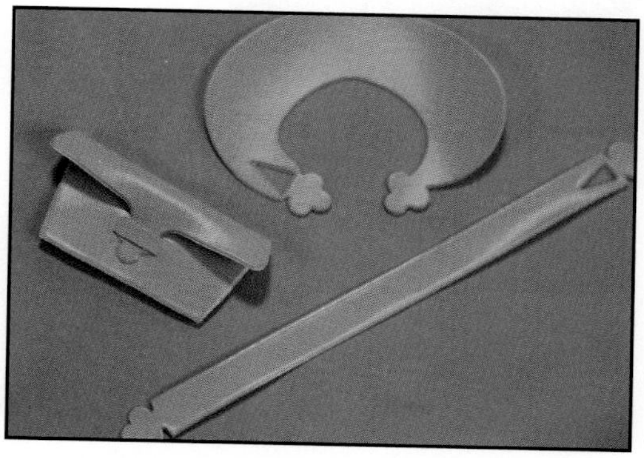

(1958) #3502, vinyl belt, bag and collar in assorted colors including green and pink.

(1958 – 1960) #3501, rhinestone shoes. Notice clear with gold flecks and black heel (in middle and on left) and (right) gold braid shoe (also came in silver). Shoes were sold in both clear tubular packaging and in hang tag packaging.

(1958 – 1960) #3503, eyeglasses in case. Courtesy Sue Johnson.

(1958 – 1960) #3510, felt tote bag with poodle on it. Also came in turquoise and pink. Courtesy Ruth and Fred Leif.

(1958 – 1959) #3557; (1960) #3567, wigs came in two styles, ponytail or angel cut in three colors, blonde, brunette, auburn. Courtesy Chree Kysar.

(1958 – 1959) #3560, straw handbags and metal headband with Jill's name on it. $45.00. Courtesy Ruth and Fred Leif.

(1958 – 1960) #3600, pearl choker and earring set. Courtesy Veronica Phillips.

(1958 – 1960) #3601, golden choker necklace and matching earrings. Courtesy Ruth and Fred Leif.

(1958 – 1959) #3602, pearl clustered bobby pin. Courtesy Laura and Ronald Colpus.

(1958 – 1960) #3603, butterfly bobby pins. Courtesy Sue Johnson.

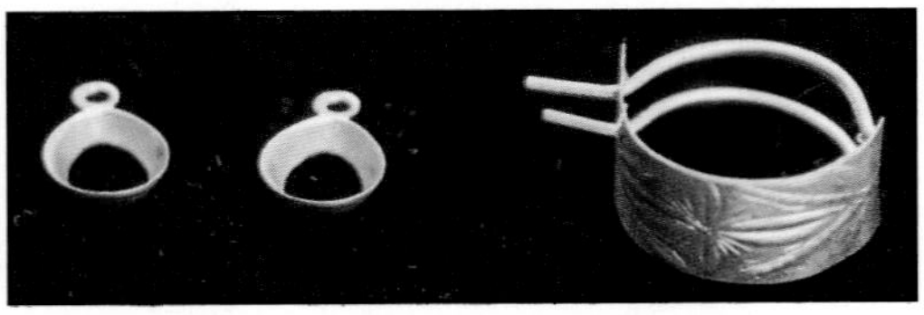

(1958 – 1960) #3604, ponytail clip with matching golden earrings. Courtesy Ruth and Fred Leif.

(1958 – 1960) #3611, rhinestone necklace and earring set. Courtesy Ruth and Fred Leif.

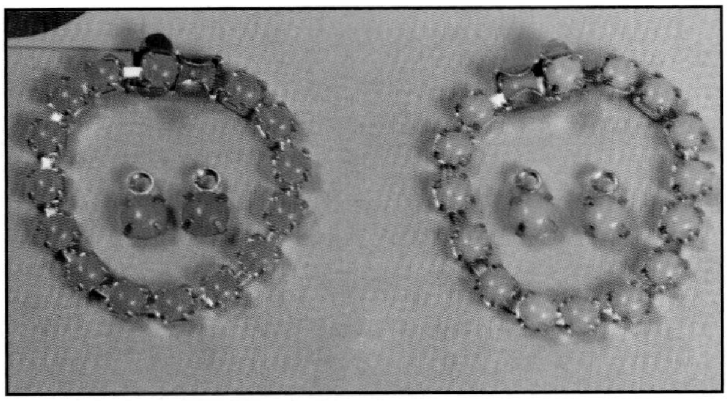

(1958) #3610, choker and earring set in rainbow colors. Courtesy Ruth and Fred Leif.

(1958 – 1960) #3650, iridescent choker and ponytail clip. Missing matching earrings. Courtesy Mary Miskowiec.

(1958) #3652, pearl hair comb and earrings. Courtesy Sue Johnson.

(1958 – 1959) #3660, pearl evening bag with handle. Courtesy Ruth and Fred Leif.

(1958 – 1959) #3563; (1960,)#3512, knit kit with instructions for three cardigan sweaters and caps for the Vogue doll family (Ginny, Jill and Ginnette). Courtesy Ruth and Fred Leif.

(1958 – 1960) #3662, ponytail clips, three to a set. Courtesy Laura and Ronald Colpus.

(1958 – 1959) #3690; (1960) #1512, child size bracelet with Ginny, Ginnette and Jill charms. Top reads, "For Ginny's mother." Courtesy Chree Kysar.

(1958 – 1960) #3750, teen togs package, Jill in leotard plus three outfits, lingerie, and accessories. Vogue dealer catalog courtesy Marge Meisinger.

(1958 – 1959) #3850, Jill's mint wooden bed with Jill's and Jan's names.

(1958 – 1959) #3851, Dream Cozy Bed Set has pillow, pillow case, two contour sheets, and bedspread. Courtesy Chree Kysar.

(1958 – 1959) #3861, mint green desk and chair set, has two drawers and a "Jill" name plate. Missing name plate. Flowers and paper not original.

(1958 – 1959) #3881, mint green wardrobe with sliding door, clothes rack, and two brass handle drawers.

1959

A full color 1959 Vogue catalog was sent to dealers and is reproduced here to show variations in outfits or when actual outfit not available. Catalog photos show outfit numbers. Dressed dolls were numbered #32+, outfits #34+.

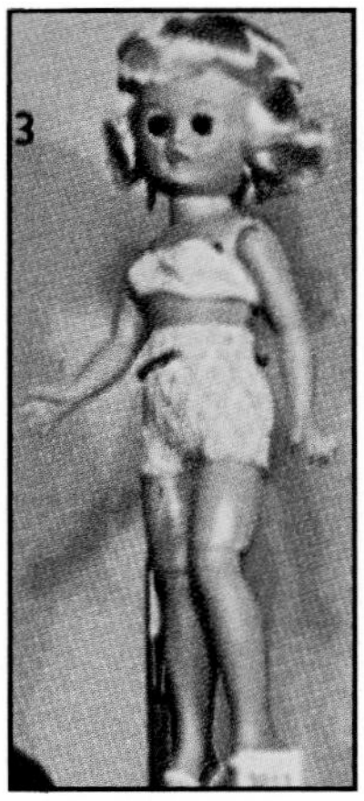

(1959) #3013, undressed angel cut dolls. Vogue dealer catalog. Courtesy Marge Meisinger.

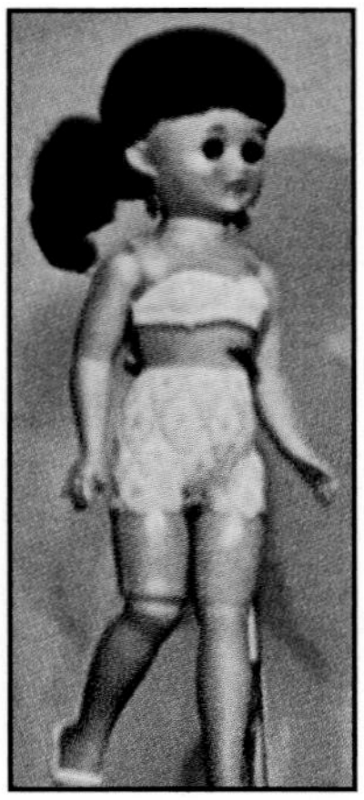

(1959) #3011, undressed ponytail doll. Vogue dealer catalog. Courtesy Marge Meisinger.

(1959) #3211, shirtwaist dress with black and white cotton skirt and white taffeta blouse with roll-up sleeves, belt. Courtesy Chree Kysar.

(1959) basic Jill (right), dressed in white panty girdle and bra (also came in black), cost $3.00. (Left) #3560, panty girdle and bra with flower, came in black or white, also came with a slip. Courtesy Mary Miskowiec.

(1959) #3212, pink strapless short gown with harem-hemmed skirt. Pink pearly choker. MIB doll, $300.00. Courtesy Ruth and Fred Leif.

(1959) #3213, black sparkly tutu with pink tulle skirt, pearl choker, silver crown, and mask. Outfit was advertised in brochure with white tulle skirt. MIB doll, $300.00. Courtesy Ruth and Fred Leif.

(1959) #3414 (#3214 dressed doll), white piqué swimsuit with plaid skirt, sunglasses and towel. Courtesy Ruth and Fred Leif.

(1959) #3215, denim jeans, yellow jersey and belt, glasses and gold hoop earrings. Matches Ginny outfit #1412 and Jeff #6431. Courtesy Ruth and Fred Leif.

(1959) #3216, strapless polished cotton pink summer dress with black beaded cluny lace, pearl choker. Courtesy Ruth and Fred Leif.

(1959) #3217, blue/green print fringed pants and cropped top, straw sailor hat. Courtesy Laura and Ronald Colpus.

(1959) #3218, orange cotton halter top dress with cluster pleated print skirt, belt. Courtesy Mary Miskowiec.

(1959) #3219, plaid Bermuda shorts with white blouse and belt, gold hoop earrings. Showing variation in plaid short's fabric. Courtesy Ruth and Fred Leif.

(1959) #3230, sheer red dotted Swiss sundress. Notice Jill necklace #3661 which did not come with outfit. Courtesy Laura and Ronald Colpus.

(1959) #3431 (#3231 dressed doll), black and white checked slacks with belt, aqua cotton top, gray wool felt blazer, gold hoop earrings. Vogue dealer catalog. Courtesy Marge Meisinger

(1959) #3432 (#3222 dressed doll), halter top two-piece cotton sailor dress in red, white, and blue with anchor motif. Jersey one-piece sleeveless top, polished cotton tie string skirt. Has a matching Ginny outfit. Vogue dealer catalog. Courtesy Marge Meisinger

(1959) #3233, pink party dress with cropped top of white embroidered cotton. Has matching Ginny and Ginnette outfits. Courtesy Ruth and Fred Leif.

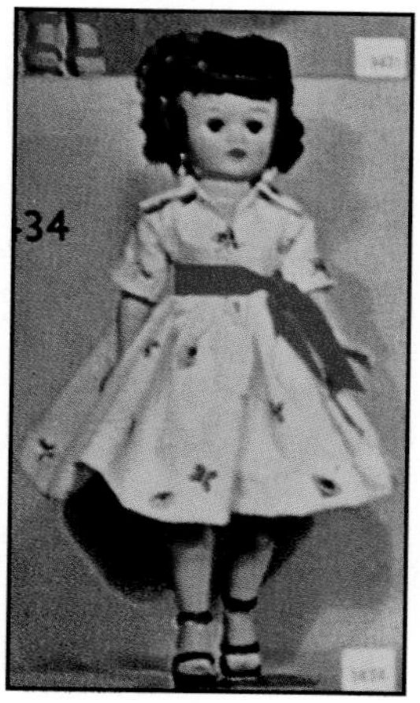

(1959) #3434 (#3234 dressed doll), yellow watercolor print cotton shirtwaist dress with orange sash. Vogue dealer catalog. Courtesy Marge Meisinger

(1959) #3235, Theater Time, aqua flowered taffeta short gown with strapless bodice and harem-hem, aqua velvety jacket. Notice embossed flowers on dress. Missing pearly choker. MIB doll, $300.00. Courtesy Chree Kysar.

(1959) #3236, fireside fashion, pants and strapless black velvet top, rabbit fur shrug and choker, earrings. Courtesy Ruth and Fred Leif.

(1959) #3237, "Wonderful for school" plaid cotton skirt, belt and white top plus cuddly soft red cardigan with gold pin. Courtesy Mary Miskowiec.

(1959) #3238, blue cotton dress banded with polka dots and white lace. Courtesy Vicki Broadhurst.

(1959) #3445, lemon yellow felt coat with flare brim cloche and clutch purse. Courtesy Sue Johnson.

(1959) #3446, blue raincoat with hood. Vogue dealer catalog. Courtesy Marge Meisinger

(1959) #3260, black silk organza short gown with pink tulle petticoat. Pink hat and pink choker. Hat is hard to find. MIB doll, $300.00. Courtesy Heather Lennon.

(1959) #3261, white felt ice skating skirt and jacket with red jersey leotard, fur hat, and white skates. Has matching Ginny outfit. MIB doll, $300.00. Courtesy Ruth and Fred Leif.

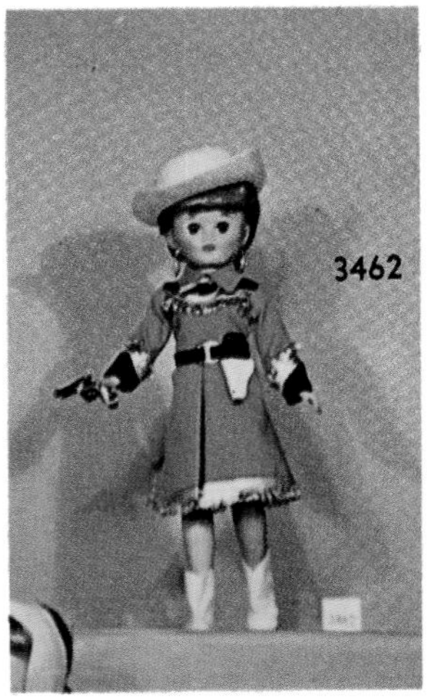

(1959) #3462 (#3262 dressed doll), blue twill rodeo outfit trimmed with silver and black, gun and holster set, white hat and boots. Has matching Ginny and Jeff outfits. MIB doll, $275.00. Vogue dealer catalog. Courtesy Marge Meisinger.

(1959) #3263, garden party dress of sheer yellow organdy over flowered taffeta, aqua sash, choker, and straw hat. MIB doll, $300.00. Courtesy Ruth and Fred Leif.

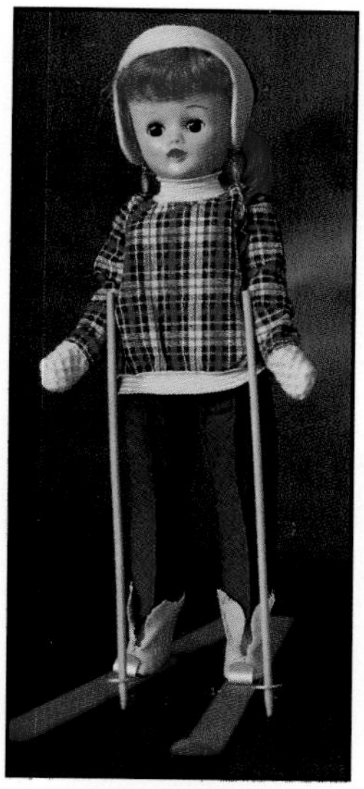

(1959) #3280, long bouffant, nylon tulle gown over pink taffeta, unsure if pink straw hat shown is original, shown in brochure with pink head wreath. Also came with pearl choker. MIB doll, $325.00. Courtesy Laura and Ronald Colpus.

(1959) #3264, green felt ski pants and plaid jacket, white earmuff cap, boots, mittens, skis and poles. Has matching Ginny and Jeff outfits. MIB doll, $275.00. Courtesy Mary Miskowiec.

(1959) #3281, bride gown in white lace over satin. Short veil may not be correct for that year, missing bouquet. Shown on Jan. MIB Jill doll, $275.00. Courtesy Laura and Ronald Colpus.

(1959) #3485, beige Dynel coat lined with taffeta, matching headband also showing. Courtesy Ruth and Fred Leif.

(1959) #3511, metal headband and two pearly covers, pocketbook in assorted colors. Vogue dealer catalog. Courtesy Marge Meisinger.

(1959) #3860, green Jill vanity with matching bench and lift-up mirror, came with plastic comb and name plate.

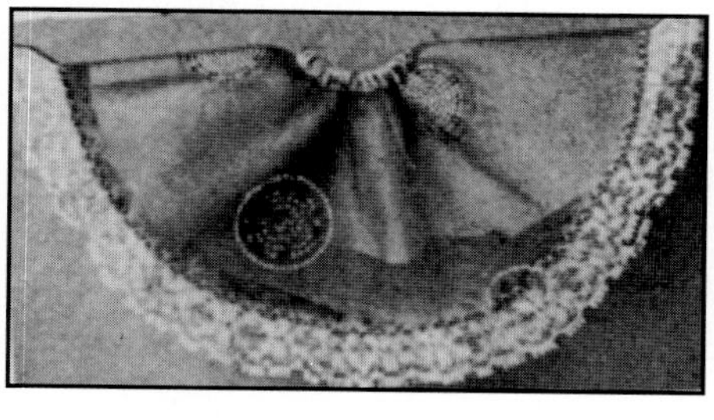

(1959) #3910, separate ruffled petticoats in assorted fabrics and colors. Vogue dealer catalog. Courtesy Marge Meisinger.

(1959) #3911; (1960) #3514; nylon tricot scanty panties. Courtesy Ruth and Fred Leif.

Not Shown

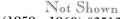

- (1959 – 1960) #3513, ruffled petticoat assorted fabrics and colors.

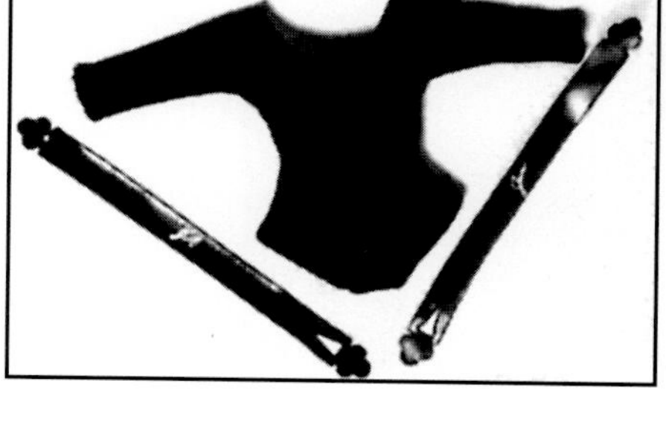

(1959) #3950, jersey leotard with two belts assorted colors. Vogue dealer catalog. Courtesy Marge Meisinger.

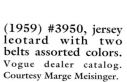

1959, #3960; 1960, #3560, panty girdle and bra, black or white, shoes and stockings (not shown). Courtesy Sue Johnson.

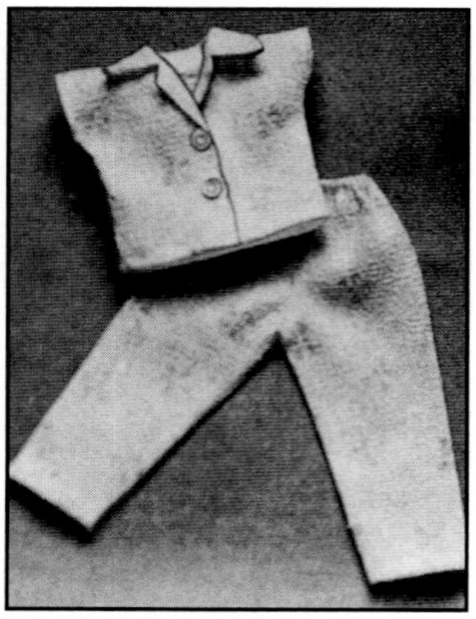

(1959) #3961, two-piece cotton p.j.s. Vogue dealer catalog. Courtesy Marge Meisinger.

(1959) #3962, print dorm robe. Vogue dealer catalog. Courtesy Marge Meisinger.

1960

Dressed dolls are numbered #31+; outfits only are #33+.

(1960) #3300, two-piece cotton p.j.s in assorted fabric.

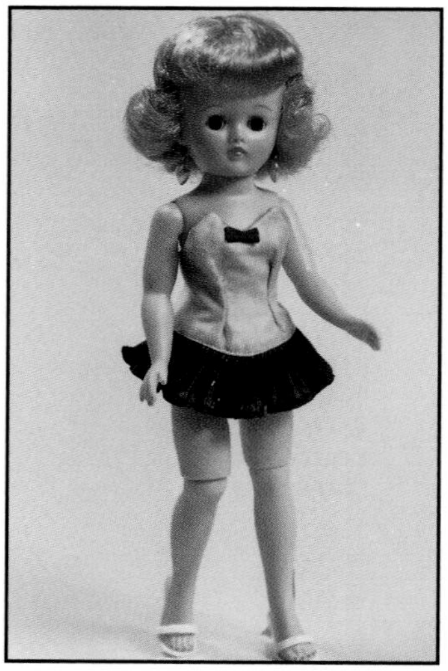

(1960) #3301, swimsuit with solid color bodice and plaid pleated skirt. Courtesy Ruth and Fred Leif.

(1960) #3302, cotton dress with print skirt with lace trimmed white yoke, and plastic belt. Dress came in assorted fabrics. Did not come with black pocketbook shown. Courtesy Sue Johnson.

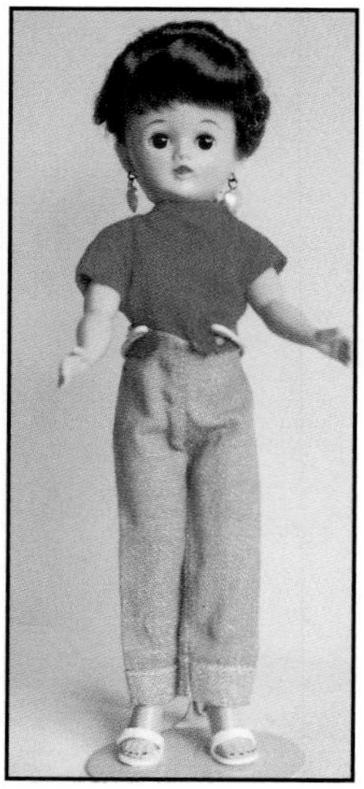

(1960) #3303, faded blue jeans and bright colored jersey, belt (shown unfastened). MIB doll, $250.00. Courtesy Chree Kysar.

(1960) #3110, aqua dress, white cropped top edged with lace, with aqua polished cotton skirt. Shown on Jan. Has matching Ginny outfit #1314. Courtesy Laura and Ronald Colpus.

(1960) #3111, Hostess with the Mostess, black velveteen slim Jim pants with striped cummerbund, white satin shirt. MIB doll, $250.00. Courtesy Chree Kysar.

(1960) #3112, off-the-shoulder summer short gown of pink checked edged with embroidered banding. Courtesy Ruth and Fred Leif.

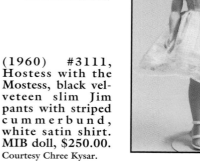

(1960) #3113, Shopping in Black and White, cotton checked with separate plastic colorful collar, matching belt and purse. Courtesy Vicki Broadhurst.

(1960) #3114, Party Time, dress with red jersey top and white lace harem skirt with velvet cummerbund. Courtesy Ruth and Fred Leif.

(1960) #3325, clear vinyl raincoat lined with print, attached hood and matching tote bag. Vogue brochure.

(1960) #3130, Could Have Danced All Night, in red cotton formal with lace banding, lace stole and velvet ribbon ties. MIB doll, $300.00. Courtesy Mary Miskowiec.

(1960) #3131, Jill Goes Visiting, plaid skirt and soft green bodice with double-breasted brown felt jacket. Courtesy Ruth and Fred Leif.

(1960) #3132, yellow sleeveless dress with white organdy band, trimmed with yellow flowers and yellow kerchief. Courtesy Mary Miskowiec.

(1960) #3133, nautical slacks outfit, blue pants, white middy with red striped V insert, white felt skimmer, matching tote bag with nautical motif. MIB doll, $275.00.

(1960) #3134, Cookout Time, sleeveless red checked dress, white apron with rooster motif, white chef's hat. Outfit is very hard to find complete. Has matching Ginny outfit #1330. MIB doll, $275.00. Courtesy Chree Kysar.

(1960) #3345, honey-colored felt coat tied with black velvet ribbon, velvet cloche. Missing clutch purse. Courtesy Laura and Ronald Colpus.

(1960) #3160, After Five outfit, black tulle and pink taffeta with low-neck black jersey top, velvet cummerbund with pearl trim matches hat. Hat and pearl trim at waist are not original. MIB doll, $300.00. Courtesy Heather Lennon.

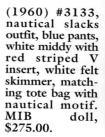

(1960) #3161, Rodeo outfit, white and red cotton with gold fringe, gun and holster, cowboy hat and boots. Has matching Ginny #1351 and Jeff #6361 outfit. MIB doll, $275.00. Courtesy Modern Doll Convention Rochester, N.Y.

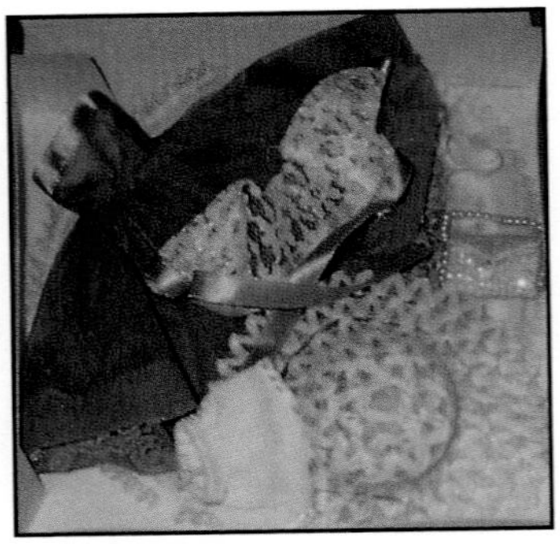

(1960) #3162, blue sheer nylon short strapless gown with white lace jacket, white straw cloche and satin sequined purse. Courtesy Tina Ritari.

(1960) #3163, aqua felt suit with short jacket and matching hat, skirt edged with black fringe. Brochure lists doll with embroidered straw handbag. Handbag shown is Vogue bag #3510. Shown on Jan. This outfit is very hard to find. MIB doll, $300.00. Courtesy Mary Miskowiec.

(1960) #3381 (#3181 dressed), bridal gown of point d'esprit and satin, chapel length veil crowned with pearl studded tiara, flower bouquet. Courtesy Ann Tardie.

(1960) #3180, red tulle bouffant prom gown, pearl trimmed velvet cummerbund, pearls in hair. MIB doll, $350.00. Courtesy Chree Kysar.

Unknown — Probably Budget Dresses

Jill in green, black and white checked dress with white stand-up collar. Vogue tag. Not in any brochure. Courtesy Nadine Steele.

Jill in red print dress with black and white flowers. Vogue tag. Not in any brochure. Courtesy Nadine Steele.

Jan in dress with pink and white checked skirt with white top. Vogue tag. Not in any brochure. Courtesy Nadine Steele.

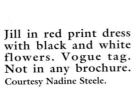

Miscellaneous Jill Items

Dress designer Joan Cornette holding Jill in 1957 outfit, #7507, she designed.

Comparison of Jill coloration. From left: early Jill without the INC mark on back, notice shiny surface, plasticizer has migrated. Also notice smaller blue irises. Jill in middle has pinker coloring. Jill on right is later Jill, notice pale almost bisque coloring.

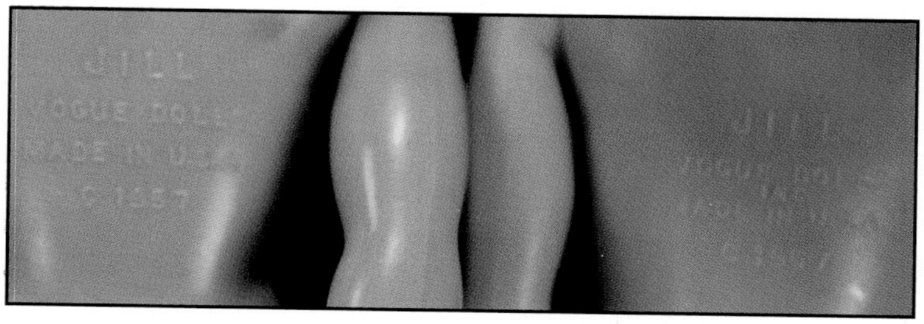

Comparison of Jill marking. On left early Jill without the INC. On right later Jill with the INC after Vogue. Courtesy Bonnie Groves.

Jill metal stand.

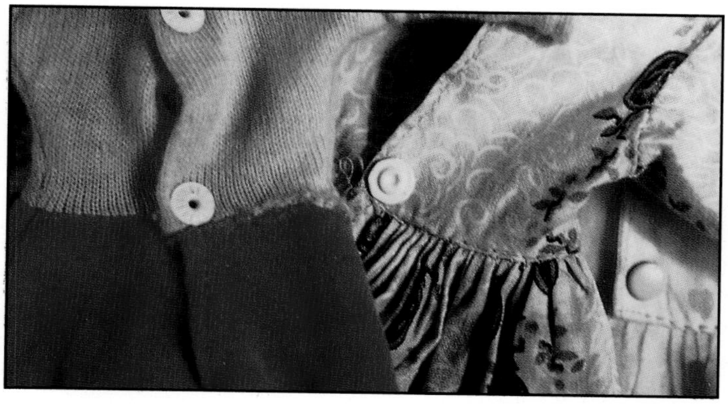

Comparison of Jill snap closings on 1957 outfits. Circle dot on left, raised squared edges, and button snap on right. All available on 1957 clothes. Most cotton dresses have middle snap.

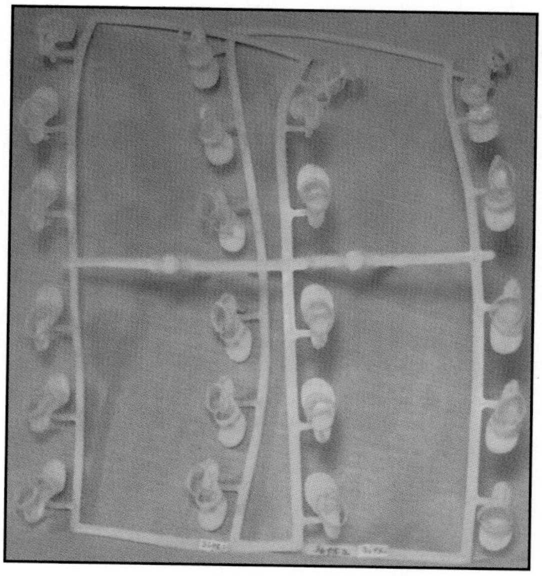

Rows of Jill shoes on form showing how they were made, probably at the Commonwealth Plastics Company. Courtesy Wenham Museum, Wenham, Mass.

Jill boxes, earlier (turquoise color) on left, and later (light blue) on right.

Jill (1957), bride outfit box. Courtesy Margie Pechet.

Jill (1960), dressed bride, came in large box. Courtesy Ann Tardie.

No Jill in 1961

All New Jill
(1962 – 1963)

Description:	10½", all vinyl, rooted blonde or brunette hair in bob in 1962, beehive in 1963, sleep eyes, high-heeled feet.
Marks:	Head: VOGUE Body: None
Outfit labels:	White twill with blue script: Vogue Dolls, Inc.
Boxes:	White box with cello window, navy and hot pink writing.

After Vogue discontinued the hard plastic Jill in 1961, there was such an outcry from the buying public calling for a teenage doll that Vogue introduced an all new Jill in 1962. All New Jill was all vinyl and had rooted hair. She had pale pink lipstick and sleep eyes. She had three lashes painted on her upper outer eye as well as molded eyelashes. All New Jill's hairdo was an angel bob, a bouffant hairdo with bangs, in brunette, auburn, and platinum. She was marked VOGUE on her head.

The doll came in the navy blue and white box with a cellophane front and she cost $3.00. Vogue marketed 10 outfits for her that year including a cute 1920s Charleston shimmy dress and a pink felt coat complete with a Jackie Kennedy inspired pillbox hat.

The 1963 Jill was the same all vinyl doll as the 1962 model except she acquired a new beehive hairdo and her lipstick was a darker shade. She was called Sweetheart Jill in the Vogue brochure. Jill's new hairdo was a chignon on top of her head in the same colors as 1962: blonde, brunette, and platinum. Eight outfits were available in 1963 with the notable ones being a green felt coat with leopard trim (copying the 1958 green velvet and leopard coat) and a cute white nautical dress. Several of her outfits matched Ginny and Ginnette.

Jill did not appear in the 1964 brochure.

Mint Prices

1962	All New Jill	$150.00 – 175.00
1963	Sweetheart Jill	$150.00 – 175.00
	Outfits Mint In Box	$35.00 – 60.00

1962

Dressed dolls are #60141+; outfits only #60340+

New Jill from Vogue 1962 catalog. Showing all outfits available that year including: #60340, baby doll lace-trimmed, sheer pajamas; 60141, outdoor sport white cotton deck pants with anchor motif, rope belt and red jersey; #60150, strapless blue batiste party dress with embroidered flower banding and lace trim. Courtesy Wenham Museum, Wenham, Mass.

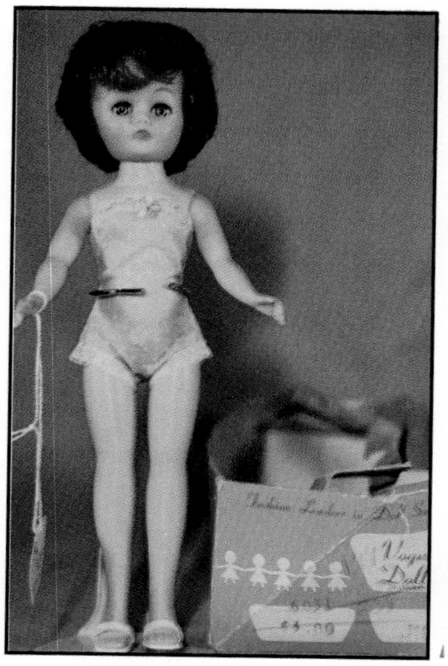

(1962) #6031, basic Jill, 10½" all vinyl with sleep eyes. Came in chemise with angel bob in platinum, brunette or auburn. Cost $3.00. Courtesy Laura and Ronald Colpus.

(1962) #60145, two-piece aqua flowered knit sheath with satin band around waist with gold motif. Courtesy Ruth and Fred Leif.

(1962) #60146, lounging outfit of rose velvety pants and pink fleecy sweater. Courtesy Laura and Ronald Colpus.

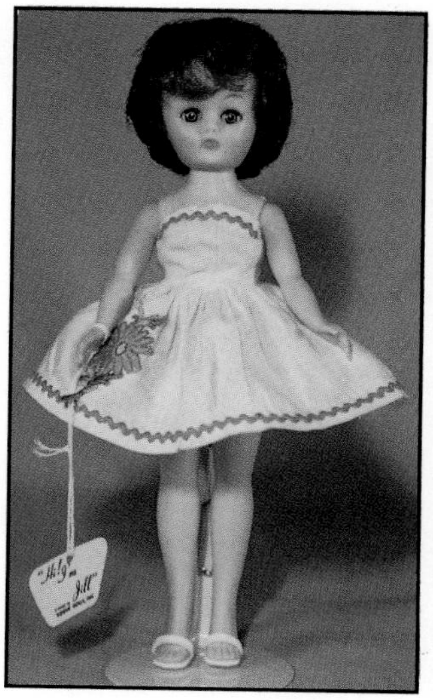

(1962) #60147, yellow strapless dress with contrasting rickrack and embroidered flower trim. Courtesy Laura and Ronald Colpus.

(1962) #60151, Dance Craze, black sheath with fringe skirt and long pearls. Courtesy Laura and Ronald Colpus.

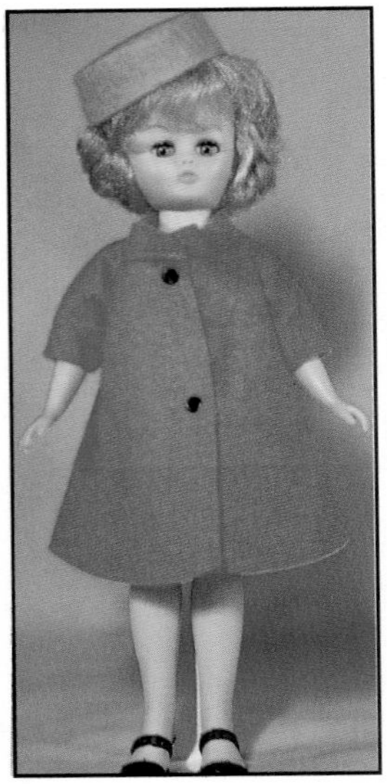

(1962) #60152, pink wool felt flair coat with pillbox hat. Courtesy Laura and Ronald Colpus.

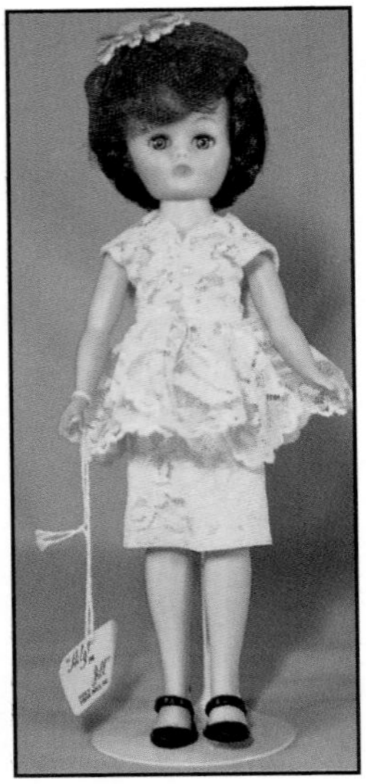

(1962) #60160, white lace sheath with overskirt and collar, net veil hat, missing handbag. Courtesy Laura and Ronald Colpus.

(1962) #60170, bridal gown in white nylon with satin sash, bouquet, and tulle veil. Courtesy Laura and Ronald Colpus.

1963 — Sweetheart Jill

Sweetheart Jill (1963), showing outfits available that year, including #60540 and #60547 not illustrated below. Vogue brochure.

(1963) Sweetheart Jill (1963), #6032, 10½", all vinyl with brunette rooted hair in a chignon. Shown with box. Courtesy Tina Ritari.

(1963) #60541, red pants with white blouse banded with lace. Pink pants also seen. Matched a Ginny outfit also available this year. Courtesy Laura and Ronald Colpus.

(1963) #60545, blue strapless gown with white lace and pink bow with wrist tag and box. This outfit matched Ginny and Ginnette outfits. Courtesy Chree Kysar.

(1963) #60546, yellow pedal pushers with pink fleecy sweater, green handbag with flower motif, sunglasses. Courtesy Nadine Steele.

(1963) #60547, white nautical dress with red white and blue. Outfit matched a Ginny outfit this year. Courtesy Mary Miskowiec.

(1963) #60550, pink strapless gown with black velvet bodice, pink rose at waist. Courtesy Laura and Ronald Colpus.

(1963) #60551, white lace sleeveless gown with blue ribbon at waist. This dress matched a Ginny, Ginnette and Miss Ginny outfit this year. Courtesy Laura and Ronald Colpus.

(1963) #60752, green felt coat with leopard print fur collar, hat and muff. Courtesy Veronica Phillips.

No Jill in 1964

Vogue Dolls From History Land

(1965)

Description: 11", all vinyl with various hair styles.
Marks: Head: numbers such as "6" or "19"
Back: VOGUE DOLLS INC
Outfit labels: Vogue Dolls from History Land/ Made in USA and #300 – 305
Name of Era, created by Vogue Dolls, Inc./ Malden, Mass. (on the other side).

In 1965 Jill appeared as "Vogue Dolls from History Land." The six outfits were a #300, Colonial Days; #301, Revolutionary Days; #302, Frontier Days; #303, Southern Belle; #304, Victorian Era; and #305, The Gibson Girl. The doll was the basic vinyl Jill but the hairdos were different. The Victorian Lady had long blonde hair with ringlet curls and straight bangs. The History Land tag reads: Vogue Dolls from History Land/ Made in USA and #300 – 305 Name of the Era, created by Vogue Dolls, Inc./ Malden, Mass (on the other side). Jill in Frontier Days wears a blue and yellow calico dress and bonnet, blue cotton apron, yellow shawl, black shoes circa 1962. These outfits are very hard to find. 1965 was the last year Vogue produced Jill. Jill was not listed under "Jill" in the Vogue price list and Jill did not appear in any other outfits that year, only as Vogue Dolls from History Land.

Mint Prices	
History Land dolls	$200.00+

History Land series (1965) #300, Colonial Days; #301, Revolutionary Days; #302, Frontier Days; #303, Southern Belle; #304, Victorian Era; and #305, The Gibson Girl. Marks are: VOGUE on head. Vogue publicity shot. Courtesy Wenham Museum, Wenham, Mass.

Frontier Days (1965), #302, History Land series, missing black apron. Courtesy Chree Kysar.

Colonial Days (1965), #300 History Land series, gray dress with white collar. Courtesy Chree Kysar.

Jan

1959 – 1960, 1963 – 1964

Description: 1959 – 1960:
10½", all vinyl, straight leg dolls, sleep eyes with molded lashes, swivel waist. Blonde, brunette or auburn ponytail or angel cut rooted hair. Metal loops on her ears for earrings. Red polish on her finger and toenails.
1963 – 1964:
All vinyl, 12", rooted blonde, brunette, auburn or platinum in bob, sleep eyes, elongated neck swivels at the base

Marks: 1959 – 1960:
Head: VOGUE (in all capitals)
Back: None
1963 – 1964:
Head: Vogue (in small letters)
Back: None

Outfit labels: 1959 – 1960:
(same as Jill) Vogue Dolls, Inc., blue script on white twill tag
1963 – 1964:
Vogue Dolls, Inc., blue script on white twill tag

Outfit closures: 1963 – 1964: Gripper style snaps with fluted metal design exposed on outside.

Jan – 1959 – 60

Teenager Jan was introduced in 1959 as Jill's friend. She is 10½" tall with a hard vinyl body and soft vinyl head. She has a swivel waist and straight legs. Her hair is rooted blonde, brunette or auburn in either angel cut or ponytail style. She has a sweet facial expression. She has blue eyes and molded lashes with four painted lashes on the outer corner of each eye.

This version of Jan was only produced two years. She can wear the same clothes as the Jill doll and does not have a separate wardrobe distinct from Jill's. She is marked VOGUE on her head.

Jan was sold at a lower price than Jill and appealed to parents who could not afford the higher priced Jill. This version of Jill is worth around $75.00 – 85.00 to collectors.

There was a Teen Togs package that came with Jan in 1959 and 1960.

There was no Jan in 1961 or 1962.

Loveable Jan – 1963

Jan underwent a drastic change in 1963. The Vogue brochure called her "Loveable Jan." Loveable Jan had a new bubble cut hairdo with bangs, a larger size (12"), a new role in the Vogue family, she was called a "new big sister to Jill," with for the first time a wardrobe separate from Jill's. The 1963 Loveable Jan has an elongated swan-like neck which swivels at the base. Loveable Jan has sleep eyes and painted lashes in the outside corner of each eye, lips of pale coral with light red cheeks. She has soft vinyl arms and rigid vinyl body and legs. Jan's feet are flat and she wears modified heels; she is a teenage doll. Her rooted hair was platinum, blonde, brunette, and auburn. She is marked VOGUE on the back of her head. Sweetheart Jan came in a white box with cello window and navy and hot pink writing

Loveable Jan had eight outfits in 1963. The basic Loveable Jan came in a red swimsuit with a white felt seahorse on the side. Her seven additional outfits are rather plain, most made of cotton, and not really fancy. Her clothes have the Vogue Dolls Inc., blue script white cotton tag. Her notable outfits include a pink fuzzy coat and a nautical clamdigger outfit, complete with sunglasses. Loveable Jan is hard to find since she was only produced for two years. Jan also came in a fitted case for $8.00.

Sweetheart Jan – 1964

In 1964 Vogue called the same 12" all vinyl doll from the previous year "Sweetheart Jan." Sweetheart Jan's hairstyle is the same as Loveable Jan, although Vogue calls it a page bob in their price list. There were six new outfits for Sweetheart Jan this year in addition to the basic doll dressed in the red swimsuit with seahorse. They included shortie p.j.s, a jersey shirt with a J on it, and jeans set complete with a Coke™ bottle, a red dot party dress, a denim school ensemble, a fleece jacket and skirt with a camera, and a blue formal dress and lace jacket. The undressed Sweetheart Jan cost $3.00. Dressed dolls cost from $4.00 to $5.00. Her separate outfits cost from $1.00 to $2.00.

The Loveable and Sweetheart Jans and their outfits remain elusive since they were not widely produced. Many collectors do not take to the new Jans, but they remain desirable since they complete a Jill and Jan collection.

Jan

Prices

1959 – 60	Mint condition doll	$75.00
	Jan MIB	$120.00
1963 – 64	Mint condition Loveable or Sweetheart Jan	$95.00
1963	Loveable Jan MIB	$150.00
1964	Sweetheart Jan MIB	$150.00
MIB outfits for Loveable and Sweetheart Jan		$50.00 – 60.00

(1959) #5010, ponytail Jan. Vogue dealer catalog. Courtesy Marge Meisinger.

#2 Jill's teen-age sister
JAN
A new 10½" teen-age doll with rooted hair! She's all vinyl with moving arms and legs and with a head that turns and eyes that close. What's more, she wears the same glamorous assortment of outfits as Jill now you have two dolls selling your teen-age outfits — and more of them! The basic Jan is made to retail at $3.00.
and...

(1958) Jan in ponytail and red nautical dress. Vogue dealer catalog. Courtesy Marge Meisinger.

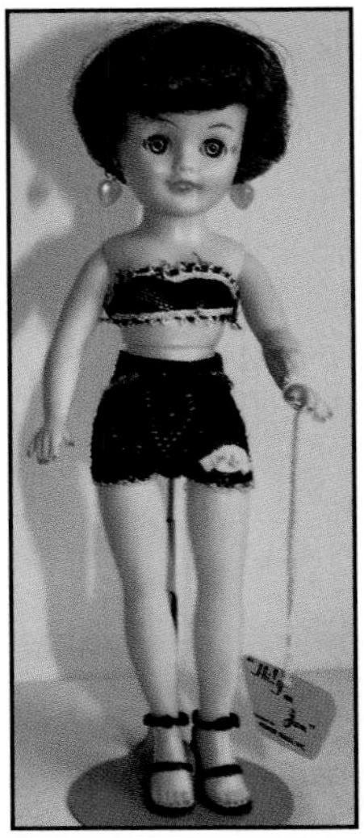

(1959) Jan, #5015, 10½", all vinyl in bra and panties. Marks: VOGUE (on head). Courtesy Chree Kysar.

Comparison of Jill and Jan body construction. Jan is all vinyl with swivel waist; Jill is all hard plastic with bending knees. Jan also came in two hairstyles a short bob and a ponytail in blonde, brunette, and auburn hair.

1963 Loveable Jan

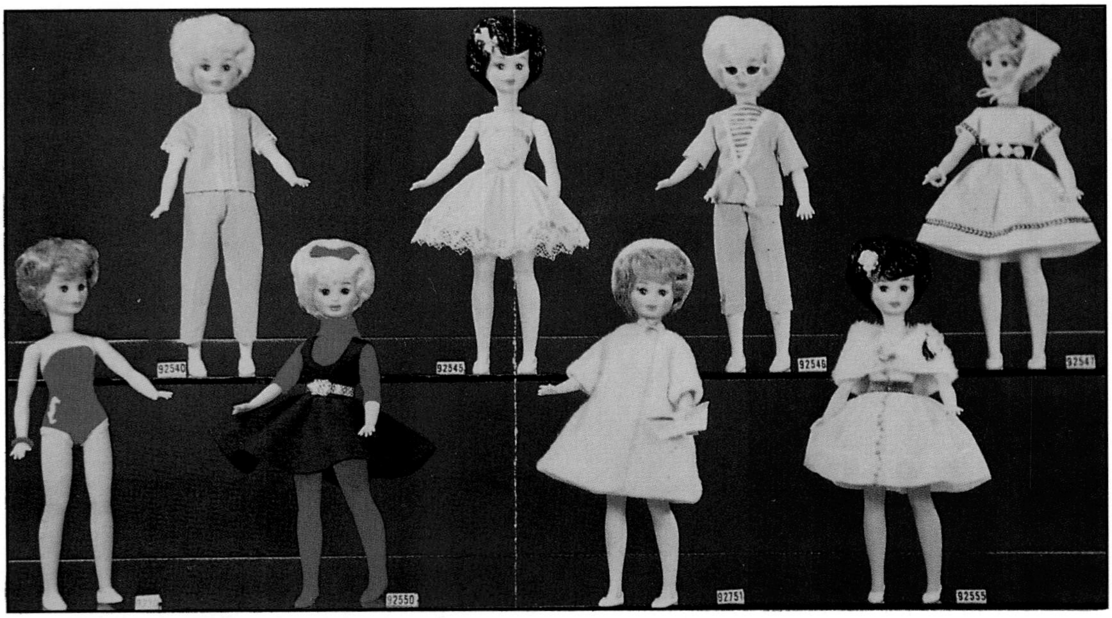

Loveable Jan (1963) in: #92540, blue cotton two-piece pajamas with white lace down front; #92545, pink strapless gown with lace at hem and pink ribbon banding on top; #92546, two-piece nautical outfit with blue pedal pushers and top with red and white V neck, sunglasses and sneakers; #92547, yellow short sleeve sundress with black embroidered banding and daisies at waist, yellow kerchief; #92550, navy jumper; #92551, pink fleece coat and hat, pocketbook; #92555, white sheer organdy short gown. Vogue brochure.

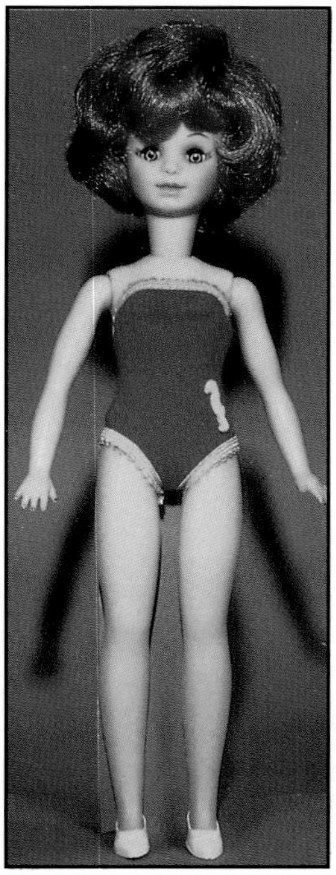

(1963) #92540, blue cotton two-piece pajamas with white lace down front. Courtesy Ruth and Fred Leif.

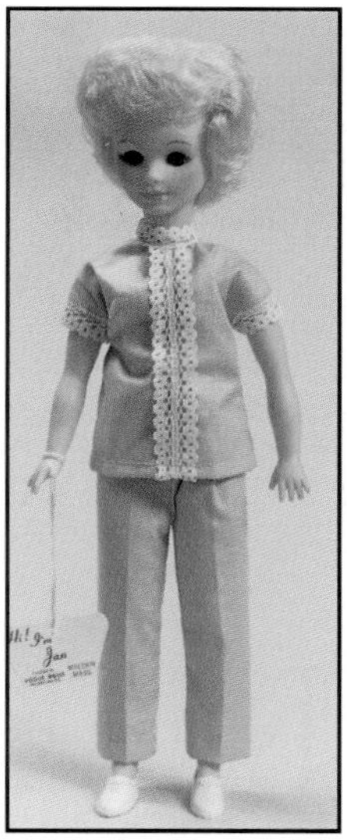

(1963) #92550, navy jumper with red tights and red turtleneck top, red bow. Shown with her box and Vogue brochure. Courtesy Tina Ritari.

Loveable Jan (1963), #9230, 12", all vinyl with long neck basic doll in swimsuit. Introduced as "new big sister to Jill." Rooted hair in bouffant style in platinum, blonde, auburn and brunette. Marked Vogue (on head); unmarked body.

(1963) #92555, white sheer organdy short gown with embroidered pink and green down center front, matching white fur shawl with pink rose, rose in hair. Courtesy Ruth and Fred Leif.

Loveable Jan in three hair shades: auburn, brunette, and blonde. Courtesy Nadine Steele.

1964 Sweetheart Jan

Sweetheart Jan (1964), the same 12" all vinyl doll as Loveable Jan, with six new outfits: #9231, basic doll in red swimsuit, has a stand with holes for her feet; #92640, baby doll pajama outfit; #92645, white T-shirt with J on it, Bermuda shorts, socks, and Coke™ bottle; #92646, strapless polka dot dress trimmed with ribbon and bow at bodice and hem; #92647, solid color school dress with black Jill belt, clutch purse, and kerchief; #92650, fleece sweater and dark skirt, headband and camera; #92651, party dress with lacy trim at bodice front, sleeves, and hem. Vogue brochure. Courtesy Marge Meisinger.

Jeff

1958 – 1960

Description: 11", all vinyl, blue sleep eyes with molded lashes, molded painted black hair.
Marks: Head: None
Back: VOGUE DOLLS
Outfit labels: Vogue Dolls, Inc. in blue script on white twill tag
Outfit closures: "Dot starlet" snaps
Boxes: 1958 – 59: Dark brown box with white writing and gold circle around Vogue Dolls (in script)
1960: Light brown box with brown print and paper doll motif on front

In 1958 Vogue introduced a teenage boy doll called Jeff. He was positioned as Jill's or Jan's boyfriend or a brother for Ginny. Jeff is an 11". vinyl doll jointed at the arms, legs, and neck. He has black painted molded hair and hazel sleep eyes. He is marked: VOGUE (on head); VOGUE DOLLS (on lower back). Jeff's head is disproportionately large for his body and he has a rather plain face. Jeff has never attained the popularity of Ginny or Jill. His interest to collectors is that he completes the Ginny family.

Jeff's ambiguous position in the Vogue family is proclaimed in the Vogue brochure to retailers. It states "We introduce this new 11", all vinyl teen-age boyfriend for Jill and Jan or a brother for Ginny." It is unclear why Vogue did not decide on his relationship to the female members of the family. Perhaps Mrs. Graves wanted the little girls to have multiple options in their play.

The 1958 brochure states: "Hi! I'm Jeff a member of the Ginny doll Family. I'm 11" tall and can stand, walk (sic) and sleep. I like school and have lots of fun at the big game...dancing...swimming in the summer...skiing in the winter. I've got clothes for all the different things I like to do". Jeff came dressed in blue or yellow striped boxer shorts and nylon slippers. He and his outfits came in a brown box. He cost $3.00. His outfits are very clever and include football and baseball uniforms, suits, dungarees, even tuxedos. His outfits have the blue print on white cotton Vogue tag. He has a skating outfit that matches Jill and even has a ski outfit complete with skis and poles that matches Jill, Ginny and Ginnette. His shoes were black, oilcloth slip-ons, and tie shoes. In 1959 he came with brown or black soft vinyl loafers. He was not a popular doll for Vogue and did not sell very well.

1958

Dressed dolls are #61+; outfits only #63+

Prices	
Mint condition	$75.00
Mint In Box	$150.00
Outfits, MIB	$25.00 – 40.00

Jeff (1958), from Vogue dealers catalog. Dressed dolls numbered #61+; outfits only #63+. Courtesy Marge Meisinger.

Jeff (1958), #6310, beige broadcloth pajamas and #6311, plaid cotton bathrobe with belt. Available as outfit only. Vogue brochure.

Close-up of Jeff tag indicating his indeterminant position in the Vogue family, "the teen-age boy."

Jeff (1958), #6311, plaid cotton bathrobe with belt and slippers. Available as outfit only. Shown with brown Jeff box.

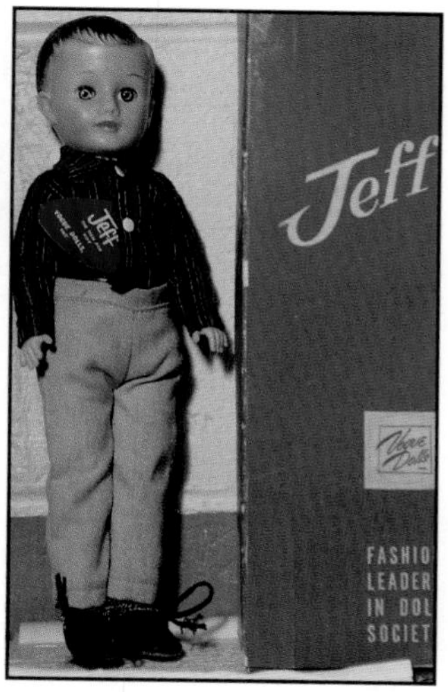

Jeff (1958), #6130, school outfit, striped shirt, tan chinos, and brown leather belt. Courtesy Kathy Tornikoski.

Jeff (1958), #6131, cabana outfit, print swim trunks with matching yellow terry cloth top, and scuffs.

Jeff (1958), #6132, blue jeans with black turtleneck, black belt, black shoes and socks. Courtesy Ruth and Fred Leif.

Jeff (1958), #6133, gray Bermuda shorts, red checked shirt, black belt, black knee socks and loafers. Courtesy Ruth and Fred Leif.

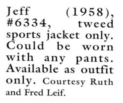

Jeff (1958), #6334, tweed sports jacket only. Could be worn with any pants. Available as outfit only. Courtesy Ruth and Fred Leif.

Jeff (1958), #6160, ski outfit of black felt ski pants, aqua sateen zipper jacket, skis and poles, earmuffs, boots.

Jeff (1958), #6361, beige nylon car coat with toggle closings and tweed cap. Notice cap is same material as #6334 tweed sports jacket. Other fabrics also seen on cap, such as red plaid. Available as outfit only. Courtesy Ruth and Fred Leif.

Jeff (1958), #6180, and (1960), #6164, navy wool felt business suit with oxford cloth shirt and bow tie, shoes and socks. Vogue brochure.

Jeff (1958) in white tuxedo outfit #6181, black pants with satin stripe, white wool jacket with white flower on lapel, black cummerbund (although booklet says plaid), white dress shirt, corsage, elastic on tie. Also plaid bowtie has been seen with this outfit.

1959

Jeff (1959) in #6010 in his blue and white shorts.

Jeff (1959), #6410, two-piece red and white dotted broadcloth pajamas and scuffs, and #6411, red flannel bathrobe with matching sash.

Jeff (1959), #6430, and (1960), #6330, striped shirt, chinos, and belt. Notice stripe color on shirt is a variation of that described in the brochure. Courtesy Ruth and Fred Leif.

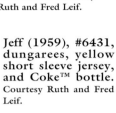

Jeff (1959), #6431, dungarees, yellow short sleeve jersey, and Coke™ bottle. Courtesy Ruth and Fred Leif.

Jeff (1959), #6461, cowboy aqua, black, and silver twill outfit with two guns, holsters, cowboy boots and hat. Matches Ginny and Jill. Courtesy Vicki Broadhurst.

Jeff (1959), #6432, navy linen Bermuda shorts with red paisley shirt, loafers and knee socks. Courtesy Ruth and Fred Leif.

Jeff (1959), #6460, football outfit, beige pants, padded jersey with letter, shoes and socks, helmet with chin guard. Notice red helmet which is different than in brochure which mentions yellow helmet. Vogue dealer catalog. Courtesy Marge Meisinger.

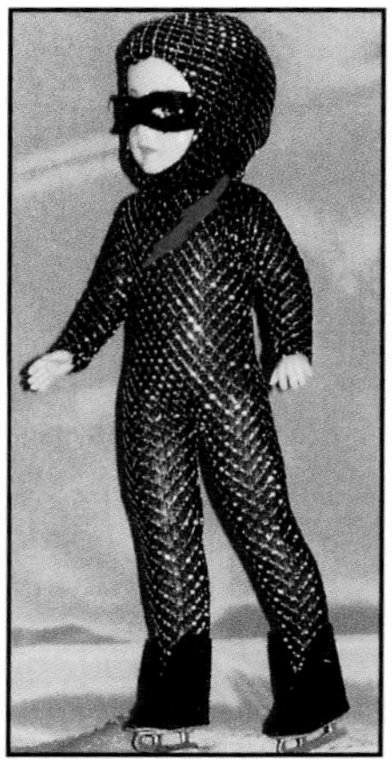

Jeff (1959), #6462, skater, black metallic jersey, mask, and skates. Courtesy Vicki Broadhurst.

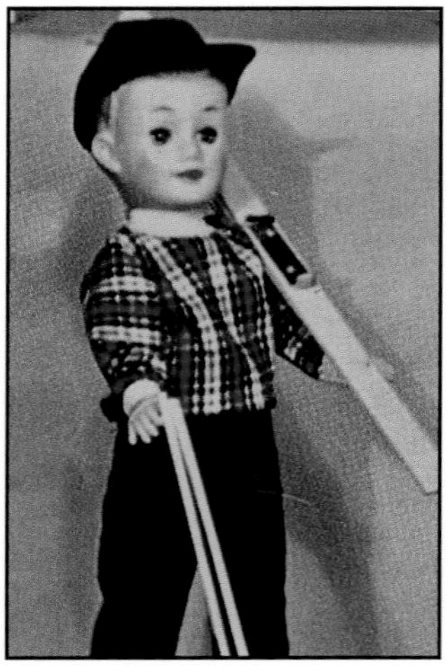

Jeff (1959), #6463, skier in plaid top, green wool felt pants, ski cap, skis and poles. Matches Ginny and Jill outfits. Vogue dealer catalog. Courtesy Marge Meisinger.

Jeff (1959). #6464, charcoal gray wool felt suit, white shirt, bowtie, belt, socks and loafers. Vogue dealer catalog. Courtesy Marge Meisinger.

Jeff (1959), #6465, tuxedo with black broadcloth pants and jacket with silk shawl collar, white shirt, black tie, belt, socks and shoes. Courtesy S. Ogilvie.

Jeff (1959 – 1960), #6510, shoes and socks in both brown and black. Courtesy Ruth and Fred Leif.

Not Shown
Jeff (1959 and 1960), #6511, cotton jersey briefs.

1960

Jeff #6010, basic doll in striped shorts showing variations of colors. Courtesy Ruth and Fred Leif.

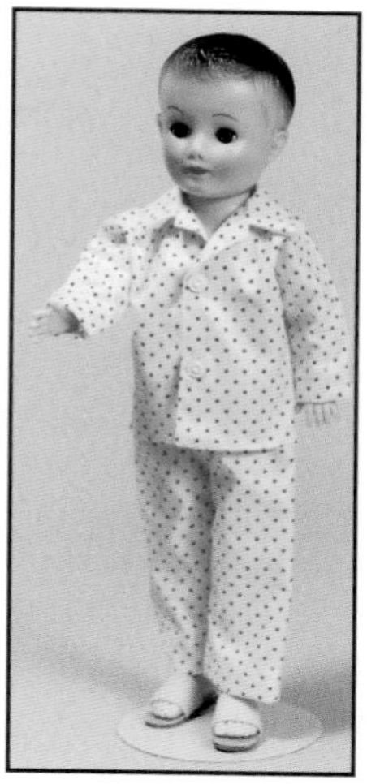

Jeff #6110, two-piece red and white dotted broadcloth pajamas and scuffs. Notice smaller polka-dots than 1959 pajamas. Also came in stripes (right). Shoes not original. Courtesy Ruth and Fred Leif.

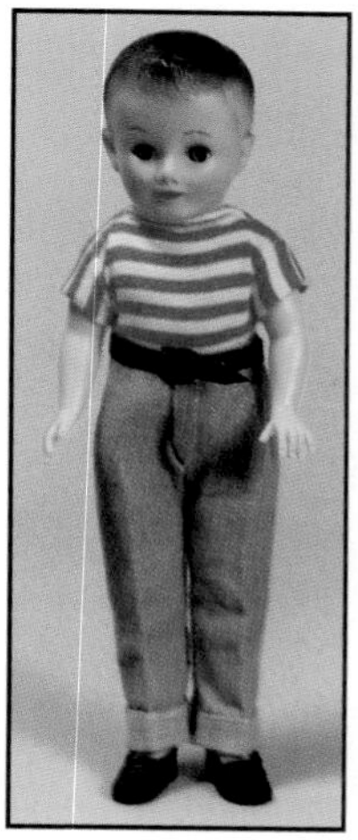

Jeff #6111, After School Fun outfit, faded blue jeans, cotton striped short sleeve jersey, and black belt. Courtesy Ruth and Fred Leif.

Jeff #6132, gray flannel baseball suit with red trim, red felt baseball cap, red and white socks. Courtesy Nadine Steele.

Jeff #6160, football outfit, royal blue jersey, beige pants, and gold helmet. Courtesy Vicki Broadhurst.

Jeff (1960), #6161, western outfit, white and red suit, cowboy hat, holster, guns, and boots. Courtesy Chree Kysar.

Jeff #6165, black broadcloth tuxedo with silk lapels, black tie, white shirt, and belt. Showing variation of brownish burgundy lapels and tie. Courtesy Laura Colpus.

Jeff (1960), #6165, tuxedo with silk lapels, black tie, white shirt, and belt. Showing lighter brown box he came in later years. Courtesy Tina Ritari.

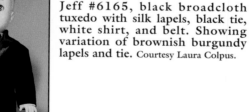

Jeff #6130, same as 1959 #6430.
Jeff #6164, same as 1958 #6380.

Jeff in plaid shirt and dungarees in unknown outfit tagged Vogue. Courtesy Jan Clanton.

Ginny and Family Matching Outfits

1955 – 1963

Mrs. Jennie H. Graves developed the concept of the "Vogue doll family," giving Ginny siblings – Ginnette in 1955 and Jill in 1957. Expanding upon the idea of the Vogue doll family, Mrs. Virginia Carlson designed several matching outfits for each year. Some of Ginny's new outfits matched sister Ginnette or Jill or both. Even Jeff, the "sometimes" brother added in 1958, had matching outfits with Ginny and the rest of the family.

Starting in 1960 there were even matching outfits with Ginny's extended family, her cousins, Littlest Angel, Wee Imp, Li'l Imp and Miss Ginny, who were added to the Vogue family line.

Ginny fans loved the idea of matching outfits for Ginny and her extended family. Vogue continued this concept from 1955 to 1963.

Matching Fabric Ginny and Ginnette 1955 outfits: Ginny (1953) wears "Party" #74 with matching nylon fabric and pink rose to Ginnette's (1955) #005.

Ginny and Ginnette in matching 1956 outfits: Ginny, #6043, and Ginnette #6510, white nylon party dress with flecks.

1957

Ginny and Ginnette in matching 1957 outfits: Ginny #7024 and Ginnette #7616, yellow print dress.

Ginny, Jill, and Ginnette in matching 1957 outfits: Ginny #7026, pink polka dot dress, Jill #7401 and Ginnette #7614. Courtesy Nadine Steele.

Ginny and Ginnette in matching 1957 outfits: Ginny #7029 and Ginnette #7615, green corduroy overalls and yellow shirt.

Ginny, Jill, and Ginnette in matching 1957 outfits: Ginny #7042, Ginnette #7627, Jill #7412, white dresses with blue ribbons. Vogue publicity shot. Courtesy Mr. and Mrs. Ted Nelson.

Ginny and Jill in matching 1957 outfits: Ginny #7043 and Jill #7407, red and gray checked tops with gray skirt. Courtesy Mr. and Mrs. Edwin Nelson.

Ginny and Jill in matching 1957 outfits: Ginny's gown is #7062; Jill's gown #7409 blue net formal gowns. Courtesy Mr. and Mrs. Edwin Nelson.

Ginny and Jill in matching 1957 bridal gowns: Ginny #7064 and Jill #7415. Courtesy Mr. and Mrs. Edwin Nelson.

Coordinated Outfits

Ginny, Jill, and Ginnette in coordinating 1957 outfits: Ginny in pink velvet #7060, Jill, #7414 pink sheer material over pink with printed blue hearts, and Ginnette in #7621, pink dress with white bonnet. Courtesy Nadine Steele.

1958

Ginny and Jill in matching 1958 outfits: Ginny #1112 and Jill #3132, aqua cotton dress with flower print skirt. Courtesy Nadine Steele.

Ginny and Jan in matching 1958 outfits: Ginny #1115, red and white candy striped dress with lace trim matches Jill and Jan's outfit #3138. Notice that Ginny's dress has a stamp on the hem indicating that this particular dress shown was a sample dress used as a home sewer's guide.

Ginny and Jill in matching outfits: Ginny #1117 and Jill #3133, dungarees and white blouses. Ginny should be a molded lash version. Courtesy Nadine Steele.

Ginny and Jill in matching 1958 outfits: Ginny #1118 and Jill #3135, Ivy League striped shorts and jersey top. Courtesy Marlene Dantzer.

Ginny and Jill in matching 1958 outfits: Ginny #1120 and Jill #3137, beige twill jodhpurs. Courtesy Chree Kysar.

Ginny and Jill in matching 1958 outfits: Ginny #1121 and Jill #3312, red pants and red and white diamond pattern blouse. Courtesy Nadine Steele.

Ginny #1154, Jill #3167, and Ginnette #2151 in matching 1958 outfits: aqua cotton snowsuit, skis and poles. May Company catalog. Courtesy Marge Meisinger.

Ginny and Jill in matching 1958 outfits: Ginny in #1138 and Jill #3161, pink cotton dress with pink jersey shrug. Courtesy Chree Kysar.

Matching Ginnette and Jimmy

Ginnette #2131 and Jimmy #4131 (1958), blue broadcloth overalls and blue and white checked shirt.

1959

Ginny and Jill in 1959 matching outfits: Ginny #1210 and Jill #3232, red and navy nautical dresses. Courtesy Chree Kysar.

Ginny and Jill in 1959 matching outfits: Ginny #1213 and Jill #3233, dress with pink skirt and white top. Ginnette's matching outfit was #2232. Courtesy Chree Kysar.

Matching Jeff and Jill

Jeff and Jill (1958), Jan in Jill's #3164 and Jeff #6462: Skater Jill's coral jersey skating dress with silver threads and Jeff's hooded black metallic jersey. Ginny had a matching outfit #1155. Courtesy S. Ogilvie.

Ginny and Jill in 1959 matching outfits: #1250 Ginny and Jill #3261, white felt ice skating skirt and jacket with red jersey. Courtesy Chree Kysar.

Ginny, Jill, and Jeff in 1959 matching outfits: Ginny #1251, Jill #3262, Jeff #6461, blue twill rodeo outfit trimmed with silver and black. Courtesy Chree Kysar.

Ginny and Jill in 1959 matching outfits: Ginny #1252 and Jill #3264, green felt ski pants and red, white, and green plaid jacket, white earmuff cap, boots, mittens, skis and poles. Jeff's matching outfit was #6463. Courtesy Chree Kysar.

1960

1960 Matching Ginny, Jill, Jan, and Jeff: Ginny #1151, Jill and Jan #3161, Jeff #6161, gold trimmed red and white cowgirl and cowboy outfits with cowboy hats and boots. Courtesy Barbara Hill.

1963

Ginny and Littlest Angel: Ginny #18536 and Littlest Angel number and year unknown, matching red and white windowpane checked dress with red apron top.

Outfits Designed with Same Fabric

Jill (1959) #3434 yellow watercolor print shirtwaist with orange sash. Vogue used the same print for a Ginny and a Littlest Angel dress. Courtesy Nadine Steele.

Matching Outfits Not Shown

Ginny and Ginnette Outfits

1956

• Ginny #6022 and Ginnette #6504, pink dress with white flecks.
• Ginny #6029 and Ginnette #6503, corduroy overalls with cat motif.
• Ginny #6048 and Ginnette #6507, polka dot swimsuit with white jacket.
• Ginny #6049 and Ginnette #6508, ski outfit, pink zipper jacket and gray pants.
• Ginny #6221 and Ginnette #6501, shortie pajamas in flower print fabric.

1957

• Ginny #7033 and Ginnette #7619, dress with lace around top of hem.
• Ginny #7048 and Ginnette #7625, swimsuit with life preserver.
• Ginny #7049 and Ginnette #7626, felt ski outfit.
• Ginny #7055 and Ginnette #7631, dress with cape.
• Ginny #7185 and Ginnette #7751, felt coat and hat.

Ginny and Jill Outfits

1958

• Ginny #1300 and Jill #3300, cotton leotard in pink, black or red.
• Ginny #1110 and Jill #3130, white cotton sundress banded with black.
• Ginny #1113 and Jill #3136, white dress with red polka dots and black ribbon beading on sleeves and neckline.
• Ginny #1114 and Jill #3134, yellow cotton dress with neckline and sleeves edged with lace.
• Ginny #1130 and Jill #3166, red cotton sailor dress with white trim, white felt hat.
• Ginny #1139 and Jill #3139, bulky knit sweater with tartan plaid slacks, straw hat.
• Ginny #1155 and Jill #3164, coral skating dress with silver threads; Jeff has a coordinating black skating outfit.

• Ginny (1958) #1164 and Jill #3192, white bridal gown of satin and tulle.
• Ginny #1116 and Ginnette #2110, gardening outfit, of pants and top with teddy bear motif.

GINNY FAMILY OUTFITS

1959

• Ginny #1212, Jill #3215, and Jeff #6431, Let's meet for a Coke™ denim jeans, jersey top, and a Coke™.
• Ginny #1231 and Ginnette #2213 sheer yellow organdy with nylon petticoat, straw hat.

1960

This year there were matching Ginny, Wee Imp, and Li'l Imp outfits (see Wee Imp chapter).
• Ginny #1114 and Jill #3110, aqua and white cropped top and aqua polished cotton skirt.
• Ginny #1130 and Jill #3134, cookout outfit of red and white checked dress, white apron with rooster motif, white chef's hat.

1962

This year there were matching outfits for Ginny, Miss Ginny, and Littlest Angel.
• Ginny #18142 and Miss Ginny #86181, aqua jersey knit slacks and kerchief with pixie felt top.
• Ginny #18145 and Miss Ginny #86100, red and white candy striped dress with white pinafore and straw hat.
• Ginny #18135 and Miss Ginny #86180, yellow cotton dress with green velvet sash and yellow rosebuds.
• Ginny #18131 and Littlest Angel #31142, white clam diggers with anchor motif with red print overblouse.
• Ginny #1815 and Littlest Angel #31160, pink organdy with felt jacket.

1963

This year there were matching outfits for Ginny, Jill, Ginnette, Littlest Angel, and Miss Ginny.
• Ginny #18531 and Jill #60541, red pants with white shirt.
• Ginny #18537, Jill #60545, Ginnette #28535, blue dress with white lace trim.
• Ginny #18538 and Jill #60547, white nautical dress with red and white stripe V front.
• Ginny #18540 and Miss Ginny #86580, white fuzzy top and pink pants.
• Ginny #18542, Jill #60551, Ginnette #28540, and Miss Ginny #86590, white dress with eyelet trim and blue ribbon at waist.
• Ginny #18545 and Miss Ginny #86500, pink nylon skirt with black velvet top and rosebud trim.

Vogue Vinyl Dolls

36" GINNY
(1960)

Description: 36", blow molded vinyl, walking doll, rooted hair, blue sleep eyes, jointed neck, arms and legs.
Marks: Head: Unmarked
Body: Unmarked
Clothing tags: No tags, unmarked
Closures: Large white circle snap with fabric in the middle, white buttons

Vogue, recognizing that Ginny's popularity was waning, attempted to broaden their market, selling a 36" Patti Playpal type doll popularized by the Ideal Toy Company. In 1960 Vogue came out with a 36" doll they called 36" Ginny. Deet D'Andrade sculpted the head and the doll was manufactured by Model Plastic Company which was formed by and supplied parts to American Character, Madame Alexander and Arranbee. There has been discussion in the literature that the 36" Ginny doll used the same parts as the 36" doll called My Angel Walking Doll sold by the Arranbee Doll Company, which was acquired by Vogue in 1958.

The 36" Ginny appears in the 1960 catalog in three outfits and had a matching 8" Ginny doll attached to her hands. There are three outfits listed: #1190, blue jeans, red and white checked shirt and straw hat; #1191, turquoise corduroy pants outfit, middy top with a V inset with Ginny's name, kerchief, black vinyl strap shoes, a dress; and #1192, a white nylon dress with tailored red velveteen jacket with pearly buttons. Dolls were sold as a set and cost $25.00. However, there is speculation that the costumes on the 36" dolls in the 1960 catalog were never distributed, nor were their 8" Ginny twins, since they are not listed on the 1960 Vogue order blank sent to dealers.

Joel Lesser, former executive vice-president of Vogue, says that the 36" dolls were sold by themselves in various costumes although they are not listed in the Vogue brochures. The 36" dolls came in outfits styled similar to Patti Playpal's dresses with pinafores. These dresses are red or coral and they have a white or red and white striped pinafore. There is a clown or apple felt motif on the pinafores and the slip is sewn into the dress. There is also a bride's outfit. These outfits are untagged which is unusual since Vogue tagged most of their clothing.

The authors have not seen any Vogue publicity photos of the doll in these outfits. Since the 36" Ginny and her clothing are unmarked, she is hard to identify. Hints for identifying the unmarked dolls are that the vinyl isn't as heavy as Patty Playpal and although her face is broad, like Patti Playpal, her mouth is in a half smile. Collectors have a challenge ahead of them in collecting 36" Ginny. They were only made for one year and are considered hard to find. The price on these dolls is relatively low, considering her rarity due to the fact that collectors haven't been able to identify the doll.

Prices

36" Ginny

Mint	$250.00
MIB	$500.00

36" Ginny (1960), short curly blonde hair with blue dress and pink sash. Courtesy Veronica Phillips.

8" Ginny doll that came with 36" Ginny #1191. Also notice matching outfit worn by 36" Ginny in background. Courtesy Wenham Museum, Wenham, Mass.

36" Ginny (1960), close-up of face. Courtesy Veronica Phillips.

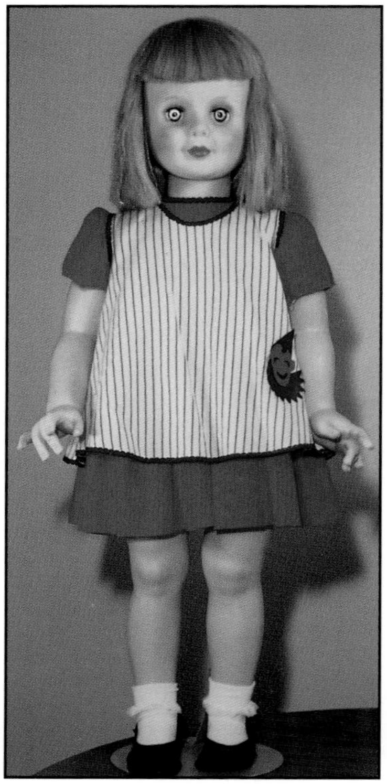

36" (1960), Ginny wearing red dress with red and white striped pinafore. Black vinyl almost oilskin like shoes, socks are replaced. Doll and dress are unmarked. Courtesy Veronica Phillips.

Hi, I'm
36"
Ginny
I AM
DRESSED 1190
$25.00 PER SET
Ginny loves to romp about in her rugged jeans of faded blue denim. Her classic tailored shirt is red checked with real buttons. On her head is a natural straw roller. In her hand — a matching 8" Ginny.
A WALKING
DRESSED 1191
$25.00 PER SET
Ginny's sooo big in her smart turquoise outfit of cotton cord. Long pants and middy top with sleeves and V-insert of jersey, printed with her very own name. She carries an 8" Ginny dressed just the same.
DOLL
DRESSED 1192
$25.00 PER SET
How beautiful Ginny is dressed in a party frock of sheer white nylon with flary skirt and taffeta petticoat. Over it a tailored cropped jacket of crimson glow velveteen with pearly buttons. And isn't little 8" Ginny sweet in her companion outfit?

Three versions of 36" Ginny holding 8" Ginny (1960). Vogue Catalog. Courtesy Wenham Museum, Wenham, Mass.

Brikette

1959 – 1961, 1979 – 1980

1959 – 1961

(Brikette)

Description: Soft vinyl head and arms, rigid vinyl body and legs. Ball-jointed twist and turn swivel waist. Elongated neck swivels at base.
22", green flirty sleep eyes, orange hair, freckles.
16", sleep eyes only added in 1960. Brunette and platinum hair also available.

Marks: Head: VOGUE INC./ 19©60
Back: None

Outfit labels: White twill with blue script: Vogue Dolls, Inc.

Outfit closures: "Dot starlet" snaps

Boxes: 1959: R and B white box with orange circles and R and B in white with blue outlining.
1960: White box with green and orange dolls logo "Brikette the red-headed imp." Clothing came in same orange, green, and white box.
1961: Clothing came in blue Vogue family box.

Brikette is a saucy, sassy 22" vinyl doll introduced in 1959. Brikette has straight orange hair, flirty green eyes, arched eyebrows, freckles, and a ball-jointed waist that can be put in many different positions. She had a soft vinyl head and arms and a hard vinyl body. Brikette is marked VOGUE INC./ 19©60 on her head. She was a licensed copy of a popular Italian doll designed by Ferruccio Bonomi of Milan, Italy. Vogue trademarked the Brikette name in August 1959.

Brikette was part of a family that included Li'l Imp and Wee Imp. They were Ginny's Impish cousins. Brikette also came in brunette and platinum hair colors. The brunette is the rarest Brikette doll. Brikette was introduced in July 1959 and first shipment of the dolls was scheduled for September 1959 in time for the big holiday selling season.

Brikette (1959) Vogue ad in *Playthings Magazine* showing striped top with green pants, and pink sleeveless party dress with white eyelet and pink ribbon. Also shows Sailor Girl, Ballerina and Li'l Imp. Courtesy Mrs. Virginia Carlson.

Wardrobe/Marketing

1959: Mrs. Virginia Carlson designed the clothes for Brikette. There were four outfits for the 22" Brikette in 1959: a navy sailor suit with red and white striped leotards and shirt; a pink sleeveless party dress; striped shirt with green denim slacks and sunglasses; and a blue ballerina tutu with flowers and ballet slippers. The outfits are tagged with the blue script Vogue Dolls, Inc. on a white cotton tag. The boxes were green and orange marked "Brikette...the red-headed imp: A member of the Original Vogue Doll Family."

1960: In 1960 Vogue introduced a 16" Brikette. The 16" version was like the 22" Brikette except it did not have flirty eyes. 16" Brikette came in platinum, brunette, and red (really orange) shaggy straight hair. There were five outfits for 16" Brikette in 1960: #8300, cotton print pajamas; #8301, sleeveless aqua and white striped polished cotton playdress; #8302, blue middy top and white pants outfit with white sailors cap; #8303, plaid pleated skirt with fuzzy gray sweater and knee socks; and #8304, black velvet and white nylon skirt party dress.

There were eight outfits available for the 22" doll in 1960: #8330, cotton print pajamas (same as 16"); #8350, aqua stripe dress (same as 16"); #8351, blue jeans and red and white checked shirt; #8360, cotton campus red and white striped pajama top with black tights and a stocking cap; #8361, blue and white sailing outfit (same as 16"); #8370, shag sweater and pleated skirt (same as 16"); #8380, tan polished cotton dress and straw hat; and #8390, black and white party dress (same as 16").

Three of these outfits were available only for the 22" Brikette in 1960: #8360, cotton campus p.j.s; #8380, tan dress and hat; and #8351, blue jeans and shirt. However, the 1960 Sears catalog featured Brikette wearing the cotton campus p.j.s in both 16" and 22" sizes. Shoes could also be bought separately for both size dolls.

1961: In 1961 there were seven outfits available for the 22" size: #82400, willow green dress; #82401, fancy frontier ensemble, a mauve cowboy outfit; #82402, the original fluffy fleece slack set; #82420, the velvety red party dress; #8361, the cool blue play set; #8431, the aqua slack and striped overblouse set; and #8441, the jaunty navy sailor suit.

There were only four outfits available for the 16" size in 1961: #86480, the willow green dress; #86481, the fancy frontier ensemble; #86482, the fluffy fleece slack set; and #86490, the velvety red party dress. The boxes for the 1961 outfits were blue-green marked "Vogue Dolls: Fashion Leaders in Doll Society. Ginny Doll Family: A member of the original Ginny Doll Family" with 16" Brikette rubber stamped on. Outfits cost in the $3.50 range for the 16" doll.

Brikette was a very popular doll due to her unique body and impish looks. There were many imitators of Brikette – one even appeared in the same Sears catalog as the original Brikette. These knock-offs included: Jolly Jinx by Jolly Toys, and Tobykins by Roberta Dolls.

Vogue only manufactured Brikette for three years. She did not appear in the 1962 Vogue catalog.

Brikette (1959), 16", platinum hair in R and B box wearing blue dress designed by Mrs. Carlson. R and B wrist tag says Hi, I'm Brikette. Vogue bought Arranbee Doll Company in 1958. Courtesy Tina Ritari.

Brikette (1959), 16", orange hair with green eyes and freckles, wearing blue dress designed by Mrs. Carlson. Starchy petticoat material sewn into skirt of dress. Soft vinyl head, hard vinyl hollow body, softer vinyl limbs, jointed waist that twists. Marks: VOGUE INC./ 19©60 (on head); None on body. No tag on dress.

1959

Brikette (1959), close-up of two-page brochure that came with 16" Brikette in R and B box.

	Prices	
16"	Mint condition	$175.00
	MIB	$275.00
22"	Mint condition	$200.00
	MIB	$300.00

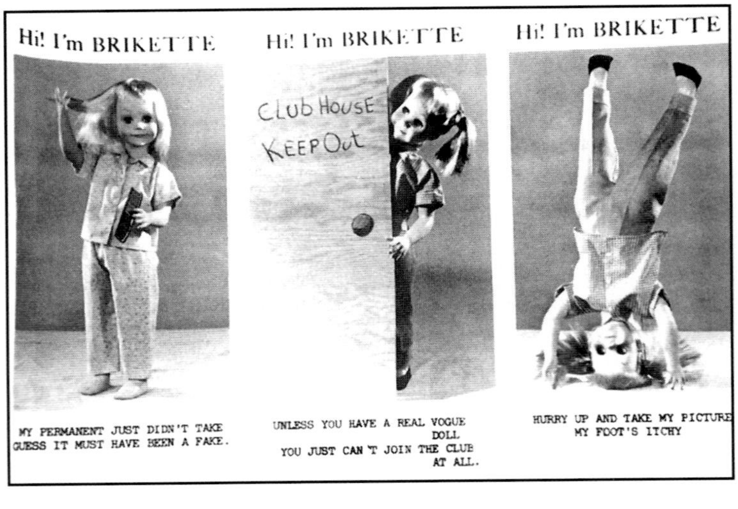

Brikette (1959), close-up of other side of two-page brochure that came with 16" Brikette in R and B box.

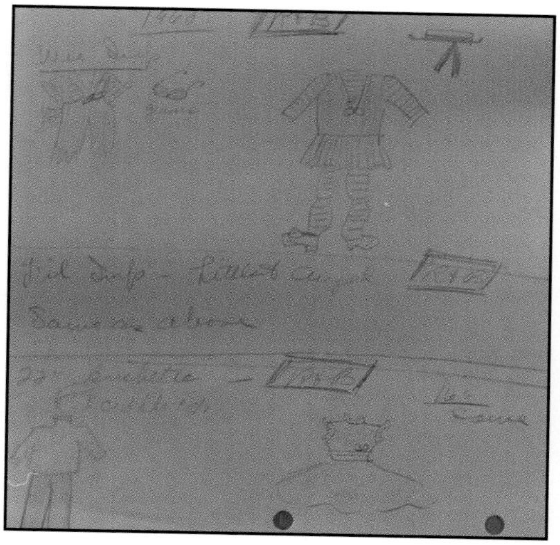

Mrs. Carlson's original drawings for the design of Brikette's clothing. Notice 1960, #8441, navy dress with red and white stripe leotights and straw skimmer; the 1959 Brikette, in blue dress with rose at waist; and 1961, #82402, for 22", white rabbit fur blouse, and cuddle cap with slacks. Also notice design of Wee Imp outfit. Courtesy Virginia Carlson.

Brikette (1959), 22", pink sleeveless party dress, pink shoes have lace trim around edges. Courtesy Joyce Zambuto.

Brikette (1959 – 1961), #8431, 22", in striped shirt with aqua (green also seen) denim slacks and sunglasses. Wrist tag says "I'm Brikette the red-headed imp." Courtesy Tina Ritari.

Brikette (1959 – 1961), #8441, 22", platinum, in nautical outfit of navy jumper with red and white striped "leotights." Tag says (front side): Hi! I'm Brikette/U.S. Pat. D-188, 118/Created by Vogue Dolls Inc./License – Bonomi, Italy/(back side): Ginny Doll/Family/FASHION LEADERS/IN DOLL SOCIETY. Missing straw hat and shoes.

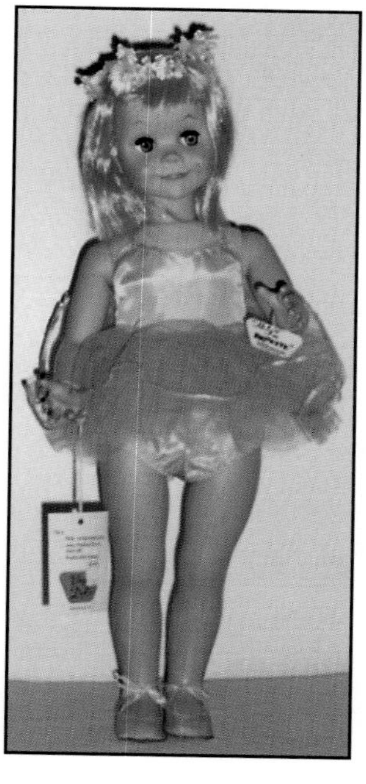

Brikette (1959), 22", in ballerina tutu, flower wreath, and ballet shoes. Notice two hang-tags. Courtesy Iris Troy.

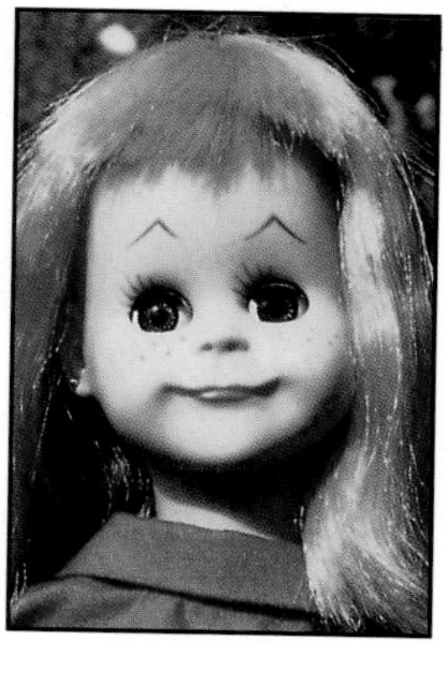

Brikette (1959 – 61), close-up of 16" Brikette's face. Marked VOGUE INC./19©60 (on head).

1960

Brikette (1960) from Vogue Catalog. Notice basic doll came in chemise, also notice denim pants outfit #8351. Dressed 22" dolls numbered #81+; outfits only #835+. Dressed 16" dolls numbered #810+; outfits only, #830+. Courtesy Wenham Museum, Wenham, Mass.

Hi, I'm Brikette
BASIC DOLL $10.00
I'm 22" tall, with impish green eyes and free-moving jointed waist. Dressed in a chemise. Available in platinum, brunette, or sassy red rooted hair.
Also available in 16" model In platinum, brunette, or sassy red rooted hair. $7.00
OUTFIT 8330 $2.00
Brikette ends the day looking like an angel as she goes to bed wearing this pair of classic styled cotton print pajamas.
Outfit for 16" Brikette 8300 $1.50
DRESSED 8150 $12.00
OUTFIT 8350 $2.50
Brikette starts another fun filled day wearing a crisp aqua and striped polished cotton dress. Skirt, sleeves and neckline are banded in white. Perky bow at waist.
Outfit for 16" Brikette 8301 $2.00
16" Brikette dressed doll 8101 $8.00
DRESSED 8151 $12.00
OUTFIT 8351 $2.50
What mischief Brikette gets into when she wears her tomboy jeans of faded blue denim. The red checked pant cuffs match the tailored shirt.

Brikette (1960), #8150 (22"), and #8101 (16"), crisp aqua polished cotton dress also showing the 1960 Brikette print box.

Brikette (1960) from Vogue catalog. Notice campus striped p.j.s, 1960, #8160 (22"). Courtesy Wenham Museum, Wenham, Mass.

DRESSED 8160 $12.00
OUTFIT 8360 $3.00
Brikette scampers about in her campus pajamas. Black tights are teamed with full top of red and white candy stripe. She wears a jaunty nightcap and matching pom-pom slippers.
DRESSED 8161 $12.00
OUTFIT 8361 $3.00
Brikette enjoys the sun and the surf in a bright blue sailing jacket with golden nautical motif teamed with whitettwill skinny pants and sassy crew hat.
Outfit for 16" Brikette 8302 $2.50
16" Brikette dressed doll 8102 $9.00
DRESSED 8170 $13.00
OUTFIT 8370 $3.50
When Brikette goes to school she's dressed in the very latest thing — grey shag sweater, pleated skirt of red plaid and black knee socks.
Outfit for 16" Brikette 8303 $3.00
16" Brikette dressed doll 8103 $9.00
DRESSED 8180 $14.00
OUTFIT 8380 $4.00
How winsome Brikette is as she takes a Sunday stroll dressed in her velvet and lace trimmed beige frock of polished cotton. On her head a saucy straw skimmer with long velvet streamers.

Brikette (1960 – 1961), #8161 (22"), 1960, #8102 (16"), sailor outfit of blue blouson jacket and white twill pants, and crew hat.

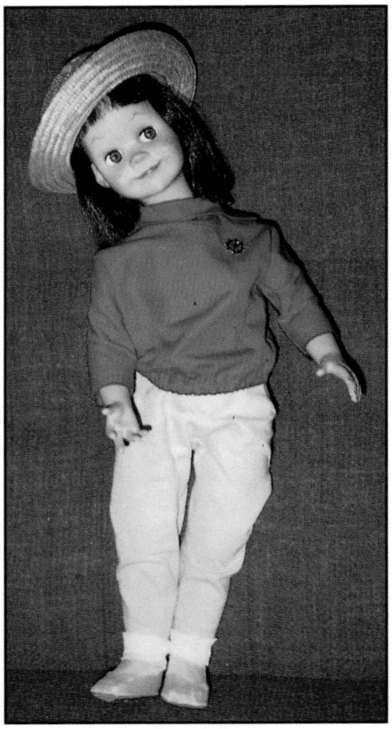

Brikette in #8161 rare brunette hair. Replaced hat. Courtesy Joyce Zambuto.

Brikette (1960), #8170 (22"), #8103 for 16", gray shag sweater, red plaid pleated skirt, and black knee socks. Originally cost $10.00 for basic 22" doll, $7.00 for 16" doll. Hair ribbon is shown on sweater.

Brikette (1960), #8180 (22" only), beige polished cotton dress trimmed in brown velvet and lace, missing straw hat with streamers. Shoes not original. Courtesy Joyce Zambuto.

Brikette (1960), #8190 (22"), #8104 for 16", platinum Brikette in a white nylon party dress with black velvet top and hat, black party shoes, white socks, complete with purse. This outfit cost $5.00. Courtesy Richard Withington Auctions.

Brikette (1960), #8300 (16"), and 8330 (22"), Brikette is getting ready for bed in her white with blue cotton print pajamas. Cost was $2.00 for outfit for 20", $1.50 for 16". Available as outfit only.

1961

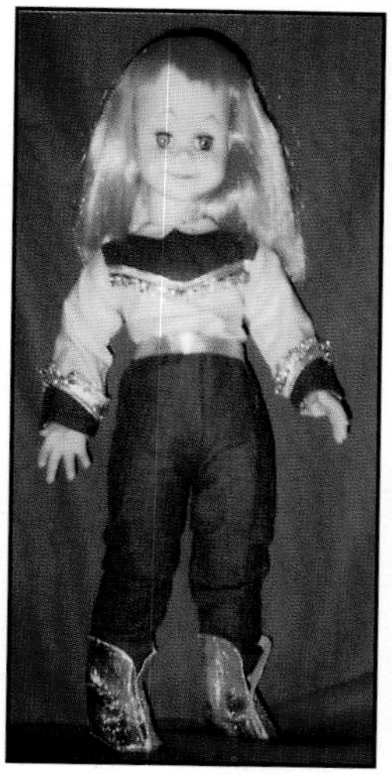

1961, #86281, for 16"; #82201, for 22", mauve Frontier Days outfit pants, rodeo blouse, silver boots. Missing felt cowgirl hat. Courtesy Joyce Zambuto.

Hi, I'm Brikette . . .

The saucy green-eyed, taffy or platinum rooted-haired imp in the "Ginny Doll Family." With my novel construction I assume many personalities in various poses. Made of vinyl, 16 in. or 22 in. tall, my wardrobe is designed especially for me.

16 in. size
280 DRESSED $8.00
480 OUTFIT $2.50
22 in. size
200 DRESSED $10.00
400 OUTFIT $3.00
kette is off to school her wispy willow en dress and kerchief h cluney trim.

16 in. size
86282 DRESSED $8.00
86482 OUTFIT $3.00
22 in. size
82202 DRESSED $10.00
82402 OUTFIT $3.50
Cool weather outings in Brikette's white bunny fur blouse and cuddle cap with aqua cord slacks.

16 in. size
86290 DRESSED $9.00
86490 OUTFIT $3.50
22 in. size
82220 DRESSED $12.00
82420 OUTFIT $4.00
Brikette is the hit of the party in her flouncy red velvety dress and headband.

22 in. size
DRESSED $10.00
OUTFIT $3.00
tte enjoys sun and in a cool blue jacket white twill pants rew hat.

22 in. size
8231 DRESSED $10.00
8431 OUTFIT $3.00
Sassy Brikette in her denim matchmates of aqua tapered pants and matching stripe overblouse.

22 in. size
8241 DRESSED $12.00
8441 OUTFIT $4.00
The "original" Brikette in red and white stripe leotights, navy dress and jaunty skimmer.

16 in. size
86281 DRESSED $8.0
86481 OUTFIT $3.0
22 in. size
82201 DRESSED $10.0
82401 OUTFIT $3.5
For "Frontier Days" Brikette wears her two-tone mauve rodeo ensemble with silver accents.

1961 Vogue catalog. Notice #86280 for 16", and #82200 for 22", willow green polished cotton dress and kerchief with cluney trim; and #86282 (for 16"), and #82202, for 22", white rabbit fur blouse and cap with aqua corduroy slacks. Courtesy Wenham Museum, Wenham, Mass.

Brikette (1961), #86290 for 16", #82220 for 22", red velvety dress and headband (which is just a strip of velveteen cloth) shown with generic blue Vogue box.

New Brikette
(1979 – 1980)

Description: 16", all vinyl, one-piece torso, rooted kinky curly short blonde hair and straight blonde and brunette hair in 1979.
In 1980 wild color pink, red or purple, kinky curly hair as well as with blonde kinky curls, sleep eyes.

Marks: Head: Lesney Prod. Corp. 1978/71679
Back: None

Outfit labels: Dress marked Vogue Dolls, Inc./ Made in USA.

Boxes: Navy, blue and white Vogue Dolls made with love

Marketing

1979: A new Brikette was introduced in 1979 after Lesney bought out Vogue. This new version of Brikette was 16" tall, and although the face was similar to the original Brikette, she did not have freckles or flirty eyes. She had blue sleep eyes and painted side eyelashes as well as top eyelashes. The new Brikette had a different body which lacked the ball-jointed twist and turn waist, slender body and bendable neck of the 1960s Brikette. This new version of Brikette looked rather stubby with her head disproportionately large for her body. This new version of Brikette was only on the market for two years.

In the 1979 catalog Brikette is shown with both kinky curly and straight blonde or brunette hair. The straight blonde or brunette hair Brikette came in four outfits: #306601, yellow long sleeved party dress with lace over top; #306602, cranberry velvet jumper with print blouse; #306603, blue dress with white polka dots with sheer organdy pinafore; and #306604, rosebud print short sleeved dress.

Three of the 1979 Brikettes had kinky curly short blonde hair. They came in these outfits: #306621, white nautical look dress with black polka dots and straw hat; #306623, plaid dress with navy bow and white straw hat; #306624, old-fashioned print dress with lacy apron and straw bonnet.

1980: In 1980, Brikette came in wild colored, kinky curly hair such as pink, red or purple as well as with blonde kinky curls. The colored hair Brikettes had color-coordinated eyes and clothing. These coordinated eyes and hair Brikettes had old-fashioned pinafore dresses and high button suedeine shoes. They were marked Lesney Prod. Corp. 1978/71679 (on head). Dress marked Vogue Dolls, Inc./ Made in USA. They were #306681, with pink hair, green eyes, and matching outfit; #306682, with purple hair, eyes and outfit; and #306683, with red hair and green eyes and matching green and red dress. The curly blonde Brikettes outfits were the same as those available on the curly hair 1979 Brikette: #306621, a black polka dot sailor girl dress; #306623, plaid dress with navy bow and white straw hat; and #306624, old-fashioned print dress with lacy apron and straw bonnet. They wore old-fashioned black and white buttoned shoes.

Brikette (1979), 16" with straight blonde hair and bangs in #306601 (#306644 on box), yellow party dress.

Brikette (1979), 16" with curly blonde hair in #306621, white dress with polka dots and straw hat.
Courtesy Ida Labaki.

Brikette (1980), 16", curly hair, in #306623, plaid coat and white hat. The box says #30667/80291 Vogue Doll Inc./subdivision Lesney Products Division, 1977/ Lesney Products Division, 141 West Common ST., Moonachie, NJ 07074.

Prices

16" New Brikette mint condition $95.00

Li'l Imp

1959 – 1960

Description: 11", vinyl head, hard plastic bending knee walker doll. Green sleep eyes, orange hair, and freckles.
Marks: Head: R and B/44
Back: R and B Doll Co.
Outfit labels: White twill with blue script: Vogue Dolls, Inc.

Li'l Imp was introduced in 1959 and first appears in the 1960 Vogue brochure. She was an adorable freckled face doll with orange hair called "Brikette's kid sister" by Vogue. Li'l Imp was an 11", bent knee walker with orange "taffy" straight hair with bangs, freckles, and green eyes. She had a soft vinyl head and hard plastic body and limbs.

Vogue had purchased the Arranbee (R and B) Doll Company of New York in 1958 and used their Littlest Angel doll for Li'l Imp. They added freckles and changed Littlest Angel's hair color to make their Li'l Imp doll.

Marketing

1959: Li'l Imp's 1959 outfits were unique and included #4230, Country Cousin, a long brown print dress with spats; #4221, Posy Ballet, green taffeta and pale pink tulle; #4210, Roveralls, green shaggy torn pants with one shoulder strap and checked shirt, holding a daisy; and #4220, Impish Elf, green wool felt outfit with bells on hat and boots with orange and white striped jersey.

1960: Li'l Imp appears in the 1960 Vogue catalog with four outfits that matched Wee Imp. She came in a Vogue green print box and her tag reads, "I'm a saucy, freckle faced tomboy, twinkling green eyed pixie; red headed little busybody." The blurb in the brochure reads: "Hi, I'm Li'l Imp and I'm always getting into mischief ...When I'm not being a tomboy, I'm very sweet and lovable!"

Li'l Imp was available undressed #4010, dressed in four outfits or the outfits could be bought separately: #4310, denim jeans and red checked shirt with straw hat; #4351, blue felt jumper trimmed with white braid with red felt sailboat motif, white jersey leotights, felt beret with red pom-pon; #4350, pink candy striped pajamas, nightcap, with pink pom-pon slippers; #4361, turquoise dotted long dress with white pinafore, bloomers and cotton stockings. All of these outfits matched Wee Imp.

Li'l Imp's shoes are marked Fairyland Doll Company on the bottom.

Prices	
Li'l Imp (1959 – 60)	
Mint condition	$150.00
MIB	$250.00
Outfits MIB	$65.00

Li'l Imp (1959) 11" tall vinyl head and hard plastic body with bent knees. Wearing outfit #4210 Roveralls green shaggy overalls, red and white checked shirt, and red hankie. Missing daisy in hand. Courtesy Iris Troy.

Li'l Imp (1959) wearing outfit #4220 Impish Elf. One-piece suit of orange and white striped cotton jersey, green wool felt vest, hat and boots, bells on shoes and hat. Courtesy Veronica Phillips.

Li'l Imp (1959) wearing outfit #4221 Posy Ballet. Green taffeta bodice and pink tulle skirt, pink ballet shoes. Courtesy Veronica Phillips.

Li'l Imp (1959) 11" tall, vinyl head and hard plastic body with bent knees. Wearing outfit #4230 "Country Cousin" dress. Marked "R and B/44" (on head); R and B Doll Co. (on back).

Hi, I'm Li'l Imp
BASIC DOLL 4010 $3.00
Hi, I'm Li'l Imp and I'm always getting into mischief. I'm 11" big with long shaggy taffy hair, sparkling green eyes and freckles on my nose! I can kneel, run and stand on my head. Sometimes I even sit still! When I'm not being a tomboy, I'm very sweet and lovable! Dressed in panties, shoes and sock
DRESSED 4110 $4.50
OUTFIT 4310 $1.50
Li'l Imp runs here and there and everywhere in her faded blue denim jeans with red checked cuffs and matching checked shirt. Her hat is a natural straw roller.
DRESSED 4150 $5.50
OUTFIT 4350 $2.50
With a hop, skip and a jump, Li'l Imp dashes to bed in her pink candy striped pajama set complete with full blown top and bold night cap. Pom-pom slippers.
DRESSED 4151 $5.50
OUTFIT 4351 $2.50
Mischievous is the way Li'l Imp looks in her white tights and jersey worn with a blue felt popover trimmed with white braid and nautical motifs. On her head, a sassy French beret with red pom-pom.
DRESSED 4161 $6.00
OUTFIT 4361 $3.00
Li'l Imp pauses a moment to be appealing in her lace trimmed pinafore and turquoise dotted dress. She wears a large bow on her head, white bloomers and long cotton stockings for a country look.
Vogue Dolls

Li'l Imp (1960) from Vogue catalog. All 1960 outfits had a matching Wee Imp outfit. Dressed dolls numbered #41+; outfits only, #43+. Courtesy Wenham Museum, Wenham, Mass.

(1960) #4110, faded blue denim jeans and red checked shirt, missing her straw roller hat. Matched Wee Imp #9113.

(1960) #4150, striped pink pajamas with original box, replaced pom-pon slippers. Outfit called "Draft Dodger" on box label. Matched Wee Imp #9135.

(1960) #4151, blue felt jumper with nautical motifs, missing her French beret with red pom-pon. Matched Wee Imp #9131, shown with doll in denim outfit.

(1960) #4161, turquoise dotted dress with white lace trimmed pinafore. Missing bloomers, long cotton stockings, and bow in hair. Matched Wee Imp #9150. Courtesy Sue Johnson.

Li'l Loveable Imp

(1964 – 1965)

Description: 11", all vinyl straight leg doll, sleep eyes, rooted blonde, auburn, and brunette hair in long and straight Dutch cut with bangs hairstyle in 1964.
In 1965 there was also blonde and brunette bobs. Vogue also marketed a separate line of black dolls in 1964 and 1965 which were the same doll except brown color with black hair and eyes.

Marks: Head: © Vogue Doll/1964.
Back: Unknown

Outfit labels: White twill with blue script: Vogue Dolls, Inc.

In 1964 Vogue marketed a redesigned all vinyl doll they called "Li'l Loveable Imp." She was 11", all vinyl, jointed at neck, shoulders, and hips. She did not have jointed knees. Her redesigned face had sleep eyes with painted lashes at the corners. Her eyebrows were painted in a straight line. Her rooted blonde, auburn, and brunette hair was long and straight Dutch cut with bangs. She is marked © Vogue Doll/1964. She cost $3.00 undressed with panties, shoes and socks, a necklace and hair bow. Li'l Loveable Imp's head was designed by Deet D'Andrade.

Marketing

1964: There were six outfits marketed for Li'l Loveable Imp in 1964: #3134, basic doll, undressed except for panties, shoes, socks, hair bow and necklace; #31640, blue footed p.j.s with appliqué lamb on front; #31645, sleeveless blue polka dot dress with flowers at waistband and green ribbon; #31646, white fleece top over red velvet pants, white hat with red pom-poms; #31647, blue and white striped sailor dress with anchor motif on bib; #31650, yellow skirt with white sheer top, yellow bow; and #31651, red and white checked dress and kerchief with blue apron with rooster motif on front.

In addition, in 1964 Vogue marketed a separate line of black dolls. They included an 11" perky Li'l Imp. The black Li'l Imp had long straight black hair with bangs and brown eyes. Her facial features and body were the same as Li'l Imp and she came in the same five outfits.

1965: L'il Imp, as she was called in 1965, also came in a black version, and had seven outfits that year. Her hairstyles in 1965 were blonde bob, brunette bob, blonde Dutch, brunette Dutch cut. The black version had a Dutch cut. She came in seven different outfits: #31140, a pink flannelette sleeper; #31145, a blue and white play suit and scarf; #31146, a pink checked topper and leotard; #31147, a lace trim blue dot party dress; #31150 a red velvety dress and lacy trim; #31151, a rose cape, hat and dress ensemble; and #31160, a brown fleece coat ensemble.

Li'l Loveable Imp was made only for two years.

Li'l Loveable Imp (1964), a redesigned 11", all vinyl doll jointed at neck, shoulders, and hips. Brochure courtesy Marge Meisinger.

Prices

Li'l Loveable Imp (1964)	
Mint condition	$65.00
MIB	$175.00
MIB outfits	$15.00+

Li'l Loveable Imp (1964), in #31645, white dress with green polka dots. Also shown is her box. Courtesy Jane Gaumond.

Li'l Loveable Imp (1965) showing her in six outfits, and black Li'l Loveable Imp. *Playthings Magazine.*

Black Li'l Loveable Imp (1964) a redesigned 11", all vinyl doll jointed at neck, shoulders and hips. Vogue brochure. Courtesy Marge Meisinger.

Wee Imp

(1960)

Description: 8", hard plastic, sleep eyes, molded lashes, bent knee walker, orange Saran wig, green eyes, and freckles. She was the same doll as 1957 – 62 Ginny except for freckles hair, and eye colors.

Marks: Head: VOGUE
Back: GINNY/VOGUE DOLLS/INC./PAT.NO.2687594/MADE IN U.S.A.

Box: White with green and orange paper doll logo

Wee Imp was an 8", hard plastic, bent knee walker Ginny doll with shaggy orange taffy hair with bangs, freckles, and green eyes. Wee Imp appeared in the 1960 catalog with four outfits that matched Li'l Imp. The Vogue brochure reads, "Hi, I'm Wee Imp. I get into all kinds of mischief but if I try real hard, I can be very, very good!" Wee Imp is marked the same as the bent knee Ginny: VOGUE (on head); GINNY/VOGUE DOLLS/INC./PAT NO.2697594/MADE IN USA (on back).

Wee Imp was part of the family that included 11" Li'l Imp, and 16" and 22" Brikette. Wee Imp was available for only one year. She is considered very desirable to Ginny collections due to her rarity.

Wardrobe

Wee Imp was available undressed, #9000, or dressed in four outfits. These were denim jeans and red checked shirt with straw hat; blue felt jumper trimmed with white braid and red felt sailboat motif, white jersey leotights, felt beret with red pom-pon; pink candy striped pajamas, nightcap with pink pompon slippers; and a turquoise dotted dress with white pinafore, bloomers and cotton stockings. These outfits were also shown in the Ginny section of the Vogue brochure for 1960. All Wee Imp's outfits matched Li'l Imps for that year.

Wee Imp (1960) from Vogue catalog, available mid 1959. Hard plastic with bending knees, green sleep eyes, "taffy" hair, and freckles. Marked the same as bent knee Ginny, VOGUE (on head); GINNY/VOGUE DOLLS/INC./PAT NO.2697594/MADE IN USA (on back). Dressed dolls numbered #91+; outfits only, #93+. Courtesy Wenham Museum, Wenham, Mass.

	Prices
Mint	$300.00 – 400.00
Outfits	$65.00 – 95.00

Wee Imp

Dressed dolls numbered #91+; outfits only, #93+.

Wee Imp (1960), came undressed, #9000, or dressed in four outfits. Outfits could be bought separately. Courtesy Chree Kysar.

Wee Imp (1960), #9113, denim jeans and red checked shirt with straw hat. Matches Li'l Imp #4110. Courtesy S. Ogilvie.

Wee Imp (1960), #9131, blue felt jumper trimmed with white braid with red felt sailboat motif, white jersey leotights, felt beret with red pom-pon. Matched Li'l Imp #4151. Courtesy Richard Withington Auctions.

Wee Imp (1960), #9135, pink candy striped pajamas, nightcap, with pink pom-pon slippers. Matched Li'l Imp #4150.

Wee Imp (1960), #9150, turquoise dotted dress with white pinafore, bloomers and cotton stockings, missing bloomers. Shows Wee Imp tag. Matched Li'l Imp outfit #4161. Courtesy Linda Gorog.

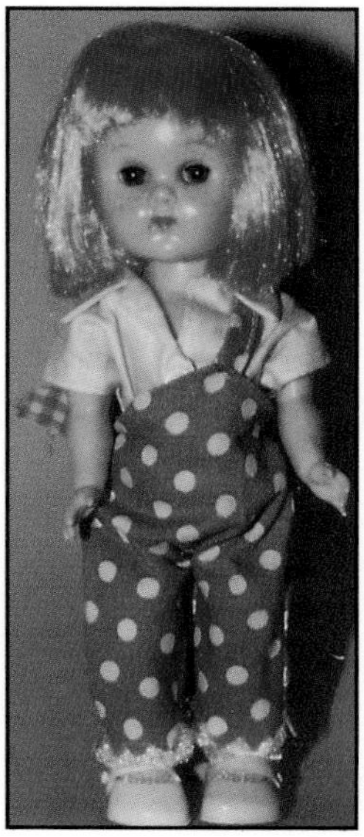

Wee Imp (1960), special Wee Imp outfit designed to match Littlest Angel outfit, blue with white polka dots and yellow short sleeved blouse, red and white checked hankie. Courtesy Kathy Schneider.

Baby Dear

1960 – 1964

Description: 18", vinyl head and limbs, cloth body baby doll.
12" size added in 1961, closed mouth, painted eyes and lashes.
Marks: Head: None
Back: VOGUE DOLLS/INC. (on a white tag with blue writing)
Left Leg 12": ©1960/E.WILKIN
Left Leg 18": E.WILKINS/©1960.
Outfit labels: White twill with blue script: Vogue Dolls, Inc.
Outfit closures: 1958 "dot starlet" snaps
Boxes: Light blue box with white paper doll on front pink script: "Ginny Doll Family" and "Fashion Leaders in Doll Society"

Baby Dear introduced in 1960 was a charming doll designed by the talented storybook illustrator, Eloise Wilkin, who had been illustrating Little Golden Books for Simon and Schuster since 1944. Mrs. Wilkin had been trying to get Vogue to produce her life-like baby doll for several years. She had worked on her sketches for the doll for many years before she was satisfied with the final design. She then made a clay model of the doll, dressed it in infant's clothing and brought it to the Vogue Company. Virginia Graves Carlson remembers the day Eloise Wilkin came in with her clay model of the doll. Jennie Graves loved it and could see the potential even though it was only a lump of clay. Jennie Graves became close friends with Mrs. Wilkin during the years they worked together.

Vogue introduced Baby Dear as an 18", lovable floppy baby with vinyl limbs and head and cloth body sculptured in the image of a one-month-old baby. Baby Dear sold for $13.00 and is first featured in the 1961 catalog that came out in summer 1960. Baby Dear had painted eyes and was distinctive from other baby dolls of the time due to her realism and sculpting of the facial features. She made a burping sound when squeezed lightly.

The original version had one sprout of rooted blonde hair on top. This topknot was glued to the top of her head but was produced for less than a year since the glue in the hair proved unsatisfactory. This topknot version of Baby Dear is hard to find today. The later version of Baby Dear had rooted blonde hair all over. Although Mrs. Graves felt that new allover rooting of the hair was too thick for an "infant look," it was the best technology at the time. Baby Dear could fit into 3-month-old baby clothes. The first Baby Dear in 1960 wore a version of a baby's undershirt designed by Carter's, cut to Vogue's specifications.

Eighteen inch Baby Dear is marked on her left leg E.WILKIN/©1960. There is also a Vogue white tag pasted on her upper back. This first version of Baby Dear was made from 1960 – 64.

Baby Dear was a huge success. Millions were sold. She was so popular that she inspired many imitations including one by the Jolly Toy Company which is unmarked. Baby Dear even had international appeal. Soviet Premier Nikita Khrushchev saw them in the window of F.A.O. Schwarz in New York in 1960 and bought 13 of them.

1960 Drawing of Baby Dear by Eloise Wilkin. Courtesy Wenham Museum, Wenham, Mass.

In 1961 Vogue introduced Baby Dear in a 12" size. She is marked ©1960/E. WILKIN (on her left leg). There were four outfits for the 12" Baby Dear: #42270, a cuddly flannelette sleeping gown; #42271, toy time topper set; #42280, bundly pink bunting; and #42290, crisp white party dress. The 18" Baby Dear came in the same four outfits except the blue flannel was a sleeper (had legs), not a gown. The 18" doll also had a separate outfit available, #48410, a baby diaper and shirt set.

A book titled *Baby Dear* was published in 1962 by Golden Books featuring Eloise Wilkin's drawings of the doll Baby Dear.

Montgomery Ward (1962) had exclusive Baby Dears available only by mail. They were a 12" wearing one-piece pink sleeping gowns which cost $4.69 and the 18" wore a two-piece sleeper costing $8.49. Extra outfits from Ward were blue batiste dresses with floral embroidery and lace trim down the middle for both the 12" and 18" dolls (costing $2.29 and $3.29 respectively), and pink hooded jackets with lace trim and matching pants for the 18" dolls ($3.79). For the 12" doll, there was a hooded jacket like bunting bag instead (cost $2.79).

The 1962, 12" Baby Dears were available in five outfits. The 1962, 18" Baby Dears were available in all of the outfits for the 12" plus #48311, a diaper and shirt set.

Vogue came out with a Moving Musical model of

Baby Dear in 1962, she is also listed on the 1963 price list. The 18" Baby Dear had a Swiss musical action mechanism inside her and played "Rock-a-bye Baby." She had a round wooden button sticking out of her lower back and sold for $10.98. Baby Dear also came in a 12" Moving Musical size that sold for $6.98. The 12" version of Baby Dear has a metal shaft with gripper surface which can be wound and plays "Lullaby and Good Night" as the doll's head moves. Both of the Moving Musical Baby Dears are marked the same way as Baby Dear. The 12" Moving Musical Baby Dear came in a white cotton two-piece outfit with tiny pink polka dots, trimmed with lace with a solid pink yoke. Another outfit was the two-piece cotton plissé sleep set with white pom-pons on front. Some 12" Musical Baby Dears do not have the mechanism to make the doll move.

The 18" Musical Baby Dear came in a red and white romper with solid red velvet on bottom and white cotton with red polka dots on top. They were both advertised with a moving mechanism in 1963. The 1963, 12" Moving Musical Baby Dear, #42550, wore a pink jersey sleeping gown. The 1963, 18" Moving Musical Baby Dear, #48580, wore a pink jersey sleeper set with pants instead of the gown.

In 1963 the 12" Baby Dear had three outfits: a pink jersey sleeping gown, a pink checked topper set, and a white embroidered ensemble. The 18" had the same outfits except her pink jersey was a sleeper set.

Vogue also produced a 12" hand puppet with Baby Dear head which is very hard for collectors to find. Baby Dear was Mrs. Wilkin's first doll.

There was even doll furniture produced especially for Baby Dear. A doll carriage was produced under a licensing agreement with the Hedstrom Union Company of Fitchburg, Masss. The carriage came in navy blue marimo and features an aluminum finish and chromed metal parts. It is 22½" long and 11¼" wide. The carriage came with a paper banner proclaiming it was for Baby Dear. There was also a Dolly Rocker lounge produced by the Bunny Bear Company of Everett, Mass. Baby Dear could sit, recline, and sleep in her lounge.

Vogue continued to sell the original 18" Baby Dear through 1968 even though they also sold a redesigned Baby Dear. Original Baby Dear listed in the F.A.O. Schwarz catalog in 1968 in her print terry cloth sleeper.

Eloise Wilkin designed two other dolls for Vogue after the Baby Dear series, 1977's Welcome Home Baby and 1980 Welcome Home Baby Turns Two.

Prices

12"	Mint	$125.00
	MIB	$250.00
18"	Mint	$225.00
	MIB	$350.00
Musical Baby Dear		
12"	Mint	$175.00
18"	Mint	$275.00
Puppet		$150.00

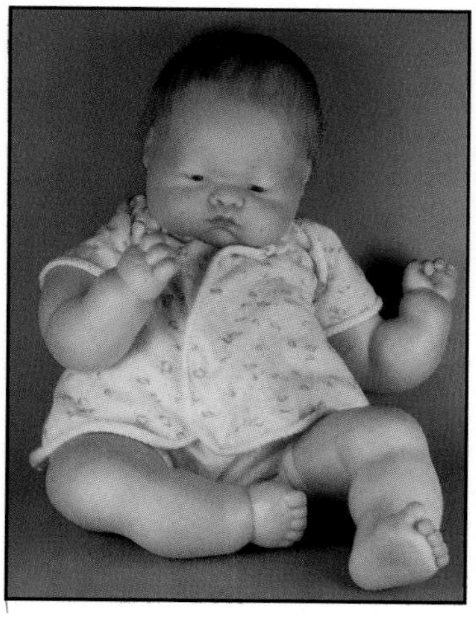

Baby Dear (1960). The first issue of Baby Dear had a "topknot" hair arrangement which was shortly changed to rooted hair by Vogue. The sacque outfit is all original with snapped flannel diaper and printed rosebud knit top with undershirt. Courtesy Kathy Barry-Hippensteel.

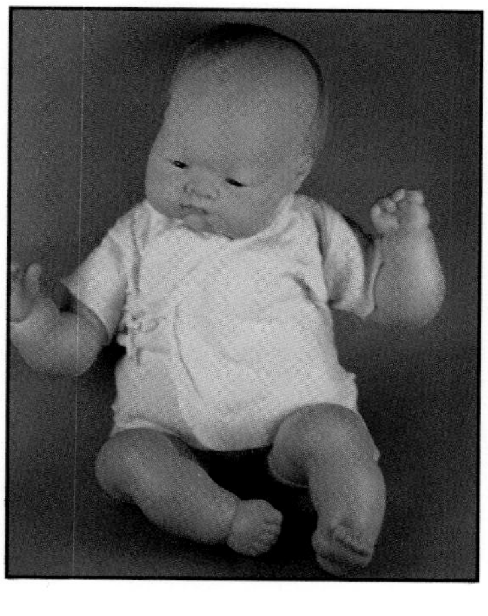

Baby Dear (1960), 18" in #48311, sacque undershirt with ties and top for the original Baby Dear were made by Carter's to Vogue size specifications. Vogue produced the flannel diaper with star snaps. This first issue of Baby Dear had a topknot hair arrangement.

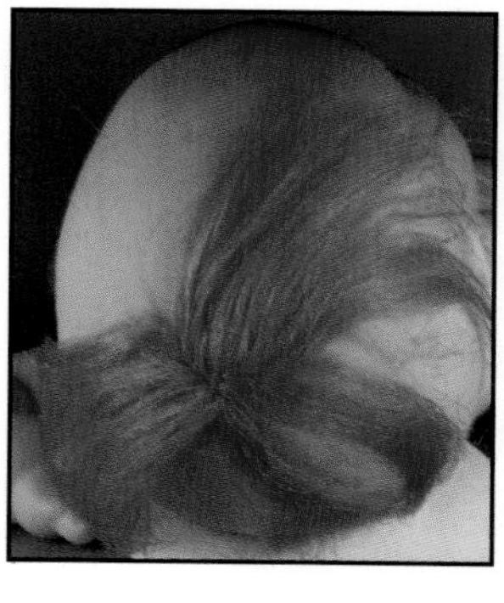

Baby Dear (1960) shows the original topknot design, with the doll's hair rooted through a small area in the head. The doll was redesigned later in the year with all-over rooted hair.

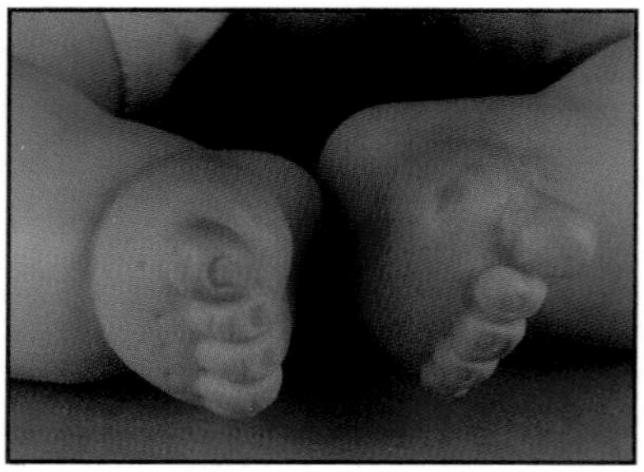

Baby Dear (1960), limbs were realistically molded. Eloise Wilkin sculpted Baby Dear's left toe sticking up.

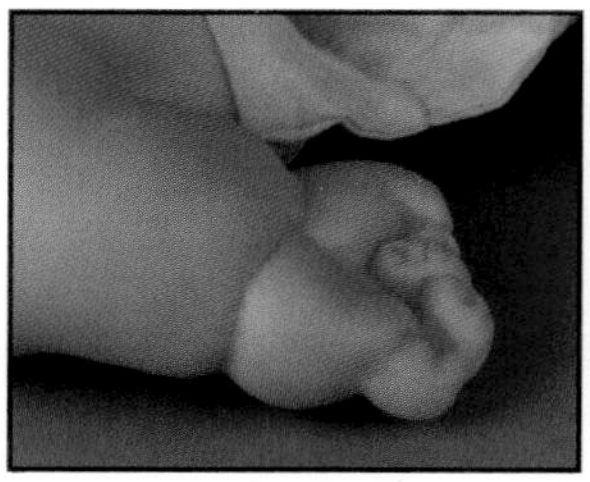

Baby Dear's realistically molded left hand in a fist.

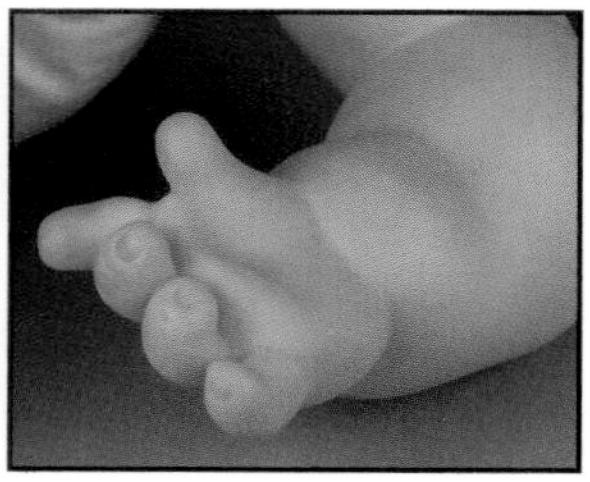

Baby Dear's realistically molded right hand.

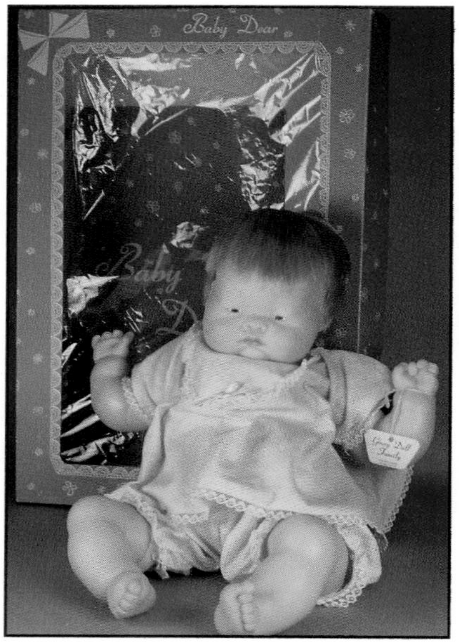

Baby Dear (1960 – 61), 18", Baby Dear with vinyl head and soft body with allover rooted hair. The cotton dress and matching pants, #48201, are tagged and all original for this doll with rooted hair. Shown with her Vogue hang-tag and box. Courtesy Kathy Barry-Hippensteel.

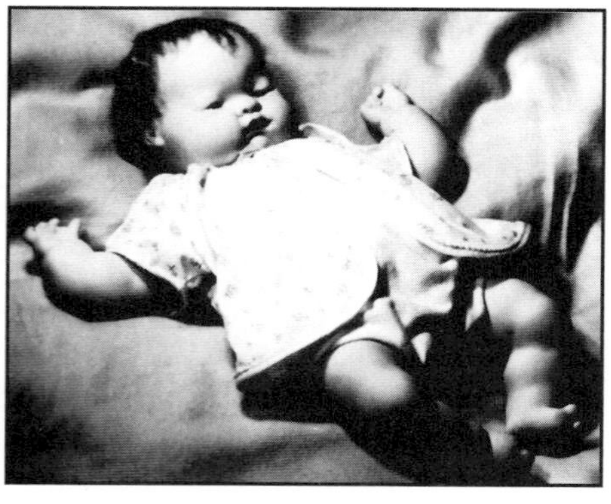

1961 Baby Dear (1961), 18", vinyl head and limbs, cloth body in rose print shirt. Courtesy Joe Kingston.

1960

18" Baby Dear

Topknot, wore a cut-down version of the white Carter's undershirt with ties.

1961

12" Baby Dear

Came as dressed doll #422+, or as separate outfit #424+.
#42270, flannelette sleeping gown.
#42271, Toy Time Topper set, pink pin dot topper with attached bib and matching panties.
#48280, bundly pink bunting, pink fleece pram bag with hood.
#42290, white batiste party dress, slip, and knit booties.

18" Baby Dear

#48200, called cuddly, blue flannel sleeper, is knit.
#48201, Toy Time Topper set, same as for 12".
#48410, diaper and shirt set.
#48212, bundly pink bunting, same as for 12".
#48220, white party dress, same as for 12".

1962

12" Baby Dear

Dressed Dolls were #421+, Outfits only were #423+.
#42100, organdy christening gown and bonnet with white slip.
#42150, pink jersey sleeping gown.
#42160, pink print on blue two-piece topper set with fluffy pom-pon.
#42170, blue batiste dress and slip with flower, embroidered banding and lace and booties.
#42180, pink lace trimmed hooded jacket and bag.

18" Baby Dear

Dressed Dolls were #481+, Outfits only were #483+.
#48100, pink print on blue two-piece topper set with fluffy pom-pon.
#48110, blue batiste dress and slip with flowered embroidered banding and booties.
#48311, diaper and shirt set.
#48120, pink hooded jacket and matching footed pants.
#48150, organdy christening gown and bonnet with white slip.
#48190, two-piece pink jersey sleeper.

1963

12" Baby Dear

#42550, pink jersey sleeping gown.
#42560, pink and white checked panties under pink and white lace top.
#42580, white short gown with bows and lace, bonnet, and booties.

18" Baby Dear

#48580, two-piece pink jersey sleeper.
#48590, pink and white checked panties under pink and white and lace top.
#48510, white short gown with bows and lace, bonnet, and booties.

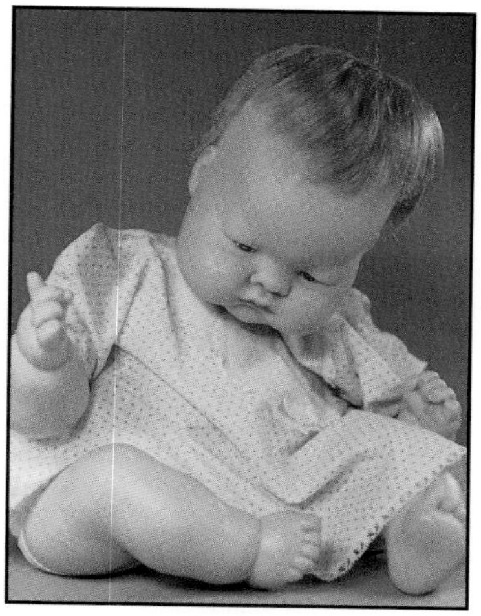

Baby Dear (1961), 18", wearing pink pin dot topper set #48201, marked E.Wilkin/ ©1960 (on left leg). The doll was designed by famous children's book illustrator Eloise Wilkin. 18" doll cost $10.00, 12" cost $7.00.

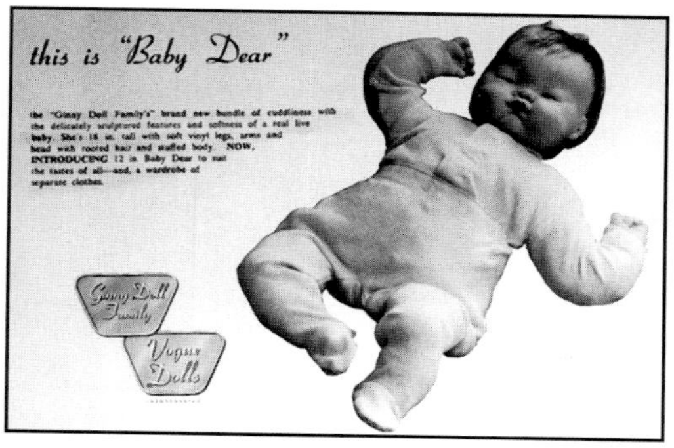

Baby Dear (1961), introducing 18" Baby Dear, wearing outfit #48200, blue cotton sleeper. Vogue brochure. Courtesy Wenham Museum, Wenham, Mass.

Inside cover of *Baby Dear* the book by Eloise Wilkin published by Little Golden Book (1961).

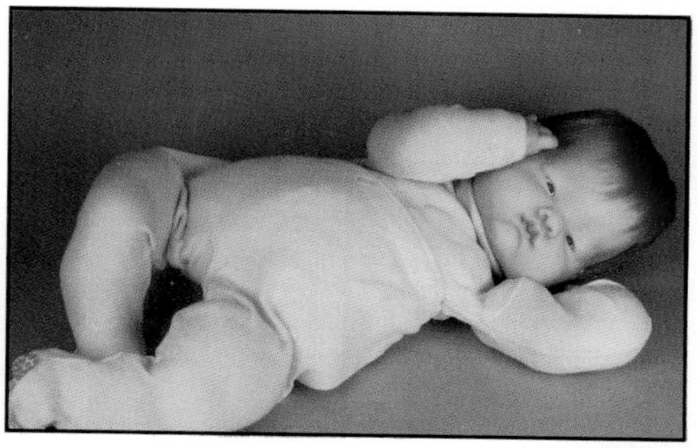

Baby Dear (1961), 18" in outfit #48200 called cuddly blue flannel sleeper. Courtesy Kathy Barry-Hippensteel.

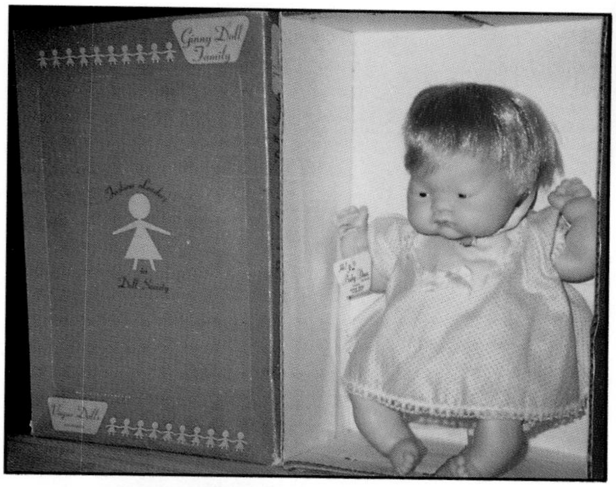

Baby Dear (1961), 12", wearing pink pin dot Toy Time Topper set #42271, mint in box. Courtesy Grace Evans.

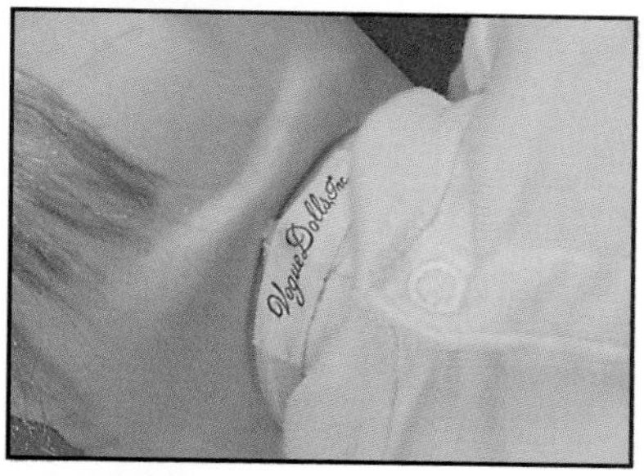

Baby Dear (1961), 18". Notice how tag is glued onto back of cloth body.

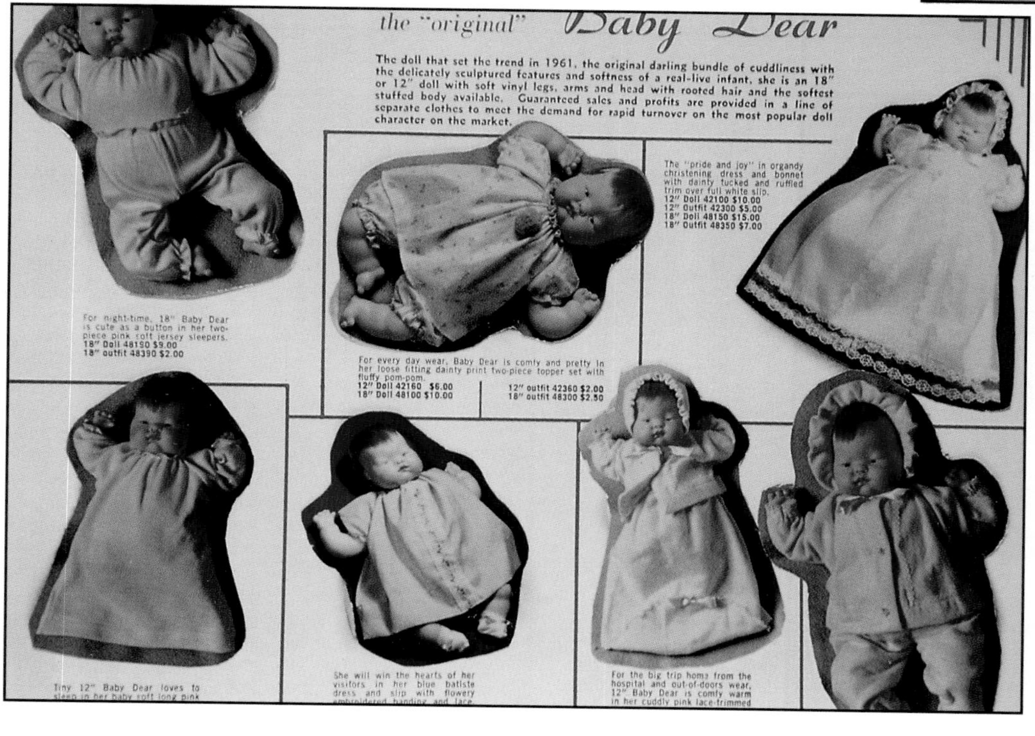

Baby Dear (1961), outfits for 12" and 18". Vogue brochure. Courtesy Wenham Museum, Wenham, Mass.

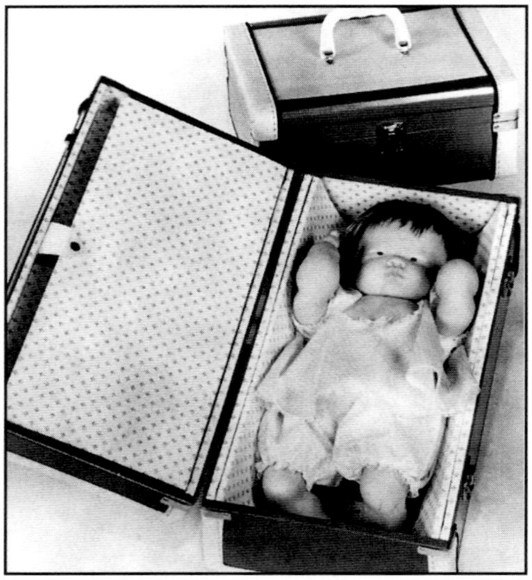

Baby Dear (1961), came in a suitcase wearing pin dot topper set. Courtesy Art Grobe.

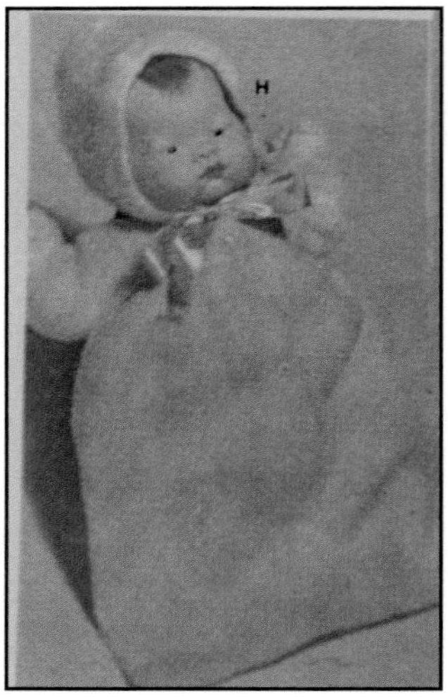

Baby Dear (1961), 12" in #42280, pink fleece pram bag and attached hood. Jordan Marsh catalog.

1962

Baby Dear (1962), outfits from Vogue catalog. Courtesy Wenham Museum, Wenham, Mass.

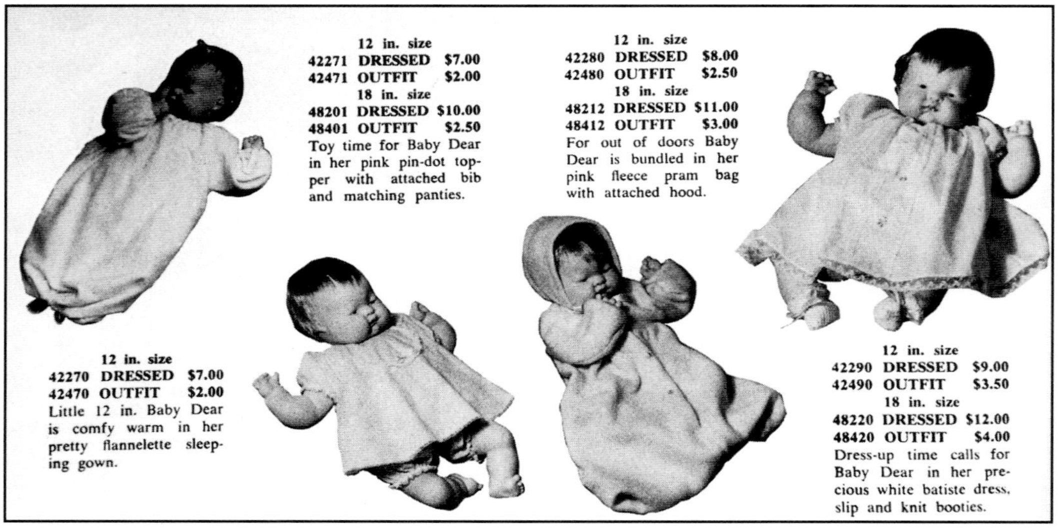

12 in. size
42271 DRESSED $7.00
42471 OUTFIT $2.00
18 in. size
48201 DRESSED $10.00
48401 OUTFIT $2.50
Toy time for Baby Dear in her pink pin-dot topper with attached bib and matching panties.
12 in. size
42280 DRESSED $8.00
42480 OUTFIT $2.50
18 in. size
48212 DRESSED $11.00
48412 OUTFIT $3.00
For out of doors Baby Dear is bundled in her pink fleece pram bag with attached hood.
12 in. size
42270 DRESSED $7.00
42470 OUTFIT $2.00
Little 12 in. Baby Dear is comfy warm in her pretty flannelette sleeping gown.
12 in. size
42290 DRESSED $9.00
42490 OUTFIT $3.50
18 in. size
48220 DRESSED $12.00
48420 OUTFIT $4.00
Dress-up time calls for Baby Dear in her precious white batiste dress, slip and knit booties.

Baby Dear (1962), 18" doll in #48110 with 12" doll in matching outfit, #42170, with replaced booties. Courtesy Kathy Barry-Hippensteel.

Baby Dear ad Montgomery Ward (1962) with 3 outfits: 12" outfit, piqué dress with braid trim down front; 12" outfit, pink pajamas; 18" outfit, pink coat with hood and pants with footies.

Baby Dear (1962), christening dress for 12" doll, #42300, mint in box. The 12" dolls had matching outfits to the 18" dolls. Courtesy Kathy Barry-Hippensteel.

Baby Dear (1962), outfit #48320, pink hooded jacket and matching footed pants, mint in box. Courtesy Veronica Phillips.

Baby Dear (1962), 18", Baby Dear, #48150, in christening gown which has the original $9.98 price tag attached. Shown with her box. Courtesy Kathy Barry-Hippensteel.

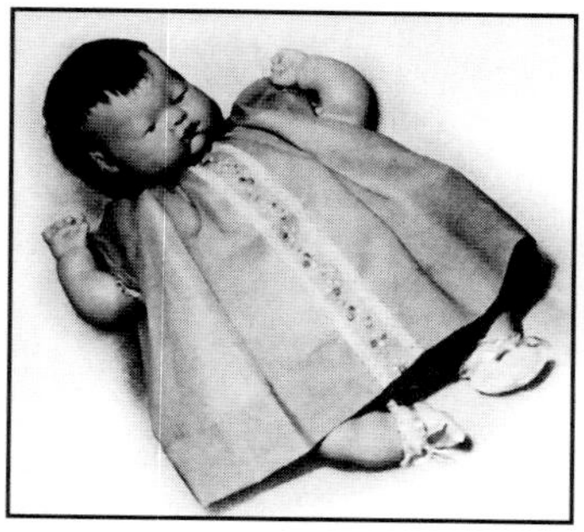

Musical Baby Dear (1962), with a Swiss music box inside. *Playthings ad.* Courtesy Wenham Museum, Wenham, Mass.

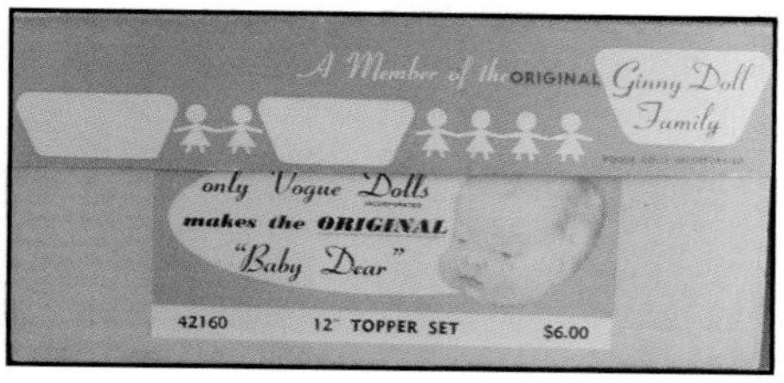

Vogue Baby Dear Box label (1962) for 12" doll, #42160, note unique perforated edge of display cut-out which is visible on top of lid. Courtesy Kathy Barry-Hippensteel.

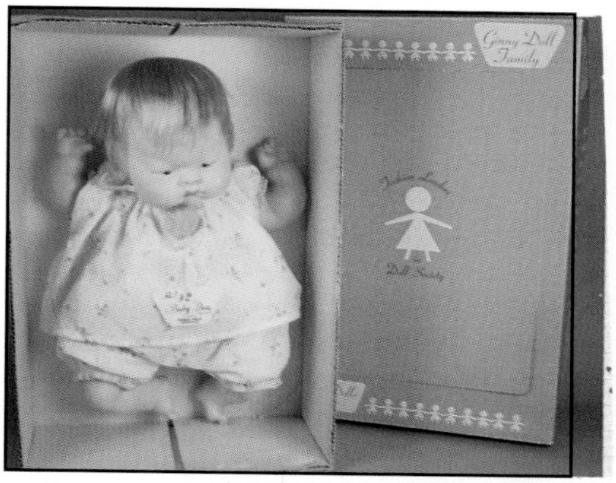

Baby Dear (1962), 12" doll in topper set #42160, all original. The doll was priced at $6.00. Courtesy Kathy Barry-Hippensteel.

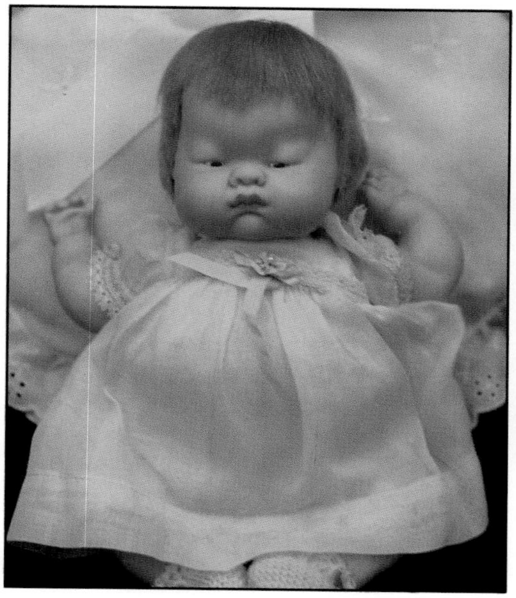

Musical Baby Dear (1962), 12", with a Swiss music box inside, wearing original white dress with flowers on front and knit booties. Courtesy Rosemary Korn.

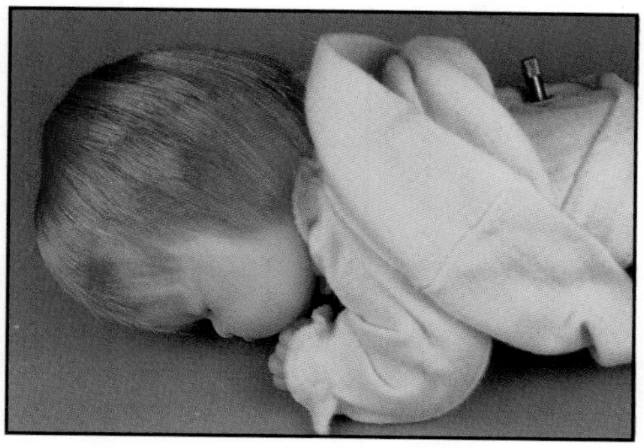

Musical Baby Dear (1962 – 63), 12", musical version of Baby Dear has a metal shaft with gripper surface which can be wound and plays "Lullaby and Good Night" as the doll wiggles. The doll is wearing 1963 sleeper outfit, #42350. (The 18" musical doll has a wooden turn key.) Courtesy Kathy Barry-Hippensteel.

Musical Baby Dear (1962), 18", with a Swiss music box inside, wearing original red footed outfit with red polka dots. Courtesy Rosemary Korn.

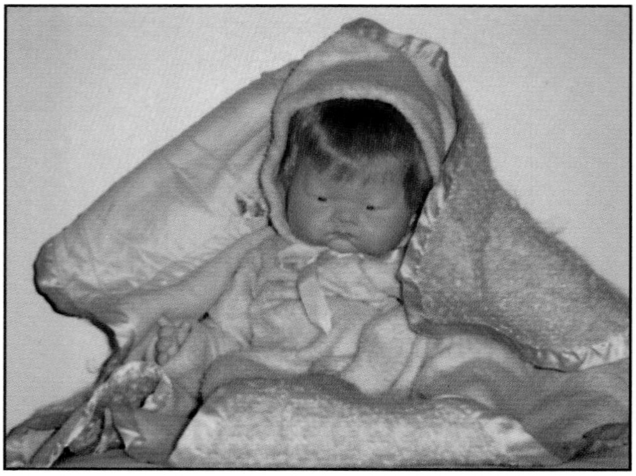

Musical Baby Dear (1962), 18", with a Swiss music box inside, wearing original lamb's wool-like blanket with Vogue tag. Pink hooded outfit not tagged. Courtesy Iris Troy.

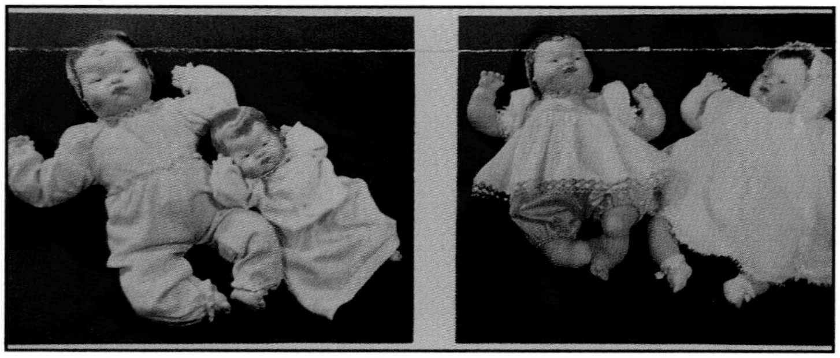

Baby Dear (1963), 12" and 18", pink flannelette sleeper, pink and white checked party dress, and white dress with bonnet. Vogue brochure.

Baby Dear (1963), 12", hand puppet. Child inserted hand inside pink fleece material to make doll's arms and head move. Courtesy Rosemary Korn.

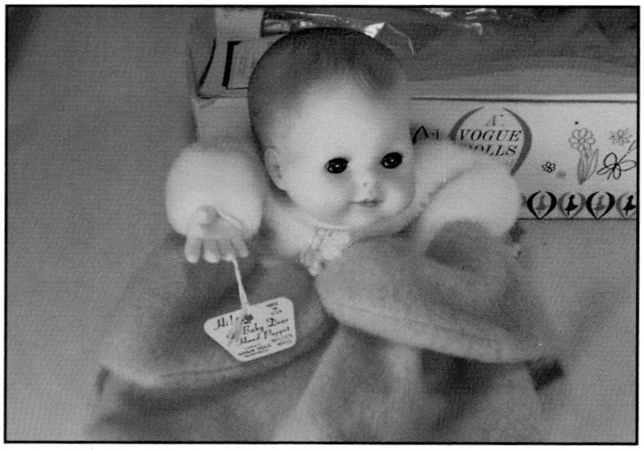

Baby Dear (1965), 12", hand puppet shown with box, came in both painted eye and sleep eye. $150.00 for either version. Courtesy Veronica Phillips.

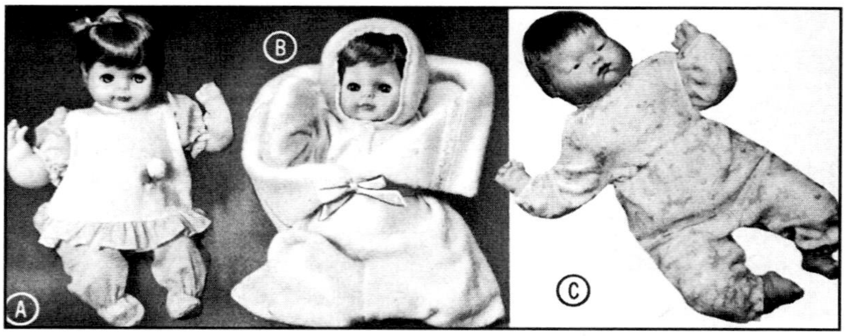

Vogue continued to sell the original 18" Baby Dear (on right) through 1968 even though they also sold a redesigned Baby Dear (two dolls on left). F.A.O. Schwarz catalog.

Redesigned Baby Dear

(1964 – 1980)

Description: 12" and 18", redesigned vinyl head and limbs, cloth body baby doll.
16" size added in 1969 – 70, open/closed mouth, sleep eyes, rooted hair.
A crier was available in 1965.
In 1969 black Baby Dear available.

Marks: Head: VOGUE DOLL/©1964
Back: None
Left Leg: ©1960/E.Wilkin.

Outfit labels: White twill with blue script: Vogue Dolls, Inc.

Outfit closures: 1958 "Dot starlet" snaps

Boxes: 1970s white box with navy and hot pink writing, cello front

Redesigned Baby Dear (1964) had a new head and sleep eyes. This broad face was only used one year. In 1965 Baby Dear's head was redesigned again and this new head was used until 1980. Vogue brochure courtesy Marge Meisinger.

Vogue redesigned Baby Dear and gave her a new head in 1964. They called this 12" and 18" doll "New, Pretty Baby Dear." She had sleep eyes and rooted hair and an open/closed mouth. New, pretty Baby Dear's body was still cloth and her limbs were floppy like original Baby Dear, however the face was a more generic baby face like other dolls. This head for this version was not designed by Eloise Wilkin. Deet D'Andrade did the wax electroplating for the mold for this later version of Baby Dear. Redesigned Baby Dear is marked VOGUE DOLL/1964 (on head); E. WILKIN (on back of leg). However, Vogue did use the same arms and legs designed by Eloise Wilkin. The 12" dressed dolls ranged from $5.00 to $7.00 and the outfits could be bought separately from $1.50 to $3.50. The redesigned 18" Baby Dear cost from $8.00 to $10.00 and her outfits cost $2.00 to $5.00.

1964: Redesigned Baby Dear had the same four outfits for the 12" and 18" except that the p.j.s were a one-piece sleeping gown for the 12" and two-piece pink pajamas for the 18". 12" Baby Dear came in a fitted case in 1964.

1965: A new head was used for Baby Dear. 12" New Baby Dear could cry in 1965. She came in two hairstyles, sculptured hair and rooted hair. She had four outfits.

The 18" New Baby Dear could cry "ma-ma" in 1965. She came in both sculptured and rooted hair, and had four outfits.

1966: No information is available.

1967: The 1967 F.A.O. Schwarz Christmas catalog shows a Baby Dear Trousseau for the 12" doll featuring the rooted hair, sleep eye Baby Dear dressed in her rose and white snowsuit with matching bonnet; with pink and white checked creeper set with duck motif; a terry cloth sleeper and a comb, brush and mirror set, packed in a 14" metal trunk. It also shows the 18" Baby Dear Doll in her pink and white checked play dress, and in her pink and white brushed wool bunting with matching bonnet and jacket.

1968: The 1968 F.A.O. Schwarz Christmas catalog features 18" Baby Dear in her two-piece fleece snowsuit with matching pom-pon hood.

In **1969** Baby Dear also came in a 16" size (as well as the 12" and 18" version) in both blonde and brunette rooted hair. She had four outfits for 12" and 16" dolls, and five for 18". 12" Baby Dear was available in a gift box featuring a pink nylon dress and bonnet, blue checked flannelette p.j.s, and a rose print topper set. Baby Dear 12", 16", and 18"also had a fitted wicker bassinet lined with taffeta and embroidered flowered nylon skirt. Black Baby Dear was available.

In **1970** Baby Dear was available in 12", 16" and 18" sizes in both blonde and brunette rooted hair. There was also a black Baby Dear. The 12" and 18" sizes also came in a sculptured molded hair version.

In **1971** the 12" Baby Dear was available with three hair choices as well as a black version. Baby Dear came in the 18" size in six outfits. She was available in blonde and brunette rooted hair as well as sculptured hair. There was also a black version.

In **1972** Vogue had the 12" and 18" versions of Baby Dear with three outfits for the 12" and six outfits for 18". However, in that year they had a cute variation. They had a 12" Baby Dear Brother and Sister in matching blue topper outfits. Brother had sculptured hair and a little bowtie on his outfit while sister had lace on her topper outfit. Baby Dear sold for $4.97.

In **1973** Vogue repeated the brother and sister variation but did not specify the name as brother for the 12" doll. They had a department store exclusive for the 12" and 18" Baby Dear as well as their regular line.

In **1974** there were five outfits for 12" Baby Dear and three for the 18" Baby Dear.

In **1975** Baby Dear was available in the 12" in four outfits. She came in both sculptured and rooted hair. The outfits available were a print nightie; red romper set; white and red topper set with teddy bear motif; and a fuzzy pink hooded jacket and footed pants outfit. She had sleep eyes and vinyl arms and legs with a foam-filled body. The 18" was available in either sculptured or rooted hair, has soft vinyl arms and legs and foam-filled cotton body, and says "ma-ma." She came in four outfits: a pink pants outfit with pastel animal print top; a white top with footed yellow pants, a fuzzy white top and navy footed bottom with a white cap; and a purple dotted sleeveless dress and bonnet. There was a Black Baby Dear in both sizes also.

In **1976** the 12" had two basic outfits, the nightie in assorted animal or floral prints or checks, and a white topper set. The 18" was available in black rooted hair but had only two outfits.

In **1977** there was only one outfit, a nightie, for 12" sculptured hair Baby Dear. There were two outfits for 18" Baby Dear brunette and blonde Baby Dear. There was new packaging that year, an angled window package with "Vogue Dolls Made with Love" and a heart on the front.

In **1978** there were three outfits for 12" Baby Dear and four for 18" Baby Dear. Her new outfits were a knit outfit and a christening dress. The dolls were available in black and blonde straight hair; 18" Baby Dear had a mama voice.

1979: Baby Dear came in 12" and 18" sizes. The 12" came only with sculptured hair and had three outfits. The 18" had black or blonde rooted hair and four outfits.

In **1980** there were three outfits for both 12" Baby Dear and 18" Baby Dear. 1980 was the last year Vogue made Baby Dear. Thus Baby Dear was one of Vogue's most successful dolls, right after Ginny, due to her popularity and longevity.

Baby Dears (1965), 12" top row, also showing Bunny Hug and Jama Baby using same arm and leg mold as Baby Dear. Vogue publicity shot. Courtesy Wenham Museum, Wenham, Mass.

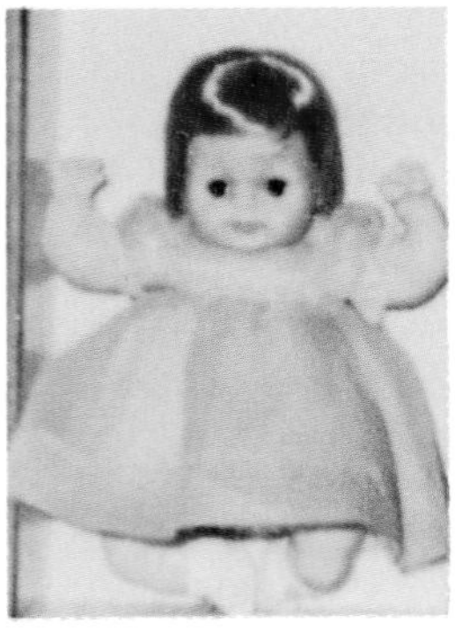

(1965) Baby Dear in case, Vogue publicity shot. Courtesy Wenham Museum, Wenham, Mass.

Prices

New Redesigned Baby Dear (1964)

12"	$150.00
12", MIB	$250.00
18"	$175.00
18", MIB	$275.00

Redesigned Baby Dear (1965 – 80)

12"	$45.00
12", MIB	$75.00
18"	$65.00
18", MIB	$95.00

1964

12" Redesigned Baby Dear – Redesigned head with sleep eyes
- Pink jersey sleeping gown
- Blue topper set with embroidered lamb and panties, booties
- Pink party dress with bows, booties
- Pink fleece baby bag and bonnet

18" Redesigned Baby Dear
- Two-piece pink jersey sleeper
- Blue topper set with embroidered lamb and panties, booties
- Pink party dress with bows, booties
- Pink fleece baby bag and bonnet

1965

12" Redesigned Baby Dear
- Pink jersey sleeper
- Blue sheer dress and bonnet
- Christening ensemble
- Pink and white eyelet outfit

18" Redesigned Baby Dear
- Pink jersey sleeper
- White fleece bunting
- Blue sheer dress and slip
- Pink and white eyelet outfit

1966

No information

1967

12" Redesigned Baby Dear
- Rose and white snowsuit
- Pink and white creeper set
- Terry cloth sleeper

18" Redesigned Baby Dear
- Pink and white checked playdress
- Pink and white wool bunting with matching jacket and bonnet

1969

12" Redesigned Baby Dear
- #4270, blue two-piece pajamas
- #4271, topper set with print teddy bear
- #4272, party dress and bonnet
- #4273, white fleece jacket and pink footed pants

16" Redesigned Baby Dear
- #4670, pastel dress
- #4671, pink dress and bonnet
- #4672, white christening gown
- #4673, white lacy dress

18" Redesigned Baby Dear
#4870, blue two-piece pajamas
#4871, topper set with print teddy bear
#4872, party dress and bonnet
#4874, white dress and bonnet
#4873, white fleece jacket and pink footed pants

1970

12" Baby Dear
#4280, maize nylon footed sleeper
#4281, pink and white checked pants and shirt outfit
#4283, pink dress and bonnet
#4284, pink and white fuzzy hooded jacket and pants
16" Baby Dear
#4780, blue sleeper, hat and blanket
#4782, pink and white fleece bunting
#4681, pink and white checked pants and shirt outfit
#4687, white christening outfit
#4689, white nylon dress with blue flowers and pillow ensemble
18" Baby Dear
#4880, maize nylon footed sleeper
#4883, pink dress and bonnet
#4882, red knit coverall
#4884, pink and white bunting

1971

12" Baby Dear
#426, pink knit pram suit with white furry hood
#424, pink brushed nylon nightie
#425, mint and white topper set
18" Baby Dear
#489, pink and white fleecy pram suit with clock on front
#488, pink lace dress and bonnet
#486, pink knit pram suit with white furry hood
#484, pink brushed nylon footed sleeper
#485, mint and white topper set with footed pants
#487, blue and white striped nylon dress and bonnet with umbrella on front

1972

12" Baby Dear
#420, pink or blue brushed nylon nightie
#422, blue topper set with white lace with horse on front (sister outfit to brother)
#423, white fleecy hooded jacket and pink footed pants
12" Brother Baby Dear
#421, blue topper set with white lace with horse on front and bowtie on sculptured hair doll
18" Baby Dear
#480, pink or blue footed sleeper
#481, pink footed topper set with bunny pushing baby carriage on front
#482, green lacy dress with bonnet
#483, white fleecy hooded jacket and pink footed pants
#487, pink lacy dress and bonnet
#488, white knit hooded sweater with pom-pon, and footed pants with cat motif

1973

12" Baby Dear
#425, pink or yellow nightie
#427, red and white checked topper with horse motif
#428, white fleecy top and blue and white footed pants
#426, red and white checked topper with horse motif, bow tie for boy doll
18" Baby Dear
#495, pink coveralls with apple and worm motif
#496, blue dress with knit sweater and cap
#490, pink or yellow p.j.s
#493, pink dress, knit sweater and cap
#491, pink and white checked topper set with face motif
#492, blue and white jacket, navy footed pants with pom-pons

1974

12" Baby Dear
#420, pink or yellow nightie
#422, green and white checked topper set
#423, white, fleecy, hooded jacket and red footed pants
#480, blue or yellow nylon pajamas
#482, green and white striped topper outfit with duck and umbrella motif
#483, navy hooded jacket and pants
#484, pink knit sweater and cap, with dress
#4855, white, lacy, long gown and bonnet
18" Baby Dear
#483, navy hooded jacket and pants
#484, pink knit sweater and cap, with dress
#4855, white lacy long gown and bonnet

1975

12" Baby Dear
#4600, print nightie
#4910, red footed pants outfit, teddy bear motif
#4620, white topper outfit with teddy bear motif, red footed pants
#4630, pink fleece snowsuit
18" Baby Dear
#4900, pink pants with pastel print blouse
#4910, white topper with duck in pocket, yellow footed pants
#4920, white fleece top with train motif, blue footed pants with white cap
#4930, pink dress with white polka dots with bonnet

1976

12" Baby Dear
#4202, nightie in assorted prints or checks
#4254, white topper set with red footed pants, teddy bear motif
18" Baby Dear
#4518, red polka dot topper with red footed pants
#4825, gingham dress with white apron

1977

12" Baby Dear
#304224, print nightie
18" Baby Dear
#304842, white cotton eyelet dress
#304843, gingham dress with white apron

1978

12" Baby Dear
#304236, pink knit two-piece outfit with cap with pom-pon ties
#304220, print nightie
#304232, long, white cotton christening gown with bonnet
18" Baby Dear
#304847, red topper set
#304849, blue dress with white polka dots
#304876, pink and white checked footed pants outfit with white apron
#304852, black, red, and yellow checked dress with white bodice

1979

12" Baby Dear
#304236, pink knit two-piece outfit with cap, pom-pon ties
#304220, print nightie
#304232, long, white cotton christening gown with bonnet
18" Baby Dear
#304803, blue nylon ribbon style dress
#304801, white dress with red pinafore with white polka dots
#304802, yellow windowpane checked dress
#304804, pink rose print long nightie with bonnet

1980

12" Baby Dear
#304220, nightie
#304224, pink knit footed outfit with pom-pon ties
#304236, white cotton christening dress
18" Baby Dear
#304809, white eyelet dress with blue trimming
#304808, pink fleece snowsuit
#304810, pink rose long dress with bonnet

Baby Dear (1969), 12" and 18", also showing black Baby Dear. Catalog courtesy Marge Meisinger.

Baby Dear (1969). Vogue added a black sleep eye Baby Dear by 1969.

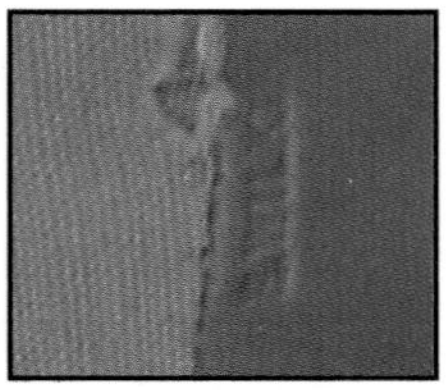

Baby Dear (1969). Although the sleep eye mold doll's head was not designed by Eloise Wilkin, it continued to carry Wilkin's mark on the limbs since the limbs were from her original 1960 mold. This is an example of a 1969 black sleep eye Baby Dear with a Wilkin mark on the leg.

Baby Dear (1970), cries "mama" soft cloth body, vinyl limbs, sleep eyes, in box. Courtesy Joe Kingston.

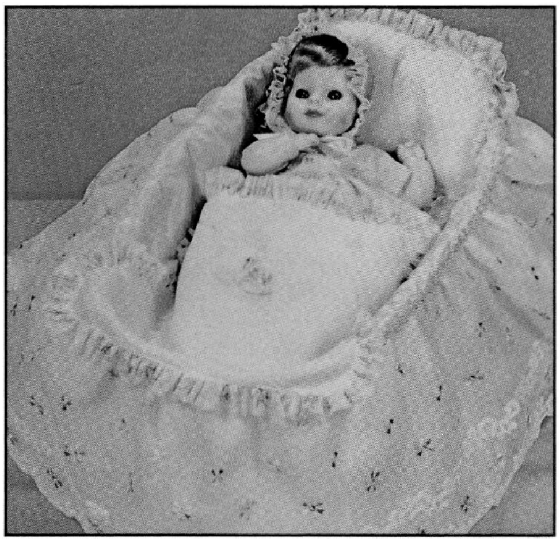

Baby Dear (1969), available in a fitted wicker bassinet lined with taffeta and embroidered flowered nylon skirt that year only. Catalog courtesy Marge Meisinger.

Baby Dear (1973), #4275, white topper set with duck and red footed pants.

Baby Dear (1975), 12", showing rooted platinum pigtails, available that year as well as sculpted hair. Catalog courtesy Marge Meisinger.

Baby Dear (1975), 18", wearing #4900, print top and pink pants, and #4910, white topper with duck in pocket, yellow footed pants. Courtesy Marge Meisinger.

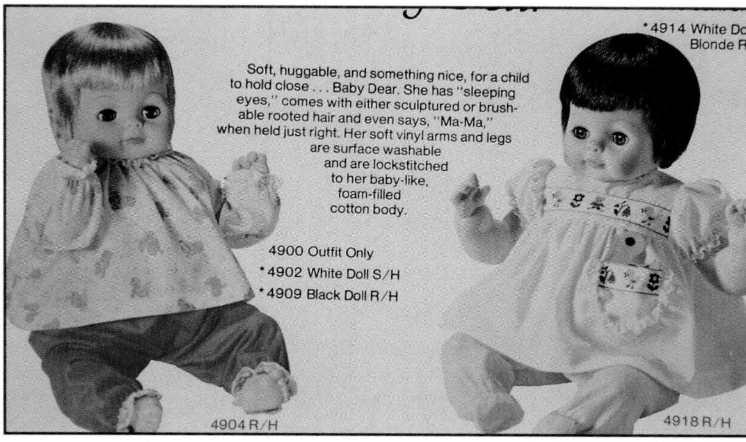

*4914 White Doll
Blonde R/H
Soft, huggable, and something nice, for a child to hold close . . . Baby Dear. She has "sleeping eyes," comes with either sculptured or brushable rooted hair and even says, "Ma-Ma," when held just right. Her soft vinyl arms and legs are surface washable and are lockstitched to her baby-like, foam-filled cotton body.
4900 Outfit Only
*4902 White Doll S/H
*4909 Black Doll R/H
4904 R/H
4918 R/H

Baby Dear-One/Bobby Dear-One

1962 – 1963

Description:	25", vinyl head and limbs, cloth body, size of a one-year-old child, open/closed mouth with two painted lower teeth, sleep eyes and lashes, chipmunk cheeks.	
Marks:	Head:	©/1961/E.WILKIN/VOGUE DOLLS/INCORPORATED
	Back:	VOGUE DOLLS/INC. (on a white tag with blue writing)
	Right Leg:	E.WILKING/©1961
Outfit labels:	1960 – 64:	White twill with blue script: Vogue Dolls, Inc.
Outfit closures:	1958:	"Dot starlet" snaps
Boxes:	White box with cello window with pastel pink around it. "A VOGUE DOLLS original" in navy and pink writing.	

Baby Dear was so successful that the following year (1962) Vogue introduced Baby "Dear-One." Baby Dear-One was a life-like, to-scale version of a one-year-old child. Baby Dear-One is described in the 1962 catalog as a "bouncy, flouncy 25" one-year-old darling." She is supposed to be Baby Dear grown up to be a one-year-old baby. A lovely poem in the 1962 catalog says, "Now that I'm one, I'm called Baby 'Dear-One'/I'm growing up and am now a big one/Please play with me and bounce me on your knee/I'll show you my two teeth and grin with glee."

Baby Dear-One has a vinyl head and vinyl limbs with a soft cloth body. Her fingers are modeled separately with the index finger pointing upwards. She weighs 4 lbs. 7 oz. She has sparkling moving eyes, rooted hair and a pudgy face with dimple and two painted front lower teeth and long, straight, blonde hair. She was designed by Eloise Wilkin and is marked on her head, 1961/E.Wilkin/Vogue Dolls.

There were three outfits in the Vogue catalog that year for Baby Dear-One. Baby Dear-One is very desirable and hard to find. She was priced $13.00 – $15.00 each.

Baby Dear-One was also advertised as an Original Vogue Doll only by mail from Montgomery Ward in

Baby Dear-One (1962) 25" vinyl head and limbs, cloth body in #55350, pink dress and bonnet, missing white vinyl shoes and socks. Notice detailed feet and toes. Marks: ©/1961/E.WILKIN/VOGUE DOLLS/INCORPORATED (on head).

Baby Dear-One (1962) Baby Dear is One 25" vinyl head and limbs. Vogue publicity photo. Courtesy Arthur Grobe.

1962. She is wearing her blue corduroy overalls with white felt duck on the front with blue and white striped shirt and cost $12.98. Perhaps the only difference was the different print on the jersey. Ward's advertisment said: "See how Baby Dear has grown, Now she's 1."

Baby Dear-One had a twin brother, Bobby Dear-One, who was the same doll with shorter hair, dressed in boy's clothes. In 1962 Vogue introduced the twins in red matching holiday outfits for the 1963 holiday selling season. They sold at $14.00 each. Bobby Dear-One did not appear in the 1962 Vogue catalog.

Baby Dear-One is shown in the 1963 catalog wearing three outfits. Bobby Dear-One wore a rose corduroy shorts outfit with lamb motif. Baby Dear-One was very successful for Vogue; hundreds of thousands of dolls were sold.

Baby Dear-One is not listed in the 1964 Vogue catalog. However, she is pictured in a newspaper dated March, 19, 1964, wearing her pink cotton batiste dress and bonnet and selling for $7.95; perhaps the store was selling left-over stock.

Prices

Baby Dear-One	
Doll in mint condition	$250.00
MIB	$350.00
Bobby Dear-One	
Doll in mint condition	$300.00
MIB	$400.00

1962

25" Baby Dear-One
#55330, pink jersey two-piece footed sleeper set
#55340, blue corduroy overalls with duck motif and blue striped jersey
#55350, pink batiste party dress and bonnet with flowered lace trim

1963

Baby Dear-One
#55530, two-piece blue footed sleeper
#55540, aqua hooded sweatshirt and pants, white shoes, sunglasses
#55541, rose jumper with rickrack and lamb appliqué, white puffy sleeves, white shoes and socks, matched Bobby Dear-One

Bobby Dear-One
#55542, pink bib shorts with rickrack and lamb appliqué, white short sleeved shirt, pink cap, white shoes and socks

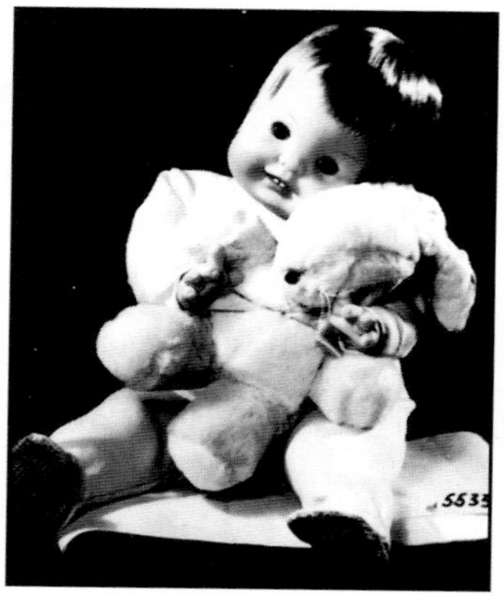

Baby Dear-One (1962), 25", outfit #55330, pink footed sleeper, too cute for words. Animal not Vogue. Vogue publicity photo. Courtesy Arthur Grobe.

Baby Dear-One (1962), 25", outfit #55340, corduroy overalls with striped jersey shirt, shoes and socks. Cost $12.98. Montgomery Ward catalog.

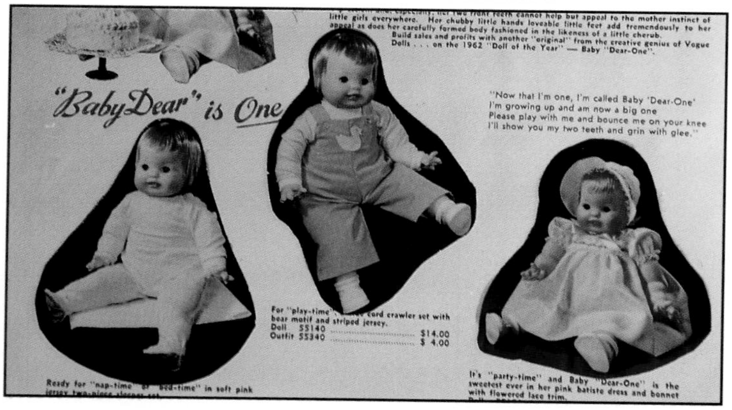

1962 Baby Dear-One (1962), 25", vinyl head and limbs, cloth body showing outfits from 1962 Vogue catalog. Courtesy Wenham Museum, Wenham, Mass.

Baby Dear-One, and twin brother Bobby Dear-One (1962), 25", red matching holiday outfits from 1962 Vogue flyer, sold at $14.00 each. Courtesy Wenham Museum, Wenham, Mass.

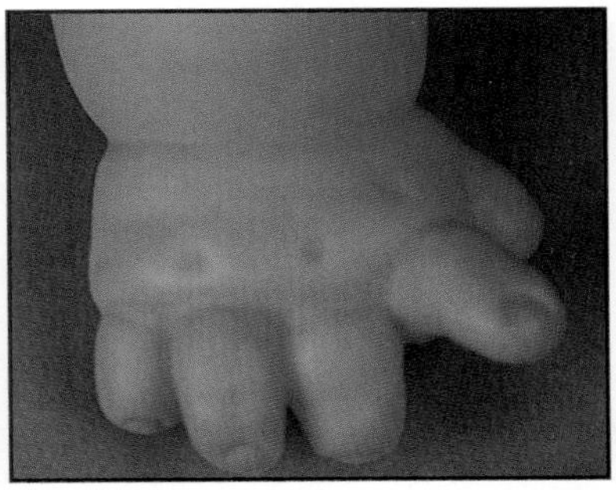

Baby Dear-One (1962 – 1963). The hands for Baby Dear and Bobby Dear were realistically molded by Eloise Wilkin. Courtesy Kathy Barry-Hippensteel.

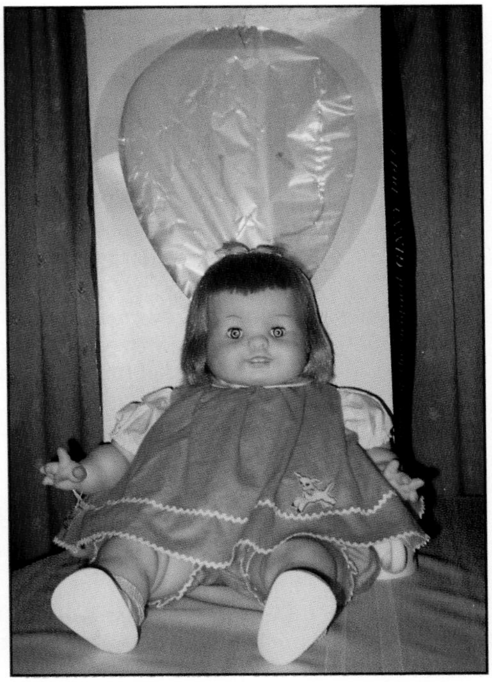

Baby Dear-One (1962), 25", #55350, pink dress and bonnet, shown with box. Courtesy Grace Evans.

Baby Dear-One (1963), 25", in #55541, rose cotton pinafore with lamb motif. Shown with box. Courtesy Grace Evans.

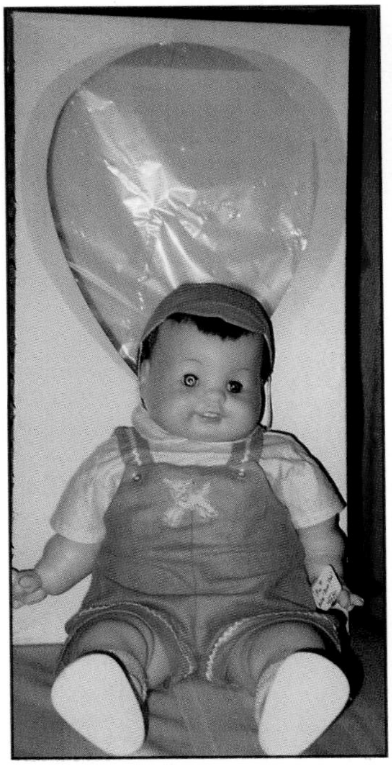

Bobby Dear-One (1963), 25", in #55542, rose cotton overall shorts with lamb motif. Shown with box. Courtesy Grace Evans.

Redesigned Baby Dear-One

(1965, 1967 – 1980)

Description: 25", redesigned vinyl head and limbs, cloth body size of a one-year-old child, closed mouth, painted eyes and lashes, sculptured or rooted hair. Cries "mama."

Marks: 1965, 1967 – 80: Head: Vogue Dolls./©1965

Outfit labels: White twill with blue script: Vogue Dolls, Inc.

Outfit closures: 1958 "dot starlet" snaps

The 1965 price list mentions a "New 25" Baby Dear-One who cries 'mama.'" She came in either sculptured or rooted hair in a pink and white eyelet outfit. This doll had a redesigned face.

It is unclear whether Baby Dear-One was produced in 1966 since the authors have not found a Vogue catalog for that year. Baby Dear-One is listed in 1967 and 1968 ads.

For the **1969** holiday season and **1970** line, Vogue came out with Baby Dear-One with a redesigned face. This doll was not designed by Eloise Wilkin. She was 25" with vinyl head and limbs, kapok stuffed cloth body, molded or rooted hair, sleep eyes, closed mouth. She had four outfits in 1970.

In **1971** she was available in three outfits. She came in blonde, brunette and sculptured hair versions as well as a black version available only in the pink knit pram suit. The F.A.O. Schwarz catalog shows her in the two-piece pink and white fuzzy pram suit.

In **1972** an added component was added to Baby Dear-One: a "mama" voice crier. She had four outfits that year.

In **1973** Vogue had an exclusive department store line of Baby Dear-One in a knit hooded pram suit.

They also had their regular line of Baby Dear-One with three outfits.

In **1974** she had three outfits.

In **1975** there were four outfits for Baby Dear-One. In addition, one outfit available from a department store was a pink lacy knit shrug and bonnet with white nylon dress. Another was a two-piece pink pajama set with ruffle down the side front. She was also available as a black doll.

In **1976** there were three outfits for Baby Dear-One who came in platinum hair that year.

In **1977** there was new packaging, an angled window package with "Vogue Dolls Made with Love" and a heart on the front.

In **1978** there were only two outfits for Baby Dear-One. Baby Dear-One still had the "mama" voice.

In **1979** there were two outfits for Baby Dear-One who had either straight yellow blonde or black hair.

In **1980** there were two outfits for Baby Dear-One. This was the last year Vogue made Baby Dear.

Mint Prices

Redesigned Baby Dear-One (1965+)	$65.00
MIB	$125.00

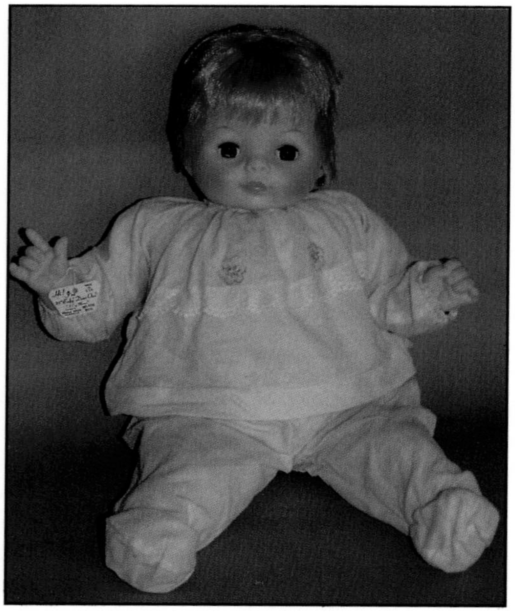

Baby Dear-One (1972) 25" with redesigned face. Vinyl head and limbs, kapok stuffed cloth body, molded or rooted hair, sleep eyes, closed mouth. Wearing #4502, pink p.j.s; #4532, three-piece hooded pram suit; and #4542, party dress and bonnet. Courtesy Shirley Niziolek.

1969
- #4553, yellow coat and bonnet

1970
- #4520, red and white overalls with white T-shirt
- #4518, blue coat and hat
- #4521, pink and white checked pants and shirt outfit
- #4524, pink and white hooded fleece jacket and footed pants

1971
- #4595, white and blue fleece pram suit with a bee
- #4522, blue print pajama set
- #4555, red knit jump suit
- #4562, pink knit pram suit with white furry hood

1972
- #4582, white knit hooded sweater with pom-pon and footed pants with cat motif
- #4502, pink footed sleeper
- #4532, white fleecy jacket with blue footed pants
- #4542, white nylon dress with yellow lace and knit sweater and bonnet

1973
- #4515, blue nylon pajamas
- #4525, white furry blouse with blue and white print footed pants and bonnet
- #4535, yellow dress, sweater and bonnet
- #4545, knit jacket and footed pants

1974
- #4500, pink two-piece p.j.s
- #4511, pink topper set with pink and white checked pocket
- #4522, pink knit sweater and cap, white dress

1975
- #4304, yellow pants with pastel animal print
- #4318, white topper with pink and white footed pants
- #4324, white fleece top with red footed pants white fleece cap
- #4335, blue dress with white sweater and bonnet

1976
- #4565, navy romper with red and white checked sleeves and bonnet
- #4574, yellow hooded sweatshirt and red pants
- #4584, gingham dress with white apron and white cap

1977
- #304575, pink p.j.s with duck motif

1978
- #304581, pink and white checked pants with white apron with rabbit motif
- #304575, pink p.j.s with duck motif

1979
- #304502, yellow flocked dress
- #304504, blue p.j.s with train motif

1980
- #304506, white eyelet dress with blue trim
- #304505, blue p.j.s with pink bib with train motif

Baby Dear-One (1969), #4553, 25", vinyl limbs and head, cloth body in yellow coat and bonnet. Courtesy Marge Meisinger.

Baby Dear-One (1975), #4304, yellow pants with pastel animal print. Courtesy Marge Meisinger.

Too Dear / Too Dear Brother

1963 – 1965 / 1963 – 1964

Description:	Vinyl head and limbs, closed mouth, sleep eyes, rooted hair, chipmunk cheeks, left arm bent, some have hole in behind. 17" and 23" available in 1963. 17" available in 1964 – 65
Marks:	23" 1963 – 65 Head: E.WILKIN/VOGUE DOLLS/1963 Inc Back: none 17" 1964 – 65 Head: ©1963/E.WILKIN/VOGUE DOLLS Back: None
Outfit labels:	1964 – 65: White twill with blue script: "Vogue Dolls, Inc."
Outfit closures:	1958: "Dot starlet" snaps
Boxes:	White box with cello window with pastel pink around it. A VOGUE DOLL original in navy and pink writing.

Vogue introduced its third doll in the Baby Dear series called "Too Dear" in 1963. In the 1963 brochure, Too Dear was shown as a 23" two-year-old likeness of the original Baby Dear. There was also a 17" version not listed in the Vogue brochure in 1963. Too Dear's face had chipmunk cheeks, sleep eyes, and rooted blonde hair. Too Dear was all vinyl, jointed at the hips, shoulders, and neck. She can stand and sit by herself. Too Dear has chubby dimpled legs. She is marked on her head: ©1963/E.Wilkin/Vogue Dolls. Unfortunately, Too Dear was not to-scale of a two-year-old child. Too Dear cost from $12.00 to $18.00.

The 1963 23" Too Dear came in four outfits: #53520, a mint jersey one-piece footed sleeper with ribbons in hair; #53540, a pink, blue, and white striped topper with pom-pons and a blue short sleeved shirt underneath, blue tights, black shoes, blue ribbons in hair; #53550, embroidered white nylon party dress with pink sash and pink slip underneath with matching bloomers, shoes and socks, pink ribbons in hair (this outfit matched Baby Dear's); and #53580, a pink fleece jacket, hat and muff, white strap shoes and socks. A pink jumper has also been seen. The 17" dolls had the same outfits; their numbers were #57500 – 57580.

Twin brother Too Dear had short, dark brown hair and was available only in 17" in 1963 as well as subsequent years. In 1963 he was wearing #57511, a pink rose velvet pants set. He is a very hard to find doll.

In 1964 and 1965 Vogue made Too Dear in only a 17" size. The 1964 Too Dear still had her straight blonde hair with bangs. The 1964 outfits for 17" Too Dear were: #57680, a yellow jersey two-piece footed sleeper; #57600, red and white striped clam diggers and blouse with red topper with appliqué face with eyes, white center snap shoes and white socks, red ribbons in hair for the girl; #57610, a pink nylon windowpane print sleeveless dress, white center snap shoes and white socks, ribbons in hair; and #57630, a brown fleece coat with brown felt hat and brown print dress underneath, white center snap shoes and white socks. The 17" Too Dear doll cost from $8.00 to $13.00 depending on the outfit. The clothes cost from $2.00 to $5.00.

Twin brother Too Dear came in only one outfit in 1964: #57601, red and white striped clam diggers and shirt with red topper with appliqué face with eyes, white center snap shoes and white socks which matched his sister's outfit. Too Dear boy had brown hair.

In 1965 Too Dear came in only the 17" size, had short curly blonde hair, and only three outfits: #57180, a pink two-piece footed sleeper; #57191, a pleated plaid skirt with red jersey shirt; and #57122, a brown fleece coat with hat and orange scarf.

Too Dear did not sell very well for Vogue, only about 50,000 dolls were sold. Too Dear is a highly prized doll to collectors and is very hard to find in original clothing. Mrs. Graves's collaboration with Eloise Wilkin on the Baby Dear line of dolls has brought joy to countless collectors of these life-like baby and toddler dolls.

Prices

Too Dear	
17" Mint	$250.00
23" Mint	$350.00
Too Dear Brother	
17" Mint	$400.00

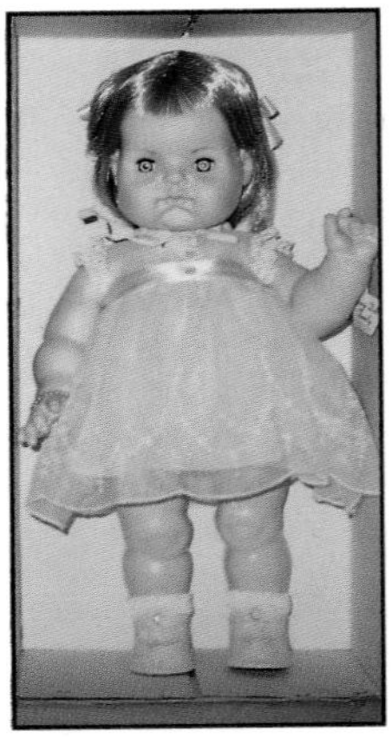

Too Dear (1963), 23", all vinyl two-year-old version of Baby Dear in #53550, party dress with pink sash. Shown in box with tag marked: Vogue Doll Family. Doll marked: ©1963/ E.WILKIN/VOGUE DOLL (on head). Courtesy Grace Evans.

Too Dear (1963), 23", in #53580 coat with fur muff and fur trimmed hat. Shown with Ted Nelson at the 200 Fifth Avenue showroom. *Playthings Magazine* Apr. 1963.

Too Dear (1963), 23", all vinyl two-year-old version of Baby Dear, #53550, showing four outfits available that year. Marks: ©1963/E.WILKIN/VOGUE DOLLS (on head). Vogue brochure.

Too Dear (1963), 17", in #57500 striped topper with pom-pons and tights. Courtesy Sherry Baloun.

Too Dear (1963), 17", all vinyl doll in tagged cotton dress #57550, with allover rosebud print and matching panties. The soft fleece pink coat with white trim is lined to match the dress. A pink bow is original to outfit. Replaced socks and shoes. Courtesy Kathy Barry-Hippensteel.

Too Dear (1963), 17" and 23", in mint sleeper #57580 (17") and #53520 (23"). Note difference in facial modeling; 23" has a rounder chin. Courtesy Veronica Phillips.

Too Dear (1963), 23", in #53540, striped topper with pompons and tights. Courtesy Veronica Phillips.

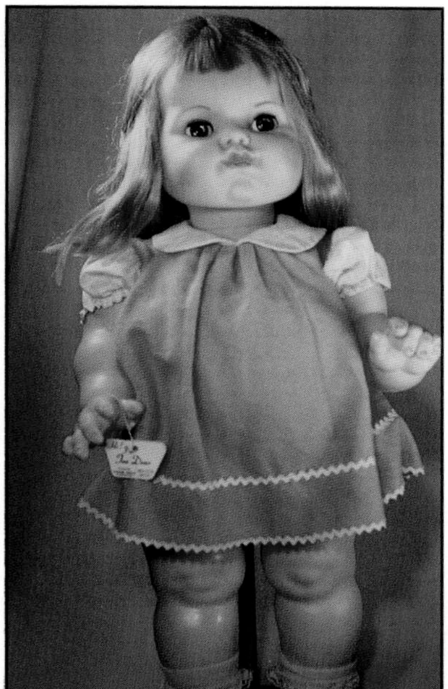

Too Dear (1963), 23", in pink jumper with white blouse, replaced shoes and socks. This outfit is not listed in the price list or brochure. Courtesy Veronica Phillips.

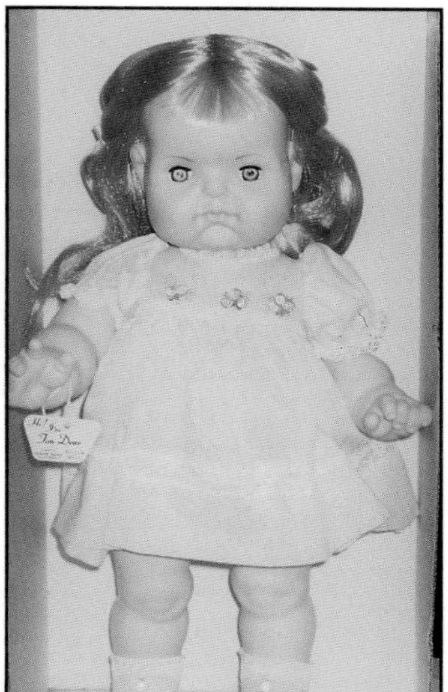

Too Dear (1963), #85 (as listed on box), white party dress with pink flower appliqué. Courtesy Sherry Baloun.

1964

Too Dear and her twin brother Bobby Too Dear (1964), 17", all vinyl in outfits #57600 – 57630. Vogue brochure courtesy Marge Meisinger.

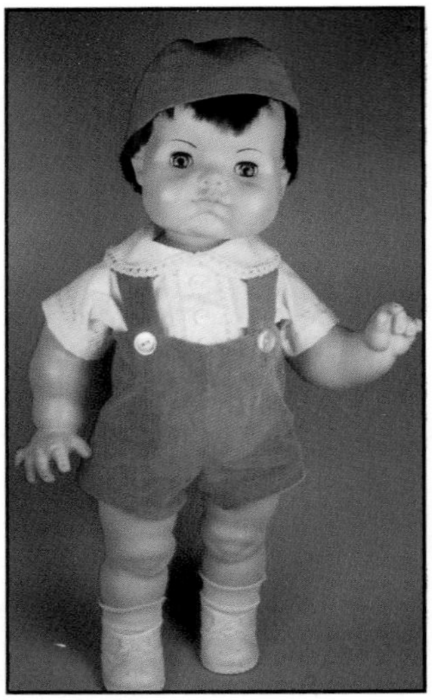

Brother Too Dear (1964) 17" vinyl doll, wears short velvet pants outfit #57511 with matching cap. Shoes are replaced. Courtesy Kathy Barry-Hippensteel.

Too Dear (1963) 17" in #57600, red and white striped pants, white top with striped sleeves, with smiley face. Courtesy Grace Evans.

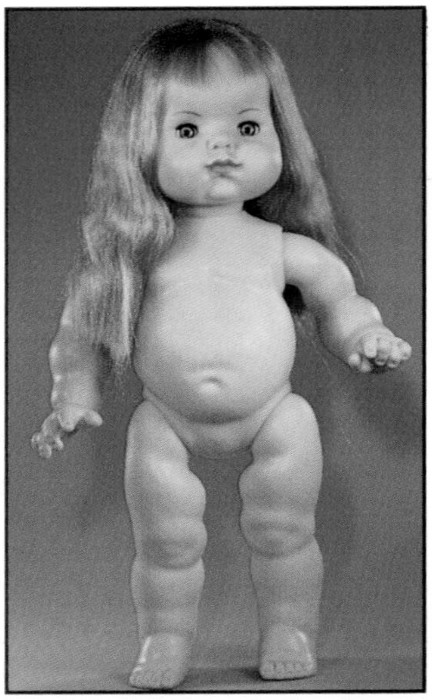

Too Dear (1963), 17", showing body construction. Notice chubby tummy and "chipmunk" cheeks and individual fingers. She also has a hole in her bottom.

1965

Too Dears (1965) 17" all vinyl. Vogue publicity shot. Courtesy Wenham Museum, Wenham, Ma.

Too Dear (1965), 17", #57191, plaid skirt and kerchief with red jersey top.

Littlest Angel
also called Saucy Littlest Angel

1961 – 1963, 1967 – 1980

Description:	1961 – 1963:	10½" vinyl head, hard plastic bent knee walker doll, sleep eyes. Vogue used the same doll as Arranbee Company's Littlest Angel Doll.
	1961:	Four different rooted hairstyles: a platinum pixie (straight hair), blonde Dutch cut, brown Dutch cut, and red shaggy hairdo.
	1962:	Hair came in two styles: a Prince Valiant straight chin length style with bangs in various colors, and a short shag hairstyle in platinum.
	1963:	Vogue called the doll "Saucy Littlest Angel." She came in two hair colors that year: straight red, really orange, hair and brunette.
	1964 – 1965:	There was no Littlest Angel.
	1966:	It is unclear whether she was available, since authors have not found a Vogue catalog for that year.
	1967 – 1974:	Littlest Angel, 11" and 15", all vinyl with jointed neck, arms and legs with rooted blonde, red, and brunette hair. The face mold for the all vinyl doll was different than the early 1960s vinyl and hard plastic version. The doll appears somewhat older, with more pronounced cheeks. She also came in a black version.
	1975:	Littlest Angel, 15", has a different face and body than previous years. Hands have spread apart fingers, legs are thinner, eyes are deeper blue.
	1976:	It is unclear whether she was available in 1976.
	1977 – 1980:	15", all vinyl.
	Marks:	
	1961 – 1963:	Head: R & B Back: R & B Doll Co.
	1967 – 1974:	Unknown
	1975:	Head: VOGUE DOLL/©1965 or ©1964
	1976 – 1980:	Unknown
Outfit labels:	1961 – 1963:	White twill with blue script: Vogue Dolls, Inc.
Boxes:	1963:	White with navy and pink print
	1969:	White with navy and hot pink print, with butterflies and flowers on side
	1975:	White with Vogue in hot pink and black writing, flowers below cello picture window

Vogue introduced Littlest Angel as part of "Ginny's Family" in 1961. She was called "Ginny's favorite cousin." Littlest Angel was the same doll as the Arranbee Little Angel (i.e., vinyl head and hard plastic bent knee body). The Littlest Angel doll is 10½" tall although described in catalogs as 11". Vogue's Littlest Angel came in four different hairstyles: a platinum pixie (straight hair), blonde Dutch cut, brown Dutch cut, and red shaggy hairdo. She cost $3.00 and came with panties and shoes and socks.

Vogue marketed Littlest Angel in an R & B box. Her clothes came in several versions of Vogue's own box with a clear front, plain color (no logo), and the cameo of the doll on the side. Vogue had a long-term relationship with Arranbee since they used some of R & B's composition 8" dolls for their Toddles line in the 1930s. The doll Littlest Angel was trademarked on June 29, 1954, and registered on May 31, 1956, by Arranbee. She is marked "R & B" on her head and back.

Wardrobe

1961: Littlest Angel had 11 outfits in 1961: #31240, a flouncy flannelette nightie; #31241, checked slacks and jacket set; #31242, a white rickrack dress with pleats; #31243, aqua play dress; #4210, sassy green roveralls; #31250, pinafore apron dress; #31251, flowered frock and leotards; #31252, crisp choir girl outfit; #31255, navy regulation coat; #31260, frilly blue nylon dress; and #31261, a pinafore and pantalettes set.

1962: In 1962 Vogue described Littlest Angel as a "cousin to the Ginny Doll Family" in its catalog. Her rooted hair came in two styles, a Prince Valiant straight chin length style with bangs in various colors, and a short shag hairstyle in platinum. The doll cost $3.00 and her outfits cost $1.00 – 3.00. Many of her outfits matched outfits for Ginny and Ginnette. There were 10 outfits available for her in the Vogue catalog: #31340, two-piece footed pajama set (matches Ginny); #31141, pink batiste sleeveless dress with lace trim; #31142, white cotton deck pants with anchor motif with red print over blouse; #31143, white piqué school dress with red, white and blue braid; #31150, blue dress with white polka dots with white pinafore and kitten motif; #31151, red dress with ruffly white lace trim; #31152, aqua corduroy slacks outfit with matching angel top;

#31153, pink and white striped apron dress with pink leotards; #31355, yellow wool felt coat trimmed with black velvet with matching cuddle cap; and #31160, pink organdy and felt ensemble with poke bonnet (matches Ginny).

She was also advertised in Montgomery Ward 1962 catalog as "original Vogue dolls only at Ward by mail." She cost $2.59 for the undressed doll wearing panties, shoes, and socks. This version was an 11" toddler with rooted hair cut in a Dutch bob, sleep eyes, fully jointed with bent knees. In the 1962 Ward catalog there were five outfits available, the only unique item being polka dot print pajamas with feet (89¢); the other outfits were available from the Vogue catalog.

1963: In 1963 Vogue called the doll "Saucy Littlest Angel" and there were six outfits for her. She came in two hair colors that year: red or really orange hair, and brunette. Her outfits were a red flannelette sleeper with a white felt duck on front, an aqua sleeveless school dress with a white and pink ribbon on front, a royal blue sailor outfit of an overblouse with a white felt anchor over red clam diggers, a yellow party dress with white apron, a red bib velvety dress with white short sleeves, and an aqua felt coat with white ribbon on front and matching hat. The dolls cost $3.00 undressed with panties, shoes and socks, and dressed dolls cost $4.00 to $5.00. Separate outfits were available from $1.00 to $2.00. This was the last year Littlest Angel had a hard plastic body.

1964 – 68: In 1964 and 1965 there was no Littlest Angel. However, Vogue issued an 11" all vinyl doll they called "Li'l loveable Imp." This new doll had a cute pug nose face and rooted long hair with bangs. L'il Loveable Imp also came in a black version, classified as a Li'l Imp.

1976:It is unclear whether Littlest Angel was available in 1976.

1977: In 1967 and 1968 she was listed in Vogue ads but the authors have not found a description of her.

1969: Littlest Angel was both 11" and 15", all vinyl with jointed neck, arms, and legs with rooted blonde, red, and brunette hair. She also came in a black version. The 11" doll came in seven different outfits: embossed cotton blue p.j.s with pom-pons, pink pants outfit with sleeveless top, white ribbed cotton dress with a red velvety skirt , blue sleeveless dress with hat, green and yellow print dress with straw hat, yellow sleeveless dress with straw hat, and navy coat and hat with white fur trim. 11" Littlest Angel was also available that year wearing a pink pants outfit with sleeveless top, embossed cotton p.j.s, with white ribbed cotton dress with a red velvety skirt in a metal trunk that had poodles on the outside and a gift box. The 15" came in four different outfits: purple and white checked long gown, blue party dress with bonnet, red jumper with white blouse and straw hat, and yellow knit sweater and pants with long knit cap.

1970: Littlest Angel was made in 1970 in all vinyl 11" and 15" sizes in both white and black versions. She had a varied wardrobe: 11" Littlest Angel came in a red playsuit with white lace; a skater with white fleece top and red skirt and a white fuzzy hat; a long pink nightie and night cap; and a blue velvet jumper with white long sleeves; and a yellow sleeveless dress. The 15" came in a red leatherette dress with white long sleeves, a blue checked skirt with suspenders and a white blouse, a yellow two-piece p.j.s set, and a white fleece coat and hat. There was also a metal trunk with the 11" doll that came with red knit playsuit, pink flannelette nightie and cap, and blue velvety school dress with panties and accessories. The trunk was pink and white had a lamb on the outside. There was also a black doll in both 11" and 15" sizes.

1971: In 1971 she also came in 11" and 15" versions. The outfits for the 11" were a red velvety skirt with white top and lamb motif, a woven woolen dress and vest, green p.j.s, blue velvet pants and white long sleeved shirt, and white fuzzy top with yellow pants. There was also two 11" Littlest Angel exclusives to department stores: pink checked nightie with white long sleeves, and a blue and white checked dress with white and blue pinafore. The 15" came in denim coveralls with white long sleeved blouse, a red print dress with white pinafore with ABCs on it, pink checked long nightie, and a blue and white snowsuit with white fur. The two department store exclusive 15" Littlest Angels wore either a yellow coverall with white sleeves and daisy motif, or a multicolored woolen dress. There was also one black doll that year.

1972: In 1972 there were five outfits for the 11" and four outfits for the 15" Littlest Angel. The 11" Littlest Angel wore a wool skirt with red jersey top, a navy pinafore with white flower motif, a pink print nightie, yellow overalls with white blouse, and a white fuzzy top with burgundy velvet pants and cap. The 15" wore a wool skirt with red jersey top, yellow overalls with white blouse, and a white fuzzy top with burgundy velvet pants and cap (all matching the 11"), and a blue checked long nightie. There was also a black doll available in the wool skirt. The 11" was available in a metal trunk with the red jersey and wool skirt, yellow overalls, and blue nightie.

1973: The 1973 Littlest Angels were available in 11" and 15" sizes. The 11" dolls had five outfits: checked long nightie, red plaid wool jumper and white blouse, blue and white checked topper set with girls on it, yellow dress with dark apron, and a red snow outfit with white bib collar and hat. The 15" dolls had the same clothes except the yellow dress which was available as an exclusive. In 1973 there was an exclusive department store line of the 15" dolls. The 15" Littlest Angels wore a long blue checked nightie and yellow short sleeved dress with dark apron. The black doll was also available as an exclusive. In the regular line, the 11" doll came in a fitted trunk with the wool jumper, blue checked pants outfit, and yellow nightie. The trunk was pink and white with a lamb motif.

1974: The 1974 line had five outfits for the 11" Littlest Angel: blue long nightie, a red and white checked pants and white topper set with strawberry motif, a white fuzzy snow top with long hat with pompon, and red pants, a yellow and white polka dot dress with white long sleeves, and a plaid skirt with white blazer with insignia. The 11" came in a trunk wearing the red and white pants and top, and came with the yellow dress and a pink nightie. The trunk was pink and white with a brown teddy bear on it. The 15" had the same clothes as the 11". There was also an exclusive department store line of a dark snowsuit with white yoke and pointed hat with white fur trim, a checked pants outfit with white topper with paper doll motif, a long checked nightie, and a plaid jumper with white long sleeved blouse. She also came in a trunk wearing the plaid jumper and came with the checked pants outfit with paper doll motif topper and a nightie.

1975: In 1975 there was a 15" Littlest Angel which came in several hairstyles: long braids, straight hair or straight side pigtails. The cutest doll that year was a throwback to Li'l Imp. She had orange side pigtails and freckles, wearing denim overalls with a watermelon motif and striped jersey shirt. Another doll with platinum pigtails wore a red dress with white polka dots a lace overskirt and daisy motif. A straight hair brunette was available in a white pinafore and red and white checked long sleeved blouse. Also an auburn straight hair doll was available in a yellow plisse dress with a matching jacket and beret. The denim overalls and red and white polka dot dress were available separately that year. 11" Littlest Angel was available in a pink Vogue trunk wearing her navy overalls with striped shirt, and a blue nightie and white dress with red and white checked sleeves. There was also a store special blonde with braided hair in white topper decorated with strawberries and red checked pants.

1976: It is unclear whether Littlest Angel was available in 1976.

1977: In 1977 there was only a 15" Littlest Angel with blonde braids wearing a pink polka dot long sleeved dress, white sheer pinafore with white tights, and another blonde wearing a crepe long floral print nightie with sleeping cap. There was also a black doll with long braids wearing the same nightie. In addition there was a 15" brunette in straight hair wearing a white pinhole lace short sleeved dress with white tights.

1978: In 1978 there was only a 15" Littlest Angel with blonde or red braids wearing a lace trimmed velvet party dress with pink bow in front with flowers in the middle, a pink long nightie, or a plaid dress with white apron. There was a 15" straight hair Littlest Angel wearing a navy and white polka dot dress with anchor motifs.

1979: In 1979 Littlest Angel came in only a 15" size and had blonde or black straight hair or in braids. These 15" dolls had painted lower side lashes. There was also a brown eye version and a black version. Her outfits were a burgundy and beige checked dress with beige apron; a white party dress with pink ribbon; a navy velvet dress with beige lace; a pink long bathrobe; a pink long nightie; and a navy with white polka dot dress with anchor motif.

1980: The 1980 Littlest Angel came only in the 15" size and had five outfits: a mint green long nightie; a red velvet dress with white lace; a dark purple velvet dress; a pink dress with tiny white polka dots; and a red plaid skirt with black velvet top and beret. She was also available in a black version. This was the last year Vogue made Littlest Angel.

Littlest Angel (1961) #31033, undressed with shaggy red hair, green eyes, and freckles (also marked as Li'l Imp); #31240, pink flannelette nightie with comb and mirror; #31241, plaid slacks and aqua felt short sleeved jacket; #31242, pleated dress with red rickrack trim; #31243, aqua and white sleeveless dress; #4210, green roveralls with jagged cuts on bottom hem and red checked shirt. Notice outfit is confused with Li'l Imp outfit.

Littlest Angel (1961) #31250, pink checked party dress with white pinafore, bow on hair; #31251, flowered frock with V yoke, bow in hair; #31252, lace trimmed choir girl top with pants; #31255, navy regulation coat and hat. Dress came on dressed doll; #31260, blue nylon dress, petticoat and bonnet; #31261, green felt jumper, print blouse with matching kerchief and pantalettes. From 1961 Vogue Catalog. Courtesy Wenham Museum, Wenham, Mass.

Prices

Littlest Angel

1961 – 63	hard plastic body, mint condition	$65.00
	MIB	$100.00
1969 – 80	11" all vinyl, mint condition	$25.00
	MIB	$45.00
	15" all vinyl, mint condition	$30.00
	MIB	$55.00
	Negro dolls add $10.00 to each price	

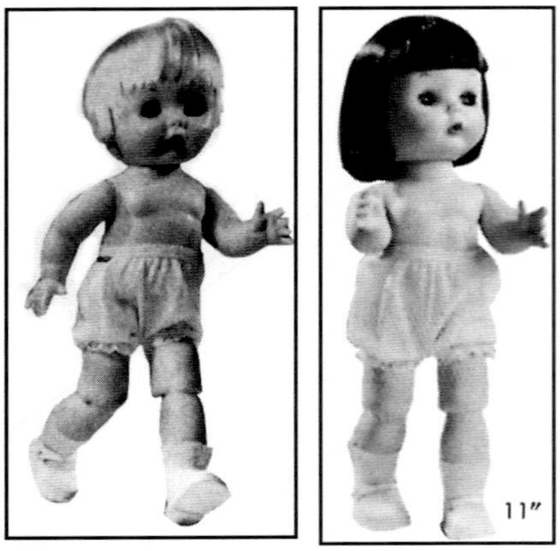

1961 – 62 (left) undressed vinyl head, hard plastic body and bent knee limbs, pixie cut hair, green eyes, and freckles; panties, vinyl button snap shoes and socks. (Right) undressed with blonde or brunette Dutch cut (bangs with chin length straight hair). Vogue catalog. Courtesy Wenham Museum, Wenham, Mass.

We dress alike with Ginny and Ginnette in our aqua cord slacks with matching angel top.
Doll 31152 $5.00 Outfit 31352 $2.00

Littlest Angel is a doll in her pink and white candy-stripe apron dress and matching pink legotards.
Doll 31153 $5.00 Outfit 31353 $2.00

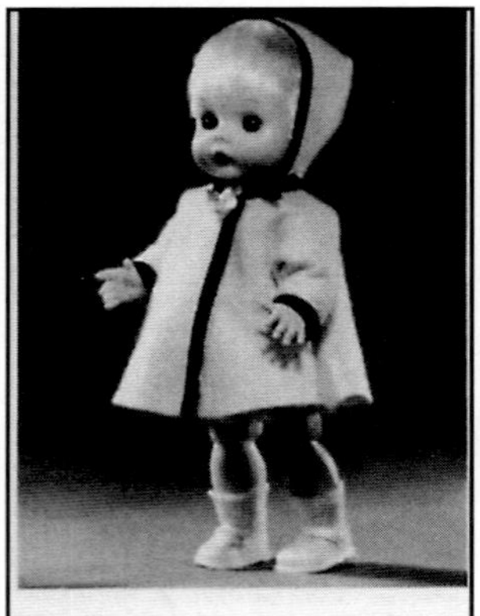

She catches admiring glances in her yellow wool felt coat and black velvet trimmed cuddle cap.
Outfit only 31355 $2.00

For a Sunday stroll with Ginny, matchmates in a pink organdy and felt ensemble with poke bonnet.
Doll 31160 $6.00 Outfit 31360 $3.00

Littlest Angel (1962) #31152 – 31160. Vogue brochure.

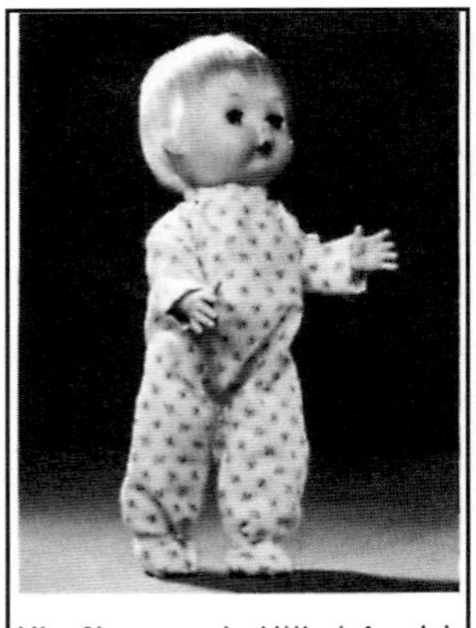

Like Ginny, cousin Littlest Angel is adorable in her matching dainty print two-piece pajammas.
Outfit only 31340 $1.00

A basic must for afternoons is a pink batiste dress with lace trim, satiny bow and rosebuds.
Doll 31141 $4.00 Outfit 31341 $1.00

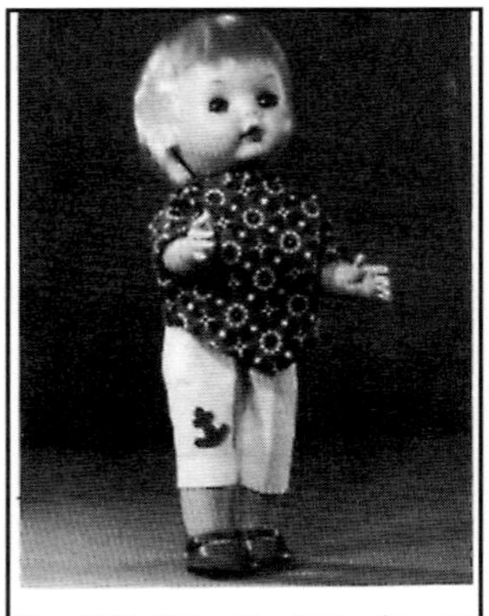

For play time or picnic fun we match Ginny's white cotton deck pants with red print over-blouse.
Doll 31142 $4.00 Outfit 31342 $1.00

For school in a patriotic motif, Littlest Angel wears a white pique with red, white and blue braid.
Doll 31143 $4.00 Outfit 31343 $1.00

For special days in school, a blue dot cotton with crisp white pinafore effect and kitten motif.
Doll 31150 $5.00 Outfit 31350 $2.00

Party-time is a success for Littlest Angel in a fiery red full-skirted dress with ruffly white lace trim.
Doll 31151 $5.00 Outfit 31351 $2.00

Littlest Angel (1962), #31340 – 31141, #31142-31151. Dressed dolls numbered #312+; outfits only, #314+. Vogue Brochure.

Littlest Angel (1962) in #31151, red dress with ruffly white lace trim.

Littlest Angel (1962), red dress with ruffly white lace trim, outfit mint in box #31351.

Littlest Angel (1962), in the Montgomery Ward catalog there were five outfits available: a white piqué dress with red, white and blue, braid trim down the front costing; polka dot print pajamas with feet; lace trimmed red party dress; blue slacks outfit with empire waist short sleeved blouse; and yellow felt coat and hat with velvet trim. Outfits cost from 89¢ to $1.79. Ward catalog.

1963

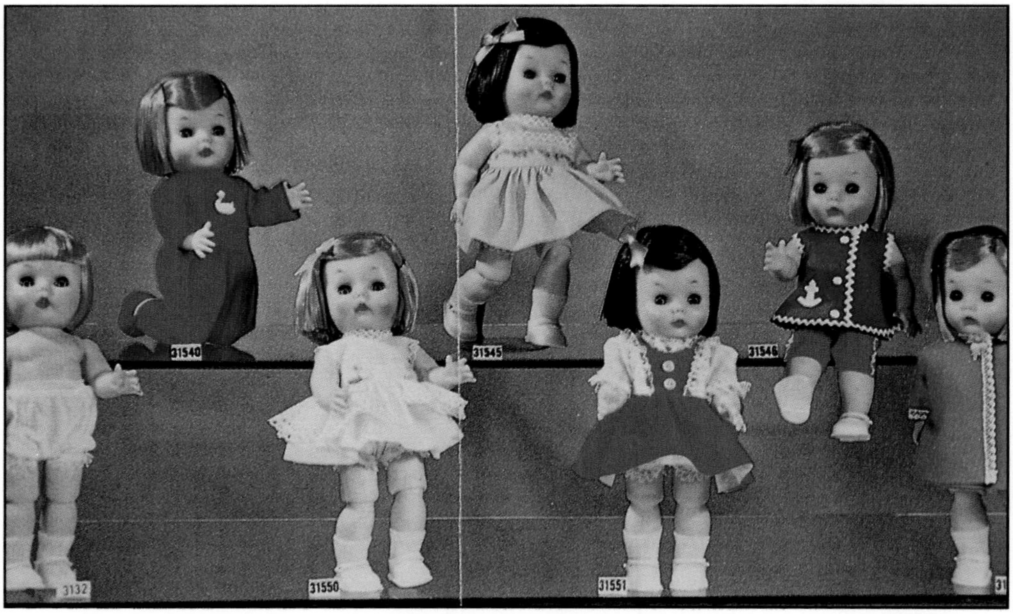

Littlest Angel (1963), outfits #31540-31753. Vogue brochure.

Littlest Angel (1961-63), 11", soft vinyl head, hard plastic bent knee body and limbs, wearing red and white checked overalls and sun hat outfit with white organdy blouse.

Littlest Angel (1961-63), 11", soft vinyl head, hard plastic bent knee body and limbs, wearing red and white checked dress with white apron, shown with coordinating Ginny outfit.

Littlest Angel (1963), 11", all vinyl, wearing blue polka dot dress with kitty motif. Doll is unmarked. Outfit is shown in 1962 brochure on hard plastic doll. Tag on clothes Vogue Dolls Inc., in blue script. Wrist tag, Littlest Angel. Missing shoes and white tights. Shown with circa 1963 box. Courtesy Ann Tardie.

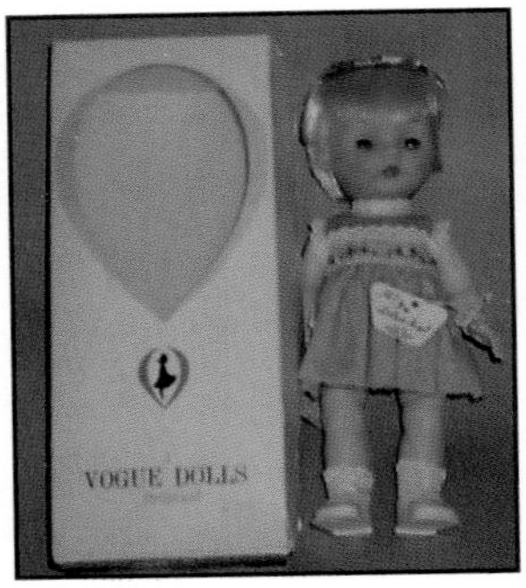

Littlest Angel (1963), 11", all vinyl, platinum blonde with blue dress with pink and yellow flowers and white tights. Doll is unmarked. Tag on clothes Vogue Dolls Inc. in blue script. Wrist tag, Littlest Angel. Private collection.

1969 – 1980

Littlest Angel (1969), 11" and 15", all vinyl with jointed neck, arms, and legs rooted blonde, red, and brunette hair. She also came in a black version. Vogue catalog. Courtesy Marge Meisinger.

Littlest Angel (1969), 11", all vinyl in blue, pink, and white piqué flowered dress with white cotton knit tights. Not pictured in Vogue catalog but shown in a store catalog.

Littlest Angel (1970), 11", in outfit #3122, blue velveteen jumper with white cotton blouse and black felt buttons.

Littlest Angel (1975), 15", #6515, pink cotton polka dot dress with white eyelet overskirt and white lace trim. Note Tonka box. Marks: Head: VOGUE DOLL/©1965.

Littlest Angel (1975), 11", in straight side pigtails, available that year only, wearing #6527, denim overalls with a watermelon motif and striped jersey shirt (a replay of the Li'l Imp). Vogue catalog courtesy Marge Meisinger.

Littlest Angel (1976) dressed in American Revolution era clothing. Probably a store special for the Bicentennial. Courtesy Joe Kingston.

Ginny Baby

1959 – 1982

Description:

1959 – 1960: 18" all vinyl baby doll, jointed at head arms and legs, sleep eyes, blonde rooted Saran hair or molded hair; a drinking and wetting doll.

1961: 12", 16", 18", 20" sizes available, all vinyl jointed at head arms and legs, sleep eyes, blonde rooted Saran hair or molded hair; a drinking and wetting doll.

1962 – 1963: 12", 16", 18," 20" sizes; 8" was added, a dry/nurser doll (i.e. nursing opening but had a closed bottom without tube through body to drain water). Used original 1955 body from 8" painted eye Ginnette (i.e., without metal squeaker in back). Molded or rooted hair in two styles: platinum pixie or blonde bob with side swept bangs. In 1963 an upswept chignon hairstyle was available. 18" available in one style, platinum pixie hair wearing pink checked gingham dress with white organdy apron.

1964 – 1965: 8", 12", 16", 18" sizes available. In 1965 rooted Saran blonde bob or platinum pixie or molded hair and black dolls in these sizes with brown bob; all sizes are advertised as "Vogue drink and wet" dolls.

1966: Three sizes; no specific documentation.

1967: Doll was available but no specific information available.

1968: All vinyl; 12" and 16" size; same description as 1964.
Black dolls advertised in both sizes.

1969: 12" and 16" all vinyl, same description as 1964. Hairstyles were flatter bobs or molded hair; black dolls advertised in both sizes.

1970 – 1975: 12", 16", 25." 25" was a drink and wet doll in 1970 only.
In 1972 a brother, #7690 (#7691 black doll), and sister #7604 (#7604 black doll) were available in matching red outfits.
12" available through 1976.
16" was drink and wet, available through 1980.

1976: No information available.

1977 – 79: 16", and 8" Ginny Baby Shower n' Bath with new mold and painted eyes; packaged with tub, hairbrush, diaper, wash cloth; drink n' wet doll.

1978 – 80: The new 8" painted eye Ginny Baby doll, #302081, with carry case and layette by Lesney.

1980: 16" only.

Marks:

1959 – 60:	Unknown.		
1961:	12":	Head:	GINNY BABY/VOGUE DOLLS INC.
		Back:	None
	16" and 18":	Head:	GINNY BABY/VOGUE DOLLS INC.
		Back:	None or VOGUE DOLL
	20":	Head:	GINNY BABY/10/Vogue Doll Inc.
		Back:	None
1962 – 1963:	8":	Head:	None or 32
		Back:	VOGUE DOLLS/INC (on lower back)

12", 18" and 20" same as 1961 – 62

Wrist Tag: White paper with black print hanging from wrist on a string;
Side 1: Hi! I'm Ginny Baby/Created by/VOGUE DOLLS INCORPORATED/MALDEN/MASS MADE IN USA;
Side 2: Ginny Doll Family/FASHION LEADERS/IN DOLL SOCIETY

Dress Tag: None or white cotton with blue print: Vogue Dolls Inc., Made In USA

1964 – 65:	8":	Back: VOGUE
	12", 18", 20":	Same as 1961 – 62
1966 – 67:	No documentation available	
1968:	12":	Same as 1961 – 62
	18":	Unknown
	Dress Tag:	Same as 1961 – 62
	Wrist tag:	Same as 1961 – 62

1969:	12":	Same as 1961 – 62
	18":	GINNY BABY/VOGUE DOLLS INC./1969
Dress Tag:	None or white cotton, Made In USA	
Wrist Tag:	Same as 1962	
1970 – 1975:	12", 16":	Same as above
	25":	Unknown
1977 – 1979:	8":	Unknown
	16":	Same as above
1980 – 81:	Head:	VOGUE

Wardrobe:

1959: A total of six outfits available either on dressed dolls or separately: blue plaid can-can romper, pink organdy dress, polished cotton topper and pants set, and white dress. Two outfits, #7430, yellow flannelette sleeper and, #7480, pink pram suit with zipper closing and white rabbit fur cloth trim and mittens, matched Ginnette.

1960: Available as dressed dolls in sleeper with slippers, #7130; pink cord coat, hat and dress, #7170; blue dot pinafore dress and hat, #7180; white dot nylon dress, #7190.
All outfits also available as separate outfits #73+

1961: 12" #72260, pink and blue nylon dress, and #72261, blue nylon dot dress.
16" #76270, assorted pink and blue nylon dress, #76271, pink fleece bunny jacket and pants.
18" #78280, assorted pink and blue nylon dot.
20" #70290, assorted pink and blue nylon dress, #70291, pink fleece bunny jacket and pants.

1962: White lace trimmed angel top over rose velvet pants available for 8", 12", 16", and 20" dolls. Blue dot topper dress with matching bloomers available for 12" doll. Aqua corduroy footed overalls with flowered trimmed white blouse available for 16" doll. Pink checked gingham dress with white organdy apron available for 8", 12", 16", and 20" dolls.
White nylon dress and bonnet over a blue slip available for 8", 12", 16", and 20" dolls.

1963: White velvet top with white pants with black ribbon trim, blue dress, white footed sleeper, pink fleece hooded jacket and pants, white dress and bonnet, pink and white topper set, polka dot dress, and bonnet.

1964: 12" and 16" only in molded hair dolls in pink topper set; pink dress and bonnet; fleece bunting. Rooted hair dolls, all sizes, came in blue dress with white apron with blue polka dots, hooded fleece jacket with animal motif and corduroy slacks; pink and white checked topper set with cat motif with pink pants; yellow party dress; red velvety and white eyelet dress-up topper; flower and lace trimmed white organdy dress; petticoat and matching bonnet. Matching outfits all four sizes.

1965: Fitted cases, #1788 and #1728 (sculpted hair), eyelet dresses, red velvety lace trimmed dresses, blue and white sheer apron dress.

1970: 12": Maize two-piece topper set, #7200; red and white fleece bunting set, #7201.
16": Pink nylon ensemble (dress and bonnet), #7224; three-piece pink dot topper set #7600; red and white topper set. #7623; maize and white pram set, #7625 (available for both sizes).
25": Pink dress and hat #7824; blue topper set, #7823; red and white coat ensemble, #7825.

1971: Pink dress and bonnet, #7202; pink and white ensemble, #7612; blue bunting set, #7280;

1972: A variety of bunting, layette, and dresses outfits. Matching Brother and Sister in red dress and pants with vest and white shirt.

1973 – 75 A variety of topper sets; fleece bunting sets; knit pram suits.

1977 – 79 Various traditional baby sleeper, play and knit outfits for the 16" doll included dresses and sun hats with ruffled edges instead of tie-on bonnets. A distinctive new Ginny Baby outfit, #307613, was introduced in 1978 with jeans and a shirt printed "Ginny's First Jeans" with pink checked cuffs and sun hat.

1981 – 1982: Cotton dresses and outfits typical of earlier styles.

Ginny Baby Marketing

The adorable 18" Ginny Baby with both rooted and sculpted hair was introduced in 1959 to broaden the Ginny Doll Family. The new 18" doll enabled Vogue to meet a popular demand for large baby dolls. Vogue stressed to dealers that, "The new 18" Ginny Baby makes it easy to order large dolls, miniature dolls and their outfits – all from one source." Ginny Baby was a reasonably priced doll, costing $9.00.

Ginny Baby developed such a following that, in addition to adding 12", 16", and 20" sizes in 1961, Vogue added an 8" version in 1962. This meant that Vogue marketed two 8" baby dolls, Ginny Baby and Ginnette (at least from 1962 – 64), in both rooted and sculptured hair versions, with many similar outfits. It is confusing for many collectors to identify these dolls without wrist tags. To further confound the issue, examination of both dolls reveals that 8" Ginny Baby and 8" Ginnette have the same face. At some point, their common head mold was changed to accommodate larger eyes, and the new mold was used for both dolls.

One of the few differences is that Ginny Baby was not a drink n' wet doll in 1962 and 1963, and was marked VOGUE DOLLS/INC. on the back, while Ginnette was a drink n' wet doll, and was marked VOGUE on the back for those same years. Identification for other years, beginning in 1964 when both are drink n' wet dolls, relies primarily on wrist tags or outfits, since the bodies appear to be the same mold with the same VOGUE mark on the back. However, collectors have a difficult time making a distinction between Ginny Baby and Ginnette dolls from the mid 1960s because at that time the dolls were selling extremely well, and to complete orders expediently, heads with hairstyles unique to one doll (i.e., Ginny Baby's 1963 chignon hairstyle) were sometimes used interchangeably between Ginnette and 8" Ginny Baby. These dolls are found that way mint in the box today. Both Tonka and Lesney continued the Ginny Baby line in 12" and 16" sizes in the early 1980s. Lesney decided that Ginny Baby was best marketed with the other Drink n' Wet dolls (i.e., Precious Penny, etc.) and featured these dolls together in the catalog. The exception to this was the 8" painted eye version of Ginny Baby which Lesney promoted heavily from 1977 – 1979 as a shower n' bath novelty doll. Generally, however, the traditional Ginny Baby introduced by Vogue in 1959 was a strong selling baby doll. It no longer appeared in Lesney catalogs in the early 1980s. Ginny Baby remains one of the most popular of Vogue's vinyl baby dolls.

Ginny Baby Doll Availability

Year	8"	12"	16"	18"	20"	25"
1959 – 60				Yes		
1961		Yes	Yes	Yes	Yes	
1962 – 63	Yes	Yes	Yes	Yes	Yes	
1964	Yes	Yes	Yes	Yes		
1964	Black dolls added to Ginny Baby Line in 8" to 18"					
1965	Yes	Yes	Yes	Yes		
1966	Three sizes available, exact sizes unclear.					
1967	Doll was available, exact sizes unclear.					
1968 – 69			Yes		Yes	
1970		Yes	Yes			Yes
1971 – 75			Yes	Yes		
1976	No information available.					
1977 – 79	Yes		Yes			
1980			Yes			
1981 – 82		Yes, other sizes not specified				

Mint Prices
Ginny Baby 1959 – 1978

8", 12" vinyl head, body, sleep eyes	$20.00 - $40.00+
16"- 20"	$30.00 - $45.00+
25"	$40.00 - $75.00+

Ginny Baby (1959) 18", vinyl doll with sculptured and rooted hair: (top) #7430, flannelette sleeper; (bottom left to right) #7460, can-can sunsuit; #7461, pink organdy dress; #7462, aqua two-piece topper set. Vogue catalog page. Courtesy Marge Meisinger.

Ginny Baby (1959), 18", dolls with rooted hair: (left) #7480, pink pram suit; #7491, white cotton dress and bonnet. Vogue catalog page. Courtesy Marge Meisinger.

I'm Ginny Baby
Ginny Doll Family

Ginny Baby (1960s), mint in box Ginny Baby outfit, #7390, white organdy with lace trim, and #7380, blue cotton with white dots for 18" doll. Courtesy Barbara Hack.

12 In.
$4.69
18

Ginny Baby (1962), exclusive outfits available only by mail from Montgomery Ward. 12" and 20" dressed in a lace trimmed white angel top with bright red velvet pants with white lace trim, shoes and socks. She drinks and wets, has rooted brown hair and soft vinyl skin, and is fully jointed. The 12" costs $4.69 and the 20" costs $7.44. Montgomery Ward catalog.

I'm cuddly Ginny Baby
Everyone loves a baby doll! Don't you! I come in several sizes—8", 12", 16", 18" and 20"—so that all little girls may enjoy at least one of me. I'm made of soft completely safe washable vinyl and love to drink from my bottle. I come dressed in several different outfits and with safe, non-toxic sculptured hair or rooted hair in two adorable styles — platinum pixie or soft blonde bob with side-swept bangs.
Ginny Baby is dressed for company in her white lace trimmed angel top over bright rose velvety pants.
8" Doll 78140 $4.00
12" Doll 72150 $5.00
16" Doll 76170 $7.00
20" Doll 70180 $8.00
For romping and gurgles, 12" Ginny Baby wears a lace trimmed blue dot topper with matching bloomers.
12" Doll 72140 $4.00
16" Ginny Baby says bounce me on your knee in my aqua cord twinkle toed overalls with separate flower-trimmed white blouse.
16" Doll 76150 $5.00

Ginny Baby (1962), #78140-76150. Vogue brochure.

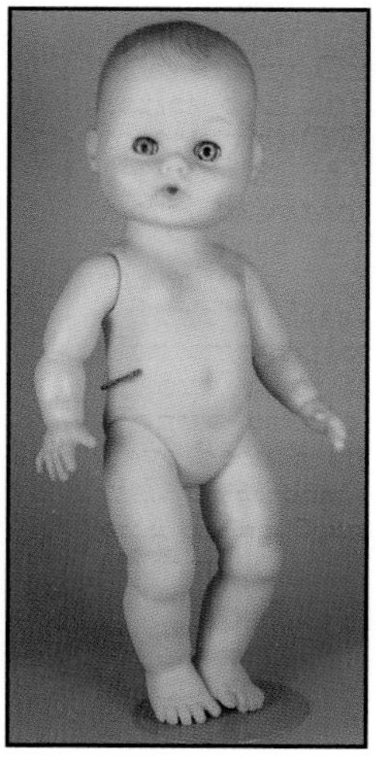

Ginny Baby (1962 – 68), basic 12" Ginny Baby, drinking and wetting doll with sleep eyes, jointed at head, neck, and arms. The 12" doll was introduced in 1962 with rooted hair or sculptured hair.

Elfin Ginny Baby with platinum pixie hair is adorable in her pink check gingham dress with white organdy apron.
8" Doll 78141 $4.00
12" Doll 72151 $5.00
16" Doll 76171 $7.00
18" Doll 78180 $8.00
Ginny Baby with her little girl bob is as pretty as a picture in her flouncy full white nylon dress and bonnet over blue separate slip.
8" Doll 78160 $6.00
16" Doll 76180 $8.00
12" Doll 72170 $7.00
20" Doll 70100 $10.00

Ginny Baby (1962) #78141-70100. Vogue brochure.

Ginny Baby (1963), 8", 12", 16", and 20" sizes. Also available in an 18" size, but not in this outfit. Note the chignon hairstyle. Vogue catalog page. Courtesy Marge Meisinger.

Ginny Baby (1963), 8", wearing rose velvety topper set, #78540, with bottle and wrist tag. Missing black shoes. Courtesy Veronica Phillips.

Ginny Baby (1963), 12" doll in #72151, white cotton dress with embroidered rose appliqué. Courtesy Sandy Johnson-Barts.

Ginny Baby (1963-68), 12" with rooted hair in dotted nylon dress with red velvet bodice and matching hat and bonnet. This particular dress was not in the Vogue catalog.

Ginny Baby (1963), 12" and 16", traditional baby styles for sculptured and rooted hair dolls. 16" outfits: (left to right), hooded pink and white fleece set, #76583; white nylon dress and bonnet, #76584; nylon dress and bonnet (sculptured), # 76565. 12" outfits for sculptured doll (second from right): pink topper set, #72545. Vogue catalog page. Courtesy Marge Meisinger.

Ginny Baby (1964), Vogue designated "Negro" dolls: (top) 8" Ginnette; (center) 11" Li'l Imp; (bottom) Ginny Baby 8", 12", 16", and 18". Vogue catalog courtesy Marge Meisinger.

Ginny Baby (1964), yellow organdy dress with lace trim, similar to 12", #72651, and 16", #76671.

Ginny Baby (1964), 8" with rooted hair, outfit red velvety and white topper. Note original wrist tag.

Ginny Baby (1964), 8", 12", 16", 18" with rooted hair in red velvety and white topper. Vogue catalog courtesy Marge Meisinger.

Ginny Baby (1964), 8", in outfit #78665, nylon flower trimmed dress with embroidered flowers and bonnet with wrist tag. Courtesy Veronica Phillips.

Ginny Baby (1964), 8", 12", 16", 18" with rooted hair, fleece jacket with animal motif and matching booties with blue cord pants. Marks: None (on head); VOGUE DOLLS INC. (on body). Vogue catalog courtesy Marge Meisinger.

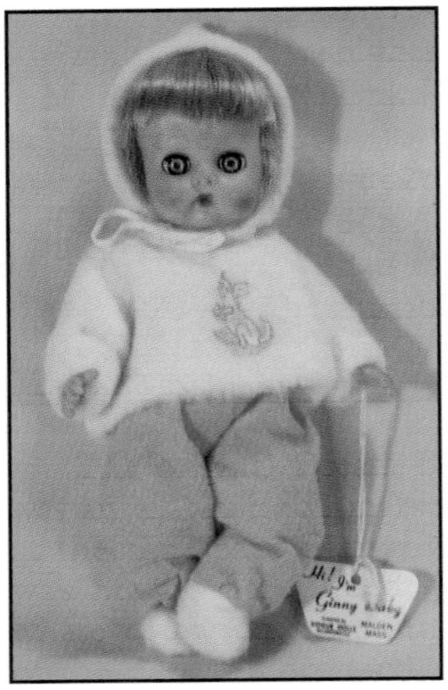

Ginny Baby (1964), 8" with rooted hair, fleece jacket with kangaroo motif and matching booties with blue pants, not corduroy as advertised. Courtesy Veronica Phillips.

Ginny Baby (1964), 8", 12", 16", 18" with rooted hair, blue dot apron dress with hair bow. Vogue catalog. Courtesy Marge Meisinger.

Ginny Baby (1964), 8" with rooted hair in blue dot apron dress with hair bow. Courtesy Audrey Fletcher.

Ginny Baby (1964), 8", 12", 16", 18" with platinum rooted hair, pink checked topper set with pink hair bow. Vogue catalog. Courtesy Marge Meisinger.

Ginny Baby (1964), 8", 12", 16", 18" with rooted hair in flower trimmed nylon ensemble with matching bonnet. Vogue catalog courtesy Marge Meisinger.

Ginny Baby (1964), 8" sleep eyes, rooted hair in yellow dress with white apron, #78547. Marks: VOGUE DOLLS INC (on lower back). Dress tagged: VOGUE DOLLS, INC. Showing Vogue navy, pink, and white box. Courtesy Veronica Phillips.

Ginny Baby outfit (1964), #78881, for an 18" doll yellow baby dress with puffed sleeves and lace trim. Courtesy Veronica Phillips.

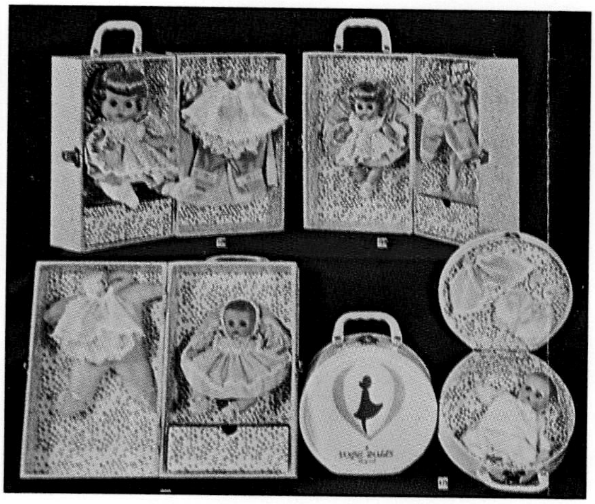

Ginny Baby (1964), (top left), Ginny Baby Fitted Case, #720, with 12" vinyl doll. (top right), Ginny Baby Fitted Case, #788 with 8". Note other cases also available for 8" Li'l Dear on bottom row. Vogue catalog courtesy Marge Meisinger.

Ginny Baby (1965), 8" white and black, rooted hair in #78342, red velvety lace trimmed dress. Marks: (White doll): S2 (on head); VOGUE DOLLS INC. (on body); black doll: None (on head); VOGUE DOLLS INC. (on body). Courtesy Veronica Phillips.

Ginny Baby (1965), designated by Vogue "Negro," 12", vinyl Ginny Baby with rooted hair, red velvety outfit similar to #78142.

Ginny Baby (1965 – 69), 12" with sculptured hair in red velvet dress with matching bonnet and lace trim.

Ginny Baby (1965 – 66), 12" with molded hair in pink dress and bonnet and knit booties. Marks: ©GINNY BABY/VOGUE DOLLS INC. (on head); 12-5 (on back). Dress tagged: VOGUE DOLLS/MADE IN USA.

Ginny Baby (1969), 12" and 16", Ginny Baby dolls with both rooted and sculpted hair. Vogue advertised "the traditional ever-popular drink n' wet basic....the prettiest anywhere...." Vogue catalog courtesy Marge Meisinger.

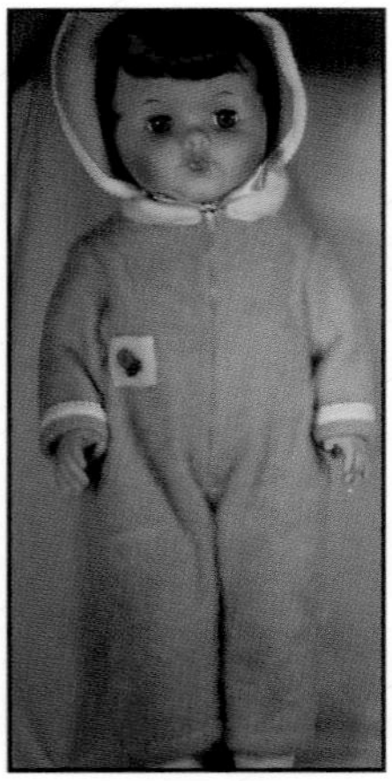

Ginny Baby (1971), 25", in #7502, blue snowsuit. Courtesy Joe Kingston.

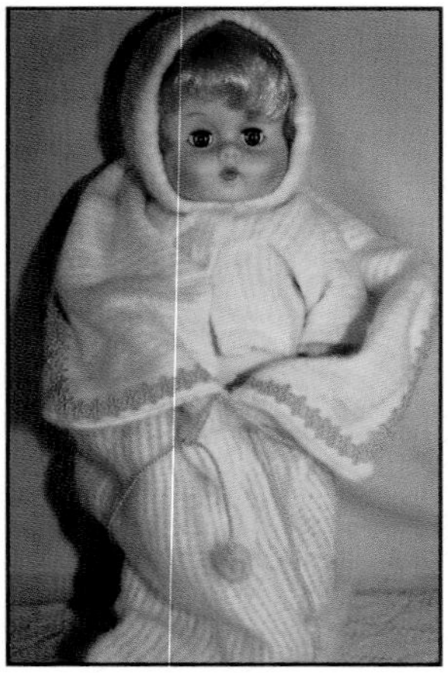

Ginny Baby (1972), 16", in #7642, knit sweater, bonnet and blanket. Courtesy Joe Kingston.

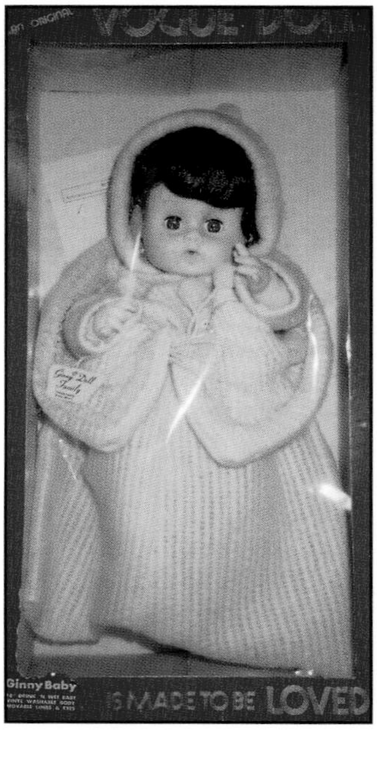

Ginny Baby (1974), 16", #76551, in a soft pink and white knit bunting with matching hood. Note the new pink box by Tonka. Courtesy Jane Gaumond.

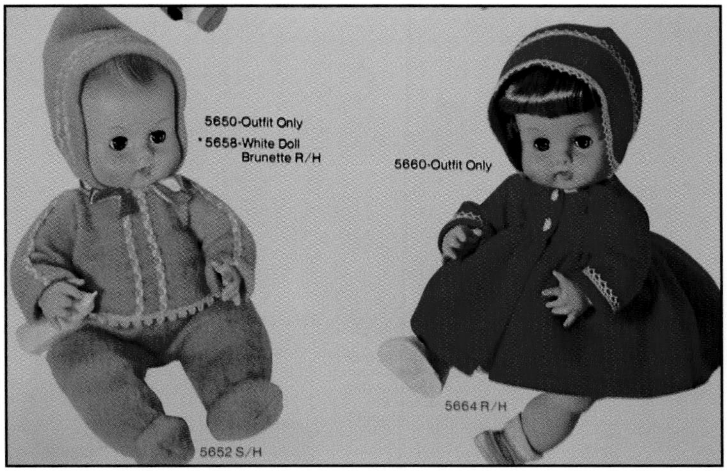

Ginny Baby (1975), 16", #5658, sculptured hair doll wearing pink fleece pram set; #5664, rooted hair doll wearing red ensemble with white lace trim. Vogue catalog courtesy Marge Meisinger.

Ginny Baby (1975), 12", #5630, carrot orange rooted hair wearing blue knit overall set; #5640, Vogue designated "Negro" doll, #5640, wearing blue and white checked apron dress and matching bonnet. Vogue catalog courtesy Marge Meisinger.

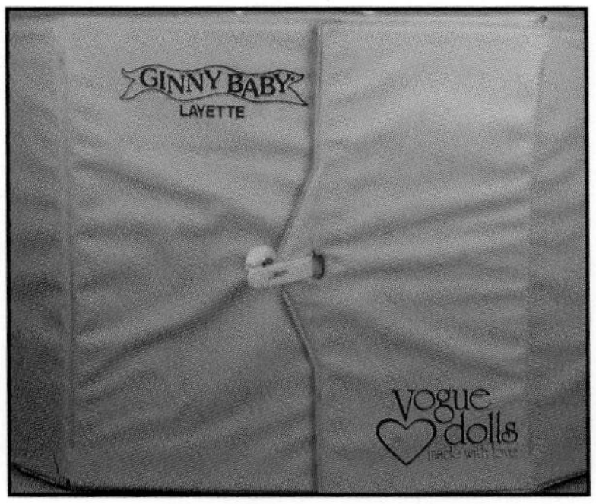

Ginny Baby Layette (1978 – 79), #302081, a pink plastic carrying case which included the 8" (new mold) painted eye, dressed in a christening dress, along with a T-shirt, panties, pink pajamas, and a dress and bottle. Vogue catalog courtesy Marge Meisinger.

Ginny Baby shower n' bath (1978), 8", with a new painted eye mold sold with a bathtub and accessories. "Just fill her bathtub with water, turn the dial and....Ginny takes a bath." Doll shown in the box. Vogue catalog courtesy Marge Meisinger.

Ginny Baby (1978-80), 16" in Ginny's First Jeans outfit, #307613. Vogue catalog courtesy Marge Meisinger.

Miss Ginny

1962 – 1965, 1967 – 1980

16" Miss Ginny
(1962 – 1964)

Description: 16" soft touch vinyl head (ball-jointed head could be tilted); jointed vinyl arms, two-piece plastic body with all jointed swivel waist (same as Brikette Doll); flat feet; sleep eyes; rooted hair in long, straight styles; pert school girl type.

Marks: Head: Unknown
Back: Unknown

Wardrobe:

1962: Three styles: #86100, candy striped dress; #86180, yellow school dress; #86181, aqua jersey and knit slacks ensemble with pixie top. All outfits matched hard plastic bent knee walker Ginny from 1962.

1963: Three outfits, including two party dresses: #86790, white embroidered eyelet dress, #86700, pink nylon with black velvet top and rosebud trim; and #86780, fleece hooded jacket and pants outfit. All outfits this year matched 8" vinyl head walker Ginny.

1964: Red checked shirt and denim skirt; yellow felt roller skater set; red velvety embroidered dress; pink lace trimmed party dress.

15" Miss Ginny
(1965 – 1975)

Description:

1965 – 1971: 15" Miss Ginny, soft vinyl head and arms; new head mold with smaller eyes; closed mouth; one-piece plastic body torso (no ball-jointed waist), and straight legs, second and third finger curled; flat feet; jointed at head, arms, and legs, sleep eyes. 1965 hairstyles were rooted in short, straight styles, and 1967, old style with long curls.

1966: It is unclear from available sources if Miss Ginny was produced in 1966.

1972 – 75: Same 15" Miss Ginny head used since 1967 but produced in hard vinyl; vinyl arms; closed mouth; previous one-piece plastic body and legs, second and third finger curled; flat feet; jointed at head, arms, and legs, sleep eyes; rooted hair in previous longer, older curled styles; sweet young debutante look. This traditional Miss Ginny was sold concurrently with contemporary Miss Ginny with a wide-eyed look in 1975. 1975 was the last year for the traditional version.

Marks:

1965 – 1967: None

1970 – 1975: None on 15" neck and body.
Wrist Tag: Hi! I'm 15" Miss Ginny/ Created by Vogue Dolls Inc.

Wardrobe:

1965: Beautiful bride doll; three outfits matching 1965 My Angel outfits: black velvety party dress and hat; red plaid school dress; brown fleece coat ensemble.

1967: Debutante styles with long Velvetex and/or linen gowns with woven trim, matching bonnets, stiff nylon or firm net petticoats, full-length hose, nylon tricot panties, and velvet slippers. Velvetex was described as "Deeply vibrant...velvet-like...soft to the touch" in a Sears advertisement, and made beautiful gowns.

1968: Debutante styles, net petticoats, full-length hose, and velvety slippers, matching hats or hairpieces; bridal gown and veil matching Ginny bridal gown, #523.
Far-Away Lands styles: Dutch, blue skirt with yellow band and eyelet apron, lace cap; Spanish, red velvet top, black lace skirt and headpiece. Nun and Stewardess, with blue suit, white lined cape, and blue hat.

1969: Debutante Collection of three long gowns with velvet, embroidery, woven, and lace trims; matching bonnets, nylons, and velvet slippers.

1970: #8527, bridal gown; and two Debutante styles: #8528, rose taffeta gown with black lace trim and matching bonnet; #8529, blue velvet gown, with lace and brocade ribbon trim, bonnet.

1971: #0850, fitted bridal trousseau trunk; also seven styles described as "tomorrow or yesterday:"
Yesterday: #8565, bridal gown and veil, #8576, red velvet gown with white brushed fleece hem, matching hat and muff; #8587, blue gown with white brushed cotton hem,

cuffs and collar with matching hat,
Tomorrow: #8515, pink and blue pajamas outfit; #8526, black and white lounger; #8537, maize knit pants suit and hat; #8548, red knit mini coat and dress set with white boots.

1972: #8522, bridal outfit; #8513 (blonde) and #8513 (brunette), yellow gown with white brushed fleece bodice and hem, yellow bonnet; #8532, black velvet gown and suspenders with white blouse and hearts and flowers braid and rickrack trim, matching velvet hat with white lining; #8552, red skirted gown with white flounce underskirt and bloused sleeves, matching red bonnet with lace trim.

1973: #8545 (white doll), #8549 (black doll), in bridal gowns. Four debutante styles: #8595, red gown, repeated from 1972; #8575, red plaid gown with white fleece hem; #8565, blue lace gown with velvet bodice; #8505 (blonde), #8508 (brunette), in teal gown with brushed fleece front panel and black velvet bodice.

1974: #8511 (blonde or brunette), in bridal gowns; #8522, yellow gown with gold braid and ruffle trim and matching hat; #8544 blonde and #85442 black doll, pink striped gown with pink velvet bodice, and matching hat; #8533, gown white piqué skirt with ruffle trim and black velvet waist coat, matching hat.

1975: #3404, bridal gown; #3419, white and blue eyelet gown with blue taffeta bonnet; #3434, pink gown with satin and lace ruffle trim, bonnet; #3425R/H, red velvet hat and gown with white organdy sleeves.

I'm sweet
Miss Ginny
Although we are in the back, Baby "Dear-One" and I are the brand new members of the famous "Ginny Doll Family." I'm 16" tall and look a great deal like my little 8" sister Ginny. Because of my two-piece body construction of rigid material, I can assume many positions. Most experts agree that my construction has the most play value built in. My arms and head are made of soft vinyl and I have moving eyes and rooted hair in three complete different styles. I hope you'll like me and play with me because I'm proud to be a member of the "Ginny Doll Family" and would love to play with you.
For school, she matches little Ginny in her sunny yellow cotton dress with soft green velvet sash and yellow rosebuds and flouncy ponytail.
Doll 86180 $8.00 Outfit 86380 $2.00
For cool weather play, she dresses like Ginny in flowered aqua jersey knit slacks and kerchief in matching pixie felt top with elfin hairdo.
Doll 86181 $8.00 Outfit 86381 $2.50
In visiting best, Miss Ginny and little Ginny are matchmates in their red and white candy-stripe pinafore dress with saucy straw skimmer.
Doll 86100 $10.00 Outfit 86300 $4.00

Miss Ginny (1962), 16", in three outfits: #86180, yellow cotton dress with green velvet sash; #86181, aqua jersey knit slacks and kerchief and felt top; and #86100, candy stripe pinafore dress. All outfits matched a Ginny outfit. Vogue catalog.

Miss Ginny – Contemporary Mold
(1975 – 1980)

Description:

1975: New 1975 Contemporaries, vinyl head mold with older wide-eyed look and long individual eyelashes, with painted lashes under eye; jointed at legs, arms, and neck; an older look; rooted hair in long straight styles or shorter, curled, or ponytail; flat feet, more sophisticated and modern, yet youthful school girl look.

1976 – 80: 15", new vinyl head mold with wide-eyed look and long individual eyelashes, with painted lashes under eye. Same mold for body, arms, and legs as 1968 – 80 Miss Ginny hard plastic body and legs; vinyl arms; jointed at legs, arms and neck; an older look; rooted hair in long straight styles or shorter, curled, or ponytail; more sophisticated, and modern yet youthful school girl look.

Marks:

1975 Head: Vogue Dolls/©1974
Back: None

1976 – 1980 Same as 1975

Wardrobe:

1975: Three slacks outfits described as "stylish, sophisticated," green tunic and gold dotted blouse, #3666R/H; rust jacket, pants, and bandanna, #3675R/H; white knit top and sweater set with blue pants.

1976 – 1980: Beautiful Debutante and Bride outfits in the "Fashion and Charm" section of the catalog.

12" Little Miss Ginny

(1965 – 1971)

Description:

1965, 1967: 12" all vinyl Little Miss Ginny was promoted as a pre-teen or sweet young girl, one-piece plastic body and legs, soft touch vinyl arms and head; open fingers palms down; closed mouth smile with two painted white upper teeth showing; jointed at neck, arms, and legs; flat feet; sleep eyes with three painted joined lines in the corners; rooted, long straight hairstyles, short bobs; turned up styles.

1966: Little Miss Ginny was not produced.

1968 – 1971: There were two types of heads used on the same body for Little Miss Ginny between 1968 – 71. One new head for Far-Away Lands dolls and the same one as the previous year for the young lady costumes as follows:

1) 12" Miss Ginny Far-Away Lands:
New head mold with closed mouth, no smile and no painted teeth showing; same 1967 one-piece plastic body and legs, with soft vinyl arms, vinyl head; open fingers, palms down (body, arms, and legs same mold as 12" Little Miss Ginny above), jointed at neck, arms, and legs; flat feet; sleep eyes; rooted hair; sweet look, but not smiling.

Note: This body was used for 12" Miss Ginny Far-Away Lands per the box label and wrist tag. Interestingly, the dealer advertisement did not mention Miss Ginny but only Collector Dolls from Far-Away Lands.

2) 12" Little Miss Ginny 1968:
Same vinyl head (smiling mouth with two painted teeth) and body as 1967 with rooted hair

1969 – 1970 12" Little Miss Ginny: Beginning in 1969 Vogue advertised a new face mold: "Now she's just as lovely as her bigger sister." In fact, the face was only slightly wider, and the mouth was still smiling, but the two teeth were no longer painted white. The vinyl body did not change.

Marks:

1965, 1967:	Head:	2071/9Eye (above indented line in the mold below hair line)
	Neck:	VOGUE DOLL/19©67(below the line)
	Back:	VOGUE DOLL
1968 – 1971:	Head:	© VOGUE DOLL/1968
	Back:	VOGUE DOLL

Dress label:

1965, 1967, 1968 – 1971: White cotton with blue writing: Vogue Dolls Inc./Made in U.S.A.

Dress closure:

1965, 1967, 1968 – 1971: Metal snap with fluted star pattern.

Tags:

1968 – 1971: Side 1: Hi! I'm 12" Little Miss Ginny/Created by Vogue Dolls Incorporated, MALDEN MASS./MADE IN U.S.A.
Side 2: Name of country, i.e.. "Switzerland."

Boxes:

1966 – 1971 Navy and white with Vogue logo "Vogue Dolls Made to be Loved."
1971: Bright fuchsia with Vogue Dolls in a block print design.

Wardrobe:

1965 and 1967:

Some short teen styles with knit tights or nylons, velveteen, knit fabrics with embroidered bands; slacks and shorts sets; long gown and debutante style matching 15" dolls; outfits with matching hats or bows and suede cloth slippers; hooded fleece coat with white boots. Some Far-Away Lands styles were available.

1968 – 1971:

Far-Away Lands: Twelve costumes: American Indian; France; Tyrolean; Ireland; Spain; Eskimo; Scotland; Switzerland; Germany; Little Dutch Girl; Far East; Mexico, Switzerland costume #8265, uses cotton skirt and blouse, braided trim, and velvet hat and vest in exact match to Hong Kong Ginny Far-Away Lands Switzerland costume, #1865. It appears that Vogue marketed these as companion outfits to Ginny's Far-Away Land series.

1968:

Special styles were promoted by stores such as Sears, who featured a red velvet Holiday Mini outfit in red Velvetex with diamond patterned mesh stockings.

1969:

Debutante Collection of three long gowns (not matching 1969 15" doll).

1970 – 71:

"Her Majesty, the Queen and her court," a collection of four dolls: Queen, in white brocade gown with purple velvet cape, #8220; Prince Consort, in white tights, velvet top and cape with matching cap with a plume, #8221; Queen's Lady (two), in blue taffeta and red Velvetex gowns with matching nylon veils, #8222, #8223. *Note:* This collection appears in Vogue's catalog, but no example has been seen to authenticate that it was ever produced.

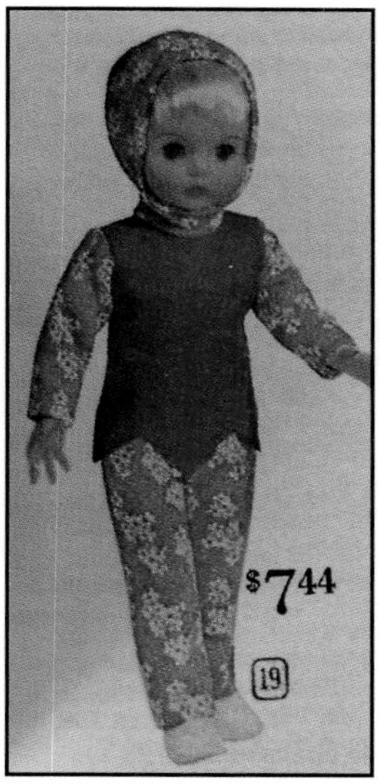

Miss Ginny (1962), 16", vinyl, jointed at waist, outfit #86181, aqua jersey knit slacks and kerchief with matching pixie felt top. Has an elfin hairdo. Montgomery Ward advertised it as an exclusive even though it appears in the Vogue brochure. She cost $8.00. Montgomery Ward catalog.

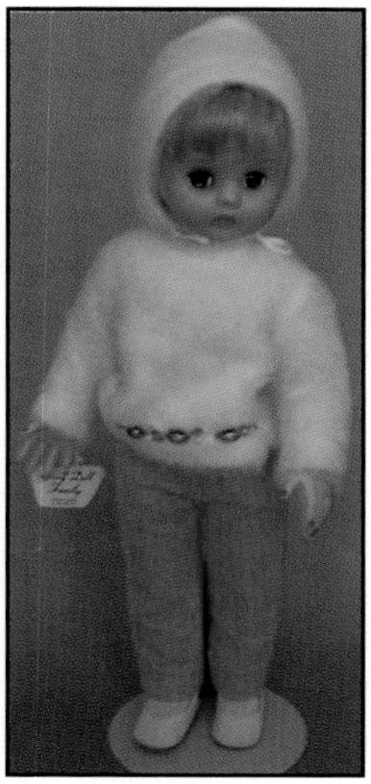

Miss Ginny (1963), 16" outfit, #86500, flower trimmed, hooded fleece jacket and hot pink cord pants. Note the Vogue Doll Family wrist tag.

Marketing

Next to Ginny herself, few Vogue dolls have undergone as many revisions in concept and design as the Miss Ginny doll. As Ginny's popularity continued to decline, Vogue created 16" Miss Ginny doll in 1962 to tap into the market for older dolls. Vogue used the ball-jointed waist body from their Brikette doll, but substituted a cute, school girl head, with a less impish look. The doll was marketed as a "sweet" girl doll. Miss Ginny was introduced as "I'm 16" tall and look a great deal like my little 8" sister Ginny. I'm proud to be a member of the Ginny Doll Family."

A new Miss Ginny doll was issued in 1965 with an older look, but still "sweet," and very much a little lady. Elegant Debutante and long gown styles were created. The Miss Ginny dolls came in a navy and white box with pink trim (the same design as a Ginny doll box of the period) with an oval cellophane window and irregular shaped Vogue logo.

Recognizing that some customers still preferred the smaller doll, Vogue came out with a 12" Little Miss Ginny in 1967. 12" Little Miss Ginny had similar fashion styles to the 15" doll, including debutante gowns and some contemporary, short styles.

By 1975, Tonka marketed the 15" Miss Ginny only with Debutante styles. Their catalog, described the doll as "an elegant sophisticate, in any of her beautiful gowns." Apparently, Tonka also recognized that this doll was still missing out on sales for stylish teen dolls. Therefore, they created Miss Ginny Contemporaries in addition to Miss Ginny Debutante, to try to capture new sales. This doll was described in the 1975 catalogue as a "Stylish, lively...Modern day, Miss...". The doll's mold was not as cute as the original Miss Ginny (the Debutante). Instead, it had a sophisticated wide-eyed look with long individual eyelashes, and was intended to be a "new, today doll."

Interestingly, when Lesney acquired the Vogue doll lines, they continued the Miss Ginny Debutante concept but dropped the cute Miss Ginny head used since 1962. Instead they used the 1974 – 1975 head from the Miss Ginny Contemporary doll. The result was a much older debutante look. The doll was described as having "fashionably styled hair, delicately sculpted faces, with radiant hand-painted color, and long curled lashes, bouffant gowns...sophisticated ladies." They continued producing this doll, adding beautiful evening gowns as well, through 1980. As Lesney began to invest most of their creative energies into promoting the Sasson Ginny doll in 1981, the Miss Ginny line was dropped altogether.

Conclusion

Miss Ginny has undergone many changes over the years. The early dolls were truly lovely, with a sweet face, detailed gowns, and coordinated outfits. The 12" Little Miss Ginny had adorable teen outfits, complete with mini skirts and boots as well as Debutante gowns that truly reflect the mid 1970s era. The later Miss Ginny dolls produced by Lesney carry the modern look to an even greater extreme, and are sought by many collectors today.

Prices

Year	Doll	Head/Body Material	Mint Price
1962 – 1964	16" Miss Ginny	Hp/Hp	$80.00
1965 – 1975	15" Miss Ginny	V/V	$25.00 – $55.00
1965 – 1975	12" Little Miss Ginny (Incl. Far-Away Lands)	V/V	$20.00 – $40.00
1975	15" Miss Ginny Contemp.	V/V	$25.00 – $45.00
1976 – 1980	15" Miss Ginny	V/V	$25.00 – $45.00

Code: Hp – hard plastic; V – Vinyl

sweet
Miss Ginny
The most reliable, pliable, playable girl doll ever made is our Miss Ginny and she is as sweet as can be. Her special two-piece body makes it possible for her to turn and tilt her head, bend or swivel her waist and assume almost any pose. Made of durable soft-touch plastic with vinyl arms and head with rooted hair, Miss Ginny will bring years of joy and play to her proud little mother. 16 inch Miss Ginny is available for from 8.00 to 10.00, with outfits from 2.50 to 4.00.

Miss Ginny (1963), three outfits for the 16" all vinyl doll with sleep eyes: (from left) # 86590, #86580, #86500, all matching Ginny outfits. The doll's body was the same as the pliable two-piece Brikette body. Vogue catalog courtesy Marge Meisinger.

Little Miss Ginny outfit (1966), Holiday Mini (see page 308).

Miss Ginny (1964), four outfits for the 16", all vinyl doll (from left), top: #86691, roller skater in yellow skirt and vest; #86601, pink party dress. Bottom left: #86690, red and white checked shirt and kerchief, denim skirt; and #86600, red velvet party dress top and white skirt. Vogue catalog courtesy Marge Meisinger.

Miss Ginny

Miss Ginny (1965), 15" new Miss Ginny doll with a vinyl body without the ball-jointed waist, and sweet new face mold, rooted hair and sleep eyes. All of these outfits matched and/or coordinated with "My Angel," a 15", little girl doll produced in 1965 by Vogue. (From left) #85160, black dress; #85161, plaid skirt and red sweater; #85182, brown coat; #85103, bride. Vogue publicity photo. Courtesy Wenham Museum, Wenham, Mass.

15" Miss Ginny and matching 12" Little Miss Ginny outfits (c. 1968), the outfits on the left use polyester blend and nylon fabrics. The two outfits on the right are later styles using soft Velvetex fabric. Dolls on far right appeared in a 1970 Sears ad. Vogue publicity photo. Courtesy Wenham Museum, Wenham, Mass

Miss Ginny (1966), this original pencil sketch was made by Mrs. Virginia Graves Carlson before her retirement in 1966 for a special Miss Ginny velvet gown for the Hudson department store. Note the front and back views, and specifications for colors, etc. Courtesy Virginia Graves Carlson.

Miss Ginny (1966), 15", vinyl, wearing red Velvetex gown with white fleece trim and muff. This outfit was featured in the 1966 – 68 Sears catalog. Courtesy Joe Kingston.

Miss Ginny (1966), 15", wearing a wedding gown patterned after wedding gown of June Nelson's son Joe Kingston's wife (shown in photo). Courtesy Joe Kingston.

Miss Ginny (1968), 15", Scotch girl. Courtesy Joe Kingston.

Miss Ginny (1968 – 70), 12", Far-Away Lands. Courtesy Modern Doll Convention, Rochester, NY.

Miss Ginny (1968), 15", in a variety of outfits made for Miss Ginny before Vogue concentrated on Debutante outfits for the doll. Top left, #8520, nurse's outfit; #8522, bride, matches Ginny bride's outfit, #523; and #8525, Dutch girl; (bottom row) #8523, stewardess; #8524, Spanish girl; and #8521, nun outfit. Vogue publicity photo. Courtesy Wenham Museum, Wenham, Mass.

Miss Ginny (1966 – 71 based on box design), 15", one-piece plastic body, blue poly/cotton blend gown with dotted nylon hem with braided trim; straw brim bonnet with matching fabric crown. Notice picture on box.

15" Miss Ginny (c. 1968 – 70) and 12" Little Miss Ginny (c. 1968). The outfits are #8229, a rich purple Velvetex fabric with pink trim, still beautiful after all this time. 12" is marked: V O G U E DOLLS/19©67 (on head); VOGUE DOLLS (on back).

15" Miss Ginny and 12" Little Miss Ginny, Debutante Collection (1969). Top, left to right: Little Miss Ginny, #8250, in pink; #8251, in yellow; #8252, in red. Bottom, from left: 15" Miss Ginny, #8557, in red with white eyelet at hem; #8558, in green velvet; #8559, in red velvet jacket and white skirt. Note the new head mold for the 12" doll was without two painted front teeth. Vogue catalog photo. Courtesy Marge Meisinger.

Miss Ginny (1970), 15" vinyl in debutante and bridal costumes. Vogue catalog photo. Courtesy Marge Meisinger.

Miss Ginny (1972), 15", all vinyl doll, rooted hair and sleep eyes. #8513, maize bonded knit gown with white fleece trim and matching bonnet. Unidentified mail order catalog. Courtesy Marge Meisinger.

Miss Ginny (1972 – 73), 15", in gown with pink skirt over cascading ruffles and bonnet and rooted wavy hair in box. 1972, #8552, and 1973, #8595. Courtesy Ida Labaki.

Miss Ginny (1973), 15", in #8575, red plaid wool with fleece trim, and #8595, pink gown. 1974 McDade catalog. Courtesy Marge Meisinger.

Miss Ginny (1972 – 1974) 15", vinyl bride doll. This box is marked with 1973 code, #8545. A black bride doll, #8549 was also available. In 1972 the dolls were coded #8522; 1974 were coded #8511; 1975, #3408, bride, and #3404, brunette bride. The gown is a beautiful brocade fabric with lace trim.

Miss Ginny (1972), 15", #8532, black velvet outfit. The Vogue catalog showed heart appliqué at the top of the skirt. Accessories included firm net petticoat, lace trimmed nylon panties, full length hose and black velvet slippers. Mint in dark pink box.

Miss Ginny (1974 and 1975), 15" (left), #8544, pink gown with pink tiers of ruffles with fleece trim. #8533, white piqué gown with black velvety jacket and matching hat. 1975 McDade catalog. Courtesy Marge Meisinger.

Miss Ginny Contemporaries (1975), new 15" vinyl doll (left), # 3666 R/H, and (right), #3675 R/H, the doll has a wide-eyed look featured as a "...new, today doll...." Obviously, the popular teen doll market influenced these styles. Vogue catalog. Courtesy Marge Meisinger.

Miss Ginny Debutantes collection (1975), 15", #3425R/H, red velvety gown with lace-trimmed panties, full length hose, and velvety slippers. Vogue catalog. Courtesy Marge Meisinger.

Miss Ginny outfit (1975), separate outfits were available for the 15" Miss Ginny such as this dungaree outfit with red jersey, #921 6433. Tag: Vogue Dolls, Inc./MADE IN U.S.A. Box label: VOGUE DOLLS INC./MELROSE MASS 02176/SUBSIDIARY OF TONKA.

Miss Ginny Debutantes collection (1975), 15" (top), #3419R/H, white gown with blue ribbon trim and (bottom), #3434 R/H, frilly gown with pink ribbon trim. Vogue catalog courtesy Marge Meisinger.

Miss Ginny Debutante (1977), 15", #303511, in a green satin gown with white braid trim and fleece accessories. Note that the new wide-eyed Miss Ginny Contemporary mold introduced in 1975 is now used on the Miss Ginny. Vogue catalog. Courtesy Marge Meisinger.

Miss Ginny Contemporaries doll and Debutante styles (1977), 15" (left), #303514, blue floral debutante gown with lace trim and matching bonnet; (right) Miss Ginny Contemporaries doll in an outfit not shown in Vogue catalog. May have been a store special. Unidentified 1977 mail order catalog. Courtesy Marge Meisinger.

Miss Ginny (1978), bride, #303501, mint in box. Courtesy Joe Kingston.

Miss Ginny Debutante (1977 – 80), 15", #303524, burgundy skirt and print top; and #303505, bride. Vogue catalog. Courtesy Marge Meisinger.

Miss Ginny (1978), cream satin gown, #303527; and #303501, bride, from Lesney. Vogue catalog. Courtesy Marge Meisinger.

Miss Ginny (1978 – 80), #303505, black bride, wears white eyelet gown and matching crown with veil.

Miss Ginny (1980), 15", in #303585 bride gown. Notice white lace trim and veil.

Little Miss Ginny

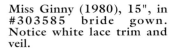

Little Miss Ginny (1966 – 68), 12", vinyl with a smiling mouth with two painted teeth. Interestingly, the outfit on the 15" Miss Ginny (on the right), is similar to those shown in the 1971 catalog. 1968 Sears catalog. Courtesy Marge Meisinger.

Little Miss Ginny, 12", with painted teeth (on the right), wears a Sears Holiday Mini from 1968. The doll on the left is a 1969 – 71 version, with a smiling mouth, but the painted teeth are not visible. Both dolls have a one-piece vinyl body, open palms, and rooted hair.

Little Miss Ginny (1969), 12", Debutante Collection, #8252, mint in box vinyl doll in red velvety gown and straw hat. Note the new face promoted in 1969 essentially the same as the previous face but without two painted teeth showing. Also, this box design was used from around 1963 until 1971 or 1972. Courtesy Sue Johnson.

12" Little Miss Ginny (1968), date based on head mold with two teeth. All vinyl doll with rooted hair in a variety of modern outfits. Top row (left to right): #8020, shorts outfit; #8021, slacks and topper outfit; #8022, slacks outfit; (bottom row) #8023, minidress outfit; #8024, hooded coat outfit; #8025, evening gown outfit, and #8026, dress and hat ensemble. Vogue publicity photo. Courtesy Wenham Museum, Wenham, Mass.

Collector Doll from Far-Away Lands (1971), 12", #8265, Switzerland with Little Miss Ginny wrist tag. Note the new vinyl head mold, with no smile used for Far-Away Lands in 1971, but sold with a Little Miss Ginny box and tag.

Special Series

Miss Ginny (1970), 12", in a fascinating collection: (center) #8221, Prince Consort; and #8220, Her Majesty, the Queen. Queen's ladies: #8222, in blue taffeta; and #8223, in red Velvetex. Production not verified. Vogue catalog photo. Courtesy Marge Meisinger.

Other Vinyl Dolls

Dream Baby

(1961, 1965, 1969 – 1973)

Description:

1961: 16" all vinyl doll with sculpted hair, sleep eyes, jointed at head, arms, and legs.

1965: In 1965 a different doll was sold with the Dream Baby name. It was a soft 12" crib doll with vinyl head, sculpted hair, sleep eyes, and kapok-filled cloth body (one piece including arms and legs). It is included in the dealer's price list as "soft cuddly doll." The head was the same as the new, redesigned Baby Dear head used during this year.

1969: The 1969 doll had the same vinyl head as the 1965 doll, and was in a semi-seated pose with thumbs cut into the pattern. The doll had a removable dress, vest or pajamas.

1971 – 1972: The 1971-72 doll had the same vinyl head, and was cut and stuffed in a sitting position, with thumbs, sleep eyes; no removable clothes.

1973: The same doll had her left arm in a downward curved position, perhaps to hold a bottle. Vogue designated black doll #4017 was introduced.

1974: The doll was shown in a different version in the 1974 Americana mail order catalog: The same vinyl head, but cut and stuffed without thumbs and with arms stretched in a higher position; no removable clothes.

Marks: Unknown

Wardrobe:

1961: #56260, aqua pram suit for the all vinyl doll similar to Ginny Baby

1969: Soft fleece, flannel, etc. removable outfits in boy, girl and romper styles, with matching hats for the soft bodied doll.

1970 – 1973: Surface washable fleece body and hood; no removable outfits for the soft bodied doll.

Marketing

The original Dream Baby was an all vinyl doll marketed at the time that Ginny Baby was newly introduced. For whatever reason, that version of the doll was dropped, but the name was recycled for a cute little soft crib doll primarily for infants.

Dream Baby (1974), this 12" soft cuddly doll has the same vinyl head as the 1969 – 1973 doll, but is cut and stuffed in a more upright, seated position, with arms stretched higher and without thumbs. Courtesy Marge Meisinger.

Dream Baby (1961), 16", all vinyl doll with sculpted hair, sleep eyes, jointed at head, arms, and legs; wears #56260, aqua pram suit with fleece trim.

Baby's first doll – Dream Baby
The perfect cribmate for the new infant is this completely safe dream of a doll with her soft, cuddly Kapok-filled cloth body and her non-toxic vinyl head with sleeping eyes and delicately sculptured hair. DREAM BABY and her removable garments are completely washable.
12" Dream Baby — one dozen 10 lbs.
#4050 romper $5.00
#4051 boy 5.00
#4052 girl 5.00

Dream Baby (1969), Vogue used the name of the 1961 all vinyl doll for this 12" soft cuddle doll with a vinyl head, advertised as "baby's first doll." The new Baby Dear head was used. (left to right) #4051, boy in plaid vest and cap; # 4050, romper; #4052, girl in plaid dress and bonnet. Outfits were removable and washable. Courtesy Marge Meisinger.

Li'l Dear
(1963 – 1968)

Description: 8", vinyl head baby doll, same head as 1962 – 1963 8" Ginny Baby; vinyl arms and legs; blue sleep eyes; stuffed cloth body. She was floppy like Baby Dear. Introduced with blonde rooted pixie hair in 1963, and in 1964 molded hair was added; open mouth, dry baby nurser. Had twin brother in matching outfit in 1963 and 1964.

Marks: Head: None

Body: White cloth tag with blue print Vogue Dolls Inc. in script glued on on her upper back near her neck.

Dress labels: Vogue Dolls Inc. in blue print on white cloth tag glued on her upper back near her neck.

Dress closures: Metal snaps with round fluted edge.

Wardrobe:

1963: Li'l Dear came in five outfits: #47530, robe; #47540, blue footed pajamas; #47541, lace trimmed topper; #47542, yellow knit topper; #47560, or fancy dress with bonnet; or #47559, rocking bassinet with topper set.

1964: #47603, pink jersey gown; #47635-6, blue knit twin set; #47640, yellow jersey sleeper set; #47641, pink checked topper set; #47642, yellow terry playsuit; #47650, blue batiste dress ensemble; #47651, fleece bunting pram set; #47600, pink velvety coat ensemble; or #47659, rocking bassinet with pink topper set.

1965: Six outfits: #47130, blue jersey sleeping gown; #47140, rose corduroy topper set; #47141, pink jersey sleeper set; #47142, cotton check romper; #47150, a white batiste dress and bonnet; and #47159, doll dressed in the pink jersey sleeper set in a rocking bassinet.

It is unclear whether Li'l Dear was produced in 1966 since the authors have not found a 1966 Vogue catalog. She was listed in 1967 and 1968 ads.

Marketing

In the mid 1960s, Vogue turned to baby dolls to broaden its line and to increase sales since the popularity of Ginny had begun to fade. Li'l Dear was patterned in the image of the newer version of Baby Dear, a dry mouth nurser. Li'l Dear's soft and cuddly body was particularly appropriate for small infants and children. Vogue sales brochures called the doll, "An irresistible wee bundle of joy." A boy Li'l Dear was introduced in 1963 with brown hair and wearing #47543, a matching knit jersey and cap. A twin outfit was also sold for him in 1964, #47636, blue knit set. Li'l Dear cost $2.50 for the undressed molded hair doll to $3.00 for the rooted hair undressed doll. Dressed Li'l Dear sold for $4.00 to $6.00. The doll was also sold in a rocking bassinet in 1963 – 65. Separate outfits were available for $1.50 to $3.00. Li'l Dear came in a fitted hat box for $5.00 and a fitted case for $8.00 in 1963.

Li'l Dear (1964), #47651, fleece bunting pram set. Mint in original box. Courtesy S. Ogilvie.

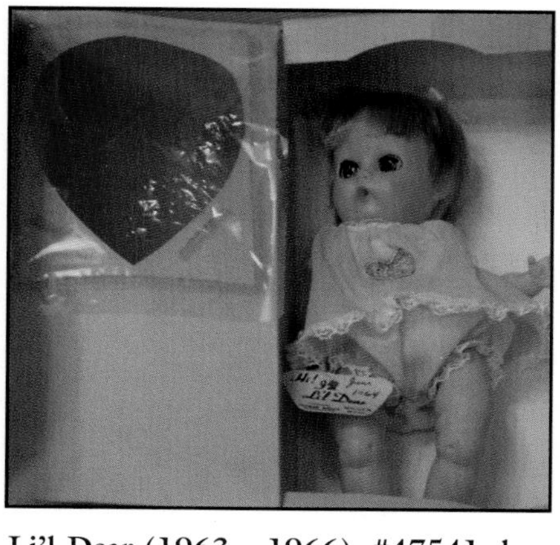

Li'l Dear (1963 – 1966), #47541, lace trimmed topper outfit, soft body, vinyl head, arms, and legs, sleep eyes, rooted hair. Mint in box with wrist tag. Courtesy S. Ogilvie.

Li'l Dear (1964), showing basic dolls, #4725 and 4730, and outfits, #47630-47642. Vogue brochure courtesy Marge Meisinger.

Li'l Dear (1964), showing cradle (right) and two outfits (above). Vogue brochure courtesy Marge Meisinger.

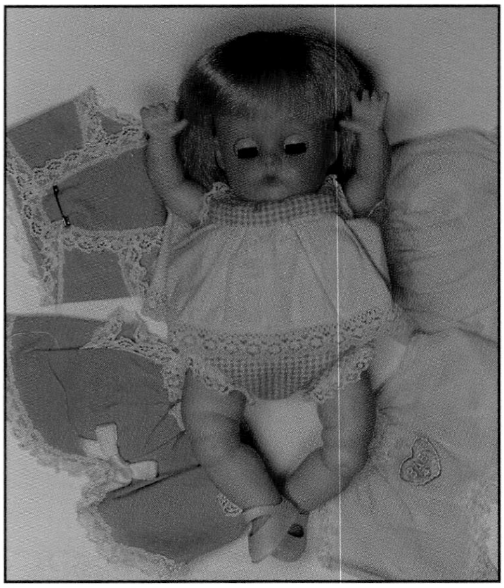

Li'l Dear (1964), #47641, pink checked topper set with outfits from Li'l Dear Fitted Case #478.

Li'l Dear (1965), vinyl head and limbs, pink cloth body, wearing blue and white dress with duck motif. Courtesy Eleanor Skinner.

Li'l Dear (1963 – 1966), Vogue introduced Li'l Dear as an 8" soft body doll with vinyl arms and legs. However, this photo shows that Vogue used various head molds, with both rooted and sculpted hair on Li'l Dear over the years: (left to right) 1964 knit suit, #47636; 1963 – 1964 (sculpted hair), pink jersey sleeping gown; 1964 – 1965 flannel gown; 1965 doll from rocking basket. Courtesy S. Ogilvie.

Li'l Dear (1964), #47636, yellow knitted boy set, rooted hair doll. Courtesy S. Ogilvie.

Li'l Dear (1965-66), blue organdy dress and lace trim, satin hair ribbon.

Bunny Hug

(1964 – 1965)

Description: 10" doll with vinyl head; sculpted hair; sleep eyes; soft fleece one-piece body (including arms and legs), stuffed with kapok.
Marks: Neck: VOGUE DOLL/1964
Wardrobe: Tie-on hood matching body fabric; undressed, no other outfit sold separately.

Marketing:

Bunny Hug (#40625) was introduced in 1964 as a soft, cuddly toy for infants and small children. It was not important to have separate outfits for this type of doll. Her number in 1965 was #40125 and she was shown with the L'il Dear series. Note: In 1969 a very similar stuffed doll, Dream Baby (p. 310) was marketed with simple one- and two-piece play outfits which were easily removable for small children.

Bunny Hug (1964 – 1965), crib doll with washable kapok filled body, vinyl head, molded hair and sleep eyes. Bunny Hug's head was the same head as 8" Ginny Baby. The doll is cut and stuffed in flat position with arms stretched out. Vogue catalog. Courtesy Marge Meisinger.

Jama Baby

(1964 – 1965)

Description: A pajama bag doll with vinyl head and cloth hands, which doubles as a bed decoration.
Marks: Unknown.
Wardrobe: The printed cotton pajama bag with ruffle trim is removable for washing.

Marketing:

Vogue's sales of baby dolls, including Ginnette, Ginny Baby, and Li'l Dear, were very strong. Jama Baby doll was developed for the same market, and, fortunately, all sold very well. However, around the time of Mrs. Carlson's retirement in 1966, a number of dolls were dropped, including Jama Baby.

Jama Baby (1964 – 1965). Vogue's "pajama bag doll" also served as a bed decoration. The pajama bag body was removable and washable. Vogue catalog. Courtesy Marge Meisinger.

Posy Pixi/Posy Baby

(1964 – 1965)

Description: 17", vinyl head and hands, foam body with poseable wire frame; large black sleep eyes with wide painted lashes in outer corners; rooted pixie cut in white and brown; smiling open/closed mouth.

Posy Baby: 17" used the same doll body as Posy Pixi but with an Angel Baby type vinyl head with blonde or reddish blonde rooted hair in short baby styles.
They were marketed together in sales literature.

Marks: Posy Pixi Head: 1964/VOGUE/ 13 (21 or 71 also seen)

Wardrobe: Posy Pixi outfits:

1. Removable red or yellow jersey knit sleeper fastened with Vogue metal snaps down the back; matching felt or knit pixie hat or hair ribbon.
2. Blue velvet topper outfit over sleeper; matching velvet pixie hat.

Posy Baby outfits:

1. Pink and white dress with metal circle snap closures down back over removable knit sleeper.
2. Sunny yellow dress over sleeper; matching tie-on baby bonnets. Most sleeper feet had felt bottoms which were silk screened with Posy Pixi logo and a flower.

Dress labels: White cloth tag with blue print: Vogue Dolls Inc.

Marketing

The 17" Posy Pixi doll was designed and sculpted by doll sculptor, Ms. Deet D'Andrade who had sculpted other dolls for Vogue. The proposal for the doll was one of many Vogue received but only one of the few that they put into production. Posy Pixi is an adorable impish little doll with a lot of play value. The child could pose the doll in many positions. Posy Pixi appeared in Vogue's 1965 doll line. Posy Baby was a variation and offered the same unique poseable body, but with a more traditional baby head and outfits. It is very difficult to find Posy Pixi in excellent condition today since her foam body has deteriorated over the years.

Posy Pixi (1964 – 1965), 17", vinyl head and hands, foam body poseable doll #676. Vogue promotional brochure. Courtesy Virginia Graves Carlson.

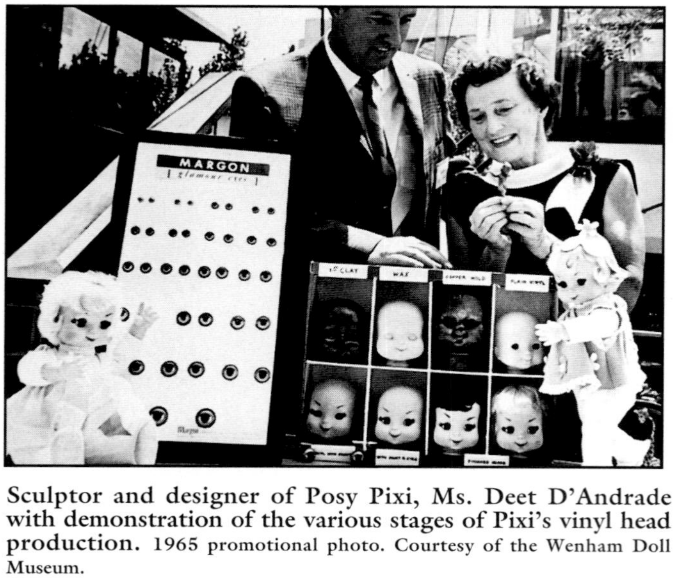

Sculptor and designer of Posy Pixi, Ms. Deet D'Andrade with demonstration of the various stages of Pixi's vinyl head production. 1965 promotional photo. Courtesy of the Wenham Doll Museum.

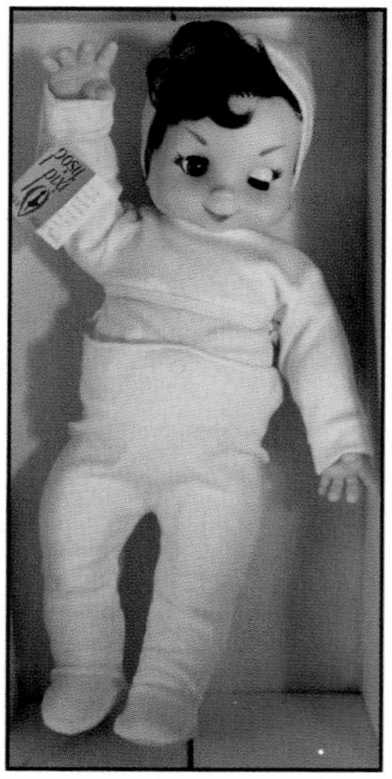

Posy Pixi (1964 – 1965), 17", in yellow knit sleeper with snaps at the waist and matching cap. Notice wrist tag and box cover. Courtesy Veronica Phillips.

Posy Pixi (1964 – 1965), 17" vinyl head and hands, foam body doll, wears a pink jumper with white daisies. Courtesy Joe Kingston.

Posy Pixi, (1964), #67800, red jersey sleeper with white pom-pons, and fleece neck and cuff trim. In 1965 the outfit was sold as #67180. Courtesy Veronica Phillips.

Posy Pixi outfit designs (1964). Mrs. Virginia Graves Carlson's 1964 design specifications for special 1964 Pixi outfits for Sears, Marshall Fields, and Montgomery Ward. Note that while the Montgomery Ward outfit (top center) is similar to Vogue's mass produced red jersey version, it would also be produced in yellow and would have multi-colored pom-pons, instead of white. Original sketches courtesy Virginia Graves Carlson.

Posy Pixi (1965), 17" vinyl head and hands, foam bodydoll. Wears a dress similar to Posy Baby's dress, #68102. Note the sleeper feet with Posy Pixi and flowers printed on bottom. Also note Vogue's box with an acetate window lid.

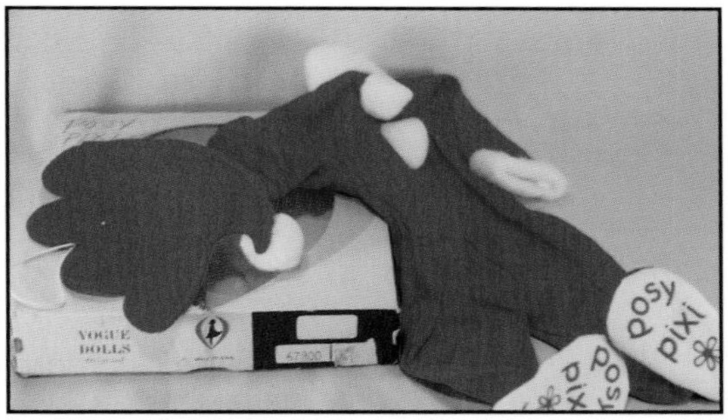

Posy Pixi (1965), #67180, red jersey sleeper with fleece collar and cuffs and pom-pon trim; red felt petal design hat.

Posy Baby (1965), 17" doll with a poseable foam body, but with Vogue's traditional Angel Baby type vinyl head instead of Pixi head. #68102, pink and white soft cotton dress and bonnet. (Far right) #68103, pink or yellow dress; both over pixi sleeper feet. Vogue promotional photo. Courtesy Wenham Doll Museum.

Love Me Linda

(1965)

Description: 16" vinyl doll, large painted eyes with heavy lids, rooted hair in long, straight styles; fully jointed at arms, legs, and neck; mouth has a wistful smile, open palms with second and third fingers molded together. Came with portrait. Also sold under the name "Pretty as a Picture" in the Sears and Montgomery Ward catalogs.

Marks: VOGUE DOLLS/©1965

Wardrobe: #86160, blue and white eyelet knee-length dress and anklets; #86171, red and black plaid dress with black tights and shoes; #86172, blue velvety knee length suit and hat, anklets.

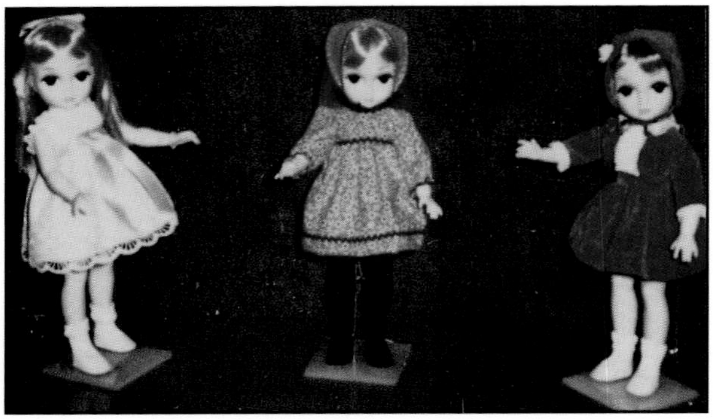

Love Me Linda, (1965), 16", vinyl doll with large painted eyes. Left to right: #86160, blue eyelet dress; #86171, red and black print dress; #86172, blue velvety suit and hat. Courtesy Wenham Doll Museum, Wenham, Mass.

The idea for Love Me Linda was taken from the popular paintings of big eyed children with a tear in their eye by artists Margaret and Walter Keane. Love Me Linda was also a copy of Lonely Lisa by Royal Doll, according to a former Vogue employee.

Marketing:

While Ginny's popularity was not as strong as it once was in 1965, Vogue's other dolls were selling very well and the doll market was strong in general. Love Me Linda was one of a number of older girl play dolls introduced to supplement their baby doll market.

My Angel

(1967)

Description: 15" all vinyl doll; jointed at head, arms, and legs; all fingers slightly curled; sleep eyes; rooted blonde hair in braids and short styles; young girl doll. Head designed by Deet D'Andrade, body by Ungaro.
While some sources report the doll was never produced, it did appear on the 1965 Vogue price list.

Marks: Head: Vogue Doll, Inc./1967
Body: VOGUE DOLL, INC./1967

Wardrobe: Three outfits appeared in 1965 dealers price sheets: # 95170, blue velvet party dress with white lace trim and blue hair ribbons; #95181, red plaid school dress with red vest and white trim; #9510, brown fleece coat and hat ensemble with red dress and scarf.
All outfits had white anklets and vinyl strap Ginny type shoes.

My Angel, (1965), 15", vinyl doll with sleep eyes and rooted hair. Outfits matched Miss Ginny in 1965: (left to right) #95170, velvety blue party dress; #95181, red plaid school dress; #95102, brown fleece coat ensemble. Vogue publicity photo. Courtesy Wenham Doll Museum, Wenham, Mass.

Marketing

My Angel was one of two young girl type dolls introduced in 1965 (along with Love Me Linda) to appeal to a market for older dolls as the popularity of their toddler doll, Ginny, declined. Both were dropped in 1966 at the time of Mrs. Carlson's retirement.

Angel Baby

(1965 – 1968)

Description: 10" and 14" all vinyl; jointed at head, arms, and legs; slightly curved baby legs; open palm hands; sleep eyes with no painted lashes; rooted hair cut short and straight in blonde and reddish blonde colors. Right foot has curled molded toes.

Marks:

10" Head:	VOGUE DOLL/1964
Back:	VOGUE DOLL/1964
14" Head:	VOGUE DOLL/©1965
Back:	VOGUE DOLL/1965

Wardrobe: Angel Baby doll outfits for 1965 were:

10" outfits: #90150, pink baby dress with baby bonnet, socks; #90151, blue baby dress with baby bonnet, socks; #90162, pink baby dress and bonnet, baby pillow and blanket with lace trim; #90163, fleece bunting and hooded sleeper.

14 " outfits: #94160, pink cotton high waist sundress with lace trim and hair ribbon, socks; #94171, pink/yellow cotton baby dress with matching baby bonnet with lace trim, socks; #94172, pink two-piece sleeper with hood.

Marketing

Angel Baby was essentially a baby version of the Littlest Angel doll. The 1965 Angel Baby type vinyl head was used on subsequent versions of Littlest Angel by Vogue beginning in 1967. Vogue catalogs document only the 1965 version of the Angel Baby. However, a 1968 Sears Christmas Catalog includes a selection of four Angel Baby doll outfits: a special red velvety holiday topper with matching bonnet, and three pajama and play outfits for the 14" Angel Baby.

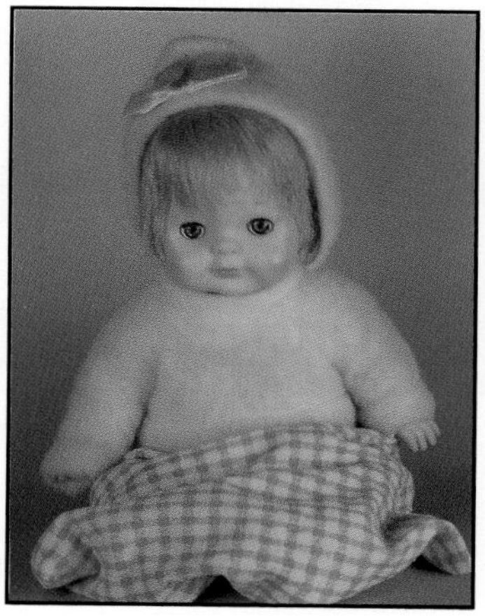

Angel Baby (1965), 10", vinyl doll in #90163, pram suit. Missing outer bunting.

Angel Baby (1965), 10" and 14", all vinyl dolls with rooted hair and sleep eyes. Vogue photo in dealer's price guide. Courtesy Virginia Graves Carlson.

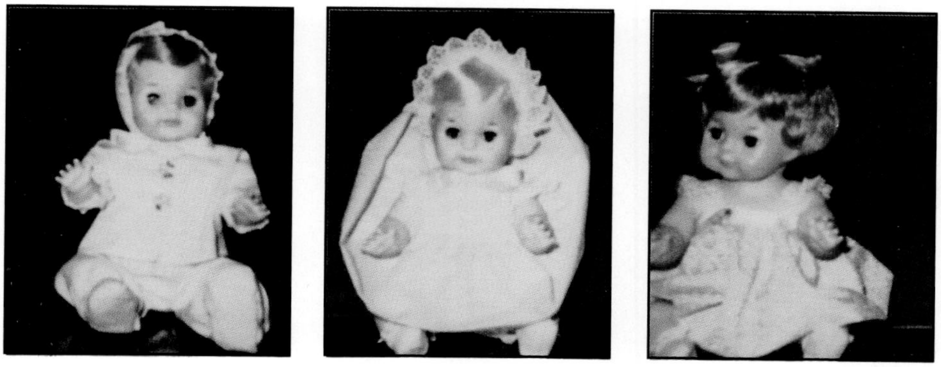

Angel Baby (1965), 14", vinyl dolls (left to right): #94160, pink and white dress; #94171, yellow dress; #94172, pink cord pram suit. Vogue photo. Courtesy Wenham Museum, Wenham, Mass.

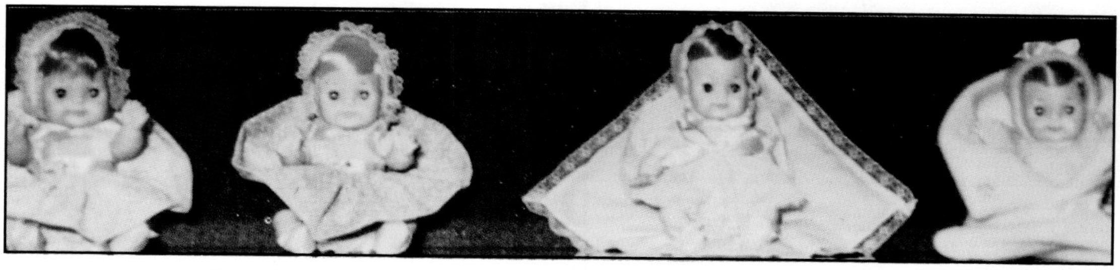

Angel Baby (1965), 10", vinyl dolls (left to right), #90150, pink dress and bonnet; # 90151, blue dress and bonnet; #90162, romper and pillow; # 90163, pram suit and fleece bunting. Vogue photo. Courtesy Wenham Museum, Wenham, Mass.

Angel Baby outfit (1965 – 1966), #49-32549 for a 14" doll is a dotted pink dress with white lace trim. Courtesy Veronica Phillips.

Angel Baby (1968), 14", vinyl dolls with rooted hair in three sleep and play outfits. Sears catalog courtesy Marge Meisinger.

Angel Baby (1968), 14" dressed in white knit outfit with pink pom-pons and pink blanket. Courtesy Joe Kingston.

Angel Baby (1968), 14", Angel Baby wearing a red Velvetex topper ensemble. Sears Catalog courtesy Marge Meisinger.

Star Bright
(1966 – 1968)

Description: 19", vinyl head and limbs, cotton body, girl doll, painted side-glancing black eyes with stars in them, rooted blonde hair, painted lashes, closed mouth. Designed by Patti Peticolus.

Marks: Head: VOGUE DOLLS/©1966

Wardrobe: Four outfits: purple and white checked nightgown with sleeping cap; blue pants outfit with bonnet; red jumper with beret; and red coat with white trim, boots, and cap.

Star Bright (1966 – 1967), 15" all vinyl body, is the same body as 1969, 15" Littlest Angel. Vogue photo courtesy of Wenham Doll Museum, Wenham, Mass.

Star Bright (1966-67), all vinyl. Notice spread apart fingers. Courtesy Mrs. Ruth Doyon.

STAR BRIGHT BABY

(1966)

Description: 18", vinyl head and limbs, cloth body, baby doll with wide faced vinyl head; jointed at neck, arms, and legs, slightly curved baby legs; painted side glancing eyes with stars for highlights and wide painted lashes in corners; rooted hair in a short pixie cut in brown, blonde, and reddish-blonde. Also was a smaller, all vinyl doll called Star Bright Baby.

Marks:

18" soft body doll:

Head: VOGUE DOLLS/© 1966

Body: NEW-KAPOK-CAL T-29/VOGUE DOLLS INC./MADE IN U.S.A. (on rayon sticker on cloth body at neck)

All vinyl doll:

Head: Unknown

Wardrobe:

18" soft body doll: Three outfits: red sleeper with feet and red print blouse with ruffle trim at neck; white baby dress and bonnet with vinyl shoes; and white fleece hooded sleeper.

All vinyl doll: Three outfits: pink and blue baby dresses; and sailor-style outfit with red skirt, white blouse, and cap with red, white, and blue trim; all had vinyl shoes.

MARKETING

Star Bright Baby was one of a number of baby dolls produced in the mid 1960s. Each had a unique character and look. As the doll's name suggests, Star Bright's particular charm was in the large sparkling eyes. She was an expansion of the concept of Star Bright the girl doll. She used the vinyl Star Bright girl head and legs, but with a cloth body, and with the vinyl wide spread arms with curved fingers of Baby Dear.

Star Bright Baby (1966), 18", vinyl head and limbs, cloth body, painted star eyes, rooted hair, wearing red sleeper outfit. Notice similarity to Baby Dear outfit from 1963. Doll came in plain cardboard box with Vogue sticker saying, "Star Bright/ Hi! I'm a soft cuddly infant with a twinkle in my eye." Courtesy Veronica Phillips.

Star Bright Baby (1966), (top), all vinyl Star Bright baby doll with large painted eyes and rooted hair shown in three outfits; (bottom) 18", Star Bright head shown on Baby Dear type soft body. Vogue photo courtesy of Wenham Doll Museum, Wenham, Mass.

DEAREST ONE

(1967)

Description: 18", all vinyl strung doll, sleep eyes, rooted short hair, open mouth nursing type.

Marks: Head: Vogue Doll, Inc./1967

Back: Vogue Doll, Inc. 1967.

Wardrobe: Cotton romper and pajama outfits.

MARKETING:

Dearest One was created at a time when baby dolls were very strong sellers for Vogue, and this doll was added to the line for that reason. She was advertised as sponge washable and drink and wet doll.

Dearest One (1967) hang tag. Courtesy Ruth Doyon.

CUTE AS A BUTTON

(1969 – 1970)

Description: 16", baby doll with cloth body, vinyl arms, legs, and head with side-glancing, painted eyes and molded hair. Uses Baby Dear arms and legs. Black version also advertised by Vogue.

Marks: VOGUE DOLLS INC, 1968

Wardrobe: #4700, white sleep gown and tie-on cap with matching blanket/pillow ensemble
#4702, pink and white fleece bunting ensemble

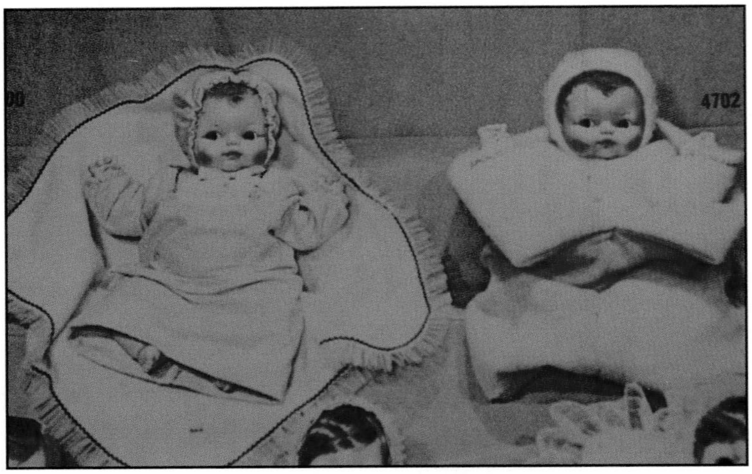

MARKETING

The doll was marketed along with the 16" Baby Dear as a "Lovable, life-like, floppy cloth body infant dolls."

Cute as a Button (1969 – 1970), 16", doll with soft cloth body, and vinyl arms and legs (same as Baby Dear); vinyl head with sculpted hair and large painted eyes; shown in #4700, baby gown, and #4702, bunting. Catalog courtesy Marge Meisinger.

WASH-A-BYE BABY

(1975 – 1976)

Description: 12" and 16", all vinyl doll; painted eye, sculpted hair with a curl on forehead; jointed at head, neck, and legs; advertised as watertight. Black doll was also available.

Marks: Unknown

Wardrobe: 1975: yellow terry cloth robe, elastic waist diaper, wash cloth, outfit also sold separately.
1976: white sacque tie blouse and shorts, red checked topper outfit.

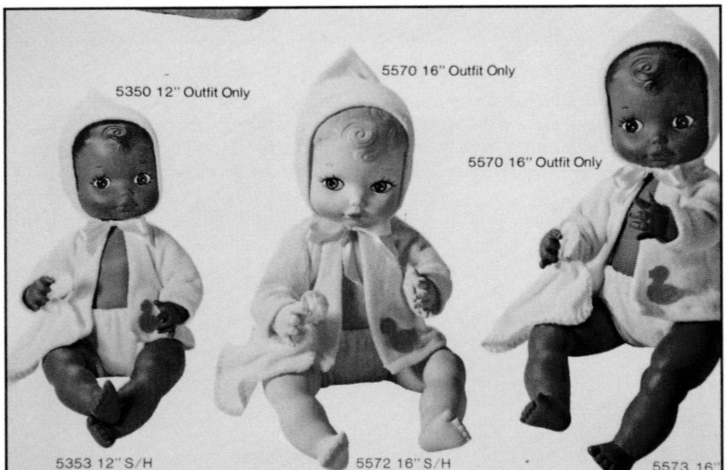

MARKETING

The doll was marketed as a playmate who could be bathed and dressed easily. This doll was produced after Tonka had bought the company.

Wash-A-Bye Baby (1975), 12" and 16", all vinyl doll with painted eyes and sculpted hair designed to be easily scrubbed in the tub. The yellow terry outfit, #5570, was sold separately. Vogue catalog courtesy Marge Meisinger.

PRECIOUS BABY/PRECIOUS PENNY

(1976 – 1980)

Description: 12", all vinyl body; jointed at arms, legs, and neck; separate fingers; wide sleep eyes with painted lashed at corners; molded hair and blonde and brunette rooted hair, Dutch boy cuts; a drink and wet doll; Vogue also advertised black dolls.

Marks: Neck: VOGUE/1975

Box: Marked Tonka Toys

Wardrobe: Knit outfits, yellow polka dot dresses and matching bonnets, denim overalls and red jerseys, tights or anklets, vinyl shoes; pink bunting.

Dress tag: Vogue Dolls, Inc./Made in U.S.A."

Marketing

Tonka introduced Precious Baby in 1975, and Lesney continued to promote the doll under the name Precious Penny as part of their Drink and Wet line, along with Baby Wide Eyes.

Precious Penny by Lesney (1978), 12" all vinyl doll, with rooted hair, large sleep eyes, formerly called Precious Baby by Tonka in 1976. 1977 outfits: (left to right) #307289; #307278, blonde; #307276, brunette. Vogue catalog. Courtesy Marge Meisinger.

Baby Wide Eyes

(1976 – 1978)

Description: 10" and 15", all vinyl toddler doll; wide, square shape face; jointed; second and third finger molded together; oversized sleep eyes with molded lashes and painted lashes on lower corners; a Drink and Wet doll. In 1977 – 1978 only the 15" available.

Mark: Head: ©VOGUE/1975
Back: ©VOGUE/1975

Wardrobe: Coat ensembles, slacks sets, knit outfits, dresses, bathing suit, vinyl shoes with anklets.

Marketing

Baby Wide Eyes was marketed by Lesney as a Drink and Wet doll. They have large, sparkling sleep eyes and unusual squared faces.

While the dates above reflect the years the doll appeared in the Vogue catalog, the doll was found in store catalogs 1976 – 1982.

Baby Wide Eyes (1977), 15", vinyl dolls in washable red coat ensembles (left), #307597, and (right) #307589. Vogue catalog. Courtesy Marge Meisinger.

Baby Wide Eyes (1976), 15" vinyl black doll showing body. Marks: ©VOGUE/1975 (on head and back). Courtesy Ruth Doyon.

Baby Wide Eyes (1978), marketed as a 15" Drink n' Wet doll.

HUG-A-BYE BABY

(1976 – 1980)

Description: 16" and 22", vinyl head, arms and legs; one-piece foam body; curled fingers on right hand, thumb and first finger touch; large sleep eyes with long lashes; rooted hair in brown, blonde, and red straight hair with bangs or pigtail styles; molded hair. Black dolls also available.

Mark: Head: VOGUE/1975

Wardrobe: Dresses with matching panties in cotton or eyelet, two-piece sleep outfits.

MARKETING

Lesney marketed Hug-A-Bye-Baby as a "huggable" baby, reminiscent of Baby Dear, but with a more whimsical face and longer lashes. This was a very strong seller for Lesney.

Hug-A-Bye Baby (1977), (left), #304615, and (center) #394613, blue checked dresses; (right) #304619, pink sleeper. 16" foam body doll with vinyl arms, legs, and head with sleep eyes and rooted hair. Also came in 22" size. Vogue catalog. Courtesy Marge Meisinger.

MY VERY BEST FRIEND

(1977)

Description: 5½", vinyl girl doll, poseable and bendable; fingers molded together; painted eyes; rooted hair in long, straight styles in blonde or brown.

Mark: Unknown

Wardrobe: Six active outfits: shopping, tennis, ice skating, ballet, horseback riding.
Accessories: Comes with a portable vinyl house with plastic furniture.

MARKETING

Promoted as a friend who is portable and can go anywhere. This doll was reportedly produced after Lesney had bought the company.

My Very Best Friend (1977), #302020, 5½" vinyl doll with painted eyes in six homemaker and activity outfits. Vogue catalog courtesy Marge Meisinger.

Baby Burps

(1977 – 1978)

Description: 16", soft vinyl; jointed at head, arms, and legs; pointing first finger of right hand; painted eyes; nursing mouth, blows bubbles and burps at random; rooted hair in short baby style.

Marks: 1975/LESNEY MADE IN HONG KONG

Boxes: "Baby Burps. Vogue Dolls made with Love."

Wardrobe: Pink dress with blue and white woven trim, hair ribbon; with plastic bottle.

Marketing

Lesney advertised this doll on television "Baby Drinks...Baby Wets...Baby Bubbles...Baby Burps!"

While the dates above reflect the years the doll appeared in Vogue catalog, the doll was found in store catalogs 1977 – 1979.

Baby Burps (1977 – 1979), 16" all vinyl Drink n' Wet doll #302000, with painted eyes and rooted hair blows bubbles and burps at random when patted on the back. Vogue catalog. Courtesy Marge Meisinger.

Baby Burps (1977 – 1979), Lesney devoted significant TV advertising revenue to promoting Baby Burps, and designed this special box for the campaign. Vogue Catalog courtesy Marge Meisinger.

Soft Sue/ Soft Sue Little Sister

(1978 – 1979)/ (1979)

Description:

Soft Sue: 16", toddler doll; vinyl head, sleep eyes with long lashes and painted lashes at outer corners; long rooted hair with bangs and ponytails; lock stitched vinyl arms with pinky finger extended; one-piece foam rubber body. In 1979, the same doll was called Soft Sue/Big Sister.

Little Sister: 8", painted eye, drink n' wet vinyl doll which came in the box with Soft Sue in 1979 only.

Marks: Unknown

Wardrobe:

1978: #304781, Soft Sue only: black and white striped smock dress, with long sleeves, red bow and white collar at the neck; white tights and white vinyl one-piece strap shoes.

1979: Soft Sue dress #304713 with an eyelet skirt; and a plaid school dress; Soft Sue as Big Sister: two dresses which match Little Sister, the 8" doll which came in the box with Sue.

Soft Sue (1978), #304781, striped smock dress and tights. 16" all vinyl doll with styleable, long, rooted hair. In 1979 she came with an 8" Little Sister vinyl doll in the same box. Vogue catalog. Courtesy Marge Meisinger.

Marketing

Soft Sue was introduced in 1978 after Lesney purchased Vogue, as Vogue's first soft bodied toddler, and was advertised as "just the beginning of a new collection."

Soft Sue was marketed alone in 1978 and 1979. However, in 1979 another version was sold with a Little Sister doll in the box. These boxes were labeled "Soft Sue/Big Sister and Little Sister." Soft Sue's hair was finely rooted to allow styling and combing. Little Sister added play value as a drink and wet doll.

Patty Cake Sings
(1978 – 1979)

Description: 17", vinyl girl doll; jointed at head, arms, and legs; arms can be clapped together activating one of two records* and Patty Cake sings; rooted hair in short straight and curly styles, painted eyes with painted upper and lower lashes.
**Note:* The door to the record player is under the dress in the doll's back. When the door is opened, one of the two plastic records is put on the player, the door is then closed, and the record plays...and Patty sings.

Marks: Head: PATTY CAKE SINGS/VOGUE DOLL/©1977
Back: 1978© LESNEY PRODUCTS CORP/PART MADE IN HONG , KONG AND JAPAN
On record player door: JAPAN PAT # 931179/, US PAT #3467393/3589735

Wardrobe: Red straight dress with plaid neck bow, white collar, and white lacy hem trim.

Patty Cake Sings (1978), 17", all vinyl doll with painted eyes. When you clap her hands, the record player hidden in the doll's back is activated, and the doll sings. Available with curly or straight hair. Vogue catalog. Courtesy Marge Meisinger.

Marketing

In 1978 and 1979 Lesney promoted Patty Cake Sings (#302091) through major media and television advertising. The cute youngster doll could sit or stand, clap and sing, providing hours of play time.

Welcome Home Baby
(1977 – 1980)

Description: 18", realistic-looking newborn baby doll; soft, vinyl head, painted blue eyes, molded hair; vinyl arms with curled fingers and pinky finger extended on right hand; one-piece cloth covered foam body; cries when turned over.
Doll designed by Eloise Wilkin, designer of Vogue's Baby Dear series in the early 1960s.

Marks: LESNEY

Wardrobe: Doll #304851 in cotton nightie gathered at the neck with embroidered design (1978, rocking horse or 1979 – 1980, rabbit) on the front and white lace trim; coordinating pink baby blanket with white crochet trim.
In 1979 – 1980 a layette outfit, #306001, was packaged and sold separately and included a white baby dress, printed kimono, panties, and knit booties.

Marketing

Lesney advertised the doll as follows: "The first doll that looks like it was born, not made...she has a life-like loveable face with delightful eyes...."

This doll is desirable to Eloise Wilkin's collectors.

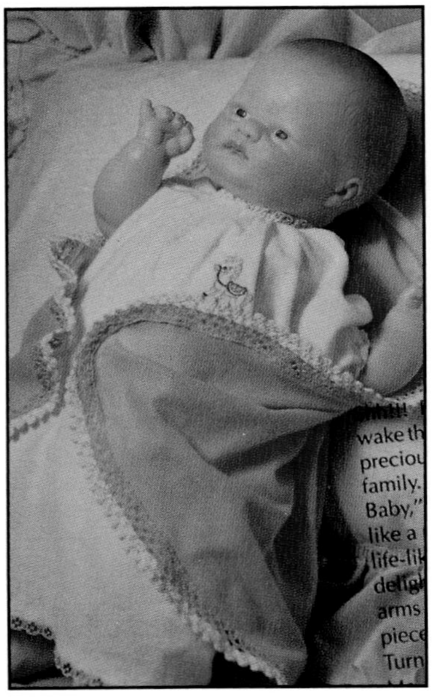

Welcome Home Baby (1978 – 1979), 18", soft body and vinyl arms, legs and head with painted eyes and molded hair; wears a newborn gown. Vogue catalog courtesy Marge Meisinger.

Welcome Home Baby Turns Two

(1980)

Description: 22", realistically detailed vinyl head arms and legs; first finger, left hand extended; soft one-piece foam body; sleep eyes; rooted short, curly hair, representing a two-year-old child. Doll designed by Eloise Wilkin, designer of Vogue's 1960s Baby Dear series.

Marks: Unknown

Wardrobe: Three puffed sleeve dress styles were available: #304906, pink and white eyelet dress; #304902, white dress with dotted apron and yoke; #304903, solid dress with eyelet and flower embroidery trim on skirt, yoke, and sleeves.

Marketing

Lesney continued to build on the popularity of Welcome Home Baby, advertising, "...the most realistic baby doll ever is now the most realistic looking two-year-old..." The doll had realistic features, and was promoted as "...another member in our growing family."

This doll is sought after by Eloise Wilkins' collectors since it is her last doll designed for Vogue.

Welcome Home Baby Turns Two (1980), 22" realistic baby doll with a soft foam body, vinyl hands, legs and head. Vogue catalog.

Winkie

(1978 – 1979)

Description: 17", soft-bodied little girl doll; vinyl head and hands; large sleep eyes that blink and wink by squeezing her hands; rooted hair in ponytail style.

Marks: Unknown

Wardrobe: Red polka dotted pinafore dress with a coordinating white dot blouse with embroidered heart and flowers and lace trim.

Marketing

The soft bodied Winkie doll was fun for younger and older children alike, as they could squeeze one hand and the doll would wink and squeeze the other hand and the doll would blink. While no example of Winkie has been seen by the authors, it is assumed that it was produced. If so, this doll undoubtedly provided Lesney with a clever doll marketing gimmick in 1978 and 1979.

Winkie (Blinkie) (1978-79), 17", soft body doll with vinyl hands and head, and rooted hair #302070. Note: The doll's name is labeled Winkie, but the Vogue catalog lists "Winkie Blinkie." Vogue catalog. Courtesy Marge Meisinger.

Miss Jill

(1978)

Description: 15", all vinyl doll with large sleep eyes and rooted hair, jointed at head, arms, and legs, flat feet.

Marks: Unknown

Wardrobe: Three dotted cotton dresses with long waists, two tier skirts, and lace edging; straw hats tied with satin ribbons.

Marketing

Miss Jill was advertised as a doll that comes adorned with the "...flavor of yesteryear." The large, sparkling eyes and lovely young lady outfits were designed to add to Lesney's teen doll line.

Miss Jill, (1978), 15", vinyl doll with large sleep eyes and rooted hair (left to right), #303535, blue dot dress; #303532, gray and white dot dress; #303531, pink dot dress. Vogue catalog courtesy Marge Meisinger.

Darling Dimples

(1979)

Description: 16", all vinyl baby doll with poseable head, arms and legs, sleep eyes, and rooted hair; a Drink n' Wet doll.

Marks: Head: LESNEY PROD.CORP. 1978; Back: VOGUE DOLL
Dress Tag: Vogue Dolls Inc/Made in USA (in blue on white script)

Wardrobe: #307634, knit sleeper outfit; #307632, quilted snowsuit with hood; #3307639, dress with lace trim and matching bonnet; #307630, dress with puff sleeves, matching hat with ruffle trim.

Marketing

Darling Dimples was made by Lesney for one year only and was marketed along with Precious Penny as a Drink n' Wet doll.

Darling Dimples (1979), 16", all vinyl Drink n' Wet doll with rooted hair, sleep eyes, and dimpled cheeks in dresses, #307639 and #307630. Vogue catalog. Courtesy Marge Meisinger.

Darling Dimples (1979), 16", all vinyl Drink n' Wet doll with rooted hair, sleep eyes, and dimpled cheeks, #307634, knit sleeper, and #307632, quilted snow suit. Vogue catalog. Courtesy Marge Meisinger.

Twinkle Baby

(1979)

Description: 15", vinyl head with painted eyes baby; vinyl arms; rooted hair in short style; stuffed body; plastic rattle in right hand lights up when arm is raised.

Marks: Complete Lesney mark unknown.

Wardrobe: Pink and yellow pajamas, ruffle trim at neck and arms.

Marketing

While the authors have not seen an example of this doll, Lesney reportedly advertised Twinkle Baby on national television not only as a soft doll to snuggle but also as a unique night light...the doll's rattle would light up when her arm was raised.

Twinkle Baby (1979), 15", vinyl head and hands, stuffed body doll with with painted eyes and rooted hair. The doll holds a plastic rattle which lights up when the arm is raised. Vogue catalog. Courtesy Marge Meisinger.

Baby Soft n' Wet
(1979 – 1980)

Description: 18", vinyl head, legs, and arms; circled fingers with pinky on left hand extended; open mouth wet nursing baby doll that wets. Rooted hair in blonde and brown hair in short straight cuts.

Marks: Unknown.

Wardrobe: Six styles: two-piece hooded knit outfit; cotton print play suit with matching ruffled sun hat; overalls and puffed sleeve blouse; quilted sleep top and pants; dotted dress with puffed sleeves and lace yoke trim; knit booties; plastic baby bottle included.

Marketing

Lesney combined a cuddly body with drink and wet play to make Baby Soft n' Wet.

Baby Soft n' Wet (1979), 18", vinyl head, arms, and legs; foam body with sleep eyes. The soft body doll is unique because it is also a Drink and Wet doll. Vogue catalog courtesy Marge Meisinger.

Miss Juliet
(1979 – 1980)

Description: 12", vinyl teen doll; fully jointed; open palm hands; sleep eyes, rooted hair in long, pulled back bun style, flat feet.

Marks: Head: LESNEY (other #s unreadable)/978/79
Back: Vogue Doll

Wardrobe: 1979: Five charming long gown styles "in the flavor of days past" with velvets and lace with matching hats, long tights or nylons, and white slippers; one matching coat and hat ensemble with a fluffy fur collar.
1980: Six gowns with velvet and lace fabrics and accents, with coordinating or matching hats.

Miss Juliet, (1979), 12", vinyl doll with sleep eyes and rooted hair. This unique doll added depth to Lesney's line of older teen dolls, and offered six costumes, including: (left) charming gown #303105, and elegant gown #303110 (second from right). Catalog courtesy of Marge Meisinger.

Marketing

Miss Juliet was Lesney's 12" version of Miss Ginny from the 1960s. The doll had a very traditional and elegant look.

Miss Juliet, (1979), #303108, coat ensemble with fur collar and matching hat, white tights, and slippers. Courtesy Ida Labaki.

CRACKER JACK®
(1979) (1981)

Description:
1979: 16" one-piece stuffed doll with white vinyl head a licensed Cracker Jack® popcorn promotional logo little sailor boy. He wears a navy cloth sailor hat and outfit. A separate cloth dog, Bingo, is packaged with the doll in a replica of the original Cracker Jack® Box.
1981: 12", licensed Cracker Jack® one-piece stuffed doll, an older looking sailor; flesh colored vinyl head with molded hat; one-piece soft body including arms and legs.

Marks:
1979: Lesney Products/Vogue Dolls, Inc.,
1981: Package: Lesney Products/Vogue Dolls Inc.

MARKETING

This doll was Lesney's first licensed doll, promoting the well-known, popular Cracker Jack® sailor, and is very popular with collectors of advertising dolls. In 1916 the little Cracker Jack® sailor was first used by Borden's Cracker Jack® Popcorn in advertising, and has been used ever since.

While the dates above relect the years the doll appeared in the Vogue catalog, the doll was found in store catalogs 1979 – 1980.

Cracker Jack® doll, (1979), #302040, 16", licensed stuffed advertising doll with a vinyl head, and removable outfit and hat. The stuffed dog, Bingo, was included in the box, which resembled the Cracker Jack® popcorn box. Vogue catalog courtesy Marge Meisinger.

Cracker Jack® doll, (1981), #302034, 12", stuffed doll with vinyl head with molded hat, presented on a card. Vogue catalog courtesy Marge Meisinger.

HILLARY
(1980)

Description: 12", baby doll; detailed vinyl head, arms, and legs; curled fingers; sleep eyes and molded hair; soft body.
This doll is very similar to the 12" soft bodied Baby Dear, but has a bisque-like finish.
Marks: Unknown.
Wardrobe: Long white christening gown trimmed in lace with ruffled baby cap.

MARKETING

Lesney marketed Hillary, #304280, as a play doll with a pale bisque-like look, but with a practical vinyl head, arms, and legs, and soft body construction.

Hillary (1980), 12", soft body doll with vinyl arms, legs, and head, with sleep eyes and molded hair. This doll is similar to the 12" Baby Dear, but the vinyl used on Hillary has a bisque-like finish. Vogue catalog courtesy Marge Meisinger.

Nicole
(1980)

Description: 17", vinyl young lady doll; jointed at head, arms, and legs; sleep eyes with painted lashes at outside corners; blonde and brunette rooted hair in long curled style with center part.
Marks: 13 EYE/93/VOGUE DOLLS,INC./1965
Dress Tag: Vogue Dolls Inc./Made in USA
Wardrobe: Six styles: mid-calf long-waisted midi dresses; dresses with long tiered skirts; very traditional, long sleeved dresses; all with white tights and patent leather strap shoes; hair ribbon.

Marketing

Nicole was introduced by Lesney as "Continental charm combined with beautifully feminine features including rooted hair in traditional dress."

Nicole (1980), #303702, blue cotton dress with continental charm. A 17", all vinyl doll with sleep eyes.

Nicole (1980), #303707, long-waisted, flowered cotton dress on a blonde Nicole. Courtesy Ida Labaki.

Glitter Girls
(1982)

Description: 5½", pocket fashion doll; poseable vinyl body and head; jointed at head, shoulders, and arms; painted eyes; rooted hair in long straight styles; a special adjustable jeweled play ring came with the doll.
Marks: Unknown.
Wardrobe: Dolls were packaged on a card in one of six metallic colored long gowns: jade, sapphire, ruby, crystal, amber, pearl. Six separate outfits were available packaged on cards: roller, western, bridal, glitter dream, dress up, and bikini.

Marketing

Lesney promoted Glitter Girls, as a doll to collect, and "Dress Her!...Pose Her!....Style Her Hair!" Also, they advertised, "A Special Offer..Dazzling Ring for you!" This doll used the same body and head mold as the 1977 My Very Best Friend doll. The doll must have been somewhat difficult to dress, as instructions were written on the back of the package of separate outfits. Instructions for hairstyles were also on the package.

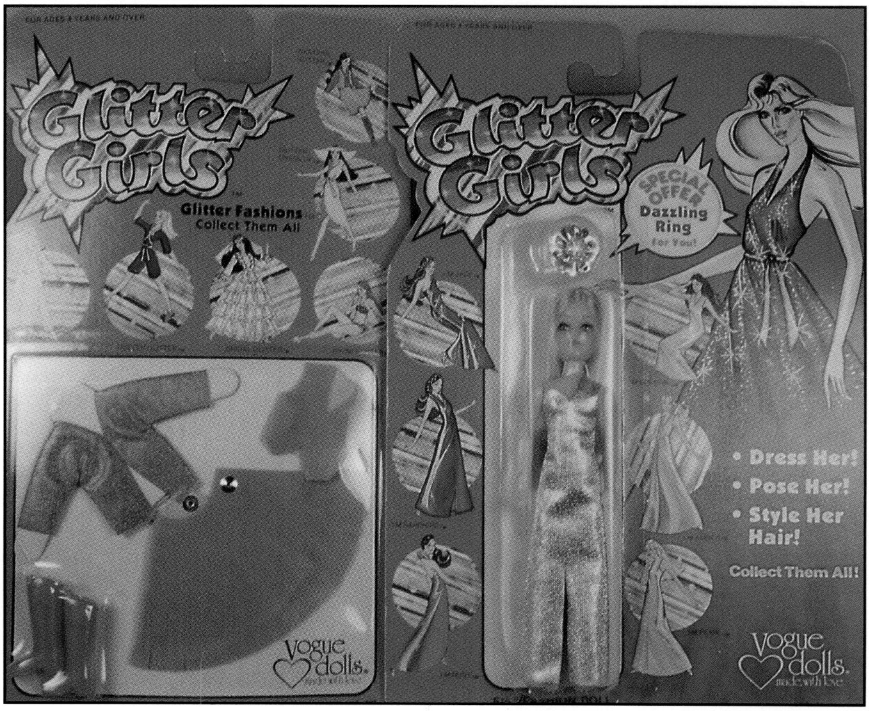

Glitter Girls, (1983), (right) card, #30-21-11, 5½", vinyl fashion doll, Amber, packaged with a play ring; (left) card, #30-22-33, with separate western fashion outfit for Glitter Girls.

Care of Dolls and Clothes

Some collectors prefer to buy mint dolls that have no defects such as soil, scrapes, or dirty clothes. Other collectors enjoy finding a doll which they can clean and restore, particularly if it had been achildhood doll. These "rescued" dolls are a great source of pleasure and pride to owners.

The rehabilitation of dolls is actually not as easy as it looks, and one is well advised to seek practical advice before embarking on any doll cleaning project. Hopefully, the following advice will be helpful on such projects, but it is not a substitute for professional assistance on dolls with great sentimental or monetary value.

Cleaning and Preserving the Doll Body

Composition: Some Vogue doll bodies in the 1930s through the 1940s were made from composition, a combination of wood pulp, sawdust, and adhesives. Composition was an improvement over bisque doll bodies, since they were not prone to breaking. However, the wood component would swell with moisture and crack the painted surface, causing crazing lines or cracks. Dolls with major cracks or chips are best left to professionals to restore and/or repaint if one desires.

However, the appearance of composition dolls with fine crazing lines and/or soiled surfaces can be greatly improved with careful cleaning and polishing. Obviously, water is not to be used, since it could actually contribute to further crazing. Instead, many collectors report satisfactory results with automobile paste wax or Westley's Concentrate Auto Polish®, available at most auto supply stores, which contains Petroleum Distillates and a negligible water component. Try whatever product you choose in an out-of-the-way spot on the doll, lightly buffing the area. If results are satisfactory, use on grimy areas, avoiding painted lines and features if at all possible. Naturally, do not store or display the doll in a humid environment or in direct sunlight.

Most composition doll bodies are strung, and sometimes the elastic becomes loose. It is not difficult to locate local doll supply shops which will sell the elastic and tools to restring the doll yourself. However, be sure to bring the doll or its measurements with you so that the correct materials can be supplied.

Plastic/vinyl: In the late 1940s, manufacturers began to use the hard plastic perfected during World War II for doll bodies. The benefits over composistion were obvious, since it would not craze from moisture. However, the older hard plastics were actually painted to achieve skin tones. Therefore, very early hard plastic dolls have to be delicately tested in a safe area before cleaning to determine if the surface can withstand the process.

Later hard plastics and vinyls mixed with skin tone pigment can be safely cleaned with the right product. One can simply use water and/or a gentle dish detergent (e.g., Dove® or Joy®) to gently wipe soiled areas. However, this treatment may not be sufficient for heavy soil or for vinyl bodies which have developed a sticky surface. Cleaning vinyl dolls with this condition, as well as all soiled hard plastic doll bodies, is best accomplished with another product made especially for cleaning doll bodies, Twin Pine's Formula 911®*. The product is used in concentrated form or diluted with water according to directions, depending on the level of soil. Repeat cleaning is necessary periodically on dolls which have had sticky surfaces to minimize any further build up. Be sure to dry the doll thoroughly, face down, according to directions.

Also, it is advisable to inspect all doll openings as well as the surface for signs of mold, etc, and to clean well before adding to your collection. Formula 911 is also excellent for this purpose. However, if this treatment does not remove dark or red mold stains or other discoloration from clothing dye transference, etc., Twin Pines REMOVE-ZIT* is a product which can accomplish this. Heavy staining may require repeated applications, but most stains will be eliminated over time with the "apply, wait, and wipe" process according to directions. The product is strong so avoid the doll's painted facial features, i.e., mouth, cheeks, etc.

Note: Some early hard plastic Ginny dolls developed a stain across the forehead, or in the eye area, from elastic bands holding the bangs in place. It is not advisable to use any product to remove these stains on any doll's face except on a truly experimental basis. Fortunately, a few of Ginny's outfits had sunglasses which come in handy in such distressed cases. Also, some of the eyebrows and eyelashes on hard plastic dolls, particularly 1953 – 1954, have faded or deteriorated to a greenish cast over time. Painting is not advised, since most attempts, even by professionals, have an unnatural look. Ginny is best left with her original paint.

Some hard plastic dolls have developed a split at the shoulder or under the arm, causing the arm itself to pull into the opening. Professionals may be able to glue with the proper tools, clamps, and heat. However, a satisfactory solution can be achieved by applying a small strip of felt-like surface with an adhesive back just inside under the split, inside the doll. Moleskin® sold as a protective product in the shoe repair section of a pharmacy or shoe repair shop works well for this purpose.

Some hard plastic dolls have developed a sour odor as the plastic material deteriorates over time. Unfortunately, this odor will likely remain even after cleaning, and no satisfactory solution is available at this time, other than to store or display the doll in a well ventilated area.

"Prettying-Up" Vogue Dolls

All of the Vogue Doll Family dolls are beautiful. However, we occasionally discover a doll that has been extensively played with and has faded that would probably be helped by a little primping.

In the area of cheek color, minimal damage can be done with the right touch. For example, some collectors like to touch up faded cheek color with a little rouge. Be advised, however, that a little goes a long way. Use a cotton puff with just a hint of pink cream rouge ever so lightly on the cheek, and then wipe off in a circular motion to avoid a dot of color look. Again, it is best to put a faded doll in a bright outfit to achieve color than to destroy her original look altogether.

The doll's hair is another area which can be greatly improved. Early mohair wigs require the most caution. If the hair is still in strands, it is best to delicately style the wig as desired when dry, using a pick, hat pin, or comb end to fashion into curls or upsweep. Start at the ends (some prefer to work up and others work down), making sure not to pull too hard, and not to pull out from the wig cap. If the hair is badly matted, the hair may only pull out when attempting to style as described above, and combing into strands may be impossible. In any case, if the wig is dirty and must be cleaned, secure the style as desired with thin hairpins or tiny rollers, wrap with a net or tulle bandanna, and then, holding the doll upside down, swish the hair only through a mild detergent, rinse and let thoroughly dry. For hard plastic sleep eye dolls, dry face down on a towel to allow any moisture inadvertently accumulated to drain from eye holes. Care should be taken with composition dolls to not get water on any body parts, and some, therefore prefer to remove the wig before washing or styling. A product called Perk* is designed especially for this purpose, and even cleans mohair. Unwrap when dry and try to leave as is to avoid pulling from the wig cap.

Synthetic wigs, even early Nutex, Dynel, and Saran, can be styled as above as well. One is tempted to apply heat from a hair dryer, which does actually help to set wig style. However, one must be very careful not to have too high a setting on the dryer, and not to have it too close in order not to melt the synthetic wigs. Again, it is wise not to work with heat without complete, comprehensive instructions from a professional or authoritative source. Peggy Millhouse, developer of the above "style it dirty" technique, has written a booklet, *Doll Wig Restoration*, giving excellent instructions regarding the use of heat in wig styling, along with reweaving techniques.**

Perking Up Your Doll's Wardrobe

Many enjoy restoring doll clothing. Although it is hard work, if done properly, a great deal of satisfaction can be gained from washing and ironing an outfit. With the proper instructions, it can look amazingly like the original mint outfit.

Nylon from the 1950s is the easiest to work with. Use a dish detergent with a degreaser such as Dawn®. Woolite® is also satisfactory. As described for wigs, above, Perk®* also works well for nylon as well as cottons and even taffeta according to instructions.

Testing for colorfast dyes, particularly some of the unstable dyes of the 1950s, is extremely important. This is a tedious task, but this is an area that must be pursued carefully and methodically. Likewise, the drying, ironing, and application of heat to washed clothing is critical to this process, and is to be carefully studied before experimenting on anything of value. Peggy Millhouse has written a booklet, *Doll Clothes Restoration*, carefully explaining details for the washing and restoration of doll clothes, providing instructions for successfully evaluating and completing a simple or complicated cleaning and/or restoration project.**.

All of the above suggestions are intended to inspire you to complete the rescue of a doll. Pick a project you will really enjoy, study and ask questions beforehand, and HAVE FUN!

Before: 1954 Candy Dandy, # 56, wears an appliqued organdy dress which has soil and age stains; also, the doll's hair is dirty. Ginny also wears the wrong hat for the outfit.
After: After washing properly, soil is removed from the dress and Ginny's hair is fluffy and beautifully set; the dress is ironed at the proper setting and is crisp again. The correct hat has also been added to the outfit. Courtesy Peggy Millhouse.

Special thanks to Peggy Millhouse and also to Nick Hill of Twin Pines for their assistance in this chapter.

*Perk, Formula 911, REMOVE-ZIT, are available at 1-800-770-DOLL or www.twinpines.com

**Booklets on doll clothes restoration and wig restoration can be ordered from Peggy Millhouse, 510 Green Hill Road, Conestoga, Pa. 17516. Ginny restoration website: www.geocities.com/Heartline/Plains/7145

These hints on restoration of dolls and clothing are suggestions only, and the authors are not responsible for any damage to dolls or clothing using the suggestions.

Chronological List of Vogue Dolls

1920s

BISQUE
Large K*R dolls

1922 – 37

RUBBER
all soft rubber

1926

COMPOSITION
Priscilla – 9½" baby
Pickaninny – 9" black baby

1930s

BISQUE
10" Just Me
8" Peggy Jean
11" Suzanne (bisque head)
Bokaye Babies
4½" Bisc Baby Doll
Valerie

Sweet Pea

1930 – 37

RUBBER
6½" all rubber child doll or
7" all rubber baby dolls

1933 – 34

CELLULOID – PYROXYLIN HEAD
K * R Dolls

COMPOSITION

1933 – 34
Baby June
Chuckles and Cuddles

mid-1930s – 40s
Dora Lee 11"

1937
Just Me, composition head

1937 – 39
Toddles Dolls 8"
Sunshine Babies 8"

1940s

CLOTH DOLLS

c.1942
7" to 24" dolls

COMPOSITION

1940 – 1948
Toddles 8"
Sunshine Babies 8"
Dora Lee 11"
Make-Up Dolls
- 13" Mary Jane
- 16" Betty Jane
- 19½" Jennie
- 20" Mary Ann

Cynthia 13" and 18"
Sportswomen series 16"
- Skater
- Golfer
- Tennis Player
- Skier

1943 – 44
WAAC-ettes and WAV-ettes, 13"

1947
Young Folks 13"
- Jean
- Judy
- Joan

Jr. Miss 17"
- Peggy
- Polly
- Lassie
- Patty
- Dixie
- Judith

Young Moderns 21"
- Gail
- Audrey
- Sue,
- Sandy
- Miss Vogue

1948
Young Folks 13"
- Joyce
- Linda
- Joan
- Ellen
- Mitzi
- Ginger

Jr. Miss 17"
- Peggy
- Polly
- Lassie
- Patty
- Dixie
- Judith

1948 – 49
Velva 15", 18" and 22", composition head, Neoprene® latex body

1948 – 49

PAINTED EYE HARD PLASTIC
Ginny 8" girl doll

1948 – 52
Crib Crowd

1949

HARD PLASTIC
Young '49ers 14"
- Peggy
- Polly
- Patty
- Penny
- Bridesmaid
- Bride

Mother

STUFFED ANIMALS

1949
Wooley Baa Baa
Wooley Baa Baa Jr.

1950s

1950 – 52
Wooley Baa Baa
Pee Wee

1951 – 1952
Honey Bunny
Scottie
Snoozie Kitty

1952
Teddy Bear

HARD PLASTIC

1950
Painted Eye Hard Plastic
Ginny 8"
Velva, hard plastic head
latex body

1950 – 1951
Velva 15", 18" and 22", hard plastic head and Neoprene® latex body

1950-1953
Strung Ginny With Painted Lash

1954
Ginny Straight Leg Walker, Painted Lash

1955 – 1956
Ginny Straight Leg Walker, Molded Lash

1957 – 1962
Ginny Bent Knee Walker

1957 – 1960
Jill

VINYL

1955 – 1969
Ginnette

1958
Jimmy

1958-60
Jeff

1959
Jan
Brikette 16" & 22"
Li'l Imp (hard plastic body)

1959-82
Ginny Baby, 8", 12", 16", 18", 20", 25"

1960s

1960
36" Ginny
Li'l Imp
Wee Imp

1960 – 1961
Brikettte

1960 –1964
Baby Dear 12" and 18"
Musical Baby Dear
Baby Dear Puppet

1960 – 1969
Ginny Baby 8", 12", 16", 18", 20", 25"

1961 – 1963
Littlest Angel aka Saucy Littlest Angel

1961
Dream Baby, also in 1965, 1969 – 73

1962 – 1963 and 1965
New Jill

1962 – 1963
Baby Dear-One
Bobby Dear-One

1962 – 1964
Miss Ginny 16"

1963 – 1964
New Jan

1963 – 1965
Ginny Vinyl Head Bent Knee Walker, hard plastic body
Too Dear
Too Dear Brother

1963 – 1966
Li'l Dear

1964 – 1965
Li'l Loveable Imp 11"
Bunny Hug
Jama Baby
Posy Pixi
Posy Baby

1964 – 1980
Redesigned Baby Dear

1965
Bunny Hug
Dream Baby
Love Me Linda
Pretty as a Picture

1965 also in 1967 – 1969
New 25" Baby Dear-One

1965 – 1968
Angel Baby

1965 – 1972
Ginny vinyl dolls, marked: USA

1965 – 1980
Miss Ginny 15"

1966
Star Bright Baby

1966 – 1968
Star Bright

1966 – 1971
Little Miss Ginny 12"

1967
Dearest One 17"
My Angel

1967 – 1968
Ginny From Far-Away Lands

1967 – 1969
Ginnette
New 25" Baby Dear-One

1967 – 1980
New Baby Dear-One
Littlest Angel 11" and 15"

1969 – 1970
Cute as a Button

1969 – 1973
Dream Baby

1970s

1970 – 1972
Vinyl Ginny Dolls, marked: USA

1970 – 1979
Ginny Baby

1972 – 1977
Ginny Dolls – Tonka

1975 – 1980
Precious Baby/Precious Penny

1976 – 1978
Baby Wide Eyes 16"

1976 – 1980
Hug-A-Bye Baby 16"
Wash-A-Bye Baby

1977
My Very Best Friend

1977 – 1978
Baby Burps 14"

1977 – 1982
Ginny, Lesney revised, slimmer body and new face

1978
Miss Jill

1978 – 1979
Patty Cake Sings
Soft Sue
Winkie

1978 – 1980
Welcome Home Baby

1979
Baby Soft N' Wet
Cracker Jack ®
Darling Dimples
Miss Juliet
Soft Sue Little Sister
Twinkle Baby

1979 – 1980
Baby Soft N' Wet
New Brikette 18"
Miss Juliet

1980s

1980
Ginny Baby
Hillary
Nicole
Welcome Home Baby Turns Two 24"

1980 – 1982
Baby Wide Eyes 16"

1980 – 1982
Ginny, Lesney revised, slimmer body and new face

1981
Cracker Jack ®

1982
Glitter Girls

1984 – 1986
Ginny Dolls, Meritus®

1985 – 1986
Ginnette (1955 – 1969), Meritus®

1986– 1995
Ginny dolls, Dakin

1990s

1990 – 1995
Ginny dolls – Dakin

1995 to current
Ginny by The Vogue Doll Co., Inc.

Bibliography

Primary Research Material

Vogue Company catalogs, original photographs, dealer price lists, publicity material: Courtesy Joe Kingston, Mrs. Virginia Carlson, Marge Meisinger, and Wenham Museum, Wenham, Mass.
Playthings magazines (1922 – 1989)
Toys and Novelties magazine (1930 – 1965)
F.A.O Schwarz catalogs
Sears catalogs
Interviews with Mrs. Virginia Carlson and former Vogue employees
Hendrickson, Robert: B.A. thesis for Harvard College, April 1954.
Howard, W.F.; Kukula, E.J.; and McDougal, A.L.; et. al. "Vogue Dolls Inc., Medford, Massachusetts, Description of Operations," written for Manufacturing Course at the Harvard Graduate School of Business Administration.

Books

Anderton, Joanne: *Twentieth Century Dolls.* Trojan Press, N. Kansas City, MO, 1971.
-----------------: *More Twentieth Century Dolls.* Wallace-Homestead, Des Moines, IA , 1983.
Johl, Janet: *Your Dolls and Mine.*
Judd, Pam & Polly: *Composition Dolls 1928 – 1955.* Hobby House Press, 1991.
-----------------: *Hard Plastic Dolls I and II.* 1990 & 1993.
Mandeville, Glenn: *Ginny... An American Toddler Doll.* Hobby House Press, 1994.
Millhouse, Peggy: *Doll Clothes Restoration; Doll Wig Restoration.* Booklets published by author: 510 Green Hill Road, Conestoga, PA 17518.
Niswonger, Jeanne: *The Ginny Doll Family.* Self-published. 1996
-----------------: *That Doll Ginny.* Self-published. 1978.
Roberts, Sue Nettleingham and Dorothy Bunker: *The Ginny Doll Encyclopedia.* Hobby House Press, 1994.
Smith, Patricia: *Modern Collectors Dolls I-VIII.* Collector Books
-----------------: *Doll Values, Twelfth Edition.* Collector Books, 1996.

Index